"The Future of Retail Banking is a thoughtful and institutionally grounded examination of how financial institutions must balance innovation, governance, customer trust, and operational resilience in an increasingly interconnected world. Dr Gulzar Singh brings the perspective of a practitioner who understands that sustainable banking institutions are built through leadership, accountability, execution discipline, and long-term public trust."

Ashok Vaswani MD & CEO, *Kotak Mahindra Bank, Former CEO, Barclays UK*

"Retail banking is evolving through a period of deep structural and technological change. In this work, Dr Gulzar Singh brings together practical banking experience, operational understanding, and institutional thinking to examine how trust, governance, resilience, and long-term accountability must shape the future direction of financial institutions."

Ram Gopal *Former Chief Executive Officer, Barclays Bank, India*

"As financial institutions evolve through AI, open ecosystems, cloud infrastructure, and interconnected digital platforms, the central challenge is no longer technology adoption alone. Dr Gulzar Singh examines the deeper institutional foundations required to govern innovation responsibly - combining operational resilience, interoperability, accountability, and trusted digital infrastructure within increasingly complex banking environments."

Olivier Poupeney *Field Chief Technology Officer (Field CTO), Developer Ecosystem & Open Source Strategy, FINOS (Fintech Open Source Foundation), The Linux Foundation, United States*

"Retail banking remains central to economic stability, public confidence, and long-term institutional resilience. In this work, Dr Gulzar Singh examines how financial institutions must balance innovation with accountability, operational discipline, and public trust while navigating increasingly complex technological, regulatory, and customer environments."

Mark Hay Academic Associate, Chartered Banker Institute, Scotland, United Kingdom

"In an environment shaped by technological disruption, operational complexity, and rising public expectations, institutions are being tested not only on performance but on resilience, accountability, and continuity. Dr Gulzar Singh brings a disciplined and globally informed perspective to how enduring institutions preserve trust, credibility, and long-term stability during periods of rapid change."

Shri Jayanto Narayan Choudhary *Former Director General, National Security Guard (NSG), Former Director General of Police (DGP), Assam, Former Special Director, Intelligence Bureau (IB), Government of India, Indian Police Service (IPS) Officer*

"Retail banking institutions today operate within an environment shaped by digital acceleration, regulatory scrutiny, operational complexity, and rising customer expectations. In this thoughtful and experience-led work, Dr Gulzar Singh examines how sustainable banking organisations balance innovation with governance, operational discipline, customer trust, and long-term institutional resilience."

Dr Rajan Pental *Executive Director, YES Bank*

"Artificial intelligence is reshaping how financial institutions operate, govern risk, and engage with customers. In this thoughtful and institutionally grounded work, Dr Gulzar Singh examines how banking organisations must combine technological advancement with governance, accountability, operational resilience, and human judgement to sustain long-term trust, credibility, and public confidence in an AI-enabled world."

Brian Charles, PhD, MBA, MS *AI Researcher and Practitioner, Chair, 2U/edX AI Advisory Council, President, SilverLead Technology, United States*

"The Future of Retail Banking presents a thoughtful and institutionally grounded perspective on leadership, governance, resilience, and public trust in modern financial systems. Dr Gulzar Singh brings together practical banking experience and disciplined institutional thinking to examine how enduring organisations are built through accountability, ethical leadership, operational discipline, and long-term responsibility."

Air Marshal K. S. Bhatia, *PVSM, AVSM & Bar, Former Air Officer Commanding-in-Chief, Indian Air Force*

"The Future of Retail Banking offers a disciplined and institutionally grounded examination of how financial systems must balance innovation with accountability, resilience, and public trust. Dr Gulzar Singh approaches banking not merely as a commercial activity, but as part of a wider architecture of governance, leadership, and long-term institutional responsibility."

Major General Surjit Singh, AVSM, VSM, FNAE, *Veteran, Engineer, Member, Indian National Academy of Engineering*

"Drawing upon extensive experience across UK banking and business relationship leadership, Dr Gulzar Singh presents a thoughtful examination of how financial institutions must balance digital transformation with trust, accountability, accessibility, and long-term customer confidence. This work offers a practical and institutionally grounded perspective on resilient banking, community leadership, and responsible financial stewardship."

Narinder Singh Dhandwar MBE, BA (Hons), *Barclays UK, MBE for Services to the Business and Financial Sectors in the West Midlands during COVID-19 (2022), Ambassador for The Albion Foundation, United Kingdom*

The Future of Retail Banking

This book provides a unique, execution-oriented institutional architecture for banking that unifies hybrid delivery, governance, trust, inclusion, and operational discipline within a single, coherent framework, with application to retail banking systems operating at scale.

Digital transformation, regulatory pressure, shifting customer expectations, and rising inclusion mandates have fundamentally altered how banking financial institutions must be designed, governed, and operated. Yet much of the existing literature treats retail banking as a technology or channel problem, rather than as a complex institutional system that must function reliably at scale. Drawing on decades of real-world banking experience across multiple geographies, this book examines how retail institutions can be deliberately designed to balance execution, trust, inclusion, resilience, and long-term sustainability. Global in perspective and grounded in execution, it serves as a reference work for those responsible for shaping the future design of modern banking institutions.

The Future of Retail Banking provides senior leaders, regulators, policymakers, and practitioners with a practical lens for navigating hybrid operating models, open finance ecosystems, ESG responsibilities, and long-term institutional resilience.

Gulzar Singh is a globally respected banking leader with three decades of executive experience across Barclays UK, HDFC Bank India, Capgemini, and broader digital transformation and financial services initiatives. He has held leadership roles across digital transformation, operations, financial crime, ESG strategy, and regulatory reform, and currently serves on several UK boards and governance institutions. He is a Chartered Fellow and Fellow of seven leading UK professional institutes and a UK Government Global Exceptional Talent recipient in digital technology, recognised for his work across banking, financial services, and institutional transformation.

The Future of Retail Banking

Institutional Architecture, Governance, and Operations

Dr Gulzar Singh

Routledge
Taylor & Francis Group
LONDON AND NEW YORK

First published 2027
by Routledge
4 Park Square, Milton Park, Abingdon, Oxon OX14 4RN

and by Routledge
605 Third Avenue, New York, NY 10158

Routledge is an imprint of the Taylor & Francis Group, an informa business

British Library Cataloguing-in-Publication Data
A catalogue record for this book is available from the British Library

Library of Congress Cataloging-in-Publication Data
A catalog record has been requested for this book

ISBN: 978-1-041-40221-3 (hbk)
ISBN: 978-1-041-40219-0 (pbk)
ISBN: 978-1-042-02176-5 (ebk)

DOI: 10.4324/9781042021765

Typeset in Sabon
by Taylor & Francis Books

Contents

	List of Figures	viii
	List of Tables	ix
	List of Boxes	x
	List of Contributors	xii
	Foreword	xiv
	Advance Praise	xvi
	Preface	xxiv
	Acknowledgements	xxvi
	Introduction	1
1	The Reinvention of Banking Institutions	3
2	The Rise of Hybrid Banking	36
3	The Trust Infrastructure Shift	77
4	The Open Finance Mandate	110
5	The ESG Banking Model	154
6	The Intelligent Branch Network	194
7	The Future of Risk	235
8	Customer Inclusion	272
9	The Institutional Design Lens	310
10	Designing the Bank of the Future	354
	Closing Reflections: The Future of Retail Banking Will Not Ultimately Be Determined by Technology Alone	396
	Index	398

Figures

0.1	The Pillars of "Trust as Institutional Infrastructure" in Financial Institutions	2
1.1	Retail Reinvention Architecture	6
2.1	Hybrid Banking Architecture	38
3.1	Trust Infrastructure Architecture	79
4.1	Open Finance as Institutional Architecture	112
5.1	ESG as Institutional Banking Architecture	156
6.1	The Architecture of the Intelligent Branch Network	195
7.1	Risk and Resilience Architecture for Hybrid Banking	267
8.1	Inclusive Customer Trust	273
9.1	Institutional Design Architecture for Hybrid Banking	312
10.1	The Architecture of a 100-Year Financial Institution	356
10.2	The Singh Framework for Designing the Bank of the Future	362

Tables

1.1	Global Illustration: Different Paths to Hybrid Retail Banking	7
1.2	Checklist: Reinvention Readiness	34
2.1	Template: Hybrid Architecture Mapping	75
3.1	Checklist: Trust Infrastructure Readiness	107
3.2	Template: Trust Infrastructure Mapping	108
4.1	Checklist: Open Finance Readiness	151
4.2	Template: Open Finance Architecture Mapping	152
5.1	Checklist: ESG banking Model Readiness	191
5.2	Template: ESG Banking Architecture Mapping	192
6.1	Checklist: Intelligent Branch Readiness	232
6.2	Template: Intelligent Branch Architecture Mapping	233
7.1	Checklist: Hybrid Risk Architecture Readiness	269
7.2	Template: Risk And Resilience Architecture Mapping	270
8.1	Checklist: Customer Inclusion Architecture Readiness	307
8.2	Template: Customer Inclusion Architecture Mapping	308
9.1	Checklist: Institutional Design Maturity Readiness	351
9.2	Template: Institutional Design Architecture Mapping	352
10.1	Checklist: 100-Year Bank Architecture Readiness	393
10.2	Template: 100-Year Bank Architecture Blueprint	394

Boxes

Framework: Retail Reinvention Architecture: Five Structural Anchors 32
Case Study: Santander Work Café—Redesigning the Branch as an Advisory and Community Anchor 52
Framework 73
Case Study: Estonia's National Digital Identity Infrastructure 80
Case Study: Open Banking Consent in the United Kingdom 84
Framework: Trust Infrastructure Architecture: Five Structural Anchors 106
Case Study: India's Account Aggregator Framework—Open Finance by Mandate 113
Framework 149
Case Study: Climate Stress Testing in UK Retail Banking (Bank of England and PRA) 159
Case Study: DBS Bank—Net Zero Branch Transformation 164
Framework 190
Case Study: BBVA Smart Branches and Real-Time Branch Intelligence 197
Case Study: State Bank of India—Integrated Branch Security Systems 198
Case Study: ICICI Bank Digital Branches and Self-Service Journeys 202
Case Study: DBS Bank—Frontline Reskilling for Hybrid Branches 214
Framework: The Intelligent Branch Network 231
Case Study: Cloud Concentration Risk and Systemic Exposure 239
Case Study: Algorithmic Opacity and Public Trust 242
Case Study: Vendor Dependency and Customer Harm 248
Framework 265
Framework 305
Case Study: Bank of England—Systemic Scenario Planning as Institutional Design 314

Case Study: HM Revenue and Customs (UK)—End-to-End Digital Service Ownership 319
Case Study: Monetary Authority of Singapore—Diversity and Supervisory Expectations 326
Case Study: NHS England—Professional Standards as System Stability 334
Framework 349
Case Study: Mitsubishi UFJ Financial Group—Banking Across Centuries 356
Case Study: Rabobank—Cooperative Purpose at Scale 365
Case Study: The Bank for International Settlements—Quiet Institutional Stewardship 370
Framework: Designing the Bank of the Future Architecture 392

Contributors

Dr Gulzar Singh is a global banking strategist, institutional architect, board-level practitioner, and international thought leader whose work spans banking, governance, technology-enabled transformation, operational resilience, and the future design of financial institutions. With more than three decades of leadership experience across global and world-class banking and consulting environments, he has worked extensively across the United Kingdom, Europe, the United States, Africa, the Gulf region, and India, contributing to large-scale institutional transformation, customer-centric operating models, governance frameworks, operational modernisation, and technology-enabled banking ecosystems.

He is the author of *The Future of Banking: A Global Blueprint for the Bank of Tomorrow*, published by Routledge / Taylor & Francis, which examined the structural, technological, and institutional transformation reshaping banking systems globally. His second book, *The Future of Retail Banking: Institutional Architecture, Governance, and Operations*, extends this institutional discussion through a deeper examination of governance, operational architecture, customer trust, resilience, digital transformation, and the long-term stewardship of banking institutions in an increasingly interconnected world.

Over the course of his international career, Dr Singh has held senior leadership responsibilities across retail banking, branch banking, operations, customer experience, digital transformation, financial crime, ESG, institutional governance, and operational resilience. His experience spans both mature and emerging financial markets, providing him with a broad perspective on how banking institutions evolve across different regulatory systems, technological environments, and societal expectations. His work focuses particularly on the relationship between trust, governance, institutional architecture, customer confidence, and long-term operational sustainability within modern financial systems.

Dr Singh is a United Kingdom Home Office Global Talent recipient in Digital Technology, endorsed through Tech Nation in recognition of his contribution to technology-led institutional transformation, banking innovation, and digital systems thinking. He holds a PhD and an MBA, is an alumnus of the Massachusetts Institute of Technology (MIT), and has also undertaken executive education and leadership programmes including advanced studies associated with the Indian Institute of Management Ahmedabad (IIM Ahmedabad).

He is a Chartered Banker from the Chartered Banker Institute, Scotland, United Kingdom, and a Fellow of the Chartered Banker Institute, Edinburgh, Scotland. He is also a Fellow of the London Institute of Banking & Finance, the International Compliance Association, the Chartered Management Institute, the Institute of Leadership, and the Institute of Consulting. His professional and academic work reflect a strong interdisciplinary approach that connects institutional governance with operational execution, leadership, compliance, management practice, and technological change.

Alongside his executive leadership work, Dr Singh serves across board, trustee, governor, governance, and advisory roles within the United Kingdom across financial services, education, sustainability, community energy, social care, and public-interest institutions. His governance contributions span cooperative and community banking, educational and multi-academy trust environments, international education, and organisations focused on long-term institutional resilience and community wellbeing.

Dr Singh also contributes internationally as an ambassador, advisor, and participant across technology, open innovation, education, healthcare, and social-impact ecosystems. He serves as an ambassador associated with FINOS and also contributes to STEM and climate-related educational initiatives linked to the Department for Education, United Kingdom. His wider work includes engagement with financial technology, digital infrastructure, institutional trust, responsible innovation, and community-focused initiatives supporting broader societal and institutional development.

Beyond books, Dr Singh writes and contributes regularly to international discussions on banking, governance, institutional resilience, financial technology, operational transformation, customer trust, and public-purpose leadership. His perspectives and articles have appeared across banking, fintech, payments, governance, and institutional leadership publications and platforms internationally, including contributions associated with global banking, retail banking, and payments discourse.

Now based in London, United Kingdom, Dr Singh continues to contribute to global conversations on banking, governance, technology, institutional trust, and the future architecture of financial systems—advocating for institutions that combine innovation with accountability, operational discipline, ethical leadership, and long-term public trust.

Foreword

Retail banking globally is entering one of the most consequential periods in its modern history. Across markets, institutions are being reshaped by digital acceleration, artificial intelligence, changing customer expectations, cybersecurity concerns, regulatory scrutiny, embedded finance, real-time payments, and rapidly evolving competitive landscapes. At the same time, banks continue to carry a much deeper institutional responsibility—maintaining trust, supporting economic activity, protecting customer confidence, and ensuring resilience through periods of uncertainty and change.

The challenge for banking leaders today is therefore not simply one of technology adoption. The larger challenge is how institutions scale responsibly while remaining trusted, customer-centric, operationally resilient, and relevant. Institutions must increasingly balance innovation with governance, speed with prudence, digital transformation with human judgement, and growth with long-term accountability.

These themes are particularly relevant in an environment where banking is becoming more interconnected across global markets. The experiences of institutions in the UK, Europe, North America, Asia, and emerging markets are increasingly influencing one another. Leadership teams today must think simultaneously about customer experience, operational resilience, data governance, risk management, inclusion, cybersecurity, technology infrastructure, and institutional trust as part of a single integrated ecosystem.

It is from this perspective that I found *The Future of Retail Banking: Institutional Architecture, Governance, and Operations* both timely and relevant.

Building on the foundations of his earlier published work, *The Future of Banking: A Global Blueprint for the Bank of Tomorrow*, Gulzar Singh continues the discussion around how financial institutions must evolve in an increasingly digital and interconnected world. While the earlier work examined the broader transformation of banking systems globally, this book moves deeper into the institutional architecture that ultimately shapes how retail banking organisations are governed, experienced, trusted, and sustained over time.

Having observed Gulzar's professional journey across banking, operations, transformation, customer experience, and institutional leadership, I particularly appreciate the balanced perspective he brings to these discussions. His work reflects the understanding that banking is not merely about products or transactions, but about building institutions that customers, regulators, employees, and society can rely upon consistently over long periods of time.

Many of the themes explored in this book resonate strongly with the realities facing banking institutions globally today. Whether one looks at large international banks, digitally transforming institutions, or rapidly scaling regional banks, the underlying issues remain remarkably similar: how to build trusted institutions at scale, how to maintain customer relevance, how to use technology responsibly, how to strengthen governance while enabling agility, and how to preserve institutional culture and accountability during periods of transformation.

These are also themes that increasingly shape leadership discussions across the global banking industry. As institutions continue investing in technology modernisation, digital capabilities, customer journeys, payments infrastructure, AI-led transformation, and operational simplification, there is an equally important need to strengthen governance frameworks, risk discipline, execution capability, and customer trust. Sustainable growth in banking can only emerge when innovation and institutional responsibility evolve together.

What distinguishes this work is that Gulzar approaches these issues from the perspective of a practitioner who has managed large-scale banking operations and transformation environments. The writing is grounded not in abstract theory, but in operational realities and institutional experience. The discussions around customer orientation, governance discipline, organisational alignment, operational resilience, and long-term trust therefore carry both credibility and practical relevance.

I also appreciate that the book avoids exaggerated predictions or fashionable narratives around disruption. Instead, it presents a measured and thoughtful perspective on how institutions evolve over time. The strongest banking institutions are rarely built through speed alone. They are built through consistency, execution discipline, trust, leadership judgement, customer understanding, and the ability to adapt responsibly to changing realities.

The Future of Retail Banking will be valuable not only to banking professionals, but also to boards, regulators, policymakers, technology leaders, governance practitioners, and those responsible for shaping the future direction of financial institutions globally. It is a serious contribution to the wider discussion on retail banking transformation, institutional resilience, operational sustainability, customer trust, and responsible growth.

Dr Gulzar Singh has written a thoughtful and institutionally grounded work that recognises both the opportunities and responsibilities that will shape the future of banking in the years ahead.

Ashok Vaswani
MD and CEO, Kotak Mahindra Bank
Former CEO, Barclays UK

Advance Praise

A Scholar's View

It gives me immense satisfaction to see Dr Gulzar Singh's continued contribution to the global banking and institutional governance conversation through The Future of Retail Banking. Having known Gulzar since his formative academic years at TAPMI, I have witnessed firsthand his intellectual discipline, clarity of thought, and sincere commitment to learning and public purpose.

Over the decades, his journey across HDFC Bank, Barclays, and international transformation environments has reflected a rare ability to combine institutional thinking with operational realism. What distinguishes this work is its balance between academic grounding and practical application. The book does not approach banking merely as a technology or product challenge, but as a wider institutional responsibility shaped by governance, trust, resilience, inclusion, and ethical leadership.

Structured across ten chapters, the work examines subjects including digital trust, ESG alignment, customer behaviour, institutional resilience, governance architecture, and the evolving relationship between technology and public confidence. It offers valuable insights not only for banking professionals and policymakers, but also for students, researchers, and academic institutions examining the future direction of financial systems.

Dr Gulzar Singh brings together practitioner experience and reflective inquiry with maturity and clarity. This book is a meaningful contribution to the wider dialogue on how modern institutions must evolve while remaining anchored in accountability, integrity, and long-term public trust.

Prof. D. Nagabrahmam
Former Institute Director and Dean
T. A. Pai Management Institute (TAPMI), Manipal
Fellow, Indian Institute of Management Ahmedabad (FPM), India

From the Desk of a Fintech Leader

I had the privilege of working alongside Dr Gulzar Singh during our early years at HDFC Bank, when customer-centric banking, branch expansion, and operational innovation were reshaping financial services across India. Even at that stage, Gulzar stood out for his clarity of thought, disciplined execution, and long-term institutional perspective.

The Future of Retail Banking arrives at an important moment for the industry. As digital transformation accelerates globally, the challenge for financial institutions is no longer technology adoption alone, but how to build systems that remain trusted, resilient, inclusive, and operationally sustainable over time.

What makes this work particularly valuable is that it comes from lived experience. Dr Gulzar Singh writes not as an external observer, but as someone who has worked through the realities of building and governing financial systems across multiple markets and institutional environments. The book thoughtfully addresses themes including customer trust, ESG, governance, hybrid banking models, operational resilience, and intelligent infrastructure.

Having worked extensively within digital banking and innovation ecosystems myself, I found the work highly relevant to the practical challenges facing modern banking leaders. It offers grounded insights for CXOs, regulators, fintech professionals, and policymakers navigating increasingly complex financial ecosystems.

More importantly, the book remains anchored in values that are becoming increasingly important globally—trust, accountability, inclusion, and institutional integrity.

Manish Boricha
SVO and Director, Wells Fargo
Alumnus, Texas McCombs School of Business
United States

A View from India's Banking Innovation Circle

In the rapidly evolving landscape of global finance, *The Future of Retail Banking* offers both strategic clarity and institutional perspective. Rather than focusing narrowly on technology trends, Dr Gulzar Singh examines the deeper transformation underway in customer relationships, governance structures, digital ecosystems, and institutional trust.

For those of us working across loyalty systems, digital engagement, and customer experience environments, the themes explored in this book are especially timely. Today's financial institutions must balance hyper-personalisation, digital convenience, ethical responsibility, operational resilience, and public confidence—often simultaneously and at scale.

What stands out in this work is its ability to connect technology with humanity. Dr Singh approaches banking not simply as infrastructure or commerce, but as a broader societal institution shaped by trust, accountability, accessibility, and long-term relevance. The book draws together insights from traditional banking, fintech innovation, policy frameworks, and emerging customer behaviours into a globally relevant and institutionally grounded framework.

The work remains practical throughout. Whether discussing embedded finance, hybrid banking models, ESG, or governance architecture, the writing reflects operational understanding rather than theoretical abstraction.

This is an important contribution for banking leaders, policymakers, fintech innovators, and governance practitioners navigating an increasingly interconnected financial environment. It provides structure, perspective, and a thoughtful roadmap for institutions seeking to evolve responsibly while preserving public trust.

Amresh Acharya
Managing Director and CEO, Loylty Rewardz
Non-executive Director, Hatio
India | United States

Public Service and Financial Futures

From the perspective of international private banking and global NRI markets, institutional trust, continuity, and long-term credibility remain central to customer relationships across global financial centres including Hong Kong, Singapore, London, and Dubai.

The Future of Retail Banking offers a thoughtful examination of how financial institutions must adapt to changing technological, regulatory, and customer environments while preserving confidence, governance standards, and operational discipline. Dr Gulzar Singh explores themes including institutional trust, ESG, customer experience, digital transformation, and operational resilience with both strategic depth and practical understanding.

What makes the book particularly relevant is its global perspective. Drawing upon experience across multiple continents and banking ecosystems, the work reflects an understanding that modern banking institutions must operate within increasingly interconnected financial, technological, and geopolitical environments.

Having known Gulzar professionally for many years, I have always appreciated his balanced and grounded approach to banking leadership and institutional governance. His perspective consistently combines strategic thinking with practical realism and long-term accountability.

This book makes a meaningful contribution to the wider conversation on how financial institutions can evolve responsibly while continuing to deliver trust, continuity, and relevance across rapidly changing global markets. It will be valuable for banking leaders, regulators, governance professionals, and those shaping the future direction of financial services internationally.

Rahul Bhandari
Executive Director—Private Banking
Global NRI and Emerging Markets, Bank Julius Baer
Hong Kong SAR

Reflections from Bangladesh's Banking Leadership

Bangladesh's banking landscape reflects many of the challenges and opportunities shaping emerging markets globally—rapid urbanisation, growing digital adoption, evolving customer expectations, and the continuing importance of trust-based banking relationships.

Working within alternate banking channels and digital financial ecosystems, I have seen firsthand how critical accessibility, innovation, and operational trust are to sustainable financial inclusion. In this context, *The Future of Retail Banking* offers a particularly relevant and practical perspective.

Dr Gulzar Singh examines the future of banking through themes including hybrid banking infrastructure, multi-channel trust models, governance, operational resilience, and inclusive financial systems. His discussion of physical-digital integration strongly reflects the realities faced across emerging markets such as Bangladesh, where institutions must balance technological advancement with accessibility and customer confidence.

What distinguishes this work is its grounding in lived institutional experience. Dr Singh brings together insights from global banking environments while remaining attentive to regional realities, operational complexity, and the importance of long-term institutional trust.

The book offers practical relevance not only for banking professionals and policymakers, but also for leaders responsible for financial inclusion, alternate banking channels, customer engagement, and digital transformation programmes.

This is a thoughtful and globally informed contribution to the wider discussion on how banking systems can evolve responsibly while remaining accessible, resilient, and trusted within diverse social and economic environments.

Nazmur Rahim
Deputy Managing Director and Head of Alternate Banking Channels
BRAC Bank PLC, Dhaka, Bangladesh

A Global Perspective from Israel

Israel has long stood at the intersection of technology innovation, cybersecurity, digital infrastructure, and advanced engineering systems. Against that backdrop, *The Future of Retail Banking* emerges as a timely and globally relevant work examining how institutions must navigate the increasingly complex relationship between technology, governance, trust, and public accountability.

Dr Gulzar Singh approaches banking not merely as a commercial system, but as part of a broader institutional architecture shaped by resilience, interoperability, ethics, inclusion, and long-term societal trust. The work resonates far beyond financial services alone and speaks directly to leaders operating across digital infrastructure, fintech ecosystems, governance environments, and public systems.

I first worked with Gulzar during his tenure at Facctum and have since followed his professional journey across Capgemini and Phoenix Empire. What continues to distinguish him is not only his clarity of strategic vision, but his ability to connect institutions, technologies, and leadership communities across sectors and geographies.

This book reflects that same institutional breadth. It combines practical banking experience with deeper reflections on governance, digital trust, operational resilience, and responsible transformation within rapidly evolving global systems.

For banking leaders, policymakers, technologists, regulators, and infrastructure professionals, this work offers a thoughtful and institutionally grounded perspective on the future direction of financial systems in an increasingly interconnected world.

Raz Caro
Senior Executive, Ab Initio
Technology Leader
Bar-Ilan University, Israel

From Nigeria's Technology Officer

Africa represents one of the world's most dynamic environments for technology, infrastructure, financial inclusion, and digital transformation. Across the continent, institutions are balancing rapid innovation with the realities of diverse populations, evolving infrastructure, and increasing demands for accessibility, resilience, and trust.

In this context, *The Future of Retail Banking* offers a particularly relevant and globally informed perspective. Dr Gulzar Singh examines not only technological transformation within banking, but also the broader institutional foundations required to sustain inclusion, operational continuity, governance, and public confidence across rapidly changing financial ecosystems.

Having followed Dr Singh's work across multiple geographies—including Barclays Africa, HDFC Bank, and his strategic leadership in the United Kingdom—I have seen firsthand the breadth of his understanding across global banking environments. His perspective reflects both operational depth and an appreciation for local realities across different markets and cultures.

The themes explored in this book strongly resonate with Africa's continuing digital and financial evolution. Whether discussing trust, hybrid infrastructure, governance, customer engagement, or operational resilience, the work remains grounded in practical realities rather than abstract theory.

The book offers valuable lessons for leaders across banking, infrastructure, technology, and public systems seeking to design resilient and inclusive institutions capable of serving increasingly diverse and interconnected populations.

Dr Col Akash Ghosh
Chief Technology Officer—Passive Infrastructure
Globacom
Lagos, Nigeria, Africa

From the World of Innovation Strategy

Having worked closely with Dr Gulzar Singh during our time at Barclays, I witnessed firsthand a leadership style grounded in clarity, operational discipline, and long-term institutional thinking. Across transformation initiatives, governance environments, and cross-functional programmes, his approach consistently balanced innovation with accountability and trust.

Over the years, I have continued to follow his professional journey through leadership roles at Facctum, Capgemini, and now Phoenix Empire. What remains consistent throughout is his ability to connect strategic thinking with practical execution while remaining deeply conscious of institutional responsibility.

The Future of Retail Banking reflects that same balance. The book examines how financial institutions must navigate digital transformation, governance complexity, operational resilience, customer trust, ESG expectations, and evolving technological ecosystems within an increasingly interconnected world.

What makes the work particularly compelling is that it does not separate technology from human judgement, organisational culture, or public responsibility. Dr Singh approaches banking transformation as a broader institutional challenge requiring leadership maturity, ethical grounding, and operational realism.

This is an important and timely contribution for banking professionals, regulators, technology leaders, and governance practitioners. It offers practical insight while maintaining strategic depth and institutional perspective throughout.

The work reflects lived experience, intellectual discipline, and a genuine commitment to responsible transformation within global financial systems.

Kaustubh Argade
Senior Vice President—Citi India

A Perspective from Public Administration and Development Leadership

Over nearly three decades in public administration and financial governance environments, I have observed how deeply institutional trust shapes the effectiveness of public systems, service delivery, infrastructure development, and long-term societal confidence.

In that context, *The Future of Retail Banking* is both timely and relevant. Dr Gulzar Singh examines banking not merely as a commercial function, but as part of a wider institutional framework connected to governance, accessibility, public confidence, operational resilience, and social inclusion.

The book thoughtfully explores how financial institutions must adapt within rapidly changing technological and regulatory environments while preserving accountability, transparency, continuity, and ethical responsibility. Its discussions around ESG, hybrid banking models, customer trust, and institutional resilience are particularly valuable for policymakers, governance professionals, and public administrators.

What distinguishes this work is its balance between strategic vision and practical realism. Drawing upon leadership experience across international banking environments, Dr Singh approaches institutional transformation with clarity, operational understanding, and a strong sense of public purpose.

I have known Dr Singh professionally for many years and have consistently respected his thoughtful approach to governance, institutional leadership, and long-term systems thinking.

This book offers meaningful insights not only for banking leaders and regulators, but also for those engaged in wider discussions around public systems, development, governance reform, and institutional trust.

S. C. Kansal
Chief Controller of Finance, Haryana Urban Development Authority (HUDA)
Advisor (Finance), Haryana Mass Rapid Transport Corporation Limited (HMRTC)
Chandigarh, India

From the Perspective of Social Care Leadership and Community Governance

The challenges facing modern institutions today extend far beyond technology or operational performance alone. Across banking, healthcare, social care, and public systems, organisations are increasingly being tested on trust, accountability, leadership behaviour, organisational culture, resilience, and their ability to sustain meaningful relationships with the communities they serve.

In *The Future of Retail Banking*, Dr Gulzar Singh examines many of these wider institutional questions with thoughtfulness and practical insight. Drawing upon extensive international banking and leadership experience, he explores how institutions preserve credibility, continuity, and operational trust while adapting to changing economic, technological, and societal pressures.

What I particularly value in this work is its grounded and balanced perspective. The book avoids fashionable prediction or exaggerated claims. Instead, it focuses on the deeper foundations that shape enduring institutions—governance, accountability, culture, ethical leadership, operational discipline, and continuity of purpose.

Although rooted in banking, the themes explored have clear relevance far beyond financial services alone. Leaders across healthcare, social care, community organisations, and public services will recognise many of the tensions and responsibilities reflected throughout the book.

At a time when institutions globally are under increasing pressure to maintain both adaptability and trust, this work offers a valuable contribution to the wider conversation around long-term stewardship, governance, and responsible leadership.

Dominic Spayne
Chief Executive Officer
Shared Lives South West
United Kingdom

Preface

Banking is again at a moment of reckoning. Not because change is new, but because the nature of change has shifted. Technology, regulation, public expectation, and global risk are no longer acting independently; they are converging. Institutions that once evolved incrementally are now required to adapt structurally, often under intense scrutiny and within compressed timeframes. In this environment, progress is not defined by speed alone, but by judgement, design, and institutional coherence.

This book is written from the conviction that the future of retail banking will be shaped less by individual innovations and more by the quality of institutional choices made today. Systems may automate processes, but institutions determine outcomes. Trust, resilience, inclusion, and accountability are not abstract ideals; they are design requirements. When they are absent, technology amplifies fragility rather than strength. When they are embedded, institutions gain the capacity to endure.

This conviction is grounded in the reality that customers encounter institutions through outcomes, not intentions. Every delay, inconsistency or failure in execution is experienced directly, shaping confidence in the system as a whole. Institutional design therefore becomes meaningful only when it translates into dependable, fair, and transparent experiences for those who rely on banking in their everyday lives.

Modern banking systems are also becoming increasingly invisible in how they shape everyday life. Customers now experience institutions through digital platforms, automated decisions, embedded financial ecosystems, and intelligent infrastructure operating continuously in the background of society. This book does not argue against technological progress. Rather, it argues that technology alone cannot sustain long-term trust, legitimacy, or institutional confidence without governance, accountability, human judgement, and carefully designed institutional architecture. As financial systems become more intelligent and interconnected, the challenge is no longer just how banks innovate, but how they remain trusted, understandable, and resilient within rapidly changing societies.

Drawing on decades of work across banking, governance, and large-scale transformation, this book is intended as a guide for those responsible for building and stewarding financial institutions. It is not a technical manual, nor is it a retrospective account. It is a practical contribution to an industry navigating regulatory pressure, societal expectation, climate risk, geopolitical uncertainty, and accelerating technological capability—all at once. In such conditions, clarity matters more than noise.

The chapters that follow are deliberately structured to reflect how institutions actually operate: across people, processes, infrastructure, and oversight. The emphasis is on execution as much as intent, and on governance as much as strategy. Throughout, the focus remains on banking as an institutional system—one that must function reliably in everyday moments, not just during periods of growth or innovation.

Whether you are shaping policy, leading transformation, serving on a board, or seeking to understand where banking is headed, this book is written with you in mind. My hope is that it serves as a reference, a companion, and at times a constructive challenge. The future of retail banking will not arrive fully formed. It will be designed—carefully, responsibly, and with long-term consequence in mind.

To support this, each chapter includes practical tools in the form of checklists and templates, enabling translation from principle to execution.

Dr Gulzar Singh
London

Acknowledgements

This book has been shaped by many influences—intellectual, professional, and personal—each leaving a lasting imprint on its ideas and intent.

I begin by acknowledging the memory of Bhai Hira Singh Ji, my great-grandfather, a poet, scholar, and pioneering figure in Sikh literature and education in pre-partition Punjab. Through the institutions he helped establish and the ideas he championed, he believed that education was not merely personal advancement, but a public duty. His commitment to learning, moral clarity, and community service continues to shape my understanding of institutions as custodians of trust across generations.

I also remember with respect my grandfathers, Major Jodh Singh and Major Balwant Singh of the Indian Army, who belonged to a generation shaped by the responsibilities of the Second World War and the formative years of the 1940s. Their friendship began during their years of service, and both carried forward a lifelong commitment to discipline, learning, and public duty. In the years that followed, they contributed to the training and selection of future officers of the Indian Army, serving as instructors at the Indian Military Academy (IMA), Dehradun, and through the Services Selection Boards (SSB) responsible for assessing candidates for military leadership. Beyond his service, Major Jodh Singh devoted himself to writing and mentoring young aspirants preparing for entry into the armed forces, while Major Balwant Singh continued to contribute to the institutional processes that shape leadership within the Army. Through their guidance and example, they nurtured values of discipline, preparation, and national service that continue to influence our family across generations.

I remember with deep respect Air Marshal Manjit Singh, my father, whose life of service to the nation instilled in me the values of discipline, integrity, and responsibility. His leadership—quiet, principled, and unwavering—shaped the foundation of my professional journey and the ethical framework that underpins this work.

I express my profound respect to General Satbir Singh, SM, my father-in-law-Chairman, IESM, and a veteran of the 1971 War. His distinguished military service, national leadership, and lifelong commitment to veterans and public institutions embody the values of duty, courage, and constitutional responsibility. His example has deepened my understanding of leadership anchored in service to the nation.

To my mother, Harbhajan Kaur, and my mother-in-law, Daljit Kaur, I owe thanks for their resilience, grace, and moral strength. Their influence is deeply woven into the character of this book.

I thank my sisters, Nuri Singh and Gunamrit Kaur, for their steady presence and support over the years.

My deepest personal gratitude is reserved for my wife, Harpreet Kaur, whose constancy and quiet support sustained this work throughout its journey.

To my daughters, Priya Singh and Preeti Singh, I am proud of the paths you are shaping with independence and purpose. You represent a generation that will inherit the institutions we design today. May you shape them with wisdom, courage, and humanity, and never lose sight of the responsibility that accompanies knowledge and influence.

Professionally, this book reflects the accumulated insight of scholars, practitioners, policymakers, and institutional leaders who continue to push the boundaries of modern finance. I am grateful to the editors, reviewers, and publishing professionals whose rigour and discipline helped bring this work to completion.

The chapters that follow have been sharpened through years of dialogue at the intersection of governance, technology, banking, and public policy. Whether through research, practice, or debate, those contributions strengthened both the argument and the intent of this book.

It is my hope that this work serves not only as analysis, but as a catalyst—encouraging students, regulators, academics, and leaders to design institutions where trust, inclusion, and public purpose are not aspirational ideals, but enduring foundations.

Introduction

Banks are among the most enduring institutions in modern society. For centuries, they have shaped economic life, mediated trust, and supported collective progress. Yet today, banking faces a different order of challenge. Technology-driven change, regulatory expansion, climate pressure, and rising expectations of fairness and inclusion are no longer peripheral concerns. Together, they are redefining what it means for banking institutions to endure, to matter, and to be trusted.

The relevance of institutional design is ultimately determined by how it is experienced by customers. Reliability of transactions, clarity of decisions, fairness in outcomes, and confidence in times of uncertainty are not abstract qualities; they are the direct result of how institutions are structured and governed. When institutional design is coherent, customers experience continuity and trust. When it is fragmented, they encounter friction, delay, and uncertainty. This book therefore approaches institutional architecture not as an internal discipline, but as the foundation of customer experience and public confidence.

Increasingly, customers interact not with visible institutions alone, but with financial systems embedded within digital and algorithmic environments. Payments, identity verification, fraud monitoring, credit visibility, and customer servicing now operate through interconnected systems that are often experienced indirectly rather than physically. In this environment, trust is shaped not only by technological capability, but by whether institutions remain transparent, accountable, and humanly responsive during moments of uncertainty. Banking therefore becomes more than a financial function; it becomes part of the wider infrastructure through which modern societies experience continuity, participation, and confidence in everyday life.

The question facing banking is no longer whether change is required, but how deliberately institutions respond. Relevance will increasingly belong to those banks that embed trust, resilience, accountability, and inclusion into their institutional design, rather than treating them as external obligations. In a world of real-time systems and heightened scrutiny, outcomes are shaped not only by innovation, but by governance, operating discipline, and institutional judgement.

This book approaches the future of retail banking as a question of institutional architecture. It argues that long-term strength will come less from individual technologies or products and more from how institutions are structured to integrate people, infrastructure, data, risk, and oversight into a coherent whole. Banking's

DOI: 10.4324/9781042021765-1

future depends on its ability to function reliably in everyday conditions, while adapting responsibly to long-term transformation.

Written from a global and practice-led perspective, the chapters that follow draw on lived experience across markets and regulatory environments. They examine how banking institutions can be designed to operate across hybrid models—combining physical presence, digital capability, and governance integrity—without losing clarity of purpose or operational control. The focus is on execution as much as intent, and on institutional capability rather than short-term advantage.

The aim of this book is not to predict a singular future, but to equip leaders, policymakers, and practitioners with the perspective required to shape one. As banks are called upon to support economies, communities, and public confidence, their role as institutions becomes more—not less—significant. The future of retail banking will not be inherited by default. It will be designed, governed, and sustained through conscious institutional choices.

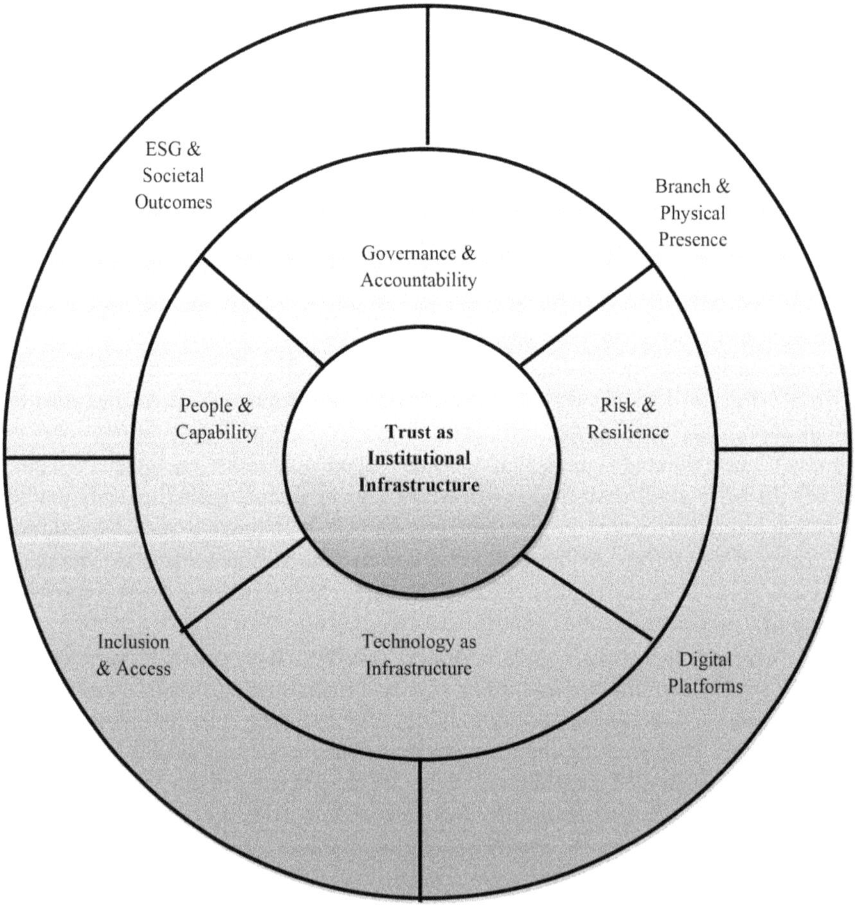

Figure 0.1 The Pillars of "Trust as Institutional Infrastructure" in Financial Institutions

1 The Reinvention of Banking Institutions

Context

Banking institutions are entering a period of structural transformation that represents one of the most significant shifts in recent decades. For decades, the industry relied on a predictable architecture: physical branches that anchored community presence, product lines built around stable customer needs, and operating models that changed only gradually. That world has receded. Banking institutions are now shaped by platforms, data flows, digital identity systems, and regulatory expectations that extend far beyond national borders. Customers interact with institutions through a constellation of channels, and their expectations are shaped not by banks alone but by the digital economy as a whole. The sector is evolving from a traditional service industry into a complex system of infrastructure, governance, and experience.

As a result, retail banking has been elevated from a transactional activity to a central part of a society's public architecture. Individuals depend on banks for identity verification, financial security, digital payments, and access to essential services. Regulators expect institutions to demonstrate transparency, resilience, and responsible conduct. Communities look to banks for inclusion, trustworthiness, and ethical behaviour. The responsibilities placed on banking institutions today are broader and deeper than in recent history. Banks are no longer evaluated only by interest rates or branch locations; they are assessed by their ability to deliver fairness, stability, and confidence in an increasingly uncertain world.

This elevation of banking into a form of public infrastructure is reflected in how customers rely on institutions not only for transactions, but for identity, security, and continuity in their financial lives.

However, the institutional foundations underpinning modern banking were not designed for this level of complexity. Many banks continue to operate on ageing technology stacks with rigid processes, fragmented data environments, and cost models heavily dependent on physical distribution. These legacy structures constrain responsiveness and limit the ability to innovate at scale. They also create a trust imbalance: customers expect transparency and control, yet internal systems and processes often lack the flexibility to deliver it. The tension between rising

DOI: 10.4324/9781042021765-2

expectations and static institutional design forms one of the core challenges facing banking institutions today.

At the same time, global demand for hybrid banking has accelerated. Hybrid delivery—where physical and digital channels work in synchrony—has become the dominant model across continents. In India, identity infrastructure and mobile platforms have reshaped customer engagement. In Africa, agent networks and community-led distribution have expanded inclusion at unprecedented rates. In the United Kingdom and Europe, open banking and regulatory alignment have pushed institutions toward greater interoperability and customer empowerment. In the United States, technology-led competition has driven banks to rethink their operating models. Across emerging and developed markets, hybrid banking has moved from optional to essential.

The outcomes that matter to customers depend on how effectively banks integrate their capabilities, not on how many channels they operate. They expect to move seamlessly between digital and physical touchpoints, receiving the same level of clarity, security, and dignity wherever they are. The benchmark for experience is no longer set by branches alone but by the responsiveness of digital interfaces, the reliability of real-time systems, and the institution's ability to provide meaningful human support when needed. The outcomes that matter to customers—confidence, convenience, transparency, and problem resolution—depend on how effectively banks integrate their capabilities, not on how many channels they operate.

This relationship between institutional design and customer outcome is often understated but increasingly decisive. Customers do not experience banking through organisational structures; they experience it through clarity, speed, fairness, and resolution. When architecture is fragmented, customers encounter delays, inconsistency, and uncertainty. When architecture is coherent, they experience continuity, confidence, and control. The effectiveness of institutional design is therefore visible not in internal efficiency alone, but in how reliably it translates into customer outcomes across everyday interactions and moments of stress.

The competitive landscape has also shifted. Banks must navigate a world shaped by cloud computing, artificial intelligence, data protection regimes, open finance mandates, and rising expectations around environmental and social responsibility. Institutions compete not only with each other but with fintech, technology platforms, alternative lenders, and emerging digital ecosystems. The intensity of this environment requires banks to move beyond incremental changes to products or processes. Competitive differentiation will come from coherent institutional design—how governance, technology, people, and purpose interact to deliver consistently reliable outcomes.

For this reason, architecture has become central to the future of retail banking; branch networks can no longer serve as the sole organising principle for operating models. Instead, banks must design their institutions around resilience, intelligence, inclusion, and customer trust. Architecture is not a technical concept; it is the alignment of strategic intent with practical capability. It determines how institutions manage risk, deploy capital, respond to disruption, and uphold their responsibilities to customers and communities. Architecture shapes how institutions think, how they behave, and how they evolve.

The next decade will demand purposeful redesign. Retail banks must balance efficiency with inclusion, automation with human judgement, innovation with stability, and scale with accountability. The systems that support customer confidence—identity, authentication, data rights, consent, and transparency—must be strengthened. The frameworks that determine risk integrity, climate responsibility, governance, and ethical AI must be embedded. And above all, institutions must become adaptive: capable of learning, evolving, and improving continuously.

This book begins from that recognition. Its ten chapters explore the architectural foundations needed to build hybrid retail institutions that are trusted, resilient, and future-ready. Each chapter considers a different dimension of institutional design, and each concludes with a reflection and a practical framework to help leaders translate insight into action.

The first pillar—Branch vs Digital Evolution—captures where the journey begins. It illustrates how the traditional branch-led model is being reshaped into an integrated hybrid architecture, and why this transformation is central to the reinvention of banking institutions.

Branch vs Digital Evolution

This section describes how the evolution of retail banking has been shaped by the longstanding interplay between physical branches and digital channels. For most of the 20th century, the branch served as the primary gateway through which individuals accessed financial services. It provided visibility, familiarity, and a sense of reassurance that was deeply embedded in local communities. As transaction volumes grew and customer expectations began to shift, digital tools emerged to support efficiency and convenience, yet the branch remained the symbolic centre of trust. Early forms of automation were designed to complement physical networks rather than replace them, extending service hours and reducing routine workloads while preserving the branch as the institution's public face.

Over time, the spread of mobile devices, internet banking, and real-time platforms altered the balance between digital and physical interactions. Customers increasingly preferred channels that offered immediacy, clarity, and control. Banks responded by modernising their digital interfaces, integrating back-end systems, and rethinking the role of branches within a wider service ecosystem. The result was not the decline of the branch but its repositioning. As digital channels absorbed transactional demand, branches began to assume a more advisory, educational, and community-focused role, forming part of a broader hybrid approach that aligns physical presence with digital intelligence.

Early digital banking extended convenience rather than redefining service structure. ATMs, phone banking, and basic online portals were introduced to reduce queues and streamline routine transactions, but the institutional architecture remained centred on the branch. Customers still saw the physical location as the definitive source of authority, and banks continued to organise their

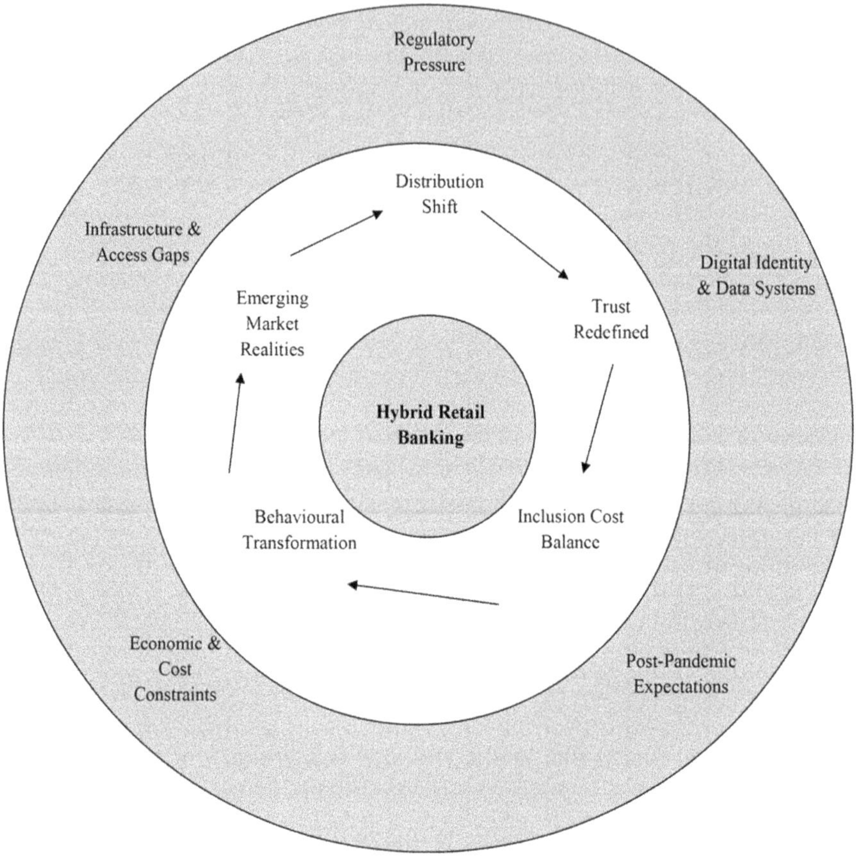

Figure 1.1 Retail Reinvention Architecture

operational models, performance metrics, and staffing structures around branch-based activity. Digital channels functioned as supplementary extensions, valued for efficiency yet not considered substitutes for in-person engagement. This period made one thing clear: technology alone does not transform institutions unless it reshapes the underlying design.

As digital capabilities matured, customer behaviour began to change more rapidly. Real-time access, mobile functionality, and intuitive interfaces created expectations that could not be met by legacy branch models. Customers no longer viewed digital tools as optional conveniences; they expected continuity, speed, and reliability across every interaction. As a result, pressure was placed on banks to reconfigure their operating models around customer journeys rather than physical locations. The branch, once the primary engine of service delivery, gradually evolved into one component of a wider ecosystem in which digital channels managed scale and immediacy while branches focused on trust, advice, and problem resolution.

Table 1.1 Global Illustration: Different Paths to Hybrid Retail Banking

Retail banking's transition toward hybrid models has followed different structural paths across regions, shaped by local infrastructure, regulation, and social context. In the United Kingdom and Europe, the shift has been driven by regulatory reform, open banking mandates, and the gradual repositioning of branches toward advisory and support roles. In the United States, market competition and technology-led challengers accelerated digital adoption while preserving large branch networks as symbols of stability and access.
In India, the emergence of national digital identity systems and interoperable payment infrastructure reshaped retail banking by enabling scale without dense physical networks, while branches evolved to support onboarding, trust, and assisted digital use. Across parts of Africa, agent banking and mobile platforms expanded inclusion by blending community presence with digital reach, creating hybrid models rooted in local trust rather than traditional branch density.
These differing paths demonstrate that hybrid banking is not a single template but an architectural outcome. While the balance between physical and digital varies by market, the underlying principle is consistent: retail banking must integrate human trust with digital capability in a way that reflects the realities of its operating environment.

As customer expectations continued to evolve, the limitations of legacy branch-centric systems became more visible. Traditional operating models were built on fixed schedules, manual processes, and fragmented technology stacks that struggled to support real-time engagement. Customers grew accustomed to the immediacy offered by digital platforms in other sectors, and any delay or friction in banking interactions appeared increasingly out of place. This gap between expectation and experience highlighted the need for deeper structural redesign rather than incremental digital upgrades. It became clear that a modern retail bank could not rely on physical presence alone to demonstrate reliability or relevance.

The widening disconnects prompted institutions to reconsider the role of branches within a digital-first environment. While branches once served as the centre of trust and authority, digital channels were now shaping customer perceptions of competence and care. The ability to resolve issues quickly, provide transparent information, and maintain consistent service standards across platforms began to matter more than the physical attributes of a location. Branches needed to evolve in both function and purpose: from handling transactions to delivering higher-value interactions. These interactions reinforce confidence, enable financial education, and support complex decisions in ways digital tools cannot replicate.

The rise of mobile banking also accelerated the realignment of customer expectations and institutional design. With smartphones becoming the primary access point for financial services, customers developed habits based on immediacy, autonomy, and seamless navigation. They expected to check balances, transfer funds, and resolve routine tasks without waiting for branch hours or navigating traditional call-centre structures. This behavioural shift placed digital channels at the centre of everyday banking, while branches took on more situational and relationship-driven roles. The change did not diminish the importance of physical locations; instead, it redefined their value. Branches became places for reassurance, guidance, and human oversight in moments where trust and clarity matter most.

For banks, this meant a reconfiguration of operations, staffing, and technology. Digital interfaces had to be intuitive, reliable, and integrated across systems. Branch staff required skills that extended beyond transactions, focusing instead on advisory capability, problem solving, and community engagement. Back-end processes needed to move from batch operations to real-time workflows to ensure that digital experiences matched customer expectations. This period marked the transition from multichannel service, where branches and digital platforms operated in parallel, to a more integrated hybrid model where each channel complements the other and strengthens the overall institutional architecture.

As hybrid models began to take shape, the distinction between digital and physical service started to blur. Customers moved fluidly between channels, initiating tasks online and completing them in branch, or seeking in-person support after facing complexity in a digital journey. Channels are not independent assets but interconnected touchpoints within a single institutional experience. The effectiveness of the branch increasingly depended on the quality of the digital pathways leading into it, while the success of digital platforms relied on the strength of human support when customers reached moments of uncertainty or risk. Banks that understood this interdependence were able to create more coherent, reassuring, and efficient customer journeys.

As a result, the branch was elevated into a strategic component of a broader design system rather than a standalone delivery point. Branch layouts, staffing models, and service flows began to evolve to complement digital usage patterns. Locations were redesigned to support advisory conversations, complex problem resolution, and interactions requiring empathy or judgement. The operational focus moved from processing transactions to strengthening trust, enabling financial understanding, and providing support at critical life moments. The branch's relevance therefore persisted not by resisting digital change but by adapting to its direction, preserving the human relationships at the heart of retail banking while aligning with a more intelligent and integrated service architecture.

Branch strategy increasingly reflects the broader shift from infrastructure that is fixed and transaction-heavy to systems that are adaptive and intelligence-led. As digital platforms assumed responsibility for routine activity, branches faced the need to specialise rather than generalise. This required banks to think more deliberately about the purpose of each location—whether it served as a community point of presence, an advisory hub, a service and onboarding centre, or a specialised support unit for particular demographics. The one-size-fits-all model that dominated retail banking for decades became unsustainable, both operationally and financially. Instead, institutions began aligning branch formats with the behavioural patterns and needs of the communities they served.

This transition also exposed the limitations of legacy cost models. Traditional branch networks were designed around predictable footfall and high transaction density. As digital behaviour reduced routine branch usage, the economic foundation of large networks weakened, forcing institutions to reconsider the balance between presence and efficiency. Yet the answer was not widespread closure. In many markets, branches continued to act as anchors of trust, especially for vulnerable customers, small businesses, and communities with limited digital access. The strategic challenge became how to redesign branch roles, footprints, and capabilities so that physical presence could remain meaningful while being supported by efficient, modern digital infrastructure.

This shows the changing economics of branch networks also prompted banks to adopt more data-driven approaches to location strategy. Instead of relying on historical footfall, institutions began analysing demographic trends, transaction migration, customer vulnerability, and regional economic activity to determine the purpose and viability of each site. This analytical discipline enabled branches to be repositioned rather than simply reduced. Some locations evolved into flagship advisory centres; others became streamlined service points or hybrid spaces that blended digital self-service with human support. The goal shifted from maintaining physical density to ensuring relevance, accessibility, and strategic coherence across the network.

At the same time, customer behaviour demonstrated that physical presence retains symbolic value that digital channels cannot fully replicate. Even when visits declined, customers derived confidence from knowing a branch was available for complex matters, dispute resolution, or sensitive financial conversations. This reassurance effect reinforced the role of branches as stabilising anchors within hybrid service models. Instead of viewing digital adoption and branch utilisation as opposing forces, banks began to see them as complementary components of a unified architecture—one that combined the efficiency of technology with the trust-building power of personal interaction.

The integration of digital and physical channels required a redesign of operational processes to ensure consistency and continuity. Many traditional workflows were built around manual verification, paper-based documentation, and sequential approval steps that did not translate easily into real-time digital environments. As customers increasingly used mobile and online platforms to initiate inquiries or transactions, branches often faced delays or discrepancies when completing those tasks in person. This fragmentation risked eroding confidence and undermining the benefits of digital transformation. To address this, banks began re-engineering processes so that data, decisions, and customer information could flow seamlessly across systems and touch points. Branch staff, once responsible for end-to-end workflows, were supported by centralised digital operations, automated decision engines, and integrated service platforms. Rather than duplicating data or repeating verification steps, branches could now access real-time information, resolve issues more quickly, and focus on higher-value interactions. The alignment of processes across channels enhanced both operational efficiency and customer experience, demonstrating that hybrid banking depends not only on technology or distribution but on the coherence of the underlying institutional architecture. The more unified these systems became, the more effectively branches could fulfil their evolving role within a modern retail bank.

This shows how, as hybrid models strengthened, branches increasingly operated as nodes within a wider institutional ecosystem rather than isolated service points. This in turn meant new expectations were required of frontline teams. Staff were no longer defined by transactional speed or operational accuracy-tasks increasingly handled by digital platforms, but by their ability to interpret customer needs, solve problems, and provide clarity in moments of uncertainty. Advisory capability, financial literacy, empathy, and sound judgement became central competencies. Branch teams were expected to navigate complex conversations, support customers facing digital barriers, and act as trusted representatives of the institution's values and purpose. The skills that mattered most were human, not mechanical.

This reorientation also altered the culture of branch environments. The traditional layout of counters and queues gradually gave way to open spaces, consultation areas, and assisted-digital zones designed to encourage engagement rather than processing. Customers visiting a branch often did so because they needed reassurance, guidance, or a resolution they could not achieve digitally. Branch spaces were therefore designed to be calmer, more deliberate, and more conducive to meaningful interaction. The physical environment became an expression of the bank's commitment to accessibility and trust. Through this evolution, branches demonstrated an enduring relevance—not as relics of the past, but as essential components of a balanced and responsive hybrid architecture.

The evolution of branches within hybrid banking has ultimately underscored a broader institutional truth: physical presence and digital capability are not competing forces but interdependent elements of a resilient service architecture. Customers value digital platforms for their speed and simplicity, yet they continue to rely on human interaction for reassurance, judgement, and support during important financial moments. The hybrid model succeeds when these strengths reinforce one another. Branches provide a sense of stability and accountability that digital channels alone cannot replicate, while digital systems extend reach, reduce friction, and enable consistent service at scale. This interdependence shows that the future of retail banking will not be defined by the dominance of one channel over another, but by the quality of integration between them. Branches will remain vital where they offer clarity, comfort, and community presence, while digital channels will continue to anchor everyday financial activity. The institutions that thrive will be those that design their architectures around this balance, ensuring that physical and digital components work seamlessly together to support customer confidence. In this way, the branch retains its relevance-not as a transactional hub, but as a cornerstone of trust within a modern, hybrid retail bank.

Consumer Confidence and Institutional Trust

Consumer confidence is retail banking's most enduring yet most fragile currency. Unlike product satisfaction or digital convenience, trust is built slowly through patterns of reliability and can diminish rapidly when expectations are not met. Over the last decade, retail customers have been exposed to a world where transparency is expected, not requested, and where the visibility of failure spreads faster than the visibility of good service. Customers no longer assess trust solely on the basis of personal interactions; they assess it through the behaviour of the institution as a whole—its governance, its digital integrity, its values, and its ability to act predictably in moments of uncertainty. In many markets, confidence has also become inseparable from the customer's daily lived experience with digital channels. A bank that is stable but slow does not inspire confidence; a bank that is innovative but inconsistent does not inspire safety. Customers now look for an equilibrium between the two: institutional steadiness and technological assurance. The accelerating pace of system outages, fraud alerts, and data breaches has heightened the stakes. Each incident becomes a referendum on the institution's credibility, shaping long-term sentiment far more than product features or marketing campaigns. In this environment, restoring and sustaining confidence is not a communications exercise but a design responsibility. It requires systems that behave consistently, decisions that reflect integrity, and leadership that signals accountability.

Trust in retail banking is increasingly shaped by what customers cannot see rather than what they can. Historically, confidence was grounded in familiar branch staff, physical records, and visible processes. Today, trust resides in invisible infrastructures: cloud resilience, cybersecurity layers, authentication journeys, and the bank's capacity to protect personal data. Customers assume these systems should operate flawlessly, yet few understand the complexity required to ensure that every login, payment, and transaction maintains integrity. This distance makes trust heavily dependent on internal discipline. Small lapses—a delayed payment, unexpected outage, failed authentication—become signals of organisational weakness, not mere technical issues. At the same time, the public is more aware than ever of how institutions manage information. High-profile data breaches in various industries have made customers far more sensitive to how their financial identity is stored, shared, and safeguarded. Confidence is no longer derived from the institution's size or heritage; it is derived from its governance. Customers increasingly judge banks on evidence of ethical handling of data, clarity around consent, and the institution's willingness to take responsibility when things go wrong. This creates a new expectation: a bank must be as transparent about its digital integrity as it is about its financial performance. In this sense, trust has moved from a relational concept to an architectural one. It is earned through design choices that demonstrate respect, reliability, and accountability at every point of interaction.

This shift also brings fraud, financial crime, and ethical conduct into sharper focus. As banking becomes more digital and distributed, the points of vulnerability increase, often in ways that are not immediately visible to customers. Identity misuse, social engineering, and transaction manipulation are no longer isolated risks but systemic challenges. Institutions are therefore required not only to prevent loss, but to demonstrate vigilance, fairness, and accountability in how these risks are managed. Trust is strengthened when customers feel protected without being constrained, and when institutions respond to incidents with clarity, responsibility, and speed.

This shows institutional trust increasingly depends on how consistently a bank behaves across every interaction, not on isolated moments of excellence. Customers now experience their bank through a mosaic of touchpoints—mobile apps, web portals, contact centres, ATMs, social-media conversations, and occasional branch visits. When these touchpoints feel coherent, customers infer that the institution itself is coherent. When they feel disjointed, customers conclude that the bank lacks control, discipline, or care. It is about doing it the same way everywhere. A secure branch is undermined by an insecure app; a helpful adviser is overshadowed by a broken digital form; a transparent message is diluted by a confusing policy. Trust collapses not because of one failure but because of a pattern that customers interpret as misalignment. This places enormous pressure on the internal organisation. Departments that previously worked in silos—risk, technology, operations, customer service, marketing—must now operate as a single system. Customers do not differentiate between them, and so the bank cannot afford to either. The quality of the experience is judged as one product, not a collection of processes. For institutions, this means governance must evolve from policing individual risks to orchestrating shared standards. When the bank's culture, technology, and frontline behaviours align, trust becomes self-reinforcing. When they diverge, confidence erodes quietly but rapidly. The institutions that recognise this pattern are rebuilding trust not through campaigns or promises, but through disciplined consistency embedded deep within their operating model.

Trust depends on how institutions manage moments of vulnerability—the points at which customers feel uncertain, exposed, or anxious. These moments include disputed transactions, failed payments, loan rejections, service breakdowns, identity verification delays, or simply a lack of clarity in communication. In the past, branches absorbed these anxieties through human reassurance. Today, most of these moments occur digitally, where emotion is harder to detect and even harder to resolve. A small error message can feel like a breach of duty; a delayed refund can seem like disregard. Customers no longer compare banks to other banks; they compare them to the most responsive digital platforms they use. When a retail bank fails to deliver that sense of clarity and control, customers begin to doubt not just the channel but the institution behind it. To rebuild trust in this new environment, banks must design for vulnerability rather than efficiency alone. Processes must anticipate confusion, misunderstandings, and emotional stress. Interfaces must communicate with certainty and offer immediate options when something goes wrong. Staff must be empowered to resolve issues quickly without procedural barriers. The institution must accept that protecting customers in their moments of highest stress is not a cost centre but a trust engine. When these moments are handled gracefully, confidence grows disproportionately; when they are mishandled, trust erodes faster than any marketing intervention can repair. The ability to recognise and respond to vulnerability is therefore becoming one of the most important capabilities in modern retail banking.

All this shows that a major driver of declining trust in retail banking is the widening gap between what customers expect and what institutions are designed to deliver. Expectations have risen dramatically because digital platforms outside the financial sector have normalised instant responses, transparent communication, intuitive navigation, and personalised engagement. Consumers now assume that any organisation—including their bank—can mirror these standards. Yet most banks still operate on legacy systems, rigid operational structures, and risk frameworks designed for a slower, paper-based era. The result is a trust deficit created not by wrongdoing but by structural lag. Customers think the bank is unwilling to improve, when in reality the institution is struggling to modernise within regulatory, operational, and historical constraints. To close this gap, banks must redesign their internal architecture around expectation management. This does not mean merely speeding up processes; it means aligning promises with capability. When institutions overpromise, trust collapses quickly. When they under promise, customers interpret it as lack of ambition. A balanced approach requires clarity about what the bank can deliver today and transparency about what it is improving for tomorrow. It also requires honest communication about constraints—security measures, regulatory obligations, fraud checks—that sometimes slow the experience but ultimately protect customers. By matching expectations to reality with precision and integrity, banks can strengthen credibility even before full transformation is complete. The act of alignment itself becomes a trust-building mechanism.

Trust in retail banking is also shaped by how institutions manage the increasing complexity of digital risk. Customers depend on banks to safeguard their identity, monitor account activity, detect anomalies, and intervene before harm occurs. Yet customers rarely see the systems that make this possible. When fraud occurs, even if resolved promptly, it creates a deep psychological disruption: a sense that the bank's protective shield failed. Conversely, when preventative measures are too aggressive, legitimate transactions may be blocked, leading customers to feel controlled rather than protected. Striking the right balance requires more than technical accuracy; it demands an understanding of how security measures affect confidence and dignity. A secure experience must feel seamless, not punitive. For institutions, this means designing risk controls that are both robust and intuitive. Alerts must be clear, guidance must be simple, and escalation pathways must be immediate. Customers want reassurance without friction, oversight without intrusion. The bank's role is to create an environment where the customer feels safe without being constantly reminded of the dangers. In this way, trust becomes a product of both safety and subtlety. The more effectively risk controls are designed into the background of everyday interactions, the stronger the customer's belief that the institution is competent, attentive, and dependable.

Another factor shaping confidence is the institution's ability to demonstrate fairness, especially in decisions involving credit, fees, disputes, and service outcomes. Customers often interpret outcomes not only on the basis of their personal situation but on perceived transparency and equity. When decisions are explained clearly and grounded in understandable logic, customers are more willing to accept unfavourable results. When explanations are vague, procedural, or overly technical, customers interpret them as arbitrary or biased. This perception gap directly influences trust. Fairness is not about agreeing with the outcome; it is about understanding it. Institutions therefore need to communicate decisions with clarity, humility, and respect. This requires rethinking how information is presented, how customers are guided through complex processes, and how frontline staff are trained to articulate rationale without sounding defensive or procedural. Fairness also extends to how institutions treat errors. When mistakes occur—as they inevitably will—a bank's willingness to accept responsibility, correct the issue quickly, and compensate appropriately becomes a defining moment in the relationship. These moments demonstrate institutional character. Customers notice when an organisation prioritises its own protection over their wellbeing, and they remember when it does the opposite. Fair treatment becomes a long-term trust asset.

Trust is also reinforced through the institution's broader social posture—what it stands for, how it behaves, and whether its actions align with its stated values. Banks are increasingly expected to contribute to societal wellbeing, support vulnerable communities, uphold environmental responsibilities, and demonstrate ethical use of data and technology. These expectations are not abstract. Customers form judgements based on visible signals: how the bank responds during a crisis, how it supports struggling households, how it treats employees, how it engages with local communities, and how transparently it communicates its commitments. A strong social posture enhances institutional credibility; a weak or inconsistent one undermines it quickly. This means trust is sustained not only by operational excellence but by behavioural integrity. Institutions must make choices that reflect long-term principles rather than short-term convenience. Consistency between words and actions is essential. A bank that speaks about inclusion but closes branches in vulnerable areas erodes its own narrative. A bank that promotes ESG (environmental, social, and governance) commitments but lacks transparency in its reporting weakens its own credibility. Trust is strengthened when customers can see evidence of alignment between the institution's purpose and its practice. In an era where public scrutiny is immediate and continuous, authenticity has become a core component of institutional trust.

In a hybrid banking environment, trust also depends on the institution's responsiveness. Customers expect issues to be acknowledged quickly, resolved efficiently, and communicated clearly. Delays, fragmented follow-ups, or repeated requests for information create frustration and the impression of internal disorganisation. Responsiveness is more than speed; it is a reflection of whether an institution cares enough to prioritise the customer's time, emotional state, and financial wellbeing. A slow response feels like indifference, while a timely one signals respect. Building responsiveness into the architecture requires redesigning internal coordination. Case handling must move seamlessly across digital, operational, and branch teams. Staff must have access to full customer histories. Systems must reduce duplication and remove unnecessary handovers. Customers must feel guided, not bounced between departments. When institutions treat responsiveness as a structural responsibility rather than a customer-service metric, trust strengthens naturally. Even complex issues become manageable if the customer senses the institution is actively engaged and accountable. Responsiveness becomes both service standard and cultural marker.

The cumulative effect of these factors reveals that trust in retail banking is now an outcome of design. It is the product of systems that behave predictably, decisions that are explained clearly, and cultures that demonstrate integrity. Customers rarely articulate trust in technical terms, yet they feel it intuitively when an institution's behaviours align across channels, contexts, and moments of vulnerability. Conversely, when systems are inconsistent or communication is unclear, trust diminishes even if individual interactions seem acceptable. This is why confidence cannot be rebuilt through branding alone; it must be earned through the coherence of the institution itself. In modern retail banking, trust functions as an operational asset, shaping customer loyalty, adoption of digital services, and willingness to engage with new products. Institutions that invest in trust architecture—strong governance, transparent communication, empathetic frontline engagement, secure digital journeys, and disciplined decision-making—build a foundation for long-term relevance. As hybrid banking becomes the norm, the ability to sustain confidence will differentiate institutions more powerfully than rates, features, or marketing campaigns. Trust, once viewed as a sentimental attribute, has become a measurable and strategic component of institutional design.

The Cost–Inclusion Dilemma

Retail banking faces a structural tension: serving customers sustainably while ensuring universal access regardless of income or geography. For decades, the economics of retail delivery relied on cross-subsidisation: higher-value urban customers, mainstream depositors, and profitable small businesses effectively covered the cost of serving low-income, rural, and vulnerable groups. As long as branch networks were the primary channel, the cost model was visible but manageable. Today, the shift toward digital channels has altered that equation. While digital transactions are significantly cheaper per unit, the infrastructure required to support secure, resilient, and compliant digital ecosystems has raised the fixed-cost baseline for institutions. Digital promises lower marginal cost, but the capital required to build and maintain the ecosystem increases structural cost. This intensifies pressure on banks to prioritise efficiency, automation, and scale, often in ways that unintentionally widen access gaps. Regulators emphasise inclusion, communities expect accessibility, and boards demand cost discipline. The dilemma sits at the centre of modern retail banking: how can a bank reduce its cost-to-serve while expanding its obligation to serve? The resolution requires a new architecture that balances economic sustainability with societal responsibility.

The unit economics of retail banking reveal the complexity of this dilemma. Branch transactions remain several times costlier than digital transactions, creating a persistent incentive to shrink physical networks. However, branches continue to anchor trust, provide critical support for vulnerable populations, and serve as stabilisers during crises. Digital channels achieve scale, but they demand significant investment in cybersecurity, cloud infrastructure, data governance, and continuous compliance. This cost is not optional; it is foundational to safety and public confidence. Emerging technologies such as AI and biometric security lower some operational expenses while increasing the cost of talent, oversight, and ethical controls. Retail banks today must therefore finance two systems simultaneously: a physical network that maintains community presence and a digital infrastructure that ensures competitiveness. This dual system exposes a structural imbalance. Customers who are technologically confident migrate rapidly to digital channels, lowering costs for their segment, while customers who need more support remain dependent on higher-cost pathways. The economic pressure to reduce legacy cost cannot ignore the moral and regulatory imperative to ensure equitable access.

Inclusion is often discussed as a moral obligation, but it is equally an economic one. When citizens remain outside the formal financial system, the cost is borne not only by households but by the broader economy. Cash dependency increases risk, slows growth, and raises the administrative burden on government and institutions. Yet inclusion requires human support, community presence, and financial literacy investment—all costly. This raises difficult questions about financial sponsorship. Who funds inclusion? Should the burden rest entirely with banks, or should governments and regulators co-design economic incentives? Some markets have introduced shared digital infrastructure, public data rails, subsidised identity systems, or community-banking partnerships to reduce costs for institutions. Others rely on market competition to drive efficiency. In practice, neither model resolves the dilemma completely. Banks must serve populations whose needs exceed their profitability, while also meeting shareholder expectations in competitive markets. This creates a structural tension that cannot be solved by cost-cutting alone. Inclusion requires a systemic model in which cost, capability, and public purpose are aligned. Without this alignment, the financial system risks leaving behind those with the greatest need for stability and support.

The move toward digital channels has created its own layers of exclusion. While digital services reduce the cost of everyday transactions, they can unintentionally raise the barriers for customers with limited digital skills, inconsistent connectivity, or low trust in technology. Many elderly customers, low-income individuals, and people with disabilities rely on physical interactions for assistance, verification, and reassurance. When branches close or shift to automated formats, the cost-to-serve may fall, but the cost to the customer—measured in effort, vulnerability, or dependence on others—increases significantly. As a result, transfers cost from institutions to individuals, widening social inequalities. In emerging markets, digital exclusion is magnified by infrastructure gaps: unreliable networks, shared devices, and linguistic barriers reduce the utility of digital banking. The cost–inclusion dilemma therefore extends beyond financial affordability; it encompasses cognitive, technological, and environmental factors. Banks must design for the full spectrum of customer capability, from the digitally fluent to the digitally fragile. Reducing cost-to-serve cannot mean reducing access. The architecture of hybrid banking must provide pathways that maintain inclusion while enabling institutions to modernise responsibly.

Regulation intensifies the dilemma through increasing expectations on banks to ensure both operational resilience and universal access. Compliance with anti-money laundering rules, data protection laws, open banking standards, and cyber-resilience frameworks raises the fixed cost of doing business. These requirements are essential for public protection and financial stability but impose significant cost on retail banks, particularly smaller institutions. At the same time, regulators expect financial inclusion strategies, fair treatment of vulnerable customers, and transparent pricing. This dual mandate—rigorous compliance and broad inclusion—creates a design challenge that legacy models cannot absorb. Banks cannot pass all compliance-related costs to customers without violating fairness expectations or driving exclusion. Neither can they reduce inclusion obligations without regulatory or reputational consequences. What emerges is a structural squeeze: cost rising from above, obligation rising from below. The institutions that will succeed are those that treat regulatory expectations as design inputs rather than operational burdens. When compliance, inclusion, and efficiency are architected together, instead of addressed separately, the model becomes both resilient and equitable.

Cost pressure reshapes the internal dynamics of retail banking. Legacy systems demand continuous maintenance, expert talent, and specialised oversight, all of which elevate cost. Migrating to modern cloud environments reduces certain operational burdens but requires new investment in cybersecurity, data controls, and system redundancy. At the same time, customer expectations escalate. They demand instant payments, invisible authentication, personalised insights, and consistent experiences across channels. Meeting these expectations requires advanced analytics, machine learning capability, and integrated data architectures. These investments shift cost from physical infrastructure to digital capability. The challenge is sequencing: institutions must carry both cost structures during transition. This dual structure is the heart of the dilemma. Banks must modernise without compromising service, maintain legacy systems while funding new ones, and reduce operational cost while increasing capability. The solution lies in designing an architecture that prioritises reusability, interoperability, and long-term cost efficiency rather than short-term fixes. Cost reduction is not achieved by shrinking capability but by redesigning its foundation.

The cost–inclusion dilemma is most visible in rural and remote regions, where low population density increases the cost of every service point. Branch operations become economically unsustainable when footfall declines, yet these communities often have the highest dependency on in-person support. Closing a branch may reduce institutional cost but increases community vulnerability. Digital channels can compensate, but only when connectivity, literacy, and reliability are strong. In many regions, these conditions are uneven or absent. Banks must therefore adapt delivery models—through micro-branches, partnership agents, mobile vans, community kiosks, or shared service hubs—to maintain presence at sustainable cost. These models are not secondary substitutes; they are essential components of a modern retail architecture. They allow institutions to preserve trust and inclusion while aligning service delivery with the economics of small communities. When designed thoughtfully, hybrid models in rural markets demonstrate that inclusion and cost discipline are not opposing forces but complementary outcomes of structural innovation.

Inclusion is not only about reaching underserved communities; it is about designing for life events and vulnerabilities that can affect any customer. Illness, unemployment, bereavement, debt spirals, or cognitive decline can place individuals at a disadvantage in navigating financial systems. These situations require human support, time, and flexibility—all of which increase cost. Banks that remove human pathways entirely in the pursuit of digital efficiency risk creating exclusion at moments when customers most need empathy and intervention. The cost–inclusion dilemma therefore demands a layered model in which human and digital capabilities complement rather than compete with each other. High-touch support should be available for those who need it, while low-touch digital pathways serve routine transactions. This segmentation must be designed ethically, with safeguards to ensure vulnerable customers are not moved into automated journeys that may cause harm. Inclusion becomes a design principle, not an accommodation. When institutions architect processes with vulnerability in mind, the cost of doing so becomes an investment in long-term trust and retention.

Market competition influences the cost–inclusion equation in ways that are often underestimated. New entrants—fintech, digital-only banks, and niche platforms—operate with different cost structures and risk appetites. They target profitable segments with low-cost digital models, eroding revenue pools that historically subsidised inclusion. Traditional banks must maintain universal obligations that their competitors do not share. This environment creates asymmetry: incumbents carry the cost of societal responsibility while challengers optimise for speed and margin. The result can be reduced ability for universal banks to fund inclusion activities. Regulators increasingly recognise this imbalance and consider policy interventions such as shared utilities, public digital rails, or targeted inclusion incentives. For banks, the strategic response must involve strengthening their role as institutional anchors—positioning themselves as essential public infrastructure rather than transactional providers. When trust, governance, and societal value become the differentiators, inclusion becomes a strategic advantage rather than a cost centre.

Resolving the cost–inclusion dilemma requires a shift from product-level optimisation to system-level architecture. Traditional levers—branch rationalisation, process automation, channel migration—can deliver efficiency but cannot address the deeper structural tensions. The future lies in integrated design: modular technology that lowers long-term cost, governance models that align capability with purpose, partnerships that extend reach without diluting trust, and multi-channel delivery systems that support both digital fluency and digital fragility. Inclusion must be embedded into core strategy, not peripheral activity. When banks treat access as a fundamental component of resilience, they build systems that serve individuals, communities, and economies across cycles. The cost–inclusion dilemma is not a barrier to progress but a blueprint for the future architecture of retail banking—an architecture where sustainability, trust, and accessibility are inseparable features of institutional design.

Post-Pandemic Behavioural Shifts

The pandemic altered retail banking's behavioural foundations far beyond temporary lockdown disruptions. It accelerated a psychological and practical shift that forced millions of customers to re-evaluate how, when, and where they engage with financial services. For many, digital channels moved from being optional conveniences to essential lifelines, creating new patterns of dependency and confidence. Customers who once preferred in-person interactions discovered the efficiency of remote transactions, while others felt heightened vulnerability navigating unfamiliar digital processes. At the same time, the crisis reshaped expectations around availability, responsiveness, and compassion. Individuals sought timely guidance, financial reassurance, and clear communication during a period of uncertainty. People came to expect that institutions should be as agile as they are stable, as accessible as they are secure. The pandemic did not simply change the channels customers used; it changed their thresholds for trust, risk, convenience, and empathy. These shifts now form a baseline for future service design. Retail banks cannot revert to pre-pandemic assumptions about behaviour. Instead, they must understand that the crisis recalibrated the entire landscape of customer expectation, anchoring hybrid engagement as both a functional and emotional requirement.

One of the most significant behavioural shifts after the pandemic was the dramatic rise in customer self-management. As physical access became constrained, customers grew accustomed to taking greater control of their financial tasks-monitoring balances, adjusting payments, managing savings, and seeking support through digital channels. This behavioural adaptation accelerated digital literacy for some but exposed gaps for others. Customers developed new habits of immediacy, expecting tasks that once required branch visits to be completed instantly through intuitive design. As a result, the perception of what constitutes "delay" or "inconvenience" changed. A two-day response time that was acceptable in a branch-based world now feels inadequate in an always-on environment. Simultaneously, the expectation of human reassurance has not diminished. Customers want digital journeys that are fast and frictionless, but they also want the option of immediate human support when facing uncertainty or financial stress. Banks must therefore design multi-modal pathways that blend autonomy with intervention. The rise of self-management does not reduce the need for personalised service; it increases the need for adaptive service models that understand when customers require independence and when they require guidance. The challenge is not replacing human support but orchestrating it intelligently around customer behaviour.

Thus, the pandemic heightened customer sensitivity to vulnerability in ways that have permanently shifted the landscape of retail banking. Financial shocks, employment uncertainty, health risks, and caregiving responsibilities exposed how quickly stable households can become fragile. Customers who never saw themselves as vulnerable began to seek support, forbearance, or flexible arrangements. This expanded the definition of vulnerability from a narrow demographic segment to a broader, situational experience. Banks were required to make rapid decisions on loan deferrals, fee waivers, and hardship support, illustrating the need for empathetic service channels and responsive risk frameworks. Post-pandemic, customers now expect institutions to recognise vulnerability not as an exception but as an integral part of lifecycle behaviour. They assume that banks will provide flexible options during periods of stress, clear communication during uncertainty, and accessible pathways for assistance. This expectation reshapes the design of hybrid services. Automated journeys must include off-ramps for customers facing distress, while staff must be equipped with the skills and authority to support individuals empathetically. The pandemic created a new behavioural norm: customers expect institutions to recognise the human realities behind financial decisions. This requires a structural shift toward designing systems that anticipate vulnerability rather than reacting to it.

Trust dynamics evolved significantly after the pandemic. Customers became more attentive to the reliability, transparency, and continuity of institutions, observing closely how banks communicated during crisis, how quickly they adapted, and how consistently they honoured commitments. The experience of uncertainty heightened the value customers place on clarity and dependability. Digital trust also gained prominence. Customers learned to evaluate not only the convenience of digital channels but their stability, failure rates, and security. System outages, slow response times, or vague communication carried more weight than before, shaping perceptions of competence. At the same time, customers placed renewed importance on human interaction as a source of reassurance. Branch staff, call-centre advisers, and relationship managers became symbols of stability in periods of disruption. Customers trust technology for speed but trust people for certainty. Banks must therefore design trust pathways that integrate both dimensions. Reliability must be demonstrated not only through secure systems but through accessible, empathetic human support. The post-pandemic trust contract is no longer based on reputation alone; it is built on lived experience during instability. Institutions that internalise as a result will strengthen their role as anchors of financial resilience.

The shift in customer expectations is mirrored by a redefinition of what counts as institutional reliability. During the pandemic, customers judged banks not only by their service delivery, but by their empathy, responsiveness, and clarity of communication. Institutions that provided transparent updates, waived penalties, and extended credit earned lasting goodwill. This goodwill continues to influence loyalty. Conversely, banks that appeared rigid or indifferent lost trust that has proved difficult to rebuild. These behavioural lessons shape the post-pandemic architecture of retail banking. Customers now expect institutions to anticipate stress, communicate proactively, and offer flexibility in moments of vulnerability. This creates a new standard for service design: products must be resilient under stress, policies must be adaptable, and frontline staff must be empowered with discretion rather than constrained by scripts. The post-pandemic customer judges a bank not only by efficiency, but by its ability to act as a stabilising presence in uncertainty. Retail institutions that embrace this expectation will strengthen their social licence; those that do not may find themselves disconnected from the emotional realities of the communities they serve.

This shows the pandemic also revealed a profound divide in digital readiness across regions and demographics. While some customers were able to transition seamlessly to online banking, others struggled due to limited connectivity, low digital literacy, or accessibility challenges. These disparities exposed a key risk within retail banking: digital transformation can unintentionally widen exclusion if it is not accompanied by support systems. The shift in behaviour therefore requires banks to redesign hybrid journeys that account for different levels of capability. Assisted digital pathways, simplified interfaces, multilingual support, and inclusive design principles must be integrated into service models. Beyond technology, the branch and contact centres must act as bridges for customers navigating new tools. The post-pandemic customer base is not homogeneous; it comprises early adopters, hesitant users, and those who depend on human support. Retail banks must therefore engineer pathways that are flexible, progressive, and inclusive. This approach not only expands access but reduces friction, ensuring that digitalisation is a catalyst for empowerment rather than a barrier to participation.

Work patterns have shifted structurally, too, influencing how and when customers engage with financial services. Remote and hybrid working have reduced weekday footfall in urban centres and increased demand for localised, community-based services. Customers are more likely to visit branches near their homes rather than near their workplaces, and they expect extended digital coverage outside traditional banking hours. This behavioural reconfiguration requires banks to rethink cost models, staffing structures, and branch networks. Traditional assumptions about peak hours, capacity planning, and location strategy no longer hold. Retail banks must therefore invest in dynamic resourcing and localised analytics to understand new patterns of movement and demand. The shift also opens opportunities for repurposing branches as advisory hubs, especially in suburban or rural areas where personal finance guidance is valued. Hybrid work has dissolved the rigid boundaries between professional time and personal time; banking must respond by offering flexible, adaptive, and context-aware services that align with this new rhythm of life.

Another lasting behavioural shift is the heightened sensitivity to financial vulnerability. The pandemic created a generation of customers who experienced sudden income shocks, credit stress, and uncertainty about their financial future. This has increased the demand for transparent products, flexible repayment structures, and proactive financial advice. Retail banks must respond by embedding empathy into their service architecture. Tools such as early warning analytics, hardship support pathways, and personalised guidance can help customers regain stability. Customers now expect banks to act as partners rather than creditors, offering foresight and flexibility when circumstances change. The nature of financial well-being is redefined as a result: customers value institutions that provide clarity, avoid surprises, and help them navigate uncertainty. By strengthening support systems and designing products that acknowledge real-life volatility, banks can reinforce trust and loyalty in an era where financial resilience is a shared priority between institutions and the communities they serve.

The rapid expansion of digital services during the pandemic has shaped new expectations around speed, transparency, and control. Customers now compare banking experiences not only with other financial institutions but with global digital platforms that offer seamless, intuitive interactions. This convergence of expectations requires retail banks to refine their service journeys to match the simplicity and clarity offered by leading technology companies. At the same time, customers demand greater visibility into how decisions are made, particularly in lending and credit assessments. The post-pandemic consumer is more aware of algorithmic processes and more concerned about fairness. To maintain confidence, retail banks must therefore explain decisions clearly, ensure transparency in criteria, and avoid jargon that alienates customers. Meeting this expectation strengthens credibility and mitigates the perception that digitalisation reduces human judgement. By combining clarity with speed, institutions can create an experience that feels both efficient and trustworthy—a central requirement in the hybrid era.

The behavioural legacy of the pandemic is not confined to customers; it extends to frontline staff whose roles have been redefined by hybrid service models. Staff now require a broader range of skills, from digital navigation to advisory capability and emotional intelligence. Their work must balance efficiency with empathy and problem-solving with regulatory responsibility. Training, support, and workplace design must adapt accordingly. Banks must recognise that frontline staff are custodians of trust who operate at the intersection of human and digital experience. When empowered, they can resolve complex issues, reinforce customer confidence, and translate institutional values into everyday actions. The pandemic demonstrated that customer satisfaction is shaped more by the quality of human support during moments of uncertainty than by the speed of routine transactions. As hybrid models become the norm, staff capability and well-being should be central pillars of institutional design. By investing in them, retail banks ensure that the behavioural shifts of the past few years become opportunities to strengthen, rather than weaken, the customer relationship.

Structural Barriers in Emerging Economies

Emerging economies face unique structural constraints shaping retail banking's trajectory. The most fundamental barrier is uneven infrastructure. In many regions, national payment rails, identity systems, and connectivity networks remain fragmented, creating large differences in service quality between urban and rural areas. Customers may have access to digital interfaces, yet lack reliable electricity, stable mobile coverage, or secure authentication mechanisms. This fragmentation forces retail banks to design operations around uncertainty rather than predictability. It also increases the cost of delivering services to communities that need them most. Financial institutions operate in an environment where technology potential is high but system reliability is low, requiring a hybrid model that blends physical presence, community outreach, and assisted digital tools. The first step toward inclusive retail banking is recognising that digital innovation must adapt to the realities of local infrastructure. Any architecture that assumes uniform connectivity risks reinforcing exclusion instead of reducing it.

This shows regulatory environments in emerging markets often evolve more slowly than technological innovation, creating gaps between what banks can build and what they are authorised to implement. Licensing regimes may be restrictive, national identity frameworks incomplete, and consumer protection rules inconsistent across regions. This regulatory misalignment introduces friction at every stage of the customer journey. At the same time, customers face uncertainty about their rights, obligations, and the safety of digital channels. These conditions make it difficult to scale hybrid models quickly. Institutions must invest in continuous regulatory interpretation, local partnerships, and adaptive risk models that can accommodate diverse legal contexts. When regulation is unclear, customers hesitate to adopt new tools, particularly those involving data permissions or digital lending. Strengthening regulatory clarity is therefore a critical enabler of hybrid banking, allowing institutions to deliver innovation without compromising trust or stability.

Another significant constraint is the persistent gap in financial literacy and digital readiness. In many emerging markets, the transition from cash-based habits to digital behaviour is not linear. Customers may adopt mobile wallets, but distrust savings products; they may receive government subsidies electronically yet withdraw them immediately in cash. These patterns reflect lived experience: economic volatility, informal lending, and reliance on personal networks. For hybrid banking to succeed, institutions must design services that align with these behavioural realities. Assisted digital models, low-tech interfaces, and community-led outreach can guide customers through incremental adoption journeys. The challenge is not only to provide tools but to build confidence in using them. The more customers understand the purpose, benefit, and safety of digital services, the more likely they are to transition from basic transactions to long-term financial engagement. Inclusion begins with literacy, and literacy must be woven into mainstream retail banking.

Economic volatility plays a major role in shaping trust in retail banking across emerging markets. High inflation, fluctuating interest rates, and irregular income patterns shape how customers perceive risk. Many individuals operate within informal or semi-formal economic systems that prioritise liquidity over long-term financial planning. As a result, they prefer products that minimise commitment and maximise flexibility. Traditional banking structures, designed around predictable customer behaviour, often do not accommodate these realities. To serve these communities meaningfully, hybrid institutions must redesign products with variable income, seasonal cycles, and price instability in mind. Flexible repayment schedules, micro-saving tools, and contextualised credit models can help bridge the trust gap. When retail banks demonstrate that their products are compatible with the volatility of everyday life, customers begin to see the institution not as an authority figure but as an accessible partner. As a result, understanding the importance of volitivity is essential for building sustainable financial inclusion.

Geographic dispersion remains one of the most difficult barriers for retail banks to overcome. Many emerging markets have vast territories with low population density, limited transport, and isolated communities. Building traditional branch networks in such geographies is expensive and often unsustainable. Digital channels offer part of the solution, but without local support structures, they cannot fully replace physical presence. Agent banking networks, community kiosks, and mobile service units become essential components of hybrid architecture. These models allow banks to extend reach while maintaining service quality. They also strengthen trust through human intermediaries who understand cultural nuances and local conditions. Geography is not simply a logistics challenge; it is a trust challenge. When customers see banking agents embedded in their communities, they are more likely to adopt formal financial services. Hybrid models that blend digital efficiency with human proximity can overcome the constraints of distance and create pathways to participation for underserved populations.

Cultural norms play a powerful role in shaping customer expectations and behaviour. In some regions, financial decisions are influenced by collective family structures rather than individual autonomy. In others, trust is built through long-standing personal relationships rather than institutional credibility. These cultural patterns can affect everything from borrowing habits to savings preferences and digital adoption. Retail banks must therefore avoid one-size-fits-all strategies. Hybrid banking must be culturally intelligent: it must adapt language, support, communication styles, and service models to the realities of each market. When digital tools replicate the relational warmth traditionally delivered in-person, customers feel confident experimenting with new channels. Culturally aligned design also prevents misinterpretation of risk and reduces friction in onboarding processes. In emerging economies, culture is not a variable; it is a structural element of the financial ecosystem. Understanding it is essential for designing inclusive and trusted retail banking systems.

Another important structural barrier is the limited depth of national credit infrastructure. Many emerging markets lack comprehensive credit bureaus, reliable scoring methodologies, or consistent data histories. This often results in large populations being classified as "thin-file" or "credit invisible," despite being economically active. Hybrid banking must therefore incorporate alternative data models that recognise non-traditional indicators of reliability, such as utility payments, transaction behaviour, or community references. These models enable institutions to widen access to credit responsibly without compromising risk standards. When customers experience fair and transparent credit processes, trust increases. The expansion of credit infrastructure is therefore a cornerstone of inclusive retail banking. It must be grounded in ethical design, with safeguards to prevent bias or misuse. By integrating alternative data and transparent criteria, retail institutions can convert invisible customers into active participants in the financial system.

Political and economic instability significantly influence the operating environment of retail banks in emerging economies. Currency fluctuations, policy reversals, and governance uncertainties can disrupt strategic planning and operational continuity. These conditions demand highly resilient operating models. Banks must invest in scenario planning, rapid response mechanisms, and diversified supply chains to mitigate volatility. Customers, meanwhile, evaluate institutions through the lens of stability. They gravitate toward banks that demonstrate consistency and protect their savings during turbulent times. Hybrid banking must therefore be anchored in operational and ethical reliability. Stability is not merely an institutional priority; it is a customer expectation shaped by lived experience. Retail banks that demonstrate resilience during shocks build lasting loyalty and position themselves as trustworthy anchors in uncertain environments.

In many emerging markets, competition from informal providers is a major structural challenge. Local moneylenders, community savings groups, and informal credit networks have deep roots and are often trusted more than formal institutions. They offer flexibility, immediate access, and relational familiarity that traditional banks sometimes lack. To compete effectively, retail banks must design models that respect and understand these informal ecosystems. Rather than replacing them, banks can integrate elements of flexibility, proximity, and cultural relevance into hybrid structures. Partnerships with community networks, simplified products, and rapid decision-making can help formal institutions gain relevance. When customers feel that formal banking aligns with their daily realities, they are more willing to transition from informal to formal participation.

The final structural barrier is the fragmentation of national digital ecosystems. In many emerging markets, fintech innovation grows faster than the banking system's ability to standardise platforms, create interoperability, or manage systemic risk. Multiple wallets, rails, and authentication methods compete simultaneously, confusing customers. Hybrid banking must play a unifying role: it must provide stable interfaces, integrated journeys, and trusted anchors that simplify the landscape. Standardisation, collaboration, and cross-sector governance are essential elements of this process. When customers see coherence across platforms, they experience digital banking as safe, predictable, and transparent. Overcoming fragmentation is therefore a foundational step toward sustainable hybrid architecture. By building systems that connect rather than divide, retail banks can transform digital ecosystems into trusted national infrastructure.

Institutional Perspective: A Global Lens on Customers, Society, and Being Human in Banking

Banking as a Civilisational Institution

Banks didn't emerge simply as financial mechanisms. They emerged because societies needed trusted systems to move value across time and between strangers. Trade, savings, lending, inheritance, and collective security all required institutional arrangements capable of reducing uncertainty between people who would never fully know one another.

Different civilisations built these arrangements differently. In Europe, banking became associated with commercial stability and governance. In the UK, it became embedded within everyday social life, carrying a sense of permanence beyond its financial function. Across Asia and the Middle East, trust was often reinforced through family, community, and state relationships rather than purely transactional ones.

These inherited expectations haven't disappeared. In some countries, digital banking has taken hold quickly because citizens already trust public systems broadly. In others, physical branches and face-to-face interaction still carry emotional weight because financial trust remains tied to visibility and human presence. Technological capability and felt legitimacy are not the same thing.

That distinction matters more as banking moves deeper into digital environments. Today, banking is experienced through interfaces, automated approvals, and invisible computational processes rather than buildings and paper. But the underlying human expectation is remarkably stable: people still want to know their savings are protected, their transactions will complete, and their institutions will hold firm when things go wrong.

Mobile-led financial systems across Africa show how quickly societies can adopt new infrastructure when traditional coverage has been limited. Latin America's history of inflation and volatility still shapes attitudes toward savings and cash. Highly integrated digital ecosystems in parts of Asia are blurring the lines between payments, identity, commerce, and banking. Meanwhile, Europe and the UK continue balancing digital transformation with long-standing expectations around regulation, privacy, and accountability.

Banking is never experienced purely as technology. It's experienced through social conditions, cultural memory, and institutional trust. As systems become more data-driven and ambient, the decisions shaping people's financial lives are increasingly made by automated processes operating in the background. Most people don't encounter these as "algorithms"—they encounter them through approvals, delays, or moments of unexplained exclusion.

This matters for legitimacy. Removing friction from banking doesn't remove the human need for reassurance or fairness. The institutions that endure will be those that combine technological capability with something harder to build: human trust, at scale.

What Human Beings Actually Want from Banking

Most people don't think about banking in terms of governance frameworks or digital infrastructure. They think about a salary arriving on time, a mortgage approved without unnecessary stress, access to savings during an emergency, or being able to speak to someone when something goes wrong. In everyday life, banking functions as a quiet structure of reassurance rather than a visible financial system.

That's why trust remains central even as products and technologies change. People rarely seek financial institutions for complexity—they seek stability, predictability, and confidence during uncertain moments. Technology can improve speed and access, but it doesn't replace the emotional expectations customers bring to financial relationships. Behind every digital interface, people are still looking for signals that the institution is reliable, fair, and capable of behaving responsibly when it matters.

These expectations surface most clearly under pressure. Fraud incidents, payment failures, sudden job loss—these expose whether customers experience a bank as supportive or distant. In those moments, people don't evaluate their bank by its technical sophistication. They evaluate whether it seems reachable, accountable, and willing to respond clearly and fairly. Trust is tested not during smooth periods, but when things break.

How this plays out varies across societies. Where banking is integrated into fast-moving digital lifestyles, customers prioritise speed and accessibility. Where older populations are large, or institutional trust has historically been uneven, physical presence and interpersonal interaction still carry real weight. Closing a branch may look like operational modernisation from one angle and feel like institutional abandonment from another.

Increasingly, customers also expect institutions to absorb complexity rather than pass it on. Open banking, embedded finance, and AI-assisted servicing may be operationally efficient, but customers still expect things to be understandable and accountable. Nobody wants to navigate a fragmented ecosystem of responsibility where no institution appears clearly answerable when a dispute arises. Simplicity and recourse become forms of trust in themselves.

This is especially important as algorithms take on more influence. Credit decisions, fraud monitoring, customer segmentation—these increasingly happen through automated systems beyond visible human judgement. Customers don't experience this abstractly. They experience it through a declined application, a frozen account, or an unexplained delay. Without meaningful explanation, these moments aren't felt as operational efficiency—they feel like opacity and lost recognition.

The tension between efficiency and reassurance may define banking's next decade. Systems will keep getting faster and more integrated. But human beings will keep expecting the same things they always have from trusted institutions: reliability under uncertainty, clarity in complexity, and the confidence that someone, somewhere, is accountable when things go wrong. The banks that endure will be those capable of delivering both.

How Banking Feels Different Across Societies

Digital transformation may look global at the level of technology, but the human experience of banking remains deeply local. Trust is shaped by history, culture, economic memory, regulation, and institutional maturity—and these vary enormously.

In the UK, banking carries a strong sense of continuity despite rapid change. Customers may criticise service standards or branch closures, yet most still interact with major institutions through inherited assumptions of permanence and systemic stability. Even when satisfaction fluctuates, structural institutional trust tends to remain embedded through regulation and historical expectation.

Across Europe, customers increasingly expect financial institutions to demonstrate ethical responsibility—around sustainability, data protection, and inclusion—alongside operational performance. Banking is not just a financial relationship; it's part of broader questions about institutional legitimacy in society.

Ireland adds another dimension. Community finance, cooperative traditions, and credit unions continue shaping how many people understand trust and accessibility. Particularly outside major urban centres, banking relationships remain tied to local visibility and community presence—expectations that differ sharply from centralised, platform-driven models.

In North America, banking is often experienced through scale, competition, and consumer credit culture. Advanced products and digital innovation coexist with a more transactional, commercially fragmented relationship between institutions and individuals—distance that becomes especially apparent during disputes or financial stress.

Singapore operates differently again. Banking, payments, identity, and public digital systems function as interconnected institutional ecosystems, creating high expectations around reliability and consistency. Customers experience banking less as a standalone relationship and more as part of a broader digitally coordinated environment.

Across the Gulf, rapid modernisation is reshaping how societies interact with financial systems—younger populations, mobile-first behaviour, and state-led transformation are accelerating change. But these shifts sit alongside strong expectations around personal trust and relationship banking. Getting the balance right between technological ambition and social legitimacy will be central to the region's financial future.

In Africa, mobile financial systems expanded not because traditional infrastructure was strong, but because telecommunications became more accessible than branch networks. Innovation often came from practical necessity rather than institutional transformation. Trust is more closely tied to accessibility and everyday usability than to brand identity or legacy structures.

Latin America carries the imprint of historical inflation, volatility, and political disruption. Many customers prioritise flexibility and liquidity not because current banking performance is poor, but because collective economic memory—passed across generations—shapes how people approach institutions today.

China represents perhaps the most integrated example of platform-based financial life. Payments, commerce, identity, and banking increasingly operate within a single digital ecosystem. Banking isn't a distinct institutional relationship; it's woven into daily life. That creates powerful efficiency, but also serious questions around data governance, concentration, and algorithmic authority.

These differences matter because trust doesn't globalise as easily as technology. A digital process considered efficient in one society can feel impersonal or exclusionary in another. The future of retail banking requires more than scalable technology—it requires understanding how different societies experience institutional legitimacy, fairness, and reassurance.

Being Human in an Age of Algorithmic Life

Banking is entering a period where many of its most important decisions are no longer visible to the people they affect. Financial access, fraud controls, credit assessments, onboarding, and risk evaluation are increasingly shaped by systems operating invisibly in the background. Customers don't encounter these as algorithms—they encounter them through moments of approval, refusal, delay, or unexplained exclusion.

This is more than modernisation. It marks a shift in how people experience institutional authority. Decisions once explained through personal interaction are now communicated through automated notifications and procedural outcomes. Many customers may no longer know—or be able to find out—whether an important financial judgement was made by a person, a policy, or a synthetic decision system.

For institutions, the advantages are real. Fraud detection runs continuously across millions of transactions. Risk systems flag anomalies in real time. Credit decisions take seconds. These capabilities improve efficiency, consistency, and scale across increasingly complex financial environments. But the human experience of these systems is often messier than the operational story suggests.

People don't evaluate institutions purely on technical accuracy. They evaluate whether the institution feels fair, reachable, and accountable when outcomes materially affect their lives. A frozen account, a declined application, or an unresolved fraud dispute carries emotional consequences far beyond the operational event. Without explanation or recourse, these experiences don't feel like efficiency—they feel like abandonment.

How people respond to automated systems also varies across societies. Where trust in coordinated institutions is already high—Singapore, parts of Northern Europe—automation tends to be accepted more readily. Where institutional trust has historically been fragile or uneven, highly automated decision-making can generate suspicion and a fear of exclusion. The same technology produces very different social reactions depending on context.

Age shapes this further. Younger people who grew up within digital ecosystems often accept automation as normal. Older and more vulnerable customers may continue associating trust with human accessibility and interpersonal reassurance. For many of them, the inability to reach a real person during financial stress doesn't just create inconvenience—it intensifies genuine feelings of confusion and institutional abandonment.

AI adds another layer. As systems become capable of interpreting behaviour, anticipating activity, and automating servicing at scale, many customers will interact more frequently with synthetic institutional systems than with identifiable human beings. This raises important questions—not only about governance, but about the future emotional relationship between institutions and the societies they serve.

People generally tolerate automation when outcomes feel fair and systems seem reliable. Trust weakens when systems feel opaque, unchallengeable, or emotionally indifferent. A negative outcome accompanied by explanation and visible accountability is far easier to accept than the same outcome delivered impersonally through a process that offers no recognition and no route to challenge.

That's the central tension banking must navigate: systems will keep moving toward greater automation because scale, fraud complexity, and regulatory pressure all demand it. At the same time, people will keep needing what is fundamentally relational—reassurance during uncertainty, dignity during vulnerability, and confidence that accountability exists when decisions become consequential.

The deeper challenge isn't whether banks become more algorithmic. That's already happening. The challenge is whether institutions can preserve human legitimacy within environments increasingly shaped by invisible systems and automated judgement.

Why Institutional Architecture Will Matter More

Technology will remain an important enabler of banking's future. But the defining question may not be technological at all. It may be institutional: which financial systems can sustain trust, resilience, and human confidence within increasingly complex digital societies?

This question is becoming more pressing because the environment surrounding financial institutions is growing structurally more unstable. Cyber threats are escalating. Fraud has been industrialised across digital ecosystems. Geopolitical fragmentation is reshaping payment systems and economic relationships. AI is accelerating capability while introducing new forms of opacity and governance risk. And customers simultaneously expect instant, seamless access to everything.

In this environment, institutional architecture—governance, accountability, resilience, risk culture, customer protection—becomes the mechanism through which institutions hold together under pressure. Customers rarely see it directly, but they experience its consequences constantly: through reliability, responsiveness, and institutional behaviour during moments of uncertainty.

Financial systems are also becoming more interconnected. Payments, identity, lending, compliance, cloud infrastructure, fraud monitoring, and embedded finance increasingly operate within integrated ecosystems rather than isolated institutional environments. A failure in one component can affect customer confidence across multiple layers simultaneously. Institutional resilience is no longer just about individual banks—it's about the stability of interconnected digital infrastructures that societies now depend on.

Different societies will face these pressures differently. The UK and Europe must balance digital innovation with governance discipline and public accountability. Parts of Asia and the Gulf will focus on scalability, infrastructure integration, and state-supported coordination. North America's highly competitive ecosystem will continue prioritising innovation speed while confronting growing concerns around cyber risk and algorithmic accountability. In emerging economies, the stakes are often highest—financial infrastructure is directly tied to inclusion, economic mobility, and public confidence in broader institutional life.

When operational failures occur—outages, fraud events, payment disruption, algorithmic bias—the consequences extend beyond immediate financial loss. They can weaken confidence in digital financial systems broadly. Trust, once destabilised, is slow to rebuild because people experience financial systems not only through logic but through emotional memory and perceived vulnerability.

AI will intensify these questions further. As it assumes greater responsibility across customer servicing, credit assessment, and risk management, institutions may become more operationally intelligent while simultaneously becoming harder for customers to interpret. The more invisible institutional systems become, the more institutional trust matters. There's a paradox at the centre of future banking architecture, and it won't resolve itself.

People rarely think about institutional architecture during stable periods. They become conscious of it the moment something goes wrong—a failed transaction during travel, a blocked account in an emergency, an unresolved fraud case, an inability to reach anyone when it matters. At those moments, invisible infrastructure becomes intensely personal. The question isn't whether the system is sophisticated. It's whether the institution is dependable, and whether accountability still exists within an automated environment.

Ultimately, the future of retail banking may rest on a deceptively simple question: can institutions continue making human beings feel economically secure within societies that are becoming progressively more digital, automated, and complex? The answer will shape not only banking, but the broader relationship between institutions, technology, and society.

Reflection

The reinvention of banking institutions is ultimately a story about recognising change before it becomes unavoidable. Across the ten sections and subsections in this chapter, a clear pattern emerges: customer expectations are evolving faster than institutional structures. Branches, once the centre of gravity, are now part of a wider ecosystem. Digital channels, once optional, have become the primary mode of engagement. Trust, once built through familiarity, must now be earned through transparency, consistency, and responsible design. These shifts are not temporary responses to technology cycles or economic shocks; they represent lasting changes in how people manage money, seek advice, and evaluate reliability.

At its core, this transformation is ultimately experienced at the level of the customer. Structural shifts in architecture, trust, inclusion, and behaviour only become meaningful when they translate into clearer decisions, safer interactions, and more dependable outcomes for individuals and communities.

The chapter highlights that the forces reshaping banking institutions are structural, not seasonal. Behavioural shifts triggered by the pandemic accelerated trends that were already visible: the rise of remote engagement, the expectation of 24/7 service access, and a stronger emphasis on financial resilience. The reinvention of banking institutions therefore requires institutions to understand context deeply and design models that respect the diversity of customer needs across geographies and demographics.

A recurring theme across the chapter is the importance of coherence. Hybrid architecture requires more than digital tools and physical touch points. It must be a unified operating model that blends efficiency, inclusion, and trust. The lessons from behavioural change, infrastructure gaps, and shifting customer priorities emphasise that retail institutions must move from reactive upgrades to deliberate structural redesign.

As banking enters a new decade of transformation, relevance will belong to institutions that recognise hybridity as a discipline, not a trend. Reinvention is not a single project; it is a continuous process of aligning purpose, capability, and trust. This chapter sets the foundation for the book's broader argument: the future of retail banking institutions will be built by organisations that design with intent, operate with resilience, and serve with humanity.

Framework: Retail Reinvention Architecture: Five Structural Anchors

Retail Reinvention Architecture: Five Structural Anchors

This framework diagnoses the structural readiness that shapes the reinvention of banking institutions. It consolidates the insights from all five pillars of the chapter into a single, practical model that senior leaders, regulators, and practitioners can use to diagnose readiness for hybrid banking.

1 Distribution Shift

Retail banking must transition from branch-centric delivery to an integrated hybrid model. Physical and digital channels must operate as one system rather than parallel infrastructures. Presence means availability, consistency, and context-aware service across all channels.

2 TRUST REDEFINED

Institutional trust is increasingly determined by transparency, data handling, operational reliability, and customer support in moments of stress. Trust requires evidence: clear decisions, fair processes, and predictable service quality.

3 INCLUSION–COST BALANCE

The legacy cost-to-serve model no longer aligns with the need for broader participation. Retail institutions must adopt architectures that allow inclusion at scale without creating economic strain. Hybrid designs must lower barriers while supporting sustainability.

4 BEHAVIOURAL TRANSFORMATION

Post-pandemic behavioural shifts have created a hybrid consumer: digital for convenience, physical for reassurance. Retail banks must design journeys that allow customers to move seamlessly between channels based on need, comfort, and complexity.

5 STRUCTURAL REALITIES OF EMERGING MARKETS

Infrastructure limitations, cultural norms, informal systems, regulatory inconsistencies, and geographic dispersion require adaptive hybrid models. Systems must recognise local constraints while enabling national participation and trust.

Purpose of the Framework

This chapter's framework establishes the foundational architecture for the rest of the book. It shows that retail banking cannot be reinvented through digital tools alone; it must be rebuilt through an integrated approach to trust, distribution, inclusion, behaviour, and structural context.

Table 1.2 Checklist: Reinvention Readiness

Template: Retail Reinvention Mapping

No.	*Dimension*	*Current State*	*Risk / Gap*	*Target State*	*Owner*
1	Institutional Structure	Product- and channel-led organisation	Fragmentation, internal silos, poor customer alignment	Customer journey–aligned operating model	CEO / COO
2	Customer Relevance	Services designed around legacy assumptions	Declining engagement, loss of relevance	Behaviour-led service design	Chief Customer Officer
3	Trust Architecture	Trust built inconsistently across channels	Erosion of confidence, reputational risk	Deliberate trust-building across journeys	CEO / Board
4	Inclusion Model	Limited focus on vulnerable segments	Financial exclusion, regulatory exposure	Inclusive, accessible service design	Head of Inclusion / Compliance
5	Cost vs Sustainability	Short-term cost optimisation focus	Long-term instability, service erosion	Balanced cost-to-serve with sustainability	CFO
6	Behavioural Alignment	Internal processes drive experience	Customer friction, drop-offs	Operating model aligned to behaviour patterns	COO
7	Channel Continuity	Disconnected channel experiences	Repetition, customer frustration	Seamless cross-channel continuity	CIO / COO
8	Institutional Adaptability	Slow response to change	Strategic rigidity, competitive disadvantage	Agile, responsive institutional design	CEO / Strategy Head
9	Governance and Accountability	Siloed decision-making	Lack of ownership, delayed execution	Clear cross-functional accountability	Board / Executive Committee
10	Readiness for Reinvention	Incremental improvement mindset	Failure to transform structurally	Willingness to redesign core architecture	CEO / Board

Bibliography

Bank for International Settlements (2021). *BIS Annual Economic Report*. Bank for International Settlements.

Deloitte (2023). *Insights on Digital Banking Maturity and Beyond Banking Models*. Deloitte Insights.

European Central Bank (2022). *The Digitalisation of Retail Banking and Implications for Supervision*. European Central Bank.

McKinsey & Company (2022). *Global Banking Annual Review 2022*. McKinsey Global Banking Practice.

OECD (2020). *The Future of Finance: Open, Connected, and Inclusive*. OECD Publishing.

Schein, E. H. (2017). *Organizational Culture and Leadership*. 5th Edition. Wiley.

World Bank (2022). *Global Findex Database 2021: Financial Inclusion, Digital Payments, and Resilience in the Age of COVID-19*. World Bank.

World Economic Forum (2023). *Insights on the Future of Global Fintech and Inclusive Growth*. World Economic Forum.

2 The Rise of Hybrid Banking

Context

Hybrid banking has become the anchor of modern retail-banking architecture because it provides what neither fully digital nor fully physical models can achieve on their own: continuity, relevance, and resilience across diverse customer needs and economic conditions. The shift towards hybrid is not a marketing idea or a technology-led trend—it is a structural response to how people actually engage with money, services, and institutions. Customers today expect the speed of digital channels, the clarity of self-service journeys, and the reassurance of human support when something goes wrong. They want flexibility in how they access their bank, but they also want predictability and trust. Hybrid banking brings these expectations together by connecting physical infrastructure, digital systems, and operational workflows into one architecture that behaves consistently across all touchpoints. It enables institutions to retain their community presence while operating with the efficiency, scale, and intelligence that digital channels provide.

This shift also reflects a deeper behavioural reality. Customers do not distinguish between channels; they expect the institution to function as one coherent system. Any gap between physical and digital delivery is experienced as a failure of the institution, not as a limitation of a specific channel. Hybrid banking therefore becomes a discipline of removing these gaps so that service feels continuous, predictable, and accountable across every interaction.

Across the world, the move toward hybridity has accelerated as regulators, governments, and central banks place stronger emphasis on accessibility, resilience, and customer protection. Markets with high digital penetration—such as Singapore, the Nordics, and the UK—are redesigning their branch strategies to ensure continued access for older adults, small businesses, rural communities, and vulnerable groups. At the same time, regions like India, Kenya, Brazil, and Indonesia are demonstrating how hybrid models can bridge infrastructure gaps through agent networks, shared digital platforms, low-cost micro-branches, and mobile-based identity systems. The common theme is clear: hybridity is emerging as the most inclusive way to deliver financial services at scale. It reduces operational pressure on branches, lowers cost-to-serve, and improves service

DOI: 10.4324/9781042021765-3

consistency across channels while maintaining the human connection that remains central to retail banking.

At the same time, regulators are increasingly focused on outcomes rather than channel presence alone. Accessibility, fair treatment, fraud protection, and service continuity are now assessed across the full customer journey. Hybrid models are therefore expected not only to extend reach but to ensure that customers are protected, informed, and supported consistently, regardless of how they access the institution.

From an institutional perspective, hybrid banking transforms how banks organise themselves internally. Traditional branch-centric structures were built for linear workflows, physical paperwork, and manual verification. Digital-only models demand advanced data governance, high investment in cybersecurity, and constant channel monitoring. Hybrid banking requires both—and more. It requires end-to-end service design where data flows cleanly across systems, where channels reinforce each other rather than compete, and where frontline staff are equipped to operate confidently in both physical and digital environments. Institutions must modernise their cores, strengthen interoperability, integrate cloud-based workflows, and ensure that risk teams, technology teams, and operational units are aligned around one architecture. This is not an IT upgrade; it is organisational redesign embedded into day-to-day operations.

This transformation also introduces heightened exposure to fraud, financial crime, and operational risk. As customer journeys span multiple channels, vulnerabilities can emerge at the points of transition, particularly where identity, authentication, or data visibility are inconsistent. Hybrid institutions must therefore embed fraud awareness, real-time monitoring, and coordinated response mechanisms into the architecture itself, ensuring that protection is continuous rather than channel-specific.

Hybrid banking also changes the economics of delivering retail services. Digital channels reduce processing cost and provide scale, but they require strong security controls, resilient infrastructure, and continuous updates. Physical channels are more expensive to operate but are essential for building trust, handling complex cases, and serving communities where digital uptake is uneven. Hybrid banking allows institutions to distribute cost intelligently—shifting simple transactions to digital platforms while preserving human-led, advisory-driven interactions in branches. This balanced model improves productivity, increases capacity, and supports more sustainable cost structures. It also gives banks the flexibility to adapt to demographic changes, economic cycles, and evolving regulatory pressures.

The chapter draws from international examples to show how hybrid models have already reshaped retail-banking strategies. Banks in India have leveraged hybrid platforms to provide millions of customers with assisted digital services in remote locations. African institutions have combined mobile money ecosystems with agent networks to create resilient, community-led hybrid systems. European banks are deploying advisory-first branches supported by omnichannel platforms and highly trained staff. Latin

American banks are using hybrid strategies to expand financial inclusion and reduce service fragmentation. These examples collectively demonstrate that hybrid banking is not a temporary adjustment but a long-term structural model suited to every market, regardless of economic maturity or technological readiness.

Hybrid banking is the natural evolution of retail finance. It aligns with customer behaviour, regulatory expectations, cost realities, and the need for resilient infrastructure. It is a design principle, not a channel strategy. The pillars in this chapter explore the operating models, infrastructure requirements, branch redesigns, cost architectures, and global case studies that define hybrid retail banking. They show why hybrid institutions outperform both digital-only and branch-dependent models, and they provide a practical blueprint for banks seeking to remain trusted, accessible, and competitive in an interconnected world.

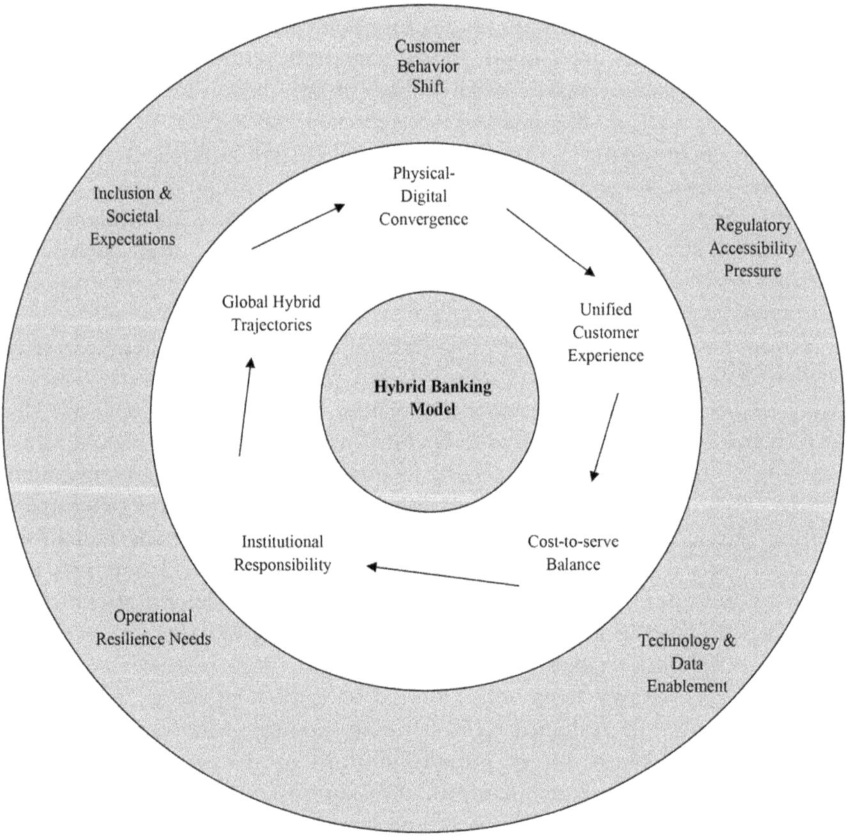

Figure 2.1 Hybrid Banking Architecture

Physical–Digital Integration Models

True physical–digital convergence requires banks to design service journeys that behave as one coherent system rather than a collection of disconnected channels. In most traditional models, the branch, call centre, mobile app, and website operate on separate platforms, supported by different teams and independent workflows. This creates friction when customers move between touchpoints—a transaction started online cannot be completed in the branch, authentication protocols differ, pricing changes across channels, and staff lack visibility of the full customer journey. Hybrid institutions correct this by redesigning the service architecture from the ground up, ensuring that data, authentication, decision logic, and service standards remain consistent regardless of the entry point. A customer initiating a request on the app should be able to complete it at the branch without repetition; a call-centre advisor should have full visibility of digital interactions; and frontline staff should access a unified interface that mirrors the customer's digital experience. This level of integration requires shared data frameworks, interoperable middleware, standardised application programming interfaces (APIs), and workflow automation that synchronises events in real time. It also requires organisational alignment—technology, operations, risk, and frontline teams working under the same service blueprint rather than isolated departmental mandates. The result is not only a smoother customer experience but also a more efficient operating model, where capacity is intelligently distributed, errors are reduced, and service requests are resolved faster. Banks that successfully achieve convergence find that customer satisfaction rises, operational costs decline, and trust improves, because customers feel recognised, supported, and understood across all channels without repeating themselves or navigating contradictory processes.

A hybrid bank can be effective only when the customer's identity is recognised instantly and consistently at all touchpoints. In the traditional setup, the customer's identity is verified in a different manner in each channel—passwords on the web, documents at the branch, voice verification at the call centre—resulting in inconsistencies, redundancies, and irritation for the customer. The hybrid model overcomes this by introducing a single identity layer that follows the customer everywhere. This implies that no matter which login method the customer uses—app, branch, video banking, or service centre—the customer's identity is recognised by the system through a single identity layer. The process becomes seamless, secure, and predictable. The single identity layer ensures that authentication rules, risk scores, preferences, and customer history are accessible to all employees and systems in real-time. This helps customer service staff to shift from mere authentication to advisory, reassurance, and problem-solving roles. It further enhances fraud prevention by closing loopholes that arise from inconsistent identity verification across multiple channels. Technically, this requires banks to invest in interoperable identity frameworks, tokenisation models, adaptive authentication tools, and carefully governed access controls. From a customer perspective, this reduces repetitive questions, unnecessary paperwork, and repeated disclosures. It also builds confidence—customers feel known, not processed. For hybrid institutions, unified identity becomes an asset that strengthens trust, supports operational resilience, accelerates service, and reduces risk across the entire ecosystem. When identity is harmonised, the whole service environment becomes more coherent, predictable, and human, reinforcing the bank's commitment to customer-centred design.

A unified identity layer also becomes a critical defence against evolving fraud patterns. Consistent identity recognition across channels reduces opportunities for impersonation, account takeover, and social engineering attacks. It ensures that risk signals are shared instantly across the institution, enabling faster detection and coordinated response. In hybrid banking, identity is not only an enabler of experience; it is a central control point for trust and security.

A defining feature of hybrid banking is the customer's ability to start a journey in one channel and complete it in another without repeating steps, re-entering information, or explaining their situation again. Journey continuity transforms fragmented service paths into a single, flowing experience that moves with the customer rather than forcing the customer to move according to the bank's structure. This requires every touchpoint—app, branch, call centre, chatbot, video desk, ATM, or kiosk—to operate on the same underlying data layer, sharing real-time updates, authentication status, and service progress. For example, a customer may begin a loan application on their mobile phone, upload documents through a web portal, seek clarification via chat, and finally visit a branch only for the final signature—each step building on the previous one without duplication. Journey continuity eliminates one of the most common sources of frustration in retail banking: repeating information. It also reduces operational costs by avoiding rework and improves risk management through consistent data handling. Technically, this relies on middleware integration, API orchestration, workflow synchronisation, and real-time data caching. Operationally, it demands well-trained frontline teams who understand exactly where a customer is in their journey at the moment of interaction. For customers, journey continuity represents respect for their time and intelligence. For the bank, it creates a coherent experience that strengthens satisfaction, trust, and conversion rates. In hybrid banking, providing journey continuity is no longer optional—it is the backbone of service reliability and a key differentiator in markets where digital fluency and expectations continue to rise rapidly.

Journey continuity also strengthens institutional accountability. When a customer's interaction is visible end-to-end, responsibility for service outcomes becomes clearer, reducing the risk of issues being passed between channels without resolution. This improves both operational discipline and customer confidence, as the institution is seen to "own" the journey rather than fragment it.

A hybrid bank cannot deliver a unified experience unless identity and authentication operate consistently across every channel. Customers expect the same level of recognition, security, and simplicity whether they walk into a branch, use an ATM, log in through a mobile app, or speak to a call-centre adviser. When security processes differ across touchpoints—for example, asking customers to remember multiple PINs, passwords, or verification steps—the experience becomes fragmented and risks increase. Consistent identity architecture ensures that the bank recognises the customer reliably, applies the same trust rules across channels, and maintains uniform fraud safeguards. This requires a layered authentication model built on device intelligence, biometrics, behavioural patterns, and risk-sensitive prompts that adjust based on context. For instance, high-risk transactions may trigger step-up verification, while low-risk interactions allow frictionless access. This consistency is what enhances customer confidence and institutional security. In the background, identity consistency uses common directories, API-connected verification processes, centralised fraud engines, and governance guidelines that outline the treatment of identity information from capture to storage and reuse. The frontline staff must also be educated to conform to digital identity processes, so that offline authentication processes are similar to online processes for customers. For customers, identity consistency provides a sense of familiarity and trust; for the bank, it eliminates discrepancies, prevents fraud, and ensures regulatory compliance for all channels. In hybrid delivery, authentication is not a layer but the glue that binds the entire service infrastructure together. A bank that masters identity consistency will create a seamless, secure, and predictable experience for the entire customer journey.

Hybrid banking requires institutions to harmonise customer journeys so that assisted channels (branch, call centre, video banking, field officers) and self-service channels (mobile app, internet banking, ATMs, kiosks) function as one continuous system rather than separate service tracks. Customers today begin a journey in one channel and complete it in another—checking eligibility on an app, seeking clarification from a call-centre adviser, uploading documents online, and finalising the transaction in a branch. When these pathways are not aligned, customers face repetition, conflicting information, and delays that undermine trust. Harmonisation demands a single view of the customer, standardised service scripts, shared data models, and real-time workflow visibility across teams so that any adviser can pick up a journey without asking the customer to "start again." It also requires unified service logic—identical pricing rules, eligibility criteria, documentation lists, and turnaround times, regardless of where the interaction takes place. Assisted channels must be equipped with the same real-time data that digital channels rely on, allowing advisers to guide customers effectively without manual checks or outdated information. Self-service tools must be intuitive enough to reduce dependency on human intervention while offering seamless escalation pathways when customers need reassurance or explanation. Harmonised journeys reduce operational burden, lower error rates, and improve customer satisfaction by eliminating friction that comes from channel fragmentation. For hybrid institutions, this is a structural discipline: every channel must reinforce the same experience, the same decisions, and the same institutional intent. When harmonisation is executed well, customers experience the bank as one integrated organisation rather than a set of disconnected departments.

Consistency in service quality is one of the defining tests of a mature hybrid institution. Customers expect the same clarity, speed, fairness, and reassurance whether they engage through an app at midnight or visit a branch on a busy weekday morning. However, many banks still operate with fragmented standards, where digital channels provide fast, rules-based decisions while physical channels rely on individual interpretation and manual judgment. This inconsistency creates confusion, erodes trust, and increases the likelihood of complaints or regulatory scrutiny. Achieving service consistency requires institutions to build a unified service framework that codifies how information is communicated, how decisions are explained, how exceptions are handled, and how vulnerabilities are identified across all touchpoints. Digital channels must embed human-centred principles such as clear language, contextual guidance, and escalation options, while physical channels must adopt the same data-driven tools and process automation used in digital journeys to reduce variation. Training becomes a critical enabler: frontline teams, call-centre agents, and digital-service designers must operate with a shared understanding of customer expectations, product regulations, and institutional values. This shared understanding is achieved through calibration meetings, journey audits, and cross-channel simulations, which help identify loopholes and ensure a consistent delivery mechanism across channels. Institutions need to develop feedback mechanisms that ensure issues identified in one channel are addressed in other channels as well. When service delivery is consistent, customers feel more confident about the integrity and reliability of the institution, no matter which door they use. Consistency is not just a superficial requirement for hybrid banks; it is a structural necessity.

Seamless transitions between channels are at the heart of a true hybrid model, yet most institutions underestimate the complexity involved. Customers want the freedom to begin a journey on one channel, pause, and resume elsewhere without repeating information, revalidating identity, or navigating inconsistent decision paths. In many banks, however, channels still operate as disconnected units, each with its own processes, data structures, and service logic. This forces customers to "start again" when moving from digital to physical or from self-service to assisted service, creating frustration and exposing operational inefficiencies. Seamless transition requires a unified orchestration layer that synchronises customer context—data inputs, documents submitted, risk flags raised, preferences captured, and previous steps completed—so that any staff member or system can pick up exactly where the journey paused. It also demands a standardised authentication framework that works smoothly across channels, reducing friction without compromising security. For frontline teams, this means having real-time visibility of the customer's digital interactions, enabling them to advise effectively and empathetically without duplication. For digital teams, it means designing journeys that anticipate moments where human support may be required and allow smooth handover without breaking the experience. Institutions must also invest in continuous testing, using real-user scenarios to identify points where transitions break or create confusion. When executed well, seamless transitions reduce dropout rates, shorten turnaround times, improve operational efficiency, and reinforce customer trust by demonstrating that the institution values their time and understands their behaviour. In a hybrid world, the ability to move effortlessly across channels is not a feature; it is a core architectural capability that differentiates mature institutions from those still operating in fragmented silos.

Unified data and context visibility is the backbone of hybrid integration, because a customer's experience is only as coherent as the information that supports it. When data sits in departmental silos—operations, risk, branches, call centres, or digital teams—service breaks down the moment the customer moves from one channel to another. They are asked to repeat information, resubmit documents, or re-explain issues that should already be visible across the institution. A hybrid-ready bank eliminates these pain points by creating a shared data fabric that captures each customer interaction in real time, regardless of where it originates. This means that when a customer uploads a document through the mobile app, a branch advisor sees it instantly; when a risk flag is triggered online, call-centre teams understand its context; and when a complaint is logged through an ATM interface or kiosk, it is reflected immediately in the customer's overall history. Such visibility needs three things: an integrated customer profile, a consistent event logging mechanism, and an intelligent orchestration engine that understands context, not just stores it. It also needs robust data governance for quality, access controls, privacy, and taxonomies so that data is meaningful and actionable. With real-time visibility, customer service representatives can make informed decisions, customers have a seamless experience, and risk teams have better visibility of emerging behaviour patterns. Unified data visibility also becomes the basis for advanced use cases like personalisation, proactive service, predictive risk analysis, and swift issue resolution. In the end, a hybrid institution that understands the customer in a consistent way across all channels is better positioned to build trust, overcome operational friction, and create experiences that feel integrated, intelligent, and human.

Human-assisted digital journeys have become a central design principle of hybrid banking because they recognise a simple truth: customers want the speed of digital systems, but they also want the reassurance of a human presence when something becomes unclear, complex, or emotionally sensitive. A hybrid-ready institution therefore blends automation with human support at precisely the right moments, making assistance a seamless extension of the digital pathway rather than an escalation or a failure point. In practice, this means embedding call back options inside apps, enabling co-browsing for complex form completions, offering video or voice advisory at key decision points, and allowing frontline teams to pick up a digital journey mid-stream with full context. Many global banks have already moved towards this model by introducing "warm-handovers" between bots and humans, designing assisted-digital kiosks inside branches, and enabling staff to guide customers remotely through authentication, onboarding, and transactions. The purpose is not to replace digital efficiency with human effort, but to ensure that customers never feel abandoned inside a system they do not fully understand. Human-assisted journeys also reduce operational errors, improve fraud detection through human intuition, and support vulnerable or digitally limited customers who might otherwise be excluded. Importantly, they help frontline teams evolve into hybrid advisors who use digital tools, behavioural data, and real-time insights to deliver more personalised service. When designed well, these journeys strengthen trust, reduce drop-off rates, and ensure that digital channels remain inclusive for all segments. By making human assistance an intentional part of the experience—not an afterthought—hybrid institutions create journeys that feel supportive, responsive, and deeply aligned with customer expectations in a world where technology and human judgement must work together.

End-to-end consistency is the ultimate test of hybrid maturity because it determines whether customers experience the institution as one coherent entity or as a collection of disconnected systems. In many banks, processes still vary by channel: different authentication steps for the app and the branch, inconsistent pricing, different documentation requirements, or uneven service responses depending on which unit handles the request. These inconsistencies erode trust, increase complaints, and create costly rework across operations. A genuinely hybrid institution removes this friction by standardising rules, policies, decision logic, and service flows across all touchpoints—digital, physical, assisted, or remote. This requires shared data foundations, unified customer profiles, centrally governed workflow engines, and cross-channel design teams that map journeys from start to finish rather than optimising channels in isolation. Leading banks achieve this through modular architecture, where the core engine executes decisions once, and every channel reflects the same outcome instantly. The front line also becomes an extension of the digital world, with employees having access to the same information that the customer views on their app, to ensure that there are no contradictions in the advice or eligibility criteria. Consistency is not just about process; it is also about tone, communication style, accessibility, and resolution options. Customers should feel the same level of clarity, transparency, and fairness whether they are interacting with a kiosk in a rural branch or a mobile app in a city centre. Consistency becomes more than just operational excellence for hybrid institutions; it becomes a promise of trust. When customers understand that the bank operates in the same way everywhere, their trust and dependence on the bank will strengthen, and their propensity to interact with the bank across channels will increase.

Hybrid Infrastructure Readiness

Hybrid infrastructure readiness begins with constructing a unified technical and operational backbone that can support both physical and digital channels with equal reliability and intelligence. Most retail banks still carry legacy cores, fragmented middleware, siloed data repositories, and channel-specific workflows that make convergence difficult. A future-ready hybrid institution must redesign this foundation around shared engines, interoperable platforms, and real-time data capability. This requires core-system modernisation—either through progressive renovation or modular replacement—so that customer journeys are not constrained by outdated batch processes or rigid product structures. The institution must also deploy strong middleware and API layers that allow systems, partners, and channels to communicate seamlessly, making it possible for the customer to start a journey on mobile, continue through assisted digital methods, and complete it in a branch without repeating steps or re-verifying information. Readiness for hybrid also requires a robust digital infrastructure, such as cloud-based ecosystems that enable elasticity, redundancy, and rapid time-to-market; cybersecurity platforms that safeguard data at every point of interaction; and workflow automation platforms that simplify high-volume processing. Governance is also essential, with technology, risk, operations, and business units needing to function under a single architecture, rather than multiple agendas. Successful institutions that build this foundation view infrastructure as a strategic asset, rather than an expense. They make investment decisions in line with customer behaviour patterns, regulatory needs, and organisational purpose, to ensure that infrastructure enables continuity, inclusion, and innovation. Hybrid banking will never be successful if the architecture is not stable, secure, interoperable, and designed to provide high-quality service across all channels.

Core modernisation is the structural engine that enables hybrid delivery to function at scale, and without it, even the most sophisticated front-end channels remain constrained by outdated architecture. Many retail banks continue to rely on legacy cores built for nightly batch processing, static product hierarchies, and paper-based control systems that cannot support real-time, multi-channel banking. Modernisation does not always require a full replacement; it can be achieved through progressive renovation, domain-based decoupling, or introducing a parallel, cloud-native core for specific product lines. What matters is that the institution moves toward a system capable of real-time data exchange, flexible product configuration, continuous deployment, and automated reconciliation. A modern core allows customer journeys to update instantly across channels, enabling branch staff, call-centre teams, and digital platforms to access the same information without delay or inconsistency. It also strengthens risk management by providing a single source of truth for credit exposures, transaction patterns, fraud indicators, and customer behaviour signals. Modernised cores support open-finance architectures through robust API frameworks, allowing banks to integrate fintech partners, regtech tools, and external data sources without compromising security. Importantly, core modernisation must be governed by disciplined change-management practices, strong migration controls, and clear board-level oversight so that risks are mitigated while benefits are realised steadily. The process is not purely technical; it reshapes workflows, team structures, and decision cycles across the institution. For hybrid banks, a modern core becomes the foundation for faster service, more accurate data, improved compliance, and the ability to innovate without destabilising operations. It is the backbone that transforms hybrid banking from a conceptual vision into a reliable, scalable institutional reality.

Data continuity is one of the most decisive factors determining whether a hybrid institution can operate with consistency, reliability, and customer confidence. In many traditional retail banks, data resides in fragmented systems—branch terminals, customer relationship management (CRM) tools, loan platforms, card systems, and digital channels—each updated at different times and governed by different rules. This fragmentation results in delays, mismatched records, duplicated queries, and service breakdowns that customers experience as friction or inconsistency. A hybrid-ready institution must treat data as a shared organisational asset rather than a departmental resource, ensuring that all channels draw from a unified, real-time data layer. This requires building an enterprise-wide data architecture that integrates core systems, middleware, analytics engines, and API gateways within one coherent framework. It also demands robust data-governance practices that clarify ownership, quality standards, lineage, retention periods, and security protocols. Seamless data continuity enables frontline teams to provide accurate information, empowers digital channels to resolve issues autonomously, and strengthens early-warning systems for credit, fraud, and operational risks. It also enables personalisation engines, workflow automation, and regulatory reporting by ensuring that the insights are timely and trustworthy. Notably, data continuity improves the customer experience by allowing customers to start a journey on mobile, modify it through call centre, and finish it in-branch without having to repeat information or face channel conflict. For hybrid banks, this continuity is not a choice but the building block for trust, efficiency, and resilience. A bank that has achieved data continuity is able to provide human and context-aware service across all channels, making it better positioned in a competitive and rapidly changing retail environment.

Data continuity also plays a critical role in fraud detection and prevention. Fragmented data environments often delay the identification of suspicious patterns, whereas unified data enables early detection, faster escalation, and more effective intervention. In hybrid institutions, data integrity therefore becomes both an operational and a risk-management priority.

Cloud migration has become one of the most important enablers of hybrid readiness because it shifts retail banks away from rigid legacy systems towards flexible, scalable, and resilient architectures. Traditional on-premise systems struggle with peak loads, real-time data needs, and multi-channel orchestration, leading to outages, delays, and limitations in service design. A hybrid-ready institution needs infrastructure that can expand or contract based on demand, support continuous deployment, and enable services to be delivered uniformly across mobile, web, branch, and partner channels. Cloud platforms—whether private, public, or hybrid—provide this elasticity, but migration must be undertaken with disciplined governance. Banks must assess application criticality, data sensitivity, latency requirements, and regulatory constraints before deciding which systems to re-platform, refactor, or retire. Cloud modernisation is not only a technical exercise; it is an operational and cultural shift requiring teams to adopt new ways of working, including automation, DevSecOps

(Development, Security, and Operations), real-time monitoring, and joint accountability between technology and risk functions. When executed well, cloud migration reduces downtime, strengthens cybersecurity controls, improves disaster recovery, and creates a backbone for API-led innovation. It also supports cost rationalisation by replacing heavy capital expenditure with more predictable operating models. For customers, the benefits are equally significant: faster service, fewer outages, smoother journeys, and more reliable access during periods of high demand. A modernised cloud-enabled infrastructure enables hybrid institutions to respond quickly to regulatory changes, competitive pressures, and evolving customer expectations. Ultimately, cloud adoption becomes a strategic foundation rather than a technology project—a prerequisite for delivering stable, trustworthy, and future-ready hybrid banking.

Interoperability is the backbone of hybrid infrastructure because a modern retail bank operates through a network of interconnected systems, channels, and external partners that must function as a single coherent environment. Legacy architectures were built in silos, with separate technology stacks for branches, ATMs, cards, mobile apps, and back-office operations. This fragmentation creates duplicated effort, inconsistent customer experiences, and operational risk. A hybrid-ready institution must instead design for interoperability at every layer—data, processes, security, authentication, and service delivery. This requires unified data models, shared taxonomies, API gateways, and middleware that allow systems to recognise and communicate with one another reliably and securely. Interoperability also extends to vendor ecosystems: cloud providers, payment networks, fintech partners, and identity-verification services must integrate seamlessly into the bank's architecture without creating single points of failure. The regulatory expectations also underscore this trend, with supervisors in the UK, EU, and Asia pressuring banks to provide end-to-end visibility over outsourced and interconnected environments. Interoperability is more than a technology challenge; it is an operating culture. It requires harmonious governance between IT, risk, operations, and product groups to ensure that any modifications in one system do not create risks or undermine service in another. When banks achieve interoperability, customer experiences become more seamless, operational expenses decrease, resilience enhances, and innovation cycles quicken. It enables the bank to deliver new services quicker, respond to market dynamics with agility, and deliver consistent quality on all touchpoints. In a hybrid world characterised by the constant interaction between physical and digital systems, interoperability emerges as a structural imperative—the engine that keeps the entire system intact and provides long-term dependability.

Cloud migration has become a defining component of hybrid infrastructure because it allows retail banks to operate with the flexibility, scale, and resilience required in a multi-channel environment. Traditional on-premise systems were built for predictable branch-centric traffic and linear processing patterns, but hybrid delivery demands capacity that can adjust dynamically to fluctuating digital volumes, real-time service expectations, and ecosystem-level integration.

Cloud adoption enables banks to deploy modular architectures, containerised applications, automated recovery protocols, and real-time monitoring dashboards that strengthen both availability and performance. However, cloud migration is not merely a technical upgrade; it introduces strategic questions around data residency, regulatory expectations, risk classification, and concentration exposure. Supervisors in the UK, EU, Singapore, and Australia increasingly expect boards to understand cloud-dependency risks and to demonstrate clear mitigation plans, including multi-cloud or hybrid-cloud arrangements to avoid over-reliance on a single provider. Operational teams must strengthen identity controls, encryption models, incident-response processes, and vendor-oversight frameworks to ensure that cloud environments remain secure and compliant. Cloud also changes the economics of technology investment: instead of large, infrequent capital outlays, hybrid institutions move toward continuous optimisation, monitoring consumption patterns and matching capacity to actual demand. Most importantly, cloud migration accelerates innovation. Banks can pilot new services quickly, scale them efficiently, and integrate emerging technologies without overhauling legacy infrastructure. For hybrid institutions, the cloud becomes the foundation that supports reliable digital services, strengthens resilience, and enables the organisation to adapt rapidly in a world where customer expectations and regulatory requirements evolve continuously.

Workflow automation is now central to hybrid readiness because it transforms fragmented, manual, and paper-driven processes into streamlined, reliable, and scalable operating flows. In a hybrid environment, customer journeys transition across digital, assisted-digital, and physical channels, and automation ensures that information moves with them seamlessly and without duplication. Modern retail banks increasingly deploy automated decision engines, straight-through-processing layers, intelligent routing systems, and rules-based workflows to reduce delays, standardise outcomes, and support frontline teams. This shift is not about removing human roles; it is about ensuring that human expertise is used where it adds the greatest value—advisory conversations, complex exceptions, financial-wellbeing support, and sensitive cases requiring judgment and empathy. Automation enhances risk control by minimising variability, ensuring auditability, and providing a uniform data trail across channels. Regulators require banks to show how automated processes are interpretable, audited for bias, and incorporated into a comprehensible governance structure. Operational resilience is enhanced as automated processes minimise reliance on specific employees, facilitate seamless scaling during peak periods, and are integrated with fraud monitoring, cybersecurity, and identity management. Notably, automation liberates employees from low-value activities and enables the organisation to redirect frontline staff to relationship-building and community outreach activities, which are critical in hybrid banking. In most cases, automation becomes the "invisible engine" that integrates physical and digital channels into a single operating system. Well-designed automation enables the creation of reliability, minimises cost-to-serve, and provides consistency that customers demand at all touchpoints.

Interoperability is one of the most difficult elements of hybrid readiness because most retail banks operate with a mix of legacy platforms, mid-life systems, and newer digital components that were never originally designed to work together. A hybrid institution requires these systems to exchange data in real time, support consistent authentication, and maintain uniform decision logic across channels. Banks are increasingly investing in middleware, API gateways, and unified data models that allow older systems to "speak" to modern architectures without compromising stability. Interoperability also reduces operational risk by ensuring that customer instructions, risk assessments, fraud signals, and service updates flow seamlessly between applications. Without it, even strong digital channels can collapse under strain because they depend on back-end systems that remain fragmented. Many institutions face the challenge of integrating vendor systems, cloud environments, branch platforms, and mobile applications into a single operational rhythm. Regulators across the UK, EU, and Asia now expect banks to demonstrate clear plans for interoperability, particularly when customer journeys rely on multiple vendors and external partners. Operational resilience frameworks increasingly include cross-system dependency mapping, latency monitoring, and failover testing across these mixed environments. Interoperability is not only a technology concern; it is a governance issue requiring joint ownership between technology, risk, and operations teams. For hybrid banks, achieving interoperability determines whether they can scale services safely, deliver consistent experiences, and respond quickly to customer needs. When built deliberately, interoperability creates an institutional "nervous system" that enables the bank to function as one integrated entity rather than as a collection of disconnected parts.

Hybrid banking depends on uninterrupted service across channels, and this requires continuous resilience testing that goes far beyond traditional annual disaster-recovery exercises. Institutions must establish operational assurance routines that simulate real-world stress conditions—cyberattacks, sudden transaction spikes, vendor outages, cloud-service degradation, and branch-level disruptions. Regulators in the UK, EU, Singapore, and Australia increasingly expect banks to demonstrate that systems can withstand concurrent failures from both internal and third-party sources. Continuous testing enables banks to identify structural weaknesses such as slow failover times, hidden system dependencies, unsupported legacy components, or lack of frontline readiness. It also strengthens operational discipline: teams across technology, risk, operations, and customer service learn how to respond with clarity and coordination during service interruptions. Modern resilience frameworks include red-team simulations, chaos-engineering exercises, real-time monitoring dashboards, and joint reviews with cloud and fintech partners. For hybrid institutions, the resilience testing process also needs to include customer-facing environments like ATMs, kiosks, call centres, assisted digital areas, and mobile apps, to ensure that service recovery plans are effective across the entire ecosystem. Operational assurance is not just about protecting uptime; it is about protecting trust. Customers trust institutions based on their ability to access funds, conduct transactions, and get support during times of stress. By integrating resilience processes into the fabric of operations, rather than viewing them as compliance activities, institutions can build the muscle memory to handle crises with a cool head and clear communication. Continuous assurance becomes a critical capability for hybrid banks to remain relevant in the long term.

Resilience must also be visible to customers. During service disruptions, the clarity, speed, and transparency of communication directly influence trust. Hybrid institutions are therefore expected to manage not only system recovery but also customer reassurance, ensuring that individuals understand what is happening and how their interests are being protected.

Effective hybrid infrastructure cannot function without governance structures that align technology, risk, operations, and frontline delivery around one shared architectural vision. This shows how traditional governance models—often siloed between IT committees, risk forums, operational leaders, and business units—are insufficient for the integrated demands of hybrid banking. To deliver consistently across physical and digital channels, institutions need governance that recognises infrastructure as a strategic asset rather than a technical function. This means establishing cross-functional bodies that review system performance, customer-journey continuity, resilience gaps, data behaviour, and vendor dependency in a single view. It also requires boards and executive committees to strengthen digital literacy and operational understanding, ensuring that investment decisions reflect long-term architectural needs rather than short budgeting cycles. Regulatory expectations, particularly in the UK, EU, Singapore, and India, increasingly emphasise board accountability for technology risk, meaning executives must demonstrate coherent oversight of cloud arrangements, API exposure, cyber posture, and system resilience. Strong governance frameworks define clear roles for technology owners, risk specialists, customer-experience teams, and third-party managers, preventing duplication, fragmentation, and gaps in responsibility. They also enforce disciplined prioritisation: resolving foundational infrastructure issues before launching new features, ensuring that hybrid delivery is stable, predictable, and safe for customers. When governance is aligned with architecture, hybrid institutions can scale confidently, integrating new partners, expanding into new markets, and modernising legacy components without destabilising operations. Governance alignment therefore becomes the final enabler of hybrid readiness—the mechanism that turns infrastructure from a constraint into a strategic advantage.

Smart Branch Configurations

In a hybrid retail-banking environment, the branch is no longer a standalone service point; it becomes an intelligent node within a wider, integrated delivery system. This section explains how modern branches must be designed to complement digital channels rather than replicate them, focusing on advisory depth, trust-building, complex problem resolution, and community presence. As routine transactions shift to mobile and online platforms, branches evolve into multi-purpose environments where customers receive human support for financial planning, complaints resolution, vulnerability-related assistance, and life-stage decisions. Smart branches rely on embedded technology—workflow engines, device orchestration, self-service zones, sensors, and data-enabled service prompts—to enhance efficiency while ensuring that human interactions remain meaningful. They serve as the physical hub for customers who want reassurance, particularly for older consumers, small businesses, and customers experiencing financial difficulties. This pillar emphasises that branch intelligence requires the integration of data in the background: advisers need to see digital footprints, transaction history, risk indicators, and customer preferences in real-time to provide personalised advice. It also discusses how smart branches help with operational resilience by acting as a crisis centre for customers during digital outages and crises. In emerging markets, smart micro-branches have a different role, acting as hybrid service delivery points where digital inclusion is complemented by assisted digital services. The guiding philosophy is that branches do not compete with digital channels but complete them. When designed smartly, they help build trust, inclusion, and visibility, leading to a hybrid architecture that balances customer needs while managing cost-to-serve.

Branch formats are no longer uniform; they are strategic assets that help banks align physical presence with local demand, behavioural patterns, and cost realities. Hybrid-ready institutions deploy a diversified network of formats—flagship advisory centres, neighbourhood micro-branches, kiosk-led touchpoints, mobile branches, co-located branches inside partner premises, and pop-up service units—each serving a distinct purpose within the overall architecture. Format diversity reduces fixed costs while increasing accessibility, enabling banks to operate in dense urban markets, underserved rural areas, transport hubs, and community locations with equal relevance. The key is intentional design: flagship centres specialise in relationship-led services and complex financial needs; micro-branches optimise throughput through automation and lean staffing; kiosks extend reach in areas with limited footfall; and pop-ups enable seasonal or event-driven presence. Also worth highlighting is how format strategy depends heavily on data—footfall patterns, demographic clusters, risk indicators, fraud patterns, customer journeys, and local economic activity. Hybrid banks use these insights to determine where advice is needed, where automation suffices, and where assisted-digital support offers the most value. Importantly, format diversity also strengthens resilience: if one channel faces disruption, alternatives remain active, maintaining continuity of service. In emerging markets, diverse formats allow banks to blend human contact with digital support, ensuring that customers with limited digital literacy are not excluded. The strategic message is clear: hybrid institutions must design a portfolio of branch formats that collectively reinforce trust, widen access, and optimise cost—a deliberate architectural decision that shapes long-term viability.

Advisory-centric branches have emerged as one of the most important anchors of trust in hybrid retail banking, offering depth, reassurance, and human clarity at moments where digital channels cannot fully resolve complexity. Such modern banks are redesigning selected branches into advisory hubs that specialise in mortgages, small-business support, financial planning, debt restructuring, and multi-generational savings needs. These hubs are configured with private consultation spaces, collaborative tools, secure document-exchange systems, and integrated appointment journeys that link seamlessly with digital pre-work carried out by customers. By moving routine transactions into automated or assisted-digital areas, advisory branches can focus more on contextual dialogue, vulnerability analysis, and advice that deepens relationships. The advisory approach also remedies a systemic flaw in purely digital models, where customers may need reassurance, risk interpretation, or guidance through regulatory or life-stage complexity. In these cases, branches serve as the organisational nexus where trust is restored, misinterpretations are clarified, and choices are made with confidence. There are many international examples, from the UK, Europe, Singapore, India, and Latin America, where banks have migrated significant numbers of their branch network into advisory-led models with robust digital integration. These branches also serve a people function, as they are home to experts, facilitate cross-training, and serve as learning spaces for frontline staff adjusting to new hybrid realities. At the end of the arc, advisory-led branches improve the hybrid offer by combining human knowledge with digital smarts, ensuring that the organisation stays relevant, understanding, and trustworthy even as customer journeys become increasingly automated.

Case Study: Santander Work Café—Redesigning the Branch as an Advisory and Community Anchor

Santander introduced the Work Café model to reposition branches away from transaction-heavy counters and towards a hybrid format combining advisory banking support with community and small-business engagement. The concept originated in Chile in 2016 and was subsequently rolled out across multiple markets, including the United Kingdom.

In the UK, Santander opened its first Work Café in Leeds in July 2019, describing it as a new branch experience designed to blend banking services with collaborative space and customer engagement. The format supports hybrid banking objectives by keeping physical presence relevant through advisory-led interactions, while digital channels handle routine servicing and self-service needs.

Branch zoning has become a core architectural principle for hybrid retail institutions, enabling banks to redesign physical spaces with precision, purpose, and efficiency. An example is how modern branches are divided into clearly defined zones—self-service areas, assisted-digital stations, advisory rooms, community spaces, and back-office micro-processing pods—each configured to remove friction and align service paths with customer intent. Self-service zones handle high-volume, low-complexity tasks using ATMs, cash recyclers, biometric kiosks, and document-upload devices, reducing queue pressure and freeing staff capacity. Assisted-digital stations support customers who can use technology but require reassurance, bridging confidence gaps without escalating workload for frontline teams. Advisory rooms provide privacy and depth for mortgage consultations, SME discussions, wealth conversations, and vulnerability-sensitive interactions. Community spaces, used in several Asian and African markets, allow branches to host workshops, financial-literacy events, and local-partnership sessions that reinforce inclusion and institutional legitimacy. Micro-processing pods replace large back-offices with compact spaces where verification, exception handling, and high-risk checks can be completed without disrupting the customer environment. Effective zoning requires meticulous workflow design: each zone must connect seamlessly with digital pre-stages, central operations, and risk-control functions. Sensors, people-flow analytics, and queue-management systems help branches anticipate demand, optimise staffing, and maintain service quality across peaks. This highlights that zoning is not a cosmetic redesign; it is a structural shift that turns branches into intelligent service ecosystems—balancing efficiency with empathy, speed with safety, and consistency with local relevance. When executed well, branch zoning reduces cost-to-serve, improves customer satisfaction, and strengthens the core hybrid architecture of the institution.

Assisted-digital workflows have become a defining feature of modern hybrid branches, ensuring that customers who are willing to use digital tools—but need reassurance or step-by-step guidance—are not left behind. Banks design these workflows by combining intuitive interfaces with highly trained frontline staff who act as digital enablers rather than transaction processors. The strongest models begin before the customer arrives: pre-staged journeys allow basic information to be captured through apps or websites so that branch teams can focus on advisory and completion rather than data entry. Once in the branch, assisted-digital desks equipped with tablets, biometric authentication, and shared-screen tools allow customers to complete onboarding, mandate updates, service requests, or loan applications with light-touch human support. Staff are trained to guide rather than take over, empowering customers to build confidence for future digital self-service. The workflow is connected to real-time system backbones so that any action taken at an assisted-digital desk reflects immediately across channels, preventing duplication or re-entry of information. For vulnerable customers - older adults, migrants, low-literacy users - these workflows reduce anxiety and create a safe transition into digital banking. The branch also benefits operationally: assisted-digital models lower physical queue volumes, reduce paper processing, and spread footfall more evenly across the day. Strong governance is essential: staff must follow data-protection protocols, escalation pathways, and accessibility guidelines to ensure consistency and safety. When well-designed, assisted-digital workflows become a powerful bridge between physical reassurance and digital autonomy, strengthening trust and enabling banks to operate hybrid models with higher quality, lower cost, and deeper customer inclusion.

Hyperlocal branch models have emerged as an essential feature of hybrid retail banking, especially in communities where trust, familiarity, and continuity still hold deep value. Such banks design compact, community-anchored branches that operate with lean staffing, high digital enablement, and strong local relevance. These branches typically occupy smaller footprints but remain strategically positioned near markets, transport nodes, or civic centres where footfall reflects daily community life. Their operating logic is simple: maintain human presence where it matters most while shifting routine transactions to digital channels. Inside, the layout prioritises advisory zones, assisted-digital desks, and flexible workstations instead of traditional counters and large back-office areas. Staff are selected not only for technical capability but for cultural fit, language familiarity, and relationship-building skills that help embed the branch in local networks. Hyperlocal branches often partner with community organisations, local businesses, and social initiatives to understand evolving needs - whether that involves financial-literacy workshops, SME guidance, or collaborative support for vulnerable customers. The model also supports more intelligent cost management, with lower rents, fewer full-time employees, extended use of multi-functional devices, and lower cash handling infrastructure. In rural or low-access areas, hyperlocal branches can be integrated with agent networks or mobile banking units, ensuring that the service continues even in areas with variable connectivity. Governance is also essential, with risk management policies, cash management, and cyber security measures needing to align with corporate requirements despite the compact nature of the model. Hyperlocal branches, when delivered effectively, become trust anchors, ensuring that the bank's presence is reinforced and that hybrid banking remains meaningfully connected to the communities it serves.

Assisted-digital branch experiences have become a defining element of hybrid retail banking because they bridge the gap between full digital autonomy and traditional counter-based service. This illustrates how banks are redesigning frontline roles, processes, and branch layouts to help customers confidently navigate digital journeys while still feeling supported by a human presence. Assisted-digital zones typically include self-service terminals, guided kiosks, and mobile-device stations where staff can coach customers through transactions, security steps, authentication procedures, or form submissions. The goal is not to push customers toward digital adoption but to ensure that the experience feels safe, personalised, and reassuring. Many customers—especially older adults, first-time users, or those with language barriers—struggle not with the technology itself but with confidence, clarity, and trust. Assisted-digital service models respond to these challenges by ensuring that digital interactions are never isolating; a frontline colleague is always available to co-navigate the journey. Banks that excel in this model invest heavily in staff capability, training frontline teams to understand user interface (UI) flows, troubleshoot common errors, and explain risks such as phishing or fraud in simple language. This approach also improves operational efficiency: assisted-digital transactions reduce wait times, free up advisory staff for more complex needs, and reduce operational strain on cash-heavy counters. Importantly, it strengthens inclusion—customers who might otherwise avoid digital channels gain confidence through guided practice, eventually becoming more independent. For hybrid banks, assisted-digital experiences embody the central philosophy of the model: use technology to enable scale and speed, but keep human reassurance at the heart of service delivery. When executed well, this approach transforms branches into learning spaces that build customer trust while easing the institution's transition toward modernised service architecture.

Smart branch design cannot be standardised across all markets; it must reflect the cultural, economic, and infrastructural realities of each region. This entails leading banks tailoring branch formats to local needs rather than replicating a single global model. In mature urban markets such as the UK, Singapore, and Western Europe, branches are shifting toward compact advisory centres, equipped with appointment-led service, video-conferencing pods, and automation-heavy layouts that minimise cash handling. These settings prioritise efficiency, privacy, and multi-channel integration, recognising that customers often begin their journeys online before seeking human guidance. In contrast, emerging and semi-urban markets across India, Africa, and Latin America often require more relationship-led formats. Here, branches remain primary trust anchors, and customers depend on face-to-face interactions for reassurance, dispute resolution, or complex financial decisions. Smart design in these regions focuses on blending automation with culturally familiar touchpoints, such as staffed service counters, community information boards, or multilingual support areas. Infrastructure challenges—intermittent internet connectivity, low digital literacy, or cash-based economies—also influence the adoption of branch technology, including offline-enabled systems, biometric authentication devices, and hybrid-energy solutions. In some markets, "hub and spoke" branch strategies are used, supplemented by micro-branches or agent networks in rural areas, to ensure that geographical challenges do not equate to exclusion. Through design adaptation, banks can avoid creating sterile or inaccessible spaces and instead design branches that reflect the tempo of the communities they serve. Differentiation in regions is thus not merely superficial; it is a deliberate approach that enhances inclusion, improves customer acceptance of hybrid models, and ensures that service architecture is aligned with actual lived behaviour in different environments.

These models have become one of the most effective ways to bridge the gap between traditional branch services and fully digital channels, particularly for customers who are willing to use technology but may not have the confidence, skills, or access to navigate it independently. Banks are thus redesigning branch environments to provide guided support that helps customers transition smoothly into digital behaviours without feeling excluded or overwhelmed. Assisted-digital zones typically include self-service kiosks, tablet stations, and biometric authentication points staffed by trained advisors who can help customers complete transactions, set up mobile banking, update KYC (Know Your Customer) details, or learn to use new features. The value of this model lies in its ability to build long-term capability: once a customer learns how to execute tasks digitally, the dependency on physical counters reduces naturally, lowering cost-to-serve and freeing frontline staff for advisory work. These models also help resolve common barriers such as language limitations, accessibility needs, or fear of making mistakes on digital platforms. Banks in the UK, EU, India, and East Africa are reporting strong outcomes when assisted-digital spaces are integrated with multilingual content, step-by-step visual guides, and queue-management systems that direct customers to the right support. Importantly, assisted-digital services also strengthen trust, as customers experience technology in a human-supported, error-free environment. This reassures hesitant customers—particularly older adults or low-digital-literacy segments—that technology is safe, reliable, and aligned with their needs. By embedding human-assisted digital pathways inside branches, banks accelerate hybrid adoption in a respectful and inclusive manner, ensuring that nobody is left behind during the transition to a more technology-enabled retail banking ecosystem.

Branches are increasingly evolving into experience-driven problem-solving centres where customers receive deeper advisory, reassurance, and resolution support that digital channels alone cannot provide. This explains why the modern hybrid branch is being repositioned as a space where complex needs are addressed through structured conversations, financial education, service recovery, and personalised guidance. As routine transactions migrate to apps and ATMs, branch staff can focus on matters that require human judgement—such as onboarding vulnerable customers, managing bereavement cases, restructuring loans, resolving fraud concerns, or assisting small businesses with documentation and compliance requirements. These interactions build trust in ways that digital channels cannot replicate, because customers associate face-to-face engagement with accountability, empathy, and institutional seriousness. To support this shift, many banks are redesigning branch interiors to include semi-private advisory pods, community-learning spaces, and flexible zones for workshops on financial literacy, digital security, or product planning. The design also incorporates smart tools—such as interactive screens, real-time dashboards, and secure document-sharing stations—to allow customers to move seamlessly between in-person and digital steps within the same visit. This reinforces the hybrid promise: customers receive the reassurance of human support with the efficiency of digital workflows. Globally, banks adopting this model report higher satisfaction scores, lower complaint volumes, and stronger loyalty among both young and older customers. By transforming branches into centres of experience and problem-solving, institutions preserve their local presence while ensuring that physical infrastructure remains relevant, purposeful, and closely aligned with the expectations of modern retail banking.

Channel Strategy and Cost Design

Hybrid banking forces institutions to rethink cost architecture from the ground up, moving away from fragmented budgeting across channels toward a consolidated model that reflects how customers actually move between digital, physical, and assisted pathways. This explains why traditional cost structures—where branches, call centres, and digital units operate with separate budgets and performance metrics—no longer support sustainable delivery. Instead, banks must design a unified cost framework that allocates investment according to customer journeys, risk exposure, infrastructure resilience, and long-term institutional purpose. Digital channels often appear cheaper at first glance, but they require continuous spending on cybersecurity, authentication layers, fraud controls, data storage, and cloud optimisation to remain reliable at scale. Physical channels carry fixed costs but remain essential for vulnerable groups, complex cases, SME advisory, and trust-building. As a result, hybrid banks combine the strengths of cost-effective automation with high-impact human service, ensuring that resources are allocated where they add the most value. Today, the best banks use analytics to identify which journeys are best automated, which need human-driven support, and which need mixed models. This enables them to remove duplication, minimise bottlenecks, and rebalance their workforce according to demand patterns, rather than historical models. Cost design becomes a strategic exercise driven by transparency: banks must be aware of the real cost-to-serve, forecast peaks and pressures, and align spending with strategic agendas such as inclusion, resilience, and trust-building. When done correctly, hybrid cost design improves financial sustainability while improving service delivery—proving that efficiency and empathy are not mutually exclusive, but rather complementary components of a unified framework.

This requires institutions to make disciplined choices about where automation delivers genuine value and where human engagement remains essential. This explains why cost efficiency cannot be achieved simply by shifting services to digital channels; instead, banks must understand the behavioural, emotional, and financial contexts that shape customer needs. Automation is highly effective for routine, low-risk, and repetitive activities such as balance checks, payments, basic credit applications, or fraud alerts. These processes benefit from speed, consistency, and lower marginal costs. However, moments of vulnerability—loan restructuring, bereavement services, financial distress, complex SME advisory, accessibility support for older customers—require human judgment, empathy, and contextual understanding. Banks that automate blindly often create hidden costs: increased complaints, regulatory scrutiny, service breakdowns, or reputational damage. Therefore, hybrid institutions allocate budgets to technology in a way that complements, rather than replaces, human capability. Many leading banks now implement "assisted digital" models where frontline teams use digital tools to guide customers who are uncertain or digitally limited, improving both experience and efficiency. Cost design also incorporates the time and resources needed to train staff to operate effectively in hybrid environments, ensuring they understand digital journeys, fraud risks, and channel interdependencies. Optimising this balance results in a blended service model where automation handles volume and people handle complexity. This reduces overall cost-to-serve, strengthens trust, and ensures that hybrid banking remains grounded in human relevance. It reinforces the principle that efficiency in retail banking is not the elimination of human contact but the thoughtful distribution of human effort where it has the most impact.

This balance also has ethical implications. Decisions that affect customers must remain explainable, fair, and accountable, particularly where automated systems are involved. Hybrid institutions must ensure that human oversight is retained where judgment, discretion, and responsibility are required, reinforcing both regulatory compliance and public trust.

This succeeds when institutions optimise capacity across channels rather than allowing each part of the system to operate independently. This also involves how banks calculate demand patterns, peak usage times, and customer behaviour to align staffing, digital workflows, and physical formats in a coordinated manner. Capacity optimisation begins with understanding the distinct roles of each channel: branches handle advisory, reassurance, due diligence, and complex problem-solving; call centres manage urgency, clarification, and exception handling; and digital channels handle routine high-volume interactions. When banks map these patterns accurately, they can reduce bottlenecks, shorten processing times, and deploy resources more intelligently. Predictive analytics is increasingly being employed by many institutions to forecast foot traffic, digital traffic spikes, seasonal credit demand, or customer churn triggers, enabling them to staff and time their opening hours accordingly. Capacity design also involves understanding interdependencies, where a rise in mobile app failures drives call centre queues, branch network closures drive digital traffic, and new fraud prevention measures drive unforeseen customer inquiries. Hybrid institutions, therefore, create buffer capacity at key system points and implement dynamic routing to enable customers to flow seamlessly between channels without duplication or irritation. This level of readiness ensures that operational resilience is not left to chance. Leading banks today integrate cost models with capacity analysis, ensuring that resource allocation is aligned with institutional purpose rather than mere cost optimisation. When done properly, capacity optimisation drives productivity, builds customer trust, and enables a service infrastructure that can absorb shocks without sacrificing experience or safety. It ensures that hybrid delivery is stable, predictable, and aligned with the actual behaviour of the people it seeks to serve.

Cost-to-serve intelligence is a central element of hybrid banking because it allows institutions to understand the true economics behind each interaction and design channels that are both efficient and fair. Modern banks analyse cost drivers across physical, digital, and assisted-digital environments, recognising that cost efficiency is not achieved by simply shifting everything online or reducing branch presence. Instead, effective cost design requires granular visibility into where value is created, where effort is duplicated, and where risks accumulate. For example, while digital transactions have low marginal cost, they require substantial investment in cybersecurity, fraud management, app stability, and system redundancy. Branches, although more expensive per interaction, deliver trust-building, identity verification, and community presence that digital channels cannot replicate. Cost-to-serve intelligence incorporates variables such as staff capacity, infrastructure load, digital adoption rates, customer vulnerability levels, and regulatory-compliance requirements. Leading institutions now use integrated dashboards that connect financial metrics with operational data, making it clear how delays, errors, or capacity gaps in one channel impact the economics of another. This helps leadership avoid blanket cost cuts and instead make targeted shifts—such as simplifying processes, relocating low-value tasks, or automating repetitive work. It also supports more informed decisions on where to open, close, or redesign branches; where to reinforce digital journeys; and where hybrid models offer the best return on effort. Ultimately, cost-to-serve intelligence ensures that hybrid banking remains sustainable, balancing the need for prudent financial management with an unwavering commitment to accessibility, inclusion, and service quality across customer segments.

Balancing investment between physical and digital channels is one of the most strategic decisions in hybrid banking, because it determines how institutions allocate capital, manage risk, and serve customers with differing levels of digital confidence. Successful banks avoid the common pitfall of treating investment as an either–or choice: instead, they recognise that physical and digital channels reinforce each other, creating a complete service architecture that supports trust, accessibility, and operational strength. Digital channels require ongoing investment in app design, cybersecurity, cloud resilience, data analytics, and AI-enabled service flows, all of which underpin speed and scale. At the same time, physical channels require thoughtful investment in modern layouts, self-service equipment, staff capability, and branch technology that reduces operating costs while enhancing the advisory role. Leading institutions allocate investment using a portfolio approach: the digital sphere receives funding for automation, predictive capacity planning, and fraud controls, while branches receive targeted capital for format optimisation, energy efficiency, and community-facing services. This well-rounded investment strategy enables banks to remain relevant across generations, from serving digitally savvy customers who value independence to catering to older or more vulnerable customers who rely on human confirmation and physical verification. It also enables banks to be resilient, such that if one channel is disrupted, the other channel will remain intact. The regulatory requirements also support this well-rounded strategy, as regulators continue to emphasise the importance of operational resilience across all channels and accessible service for all segments. By using the hybrid perspective in designing investment decisions, banks can mitigate risks associated with single-channel exposure.

Optimising cost-to-serve across customer segments is central to hybrid banking because different groups use channels in fundamentally different ways, creating variations in operational load, service expectation, and economic contribution. Successful institutions move away from uniform cost assumptions and instead design nuanced cost models that reflect real patterns of behaviour. Younger, digitally fluent customers often prefer app-based interactions, reducing branch footfall but increasing demand for real-time support, cyber protection, and automated journeys. Older adults, small businesses, migrants, and financially vulnerable customers may require deeper advisory engagement, in-person verification, and multilingual or assisted-digital services. Each of these needs carries a different cost structure. Leading banks analyse transaction-level data, behavioural clusters, and customer-journey friction points to understand where costs are generated and where efficiencies can be gained without compromising fairness or access. They redesign processes so that simple, predictable tasks move into automated flows, while human capital is focused on complex queries, relationship building, and reassurance. Institutions also calibrate fees, service tiers, and advisory models based on transparent value exchange rather than blanket pricing. Importantly, cost optimisation is not about reducing service options; it is about rational allocation. Hybrid design enables banks to shift capacity dynamically—digital for scale, physical for trust—ensuring that each segment receives the right support at the right cost. Regulators increasingly expect this clarity, especially for vulnerable groups. By optimising cost-to-serve intelligently, banks create a balanced economic model that supports inclusion, enhances customer satisfaction, and strengthens long-term institutional health.

Balancing automation with human advisory capacity is one of the most critical design choices in hybrid banking, because it determines how institutions manage scale while preserving the human touch that underpins trust and confidence. An important distinction is how banks assess which customer interactions can be shifted to automated or self-service channels without diminishing quality, and which interactions must remain advisory, relationship-led, and judgement-based. Routine activities—balance checks, basic queries, document uploads, product information, status tracking—can be automated reliably, reducing wait times, operational workload, and error rates. However, moments that involve vulnerability, financial stress, regulatory sensitivity, or long-term planning require human presence, empathy, and reassurance. Leading banks build capacity models that map emotional, regulatory, and financial complexity across journeys to determine the right mix of automation and human advisory. Automation is not treated as a cost-cutting instrument but as a tool that frees frontline staff to focus on higher-value roles: supporting vulnerable customers, giving personalised guidance, resolving complex cases, and strengthening relationships. This balance also requires redesigning training models: staff must be equipped to handle escalations from digital channels, interpret data insights, and guide customers across blended journeys. Institutions that get this balance right see measurable improvements in satisfaction, operational resilience, and financial performance. Those that automate indiscriminately risk alienating customers, increasing complaints, and losing the trust that differentiates successful retail banks from purely digital alternatives. An effective hybrid model therefore deploys automation strategically, strengthening—not replacing—the human advisory capability that sustains long-term institutional legitimacy.

Optimising channel costs through capacity alignment is central to the long-term viability of hybrid retail banking, because it determines how institutions distribute workload, manage peak demand, and prevent unnecessary duplication across physical and digital environments. Pertinent here is how banks use data-driven capacity modelling to understand when and where customers prefer digital access, when they require assisted support, and when branch-based engagement delivers the highest value. Rather than reducing physical channels blindly, leading institutions study hourly, daily, and seasonal demand patterns to design staffing, routing, and automation flows that match real customer behaviour. Digital channels may absorb high-volume, low-complexity interactions, but they also generate new types of demand—clarifications, escalations, and assisted journeys—that must be planned into capacity models. Branches remain essential for advisory services, complex transactions, SME support, KYC verification, and customer segments that rely on human reassurance. Cost optimisation, therefore, is not about pushing customers into one channel but aligning the nature of demand with the capability of each channel. Banks use unified dashboards to monitor wait times, abandonment rates, digital drop-offs, and assisted-service triggers so they can reassign workloads dynamically across teams. A well-designed hybrid model avoids the trap of underutilised branches, overloaded call centres, or stretched digital teams, all of which inflate cost-to-serve. Instead, it builds an adaptive system where capacity flexes intelligently based on demand signals. When executed well, this approach reduces operating costs, improves service quality, and enhances institutional resilience, demonstrating that financial efficiency in hybrid banking is achieved not through cuts, but through precise architectural alignment between customer needs and channel capability.

Cost transparency has become a strategic discipline for hybrid retail banks because it clarifies the true economics of service delivery across every channel and forces institutions to confront inefficiencies that were previously hidden within departmental budgets. Modern banks are thus moving away from aggregated cost centres—where branch, digital, call-centre, and back-office expenses are often blended—toward granular, activity-based costing that reveals the precise cost of account opening, cash transactions, onboarding journeys, complaint resolution, digital escalations, SME advisory, and other key service flows. When leadership has this level of visibility, they can redesign processes with accuracy rather than assumptions. In many markets, institutions have discovered that badly designed digital journeys inflate total cost because they generate repeat contacts, branch rework, or manual verification. Conversely, some physical interactions remain highly efficient when tied to local knowledge, trust, and advisory depth. Cost transparency enables banks to strike the right balance, shifting investment from low-impact activities into areas that strengthen trust, inclusion, and institutional credibility. It also supports board-level decision-making: directors can challenge cost patterns, understand channel-level return on investment, and assess whether hybrid delivery is being executed responsibly. Regulators increasingly expect banks to demonstrate that pricing, accessibility, and service levels reflect fair cost structures—particularly for vulnerable groups and rural communities. Transparent cost architecture also helps frontline leaders, who gain a clearer understanding of how operational choices influence financial sustainability. When adopted as a disciplined management practice, cost transparency transforms hybrid banking from a set of disconnected channels into a coherent, financially responsible system where decisions are evidence-led, customer-centric, and aligned with long-term institutional health.

Hybrid retail banking succeeds only when efficiency and accessibility are treated as equal design priorities, rather than competing objectives. Thus, institutions must build cost models that protect universal access while enabling operational discipline across channels. In many markets, digital pathways deliver lower marginal cost but require substantial ongoing investment in cyber controls, authentication models, cloud resilience, and fraud-prevention capabilities. At the same time, branches—although more resource-intensive—remain essential for advisory interactions, vulnerable populations, SMEs, and communities that depend on human judgment and reassurance. Balancing these realities means banks must carefully design which services belong where: routine, high-volume processes should migrate to self-service and assisted-digital flows, while complex or emotionally sensitive interactions remain anchored in physical or hybrid formats. Accessibility also varies geographically: rural regions, low-connectivity markets, and ageing populations require tailored branch formats, community anchors, or partner networks to maintain trust and inclusion. This highlights that efficiency should never be achieved by withdrawing service from those who rely on it most. Instead, leading banks across Asia, Europe, and Africa are adopting segmented delivery models that match cost structures to actual customer needs, behaviours, and risk profiles. Boards play a critical role in ensuring that efficiency programmes do not erode a bank's social licence, long-term reputation, or regulatory standing. When executed thoughtfully, hybrid delivery aligns cost optimisation with institutional purpose, allowing banks to sustain profitability while meeting their responsibilities to all customer groups. The result is a balanced, future-ready architecture where efficiency strengthens—rather than weakens—a bank's commitment to fairness, accessibility, and public trust.

Global Case Studies in Hybrid Success

India offers one of the clearest demonstrations of hybrid banking at population scale. Large public and private sector banks have learned to combine digital public infrastructure with high-density branch and ATM networks, business correspondents, and local partner outlets. Unified Payments Interface (UPI), Aadhaar-based identity, and account aggregators sit on one side of the hybrid equation; small branches, rural service centres, and feet-on-street relationship teams sit on the other. The result is an ecosystem where a customer may open an account using e-KYC, receive government benefits directly into their account, transact through QR codes, yet still walk into a small branch or service point for reassurance, dispute resolution, and more complex needs. For banks, the Indian experience shows how hybridity can dramatically reduce cash-handling costs and improve reach without abandoning physical presence. It also underlines the importance of disciplined process design: the strongest institutions have built clear escalation paths, shared data flows across channels, and robust fraud controls that protect both low-income and affluent customers. India proves that hybridity is not a luxury for rich markets; it is a necessity for large, diverse populations where digital and human channels must work in tandem to achieve inclusion.

Kenya's experience with mobile money, especially M-Pesa and related services, is often cited as a digital success story, but its real strength lies in its hybrid structure built around human anchors. Telecom-led platforms provide the digital rails for payments, remittances, and basic savings, yet the system depends on thousands of agents located in shops, kiosks, and market stalls. These agents handle cash-in, cash-out, and customer support, effectively functioning as micro-branches embedded in local communities. Banks that have partnered with mobile-money ecosystems have extended credit, savings, and insurance products using transactional data, while continuing to operate traditional branches for SMEs and higher-value customers. The Kenyan case demonstrates how hybrid models can emerge from non-traditional starting points: a telecom operator, not a bank, provided the initial digital backbone, and banks adapted by layering regulated financial services on top. It also shows that trust in digital services is often built through face-to-face interactions, especially in low-literacy or cash-heavy environments. For global retail institutions, Kenya's lesson is clear: hybrid success depends less on who owns the channel and more on how effectively banks integrate with local networks, share risk, and maintain a strong human interface alongside fast, ubiquitous digital rails.

In the United Kingdom, hybrid banking has developed through careful branch rationalisation combined with commitments to service continuity. Major banks have reduced high-street branch footprints in response to changing customer behaviour and cost pressures, but they have also invested heavily in mobile apps, online banking, contact centres, and specialist hubs for vulnerable customers. Shared-banking hubs and community access points have begun to emerge, where multiple institutions provide face-to-face services from a single location. Regulatory expectations around access to cash, consumer protection, and operational resilience have forced banks to design structured transition plans rather than purely cost-driven closures. The UK model shows how hybrid banking in mature markets must address legacy infrastructure, long-standing customer habits, and strong regulatory scrutiny. Banks that have managed the shift well typically combine clear communication, phased migration of services, and targeted support for those less comfortable with digital tools. They invest in "assisted digital" roles within branches and call centres to help customers build confidence. The UK experience underlines that hybrid success in developed economies is judged not only by efficiency gains but by how fairly institutions manage change for older adults, rural communities, and financially fragile households.

Singapore illustrates how a small, highly connected market can use hybrid banking to build sophisticated ecosystem platforms. Leading banks operate flagship branches that provide advisory, wealth management, and SME services, while day-to-day transactions have moved decisively to digital channels. National initiatives such as PayNow, Singpass identity, and shared infrastructure for instant payments give institutions a common digital foundation. Banks differentiate themselves through integrated lifestyle platforms that blend banking, e-commerce, transport, and public-service access within a single app environment. Yet physical presence has not disappeared: branches and experience centres are used for complex conversations, cross-border needs, and relationship building with SMEs and affluent customers. The Singapore model shows how hybrid banking can be tightly integrated with national digital strategies, creating an ecosystem where banks, technology providers, and government agencies collaborate on common rails. It also demonstrates the value of disciplined risk management and cyber-resilience; regulators expect banks to treat digital operations with the same seriousness as core balance-sheet risks. For global institutions, Singapore's lesson is that hybrid success at the premium end of the market depends on deep ecosystem integration, seamless digital journeys, and selective but high-quality physical touchpoints.

Brazil offers a vivid example of hybrid banking in a large, volatile market with significant inequality. Traditional banks historically operated dense branch networks in urban centres, while many rural areas and low-income communities were underserved. Over the past decade, a wave of digital-first challengers has emerged, using low-cost apps and simplified accounts to attract millions of customers. Established banks responded by upgrading digital channels, partnering with agent networks, and redesigning branch formats into leaner service hubs. Regulatory support for open banking, instant payments (PIX), and financial inclusion has accelerated competition and encouraged interoperability. In practice, a Brazilian customer might open an account via a digital onboarding process, receive their salary into an app, and still rely on local agents or branches for cash transactions, dispute resolution, or credit discussions. The Brazilian case shows how hybrid models can thrive in markets with currency volatility, inflationary pressures, and complex risk profiles. Successful institutions combine strong digital propositions with flexible, community-based distribution and robust risk analytics. The lesson for global retail banks is that hybrid architecture can stabilise service delivery in uncertain environments, while opening new routes to previously excluded or informal-economy customers.

Across continental Europe, many cooperative and regional banks have adopted hybrid strategies that rely on shared infrastructure and strong local presence. Banking groups in countries such as Germany, France, and the Netherlands operate federated models where local institutions share central IT platforms, payment rails, and regulatory functions while retaining community-level governance. Hybrid delivery here combines well-equipped branches, regional decision centres, and comprehensive digital platforms that support everyday transactions, SME services, and cross-border payments. These banks use their cooperative identity and long-standing local relationships to maintain trust, while digital tools allow them to standardise operations and compete with larger commercial players. The European experience shows that hybrid banking does not always mean radical physical downsizing. Instead, it can mean re-purposing branches as advisory and SME hubs, supported by centralised processing and digital self-service for routine tasks. It also highlights the role of industry utilities and shared platforms in reducing technology costs. For global practitioners, Europe demonstrates how hybrid models can protect community banking values while delivering modern, digital convenience, especially when institutions are willing to collaborate on back-end infrastructure and risk management.

In the Gulf and wider Middle East, hybrid banking has evolved within relationship-centric cultures where physical presence and personal interaction remain highly valued, especially for affluent and corporate segments. Banks have invested heavily in mobile and internet banking for retail customers, enabling real-time transfers, bill payments, and remote account management. At the same time, flagship branches, lounges, and relationship-manager offices continue to play a central role in customer experience and brand positioning. Many institutions offer appointment-based advisory sessions, video-enabled relationship meetings, and blended service models where customers start a journey digitally and complete it face to face. Regulatory programmes around instant payments, digital identity, and open finance are gradually deepening the digital foundation. The regional lesson is that hybrid success in relationship-driven markets must honour cultural expectations around hospitality, privacy, and trust. Banks that perform well typically segment their networks carefully, using the digital arena for mass-market convenience while preserving high-touch channels for key customer groups. This reinforces the wider theme of the book: hybrid banking is not a single template, but an adaptive architecture that reflects local culture, economic structures, and regulatory maturity.

In North America, especially the United States, hybrid banking has been shaped by intense competition between large incumbents, regional banks, credit unions, and digital-only players. Big banks operate extensive branch networks alongside sophisticated mobile apps, integrating ATM fleets, call centres, and online platforms into unified service environments. Regional banks and credit unions often differentiate through community presence and personalised service, while investing in third-party digital platforms to keep pace. Fintechs have pushed the market towards faster account opening, fee transparency, and intuitive user experience (UX), forcing incumbents to modernise legacy systems and simplify products. The hybrid pattern that emerges is one where customers use apps for routine tasks, ATMs for cash and basic services, branches for advice and problem resolution, and contact centres for complex or urgent issues. The North American case demonstrates how competitive pressure can accelerate hybrid evolution but also expose weaknesses in operational resilience and customer protection when systems are fragmented. Institutions that manage the transition well invest heavily in API-based integration, data-driven insight, and streamlined processes, ensuring that every channel reinforces a consistent, trusted experience rather than operating as an isolated product silo.

Looking across India, Kenya, the UK, Singapore, Brazil, Europe, the Gulf, and North America, common patterns emerge that define successful hybrid banking. First, every strong case combines clear institutional purpose with practical design choices: hybridity is not pursued as a technology trend but as a way to serve communities more reliably and inclusively. Second, governance and risk management are consistently strong in high-performing examples; institutions treat digital operations, third-party dependencies, and data flows as core risk domains, not peripheral IT issues. Third, frontline capability is always central. Banks that invest in staff training, assisted-digital support, and clear escalation paths deliver smoother journeys than those that rely solely on self-service. Fourth, local context matters: agent networks in Kenya, open-data platforms in India, cooperative structures in Europe, and ecosystem apps in Singapore each show how hybrid design must be tailored to infrastructure, regulation, and social norms. These patterns distil into a simple message for practitioners: hybrid banking succeeds when technology, people, and governance are aligned around real customer lives, not internal product structures.

The global evidence on hybrid success carries clear implications for future retail-bank architecture. Institutions that wish to remain relevant over the next decade must move beyond pilot projects and isolated digital initiatives toward fully integrated structural design. This means building core systems and data platforms that treat every channel—app, web, branch, call centre, ATM, agent, and partner platform—as part of one coherent service fabric. It means designing branch networks as strategic assets rather than cost liabilities, with formats calibrated for local need, advisory depth, and inclusion goals. It also means adopting open standards, API-driven integration, and disciplined vendor governance to support ecosystem partnerships without losing control of risk. Finally, the case studies show that hybrid banking is a long-term commitment rather than a one-off transformation. Leadership teams must maintain a continuous improvement mindset, learning from incidents, customer feedback, and external shocks. When institutions internalise these lessons, hybrid architecture becomes more than a response to digital disruption; it becomes the backbone of resilient, trustworthy retail banking that can adapt to new technologies, regulations, and societal expectations over many years.

Institutional Perspective: A Global Lens on Customers, Society, and Being Human in Hybrid Banking

Why Human Beings Still Seek Physical Reassurance

Digital banking has transformed how people interact with financial institutions—mobile apps, real-time payments, biometric authentication, automated onboarding. Yet physical reassurance hasn't disappeared. That persistence isn't about slow adoption. It reflects something more enduring about human behaviour.

Financial decisions are bound up with security, identity, family, and vulnerability. During moments of stress or uncertainty, many people still seek visible institutional presence and human interaction, even within highly advanced digital systems. Convenience shapes routine behaviour, but reassurance matters more when circumstances become complicated or emotionally significant. Mortgage discussions, fraud disputes, bereavement cases, financial hardship—these carry psychological dimensions that transactional efficiency alone can't address.

This helps explain why fully digital banking hasn't displaced hybrid models across most markets. Customers may handle everyday transactions on their phones while expecting human support when situations get serious. Branch closures in the UK and Europe have sparked broader societal debates precisely because, for many customers—particularly older or vulnerable individuals—the local branch represents continuity and institutional visibility, not just a service point. Its disappearance can feel like withdrawal, even where digital alternatives technically exist.

The meaning of physical presence varies across societies. In Ireland, community finance and credit unions reflect trust grounded in local familiarity. Across parts of Africa, physical banking may remain important not only for trust reasons but because connectivity and digital infrastructure remain uneven. In Asia and the Gulf, rapid digital adoption coexists alongside relationship-based cultures where institutional reputation and personal confidence carry significant weight.

The pandemic made this clearer. Digital systems stayed operational, yet customers still sought direct confirmation from institutions during the uncertainty. Call centres, branches, and relationship managers became psychological anchors. Technological functionality didn't resolve emotional uncertainty—it just meant the infrastructure kept running.

As AI-assisted servicing and automated customer journeys become standard, this tension will grow. Automated systems handle procedural tasks well. They struggle with situations requiring explanation, discretion, or emotional reassurance. People continue seeking recognisable accountability when financial outcomes materially affect their lives.

Hybrid banking, then, isn't simply a transitional state between physical and digital. It reflects a recognition that trust operates across multiple forms of interaction. Customers move between apps, contact centres, branches, and relationship managers depending on the complexity or emotional stakes of a situation. The challenge for institutions isn't choosing one channel over another: it's ensuring trust moves coherently across all of them.

The Social Meaning of Banking Access

Banking access is typically measured through account ownership, digital penetration, branch density, or transaction volumes. These indicators matter, but they don't capture how access is actually experienced. Financial access isn't just about whether a service technically exists—it's about whether people feel capable of participating confidently, safely, and with dignity.

That distinction becomes more important as banking moves further into digital environments. For digitally fluent customers, digital banking feels intuitive. For others, access is shaped by age, confidence, education, geography, language, disability, or simple familiarity with financial systems. A service that appears accessible may still feel socially inaccessible to large parts of the population.

Ageing populations are reshaping what accessibility means in developed economies. Older customers may carry significant financial experience while struggling with authentication procedures, evolving interfaces, fraud alerts, and AI-driven customer journeys. In these situations, accessibility becomes about reassurance and institutional patience, not just technological availability.

Geography still matters too. Rural communities and smaller towns experience the withdrawal of physical banking infrastructure differently from urban centres. In parts of the UK and Ireland, branch closures carry symbolic weight—local institutions were never just service providers; they were visible parts of community and commercial life. For small businesses, elderly residents, or people with limited transport, reduced physical presence creates both practical and psychological distance.

In emerging markets, access carries deeper implications. Across Africa, mobile financial systems have expanded inclusion significantly by reducing dependence on branch networks. But access still depends on infrastructure reliability, device affordability, and trust in digital systems themselves. Financial inclusion here connects to telecommunications infrastructure and broader economic development as much as institutional strategy.

Migrants and internationally mobile people face a different set of barriers: unfamiliar regulatory environments, identity requirements, language obstacles, and documentation hurdles. For these individuals, banking access is intertwined with feelings of legitimacy and belonging. Administrative delays aren't just inconvenient; they can feel like exclusion from everyday economic life.

Vulnerability adds another layer of complexity. Customers facing financial distress, bereavement, health challenges, or sudden instability need flexibility and human judgement, not just efficient processing. As systems become more automated, institutions face real pressure to ensure that efficiency doesn't quietly erode compassion or procedural fairness.

This matters more as financial systems become increasingly interconnected. Payments, identity, credit scoring, fraud monitoring, and government services now overlap within complex institutional ecosystems. Someone struggling to navigate one part of the system can encounter cascading exclusion affecting employment, housing, or healthcare. Banking access becomes inseparable from broader social participation.

The future of retail banking will partly depend on how institutions redefine inclusion. Access can no longer be measured by physical reach or technological capability alone. It increasingly means being understandable, navigable, responsive, and emotionally accessible across a diverse customer population. In the long run, institutions may be judged not only by how intelligently they operate, but by how effectively they allow different human beings to participate confidently in financial life.

How Hybrid Banking Feels Different Across Societies

Hybrid banking is often described operationally as the integration of physical and digital channels. In practice, it's experienced very differently across societies—because trust, convenience, and the meaning of institutional presence are all shaped by culture, demographics, infrastructure, and history. Technology scales globally; customer expectations don't.

In the UK, hybrid banking balances digital efficiency against expectations of institutional continuity. Mobile banking and contactless payments are widely adopted, yet accountability, branch accessibility, and human support remain important—especially for older populations and vulnerable communities. The ongoing debate about branch closures reflects something real: many people still see banking institutions as civic infrastructure, not just service providers.

Across Europe, hybrid models operate within stronger expectations around governance, consumer protection, and social responsibility. Customers increasingly expect digital innovation to sit alongside privacy safeguards and genuine inclusion. Hybrid banking becomes connected to broader societal questions about fairness and institutional accountability, not just customer convenience.

Ireland offers a distinctive case. Cooperative traditions and the enduring role of credit unions reinforce visible, community-based institutional presence. For many customers outside major cities, the shift to hybrid banking isn't just a technological transition, it's an effort to preserve human accessibility while adapting to changing behaviour.

In North America, scale and competition define the experience. Customers expect seamless digital capability across products while simultaneously demanding rapid, personalised intervention during disputes or disruptions. The hybrid experience often reflects tension between operational efficiency and the need for human escalation within highly scaled systems.

Singapore—one of the most digitally integrated financial environments in the world—sits at the other end of the spectrum. Banking operates within coordinated ecosystems connecting payments, digital identity, and public infrastructure. Hybrid banking here involves fewer traditional branch interactions, yet institutional confidence remains high because trust extends into broader national infrastructure coordination.

Across the Gulf, hybrid banking is evolving rapidly alongside relationship-based commercial cultures. Digital adoption has accelerated through younger populations and state modernisation programmes, but personal trust and institutional reputation remain influential. Digital channels are extending human relationships, not replacing them.

In much of Africa, hybrid banking emerged through different conditions entirely. Mobile platforms reached communities that traditional branches never did. Customers experience hybrid banking through combinations of mobile apps, local agents, and community intermediaries. Trust depends less on institutional heritage and more on everyday usability and transaction reliability.

Latin America carries the weight of economic memory—inflation, currency instability, institutional volatility. Financial behaviour is shaped by history as much as present conditions. Hybrid banking here often involves stronger preferences for flexibility, visible access, and quick availability of funds, even as digital adoption grows.

China represents perhaps the most integrated case. Finance, commerce, communication, and identity increasingly operate through continuous platform ecosystems. Hybrid banking becomes less about switching between branch and app, and more about navigating an environment where financial interaction is simply embedded in daily life.

These differences matter because hybrid banking is ultimately about human adaptation, not channel architecture. People don't experience financial systems through technology alone—they experience them through emotional confidence, cultural expectations, and perceptions of accessibility when they need support. A process that feels efficient in one society can feel impersonal or exclusionary in another.

As institutions continue redesigning customer journeys around digital platforms, hybrid banking may prove not to be a transitional phase at all but the long-term reality of modern banking itself.

Human Behaviour in an Increasingly Digital Financial World

Digital transformation has changed not just how financial services are delivered, but how people behave within financial systems. Banking has become less visible as a distinct activity and more embedded in broader digital life—payments, savings, borrowing, authentication, all running continuously in the background.

This has shifted expectations sharply. Speed, convenience, and continuous accessibility are now treated as baseline features, not premium service. Delays that were once accepted as part of institutional process are increasingly experienced as failures. The bar has moved, and institutions that don't keep up feel unreliable rather than simply traditional.

At the same time, digital dependency has created new forms of psychological tension. People increasingly rely on systems they don't fully understand and can't directly control. Fraud monitoring, authentication protocols, AI-assisted servicing, and algorithmic risk controls shape financial life invisibly. Most people don't encounter these as technology—they encounter them through transaction approvals, account verifications, payment interruptions, or sudden access denials.

This quietly reshapes the relationship between individuals and institutions. Traditional banking involved identifiable human interaction. Digital systems operate through procedural authority. Customers may find institutions efficient while feeling uncertain about where accountability actually resides when something goes wrong.

Fraud is perhaps the clearest example of this new environment. As financial systems have become more digital, fraud has industrialised across multiple channels simultaneously. Customers must now stay continuously alert to phishing, impersonation, identity theft, and behavioural manipulation. Part of the security burden has effectively shifted onto the customer, creating digital anxiety even as institutional protections improve.

Generational differences shape how this is experienced. Younger customers accept continuous authentication and automated notifications as routine. Older customers may find the same systems cognitively exhausting or difficult to navigate. Vulnerable customers often struggle not because technology is unavailable, but because increasingly procedural systems reduce opportunities for reassurance or contextual human support when they need it most.

AI deepens this shift further. Systems can now predict behaviour, automate service interactions, identify anomalies, and recommend financial actions at scale.

Financial experiences may increasingly become anticipatory—institutions intervening algorithmically before customers even initiate interaction. These capabilities improve efficiency and risk management, but they raise serious questions about transparency, behavioural influence, and institutional responsibility.

Despite rapid adaptation, the emotional foundations of trust change slowly. Customers still seek reassurance during uncertainty, fairness in disputes, clarity in complexity, and confidence that accountability exists when systems fail. Digital adoption doesn't eliminate human vulnerability—it just changes the environment in which vulnerability is experienced.

The challenge for retail banking isn't only technological advancement. It's managing both forms of transformation simultaneously: continuing to innovate in response to competition and fraud complexity, while preserving forms of trust and human legitimacy capable of supporting people living within increasingly automated financial systems. Institutions that succeed technically but fail behaviourally will struggle to hold long-term trust. Those that combine intelligent infrastructure with transparency and human accountability may find that becomes their most durable competitive advantage.

Why Hybrid Institutions May Become the Most Trusted

The future of retail banking is often framed around digital acceleration, automation, and AI. These forces are real and consequential. But long-term institutional success may depend less on becoming fully digital and more on becoming institutionally balanced. In complex societies, trust may emerge not from eliminating human interaction, but from combining technological capability with human reassurance across multiple forms of engagement.

Hybrid institutions may ultimately become the most trusted precisely because they can move across both environments. Customers expect digital convenience for routine activity, but they continue seeking visible accountability and human accessibility during uncertainty, vulnerability, or complexity. Institutions capable of operating effectively across both may develop deeper legitimacy than those designed exclusively around either model.

Hybrid banking is often misread as a transitional state. It may instead be a permanent one, shaped by the uneven complexity of human behaviour. Financial life doesn't unfold uniformly. People move between moments of confidence, confusion, urgency, and vulnerability. A customer perfectly happy with fully digital payments may need genuine human reassurance during a fraud incident, bereavement, or major life decision. No single channel design serves all of that.

This becomes more significant as societies grow more fragmented in their relationship with technology. Younger generations may embrace automation comfortably; ageing populations continue valuing accessible, interpersonal support. Urban customers adapt quickly to digital ecosystems; rural and vulnerable communities depend more heavily on physical infrastructure. Hybrid institutions aren't necessary because technology is incomplete—they're necessary because human adaptation is uneven.

Growing digital risks reinforce this further. Cyberattacks, impersonation technologies, synthetic identity manipulation, and AI-generated deception are eroding public confidence across digital environments. As these threats evolve, customers will place growing value on institutions that offer not just technological protection, but recognisable accountability and reliable human intervention when systems fail.

This represents a meaningful strategic shift. Competitive advantage in banking used to mean scale, product breadth, or branch networks. Increasingly, it may mean trust continuity across fragmented customer journeys—being understandable, reachable, and dependable at the moments when financial outcomes become personally significant.

AI will intensify this dynamic rather than resolve it. More intelligent systems may make institutions operationally stronger while simultaneously making customers more sensitive to transparency and recourse. The paradox of future banking is that the more technologically sophisticated systems become, the more important human legitimacy may be.

Hybrid institutions may also prove more operationally resilient and less exposed to single points of failure across channel, technology, or behavioural assumptions. The ability to maintain continuity across physical, digital, assisted, and automated environments better positions institutions to absorb disruption when cyber incidents, infrastructure failures, or sudden behavioural shifts occur. Hybrid capability is both a customer strategy and a resilience strategy.

Over time, the physical versus digital distinction may matter less than institutional coherence. Customers won't think in terms of channels—they'll judge whether institutions feel dependable across different moments and forms of interaction. Trust will become increasingly connected to consistency of experience, not delivery mechanism.

The institutions that endure won't be those that went fully digital fastest. They'll be those that combined technological intelligence with human confidence at scale—operationally advanced, yet capable of making people feel supported, recognised, and secure within an increasingly automated financial world.

Reflection

Hybrid banking has emerged as the quiet but decisive shift that is redefining how retail institutions serve their communities. The examples and structural pillars explored in this chapter show that hybridity is not simply the merging of physical and digital channels; it is a fundamental redesign of how banks think, operate, and remain present in people's lives. What becomes clear is that hybrid banking succeeds when it is treated as an institutional philosophy rather than a technology trend; when banks that align their purpose, infrastructure, branch strategy, and frontline capability build models that are both efficient and reassuring; and when they are able to support customers who want digital speed without compromising those who still value human guidance. The global case studies reinforce the same lesson: hybrid banking adapts itself to the realities of each society—whether through agent networks in Kenya, open digital rails in India, cooperative structures in Europe, or ecosystem platforms in Singapore. Yet despite these differences, the underlying principles remain universal: shared data, seamless journeys, operational resilience, and meaningful human contact at the moments that matter. This chapter also highlights how hybridity strengthens trust by reducing the distance between the institution and the customer. It allows banks to be present everywhere without losing their sense of responsibility to the local community. As retail banking enters the next decade of transformation, hybrid architecture stands out as the most durable, inclusive, and strategically balanced model. It gives institutions the flexibility required to respond to technology cycles and economic volatility while preserving the humanity, stability, and continuity that define the core of banking.

Ultimately, hybrid banking is judged not by its structural design alone, but by how it is experienced by customers in moments that matter. The ability to provide consistent, secure, and reassuring service across channels becomes the true measure of institutional effectiveness in a hybrid world.

Framework

Framework Overview

This framework summarises the core structural elements that define hybrid retail banking. It brings together the insights from all five pillars in this chapter to show how physical and digital systems can operate as one unified architecture. The framework highlights how customer journeys, data flows, branch formats, and operating models must be re-designed to support seamless movement across channels.

1 Physical–Digital Convergence

Hybrid banking requires a unified service system where physical and digital journeys connect without friction. Convergence ensures that authentication, data, decisions, and customer experience remain consistent regardless of entry point. Branches, apps, call centres, and assisted-digital channels operate as one continuous environment rather than separate departments.

2 INFRASTRUCTURE READINESS

Hybrid delivery depends on modern, interoperable infrastructure. Core systems, cloud layers, workflow automation, data integrity, and cyber controls must work together to support reliability across all channels. Infrastructure readiness becomes the backbone of service continuity, operational resilience, and customer trust.

3 SMART BRANCH INTEGRATION

Branches evolve into intelligent nodes within the hybrid ecosystem. They balance automation with advisory support, reduce operational load through smart devices, and reinforce trust where human reassurance matters. Branch formats adapt to geography, demographics, and institutional purpose.

4 CHANNEL STRATEGY AND COST ALIGNMENT

Hybrid banking reshapes the economics of retail delivery. Institutions must design channel strategies that balance capacity, cost-to-serve, inclusion, and customer preference. Effective cost alignment reduces duplication, improves efficiency, and supports long-term financial sustainability while protecting accessibility.

5 GLOBAL HYBRID MODELS

Real-world examples from Asia, Africa, Europe, and Latin America show how hybrid banking adapts to local realities. Successful models share common features: governance discipline, strong infrastructure, clear service mapping, frontline capability, and a balanced mix of digital convenience and human presence.

Purpose of the Framework

This framework shows how hybrid banking must be engineered deliberately rather than implemented as a collection of disconnected initiatives. It demonstrates that presence, reliability, and accessibility arise from structured design choices—not from digital expansion alone. By consolidating principles across integration, infrastructure, branch design, channel strategy, and global learning, the framework gives leaders a practical reference for building hybrid retail institutions capable of long-term relevance, customer trust, and operational durability. The framework should also be read through the lens of customer outcome. Each structural element—integration, identity, continuity, infrastructure, and governance—must translate into clearer, safer, and more reliable experiences for customers. Without this linkage, architectural strength does not convert into institutional trust.

Table 2.1 Template: Hybrid Architecture Mapping

No.	*Dimension*	*Current State*	*Risk / Gap*	*Target State*	*Owner*
1	Channel Integration	Channels operate in silos with limited coordination	Fragmented journeys, duplication, customer frustration	Fully integrated omnichannel architecture with seamless transitions	CIO / COO
2	Customer Identity Layer	Multiple authentication processes across channels	Inconsistent verification, fraud exposure, poor experience	Unified identity layer across all touchpoints	Chief Risk Officer / CIO
3	Journey Continuity	Customers restart journeys across channels	Drop-offs, rework, operational inefficiency	End-to-end journey continuity across channels	COO
4	Service Consistency	Varying service quality and decisions across channels	Trust erosion, complaints, regulatory risk	Standardised service framework across all channels	Head of Operations
5	Data Visibility	Data fragmented across systems and teams	Lack of context, delayed decisions, errors	Real-time unified customer data visibility	Chief Data Officer
6	Assisted Digital Capability	Limited support for digitally uncertain customers	Exclusion, increased dependency on branches	Embedded assisted-digital journeys across channels	Head of Customer Experience
7	Infrastructure Readiness	Legacy systems with limited interoperability	Slow processing, integration constraints	Modern, API-driven, cloud-enabled architecture	CIO
8	Operational Resilience	Periodic testing with limited cross-channel scenarios	Service disruption, recovery delays	Continuous resilience testing across all channels	Chief Risk Officer
9	Branch-Digital Alignment	Branch and digital teams operate independently	Misaligned service experience	Branches integrated as part of hybrid ecosystem	Head of Retail Banking
10	Governance Alignment	Siloed decision-making across functions	Conflicting priorities, delayed execution	Unified governance across technology, risk, and operations	CEO / Board

Bibliography

Accenture (2023). *Insights on Platformisation and Customer Experience in Banking*. Accenture Banking Research.

Bank for International Settlements (2022). *Operational Resilience and Third-Party Risk in Financial Services*. BIS.

Deloitte (2023). *Insights on Hybrid Banking and Digital Customer Transformation*. Deloitte Insights.

European Banking Authority (2021). *Guidelines on ICT and Security Risk Management*. EBA.

European Central Bank (2022). *Digitalisation and the Future of Bank Branches in Europe*. European Central Bank.

International Monetary Fund (2023). *Digital Financial Services and Financial Inclusion: Global Trends and Policy Challenges*. IMF.

KPMG (2022). *Research on Human-Centred Hybrid Banking Models*. KPMG International.

McKinsey & Company (2023). *Global Banking Annual Review 2023*. McKinsey Global Banking Practice.

OECD (2021). *Digital Transformation in Financial Services and Consumer Protection*. OECD Publishing.

PwC (2023). *Insights on Retail Banking Ecosystems and Future Financial Services Models*. PricewaterhouseCoopers.

Schein, E. H. (2017). *Organizational Culture and Leadership*. 5th Edition. Wiley.

World Bank (2022). *Global Findex Database 2021: Financial Inclusion, Digital Payments, and Resilience in the Age of COVID-19*. World Bank.

World Economic Forum (2023). *Insights on Global Fintech and Inclusive Financial Growth*. World Economic Forum.

World Economic Forum (2022). *Digital Identity Systems and Financial Inclusion*. World Economic Forum.

3 The Trust Infrastructure Shift

Context

Trust in retail banking is no longer anchored in physical presence, paper-based verification, or familiar branch interactions. It is increasingly produced through a distributed network of digital infrastructures that operate silently beneath every customer journey. Identity frameworks, authentication systems, consent layers, encryption standards, data-handling mechanisms, cloud environments, and cross-institution governance now determine how individuals experience safety and reliability. This shift marks a fundamental redefinition of trust: from something earned through relationships to something demonstrated through system performance. Customers rarely meet bank employees, but they continuously interact with digital traces of the institution. Each login attempt, each transaction, each permissions screen, and each authentication request become a trust event. In this environment, the architecture that underpins digital interactions is no longer a technical function: it is the institution's public face.

Customers do not engage with trust as an abstract concept; they experience it through moments of interaction. A failed authentication attempt, a delayed payment, or an unclear consent request immediately translates into doubt about the institution. Conversely, smooth and predictable journeys reinforce confidence without conscious effort. Trust in hybrid banking is therefore behavioural and cumulative, built through repeated system performance rather than isolated assurances.

This new reality also places retail banks inside broader ecosystems they do not fully control. Payments routes involve multiple gateways; identity checks rely on telecom networks and device protocols; open-banking journeys depend on API performance; cloud-based applications share operational responsibility with external providers; and fintech partners deliver key components of customer experience. As a result, trust is now shaped by interconnected systems operating across institutional boundaries. A failure in any one layer—authentication, connectivity, fraud screening, data-sharing protocols, API standards, or vendor security—can immediately undermine confidence regardless of where the failure originated. Banks must therefore strengthen governance models that span third parties, vendors, and cross-border infrastructures, ensuring every component of the ecosystem reflects consistent standards of transparency, resilience, and accountability.

DOI: 10.4324/9781042021765-4

Regulatory expectations have accelerated this shift. Frameworks such as GDPR, PSD2, open finance standards, national identity schemes, and operational-resilience regulations have elevated data rights and infrastructural responsibility to the level of core institutional obligations. Retail banks must now demonstrate how customer data is accessed, stored, protected, shared, and audited. Consent journeys require clarity; authentication pathways must adapt to risk; and data-sharing systems must be transparent and interoperable. These regulatory developments are reshaping the internal structure of banks, compelling them to invest in governance, operational assurance, third-party controls, and real-time monitoring. The responsibility for trust can no longer sit with frontline teams alone; it must be embedded into the architecture itself.

The hybrid era adds further complexity. As digital interactions dominate transactional demand, customers expect seamless movement between channels, consistent identity recognition, and personalised experiences that do not compromise privacy or security. At the same time, the rise of cyber threats, synthetic identities, and advanced fraud techniques has increased the need for stronger safeguards. This combination of rising expectations and rising risk creates a new trust equation: institutions must deliver speed, convenience, and personalisation without sacrificing integrity, fairness, or resilience. Achieving this balance requires a redesign of the systems, partnerships, governance structures, and operating practices that underpin hybrid banking.

This environment also amplifies exposure to financial crime. Fraud patterns now exploit gaps between systems, channels, and partners, particularly where identity signals, transaction monitoring, or data-sharing controls are not fully synchronised. Institutions must therefore design trust infrastructure with embedded fraud intelligence, ensuring that detection, prevention, and response operate continuously across the entire ecosystem rather than within isolated control points.

Trust has therefore become a structural capability, not a marketing attribute. It is engineered into infrastructure, reinforced through governance, and demonstrated through consistent performance across every interaction. Retail banks must now think of themselves not only as financial institutions but as custodians of identity, stewards of data, and participants in a broader public infrastructure. The chapters that follow examine how digital identity, consent architecture, ecosystem governance, collaboration frameworks, and open-source standards collectively define the trust foundation of the future retail bank.

Digital Identity and Authentication

Digital identity has become the primary entry point into modern financial systems, replacing the physical checks and in-person verification that once anchored customer onboarding. In today's hybrid environment, a customer's identity is confirmed, authenticated, and monitored through layers of signals that operate silently in the background. These include device credentials, biometrics, behavioural patterns, and network intelligence. Each signal contributes to a single question: can this person be trusted to access financial services securely? Banks must now

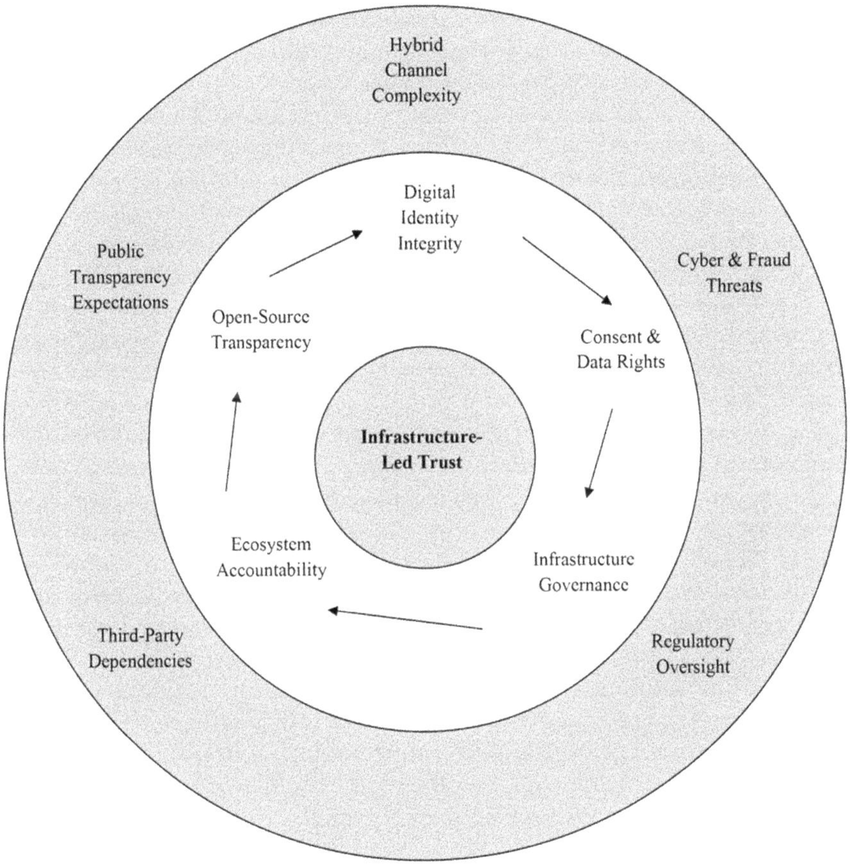

Figure 3.1 Trust Infrastructure Architecture

manage identity not as a one-time event, but as a continuous relationship between the customer and the institution. This shift requires stronger authentication frameworks that balance convenience with institutional responsibility. A frictionless login experience must coexist with robust controls, fallback mechanisms, and continuous assurance. In this new environment, identity is no longer a documentation process; it is a living architecture that supports safety, accountability, and seamless multichannel engagement.

The history of authentication has brought about a paradigm shift in the way banks are able to confirm the intentions of their customers and ensure security. The traditional methods of authentication were dependent on passwords, PINs, and manual verification, which had inherent risks of loss, duplication, and social engineering attacks. Contemporary authentication methods move away from static credentials and towards dynamic trust indicators. Biometric authentication through facial recognition and fingerprint scanning is more secure, and device binding enables the linking of identity to a particular mobile device or hardware token. Behavioural analysis looks at habits like typing rhythm, geolocation, and transaction patterns to identify anomalies in real-time. Such methods make authentication less dependent on remembered credentials and more secure through layered security, which increases the resilience of institutions. However, the complexity of these systems needs to be managed through proper governance, customer communication, and biometric data management.

A defining feature of modern identity architecture is the shift toward continuous authentication. In earlier banking models, verification occurred at the point of login or during high-risk transactions; once authenticated, a user's session was largely trusted. Today, hybrid banking demands uninterrupted assessment of risk. Continuous authentication evaluates identity across the entire customer journey by analysing device integrity, network patterns, behavioural signals, and transaction context. If any deviation appears unusual, the system can request step-up verification, restrict functionality, or temporarily suspend access. This approach significantly reduces fraud by detecting compromised sessions long before a customer is aware of suspicious activity. For institutions, continuous authentication builds a dynamic trust profile that grows more accurate over time. The challenge lies in striking the correct balance between security and user experience. Excessive prompts may frustrate customers, while insufficient controls may expose them to harm. Effective implementation therefore requires calibrated thresholds, clear fallback options, and transparent communication that preserves confidence while protecting the customer.

Continuous authentication also strengthens institutional accountability by ensuring that risk is assessed dynamically rather than assumed after initial verification. This reduces the likelihood of prolonged exposure during compromised sessions and reinforces the perception that the institution is actively protecting the customer throughout the interaction.

Case Study: Estonia's National Digital Identity Infrastructure

Estonia: Public Digital Identity System

Estonia implemented a nationwide digital identity framework that allows citizens to authenticate themselves securely across banking, government, and commercial services using a single trusted credential. The system supports continuous verification through cryptographic keys, device-based authentication, and real-time validation rather than one-time identity checks.

Banks operating within this framework rely on infrastructure-level trust rather than repeated customer verification, enabling seamless digital onboarding, transaction authorisation, and cross-institution service access. The model demonstrates how continuous, infrastructure-led identity assurance can reduce fraud, simplify customer journeys, and strengthen trust across an entire financial ecosystem.

Hybrid banking is made possible by the use of identity infrastructure that can work well in multiple channels, devices, and touchpoints. A customer can start the process using a mobile app, submit documents using a web portal, and finalise the verification process using a branch or call centre. Each of these processes has to work well together so as to avoid duplication of effort, errors, and conflicting identity states. This calls for high levels of interoperability between the internal systems, third-party identity providers, and national digital ID infrastructure, if it exists. Interoperable identity infrastructure ensures that once a customer has been verified, their identity state is consistent across products and channels without the need for repeated verification. This enhances efficiency, reduces the cost of onboarding, and increases completion rates. It also enhances security by ensuring that all channels rely on a single source of truth instead of working with parallel systems that have inconsistent data. Banks will have to invest in identity orchestration platforms that bring all these processes together, allowing for the controlled sharing of identity attributes and a consistent risk profile across the entire organisation.

Authentication in hybrid banking must balance strength with fluidity. Traditional security models relied on static credentials such as passwords, PINs, or security questions, all of which are vulnerable to compromise and place cognitive burden on customers. Modern authentication replaces these with layered, risk-sensitive approaches that adapt to context. For low-risk actions, device recognition or biometric matching may be sufficient; for higher-risk transactions, banks can add step-up authentication using behavioural signals, possession factors, or out-of-band verification. This adaptive model protects customers without disrupting the flow of everyday tasks. It also reduces friction for vulnerable or digitally hesitant groups who may struggle with complex security procedures. Strong authentication is not simply a technical requirement; it is a contributor to institutional trust. Customers form their perception of safety based on whether authentication feels reliable, predictable, and respectful of their time. Banks that design smooth, intuitive authentication journeys reinforce confidence and enable customers to use digital channels more fully.

Clarity also plays a critical role. Customers must understand why additional authentication is requested and how it protects them. When security measures appear arbitrary or excessive, they create friction and uncertainty. When they are predictable and well-explained, they reinforce confidence and acceptance.

Identity systems are becoming more sophisticated, and retail banks must prepare for a future in which authentication is decentralised, portable, and managed by customers. Customers are given more control over their identity with new methods like decentralised identifiers, verifiable credentials, and token-based identity wallets, which means that institutions no longer own the identity. Rather, customers hold cryptographically secured credentials on their own devices and decide when and where to share them with different banks, platforms, and service providers. This method decreases the necessity for centralised databases, lowers the risk of breach for institutions, and enhances privacy by limiting the volume of personal data that any organisation stores. However, decentralised identity also brings fresh challenges to operations: banks need to establish verification bridges to authenticate credentials issued by third-party authorities; they need to set up trust registries, credential revocation systems, and create an interoperable infrastructure that is in line with both national and international standards.

Therefore, new technology, worker training, and customer education will have to be funded so that customers understand how to use their digital wallets effectively. Above all, banks have to embed these systems in reliable anti-fraud measures as decentralised systems alter the types of threats by shifting the attack surface to endpoints and user devices. Properly implemented,

hybrid banking requires identity systems that operate seamlessly across physical, digital, and assisted channels, ensuring that customers encounter a consistent level of trust wherever they interact. The architecture behind omnichannel identity orchestration, where a customer authenticated on one channel can move fluidly to another without repeating verification steps or exposing additional risk, requires banks to integrate device intelligence, behavioural analytics, and continuous authentication into a single identity engine capable of assessing risk dynamically. For example, a customer who begins a loan application online should be able to continue it in a branch or contact centre with their authentication state preserved securely through encrypted session tokens. This reduces friction, improves accessibility, and reinforces institutional credibility by demonstrating that trust is embedded into the operating fabric rather than restricted to isolated systems. The challenge lies in aligning legacy platforms, cloud services, and regulatory constraints into a coordinated framework that can authenticate, reauthenticate, and escalate controls with precision. When executed effectively, omnichannel identity orchestration strengthens trust by showing customers that the institution recognises them consistently, protects them continuously, and supports them wherever they choose to bank.

As hybrid banking gains more ground, the banking sector will have to equip itself to face identity risks which will arise due to complex digital behaviours. This environment highlights the growing incidence of synthetic identities, impersonation via deepfakes, and automated fraudulent attacks that exploit legacy verification processes whilst taking advantage of modern digital channels. Traditional identity checks that were enough to verify customer's credentials in face-to-face interactions are no longer sufficient in an era where attackers can forge biometric data, trick voice authentication systems and create entirely new identities through AI tools. Therefore, in addition to static verification, banks should rely on anomaly-driven identity intelligence that performs continuous monitoring of behavioural cues such as typing styles, transaction frequencies, device fingerprints, and network locations. When these behavioural factors are analysed together, banks can spot identity frauds at their onset, facilitate protective measures automatically, and eliminate the necessity for genuine customers to be inconvenienced in the process of avoiding unauthorised intrusions. Such a dynamic way of protecting oneself is a clear indication to the community that banks have the capacity to foresee and prepare for threats rather than just dealing with them afterwards, thus, increasing the level of confidence in the banks in a world where identity is both a valuable possession and a target.

The final dimension of modern identity design is resilience: ensuring customers can authenticate themselves even when technology fails, devices are lost, or digital credentials become inaccessible. There is thus a need for robust fallback mechanisms that preserve both security and dignity. Customers may face hardware failures, network outages, biometric mismatches, or accessibility constraints, and a rigid digital-only pathway can unintentionally exclude the very individuals hybrid banking aims to support. Banks must therefore implement layered recovery options such as secure human-assisted verification, time-bound recovery codes, secondary trusted devices, or identity re-verification through regulated third parties. These pathways must be governed carefully to avoid social-engineering risks, yet designed with empathy so customers do not feel trapped at moments of vulnerability. A well-constructed resilience model ensures that identity is not a single point of failure, and it reinforces public confidence that hybrid banking remains reliable even under stress.

A final strategic consideration is the shift toward interoperable identity ecosystems, where customers can authenticate seamlessly across banking, government, and commercial services using a unified credential. Banks must prepare for an environment in which identity is portable, standardised, and governed through shared public–private frameworks. Interoperability reduces duplication, lowers onboarding cost, and strengthens fraud prevention by enabling consistent verification across multiple domains. However, it also requires banks to align with national digital ID schemes, global standards, and trust frameworks that define assurance levels, metadata rules, authentication protocols, and dispute mechanisms. Participation in these ecosystems demands strong technical integration, transparent governance, and readiness to collaborate with regulators, fintechs, and identity providers. When executed well, interoperable identity elevates customer experience, enhances systemic security, and positions retail banks as integral pillars of a broader societal trust infrastructure.

Consent Architecture and Data Rights

Responsible handling of customer data is at the core of modern retail banking; therefore, consent architecture forms a core part of the institutional trust framework. In the hybrid setup, customers not only want to know what data is collected about them but also demand transparency when their data is processed and shared via different digital channels, partner ecosystems, and regulatory networks. This section explores how consent should be changed from a mere compliance formality to a transparent, user, driven experience that gives the users more control to decide and even lessens misunderstanding. Customers have an increasing tendency to use banking services via app interfaces, embedded journeys, and third, party platforms; every such contact results in the creation of data that is to be used only with the customer's complete and continuous consent. Thus, banks need to create consent paths that not only clarify what the data is used for (its "purpose", duration, and the "benefit" resulting from it) but also that very naturally offer the customers the possibility of "pausing" or "revoking" their consents or "modifying" them anytime they want. Such a change requires the use of simple language, the logical design of the user interface, and one single consent ledger that constantly keeps track of data permissions for customers across different products and systems. Gaining knowledge about and having control over the use of their data is how customers get empowered—trust is then deepened. Henceforth, consent architecture is not only an arrangement for legal safety but also a trust strategy in hybrid banking.

Consent architecture also carries an ethical responsibility. Institutions must ensure that permissions are not obtained through complexity, inertia, or customer fatigue, but through genuine understanding. This distinction separates compliance from trust and defines whether customers feel respected or managed.

As banking journeys spread across multiple channels and third-party ecosystems, customers require greater visibility into how their data moves beyond the institution's boundaries. There is a need for transparent data-sharing frameworks that allow individuals to understand not only what information is collected but where it flows, who receives it, and for what purpose. Traditional consent notices rarely provide this level of granularity, leading to confusion, mistrust, or blanket refusals that limit the value of personalised services. In a hybrid banking environment, consent must therefore be designed as a real-time, contextual experience. When customers initiate payments, connect external accounts, or access embedded financial tools, the system should surface clear requests that explain the specific data required and how it will be used. Banks must integrate these consent prompts into frictionless, well-timed interactions that respect customer attention while meeting regulatory expectations. To support this, institutions need robust back-end infrastructure that logs consent events, enforces expiry rules, and synchronises permissions across partner platforms. This ensures that data is accessed only with valid, verifiable approval and that customers retain meaningful control over their personal information. By combining clarity, timing, and strong governance, transparent consent journeys reinforce the institution's commitment to respecting data rights.

Case Study: Open Banking Consent in the United Kingdom

United Kingdom: Open Banking Framework

The UK's Open Banking initiative introduced standardised consent mechanisms that allow customers to explicitly authorise data sharing between banks and licensed third-party providers. Customers can see which organisations have access to their data, for what purpose, and for how long, with the ability to revoke consent at any time through their bank interface.

This framework shifted trust from bilateral agreements to regulated infrastructure, where transparency, auditability, and customer control are embedded into the system design. The UK experience shows how clear consent architecture can enable ecosystem innovation while preserving customer confidence and data rights.

Effective consent architecture in hybrid banking entails that the banks do not merely disclose information but also implement consent mechanisms that allow permission to be truly meaningful and capable of being enforced. This illustrates that banks need to establish structured consent governance which keeps a record of every situation when data is accessed, processed, or shared, thereby, permission is honoured accurately across complex technical environments. Still, a lot of banks rely on fragmented systems whereby consent is captured in one platform, stored in another, and is being inconsistently implemented in downstream processes. This gives rise to operational blind spots and customers are exposed to the risk of unauthorised data usage. A unified consent governance model discards this fragmentation and introduces a single source of truth: a central ledger where the scope, validity, and conditions of the permissions are recorded. This ledger should be connected with APIs, partner systems, and internal databases so that access control can be automatically enforced in real time. Besides, governance involves institution discipline, routine audits, expiration confirmations, handling of revocations, and clear reporting where regulators and customers are shown that the data is responsibly managed at every stage. Embedding governance into the design of consent by banks instead of treating it as a mere chore enables them to create systems where the rights of customers are protected structurally. This increases the level of trust.

As data-driven services expand, customers increasingly expect consent to operate as a flexible, ongoing relationship rather than a one-time decision. The need is apparent for dynamic consent mechanisms that empower individuals to adjust their permissions as their needs, preferences, or risk perceptions evolve. Traditional static consent models do not match the realities of hybrid banking, where customers shift between channels, update personal information, activate new products, and engage with third-party services. Dynamic consent enables users to review, modify, or withdraw permissions at any point through intuitive dashboards or contextual prompts. Building this capability requires banks to integrate real-time consent orchestration into their digital infrastructure, ensuring that any change is reflected immediately across all internal systems and partner networks. It also requires thoughtful interface design that avoids overwhelming users while providing sufficient granularity to make meaningful choices. Dynamic consent strengthens accountability: it forces institutions to maintain accurate permission records, manage data exposures responsibly, and treat customer preferences as living instructions rather than archived forms. By giving customers greater agency over their data, dynamic consent builds confidence and strengthens trust in digital interactions.

In hybrid banking, consent must be accessible to all customers, regardless of literacy levels, digital comfort, or cognitive ability. Herein lies the importance of inclusive consent design, where information is presented in formats that all users can understand and act upon. Many individuals struggle with dense legal language, multi-step processes, or rapidly presented prompts embedded within digital journeys. An inclusive model replaces complexity with simplicity, using clear wording, visual cues, layered explanations, and multilingual support to ensure customers genuinely comprehend the choices they are making. This is especially important in markets with linguistic diversity, limited digital literacy, or vulnerable populations who may depend on branches or assisted channels. Banks must ensure that consent pathways work consistently across mobile apps, branch interactions, call centres, and agent networks, so customers can manage their data rights wherever they feel comfortable. Inclusive consent is not only a fairness issue; it is a strategic necessity for maintaining broad participation in digital ecosystems. When customers feel respected, informed, and in control, they are more willing to adopt digital services and share data responsibly. This strengthens trust and reinforces the institution's commitment to protecting the rights of all users.

Data-sharing partnerships have become more prevalent in hybrid banking, and third-party governance has become an essential aspect of consent architecture. Banks need to ensure that each third-party provider handling customer data, whether it is a fintech firm, payment service provider, cloud service provider, or analytics firm, also complies with the same consent principles that the bank follows. Customers expect that once they have given consent to a bank, their data will be protected throughout its entire lifecycle; otherwise, any vulnerability in a third-party system will also be a vulnerability in the bank's trust score. To ensure this, banks need to set up strict governance structures: legal agreements outlining the terms of data handling, real-time monitoring of API usage, automated enforcement of consent limits, and regular audits to ensure that third-party providers are in compliance. Banks also need to keep comprehensive lists of all third-party providers who handle customer data, tracing the flow of data through various systems so that consent is never overstepped or otherwise compromised. When customers withdraw consent, third-party systems need to receive and act on this request immediately, proving that customers always retain control over their data.

Weak consent enforcement can also create indirect fraud exposure, where data accessed legitimately is later misused or insufficiently protected within partner environments. Strong governance ensures that consent integrity is maintained throughout the data lifecycle, reducing both operational and reputational risk.

The effectiveness of consent systems increasingly depends on how well banks communicate the value exchange behind data use: why information is requested, how it enhances the customer's experience, and what safeguards are in place to prevent misuse. With regard to this concept of transparent value articulation—where institutions explain the tangible benefits that arise from sharing specific data elements, such as faster onboarding, personalised financial insights, simplified payments, or improved fraud protection—customers are more willing to grant consent when they clearly understand the purpose and when the outcome aligns with their own interests. However, banks must also avoid overstating the benefits or burying risks in vague language; credibility hinges on striking an honest balance between utility and responsibility. This requires close coordination between product teams, risk functions, and customer-experience designers to ensure that messaging is accurate, contextual, and free of technical jargon. Clear articulation of value also supports regulatory expectations for fairness and accountability, demonstrating that consent is obtained through informed understanding rather than passive acceptance. When customers perceive consent as a choice grounded in mutual benefit rather than institutional convenience, trust deepens and engagement increases across hybrid banking channels.

Modern consent systems must account for the fact that customers operate across multiple devices, platforms, and environments, each generating its own data trail and set of permissions. Such systems need cross-channel synchronisation, where any change a customer makes to their consent settings is propagated instantly across all systems—mobile apps, web portals, branch terminals, call-centre interfaces, and partner APIs. Without this synchronisation, customers may unknowingly grant or revoke permissions in one channel while outdated settings persist elsewhere, creating operational inconsistencies and undermining trust. Achieving real-time alignment requires banks to implement centralised consent registries, event-driven architectures, and governance controls that ensure every channel reads from the same authoritative record. It also demands rigorous testing of dependency systems to prevent scenarios in which downstream platforms continue to access data after consent has expired or been withdrawn. Cross-channel synchronisation strengthens accountability and protects customers from unintended exposures, while also reducing the risk of regulatory breaches linked to inconsistent data handling. When customers see that their preferences are honoured universally—not just within a single touchpoint—they gain confidence in the integrity and reliability of the institution's hybrid service model.

With the increasing complexity of hybrid banking, it is essential that consent systems be designed with resilience and continuity in mind, particularly in the event of outages, cyberattacks, or emergency scenarios. The importance of having effective fallback solutions that safeguard data rights even when regular digital operations are interrupted is clear. Banks need to develop consent system architectures that incorporate redundant storage, duplicate registries, and secure offline verification channels to ensure that permissions are still enforceable irrespective of system conditions. This prevents scenarios where, during temporary failures, outdated permissions are applied, data is shared inadvertently, or customers are forced into blanket acceptance simply to access essential services. Resilience also requires clear escalation protocols so that frontline staff, call centres, and branch teams know how to manage data requests safely during disruption. Regulatory expectations increasingly demand that institutions demonstrate not only normal governance but crisis governance—showing that customer rights remain protected under stress. When customers trust that their data will not be exposed during unpredictable events, it reinforces the perception that the institution's commitment to consent is structural rather than conditional. Such resilience strengthens institutional legitimacy in a hybrid environment where continuity and trust are inseparable.

The final dimension of modern consent architecture is interoperability: ensuring that data rights are portable and meaningful across ecosystems, not confined to a single institution. Hybrid banking increasingly depends on shared standards that allow customers to carry their permissions seamlessly across banks, fintech platforms, government services, and cross-border environments. Interoperable consent frameworks prevent fragmentation by aligning terminology, metadata, authorisation protocols, expiry rules, and revocation mechanisms so that permissions hold the same meaning wherever they are applied. This reduces customer confusion, strengthens regulatory oversight, and prevents inconsistencies in how data is accessed or interpreted by different systems. Interoperability also supports competition and innovation by allowing customers to move between providers without repeating lengthy consent journeys or exposing new risks. For banks, participating in interoperable consent networks requires disciplined governance, robust technical integration, and readiness to collaborate with industry bodies and regulators that define shared rules. When executed well, interoperability transforms consent from a local compliance function into a universal data-rights framework, reinforcing customer agency and strengthening public trust in the broader financial ecosystem.

Infrastructure Governance Models

Hybrid retail banking depends on a technology landscape that is no longer contained within a single institution. Cloud platforms, API networks, third-party service providers, artificial intelligence tools, and cross-border data infrastructures now form an interconnected ecosystem through which financial services are delivered. Governance must evolve to match this complexity: traditional oversight models, built for closed, on-premise systems, are insufficient in a world where critical processes run on external environments governed by different standards, jurisdictions, and risk cultures. Banks must therefore adopt governance frameworks that map the entire operating estate, classify systems according to criticality, and apply controls proportionate to the risk each component carries. Governance must be proactive rather than reactive, integrating continuous monitoring, auditable decision-making, and clear accountability lines from operational teams up to the board. Strong governance is no longer an administrative requirement; it is the architecture that ensures technology supports institutional reliability rather than undermining it. In the hybrid era, a bank cannot claim to be trustworthy unless its infrastructure governance is transparent, disciplined, and aligned with the expectations of regulators and the public.

This shift elevates governance to a board-level responsibility. Leadership must understand not only financial risk but also infrastructural risk, ensuring that technology decisions align with institutional resilience, regulatory expectations, and long-term trust.

As hybrid banking expands, governance must address the increasing dependency on third-party and outsourced infrastructures, many of which operate beyond the bank's direct line of control. Institutions must build governance models that extend oversight across cloud service providers, API aggregators, fintech partners, data analytics vendors, and cross-border processing environments. This requires a shift from contract-based assurance to continuous, risk-sensitive monitoring that evaluates performance, compliance, security posture, and resilience in real time. Banks must maintain detailed inventories of all external dependencies, categorising each according to criticality, failure impact, and regulatory sensitivity. Governance also demands robust exit strategies, ensuring that the institution can migrate services or revoke access swiftly if a provider fails, becomes non-compliant, or introduces systemic risk. Clear roles, escalation paths, and audit trails must be established so accountability remains unambiguous even when operations span multiple organisations. In hybrid banking, third-party governance is not an add-on; it is a structural necessity that protects customers, reinforces institutional credibility, and maintains operational continuity across a distributed ecosystem.

Effective governance also requires institutions to embed resilience and recovery principles into every layer of their technology estate, ensuring that hybrid banking services remain reliable even under stress. It focuses on the need for banks to design governance structures that account for system outages, cyber incidents, vendor failures, and unexpected surges in demand. Resilience governance begins with thorough mapping of dependencies: understanding which systems must be restored first, which data flows are most vulnerable, and which customer journeys are most sensitive to disruption. Institutions must implement robust backup mechanisms, redundancy across critical components, and clearly defined recovery-time objectives that align with regulatory expectations and customer tolerance. Governance must also include crisis protocols that outline how decisions are made, who authorises emergency actions, and how communication flows internally and externally. These protocols ensure that response is coordinated rather than improvised. By embedding resilience into governance rather than treating it as an operational afterthought, banks enhance their ability to deliver stable, trustworthy services that reinforce public confidence in the hybrid model.

Resilience must also be visible in customer communication. During disruption, timely and transparent updates influence how customers perceive institutional reliability. Silence or ambiguity during incidents can undermine trust more quickly than the disruption itself.

Resilient governance in hybrid banking must account for the reality that systems will fail, disruptions will occur, and recovery must be assured without compromising customer trust. Robust resilience governance defines how institutions prepare for, respond to, and learn from operational incidents; this includes establishing clear thresholds for service degradation, setting recovery-time objectives, maintaining redundancy across critical systems, and designing failover mechanisms that activate without noticeable friction for customers. Governance must also extend to incident communication, ensuring stakeholders—customers, regulators, partners, and internal teams—receive timely, accurate updates that reinforce transparency and trust. After-action reviews are essential to identify root causes, strengthen controls, and refine resilience plans across the hybrid estate. As retail banking becomes more dependent on cloud infrastructure and third-party platforms, resilience cannot be outsourced; it must be governed centrally, with banks retaining ultimate accountability for continuity. A mature resilience framework demonstrates that the institution is prepared not only to prevent disruptions but to manage them with discipline and clarity, preserving confidence even under stress.

Effective governance in hybrid banking requires a disciplined approach to change management, ensuring that every modification to systems, interfaces, codebases, and data pathways is executed safely and predictably. It examines how uncontrolled or poorly coordinated changes—whether triggered by software updates, vendor integrations, regulatory adjustments, or internal optimisation projects—can introduce instability, outages, or security vulnerabilities that erode customer trust. Modern governance therefore demands a structured change lifecycle: rigorous impact assessments, segregation of duties, controlled testing environments, rollback procedures, and transparent documentation that allows every change to be traced and verified. In hybrid ecosystems where multiple teams, vendors, and platforms contribute to the operational stack, coordination becomes as important as technical execution. Banks must establish change councils, cross-functional oversight mechanisms, and automated validation tools to ensure alignment across the enterprise. The objective is not to slow innovation but to safeguard it, allowing institutions to evolve confidently without exposing customers to avoidable risk. Predictable change management signals institutional maturity and reinforces the integrity of the hybrid banking architecture.

Hybrid banking adds a new layer of complexity to data governance, requiring institutions to manage information that flows across channels, jurisdictions, and external service environments. It explores how banks must build governance structures that ensure accuracy, integrity, and accountability across increasingly fragmented data ecosystems. Traditional data governance focused on central repositories and controlled internal processes, whereas hybrid models demand real-time synchronisation, lineage tracking, and consistency across mobile apps, cloud systems, branch platforms, API exchanges, and partner networks. Banks must maintain a single source of truth through master data management, enforce strict ownership models for every dataset, and apply automated controls that detect anomalies or unauthorised changes. Cross-border operations introduce additional obligations around localisation, residency, and privacy regulation, requiring governance frameworks that adapt to multiple regulatory regimes without fragmenting oversight. Strong data governance also supports analytics, risk models, and customer experience by ensuring that insights are built on reliable foundations. In hybrid banking, effective data governance becomes a core enabler of trust, ensuring that information is correct, protected, and used responsibly wherever it travels.

This requires governance structures that are capable of operating at the pace of real-time digital systems. It examines how traditional governance processes, built around quarterly reviews and static controls, must be re-engineered for continuous oversight. As institutions depend on cloud services, API gateways, AI-driven decision engines, and vendor-operated platforms, the governance environment must incorporate live dashboards, automated alerts, behaviour-based thresholds, and near-real-time intervention protocols. This shift demands a redesign of roles and responsibilities: operational teams must escalate incidents faster, second-line functions must oversee dynamic risk patterns, and boards must receive timely, intelligence-driven updates rather than retrospective summaries. Governance is strengthened through clear accountability maps that define who owns each system, dataset, and failure point across the hybrid ecosystem. External partners must also be embedded into the governance cycle, with agreed reporting standards, test schedules, and event-management procedures. When governance aligns with real-time architecture, institutions become more predictable, resilient, and transparent—qualities that customers and regulators increasingly expect from modern retail banks.

Governance in hybrid banking increasingly depends on disciplined integration between internal systems and the wider ecosystem of partners that support everyday services. As banks rely on payment processors, identity providers, cloud platforms, and specialist fintech vendors, governance must ensure that every component meets consistent standards of security, resilience, and ethical behaviour. This requires institutions to harmonise controls across environments that they do not fully own. Vendor contracts must embed clear expectations on uptime, data handling, incident notification, and regulatory compliance, supported by independent audits and transparent evidence-sharing. Internally, banks must maintain unified policies that apply uniformly across legacy systems and new cloud-native platforms, avoiding the fragmentation that undermines reliability. Effective governance also depends on the ability to trace responsibility across the chain: who operates a system, who monitors its behaviour, who intervenes when risks escalate, and who is accountable to customers and regulators. When these elements work coherently, governance becomes an architecture that ensures consistency, continuity, and accountability across the entire hybrid environment.

Hybrid banking demands governance structures that can anticipate failure rather than merely respond to it. Systems now operate in real time, with interdependencies that amplify the impact of disruptions across channels and partner networks. This environment requires continuous monitoring of operational health using automated alerts, behavioural baselines, and predictive analytics that detect anomalies before they escalate. Governance must also account for the differing risk profiles of various technologies: cloud workloads, API gateways, customer-facing apps, and legacy cores each carry distinct vulnerabilities and recovery constraints. A mature governance model therefore establishes differentiated controls, tiered risk classifications, and clear thresholds for escalation. It ensures that incidents are not managed in isolation but examined through a systemic lens, capturing upstream causes and downstream effects. Equally important is disciplined documentation, which allows institutions to reconstruct events during audits, regulatory reviews, or customer claims. By embedding foresight into oversight, governance becomes a stabilising force that strengthens operational integrity across complex, continuously evolving systems.

Effective infrastructure governance also depends on cultivating institutional clarity about who is accountable for what. As systems become more distributed across cloud providers, fintech collaborators, outsourced service centres, and internal technology teams, ambiguity can creep into even the most critical processes. This emphasises the importance of clearly defined ownership across all components of the hybrid stack, from authentication services and data pipelines to customer interfaces and incident-response workflows. Strong governance assigns responsibility not only for operations, but also for resilience testing, vendor oversight, and continuous improvement. This includes formalising joint-responsibility arrangements with external partners and ensuring that contractual frameworks reflect operational realities rather than legacy assumptions. Institutions must also build governance forums that bring together technology, risk, compliance, and business leaders to maintain a unified understanding of system behaviour. When accountability is explicit and cross-functional coordination is routine, governance evolves from a safeguard into an enabler of trust, allowing retail banks to innovate confidently without compromising reliability.

Fintech–Bank Collaboration Models

Fintech–bank collaboration has matured from a tactical convenience into a structural requirement for hybrid retail banking. Banks no longer attempt to build every capability internally—the pace of innovation, regulatory complexity, and customer expectations far exceed traditional product-development cycles. Fintechs bring speed, modular technology, and strong behavioural design; banks bring governance, stability, and long-term accountability. When these strengths align, collaboration becomes an architectural advantage rather than an optional partnership.

Payments, credit scoring, identity verification, onboarding flows, and budgeting tools are increasingly operated by specialist providers embedded inside banking platforms. The customer sees none of this—they experience only seamlessness or friction. That experience depends entirely on how well banks and fintechs integrate their systems, safeguard data, and share responsibility. The pressure on institutions is therefore not to collaborate more, but to collaborate intelligently. Poorly governed partnerships create operational risk; well-designed models improve inclusion, efficiency, and adaptability.

From the customer's perspective, the distinction between bank and partner is largely invisible. Responsibility for outcomes remains with the bank, regardless of how services are delivered. This makes governance of collaboration a central component of trust architecture.

These services now sit inside critical transaction paths, meaning any weakness in their systems becomes a weakness in the bank's promise to its customers. This interdependence requires banks to evaluate partners not just on technology features and cost, but on resilience, ethical data use, operational continuity, and regulatory alignment. A fintech may excel in product design, but without disciplined engineering practices, sustainable funding, and transparent governance, the bank inherits substantial risk.

Successful collaboration begins long before contracts are signed—with due diligence examining security posture, code quality, integration maturity, contingency processes, and ownership models. As retail banking evolves into a network of interconnected services, the strength of each component becomes a determinant of institutional trust. Customers rarely distinguish between bank and partner; they expect reliability from the system as a whole.

Failures within widely used fintech components can propagate across multiple institutions simultaneously, increasing the importance of shared standards, coordinated response mechanisms, and sector-wide resilience planning.

Banks and fintechs operate with fundamentally different mandates and incentives. Banks are built for continuity, prudential regulation, and long-term stability. Fintechs operate with compressed innovation cycles, narrower product scopes, and an optimisation mindset centred on speed. When these cultures interact without a structured operating philosophy, delivery slows, governance strains, and trust deteriorates.

Effective collaboration requires explicit frameworks that help both sides contribute their strengths without exposing each other to unmanaged vulnerabilities. Banks must define clear onboarding expectations—data boundaries, integration protocols, incident-handling procedures, and realistic review cycles. Fintechs must adopt enterprise-ready behaviours—structured release management, transparent performance reporting, predictable change windows, and compliance readiness. Well-governed API standards, version controls, sandbox environments, and consistent data definitions prevent the ambiguity that causes downstream service failures.

Cultural alignment reinforces this through joint steering forums, shared escalation routes, and collaborative resolution mechanisms that prevent issues from turning adversarial. When both organisations recognise their interdependence and operate within a matured engagement model, partnerships shift from tactical experiments to strategic capabilities.

Hybrid customer journeys span multiple infrastructures, regulatory obligations, and operational pathways. When responsibility isn't allocated explicitly—across onboarding, data handling, transaction processing, and customer support—small coordination gaps can escalate into systemic failures. Banks must map the full-service pathway and identify moments where a failure in a fintech-controlled module affects the bank's regulatory obligations. Audit trails, performance logs, encryption keys, and error-handling records must be jointly visible. A shared journey cannot rely on opaque vendor-driven reporting.

Equally important is clarity around customer communication. When an outage occurs or a transaction is delayed, customers should not be caught between two institutions claiming limited responsibility. Mature collaboration models embed unified service-level expectations, shared incident response protocols, and pre-agreed recovery parameters, ensuring that when something goes wrong, accountability is clear and response is swift.

Data boundaries deserve the same rigour. Hybrid financial journeys typically involve multiple systems touching the same customer record. Strong models specify who collects, processes, stores, enriches, and transmits customer data—and who bears responsibility for breaches or inaccuracies. When data boundaries are jointly designed, documented, and embedded into operating rhythm, collaboration becomes more stable, regulatory compliance is easier to maintain, and customers retain visibility and control over how their information is used.

Trust within collaboration is reinforced when both organisations maintain transparency in performance, risk posture, and operational behaviour. Banks historically operated with closed internal systems, but partnerships now require shared dashboards, common KPIs, and joint reporting routines. Fintechs often prioritise speed over documentation, creating visibility gaps around change management, model updates, vendor dependencies, or data-handling practices. Effective collaboration demands real-time service metrics, open disclosure of system changes, structured incident communication, and alignment on how emerging risks are identified and mitigated.

Collaboration at scale also requires structured learning loops. Many early partnerships fail not because of technical flaws but because lessons aren't captured—gaps in onboarding, mismatched expectations, unclear risk boundaries, or unforeseen customer-experience issues. By documenting these insights and integrating them into governance handbooks, vendor scorecards, and due-diligence workflows, banks create a repeatable, predictable collaboration architecture. Fintechs benefit too, gaining clarity on regulatory expectations and enterprise-grade risk controls. When insights are embedded into organisational memory rather than remaining with individual project teams, partnerships become smoother, faster, and safer.

Sustaining trust in fintech–bank collaboration ultimately depends on the bank's ability to treat every partnership as part of its own operating fabric rather than a peripheral add-on. When external capabilities sit outside mainstream structures, they create fragmentation. When they're embedded into core processes, they strengthen flexibility and innovation.

This requires banks to align partnership models with enterprise priorities—financial inclusion, cost transformation, and accelerated digital adoption. It also requires transparent communication with customers so they understand which services are delivered jointly and how their data flows across organisations. Risk cultures must be actively bridged: banks need mechanisms allowing fintechs to innovate without breaching regulatory thresholds; fintechs need frameworks that translate banking requirements into design principles rather than constraints.

As hybrid ecosystems expand, the banks that succeed will be those building partnerships grounded in clarity, shared accountability, and continuous alignment with institutional purpose. Collaboration is no longer about procurement contracts or vendor management. It's about engineering trust across institutional boundaries—and sustaining it at scale.

Open Source and Public Trust

Open-source technology is reshaping the foundations of trust in modern retail banking by shifting credibility away from hidden proprietary systems toward transparent, publicly verifiable code. In a hybrid environment where customer interactions depend on digital interfaces, API networks, and distributed infrastructure, institutions must anchor reliability in systems people cannot see but must still be able to trust. Open-source frameworks offer this assurance by allowing a broad community of engineers, academics, regulators, and security specialists to examine how a system behaves, how vulnerabilities are discovered, and how updates are managed. Unlike proprietary software, which confines oversight to limited groups under non-disclosure constraints, open-source ecosystems invite scrutiny from thousands of contributors who bring diverse perspectives and expertise. This community-driven verification strengthens resilience and reduces the likelihood that critical risks remain undiscovered. For banks, this transparency is not only a technology decision; it is a governance commitment. It signals to customers, regulators, and partners that the institution is willing to subject its infrastructure to open examination rather than relying solely on brand reputation or marketing assurances. In a world where digital interactions dominate and customers rarely see a human representative, trust must be built through systems that operate consistently, securely, and predictably. Open-source adoption provides the structural confidence required for hybrid banking, ensuring that reliability comes not from claims but from verifiable integrity.

However, transparency alone does not guarantee trust. Without disciplined implementation, clear ownership, and ongoing maintenance, open systems can introduce fragmentation or unmanaged risk. Governance remains essential to translate openness into reliability.

This adoption goes beyond software selection; it represents a structural shift in how retail banks think about transparency, accountability, and systemic reliability. When an institution adopts open standards for identity, payments, encryption, or data exchange, it moves away from dependency on closed, proprietary systems whose internal logic cannot be independently verified. This matters because modern retail banking operates within an expanding web of partners—payment gateways, cloud providers, fintech collaborators, and regulatory data networks—and the integrity of every customer experience depends on how these systems interact. Open-source frameworks reduce uncertainty by allowing banks and regulators to understand exactly how processes function, how data moves, and how safeguards are embedded. They also create a more resilient environment, because vulnerabilities discovered anywhere in the ecosystem become visible and fixable for everyone using the same standard. For customers, this shift builds a form of trust that does not rely on physical presence or brand familiarity; it rests on the knowledge that the institution is using infrastructure which is open to inspection, tested globally, and strengthened continually through shared learning. For regulators, open-source adoption reduces supervisory blind spots and enhances the ability to assess whether institutions meet common safety, performance, and compliance expectations. In this sense, open-source frameworks serve as a public good—a shared reliability layer underpinning the hybrid financial system.

Interoperability lies at the heart of hybrid banking, and open-source frameworks provide the most stable foundation for achieving it at scale. As retail banks operate across multiple channels, devices, partners, and regulatory environments, they must ensure that systems can communicate reliably without introducing friction into customer journeys. Open standards—whether in payments, identity, data portability, or API architecture—allow institutions to integrate new capabilities without rebuilding entire technology stacks. This reduces operational risk and accelerates innovation because modular, interoperable components can be upgraded independently. Open-source interoperability also prevents lock-in to single vendors, which can create hidden vulnerabilities when one provider controls critical infrastructure. By adopting open frameworks, banks gain strategic flexibility: they can adapt their architecture rapidly as customer expectations shift, regulatory demands evolve, and new players emerge. Moreover, interoperable systems strengthen trust because predictable, well-documented behaviour reduces the likelihood of failures during cross-platform transactions. For customers, this translates into smoother digital journeys and consistent service quality, regardless of how they access the bank. For institutions, it reduces the cost and complexity of managing multiple systems and ensures that hybrid delivery rests on a dependable, future-ready infrastructure.

One of the strongest advantages of open-source ecosystems is the depth and diversity of community-driven scrutiny they attract, which significantly improves the security posture of hybrid retail banking. In traditional proprietary models, code is reviewed by select internal teams or contracted auditors who operate within fixed schedules and limited visibility. By contrast, open-source projects benefit from continuous observation by global contributors—engineers, researchers, security analysts, and academics—who spot vulnerabilities that may never surface in closed environments. This type of distributed oversight accelerates detection, enhances patch quality, and reduces the window of exposure for institutions. For retail banks operating within increasingly connected ecosystems, this continuous assurance becomes crucial. Hybrid banking expands the attack surface through APIs, cloud dependencies, and third-party integrations, making early detection and rapid remediation essential. Community-based scrutiny strengthens resilience not only by identifying issues but also by sharing solutions across jurisdictions and sectors. A vulnerability discovered in one geography quickly becomes a lesson for institutions elsewhere, raising collective safety levels. For regulators, this model provides confidence that critical systems are not dependent on the capacity of one organisation alone but benefit from a broader defence network. Ultimately, this collaborative security model reinforces public trust by showing that the infrastructure behind hybrid banking is subject to ongoing, credible, and transparent examination.

The benefits of open-source adoption can only be realised when banks complement technological openness with disciplined internal governance. Without structured oversight, open-source components may be integrated inconsistently, updated irregularly, or layered onto legacy systems in ways that create unintended vulnerabilities. This emphasises the need for banks to establish clear policies for selection, evaluation, integration, and lifecycle management of open-source tools. Governance should include mandatory security audits, compatibility assessments, version control protocols, and well-defined ownership for maintaining each component. Importantly, institutions must treat open-source adoption not as a cost-saving shortcut but as a strategic capability requiring skilled teams who understand both the opportunities and the risks. When supported by strong governance, open-source frameworks enhance operational resilience and transparency, reinforcing customer trust. But when governance is weak, the same openness that strengthens security can become a channel for fragmentation or accidental exposure. Effective open-source governance therefore becomes a visible part of the institution's commitment to safety, accountability, and predictable performance—values that define the credibility of hybrid retail banking.

Open-source frameworks also encourage a more collaborative form of innovation that strengthens hybrid banking's long-term adaptability. In proprietary environments, innovation is typically constrained by vendor roadmaps, commercial priorities, and contractual cycles that determine when upgrades are released and which features are prioritised. Open-source ecosystems operate differently: improvements emerge from collective problem-solving, academic research, community dialogues, and real-world use cases contributed by institutions across sectors. This diversity of inputs accelerates the development of features that matter—stronger encryption, more efficient data-exchange protocols, improved identity modules, and better resilience tools. For retail banks, this means they benefit from advancements created far beyond their internal R&D capabilities, reducing the cost and time associated with maintaining modern infrastructure. Moreover, open innovation strengthens transparency because every enhancement, modification, or fix is recorded publicly, allowing institutions and regulators to understand precisely how systems evolve. This continuous, community-driven evolution aligns with the needs of hybrid banking, where customer expectations and regulatory requirements change rapidly. By participating in open-source ecosystems, banks position themselves within a broader innovation economy that enhances their ability to adapt, respond, and improve in ways that proprietary systems alone cannot support.

This also redefines how retail banks manage systemic risk, particularly in interconnected financial ecosystems where failures in one institution can quickly cascade across networks. Because open-source frameworks allow full visibility into how systems are structured and how components interact, they reduce the uncertainty that often accompanies proprietary black-box solutions. This visibility is critical for hybrid banking, where resilience depends on understanding the dependencies between cloud providers, API layers, fintech partners, and internal systems. When banks use open-source components with transparent architectures, regulators and internal risk teams can more accurately model failure scenarios, stress-test systems, and identify where safeguards must be reinforced. In addition, open-source tools often come with extensive testing suites and global user feedback, helping institutions anticipate risks earlier in the development cycle. This makes systemic risk more measurable and therefore more manageable. For customers, the payoff is stability—fewer outages, fewer hidden vulnerabilities, and more predictable service across channels. For the institution, it strengthens risk governance and aligns operational resilience with public expectations, regulatory standards, and long-term trust.

The use of open-source technologies also enhances regulatory confidence by giving supervisors clearer oversight into the systems that underpin retail banking. Regulators are increasingly required to assess not only financial soundness but also the operational resilience, data integrity, and cybersecurity posture of institutions operating within hybrid delivery models. Proprietary technologies often limit transparency, forcing regulators to rely on vendor attestations or partial documentation. In contrast, open-source frameworks allow regulators to examine source code, understand architectural decisions, evaluate update histories, and verify whether controls have been implemented correctly. This reduces supervisory blind spots and strengthens the alignment between institutional behaviour and regulatory expectations. For banks, this transparency lowers compliance friction: approvals become faster, audits more predictable, and regulatory relationships more collaborative. When a regulator can clearly see how a system works, confidence increases—and with it, the institution's standing in the broader market. The resulting dynamic benefits customers indirectly as well, as stronger regulatory assurance increases overall trust in digital and hybrid banking channels.

Open-source adoption also strengthens customer empowerment by aligning financial infrastructure with modern expectations of choice, clarity, and control. In a hybrid banking environment where customers use multiple channels and interact with diverse service providers, trust increasingly depends on whether institutions demonstrate openness rather than secrecy. Open-source frameworks contribute to this expectation by enabling clearer communication about how systems behave, how data is processed, and how security is maintained. Even if customers never examine the underlying code, the knowledge that a bank operates on transparent, publicly verifiable foundations creates a psychological sense of safety that closed systems cannot easily replicate. This transparency helps customers feel more confident when authorising data-sharing, adopting new digital services, or engaging with fintech-powered experiences. It reduces the perceived risk associated with hybrid journeys and reinforces the idea that trust is being built into the infrastructure itself rather than demanded through brand reputation alone. For institutions, this shift toward customer-centred transparency becomes a long-term advantage, as confidence built on structural integrity tends to be more durable than confidence built on marketing assurances or legacy familiarity.

Ultimately, the strategic value of open-source adoption in hybrid retail banking lies in its ability to align institutional purpose with public expectations of fairness, accountability, and shared progress. In an era where financial services are delivered through invisible digital layers rather than physical interactions, customers increasingly judge institutions by how responsibly they design their systems and how openly they communicate those design choices. Open-source frameworks embody this philosophy by making the underlying mechanisms of trust visible, testable, and collectively maintained. They allow banks to participate in broader innovation communities, strengthen resilience through shared knowledge, and demonstrate a genuine commitment to transparency. For regulators, this visibility reduces uncertainty and builds confidence in the stability of hybrid financial ecosystems. For society, it ensures that essential banking services are built on infrastructure that prioritises security, integrity, and public benefit. As hybrid models expand and reliance on third-party platforms deepens, banks that adopt open-source principles will be better positioned to deliver trustworthy, adaptable, and future-ready services—not because they claim to be transparent, but because their architecture makes transparency real.

Institutional Perspective: A Global Lens on Customers, Society, and Being Human in an Age of Invisible Trust

When Trust Becomes Invisible

For most of modern banking history, trust was something people could see. Large branches, printed statements, signatures, formal procedures, and face-to-face conversations all reinforced the idea that institutions were stable, accountable, and present. Banking felt tangible because trust was rooted in the physical world.

That visibility has largely disappeared.

Today, customers interact mostly through apps, biometric logins, authentication prompts, encrypted payment systems, and automated platforms running quietly in the background of everyday life. The institutional experience now happens through systems most people rarely see or fully understand. Yet modern society depends on those systems constantly—for salaries, savings, payments, commerce, identity, and participation in the economy itself.

This represents a major shift in how trust operates. In the past, trust was reinforced through human familiarity and visible continuity. Now it is maintained through the reliability of invisible infrastructure. A payment clearing instantly, an account opening smoothly, or fraud being blocked without disruption all strengthen confidence even when customers have no idea how the system works underneath.

Trust has become infrastructural rather than interpersonal.

Most people don't think about this when systems work normally. But invisible trust becomes suddenly visible when something fails. A system outage that blocks salary access, an authentication failure while travelling, or an identity theft incident quickly turns abstract infrastructure into a deeply personal experience. Customers become aware of how dependent modern financial life is on technological systems operating beyond their control.

That dependence now extends far beyond banking. Payment rails, digital identity systems, cloud providers, government platforms, and financial services increasingly function as interconnected layers of broader social infrastructure. Banking is no longer a standalone activity. It is embedded within systems supporting employment, healthcare, housing, taxation, and daily economic participation.

Different societies experience this transition differently. In places where institutional coordination and public trust are already strong—such as Singapore or parts of Northern Europe—invisible digital systems are often adopted confidently. In countries where trust in institutions has historically been weaker or more fragmented, invisible systems may generate more scepticism even when the technology itself is advanced. China presents another model, where trust is shaped more by the continuity of integrated digital platforms than by traditional institutional relationships. Across parts of Africa, trust tends to grow from practical reliability and usability rather than institutional legacy.

This shift also changes the emotional relationship between people and institutions. Digital convenience can feel empowering while simultaneously increasing dependence on systems customers cannot independently verify. Access to savings, identity recovery, or fraud resolution increasingly relies on algorithmic systems and infrastructure providers operating far from visible human interaction.

As financial systems become more intelligent and interconnected, institutional trust may depend less on reputation alone and more on operational integrity. A well-known brand can still lose confidence quickly through repeated outages, opaque data practices, or poor crisis response. Invisible systems must work not only technically, but psychologically and socially.

People are generally comfortable with complexity when systems appear reliable and fair. Trust weakens when systems feel unpredictable, opaque, or impossible to challenge. Trust may now be engineered through infrastructure, but it is still experienced in deeply human ways whenever continuity or security is tested.

Digital Identity and the Future of Personhood

For most of modern history, banking identity was physical and visible. People proved who they were through documents, signatures, passports, and face-to-face interaction. Identity was stable, observable, and tied directly to physical presence.

That model is changing rapidly.

Identity is becoming digital, distributed, and infrastructural. Customers now authenticate themselves through biometrics, devices, behavioural patterns, transaction histories, and evolving digital footprints. Increasingly, institutions know people less through direct interaction and more through the data environments generated by everyday activity.

This is more than technological modernisation. It represents a deeper shift in how institutions recognise personhood itself. Access to banking, healthcare, employment, payments, and public services increasingly depends on trusted digital identity across interconnected systems. Identity is no longer simply personal—it is becoming infrastructure.

For most people, this remains invisible during normal use. A biometric login works instantly. A payment clears without friction. An account opens in minutes. Behind those simple experiences sit complex systems of authentication, behavioural analysis, and data matching operating continuously in the background. Institutions increasingly judge legitimacy not only by what customers provide directly, but by how digital systems interpret behavioural consistency across multiple environments.

The opportunities are significant. Digital identity can reduce fraud, simplify onboarding, expand inclusion, and provide access at enormous scale. Across Africa and Asia, mobile identity systems have already widened participation beyond traditional branch-based banking. India's digital public infrastructure—linking identity, payments, and public services—has accelerated financial participation dramatically while also raising important debates around privacy, governance, and long-term dependence on centralised systems.

Singapore has integrated digital identity into broader national infrastructure, creating seamless interaction across banking, healthcare, payments, and government services. Europe, meanwhile, approaches digital identity through stronger concerns around privacy, consent, and data protection, reflecting different historical relationships between citizens and institutions.

These differences matter because digital identity is not just technical infrastructure. It is a social relationship built on trust. People need confidence that identity systems are secure, fair, recoverable, and accountable when problems occur. A failed authentication may appear minor technically, but for the individual it can temporarily block access to salary payments, travel, healthcare, or housing.

AI adds another layer of complexity. Institutions increasingly evaluate identity through behavioural patterns—movement, spending activity, typing rhythms, and device interaction—rather than static verification alone. Identity becomes dynamic and continuously assessed through algorithmic interpretation.

In these systems, customers may face situations where their legitimacy is judged through processes they cannot fully understand or challenge. A frozen account or failed verification may feel less like an inconvenience and more like temporary institutional invisibility.

The emotional stakes are high because financial identity increasingly determines participation in digital society itself. Identity systems now influence economic inclusion, mobility, and social continuity in ways that extend far beyond authentication.

The future challenge lies in balancing security, efficiency, inclusion, privacy, and fairness at the same time. Institutions need stronger digital identity systems to manage fraud and expanding digital ecosystems, but they also need clear mechanisms for explanation, recovery, and accountability when systems fail.

The underlying expectation remains simple: people want confidence that institutions can recognise them fairly, protect them securely, and restore trust quickly when something goes wrong.

How Different Societies Experience Invisible Systems

Invisible digital systems do not create trust in the same way everywhere. Financial technologies may rely on similar infrastructure globally, but how people interpret automation, reliability, and data-driven systems depends heavily on local history, governance, economic experience, and institutional confidence.

Trust may operate through invisible systems, but its emotional meaning remains deeply local.

In the UK, digital banking adoption is high, yet customers still expect accountability and clear recourse when problems arise. Automated systems are accepted during normal activity, but disruptions quickly revive expectations for visible institutional responsibility.

Across Europe, digital systems are shaped by stronger expectations around privacy, transparency, and regulatory oversight. Customers may appreciate convenience while demanding safeguards around data usage, explainability, and procedural fairness. Historical concerns about concentrated institutional power continue influencing attitudes toward AI and behavioural monitoring.

Singapore is one of the clearest examples of high-trust invisible infrastructure operating at national scale. Banking, payments, public services, and identity systems function as tightly integrated ecosystems embedded into daily life. Confidence in invisible systems is reinforced by confidence in institutional coordination itself.

China represents a different model, where payments, commerce, communication, mobility, and identity are deeply integrated within large digital platforms. Customers experience invisible infrastructure less as abstract institutional systems and more as seamless continuity woven into everyday activity.

North America operates within more fragmented and competitive ecosystems. Customers often experience advanced innovation and personalisation, but trust is shaped heavily by concerns around cybercrime, data breaches, and platform fragmentation. Digital systems can feel highly sophisticated while still appearing institutionally disconnected during disputes or disruptions.

Across the Gulf, digital finance is growing rapidly alongside national modernisation efforts. Mobile-first behaviour and younger populations are accelerating adoption, but personal relationships and institutional reputation remain central to trust. Invisible systems are expected to complement visible credibility, not replace it.

In Africa, digital financial ecosystems expanded largely out of practical necessity. Mobile finance developed where telecommunications infrastructure arrived before traditional banking networks. Trust therefore depends heavily on reliability, accessibility, and usefulness rather than institutional heritage.

Latin America's relationship with invisible systems is strongly shaped by memories of inflation, volatility, and institutional instability. Customers may adopt digital systems enthusiastically while still remaining cautious about long-term institutional dependence.

These differences create a challenge for global institutions. Operational consistency alone does not create emotional legitimacy. Systems built around automation and efficiency must still adapt to local expectations around transparency, recourse, and reassurance.

Trust cannot simply be exported from one market to another. It must be earned within the social realities of each society.

Being Human Inside Algorithmic Infrastructure

Modern financial systems increasingly operate through algorithms running continuously in the background of daily life. Fraud detection monitors transactions in real time. Credit models analyse financial patterns automatically. Authentication systems evaluate behaviour, geolocation, and device usage within seconds.

Banking is no longer shaped primarily through direct human interaction. It is increasingly mediated through invisible infrastructure.

Most customers barely notice these systems when they work well. Payments clear instantly. Fraud is stopped automatically. Services adapt smoothly across devices and channels. Beneath that simplicity, however, lies a profound change:

institutions increasingly understand customers through data patterns before any human interaction occurs.

Historically, financial judgement was tied to identifiable people—branch managers, underwriters, advisers, or investigators. In algorithmic systems, judgement emerges through behavioural interpretation generated by automated systems trained to detect patterns, anomalies, and predictive signals across enormous datasets.

The benefits are substantial. Algorithmic infrastructure allows banks to manage fraud, cyber threats, compliance, and operational complexity at scales impossible through manual systems alone. AI-driven monitoring can identify suspicious activity within milliseconds, while predictive systems can detect operational stress before visible disruption occurs.

These capabilities are becoming essential.

But algorithmic efficiency also changes how people experience institutional authority. Customers may no longer understand how decisions are reached, what variables influenced outcomes, or whether a problem reflects genuine risk or system error. A delayed payment, failed onboarding, or blocked transaction can feel confusing and inaccessible even when technically justified.

That opacity matters because trust depends not only on accuracy, but also on emotional understanding and perceived fairness. People accept complexity when outcomes feel explainable and recoverable. Trust weakens when systems feel arbitrary or impossible to challenge through meaningful human interaction.

A technologically advanced institution can still feel emotionally distant if customers cannot understand how decisions affecting their lives are being made.

Different societies experience this unevenly. In countries where institutional trust is already high, automated systems are generally accepted more easily. In environments where trust is fragile or economic insecurity is greater, algorithmic systems can trigger deeper fears around exclusion, surveillance, or loss of personal agency.

AI intensifies these tensions further. Institutions may become more operationally capable while becoming emotionally less visible. Customers may rely heavily on systems they only partially understand while remaining uncertain about where accountability exists when things go wrong.

This condition reflects what might be called algorithmic life. Financial behaviour, identity verification, fraud detection, and service access are increasingly interpreted through automated systems that continuously shape participation in economic society. Most people rarely see these systems directly, yet they are influenced by them constantly.

The central challenge is clear. Financial systems must continue becoming more automated because modern operational complexity and cyber risk demand it. At the same time, institutions must preserve human reassurance, transparency, and accountability strong enough to maintain legitimacy within increasingly invisible systems.

The issue is no longer whether algorithmic infrastructure will expand. It already is. The real question is whether people will continue feeling recognised, protected, and fairly treated inside systems increasingly governed by automated interpretation rather than visible human judgement.

Why Trust Architecture Will Define Institutional Legitimacy

As banking becomes more digital, interconnected, and algorithmically driven, institutional legitimacy may depend less on physical scale and more on the integrity of the systems operating beneath the surface.

Historically, trust in banks came from physical presence, reputation, and long-standing relationships. Increasingly, institutions will be judged by the resilience, transparency, and reliability of the infrastructure through which financial life actually functions.

This is a major shift.

Most customers will never see the systems governing authentication, fraud detection, payments processing, or AI-driven decisions. Yet these invisible systems increasingly determine whether banking feels secure, fair, and trustworthy. Trust architecture becomes more than technical infrastructure—it becomes the environment through which society interprets institutional legitimacy itself.

The stakes are rising because financial ecosystems are becoming deeply interconnected. Banks now depend on cloud providers, fintech partnerships, open banking frameworks, cybersecurity networks, payment platforms, identity systems, and data-sharing environments operating across borders.

Trust can no longer depend solely on the strength of individual institutions. It increasingly depends on the resilience of the wider ecosystem.

A cyberattack, cloud outage, authentication failure, or algorithmic error can now affect millions of people simultaneously. Invisible infrastructure carries consequences that extend far beyond technical operations.

People rarely think about trust architecture during stable periods. They notice it when continuity breaks—when salaries are delayed, transactions fail during emergencies, fraud remains unresolved, or systems stay offline too long. In those moments, invisible infrastructure becomes deeply personal.

Customers are not only judging operational competence. They are judging whether institutions appear accountable and capable of restoring confidence under pressure.

That is why governance will become central to future banking legitimacy. Advanced technology alone cannot sustain trust if systems appear opaque or impossible to challenge when errors occur. Automated systems must remain explainable, recoverable, and aligned with public expectations of fairness.

Different societies will approach this differently. Europe is likely to focus heavily on balancing innovation with privacy and accountability. Singapore and parts of Asia may continue building legitimacy through coordinated digital infrastructure. North America is increasingly focused on cyber resilience, platform concentration, and data governance. Across Africa and Latin America, practical reliability, inclusion, and usability remain critical to how trust is experienced day to day.

AI will intensify these issues. While AI can strengthen fraud prevention and operational efficiency, it also increases public sensitivity around transparency and accountability. The future of trust may depend not only on whether systems are intelligent, but on whether that intelligence is governed responsibly.

Institutions are taking on a broader role. Invisible systems now influence identity verification, transaction legitimacy, fraud classification, and access to economic participation itself. Over time, customers may judge banks less by products and more by whether systems remain dependable when it matters most.

The institutions that endure will not necessarily be those with the most advanced technology alone. They will be the ones capable of combining technological sophistication with resilient governance, transparency, accountability, and human legitimacy at scale.

The future ultimately comes down to a simple question: can people continue feeling secure inside systems they increasingly cannot see? The answer will shape not only banking, but the broader relationship between technology, institutions, and society.

Reflection

The shift from reputation-based trust to infrastructure-based trust marks one of the most significant turning points in the history of retail banking. For more than a century, customer confidence rested on physical presence, branch familiarity, personal interactions, and institutional longevity. In the hybrid era, these foundations have moved into digital systems that must earn trust through reliability, clarity, and integrity rather than visibility. This chapter has shown that modern trust is not an abstract sentiment; it is an engineered capability shaped by identity systems, authentication layers, consent architecture, governance models, and collaborative digital ecosystems. Institutions that once relied on brand equity must now demonstrate operational transparency, predictable behaviour across platforms, and disciplined stewardship of customer data. The financial system has become too interconnected for any single organisation to carry the entire weight of trust. Banks now share responsibility with fintech partners, cloud providers, identity networks, and regulatory infrastructures, making cooperation as important as compliance. Open-source frameworks underline this shift by reinforcing transparency, collective scrutiny, and public accountability in ways proprietary systems cannot easily match. As institutions design for the next decade of hybrid banking, trust must be embedded into architecture rather than appended as a message. The lesson is clear: resilience, fairness, and transparency must be built deliberately into the systems that customers depend on but rarely see. Trust cannot be requested—it must be designed, demonstrated, and maintained through the architecture that supports every digital experience. In this new environment, banks that recognise trust as a structural capability will be better positioned to lead in a world where confidence is earned not through proximity, but through integrity in design. What ultimately matters is how this architecture performs under pressure. Moments of stress—fraud attempts, system outages, or unexpected demand—reveal whether trust has been structurally embedded or only superficially designed. Institutions are judged most clearly when conditions are least stable.

Framework: Trust Infrastructure Architecture: Five Structural Anchors

Framework Overview

This framework explains the structural components that enable trust to function reliably in hybrid retail banking. It consolidates insights from all five pillars to show how institutions can embed transparency, security, ethical safeguards, and operational integrity into a unified trust architecture that works consistently across digital and physical environments.

Trust Infrastructure Architecture

IDENTITY INTEGRITY

Hybrid banking requires identity systems that remain consistent, secure, and continuous across channels. Strong identity foundations ensure that authentication, access, and fraud controls adapt to customer risk profiles while maintaining ease of use.

CONSENT AND DATA TRANSPARENCY

Customers must be able to understand, control, and revoke data permissions. Trust increases when consent journeys are simple, predictable, and transparent, and when institutions clearly explain how data is used to deliver value, safety, and personalisation.

GOVERNANCE OF INTERCONNECTED SYSTEMS

Hybrid delivery relies on cloud platforms, APIs, fintech partners, and third-party vendors. Governance must extend across the entire ecosystem, ensuring service reliability, accountability, and risk integrity across all operating layers.

THIRD-PARTY TRUST ALIGNMENT

Banks now share responsibility for customer journeys with technology partners. Trust depends on evaluating third parties for security, resilience, sustainability, cultural alignment, and operational readiness, supported by continuous audits and joint controls.

OPEN-SOURCE CONFIDENCE

Open-source systems strengthen trust by enabling transparency, independent review, and shared innovation. When supported by disciplined governance, open standards improve interoperability, code reliability, and public assurance across hybrid channels.

Purpose of the Framework

This framework shows how trust in hybrid banking must be engineered, not assumed. It demonstrates that reliability, transparency, and accountability arise from deliberate architectural choices, and it provides leaders with a clear structure for diagnosing trust gaps and strengthening institutional credibility. Each element of this framework must translate into tangible customer outcomes: secure access, clear data control, reliable service, and consistent experience across channels. Without this translation, structural strength does not convert into institutional trust.

Table 3.1 Checklist: Trust Infrastructure Readiness

1	Identity Do our identity systems continuously verify users across journeys, or rely on one-time authentication?
2	Authentication Are our authentication methods adaptive to risk, or static and uniform across all interactions?
3	Continuity Does trust persist across channels, or reset when customers move between digital and physical touchpoints?
4	Consent Do customers clearly understand and control how their data is used, shared, and revoked?
5	Transparency Are our systems explainable in how decisions are made, or opaque to customers and regulators?
6	Resilience Can trust be maintained during system failures, cyber incidents, or service disruptions?
7	Ecosystem Do we govern third-party dependencies with the same discipline as internal systems?
8	Governance Is accountability for trust distributed clearly across technology, risk, and business functions?
9	Security Are we anticipating evolving threats such as synthetic identity and AI-driven fraud?
10	Integrity Is trust deliberately engineered into our architecture, or assumed through brand and legacy?

Table 3.2 Template: Trust Infrastructure Mapping

No.	*Dimension*	*Current State*	*Risk / Gap*	*Target State*	*Owner*
1	Identity Integrity	Fragmented or session-based identity checks	Identity gaps, fraud exposure	Continuous, multi-layered identity verification	CIO / CISO
2	Authentication Model	Static credentials and uniform controls	Vulnerability to attack, poor UX	Adaptive, risk-based authentication	CISO
3	Channel Trust Continuity	Trust resets across channels	Customer friction, inconsistency	Seamless trust across all touchpoints	COO / CIO
4	Consent Architecture	Legalistic, unclear consent flows	Customer confusion, regulatory risk	Transparent, dynamic consent control	Chief Data Officer
5	Data Transparency	Limited visibility of data usage	Loss of confidence, compliance gaps	Clear, explainable data practices	Chief Data Officer
6	Infrastructure Resilience	Basic recovery mechanisms	Trust breakdown during failure	Embedded resilience and fallback pathways	COO / CIO
7	Third-Party Governance	Contract-led oversight	Hidden systemic risk	Continuous ecosystem governance	CRO / COO
8	Governance and Accountability	Siloed ownership	Delayed response, weak control	Clear cross-functional accountability	Board / Executive Committee
9	Cyber and Fraud Defence	Reactive fraud controls	Exposure to advanced threats	Predictive, intelligence-led defence	CISO
10	Trust Architecture Maturity	Trust treated as outcome	Inconsistent delivery	Trust engineered as core capability	CEO / Board

Bibliography

Bank for International Settlements (2023). *Principles for Operational Resilience in Financial Services*. BIS.

European Banking Authority (2021). *Guidelines on ICT and Security Risk Management*. EBA.

European Commission (2022). *Digital Operational Resilience Act (DORA)*. European Union.

Gillespie, T. (2018). *Custodians of the Internet: Platforms, Content Moderation, and the Hidden Decisions That Shape Social Media*. Yale University Press.

International Monetary Fund (2023). *Research on Digital Trust and Financial Stability in Platform Banking Environments*. IMF.

Klapper, L., Singer, D., Ansar, S., and Hess, J. (2022). *The Global Findex Database 2021: Financial Inclusion, Digital Payments, and Resilience in the Age of COVID-19*. World Bank.

National Institute of Standards and Technology (2023). *Digital Identity Guidelines (NIST SP 800–63)*. U.S. Department of Commerce.

OECD (2021). *Enhancing Access to and Sharing of Data: Reconciling Risks and Benefits for Data Re-use across Societies*. OECD Publishing.

OpenID Foundation (2022). *OpenID Connect Core Specifications*. OpenID Foundation.

PwC (2023). *Insights on Trust, Security and Transparency in Digital Banking Ecosystems*. PricewaterhouseCoopers.

Schneier, B. (2015). *Data and Goliath: The Hidden Battles to Collect Your Data and Control Your World*. W. W. Norton & Company.

The Linux Foundation (2023). *Research on Open Source in Financial Services and Digital Trust Frameworks*. Linux Foundation Research.

World Economic Forum (2022). *Digital Identity Systems: Balancing Innovation, Security and Privacy*. World Economic Forum.

World Economic Forum (2023). *Global Cybersecurity Outlook 2023*. World Economic Forum.

Zuboff, S. (2019). *The Age of Surveillance Capitalism*. Profile Books.

4 The Open Finance Mandate

Context

Open finance represents one of the most far-reaching shifts in the modern financial system, extending well beyond the initial ambitions of open banking. While open banking introduced the idea that customers should be able to share their payments and account data securely with authorised third parties, open finance broadens that principle to include the entire spectrum of financial relationships: mortgages, savings, pensions, insurance, investments, credit histories, tax information, and in some markets, even telecom and utility data. This evolution marks a structural redefinition of how financial institutions operate. It shifts customer information from being a proprietary institutional asset to a consumer-owned resource that flows across ecosystems through secure, consent-driven frameworks. In practical terms, open finance requires banks to design systems that can communicate externally, manage permissioned data flows, and maintain consistent security and conduct standards across multiple interfaces they do not directly control.

Customers do not distinguish between institutions when interacting across an open-finance ecosystem. A delay, failure, or inconsistency at any point in the journey is attributed to the overall system rather than a specific provider. Trust therefore becomes collective and cumulative, shaped by repeated interactions rather than individual institutional performance.

This shift demands a deep architectural change inside retail institutions. Legacy systems, once designed for internal control, must now support external interoperability. Data architectures built around product silos must transition toward unified models that allow information to be retrieved, verified, processed, and shared in real time. Governance structures that previously focused on internal audit and compliance must now accommodate ecosystem-level risks, third-party dependencies, and cross-jurisdictional regulatory requirements. For hybrid banks—institutions that combine physical presence with digital delivery—these adjustments require careful coordination across technology teams, product lines, risk units, operational centres, and customer-facing channels. The move toward open finance effectively rewires how a bank thinks about trust, transparency, and customer empowerment.

DOI: 10.4324/9781042021765-5

The expansion of data-sharing also increases exposure to financial crime. Fraud patterns now exploit gaps between institutions, particularly where identity signals, consent frameworks, or monitoring standards are not fully aligned. Open finance therefore requires embedded fraud intelligence that operates across the ecosystem rather than within isolated institutional boundaries.

At the same time, open finance is accelerating a broader cultural and competitive realignment. Customers expect consistent experiences across platforms—whether interacting with a bank's app, a fintech partner, a pension provider, or an e-commerce platform offering embedded financial services. This expectation forces banks to modernise their user journeys, consent processes, authentication layers, and data-sharing flows. It also means that institutions can no longer rely solely on brand loyalty or distribution networks; value shifts toward reliability, speed, personalisation, and the ability to orchestrate cross-sector services. Banks that adapt early can position themselves as trusted coordinators within open ecosystems. Those that resist may see parts of their traditional value chain absorbed by more agile providers—particularly in lending, savings, wealth management, and small-business services.

Global regulatory trajectories reinforce the inevitability of this transformation. The UK continues to expand consumer-data rights, the EU is driving standardisation through PSD2, PSD3, and the Financial Data Access Regulation, and India has pioneered account-aggregator frameworks built on digital public infrastructure. Australia, Singapore, Brazil, and Indonesia have adopted variations of open finance to promote competition, customer empowerment, and financial inclusion. While each region follows its own path, the direction is consistent: interoperable systems, explicit data-sharing rules, secure APIs, strong liability frameworks, and clear consent architecture. This global momentum creates a new expectation for retail institutions: open finance is not an experiment, but a baseline requirement for long-term competitiveness.

For bank leadership, the implications are structural and strategic. Open finance forces boards and executive teams to oversee new forms of risk, from data-flow liability to ecosystem conduct breaches. It also requires strategic clarity about the bank's role: platform orchestrator, infrastructure provider, ecosystem partner, or specialised service leader. These choices influence investment, capability building, talent requirements, customer-journey design, and partnership models. The shift toward openness is not merely about complying with regulators; it is about positioning the institution for relevance in a marketplace where information symmetry, transparent governance, customer control, and ecosystem participation define competitive advantage.

In this chapter, the five pillars explore the essential components of open finance architecture: regulatory mandates, data portability, platformisation, embedded-finance ecosystems, and board-level strategic challenges. Together, they establish a blueprint for how future-ready retail banks can build secure, interoperable, and inclusive systems capable of meeting both regulatory expectations and customer needs in an increasingly interconnected financial world.

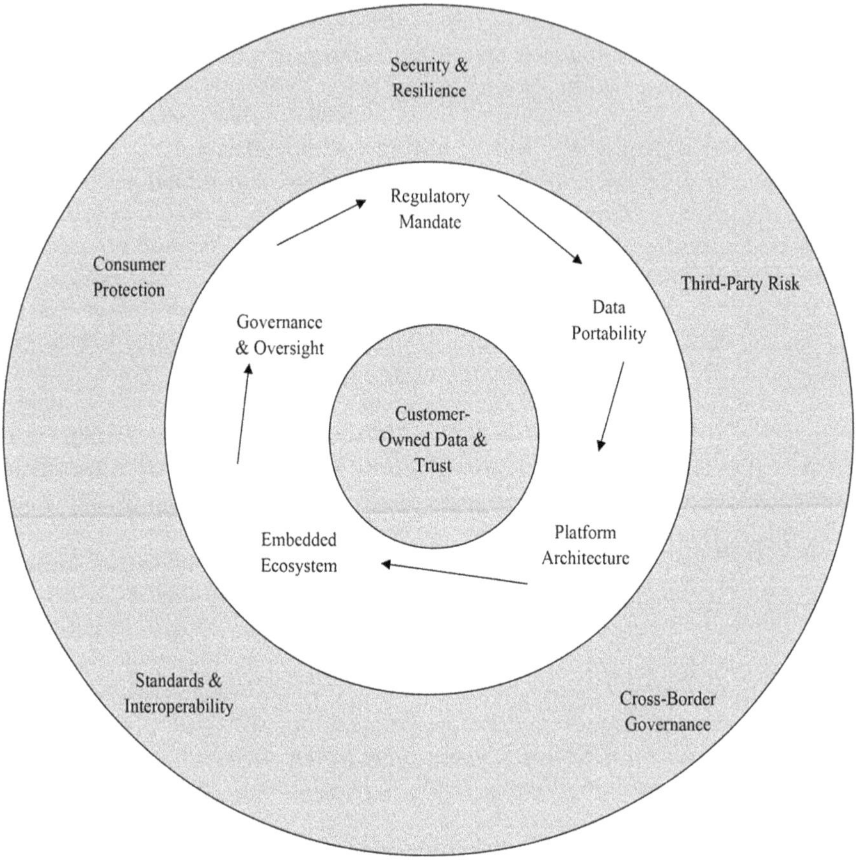

Figure 4.1 Open Finance as Institutional Architecture

Regulatory Mandates

Regulatory mandates are now the primary force shaping the architecture of open finance, defining the rules, standards, and safeguards that determine how financial data moves across banks, insurers, pension providers, fintechs, and non-financial platforms. In the UK and EU, regulators have shifted decisively from encouraging data sharing to enforcing it as a legal right grounded in consumer empowerment and market transparency. The UK's transition from Open Banking to the broader Financial Data Access Framework signals a structural expansion: payments and current-account data were only the beginning, and the next phase brings mortgages, investments, savings, credit, and even loyalty data into a regulated, permission-based ecosystem. The European Union's progression from PSD2 to PSD3, alongside the new Financial Data Access Regulation, strengthens liability rules, clarifies data-holder responsibilities, and embeds higher technical-security thresholds for API interactions; these changes require banks to redesign both the technical and governance components of their open finance stack. India's approach, built on digital public infrastructure rather than purely market-driven incentives, has become a global standard for consent-based financial data flows, with Account Aggregator meeting this challenge by providing citizens with the facility to securely share verified information instantly with lenders, wealth managers, insurance companies, and government agencies. This technology stack, underpinned by standardised application program interfaces, protocol layers, and consent executive architectures, represents one way in which public policy can create an environment that is conducive for financial technology innovations while still respecting the rights of citizens. Australia, Singapore, and Brazil all utilise a regulated financial ecosystem of this nature, further strengthening the international push for open finance. In financial retail banking organisations, regulatory directives of this type require organisations to implement more than just compliance actions. They drive fundamental technological architectures in API gateway landscapes, taxonomies, liability models, third-party management, and consent accountability layers.

Case Study: India's Account Aggregator Framework—Open Finance by Mandate

India's Account Aggregator (AA) framework represents one of the world's most advanced implementations of open finance as a regulatory mandate rather than a market-led initiative. Introduced and regulated by the Reserve Bank of India, the framework enables individuals to securely share verified financial data such as bank accounts, loans, insurance policies, investments, and tax records across institutions through explicit, time-bound consent.

Unlike early open banking models that focused narrowly on payments, the AA system was designed from inception as a full-spectrum open finance architecture. Licensed Account Aggregators act as consent managers, while regulated Financial Information Providers and Financial Information Users exchange data through standardised APIs without storing customer information. This separation of roles embeds accountability, traceability, and consumer control directly into the infrastructure.

The framework has enabled faster credit assessment, reduced documentation burdens for consumers and small businesses, and supported cross-sector use cases including lending, wealth management, insurance, and government-linked services. Importantly, participation is not optional for regulated entities, making interoperability and data portability a baseline obligation rather than a competitive differentiator.

India's Account Aggregator model is now referenced by global regulators and policy bodies as a blueprint for population-scale open finance, demonstrating how regulatory mandates can create trusted, interoperable ecosystems while preserving consumer rights and institutional accountability.

Institutions operating in open finance are increasingly functioning as architectural blueprints rather than compliance checklists, forcing retail banks to redesign systems, decision pathways, and customer journeys from the ground up. Supervisors across the UK, EU, India, Australia, and Singapore are signalling that data mobility, customer rights, interoperability, and liability clarity are now structural expectations embedded directly into the financial ecosystem. As a result, banks must transition from treating regulation as an end-stage obligation to viewing it as the design logic that shapes how their technology stacks, API gateways, authentication layers, and consent mechanisms operate. When regulators mandate standardised APIs, for example, banks must reorganise their internal data models to ensure consistent formatting, secure transmission, and predictable performance across multiple external interfaces. When consent rules become more granular, institutions must rebuild customer-facing flows so that permissions are meaningful, revocable, and aligned with local data-protection expectations. In a similar vein, cross-border regulatory frameworks force banks to reconsider their choices of vendors, cloud-hosting options, and plans for operational resilience in ways that ensure compliance for multiple jurisdictions at once. Regulation is also hastening the shift away from proprietary, closed systems and toward interoperable, modular architectures that can be supervised consistently. In India, the Account Aggregator framework forces banks to adopt unified API standards; in the UK and EU, upcoming PSD3 and the Financial Data Access Framework require banks to open additional datasets while maintaining strong security and monitoring. These mandates are structurally significant because they shift institutional responsibility from what a bank controls internally to how it participates in a broader data-sharing ecosystem. For hybrid institutions, regulatory alignment becomes a design principle-ensuring that every digital component is transparent, accountable, and capable of operating within an interconnected financial network.

Customer data rights have become the centrepiece of regulatory thinking in open finance, transforming how retail banks must collect, use, store, and share information across increasingly complex digital ecosystems. Regulators in the UK, EU, India, Australia, Brazil, and Singapore are converging on the principle that individuals—not institutions—own their financial data, and this shift requires banks to redesign long-standing assumptions about data control. Instead of viewing customer information as an internal asset, banks must now treat it as a permissioned, purpose-bound resource that can only be accessed with clear, informed, and revocable consent. This regulatory expectation compels institutions to rebuild their consent journeys so they are explicit, contextual, and easy to understand, with customers able to see precisely which entities have access to their data and for what purpose. Supervisors are also widening the definition of financial data to include non-traditional sources such as utility payments, payroll records, insurance history, investment portfolios, pension information, and certain categories of behavioural data when linked to financial decision-making. As the scope expands, banks must create stronger governance models to prevent over-collection, misuse, or unauthorised sharing. The EU's upcoming Financial Data Access Framework, for example, requires consistency across data formats, retention rules, and consent withdrawal, while India's account-aggregator model enforces strict purpose limitation and end-to-end encryption. These rights reshape architecture by requiring unified data taxonomies, consistent metadata, and real-time auditability across all internal systems. For hybrid banks, this means adopting design philosophies where privacy is structural, not optional, and where all customer-facing journeys must reflect fairness, transparency, and control. Data rights have therefore moved beyond regulatory compliance—they are redefining the ethics, responsibilities, and operating logic of modern retail institutions. Clarity in consent is equally critical. Customers must understand what they are agreeing to, how their data will be used, and how they can withdraw access. Where consent becomes complex or opaque, regulatory compliance may be achieved, but trust is weakened.

As open finance expands across sectors and jurisdictions, regulators are placing far stronger emphasis on liability and accountability frameworks that determine who is responsible when data flows across multiple intermediaries. Traditional banking operated within closed systems where responsibility was clearly held by the institution managing accounts and transactions. Open finance disrupts this simplicity by introducing fintech partners, API aggregators, third-party processors, digital-public-infrastructure entities, and cross-border service providers, each of whom touches customer data at different points. Regulators in the UK, EU, India, Singapore, and Australia are therefore redefining accountability to ensure that when something goes wrong—whether a data breach, service outage, privacy failure, or incorrect decision—it is clear which party is liable and how customers are protected. The EU's PSD3, and additionally the Financial Data Access Framework, emphasises and enforces strict allocation of responsibility between data holders and data users, with contracts outlining liability for misuse, delays, unauthorised access, and inaccuracies in data transmission. Other notable realities in relation to data use include India's account aggregator, which seeks to ensure real-time consent, encrypted data, and clearly outlined resolution of disputes, making it impossible for institutions to shift responsibility to data aggregators. In regard to fintech, which has often used third-party data indirectly, the FCA of the UK emphasises the need for financial institutions to control all third-party dependencies, with boards being forced to ensure they comprehend and mitigate all ecosystem risks. In all cases, these realities necessitate a shift in retail banking structures, with institutions being forced into redesigned structures every day, with accountability being an integral part of API management, vendor selection, and reporting systems. In essence, there is an emerging regulated financial constituency where institutions ensure accountability in their systems, focusing on protecting customers as data use becomes more interconnected and data-driven. This redistribution of responsibility elevates accountability to the board level. Directors must ensure that liability is clearly understood, contractually defined, and operationally enforceable across all ecosystem participants.

Regulators worldwide are accelerating the shift from open banking to full open finance because the original scope—limited largely to payments and basic account data—is no longer sufficient to support modern consumer needs or competitive market structures. Customers now interact with a far wider financial ecosystem that spans savings, pensions, insurance, investments, credit platforms, wallets, wealth-advisory tools, and non-bank digital services, all of which generate meaningful behavioural and financial data. Regulators in the UK, EU, India, Australia, and Singapore recognise that restricting data rights to current accounts creates artificial silos that impede customer mobility, limit innovation, and concentrate power among incumbent institutions. Open finance therefore aims to expand access so that consumers can view, share, and manage their full financial life through a unified ecosystem governed by clear rights, transparent consent, and secure infrastructure. In the UK, the transition is being formalised through the Smart Data Initiative and strengthened by the FCA's focus on interoperability and competition. The EU's Financial Data Access Framework reinforces this approach: access rights across a broad portfolio of products, underpinned by shared standards to which banks, insurers, pension providers, and investment firms will be subject. India's Digital Public Infrastructure extends that logic one step further: account aggregators enable cross sector data movement that empowers citizens—rather than institutions—to make decisions about how their information is used. For regulators, open finance offers a mechanism to entrench inclusion, lower switching costs, unlock personalised credit, and stimulate responsible innovation across markets. This extended regulatory vision demands that retail banks revisit their operating systems, data governance, and partnership models. The direction of travel is clear: open finance is not a technology upgrade but a structural mandate that remakes power dynamics, customer expectations, and competitive design across global financial services.

Supervisors across major jurisdictions are tightening expectations around security, liability, and consent because open finance dramatically expands the number of participants handling sensitive financial data. Regulators in the UK, EU, India, and Australia now require banks and third-party providers to operate within clearly defined accountability frameworks that specify who is liable when data is misused, breached, or inaccurately transmitted. The FCA and PRA emphasise that liability cannot be diluted across partners; institutions must prove that risk controls, encryption standards, and authentication layers are consistently enforced across all connected systems. The EU's Financial Data Access Framework goes further by requiring "permissioned APIs", meaning that every data call must reflect explicit, time-bound, revocable consent that customers can monitor and withdraw at any moment. India's account-aggregator ecosystem embeds consent directly into digital public infrastructure: users issue granular permissions for each data flow, and providers must maintain immutable logs that demonstrate compliance. Supervisors also expect banks to minimise data sharing, ensure that only essential fields are transmitted, and provide customers with transparent dashboards showing how their information is used. From a security standpoint, the importance of real-time monitoring, multi-factor authentication, and endpoint security is considered immutable. Regulators are also demanding continuous assurance such as penetration tests, security audits, and oversight of partners instead of periodic assurances. This move mirrors a broader regulatory philosophy as well. In an environment where data is constantly in motion across dozens of platforms, transparency is needed for customer trust, ultimately providing accountability and unwavering security assurances. For retail banking institutions especially, it demands a rebuild in terms of providing consent experiences, partners, and infrastructure that is secure enough to enable continuous permission-based data flows. The message sent by regulators couldn't be clearer—transparency, liability clarity, and security are no longer niceties for the regulated but are foundational elements of open finance architecture. Security measures must also be visible to customers in a meaningful way. When protection mechanisms are understood and predictable, they reinforce confidence; when they appear inconsistent or unexplained, they introduce uncertainty.

Open-finance regulation is evolving along two parallel paths: a trend toward global convergence around core principles, and a clear divergence in how different jurisdictions interpret implementation. Convergence is visible in the shared emphasis on consumer rights, explicit consent, transparent API standards, and strong liability frameworks. Whether it is the UK's Data Protection Act, the EU's GDPR and FIDA proposals, India's Digital Public Infrastructure model, or Australia's Consumer Data Right, regulators consistently reinforce that individuals—not institutions—own their financial information. Yet beneath this shared philosophy, divergence remains substantial. The UK's model is industry-driven and iterative, allowing market participants to shape standards through collaborative working groups. Europe adopts a more prescriptive legislative model, defining everything from API taxonomies to security baselines within binding regulations. India's approach is unique: it embeds open finance into national digital infrastructure, relying on federated consent artefacts and licensed intermediaries known as account aggregators. Meanwhile, Singapore and Australia have taken an innovation-first approach to a regulatory sandbox meant to foster ecosystem experimentation. Such variations give rise to differences in institutional architecture. A UK/European bank will need to heavily invest in compliance engines and auditability, while an Indian bank will need to focus on high-volume, low-cost data flows through public platforms. Regulators in Africa and Latin America are adopting elements from these examples to spur financial inclusion. They're starting with open payments before moving into open finance. For a global institution, dealing with these differences means having adaptive compliance systems, a version of API stack, and a corresponding governance structure able to accommodate these different regulatory approaches at the same time. The fact is, these differences aren't a step backward from the innovation in global open finance; rather, this shows that local interpretation is key to a global standard on rights, transparency, and customer empowerment.

Supervisory expectations under open finance are moving from periodic compliance to real-time, continuous oversight, fundamentally reshaping how retail banks must design their internal systems. Regulators in the UK, EU, India, Singapore, and Australia are increasingly signalling that open-finance environments require visibility into live data flows, API uptime, third-party behaviour, and consent-management performance. This evolution reflects the nature of open finance itself: once customer data moves across multiple institutions and intermediaries, traditional annual audits or quarterly compliance reviews become insufficient to detect breaches, misuse, or operational failures. Supervisors now expect banks to maintain real-time monitoring dashboards, automated alerts, and evidence-ready audit trails that can be produced on demand. The UK's FCA emphasises operational resilience and obliges firms to demonstrate that critical services remain within defined impact tolerances even under stress. The EU's emerging FIDA and DORA frameworks reinforce continuous oversight of ICT risks, vendor governance, and cross-border dependencies. India's RBI and MeitY expect regulated entities to maintain real-time consent logs and tamper-proof data rails through the Account Aggregator framework. Such demands require banks to re-architect the compliance activity to accommodate automation, telemetry, and proactive governance instead of solely relying on human verification. Such demands also influence the way banks approach the risk culture. This influences compliance teams to bond more meaningfully with technology, cyber security teams, as well as API operating teams for the maintenance of regulatory hygiene. However, for hybrid banks, real-time compliance is a competitive advantage. Banks that live by transparent governance and riskiness have more opportunities for trust-building. For retail banks across the globe, as the demands acting as supervisors become more strenuous, real-time compliance is not viewed as a disclosure but as an architecture of all aspects of open finance.

Liability in an open-finance environment becomes far more complex because customer data, transactions, and service decisions often move across multiple institutions, platforms, and intermediaries rather than remaining within a single bank. Regulators in the UK, EU, India, Singapore, and Australia are therefore reshaping liability rules to ensure that consumers are protected even when financial journeys are distributed. Under PSD2 and the emerging PSD3/FIDA framework, European banks remain responsible for compensating customers in cases of unauthorised transactions, even if failures occur at a third-party provider, unless negligence can be clearly demonstrated. The UK's regulatory architecture reinforces similar principles: accountability follows the entity best positioned to manage the risk, not the entity that happens to be closest to the customer interface. India's Account Aggregator system defines granular responsibilities across data fiduciaries, user-consent artefacts, and financial-information providers, ensuring that customers retain predictable rights even when multiple participants are involved. These evolving liability structures require banks to maintain rigorous third-party governance, clear contractual safeguards, and continuous assurance that partners adhere to security, privacy, and operational-resilience standards. Consumer protection provisions now emphasise timely grievance resolution, transparent communication, and data use disclosures, and regulators expect banks to assume ownership of outcomes even when working with external partners. Henceforth, open finance liability is a strategic issue that underlines consumer risk management, and banks have to incorporate traceability and dispute resolution mechanisms into their open banking infrastructure so that customers are protected. For a hybrid bank, it is not just a liability that needs to be managed; it is a trust factor that different customers are protected even though they are connected to a bank.

Supervisory convergence is emerging as one of the most influential forces shaping the future of open finance, as regulators across the world recognise that fragmented standards limit innovation, weaken consumer protection, and create operational friction for cross-border financial institutions. The UK, EU, and India represent three distinct but gradually converging approaches: the UK emphasises outcome-based supervision with strong accountability principles; the EU focuses on harmonised rules, mandatory reporting, and prescriptive oversight through PSD2, PSD3, and the Financial Data Access framework; and India's digital public-infrastructure model prioritises secure, standardised APIs with unified consent artefacts. Increasingly, supervisory bodies are coordinating through global platforms such as the G20, FSB, BIS, and IOSCO to align their expectations around data governance, interoperability minimums, algorithmic transparency, and cross-sector risk oversight. This convergence is being driven by shared challenges: global fintechs operating across jurisdictions, cloud concentration risk, rising cybersecurity exposures, and growing pressure to ensure that customers experience consistent protection irrespective of where a service provider is headquartered. For banks, supervisory convergence means a set of new obligations: harmonisation of data taxonomies, alignment of API standards, adoption of global assurance models, and preparations for "real-time" regulatory access to logs and risk indicators. For banks, supervisory convergence also offers an opportunity: banks that move early to align to global data taxonomies will unlock operational scale and branding opportunities as trusted nodes within a global open finance system. As standardisation continues to drive supervisory requirements, banks will need to think anew about the technology and governing models that keep pace with these shifts—structurally embedding rather than "bolting on" regulatory requirements. At its heart, the future of open finance will belong to organisations that see supervisory convergence as an opportunity rather than a barrier, fully integrating global requirements within a unified platform that unlocks trust, security, and customer experience at scale.

Data portability sits at the heart of open finance because it redefines who truly owns financial information and how that information can be used to create value. For decades, banks operated as custodians of customer data, storing it in siloed systems and limiting its movement across products or institutions. Open finance reverses this logic by placing full rights and control in the hands of customers, who can now permit their data to move, be shared, or be withdrawn across banks, fintechs, insurers, pension providers, and non-financial platforms. This shift is more than a regulatory requirement; it is a structural redesign of power, trust, and competition. Portability demands that institutions move away from proprietary formats and legacy databases and towards standardised taxonomies, modular API architectures, and interoperable data models. Where data is universally portable, customers can benefit from the smooth transition of products, faster service onboarding, and personalised service. However, this has significant implications for banks. While banks can call data accurate, secure, minimalised, and with clear consent in the presence of data portability, they can never overlook the fact that this creates an accountability model where all the operational risks have already been considered. Data portability can trigger competition in the banking sector, since customers can change banks easily and banks have to keep providing better service. However, data portability is not just a customer benefit; it enables innovation in the market. This means fintechs can use the data of banks to develop applications, banks can partner with external organisations from other sectors and fulfil the overall requirement of data privacy and security. Only the organisations that keep the data portability feature in mind will thrive in the next form of hybrid financial systems in the future. For customers, portability is meaningful only when it reduces effort, improves access, and enables better decisions. Without these outcomes, the structural shift does not translate into practical value.

Interoperability is the technical and governance backbone that allows open finance to function as a connected ecosystem rather than a collection of isolated experiments. It ensures that data can move across institutions, sectors, and jurisdictions without being distorted, delayed, or exposed to unnecessary risk. For banks, interoperability demands far more than building APIs; it requires harmonised data standards, consistent taxonomies, secure transmission rules, and shared validation protocols that guarantee accuracy when information flows between entities. In practice, this means replacing fragmented legacy systems with middleware layers, API gateways, and unified data models capable of recognising and processing diverse data sources. Interoperability also forces institutions to align on identity verification, encryption methods, access controls, and audit trails so that data sharing does not create operational vulnerabilities or regulatory breaches. Its effective implementation creates opportunities for customers, which otherwise would have been hindered by friction, particularly where customers seek credit, move savings, or verify themselves across various players who have adopted interoperability strategies. It also creates opportunities for players, regardless of their size, who can compete within the market provided they have fulfilled security and governance requirements. Yet, strategy accompanies interoperability, and banks have the duty of managing issues around liability allocation, latency management, consent portability, and real-time monitoring of third-party conduct. It will also require banks to cope with international fragmentation, where standards in jurisdictions such as the UK, EU, India, Australia, and Singapore are evolving at dissimilar rates. Indeed, interoperability is not merely a technological shift; it has the capability of transforming open finance from vision to reality for hybrid institutions offering trusted, scalable, and converged services in a highly distributed environment.

Data portability is the principle that empowers customers to move, share, or withdraw their financial information across institutions with ease, transparency, and full control. In open finance, portability is not a technical convenience; it is a structural shift in power from banks to individuals. When customers can carry their transaction history, savings behaviour, credit performance, insurance patterns, or pension data across providers, they are no longer locked into institutions because of legacy data barriers. This forces banks to compete on service quality, trust, value, and responsiveness rather than customer inertia. Delivering portability, however, demands deep architectural readiness. Banks must maintain clean, standardised data sets, clearly defined schemas, and consistent metadata so that information remains accurate and meaningful when transferred outward. But this also demands robust consent-management systems that allow customers to approve, revoke, or time-limit access without confusion. Importantly, data portability must be implemented with privacy-by-design principles; customers should never be exposed to unnecessary risk when exerting their data rights. Regulators around the world are increasingly viewing portability as a catalyst for market competition: the UK's FCA, the EU's financial data access framework, India's Account Aggregator model, and Australia's Consumer Data Right all place portability at the centre of consumer empowerment. For hybrid banks, this shift brings strategic implication: to wit, institutions that master portability can build integrated, multi-product journeys, improve risk assessment through richer external data, and participate confidently in cross-sector ecosystems. Those that struggle risk being marginalised as platforms, fintechs, and digital public infrastructures unlock more fluid customer movement. At bottom, portability represents a decisive move toward a customer-owned financial future, and banks must redesign their systems, governance, and engagement logic to fit this new paradigm.

Interoperability is the technical and governance backbone that makes open finance function reliably across institutions, sectors, and jurisdictions. It is the capability of disparate systems to recognise, validate, exchange, and use financial data without friction or ambiguity. Without interoperability, data portability is merely a theoretical right; customers can request their data, but institutions cannot interpret it consistently or plug it into decision-making systems meaningfully. True interoperability requires shared API standards, uniform taxonomies, common data definitions, and aligned security protocols. Around the world, this remains a significant challenge: legacy banking platforms often store data in fragmented formats, with inconsistent identifiers, outdated file structures, and siloed operational workflows. Fintechs, by contrast, operate on modular, cloud-native architectures that rely on standardised APIs and agile integration layers. To bridge these different worlds, investment is necessary in middleware, orchestration platforms, and associated data governance disciplines that guarantee their accuracy, timeliness, and auditability. Furthermore, regulatory bodies are increasingly demanding such interoperable structures, ranging from the EU's proposed Data Act to India's specifications around its digital infrastructure, and even the UK's extensions to its open banking landscape. From a strategic point of view, one of the most critical effects of interoperability is its ability to redraft the competitive landscape itself—where banks adopting such standard structures are able to take advantage of multi-institution journeys, embedding their propositions within other institutions' ecosystems, and leveraging such richer, more timely data sets to better inform underwriting activities, prevent fraud, and enhance their understanding of customers. Conversely, by resisting such a push towards a more unified model, they will increasingly be forced to be a sole actor within a fragmented landscape. Interoperability is not simply a commercial activity; it is a means by which trust, consistency, and fairness are injected into the open finance landscape. It is a reality that hybrid banks will be expected to master if they hope to deliver on scales that reduce friction and maintain a seamless customer experience.

Data portability cannot succeed without a strong governance framework that clarifies who is responsible for accuracy, security, and continuity across the full lifecycle of shared information. In open finance, data rarely travels in a straight line; it moves through banks, fintechs, account aggregators, insurers, credit marketplaces, analytics platforms, and sometimes non-financial service providers. Each point of transfer introduces obligations around authentication, encryption, consent validation, error correction, and dispute handling. Regulatory regimes in the UK, EU, India, Singapore, and Australia now expect institutions to document precisely how they manage these responsibilities—including how liability is allocated when data is misused, misinterpreted, or exposed. Legacy governance models are no longer adequate; annual vendor reviews cannot manage real-time API interactions, and traditional IT controls cannot oversee multi-party data routing. Hybrid banks must therefore adopt continuous monitoring systems that detect anomalies, verify data integrity, and track usage against agreed permissions. They also need contractual structures with partners that specify data-quality thresholds, incident-response duties, and audit rights. Cybersecurity becomes central to governance because even a single vulnerability in an external partner can compromise an entire ecosystem. Governance also extends to minimisation and proportionality: institutions must ensure that only the necessary data moves, that retention limits are respected, and that individuals retain the right to withdraw access at any time. By embedding stronger governance across data flows, hybrid banks create a transparent, predictable, and secure environment for customers—reinforcing trust while reducing regulatory risk. In an open-finance world defined by shared responsibility, governance is the mechanism that converts portability from a regulatory requirement into a safe, reliable, and customer-centric experience.

Legacy systems remain one of the biggest structural barriers to achieving true data portability, and hybrid banks must confront this challenge directly if they want to participate effectively in open finance. Many core banking platforms were designed decades ago, built around batch processes, rigid file structures, and siloed data architectures that cannot easily support real-time API exchanges. When these systems attempt to interact with modern fintech platforms or cross-sector data networks, delays, inconsistencies, and reconciliation errors become common. This undermines customer confidence and creates operational friction across journeys such as account switching, income verification, affordability checks, investment-linked advice, and insurance underwriting. To overcome these constraints, hybrid banks are increasingly adopting middleware solutions, data-virtualisation layers, and APIs that enable a disassociation between customer-facing innovation and legacy platforms, together with a gradual modernisation of the legacy platforms themselves. This will enable institutions to engage in open finance in a safe and open manner without increasing the level of driven risk for internal systems from unfettered external requests. Even though technology has been deemed crucial in addressing legacy constraints in the field of open finance, other factors such as governance structures and documentation and mutual testing have been deemed important as well. Indeed, institutions should ensure that they have created an inventory of all existing data sources and eliminate any level of data duplication, perhaps ensuring consistency and distinction between internal partners and other players, such as third-party participants, who are engaged in interpreting such kinds of data on a business unit level. Under legacy constraints, we can equate culture more so because the majority of teams are viewed as being constructed based on closed architectures and institution-centric innovation; open finance features will, therefore, require teams to work more with third-party software and development teams and other agile release methods, which are constantly changing and integrated iteratively. This business strategy can be viewed in a world where customers can move instantly on a data point and is, therefore, more transformative than estimations themselves.

Unified data models form the backbone of any interoperable financial ecosystem, enabling institutions, fintechs, insurers, pension providers, and non-financial platforms to interpret and process information consistently. Without a shared data language, every exchange becomes prone to misclassification, mismatched fields, and inconsistent interpretations of customer identity, transaction history, affordability indicators, or behavioural insights. Hybrid banks must architect data models that simplify complexity by harmonising taxonomies, definitions, and metadata across multiple product lines and external partners. Unified data models also reduce operational risk by eliminating redundant fields, improving validation logic, and enabling APIs to deliver clean, structured data irrespective of source-system variation. But developing such models requires sustained internal alignment: business units must align on standardised definitions; technology teams must reimagine schemas to support modularity; and risk, compliance, and audit functions must collectively validate the data lineage. Once in place, unified data models unlock new capabilities. They make customer journeys seamless by ensuring that information captured in one channel is instantly usable across others. They allow for advanced analytics, enabling predictive risk modelling, more precise offers, and more accurate fraud detection. They reinforce external collaboration by allowing fintech partners to integrate faster, test more efficiently, and maintain consistent service delivery. Beyond technology, unified data models foster trust: customers develop more confidence when their information is handled both accurately and consistently across providers, reducing frustration, errors, and complaints. By treating the standardisation of data models as a core architectural investment rather than a compliance obligation, hybrid institutions can establish a bedrock for open finance ecosystems that depend on clarity, precision, and shared understanding.

API governance is the structural discipline that keeps data exchange predictable, secure, and trustworthy across open-finance ecosystems. As hybrid banks expose more services through APIs—KYC verification, account information, payments initiation, lending data, affordability signals—the risks associated with weak governance multiply rapidly. Institutions must move beyond basic API publishing and adopt a governance framework that covers version control, performance monitoring, security testing, partner onboarding, and lifecycle management. A well-governed API environment ensures that data flows are consistent, that every request is authenticated, and that downstream services do not break whenever upstream systems change. It also prevents fragmentation: without strict governance, different teams may create multiple APIs that serve similar purposes but behave differently, creating operational risk and partner confusion. API governance further demands clear oversight roles: product teams must document functionality; security teams must test vulnerabilities; compliance teams must validate data-usage rules; and technology teams must enforce throttling, logging, and audit trails. For ecosystem partners, governance signals credibility. Fintechs integrate more confidently when they know that APIs will not change unpredictably, that documentation is accurate, and that support processes are responsive. Strong governance also enables institutions to track performance metrics—latency, uptime, error rates—that directly affect customer experience. In an open-finance environment, APIs become public-facing infrastructure, and governance becomes a determinant of trust: poorly governed APIs lead to broken journeys, inconsistent data, and regulatory exposure. By institutionalising governance as an architectural requirement rather than an IT function, hybrid banks can deliver resilient, standardised data exchange that strengthens operational reliability and deepens partner confidence across the financial ecosystem.

Data quality becomes exponentially more important in an open-finance environment because information flows across multiple systems, partners, and regulatory jurisdictions. This explains why hybrid banks must treat data quality as a strategic capability rather than a back-office function. When customers share their financial information through portable and interoperable channels, the receiving institution relies entirely on the accuracy, completeness, and timeliness of that data. Any inconsistency—a delayed balance update, an outdated credit line, a mislabelled transaction—can lead to incorrect affordability assessments, inappropriate product recommendations, or flawed risk decisions. Distributed ecosystems intensify these dangers as fintech organisations might utilise divergent classification criteria, while insurance organisations might interpret fields in different ways, and legacy frameworks might hold transactional data in formats altogether incompatible with current classification frameworks. For data integrity, banks need to put resources into standardised data models, validation systems, and data reconciliation processes that reliably survey information for lacunas, mistakes, and duplication during its way through different frameworks. Better data governance implies recognising data possession, refresh cycles, and supervising frameworks for mistakes and irregularities. While machine learning projects can help data validation, human administration is fundamental during cases wherein context plays an essential part, for example, incorrectly classified vendor classifications or erratic pay streams. Data source is another developing region of focus for controllers, requesting banks to prove data sources, processing, and dealings. High-quality data is, in this sense, as much a matter of trust as of technology; clients, accomplices, and controllers anticipate exactness. Yet, by structuring data quality into open finance banks, they can guarantee portability and interoperability yield precise, undeceiving, and equitable monetary results.

Transparent data-sharing practices are essential for sustaining customer trust in an open-finance ecosystem where information moves fluidly across institutions and platforms. As individuals gain the ability to transfer, revoke, or limit access to their financial data, hybrid banks must demonstrate that every data exchange is purposeful, secure, and visibly governed. This outlines how transparency becomes an operational discipline, not a communication exercise. Customers want to know exactly what data is being shared, why it is necessary, how long it will be retained, and which third parties will have access. Modern open-finance frameworks already demand explicit consent, but transparency goes further: institutions must provide plain-language explanations, real-time dashboards showing active permissions, and clear pathways for customers to modify or withdraw access. Furthermore, when transparency is built into the system design, there is less friction, fewer complaints, and increased trust within digital channels. For partners within the ecosystem, transparency means that there is clarity regarding liability. They understand the extent of liability, audit requirements, and rules surrounding the use of shared data. Without transparency, there is often a lack of trust within a system, often compounded by a lack of transparency with regulatory bodies when evidencing transparent working practices. For consumers, a lack of transparency means that trust is breached when it is perceived that shared data is being utilised beyond their knowledge or without their expectation. For banks, a transparent approach to identity and system interactions is built into complex open finance using identity flows, API interactions, data classification models, and consumer interfaces. The transparent use of shared data is, therefore, less about a regulatory requirement and more about a key component of building trust within a financial system, enabling consumers to engage with a connected world with trust.

Platform Setup of Retail Banks

Platformisation requires hybrid retail banks to rethink their core architecture from the ground up, shifting away from tightly coupled legacy systems toward modular, interoperable, and API-driven environments. This section explains how the transition starts with decoupling monolithic cores and creating service layers that can support multiple partners, channels, and product flows simultaneously. A platform bank must provide a stable foundation—payments, identity, compliance, onboarding, and data-processing engines—while allowing external providers to plug into its environment without compromising security or performance. This demands investment in microservices, orchestration engines, event-driven design, and real-time messaging layers so that the institution can operate like a technology platform rather than a closed financial utility. The architectural redesign also includes redesigning data and information management—for instance, unified data models and scalable cloud infrastructure allow internal teams and partners to access data and information in a unified manner through API gateways. Other processes that need to be put in place include developing partner governance protocols for the overall administration and management of services and data within a retail banking setup and ensuring that there are no structural vulnerabilities or weaknesses when there is a move towards expanding the scale and scope of banking platforms. Perhaps most significantly, the architecture design for a retail banking system nowadays also promotes agility—for instance, time-to-market for new and innovative products is shortened and customer experience for existing and new customers is also redesigned without affecting architectural layers—this being maybe the only way that retail banking will scale and remain relevant given rising customer needs and platforms. From the customer's perspective, the platform remains the bank, regardless of how many external providers are involved. Responsibility for outcomes therefore remains anchored with the institution.

This changes how retail banks design and deliver services by shifting from vertically integrated product silos to modular, composable building blocks that can be assembled, combined, or replaced without disrupting the wider system. Modularity allows banks to break down products—such as loans, payments, savings, insurance, and investments—into discrete components like identity verification, credit scoring, risk pricing, disbursement, and servicing. Each component becomes a "service module" that can be orchestrated internally or delivered through ecosystem partners. This structural change reduces duplication of effort, lowers operational cost, and increases the consistency of customer experience across channels. Modularity also enables rapid innovation: banks can experiment with new customer journeys, introduce new features, or partner with fintechs without needing to rebuild entire systems. For example, a financial institution might incorporate an external credit decision engine or a third-party risk scoring service into its current lending process. With modular service design, banks also reap benefits in terms of stronger operation resilience, as malfunctions in the service modules do not impact other modules of the overall product suite. Moreover, banks reap benefits in terms of efficient governance, where compliance and risk rules can be uniformly applied to the entire service suite, without having to retrofit rules into individual product suites. Hence, for hybrid retail banks, moving away from product-centric design to service design is the key to scaling up their platform-based ecosystems, thereby allowing banks to achieve their position as orchestrators rather than producers of value. This, in turn, enables banks to achieve agility in meeting evolving market, regulatory, and customer demands in terms of precision, speed, and reliability.

API management has become the structural backbone of platform-based retail banking, enabling institutions to expose services securely, onboard partners efficiently, and orchestrate customer journeys that extend beyond the bank's own channels. Mature API management frameworks allow banks to standardise how data is shared, authenticate who can access it, monitor usage patterns in real time, and enforce governance controls across every interaction. In a platform environment, APIs are not just technical connectors; they are strategic assets that determine how quickly a bank can launch new partnerships, integrate third-party capabilities, or support embedded finance propositions. A strong API layer includes developer portals, automated testing environments, version-control mechanisms, throttling rules, analytics dashboards, and consent-management integration, ensuring that every data call is compliant, predictable, and resilient. Effective API governance also protects the bank from fragmented integration practices that can lead to cybersecurity or operational issues. Thus, banks have standardised approaches in terms of authentication, encryption, onboarding, and monitoring, ensuring that they have visibility into the entire ecosystem, including the fintech or other business domains. Furthermore, banks also have the opportunity to leverage these APIs to enable monetisation, such as by providing different access levels or usage-based pricing. Finally, in hybrid retail banking models, banks are able to leverage this seamless transition between digital and physical channels, enabling their frontline teams to view real-time data, including data that is being extracted in real-time from multiple external systems. In other words, effective API management, therefore, turns an isolated bank into a platform entity, providing them with the much-needed structural advantage to operate in an environment where hybrid ecosystem issues arise.

Real-time data orchestration is the engine that enables platform-based retail banks to deliver seamless, context-rich customer experiences across channels, partners, and product lines. Hybrid institutions must move beyond periodic batch processing toward continuous data flows integrating customer interactions, risk signals, and transactional activity at the moment they occur. Real-time orchestration lets a bank pull together multiple data sources—internal systems, third-party APIs, device metadata, behavioural indicators, and ecosystem partners—into one coherent layer supportive of decisioning, personalisation, fraud detection, and operational responsiveness. Without this capability, platformisation gets fragmented as customer journeys break at every turn because data cannot move quickly enough between systems. Good orchestration requires more than technology; it demands clarity on governance over what data is used, how it is validated, who is allowed access, and how different systems interpret it. Banks must invest in event-driven architectures, message queues, streaming analytics, and data-quality pipelines that ensure accuracy across every interaction. Real-time integration also enhances risk management by providing dynamic insights into spending behaviour, credit performance, or unusual activity, enabling timely interventions. For customers, this translates into intuitive service experiences—instant loan approvals, proactive alerts, frictionless authentication, and personalised recommendations that reflect current needs rather than historical snapshots. In a platform ecosystem, real-time orchestration is equally critical for partner collaboration: insurers, fintechs, retailers, and service providers rely on timely data exchanges to deliver embedded services. By mastering real-time orchestration, banks shift from reactive operators to proactive designers of customer journeys, strengthening trust, operational efficiency, and competitive positioning in an increasingly interconnected marketplace.

Modular architecture is a foundation upon which platform-based retail banks are built, inheriting a capacity to innovate, integrate, and adapt without jeopardising stability. This will trace the path which hybrid banks must take to move away from monolithic architecture, in which every element is tightly coupled to others, to a more flexible modular structure where systems are loosely coupled, allowing for easier innovation. A modular bank enables the integration of new features or functions like fraud detection, KYC, lending, or payment solutions, allowing banks to add these in a cost-effective manner without having to redesign large swathes of code. In effect, this also allows them to innovate without fear, taking risks with a service or feature without affecting others. Modular systems support platformisation by allowing banks to orchestrate multiple services in parallel, each performing specialised tasks yet functioning cohesively through API gateways and shared data models. Governance becomes critical: version control, service registries, architectural guardrails, and rigorous testing frameworks ensure that each module performs reliably within the wider ecosystem. Modular design also enhances resilience by containing failures—if a single service experiences downtime, it can be isolated while the rest of the system continues to operate. For customers, modular architecture results in faster feature releases, more personalised services, and smoother journeys across digital and physical channels. In a competitive open-finance landscape, modularity is not simply a technology upgrade; it is a strategic enabler that positions retail banks to evolve constantly, engage deeply with partners, and maintain operational integrity in a dynamic and distributed financial ecosystem.

Governance complexity increases manifold for retail banks when they change their operating model from closed to platform, bringing together multiple fintech, tech, data, and non-financial institutions. In this arc, we will traverse through the process of re-designing their governance structures for managing shared accountabilities, fluctuating risk scopes, and decentralising operational accountabilities, which become important as we move into a new structure, unlike the past where governance, internal controls, and departmental oversight were enough for managing an entity. In platforms, where services are collaborative and data and customers cross organisational boundaries, there is an urgent need for partner onboarding mechanisms, service level expectations, joint risk assessment, and ongoing compliance tracking within APIs. Every partner must be evaluated not only for innovation capability but also for data governance maturity, cyber posture, audit readiness, financial stability, and operational resilience. Banks must also establish decision rights: who has authority to change a product journey, halt a data flow, adjust an algorithm, or escalate an incident affecting a shared customer experience. Governance councils that include technology, risk, legal, data, and product leaders become essential for evaluating ecosystem changes. Regulatory compliance must be treated as a collective responsibility, especially when platforms span jurisdictions. Effective ecosystem governance enables trust, reduces friction, and ensures that external innovation does not introduce internal vulnerabilities. For customers, this results in safer, more consistent experiences across all embedded and partner-delivered services.

Overall, the risk management process becomes far more difficult for retail banks as they operate via an API platform that seeks to integrate various external service providers, data entities, and service layers. Overall, the above arcs seek to identify the various steps taken towards the redesigning of the risk profile of hybrid retail banks that embody the concepts of distributed operating systems rather than the traditional or contemporary siloed environments. In the case of the API operating platform of the hybrid retail bank, in the event of failure in the API systems of the retail bank, thousands of customers could be affected due to the failure of the API systems of a partner organisation seeking to execute payments on its part via the API systems of the retail bank. Traditional vendor-assessment cycles—annual reviews and checklist audits—are inadequate for environments where consumer-facing services depend on dynamic integrations that change weekly. Platform risk management must include behavioural analytics for partner performance, proactive anomaly detection, joint-incident simulations, and cross-organisation post-mortems to strengthen collective resilience. Regulatory expectations are also shifting: supervisors increasingly require banks to demonstrate control over third-party risk, data lineage, API authentication standards, and ecosystem-wide operational resilience. For customers, distributed risk must be invisible; trust is maintained only when services remain seamless, even when external components fail. Effective risk management in platform banking therefore requires a combination of technological vigilance, governance maturity, and collaborative discipline, ensuring that innovation does not compromise stability or institutional credibility. Interconnected platforms also introduce systemic considerations. Failures within widely used components can propagate rapidly across institutions, making resilience a shared responsibility rather than an individual one.

Governance in a retail banking business leveraging platforms has to evolve from the simple task of managing internal operations to managing a wide, diverse, and distributed network of external contributors whose behaviours have direct impact in terms of customer experience, regulatory compliance, and firm-wide reputation. This tracks how governance will need to be re-designed to ensure clarity, accountability, and discipline in multi-party systems. In platforms, partners might originate credit, make payment, provide identity services, deliver analytics, or incorporate banking services into their own platforms, each with its own regulatory issues, risks, and impact on customers. Banks, therefore, need to develop partner governance structures that require rigorous due diligence, tiering of onboarding criteria, continuous compliance, and contractual clarity. Traditional outsourcing guidelines are insufficient, because platform partnerships operate with higher velocity, greater interdependence, and more fluid data movement. Boards and senior executives must also strengthen their oversight capabilities, ensuring that governance committees understand API policies, consent flows, third-party authentication methods, and cross-border data considerations. Partner scorecards, performance heat maps, and joint-governance councils create transparency and alignment, enabling banks and partners to resolve issues before they escalate. The regulator's perspective is equally important: supervisory bodies now expect banks to demonstrate full accountability for outsourced or co-branded services, even when executed by external providers. Effective governance therefore requires not only contractual controls but a cultural commitment to shared standards and ethical conduct. As platform ecosystems grow, governance becomes the differentiator that determines whether innovation leads to sustainable value or systemic vulnerability—positioning disciplined oversight as a central pillar of platform-era institutional strength.

Platformisation also changes the revenue model of retail banking from being product-based to being ecosystem-based, involving value creation, thus driving retail banks to consider how their revenues are generated, distributed, and made secure in their wide network partnerships. This thus links to the evolution of retail banks' overall revenue architecture in moving towards delivering services offered by multiple providers, facilitated by APIs, embedded journeys, and curated services offered by third-party providers. Although traditional retail banks' sources of revenues, or balance sheet-based revenues, remain relevant, other forms of revenues, such as revenues generated by partnerships, APIs, data-based revenues, subscription revenues, marketplace revenues, and cocreated product revenues, become more relevant to driving their platforms. What becomes difficult in this adjustment is ensuring that retail banks develop architectures in their revenues that ensure innovation is balanced with caution, yet at the same time, ensure that fee structures remain transparent, reasonable, and do not foster mis-selling or risky conduct by their partners or sales teams. Profitability also depends on how well cost structures are realigned; platform banking reduces distribution costs but increases spend on governance, cyber resilience, partner oversight, and technology integration. Banks must therefore create dynamic revenue models that reflect partner performance, customer lifetime value, and ecosystem contribution rather than simplistic product yields. A robust economic model also requires scenario planning to anticipate volatility—such as changing partner incentives, regulatory pricing caps, data-usage restrictions, or competitive shifts from big-tech platforms. Boards and senior management must understand that platform banking produces ecosystem economics, where value is co-created and interdependent, and margins depend on the strength of collaboration rather than the performance of isolated units. In this environment, revenue architecture becomes not just a financial design challenge but a strategic question of positioning: institutions that build transparent, sustainable, and inclusive revenue models will gain trust, attract high-quality partners, and secure long-term stability in a rapidly evolving financial landscape.

As the importance of platformisation becomes integral to retail banking strategies, governance and long-term stewardship are the critical determinants for ensuring that the viability, trustworthiness, and socially responsible natures of such ecosystem platforms are successfully maintained. The trajectory of this will mean that increased platforms governance should now spread beyond internal structures to ensure overall accountability for fintech partners, API providers, data intermediary facilitators, cloud architectures, and multiple other non-traditional banking ecosystem players. This is because existing traditional governance structures are simply insufficient when the operational landscape of such platforms includes increasing instances of decentralised decisions, dynamic data sharing activities, asymmetrical information flows, and constantly shifting risks. Therefore, such governance structures need to be instituted within banking boards to ensure overall accountability for operational integrity among fintech partners based on defined thresholds for performance, settling disputes between multiple players, and ensuring responsible data handling across all constituents within the ecosystem platform. Long-term stewardship also requires designing incentive structures that reward ethical behaviour, sustained service quality, and customer-centric innovation rather than short-term volume gains. The governance remit must include monitoring how platform design affects vulnerable customers, ensuring that embedded experiences remain fair, accessible, and free from manipulative nudges. Resilience planning is equally critical: contingency arrangements for partner failures, cyber incidents, or regulatory interventions must be embedded into the platform's operational architecture. Ultimately, the credibility of a platform bank depends on its ability to govern not just its own operations but the conduct and reliability of the entire ecosystem it orchestrates. Institutions that treat governance as a strategic enabler—rather than a compliance formality—will establish themselves as trusted anchors capable of shaping stable, transparent, and socially aligned financial platforms for the future.

Embedded Finance and Ecosystem Design

Embedded finance, at its core, is reshaping retail financial distribution by bringing financial services deeply into the natural flow of consumers and businesses. In other words, instead of asking consumers and businesses to find their way to financial services through financial institutions, apps, or the internet, embedded finance puts financial services such as lending, payments, insurance, and savings/credit access inside retail markets, delivery, communities, healthcare systems, and mobility apps. This change moves financial distribution from (or beyond) channel-based thinking into an orchestrated model where financial services are invisible in their delivery, as opposed to something that must be actively pursued. Embedded finance decreases friction, removes unnecessary steps, and connects customers where and when they need it, in whatever experience they need it, such as checking out on an online retail site, managing supply-chain invoices, hailing a cab, or healthcare services, and so forth. For banks, this redefining of distribution offers lower cost-to-serve, broader reach into underserved communities, and the ability to build more contextual and personalised financial pathways. However, embedded journeys demand meticulous architectural design: seamless API connectivity, shared identity layers, robust transaction monitoring, and real-time risk engines that function reliably outside the bank's proprietary environment. Governance becomes essential because customer experiences in embedded environments reflect back on the bank, even when delivered through partners. This also highlights that embedded finance is not just a technology development but an institutional shift, requiring banks to understand partner ecosystems deeply, standardise onboarding, and align risk, compliance, and customer-protection expectations across distributed networks. Banks that master embedded distribution will shift from being service providers to becoming financial infrastructure embedded in the core fabric of daily life, strengthening relevance and expanding inclusion across demographics and geographies.

As embedded finance grows the extension of finance beyond traditional bank environments, one of the key areas that presents the biggest challenge in ensuring institutional credibility and a safe experience for all involved parties lies in governance. Thus, this seeks to examine issues that surround a proliferation of accountabilities as any financial product moves beyond the traditional bank environment and into the domain of retail partners, e-commerce, gig economy apps, community groups, and/or industry-specific digital hubs. Overall, this presents a unique governance structure that seeks to resolve issues that are not entirely under the control of the bank, contrasting with traditional structures that have a straight-up customer experience chain and where the bank retains all accountabilities. Banks must establish transparent service boundaries, codified responsibilities, and continuous monitoring frameworks that capture data quality, behavioural anomalies, partner performance, and emerging vulnerabilities in real time. Governance teams must also account for cross-jurisdictional complexity, as embedded finance often spans sectors with different regulatory regimes, privacy obligations, and operational standards. This emphasises that governance cannot rely solely on contracts; it must be embedded into technology—through automated controls, consent dashboards, real-time alerts, and shared audit trails. Customer-protection measures, including clear disclosures, grievance pathways, and consistency in service experience, must remain intact even when the customer never interacts directly with the bank. The success of embedded finance rests on the bank's ability to maintain trust across distributed delivery systems without diluting compliance standards. Institutions that build strong, adaptive governance architectures will be able to scale embedded partnerships confidently, safeguard brand reputation, and ensure that innovation does not compromise the rights, safety, or expectations of customers using financial services in an unfamiliar environment. Embedded environments must not prioritise convenience at the expense of informed decision-making and customers should not be led into financial commitments without adequate understanding, regardless of how seamlessly services are delivered.

Therefore, the field of finance is altering in terms of its distribution by embedding financial services within the context in which customers make decisions, are transacting, and/or seek assistance. Figure 4.1 illustrates the benefits of contextual integration, demonstrating how banks can distribute credit, payments, insurance, and savings products far beyond the traditional boundaries of branches, apps, and online platforms, towards meeting their customers across the context of retail, logistics, health, agriculture, and mobility, among many more points. The potential benefits in terms of acquisition, convenience, and decision-making, therefore, are enormous, but care must also be taken regarding an appropriate digital foundation, including the likes of data synchronisation, underwriting, KYC, and consent. In this context, the delivery of financial services becomes dependent on an appreciation of the role of behavioural psychology as a means of creating a profound understanding of the way in which customers are behaving at points of non-bank platforms and identifying instances in which financial assistance can actually make a material contribution. This also highlights the operational challenge of maintaining consistent service standards when customers may never enter a bank channel; customer journeys must remain transparent, fair, and easy to navigate regardless of the partner environment. For financially underserved communities, contextual finance creates new pathways for participation—farmers accessing working capital through agri-platforms, small merchants receiving loans through payment aggregators, or gig workers obtaining insurance through ride-hailing ecosystems. The success of contextual distribution depends on institutional discipline: banks must balance innovation with responsibility, ensuring that embedded services enhance customer outcomes rather than encouraging excessive borrowing or product mis-selling. In hybrid retail banking, contextual finance becomes a strategic lever that deeply aligns distribution with real-world behaviour, positioning the bank as an invisible yet reliable infrastructure within the customer's daily ecosystem.

As the reach of embedded finance grows in retail, mobility, healthcare, agricultural, and online platforms, the governing responsibility falls squarely on retail banks. This shift, therefore, means hybrid banks have to remodel their governing structures in order to effectively manage risks that do not fall within their primary line of operation. As financial services are offered, and they are offered through non-banking platforms, the consumer, in most instances, is unaware of when he or she is being handled by either of them, thereby making governance a collaborative responsibility, albeit an uneven one. Banks have to, therefore, put in place structures that clearly outline liability, that is, who to hold responsible in cases such as on-boarding, KYC, credit decisioning, communication, and so forth, lest mistakes by one side at the interface result in damage to their overall brand, without them being in control of the entire journey. This also emphasises the rising regulatory expectation that banks perform continuous due diligence across partner ecosystems, not just at the point of contract signing. Supervision now requires real-time monitoring of data flows, product suitability, consent management, and conduct patterns within embedded channels. Boards and risk committees must assess partner resilience, cultural alignment, compliance maturity, and incident-response capability before approving large-scale ecosystem integration. The operational challenge is substantial: governance teams must coordinate with legal, technology, compliance, and customer-experience units to maintain consistent standards across multiple partner environments. For banks that manage these complexities effectively, embedded finance becomes a competitive differentiator—creating a trusted, well-regulated ecosystem in which customers can confidently engage. For institutions that underestimate the governance dimension, embedded finance can expose them to silent risks that are difficult to detect and even harder to control.

As more of the financial service scope enters the non-bank world, existing risk assessment and KYC techniques must be re-engineered to work effectively and seamlessly. This has been the thinking behind why embedded finance cannot work with legacy risk scores developed traditionally. Notably, customer engagement has become so fluid, contextual, and even spontaneous. Such interactions can occur on a page like a check-out button, a logistics site, the reception desk at a clinic, or even the inventory page of a small business. As a result, banks must create more malleable systems that reflect customer behaviour and different forms of data, including contextual information. They must be able to account for speed while maintaining prudence to adhere to compliance requirements. For instance, traditional risk assessment techniques must not just be modified but completely reconfigured to suit embedded engagements. Similarly, KYC techniques also have to be revised, as they usually involve static processes that are not appropriate for embedded engagements. Static processes cannot work for instant engagement. Banks must adopt modular identity checks, biometric authentication, and risk-sensitive tiering that adjusts verification intensity based on product type, exposure, and customer history. This emphasises that distributed KYC increases the risk of inconsistency—different partners may interpret guidance differently or fail to escalate anomalies. To mitigate this, banks must implement centralised decision engines, unified KYC rulebooks, and supervised partner workflows that maintain regulatory equivalence across all embedded touchpoints. The redesign effort also requires strong auditability: every decision, data exchange, and verification step must be traceable for regulators and internal assurance teams. When executed well, new underwriting and KYC models allow banks to acquire customers more efficiently, personalise offers based on real-time context, and extend credit responsibly in ecosystems where formal banking interactions were previously rare.

As financial services become embedded in retail, healthcare, mobility, and digital commerce platforms, responsibility for consumer protection extends well beyond the bank's own channels. This helps explain why hybrid institutions must redesign their safeguards for environments where customers interact with financial products through third-party interfaces that may not fully understand regulatory nuance, disclosure standards, or vulnerability protocols. In these embedded settings, the risk of mis-selling, incomplete information, or confusing product presentation is much higher, because non-bank partners usually prioritise speed and conversion over regulated advice. Banks have to create partner-ready consumer-protection frameworks comprising product simplification disclosures, standardised risk explanations, tested interface designs, consent prompts, and triggers to escalate vulnerable behaviours. These protections must work in the background without customers even feeling them: automated alerts should detect rushed decisions, unusual borrowing patterns, or friction points that may indicate misunderstanding. This highlights the governance challenge as well: banks are legally accountable even when the interaction occurs elsewhere. Therefore, rigorous training programmes, partner onboarding protocols, certification requirements, and continuous compliance monitoring become essential elements of embedded finance. Banks must also maintain clear audit trails of how customers were informed, how choices were presented, and how partner interfaces performed in live environments. Consumer protection cannot be retrofitted after a complaint; it must be architected into the ecosystem from the start, ensuring that every embedded interaction meets the same standards of fairness, clarity, and empathy that regulators expect from traditional channels. When consumer-protection design is robust, embedded finance becomes a source of trust, widening access without diluting responsibility.

As finance gets embedded in consumers' checkout experiences, logistics services, mobility services, and community commerce experiences in particular, underwriting styles are increasing from static document-intensive approaches to more adaptive decision systems. Related to this is the challenge of serving customers in distributed systems, where consumers are applying at the moment of purchase with limited time, mixed purchasing intent, and through channels that offer varying degrees of visibility into customer behaviours. In embedded systems, banks must create an underwriting engine that incorporates various inputs such as transaction history, behavioural signals, device trust score information, partner platform information, and the ability to make affordability determinations in a way that still meets regulatory requirements related to fairness, equity, and transparency. This paragraph also highlights how hybrid institutions must introduce friction intelligently: small-ticket loans may be auto-approved, while higher-risk categories trigger additional checks, micro-interactions, or delayed decisions. Importantly, embedded underwriting must remain explainable; customers must understand why an approval or rejection occurred, and banks must document decision logic in a way that withstands supervisory scrutiny. Because risk exposure increases when applications originate outside the bank's-controlled environment, continuous monitoring becomes essential—reviewing partner flows, recalibrating thresholds, and conducting periodic stress tests to ensure the distributed model behaves consistently across markets. Ultimately, this positions redesigned underwriting as a strategic enabler of embedded finance: when credit risk is managed intelligently at the point of need, banks can expand access, reduce fraud exposure, support inclusion, and protect institutional integrity in a rapidly evolving ecosystem.

As banking products become embedded, consumer risk becomes more complex and more critical at the same time. This has sought to explore the risk that can arise at some points as a result of making choices within non-banking interfaces, since the consumer might not even realise they are entering into a regulated credit product, insurance scheme, or making a payment. As hybrid institutions grapple with providing embedded journeys as banking products are pushed into new interfaces and among retailers, e-commerce sites, and service providers, the hybrid bank has to ensure that they provide information on the product that is not hidden behind quick-purchase options, while at the same time providing clear differentiation between what the customer must do and what they can do. Banks must also protect customers from high-pressure marketing techniques in embedded environments, where behavioural nudges from non-bank partners may encourage over-borrowing, impulse-led credit use, or poorly understood insurance add-ons. Regulatory scrutiny is increasing in this area, with supervisors in the UK, EU, Australia, and Singapore expecting banks to demonstrate that embedded partners meet conduct standards equivalent to those of a core banking channel. To achieve this, institutions must implement governance structures that include periodic mystery shopping, partner training, regular audits of interface design, and clear escalation paths for complaints originating through partner platforms. Embedded journeys must also be designed to support vulnerable customers by offering cooling-off periods, simplified explanations, and easy access to support tools regardless of the platform used. Ultimately, this argues that responsible design in embedded finance is not just a compliance requirement; it is fundamental to safeguarding institutional trust and ensuring that the convenience of distributed banking does not compromise customer wellbeing or long-term financial stability.

As embedded finance brings banking services into external platforms, operational alignment becomes a core determinant of reliability, safety, and customer experience. Hybrid institutions must thus synchronise data flows, transaction triggers, authentication signals, and service-level expectations across partners whose systems operate at varying speeds, maturities, and risk standards. Real-time data integrity is essential: an embedded loan offer, payment approval, or insurance confirmation must reflect accurate, up-to-date information on credit limits, account balances, fraud alerts, and identity verification. Any delay or mismatch between the bank's systems and the partner's platform can create customer dissatisfaction, financial loss, or conduct risk. For example, a retailer may approve a purchase based on outdated balance data, or a logistics partner may initiate a lending workflow when a customer's risk profile has materially changed. To avoid such failures, banks must establish rigorous operational protocols that include synchronised API refresh cycles, event-driven notifications, automated reconciliation processes, and near-real-time exception handling. Institutions also need strong business-continuity structures that define failover scenarios when a partner system becomes unavailable or inconsistent. Operational risk increases when embedded environments span multiple geographies or regulatory zones, making transparent data lineage and auditability essential for supervisory assurance. Accordingly, the success of embedded finance depends not just on front-end innovation but on disciplined operational engineering. Banks that invest in unified data models, resilient API gateways, cross-platform monitoring tools, and clearly defined operational responsibilities will deliver embedded journeys that are reliable, intuitive, and trusted—protecting both the customer and the institution in a distributed financial ecosystem.

For example, as embedded finance continues to infiltrate retail, mobility, healthcare, logistics, and community platforms, its boundaries may blur in terms of ensuring customer protection, hence increasing the potential for customer confusion and resulting conduct risks. The aforementioned narrative highlights the importance of emphasising the role of consumer protection in the embedded finance journey, ensuring that at all times, the customer receives the same level of transparency and product protection as they would within a bank's platform. Moreover, as a customer uses a non-bank channel for a loan, an insurance product, a payment plan, or a deposit product, they may not understand what bank is responsible, what data is shared, and what the terms and conditions of the transaction are, for example. Therefore, banks may unintentionally create a conduct risk as a result of embedded finance if they are not explicit in transparency, and this can further lead to a customer being misguided, put under pressure at the point of sale, and/or being unaware of how to resolve a dispute. Therefore, banks must establish how they will create a disclosure standard, brand attribution, product explanation, and customer choice at every step in the embedded finance journey. They must also ensure that grievance-handling mechanisms extend seamlessly into partner environments so that customers are not left navigating fragmented support systems when issues arise. This includes standardised complaint-routing, real-time case visibility, and multilingual support for diverse user groups. Regulators across regions are increasingly scrutinising embedded setups for suitability, fairness, and data-handling discipline, placing accountability squarely on banks even when the customer interacts through third-party channels. We can conclude that responsible embedded finance requires a blend of protection, clarity, and institutional discipline: banks must design journeys that are simple, transparent, and respectful, ensuring that customer wellbeing is preserved wherever financial services appear. Customers must always be able to identify the responsible institution, understand the product, and access support without confusion. Clarity of ownership is essential to maintaining trust in distributed environments.

Strategic Challenges for Bank Boards

As open finance reshapes the competitive landscape, board accountability must expand beyond the traditional oversight of internal operations to include ecosystem-wide responsibilities that were not previously part of a bank's governance remit. In an interconnected environment where financial services are delivered through APIs, third-party platforms, embedded journeys, and cross-sector data exchanges, the board is now accountable for risks, performance, and customer outcomes that originate outside the institution's physical and digital boundaries. This requires directors to strengthen their understanding of data governance, interoperability requirements, consent frameworks, cybersecurity dependencies, and partner-level operational resilience. Boards must move from a siloed supervisory style toward an integrated architectural lens-overseeing architectural choices such as modular technology stacks, shared data models, onboarding protocols for fintech partners, and the monitoring of external interfaces. At the same time, directors must be equipped to navigate new regulatory expectations that emphasise customer data rights, incident transparency, and cross-entity accountability during outages or systemic failures. This emphasises that traditional board expertise in credit, audit, or compliance is not enough; directors must build fluency in digital ecosystems, platform economics, and real-time risk management to provide meaningful strategic direction. This shift also requires boards to adopt a more proactive posture, challenging management not only on growth and profitability but also on the integrity and interoperability of the institution's infrastructure. Future-ready boards will be those that embrace this expanded mandate—balancing innovation with protection, supporting experimentation while safeguarding customer confidence, and shaping an institution that can operate responsibly in an open, interconnected financial world. Board oversight must extend beyond institutional boundaries to include ecosystem performance, ensuring that customer outcomes remain consistent across all participating entities.

Open finance deepens the reach of data exchanging among banks, fintech, insurance, retailers, and public platforms, with the importance of the board's data governance becoming one of the key determinants in leading an institution forward. Directors, therefore, have to guarantee that data regarding customers is dealt with, not merely as an extra tool, but also as a right that is subject to legal, philosophical, and reputation-based obligations. This calls upon boards to oversee data responsibility structures that, among other things, clearly define data collection, categorisation, storage, minimisation, anonymisation, sharing, and erasure at every point in contact with an increasingly intricate data ecosystem. The catch, therefore, is that data now flows through external interfaces, processing centres, analytical engines, partner platforms, and other clouds, posing risks that cannot be contained using internal policies. Boards, therefore, have to call upon one unified data design that lays out common taxonomies, tracking, encryption, and real-time management across every associated entity. They must also ensure the institution maintains transparent consent practices aligned with emerging global standards, enabling customers to understand how their information is used and to revoke access when required. Beyond compliance, the board must recognise that data governance is foundational to trust: any breach, misuse, or opaque sharing practice can undermine customer confidence for years. This requires directors to scrutinise management's reporting mechanisms, validate incident-response plans, and ensure that third-party partners operate under contractual and technical safeguards equivalent to the bank's own standards. By embedding data responsibility into strategic decision-making, boards position the institution to operate confidently in an environment where data flows drive innovation, but also carry heightened risk and far-reaching accountability.

Open finance also blurs boundaries between banks and their external partners; boards must move beyond overseeing internal risks and effectively start governing external risks in relation to fintechs, cloud infrastructure, data intermediary services, and cross-sector platform initiatives. In such an interconnected landscape, boards face challenges linked to an open finance network, where any weakness among external dependencies, such as fintechs, cloud services, data services, and cross-sector platform initiatives, may mean an avalanche of failures in terms of service reliability, customer safety, legal compliance, and organisational reputation. A board of directors, therefore, has an imperative for assurance of dependencies well beyond internal systems, raising requirements for structured oversight of partner governance, resilience, and operating interlocks, including an understanding of their external dependencies in relation to user authentication, data handling, outages, and cyber breaches, all of which should be at or above an acceptable threshold for the bank. Indeed, directors should insist on clearly defined accountability frameworks for incident escalation, liability assignment, and communication pathways when a disruption originates within a partner's environment. Traditional vendor scorecards are insufficient; ecosystem-wide risk oversight requires periodic resilience testing, API-level monitoring, and integrated dashboards that track service dependencies in real time. Boards must also consider geopolitical exposure, given that data hosting, cloud operations, and fintech partners may operate across multiple jurisdictions with varied legal protections. The goal is not to restrict innovation but to ensure that participation in open ecosystems does not introduce unmanaged vulnerabilities that undermine customer trust or regulatory expectations. Ultimately, open finance gives the board a new role: stewarding the institution's position within a wider, interconnected system where risks are shared, consequences are amplified, and oversight must be both forward-looking and technically informed.

As open finance accelerates the convergence of technology, data, regulation, and customer experience, boards must strengthen their collective digital and data literacy to govern effectively in a structurally altered environment. Traditional governance expertise—finance, compliance, operations, legal—is no longer sufficient when the institution's competitiveness depends on API performance, interoperability, cloud resilience, algorithmic fairness, and real-time data governance. Directors increasingly face decisions that require understanding complex architectural concepts such as data lineage, tokenisation, consent artefacts, encryption standards, and partner API dependencies. Without foundational fluency, boards risk becoming dependent on management narratives, unable to challenge assumptions, ask probing questions, or detect early-stage vulnerabilities in technology strategies. Strengthening literacy does not mean turning directors into technologists; it means building the capacity to interpret risk dashboards, understand the strategic implications of architectural choices, evaluate digital-governance frameworks, and scrutinise data-protection practices with confidence. Leading regulators—including the PRA, FCA, MAS, ASIC, and European supervisory bodies—now expect boards to demonstrate informed oversight of technology and data-related decisions, placing direct responsibility on directors for failures involving poor digital governance or inadequate partner controls. This shift requires structured induction programmes, ongoing briefings, scenario-based workshops, and independent technology reviews that give directors a clear line of sight into emerging risks and innovation pathways. Boards must also diversify their composition to include directors with experience in digital ecosystems, cyber resilience, data management, and customer-centric service models. In an open-finance world, digital and data literacy becomes a governance competency on par with financial expertise—it is essential for safeguarding trust, ensuring regulatory alignment, and guiding the institution through an increasingly interconnected financial landscape.

As retail banking shifts to a distributed ecosystem facilitated through APIs, boardroom accountability is not only concerned with internal bank operations but with the complex array of third-party providers, fintech partners, data sharing environments, and inter-sectorial service environments that are all stitched together. This fundamental shift impacts how boards think about institutional risk in a significant way: a services outage because of a cloud provider, a fintech partner failing to comply with regulations appropriately, or a data-handling issue within an embedded fintech environment all have far-reaching operational and reputational consequences for the bank itself, despite these causes being entirely outside the bank's direct control chain. Thus, it is imperative that boards move beyond an ecosystem or third-party risk understanding and think through how they can address risk and opportunities at a much greater scale: this means not only understanding and monitoring how they manage risk within their institution but also having a grasp on how their third-party vendors and fintech partners operate and maintain institutional resiliency and risk management capabilities through open finance channels or third-party interfaces and environments. Regulators now hold directors accountable for, demonstrating awareness of dependency chains, fourth-party exposures, and the implications of interoperability failures, reflecting the broader accountability embedded in open-finance policy design. Boards must ensure that management teams conduct rigorous due diligence, maintain continuous monitoring, and embed contractual obligations that preserve data integrity, consumer protection, and operational continuity. Accountability must also extend to strategic decisions: whether to act as ecosystem leader, infrastructure provider, or participant—each carries different risk horizons and governance expectations. Ultimately, board oversight in an open-finance era is about protecting institutional integrity in a world where customer journeys span multiple entities. Directors must recognise that accountability now stretches well beyond the balance sheet, requiring a governance mindset prepared for interconnected risks, shared responsibilities, and collaborative resilience across the entire financial ecosystem.

Therefore, unless they have a high level of understanding and familiarity with the digital world, open finance, data rights, API management, cybersecurity threats, and partner-centric operating systems, they will not be able to effectively oversee the developing world of open finance. For instance, while classic dimensions of board powers—such as understanding the finances, regulations, audit processes, and the overall organisation and management of the company—remain vital, they are no longer deemed satisfactory if considering operating in a world where data portability choices, consent infrastructures, cloud dependencies, and even fair algorithmic behaviours are shaping competitiveness and risk landscapes as never before. For instance, directors need to be able to think through architectural assumptions, challenge supporting technological premises, and even understand the implications of interoperability challenges—or even what might be deemed ecosystem-level cybersecurity breaches. Thus, many institutions are slowly appointing technology-related experts to their boards or even committees, but what does this really mean? Beyond adding specialists; it requires all directors to understand how open-finance systems work in practice and how weaknesses in one layer—consent journeys, vendor pipelines, encryption standards, or data-retention policies—can propagate into systemic vulnerabilities. Strengthening board literacy also improves decision quality: directors can better evaluate investment proposals, challenge unrealistic transformation timelines, and scrutinise governance designs for fintech partnerships or embedded-finance arrangements. Regulators across the UK, EU, Singapore, and Australia increasingly expect boards to demonstrate informed oversight of digital operations, not simply rely on management representations. For hybrid banks, this literacy becomes a competitive differentiator. Boards that understand technology deeply can anticipate risks earlier, shape architectural strategy more confidently, and guide institutions through complex transitions with greater clarity and integrity.

Boards face a structural tension in the open-finance environment: they must encourage innovation to remain competitive while simultaneously upholding their prudential responsibility to protect consumers, safeguard data, and maintain systemic stability. This balance is far more complex in an interoperable ecosystem where product launches, data partnerships, and new API connections can introduce risks that extend beyond the institution's own perimeter. Boards must therefore develop disciplined mechanisms to evaluate innovation proposals through a dual lens—commercial upside and systemic impact. This includes understanding how new journeys alter data flows, how embedded-finance partners manage customer interactions, and how algorithmic decisions may affect vulnerable groups or trigger regulatory scrutiny. Innovation cannot be treated as an isolated function overseen solely by product teams; it must be integrated into the broader risk, compliance, and operational-resilience framework. At the same time, overly conservative oversight can stifle the bank's ability to adapt, respond to evolving customer expectations, and compete with fintechs that move at speed. Effective boards establish structured pathways that allow experimentation within protected sandboxes, mandate early-stage risk assessments for all digital propositions, and demand clear escalation processes for any changes affecting customer consent, financial advice, or data sharing. They also reinforce cultural expectations—innovation must advance institutional integrity, not circumvent it. As regulators worldwide shift towards outcomes-based supervision, boards are increasingly accountable not just for approving new models but for anticipating the second-order effects those models may create across the ecosystem. Institutions that manage this balance well emerge with stronger reputations, more resilient architectures, and innovation strategies that command regulatory and public confidence.

Boards cannot oversee open finance effectively without a deep and continuously evolving understanding of digital infrastructure, data governance, cybersecurity, and ecosystem-level risk. The shift from institution-centric banking to interconnected financial platforms demands that board members move beyond traditional financial oversight and build competence in areas such as API architecture, consent frameworks, cloud-operating models, algorithmic decisioning, and partner-dependency risks. This is not about turning directors into technologists; it is about enabling them to ask the right questions, challenge management assumptions, and recognise early signs of structural vulnerability. Many global regulators now expect board committees to demonstrate digital literacy as part of their supervisory capability—reflected in board-effectiveness reviews, regulatory interviews, and internal audit assessments. The challenge is compounded by the cross-sector nature of open finance: retail banking is increasingly dependent on non-bank providers such as telecom operators, payment aggregators, cloud vendors, fintech partners, health-tech platforms, and mobility networks. Boards must therefore broaden their worldview beyond the financial sector, understanding how data governance or cyber practices in adjacent industries can directly influence the bank's risk profile. Forward-looking boards establish structured learning pathways, invite external experts for periodic briefings, commission independent technology audits, and maintain dedicated committees for digital and ecosystem oversight. They also encourage diverse board composition, ensuring representation from technology, consumer-protection, behavioural-science, and public-policy backgrounds. With open finance accelerating, digital literacy is no longer an optional advantage but a core governance requirement. Boards that invest in strengthening this capability are better positioned to provide meaningful oversight, support responsible innovation, and guide institutions through complex cross-sector dependencies with confidence and authority.

Long-term accountability becomes a defining responsibility for bank boards as open finance reshapes how data flows, how risks propagate, and how customer outcomes are produced across interconnected platforms. Unlike traditional banking, where most operational activity sat within the institution's own perimeter, open finance distributes accountability across fintech partners, third-party processors, API cohorts, cloud providers, and cross-sector collaborators. This makes it difficult to isolate ownership when a failure occurs, and many institutions underestimate the reputational and regulatory consequences of these gaps. The leading boards recognise that accountability cannot be left to the operation of contracts; it needs to be inculcated through governance design, clear escalation hierarchies, and transparent decision-rights. This includes defining which committee owns which aspect of ecosystem risk, ensuring that management maintains complete visibility of external dependencies, and mandating that impact assessments account for downstream and upstream effects. Regulators in the UK, EU, Singapore, and Australia are beginning to assess board accountability for data-sharing models, third-party failures, and algorithmic decisions, meaning that boards can no longer rely on management assurances without independent verification. Leading boards also link long-term accountability to culture, promoting behaviours that prioritise transparency, responsible innovation, and customer fairness even when working with external partners. They insist on regular reporting that highlights structural vulnerabilities rather than operational successes, create board-level dashboards for dependency risks, and ensure that customer harm—whether arising internally or through partners—is addressed with the same seriousness. By embedding long-term accountability into governance, boards strengthen institutional resilience, reduce regulatory exposure, and build public trust in a financial environment where responsibility is increasingly shared but expectations remain firmly centred on the bank.

Boards overseeing retail banks in an open-finance environment must prepare for a future in which regulatory frameworks no longer evolve through large, infrequent directives but through continuous, standards-driven adaptation. This shift is already visible across leading jurisdictions: the UK is moving from prescriptive PSD-style rules toward dynamic technical standards, the EU is embedding ongoing interoperability requirements through the Financial Data Access Framework, and India's Account-Aggregator ecosystem evolves through rapid iteration rather than long policy cycles. For boards, this means the traditional approach of relying on compliance teams to monitor periodic regulatory changes is rendered insufficient. Instead, they need to anticipate a world where regulatory expectations are increasingly embedded in API standards, consent schemas, security protocols, and data-exchange specifications—many of which are updated multiple times per year. This requires boards to strengthen their oversight of technological infrastructure, ensure that management invests in adaptable systems, and demand forward-looking regulatory intelligence rather than backward-looking compliance reports. It also means cultivating a governance culture that sees regulatory evolution as an opportunity to modernise architecture, reduce operational drag, and improve customer outcomes. Boards must encourage management to participate in standards bodies, collaborate with peer institutions, and engage with ecosystem working groups so that the bank can influence—rather than merely react to—emerging rules. They also need to ensure that the organisation's risk appetite reflects the realities of continuous change, with buffers built into technology budgets, vendor strategies, and workforce capability. Ultimately, boards that prepare for this post-regulatory, standards-driven landscape will position their institutions not merely to comply, but to compete effectively in a future where trust, interoperability, and agility define institutional advantage.

Institutional Perspective: A Global Lens on Customers, Society, and Being Human in an Open Financial World

When Banking Stops Living Inside Banks

Banking used to have clear boundaries. Customers visited branches, completed transactions through identifiable channels, and knew exactly which institution they were dealing with. The bank was a visible destination.

That's changing fundamentally.

Financial services are now embedded into retail platforms, e-commerce journeys, mobility apps, healthcare systems, and social platforms. Payments happen invisibly during online purchases. Credit appears at checkout. Insurance surfaces during travel bookings. Customers increasingly encounter finance not as a separate process, but as an invisible layer woven into daily digital life.

This matters because institutional visibility changes when banking becomes embedded. Historically, customers knew who was responsible for financial decisions and dispute resolution. In embedded environments, those boundaries blur. A customer might receive credit through a retail platform, make payments through a technology ecosystem, and access insurance through a mobility app—without knowing which regulated institution underpins any of it.

The opportunities are real—embedded finance improves accessibility and inclusion by delivering financial services at moments of genuine relevance. But when things go wrong, blurred accountability creates confusion. A declined transaction or disputed loan may involve multiple institutions simultaneously, leaving customers uncertain about where responsibility actually sits.

Different societies will adapt differently. Singapore and East Asia may move quickly given existing comfort with integrated digital environments. Europe's expectations around transparency and regulatory accountability will produce more cautious integration. Across developing economies, embedded finance will emerge more pragmatically around mobile infrastructure and economic participation.

The emotional consequences matter. Banking historically carried identifiable institutional relationships—familiarity, reassurance, visible accountability. Embedded systems transform banking into an environmental condition operating continuously in the background. Customers gain convenience while becoming less aware of the institutional structures shaping financial decisions around them. The future of retail banking may depend less on physical scale or digital channels, and more on whether institutions can maintain trust and accountability within ecosystems where finance increasingly disappears into everyday human experience.

Customer Data, Human Agency, and the New Ownership Question

For most of modern banking history, financial institutions controlled the majority of customer data. Transaction records, payment histories, and financial profiles remained inside institutional systems, reinforcing banks as central custodians of financial knowledge.

Open finance changes this balance fundamentally.

Customers are increasingly positioned not just as users of financial systems but as owners of their own financial data. Through APIs, consent frameworks, and portability standards, individuals can move financial information across institutions and service providers in ways previously impossible.

The operational benefits are genuine—more personalised services, simplified onboarding, improved lending visibility, and more competitive ecosystems. But beneath these efficiencies sits a deeper question: who ultimately controls financial identity in a connected digital world?

Open finance redistributes informational power across wider ecosystems—banks, fintechs, platforms, payment providers, analytics firms, cloud environments, and AI-driven systems. Customers may theoretically possess greater control over their information yet operate within increasingly complex ecosystems where consent and understanding become harder to interpret clearly. Many individuals technically approve data sharing without fully understanding how information flows or how behavioural insights are operationally used.

Different societies interpret this differently. In Europe, consent and transparency are non-negotiable foundations of public trust. In the UK, open banking balances competition with institutional accountability. Across Asia, convenience and infrastructural integration are prioritised strongly. In China, data sharing is experienced as part of broader digital participation rather than isolated institutional exchange. In emerging markets, alternative behavioural data—mobile payments, telecommunications activity—may expand inclusion for populations historically excluded from traditional banking, alongside genuine questions about fairness and explainability.

AI deepens all of this. Systems increasingly derive value from patterns and predictive insights across interconnected data environments rather than static financial records. Recommendation engines, embedded offers, and personalised pricing may shape financial behaviour in ways customers experience as helpful while remaining only partially aware of how deeply algorithmic interpretation is shaping their interaction.

The future challenge is balancing openness with legitimacy. People may accept highly connected financial environments, but they still expect dignity, agency, and accountability within systems handling deeply personal economic information. The future of trust may depend not only on who legally owns customer data, but on whether individuals continue feeling psychologically secure within environments where financial identity is continuously shared and interpreted across invisible digital ecosystems.

How Different Societies Will Experience Open Finance

Open finance is often presented as straightforward progress toward greater connectivity and empowerment. In practice, societies will experience it very differently because trust, institutional maturity, regulatory culture, and customer behaviour vary significantly. The technology may be global; the human experience of openness is local.

In the UK, open banking has evolved within a regulated environment emphasising competition, consumer protection, and accountability. Expectations around governance, fraud protection, and recourse remain high—open finance here operates as a carefully managed institutional transition requiring continued public trust in regulatory oversight.

Across Europe, historical sensitivity toward data concentration has produced a regulatory culture where consent, explainability, and accountability sit at the centre of legitimacy. Customers may embrace interoperability while expecting robust safeguards around behavioural profiling and algorithmic decision-making.

In North America, rapid innovation and personalisation coexist with growing concerns around data aggregation, platform concentration, and cybersecurity. Ecosystems may evolve quickly while generating ongoing governance debate.

Singapore represents highly coordinated digital infrastructure where payments, identity, government services, and commercial platforms operate through integrated frameworks. Customers experience open finance as an extension of already-coordinated digital life rather than disruption.

China's model is different: financial ecosystems function through deeply integrated platform environments connecting commerce, communication, identity, and mobility. The ecosystem is the institution.

Across the Gulf, ambitious modernisation agendas and rapidly digitising populations are accelerating ecosystem development, yet institutional reputation and relationship trust remain powerful social forces. India represents one of the most significant large-scale experiments in digital public infrastructure, connecting payments, identity, and digital services at extraordinary scale, raising important questions around governance, resilience, and long-term institutional dependency.

In much of Africa, openness is experienced pragmatically around accessibility, transaction continuity, and everyday utility rather than formal institutional frameworks. In Latin America, economic memory—of inflation, volatility, and uneven institutional confidence—continues shaping cautious attitudes toward financial systems regardless of digital adoption.

The core insight is this: open finance ultimately depends on trust scaling alongside connectivity. Financial systems can become highly connected operationally while still requiring locally grounded forms of trust and human reassurance. The future of open finance will depend not only on how effectively systems exchange information, but on whether societies continue feeling confident living inside increasingly interconnected financial environments.

Being Human Inside an Embedded Financial Society

As open finance expands, banking gradually disappears into the background of everyday life. Payments occur automatically. Lending decisions emerge within online purchases. Insurance integrates into travel apps. Financial interaction increasingly happens without deliberate engagement with a traditional banking institution at all.

This creates an embedded financial society—an environment where financial systems are woven continuously into commerce, technology, communication, and daily behaviour. Banking becomes less a separate institutional activity and more an invisible layer integrated into the fabric of digital life.

The convenience is real. Frictionless payments, instant approvals, personalised recommendations, and seamless digital journeys reduce interruption and cognitive effort. But the psychological consequences are more complex than convenience alone suggests.

Historically, financial decisions carried moments of pause and conscious engagement. Visiting a branch, reviewing a statement, signing documents—these were visible, identifiable processes. Embedded systems progressively remove these moments. Decisions become continuous, ambient, and behaviourally integrated into digital environments designed to feel effortless.

When finance becomes invisible, people may no longer distinguish clearly between consumption, technology interaction, and financial decision-making. Embedded systems also introduce subtle behavioural influence—personalised recommendations, algorithmic prioritisation, dynamic pricing, and predictive offers operate continuously across digital platforms. AI intensifies this significantly, interpreting behavioural data to anticipate needs and automate recommendations before individuals consciously initiate financial decisions.

What happens to human agency when financial life becomes frictionless, continuous, and algorithmically mediated? Friction has historically performed important psychological functions—deliberation, pause, and visible process created opportunities for awareness and conscious judgement. Embedding removes many of these moments.

Different societies will respond differently. Europe's sensitivity around privacy and data governance will produce stronger expectations for transparency and customer control. In Singapore and East Asia, embedded financial life may feel like a natural extension of existing digital ecosystems. Across developing economies, embedded systems may significantly improve access while increasing dependency on platform infrastructure, operating beyond direct customer understanding.

The emotional implications are significant. As banking becomes less tangible, customers continue expecting reassurance that institutions remain accountable and recoverable when problems occur. Fraud incidents, subscription disputes, or automated financial errors become psychologically harder to navigate precisely because the institutional structures involved are invisible beneath layered digital ecosystems. Preserving human agency may become just as important as expanding technological capability.

Why Trust Will Become the Ultimate Infrastructure of Open Finance

Open finance promises seamless connectivity, interoperable systems, personalised services, and expanded financial participation. But beneath this growing connectivity lies a more fundamental reality: open systems only function sustainably when trust scales alongside openness.

Historically, trust in banking was concentrated within identifiable institutions—a branch, a brand, a regulated entity operating within visible boundaries. Open finance changes this architecture. Financial activity increasingly flows across multiple organisations simultaneously, often invisibly. A single customer interaction may involve banks, payment processors, cloud providers, fintech applications, identity systems, analytics platforms, and AI-driven decision environments—all operating beneath one seamless experience.

Trust therefore becomes distributed. Customers no longer evaluate confidence through one institution alone. They assess whether entire ecosystems feel reliable, secure, transparent, and accountable during moments of uncertainty.

The opacity problem is real. Customers appreciate frictionless experiences during normal operation but become deeply uncertain about accountability when disputes or failures occur. A customer experiencing fraud through an embedded payment environment may not know whether responsibility sits with the bank, platform, payment provider, or infrastructure intermediary. Open ecosystems require new forms of institutional clarity capable of preserving customer confidence even when operational structures become increasingly distributed.

Different societies will navigate this differently. In Europe, trust depends on governance discipline, privacy protection, and strong regulatory oversight. In Singapore and other coordinated digital environments, trust derives from integrated infrastructure reliability and institutional coherence. Across emerging markets, practical accessibility and inclusion remain central. In North America, concerns around platform concentration, data control, and cybersecurity will increasingly shape public perceptions.

AI intensifies all of these dynamics. The more capable systems become, the more important it is that their governance remains visible and accountable. Technology alone cannot sustain legitimacy indefinitely. Open ecosystems require customers to believe that systems are fair, information is protected, consent remains meaningful, institutions remain accountable, and recovery is possible when things go wrong.

The stakes extend beyond customer experience. Open financial ecosystems increasingly support broader societal infrastructure—payments, commerce, identity, mobility, healthcare, and government services now intersect continuously through shared digital environments. Trust failures within financial infrastructure can produce consequences extending well beyond banking into wider social and economic stability.

Connectivity creates capability. Trust creates legitimacy. Open systems may process transactions technically, yet societies only continue depending on them when human beings believe those systems will remain dependable during vulnerability and uncertainty. The institutions that endure will be those ensuring that openness strengthens trust rather than diluting it.

Reflection

Open finance represents one of the most consequential structural shifts in the architecture of modern retail banking, not because it introduces new technologies, but because it redefines long-standing assumptions about ownership, control, oversight, and institutional responsibility. For decades, banks operated in closed environments where information asymmetry shaped competitive advantage, and customer relationships were defined by proprietary products and inward-facing systems. Open finance dismantles these assumptions by placing the customer—not the institution—at the centre of the data ecosystem. It assigns banks a new role: custodians of trust within a transparent, multi-institutional architecture where interoperability, governance alignment, and ecosystem accountability determine long-term relevance. For hybrid institutions, this shift requires more than API readiness; it demands new leadership behaviour, stronger governance literacy, and cultural openness to collaboration at scale.

The resilience of open finance is most visible during moments of stress. System outages, fraud attempts, or data failures reveal whether architecture, governance, and coordination have been structurally embedded or remain fragmented.

At the operational level, open finance forces retail banks to integrate their internal architectures with external partners in ways that are predictable, resilient, and safe. Data portability means banks must reduce fragmentation across systems, align taxonomies, and adopt consistent security models. Embedded finance requires them to govern risk across boundaries they do not fully control. Platformisation introduces service dependencies that test continuity planning and crisis-management arrangements. Each of these pressures expands the scope of board oversight, requiring senior leadership teams to think beyond their historical remit and adopt a system-wide perspective. Boards must understand API-driven business models, regulatory interdependencies, and the vulnerabilities introduced through third-party infrastructure. They must also navigate the tension between innovation momentum and institutional integrity, ensuring growth does not come at the expense of safety, fairness, or ethical conduct.

Ultimately, open finance is not a competitive strategy. It is a public-infrastructure reality that will shape customer expectations, regulatory frameworks, and industry behaviour for the next decade. Institutions that embrace this shift proactively—with clarity, discipline, and responsible governance—will emerge as trusted anchors in an increasingly interconnected financial ecosystem.

Framework

Framework Overview

This framework consolidates the structural forces that define the open finance mandate for retail banking. It brings together insights from all five pillars to show how interoperability, consumer data rights, regulatory alignment, and ecosystem-based service design are reshaping institutional architecture. It highlights how API-driven exchanges, platform governance models, and cross-sector data portability now underpin customer journeys, operational resilience, and competitive positioning. The framework shows that open finance is not simply a compliance requirement; it is the backbone of a transparent, participatory, and collaborative financial system.

Open Finance Architecture

REGULATORY COHESION

Global regulatory frameworks increasingly set the direction for open finance. Clear mandates around data access, security standards, and consent mechanisms define how institutions must design their internal systems and external interactions. Regulatory cohesion ensures that customer rights are protected while enabling competitive innovation across markets.

DATA PORTABILITY AND INTEROPERABILITY

Open finance depends on seamless data movement across banks, fintechs, insurers, and non-financial platforms. Standardised APIs, unified taxonomies, and interoperable data models allow institutions to exchange information reliably while maintaining privacy and security. Interoperability becomes the structural foundation for customer choice and transparent service delivery.

PLATFORM-BASED OPERATING MODELS

Retail banks are transitioning from product-centric institutions to platform orchestrators. Platformisation enables them to integrate third-party services, manage real-time data flows, and deliver modular customer journeys. This anchor reflects how platform models reshape operating structures, revenue logic, and service design.

EMBEDDED FINANCIAL ECOSYSTEMS

Open finance allows banking services to be delivered within non-bank environments—retail, mobility, healthcare, logistics, and community platforms. Embedded ecosystems expand reach, lower distribution costs, and create context-rich service experiences. They require strong governance, shared risk protocols, and adaptive compliance.

STRATEGIC OVERSIGHT AND BOARD READINESS

Boards now hold responsibility for ecosystem risks, data-governance decisions, third-party partnerships, and regulatory alignment. Strong oversight ensures that open finance is implemented with accountability, resilience, and long-term vision. Governance capability becomes a differentiator that shapes institutional trust and competitive advantage.

Purpose of the Framework

This framework clarifies how open finance must be engineered into the institutional architecture of modern retail banks. It demonstrates that data mobility, ecosystem collaboration, and regulatory alignment must operate as integrated structural capabilities. The framework provides leaders with a clear model for diagnosing readiness, strengthening operational design, and building open-finance strategies that are trustworthy, adaptive, and globally aligned. Each component of this framework must translate into tangible customer outcomes: clear data control, secure access, reliable service delivery, and consistent experience across institutions.

Table 4.1 Checklist: Open Finance Readiness

1	Data Ownership Have we structurally recognised that customer data belongs to the individual, not the institution?
2	Consent Architecture Are our consent mechanisms clear, granular, revocable, and auditable in real time?
3	Data Portability Can customer data move seamlessly across institutions in standardised, usable formats?
4	Interoperability Do our systems align with external API standards, taxonomies, and data models across ecosystems?
5	Regulatory Alignment Are we prepared for evolving mandates such as UK Smart Data, EU PSD3/FIDA, and similar frameworks globally?
6	Third-Party Governance Do we have continuous oversight of fintechs, aggregators, and partners accessing our data?
7	Liability Framework Is accountability clearly defined when data flows across multiple entities and platforms?
8	Security and Resilience Are we able to maintain secure, real-time data exchange across internal and external systems?
9	Platform Readiness Can we operate as part of a broader ecosystem rather than as a closed financial institution?
10	Board Oversight Does the board understand and actively govern open finance risks, dependencies, and strategic positioning?

Table 4.2 Template: Open Finance Architecture Mapping

No.	*Dimension*	*Current State*	*Risk / Gap*	*Target State*	*Owner*
1	Customer Data Ownership	Data treated as institutional asset	Misalignment with regulation and trust	Fully customer-owned, permission-based data model	Chief Data Officer
2	Consent Management	Static, legalistic consent flows	Poor transparency, regulatory risk	Dynamic, real-time consent dashboards	Chief Data Officer / CIO
3	Data Portability	Fragmented, non-standard formats	Limited mobility, competitive disadvantage	Standardised, API-enabled portability	CIO
4	Interoperability	Partial API capability	Inconsistent data exchange, integration risk	Fully interoperable systems with shared standards	CIO / CTO
5	Regulatory Compliance	Reactive compliance approach	Delays, penalties, strategic misalignment	Regulation embedded as design principle	CRO / Compliance Head
6	Third-Party Ecosystem	Contract-based oversight	Hidden operational and conduct risks	Continuous monitoring and governance	COO / CRO
7	Liability and Accountability	Ambiguous ownership across partners	Customer harm, dispute complexity	Clear liability frameworks across ecosystem	Legal / CRO
8	Security and Data Protection	Perimeter-focused security	Exposure in distributed environments	End-to-end ecosystem security model	CISO
9	Platform Capability	Closed, product-centric model	Loss of relevance in open ecosystem	Platform-based, partner-integrated architecture	CIO / COO
10	Board Readiness	Limited visibility of ecosystem risks	Weak oversight of open finance exposure	Active board-level governance and literacy	Board / CEO

Bibliography

Australian Competition and Consumer Commission (2025). *Consumer Data Right Framework and Open Banking Developments*. ACCC.

Bank for International Settlements (2021). *Principles for Operational Resilience*. BIS.

Cambridge Centre for Alternative Finance (2024). *Research on Open Banking and Open Finance Ecosystems*. University of Cambridge Judge Business School.

European Commission (2023). *Financial Data Access and Payments Package*. European Commission.

European Commission (2023). *Proposal for a Regulation on a Framework for Financial Data Access*. European Commission.

Financial Conduct Authority (2025). *Open Finance and Smart Data Developments*. FCA.

Financial Conduct Authority (2025). *Research and Guidance on Open Banking and Open Finance in the UK*. FCA.

Government of India, Department of Financial Services (2025). *Account Aggregator Framework and Digital Financial Infrastructure*. Ministry of Finance.

Ministry of Electronics and Information Technology, Government of India (2023). *India's Digital Public Infrastructure*. Government of India.

OECD (2020). *The Future of Finance: Open, Connected and Inclusive*. OECD Publishing.

Reserve Bank of India (2016). *Non-banking Financial Company – Account Aggregator (Reserve Bank) Directions*. Reserve Bank of India.

World Bank (2022). *The Global Findex Database 2021: Financial Inclusion, Digital Payments, and Resilience in the Age of COVID-19*. World Bank.

World Economic Forum (2022). *Digital Identity Ecosystems: Unlocking New Value*. World Economic Forum.

World Economic Forum (2023). *Insights on Global Fintech and Inclusive Financial Growth*. World Economic Forum.

5 The ESG Banking Model

Context

Environmental, social, and governance (ESG) expectations have fundamentally transformed retail banking. For decades, sustainability sat on the periphery—expressed through annual reports or isolated community programmes. Today, regulatory pressure, climate volatility, digital transparency, and investor scrutiny have pushed ESG into the heart of institutional design.

This shift is structural, not cosmetic. Banks are now required to integrate climate-adjusted risk models, responsible lending frameworks, ethical technology deployment, and transparent reporting into everyday operations. Governments, supervisors, and communities increasingly expect institutions to serve not only as financial intermediaries but as stewards of societal resilience and environmental stability. The hybrid banking era intensifies this responsibility—digital delivery widens reach, accelerates decisions, and exposes institutions to real-time public judgement.

Despite strong policy frameworks, the gap between ESG intent and operational execution remains material. Institutions often demonstrate maturity in reporting and commitments, but inconsistency emerges at the point of customer interaction, where processes and behaviours determine real outcomes.

Multiple forces are driving this simultaneously. Climate change is producing immediate, measurable financial effects—mortgage impairment in flood-prone regions, higher credit volatility among households exposed to rising insurance costs, and growing agricultural risk. Regulators across the UK, EU, US, and Asia now require climate scenario analyses, environmental risk integration into credit underwriting, and structured disclosure through frameworks such as the ISSB (International Sustainability Standards Board) and TCFD (Task Force on Climate-Related Financial Disclosures). At the same time, rising expectations around ethical AI, conduct fairness, and inclusive access are reshaping institutional obligations. A misaligned algorithm, unclear grievance process, or poorly designed digital journey can quickly escalate into reputational damage and regulatory intervention.

Trust becomes the integrating measure across all of this. Customers, regulators, and investors don't assess ESG in isolation—they evaluate whether institutional behaviour remains consistent under pressure, complexity, and scale.

DOI: 10.4324/9781042021765-6

Hybrid banking models deepen ESG complexity by expanding the environments in which responsible behaviour must be demonstrated. Digital channels raise questions of data rights, accessibility, algorithmic fairness, and digital safety. Branch networks raise considerations of energy efficiency and community presence. Fintech partnerships require alignment on ethical standards and customer protection. Institutions are expected to maintain consistency across all these layers—offering customers a safe, transparent, and inclusive experience whether they interact through a mobile device or walk into a branch.

The global dimension intensifies this further. Retail banks operate across markets with different climate exposures, cultural expectations, and regulatory regimes. Green financing in Europe may focus on energy-efficient homes and electric vehicles, while banks in South Asia or Africa may prioritise microfinance for climate-vulnerable households or resilience lending for small businesses affected by extreme weather. Digital inclusion challenges differ just as widely—elderly customers in the UK may struggle with authentication journeys, while rural communities in emerging markets may lack stable connectivity or face language barriers. ESG integration demands granular understanding of local customer behaviour, infrastructure, and cultural norms. A one-size-fits-all approach is insufficient. Measurement discipline is therefore critical: ESG requires consistent metrics, verifiable data, and repeatable processes that allow institutions to move from narrative to evidence.

The governance implications are equally far-reaching. Boards and executive teams now face direct accountability for environmental and social outcomes, not only financial results. Supervisors expect directors to understand climate risk, AI ethics, digital conduct, and social impact—and to incorporate these into strategy, capital planning, and risk oversight. Retail banks must appoint sustainability leads, upgrade risk frameworks, improve data architecture, and establish cross-functional committees ensuring transparency and timely action. ESG reporting has become more rigorous, demanding accurate data, consistent metrics, and independent assurance. Weaknesses in reporting or accountability can lead to regulatory penalties, investor mistrust, and reputational erosion. Strong governance, by contrast, reinforces confidence and positions banks as credible partners in national and global sustainability agendas.

At the centre of all these expectations is a profound shift in how society views the role of retail banking. Banks are no longer measured only by efficiency or profitability—they are evaluated by their contribution to environmental stability, social wellbeing, and responsible governance. ESG therefore becomes the operating philosophy guiding how banks design services, engage customers, allocate capital, manage risk, and build trust. Institutions that embed ESG deeply into their processes will be better positioned to withstand volatility, attract long-term investment, retain customer confidence, and deliver meaningful societal value.

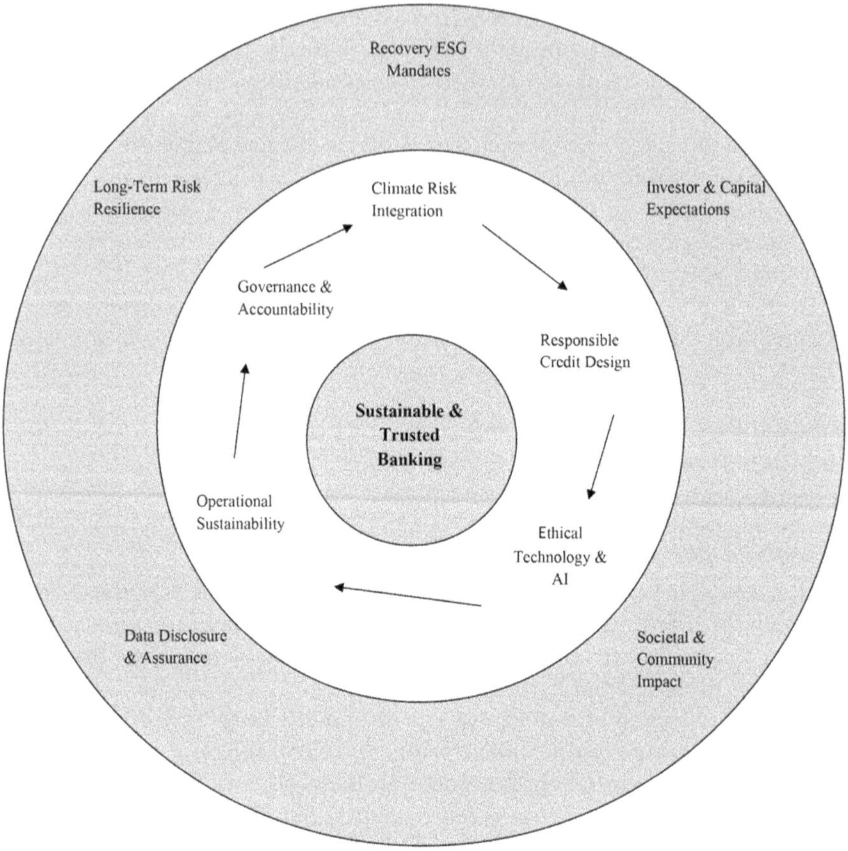

Figure 5.1 ESG as Institutional Banking Architecture

Climate Risk and Retail Portfolios

Climate risk has moved from a theoretical concern to a concrete financial reality that shapes the everyday decision-making of retail banks, influencing mortgage portfolios, unsecured lending, small-business credit, and long-term customer stability. Physical risks such as floods, storms, droughts, coastal erosion, and extreme heat now carry measurable implications for collateral values, insurance availability, and repayment capacity. Homes located in flood-prone areas face rising premiums or loss of insurability; agricultural borrowers are exposed to unpredictable crop cycles; and small businesses dependent on transport or energy infrastructure face higher volatility. At the same time, transition risks—policy changes, carbon taxes, emission standards, zoning requirements, and the rapid shift toward low-carbon technologies—create new uncertainties for households and micro-enterprises trying to adapt. Regulators in the UK, EU, and Asia increasingly expect retail banks to integrate climate-adjusted probability-of-default metrics, forward-looking scenario analyses, and geographic heat-mapping into credit processes, rather than relying on historical models which do not reflect the risks of a climate-change world. For hybrid banks, this requires integrating climate information into the systems used by branch staff, risk managers, and underwriting centres, so climate risks are understood at the time of decision-making. Finally, the process of diversification, as seen with concentration risks of regions dominated by single industries, with coastlines at risk, or cities threatened by heatwaves, requires differentiated approaches to capital allocation. When moving beyond compliance and considering how climate intelligence informs engagement with customers, it helps customers too, as families want banks to help them understand their climate risks and opportunities for resilience, energy savings, and adaptation to the risks of climate change. As such, it is not just reactive financial service providers, such as banks, which serve customers; it is financial service providers actively working towards the well-being of their customers.

Banks must also translate climate intelligence into practical customer guidance, helping households understand risk exposure, financing options, and resilience measures in simple terms.

Retail portfolios are increasingly exposed to climate-driven volatility because household finances are directly affected by environmental disruption, rising energy costs, and shifting insurance dynamics. As extreme weather becomes more frequent, families face unexpected expenses such as home repairs, temporary relocation, or loss of income due to business interruption. These pressures influence credit behaviour, increase short-term liquidity needs, and can heighten delinquency risks even among historically reliable borrowers. For retail banks, the challenge is not only to predict default probabilities but to understand how environmental stress interacts with local employment patterns, property markets, and household resilience. Mortgage lending becomes more complex when property values fluctuate due to flood-zone reclassification or when entire regions face affordability challenges linked to extreme heat or water scarcity. The transition to low-carbon living also adds financial pressure on consumers who must invest in energy-efficient homes, electric vehicles, or new heating systems—often requiring tailored financing solutions. Regulatory bodies now expect banks to incorporate these socioeconomic dimensions into risk assessments and to demonstrate that climate considerations are embedded into credit policies rather than treated as post-approval checks. This creates a compelling need for internal data integration: climate mapping, land-use data, satellite imagery, and insurance-risk indicators must flow seamlessly into retail credit models. It also reinforces the importance of frontline capability, as branch officers need simple tools to interpret complex climate data when advising customers on mortgages, refinancing needs, or adaptation loans. A bank that understands local climate realities and proactively supports households builds long-term loyalty, reduces unexpected losses, and contributes meaningfully to community resilience.

Yet another area where climate risks could be changing the risk management approaches of retail banks would be their views on collateral stability, especially for those types of collateral where their valuation does tend to depend particularly heavily upon their environment. Properties, for instance, in flood-vulnerable coastal areas, those in high-temperature urban centres, or those in water-scarcity zones, may now be showing early signs of withdrawal from risk pools, of weaker resale ability, and of slower rates of annual capital growth. Consequently, this would directly impact LVR (Loan to Value Ratio) calculations, refinancing options, and capital management strategies. In short, retail banks would no longer be able to bank upon past collateral behaviour being predictive of future behaviour, but would need to factor in forward-looking data like climate-resilience premiums, regional planning initiatives, and critical infrastructure resilience scores, among others. This means retail lenders must build climate sensitivity into cash-flow models and credit-monitoring routines, identifying early warning signals when local economies face environmental stress. Regulatory expectations in the UK, EU, and Asia increasingly require banks to demonstrate how climate scenarios influence both asset quality and portfolio migration trends. This demands a more dynamic form of risk management: regular portfolio heat-mapping, climate-aligned stress tests, and active engagement with customers whose assets or incomes are vulnerable to environmental volatility. By embedding these considerations into everyday lending practices, retail banks strengthen their ability to anticipate losses, safeguard customer stability, and align credit strategy with long-term sustainability goals.

Climate volatility is also transforming the way retail banks evaluate household vulnerability, as families increasingly face income instability driven by extreme weather events, rising energy costs, and shifting labour patterns in climate-exposed sectors. Households employed in agriculture, logistics, construction, hospitality, or small local services often experience abrupt financial stress when weather patterns disrupt seasonal work, damage community infrastructure, or raise operating costs for employers. This creates a cascade effect on personal loans, credit-card repayments, and mortgage servicing capacity. For hybrid retail banks, the challenge is not only detecting these shifts but building climate-aware affordability frameworks that recognise how environmental pressures amplify traditional credit risks. This requires deeper engagement with local economic data, insurance trends, and municipal adaptation plans to understand how climate disruption affects household cash flows. Regulators are increasingly signalling that retail banks must incorporate climate vulnerability into credit scoring, hardship frameworks, and early-intervention mechanisms. Practical steps include proactively identifying customers in high-risk zones, offering flexible restructuring options after climate events, and designing financial-wellbeing programmes tailored for communities experiencing chronic environmental stress. The most resilient retail banks will not rely solely on portfolio-level climate analysis; they will integrate climate awareness into frontline conversations, customer-support journeys, and product suitability assessments. By aligning climate intelligence with household-level behaviour, banks help reduce defaults, support community resilience, and demonstrate that ESG principles are embedded in day-to-day risk decision-making rather than confined to sustainability reporting.

Early identification must be matched with structured intervention pathways, ensuring that customers receive timely support rather than reactive remediation after stress materialises.

The climate-related regulations are changing at breakneck speeds, significantly affecting how banks' risk modelling, pricing, and management are conducted. All these are changing the entire banking compliance environment, which moves well beyond the traditional world of credit risk. Today, banks' supervisors in the UK, EU, and APAC, as well as those in various emerging markets, require retail banks to show how they are governing and managing climate-related risks using techniques such as scenario analysis, stress tests, and board or transparent management oversight. Furthermore, retail banks today are needed to link these new types of analysis to bank portfolio exposure profiles such as those based on geography, asset types, and customer types, as well as those related to various types of customer vulnerabilities. As such, banks' risk data requires this much higher level of granularity to understand how such climate-related events impact borrowers' stress and collateral, as well as local economies. However, there are still pressures from emerging issues such as carbon taxes, zoning regulations, insurance withdrawals, and energy efficiency, which put additional stress on banking underwriting criteria, such as those for mortgages and commercial lending, especially for long-tenor products like mortgages. Regulators are signalling that climate risk must sit within the core enterprise-risk framework rather than remain a specialist ESG function. This compels boards and executive teams to build stronger governance routines, including clear escalation paths, cross-functional climate committees, and routine reporting that links environmental trends with credit and operational metrics. For hybrid banks, regulatory alignment also intersects with customer trust: transparent climate governance demonstrates institutional responsibility, strengthens community relationships, and positions the bank as a long-term partner in resilience. By embedding regulatory expectations into everyday processes—rather than treating climate compliance as an annual reporting cycle—retail banks signal maturity, preparedness, and a commitment to safeguarding households and local economies in an increasingly volatile world.

Case Study: Climate Stress Testing in UK Retail Banking (Bank of England and PRA)

The Bank of England and the Prudential Regulation Authority (PRA) conducted the Climate Biennial Exploratory Scenario (CBES) to assess how physical and transition climate risks could affect UK banks' retail mortgage and consumer portfolios. Major retail banks were required to model long-term impacts of flooding, heat stress, carbon pricing, and policy transition on household affordability, collateral values, and default probabilities. The exercise revealed that climate risk manifests first at the retail level through property exposure, insurance availability, and regional income volatility, long before it appears as systemic loss. As a result, UK supervisors have pushed banks to embed climate-adjusted assumptions into mortgage underwriting, portfolio concentration limits, and governance oversight. This case demonstrates how ESG has moved from disclosure into binding retail risk architecture.

Retail banks face a growing operational challenge as climate volatility disrupts local economies, household stability, and community-level financial behaviour in ways that traditional credit models were never designed to capture. Extreme weather events increasingly reshape the daily realities of customers: families face rising insurance premiums, businesses struggle with intermittent operations, and vulnerable communities bear the brunt of infrastructure breakdowns and employment instability. These shifts translate into higher delinquency risks, reduced savings capacity, unpredictable cash flows, and greater demand for short-term liquidity. For banks, this means frontline teams must be trained to recognise climate-linked stress signals—from seasonal income fluctuations to localised supply-chain disturbances—and adjust interactions with empathy and accuracy. Mortgage portfolios require far more nuanced assessments of long-term property resilience, while small-business lending must account for changing operating environments and access to climate-proof utilities. Hybrid banks also have the added complexity of digital-first engagement: customer distress may surface through behavioural data before it appears in financial statements, requiring integrated analytics that combine local climate alerts, transaction patterns, and service-usage anomalies. Internally, risk teams need frameworks that connect physical climate data with customer vulnerability profiles, allowing for early intervention, tailored restructuring, and proactive communication during climate events. Banks that adapt in this way strengthen both resilience and trust, demonstrating an understanding of the lived realities of the communities they serve. By treating climate-driven household and business instability as a core component of retail banking—not an occasional anomaly—institutions position themselves as responsible, adaptive, and community-anchored partners in an era where environmental volatility increasingly shapes financial well-being.

Also, these are increasingly expected to integrate forward-looking climate intelligence into everyday decision-making, moving beyond static risk assessments toward dynamic models that track how environmental pressures evolve over time. Traditional credit frameworks largely assume stable economic conditions, but climate-linked disruptions such as crop damage, heat stress, supply-chain delays, and urban-infrastructure failures make customer behaviour far more volatile and geographically uneven. Key in this regard is how hybrid banks redesign portfolio monitoring so that risk signals are sensitive to regional climate patterns, seasonal variations, and the financial fragility of households and small businesses exposed to environmental stress. For instance, heatwaves can reduce productivity and raise living costs, indirectly affecting repayment capacity; floods can interrupt trading for micro-enterprises; and rising insurance premiums can change affordability for families on fixed incomes. These factors require continuous recalibration of credit scoring, probability-of-default estimates, and early-warning mechanisms. It is important also to highlight the need to mainstream climate indicators within customer support systems such as restructuring options, moratorium options, emergency access to credit lines, and specific advice; these need to be specific to local climate conditions as opposed to generalised policies. The importance of understanding the concentration of climate exposure within segments, cities, and income cohorts at the board level also needs to be highlighted, in order to better buffer, allocate capital, or design products accordingly. Institutions with a hybrid approach, complimented by robust data capabilities, are better positioned as they can utilise climate data, behavioural analytics, and channel data to inform an evolutionary perspective of risk. Banks who adopt this perspective of incorporating climate intelligence within portfolio management are better prepared to handle the current environmental uncertainties with certainty and stability.

Boards must maintain clear visibility of climate concentration risks, ensuring that portfolio exposure aligns with long-term sustainability and capital strategy.

Retail portfolios are becoming increasingly sensitive to climate-driven insurance dynamics, as insurers reassess pricing, coverage limits, and risk appetite across geographies affected by flooding, wildfire exposure, coastal erosion, and extreme weather trends. These insurance shifts create second-order financial risks for households and small businesses, which in turn influence loan affordability, collateral stability, and repayment behaviour. When premiums rise sharply or coverage becomes restricted, customers face higher outgoings and greater vulnerability, often without fully understanding the long-term financial implications. Mortgages on properties in high-risk zones may become harder to refinance; small businesses may struggle to absorb unexpected insurance costs; and informal enterprises may operate without sufficient protection, increasing the likelihood of financial shocks. Banks must incorporate insurance trends into lending models, recognising that climate resilience is now intertwined with the availability and affordability of insurance. This requires alignment between risk teams, credit committees, and frontline staff so they can anticipate customer strain earlier and design appropriate mitigation strategies. For regulators, the linkage between insurance and banking risk is becoming a priority, with expectations that institutions conduct joint scenario assessments and maintain clear visibility of insurance exposures within their portfolios. Hybrid institutions are uniquely positioned to integrate these insights: branch teams understand local patterns, digital systems monitor behavioural changes, and data models can track premium shifts in real time. By proactively embedding insurance dynamics into portfolio oversight, banks strengthen resilience, support customer stability, and build a more accurate understanding of climate-adjusted financial risk.

Climate-driven migration is a new and major risk factor for retail banking. It reshapes household stability, income continuity, property markets, and credit behaviour over the long term. Due to unproductive weather, lack of water, and higher temperatures, livelihoods become disrupted in millions of families, especially in South Asia, Sub-Saharan Africa, Southeast Asia, and Latin America. People affected are moving from those rural areas that are really vulnerable and coastal areas into town centres. Local credit dynamics are altered as borrowers abandon properties, interrupt repayment cycles while relocating, or move to informal housing structures where collateral structures weaken. Large inflows to receiving urban areas bring pressure on infrastructure and rental prices, raising short-term financial stress on the migrant families. These changes complicate traditional underwriting models because residency, income patterns, and household composition may become less predictable for banks. Hybrid institutions must integrate mobility indicators, geospatial risk, and socioeconomic resilience factors into portfolio monitoring. Branch teams in affected regions play a critical role by detecting early signs of migration-related strain—irregular instalments, withdrawals linked to relocation expenses, or requests for restructuring. Digital channels complement this by tracking behavioural signals, such as sudden address changes or concentration shifts in transaction patterns. Regulators across emerging markets are beginning to recognise climate migration as a systemic concern, encouraging banks to incorporate adaptive repayment structures, relocation-support products, and stress-tested portfolio scenarios. By acknowledging climate-driven mobility as a mainstream risk rather than an exceptional event, retail banks can design more resilient lending practices, protect vulnerable communities, and maintain long-term portfolio stability in markets where climate volatility is reshaping demographic realities.

Climate change, through the withdrawal of insurance, is turning into one of the most impactful disruptive events for retail banking, which is completely changing the way collateral values, risk, and household riskiness are being evaluated and revaluated. With the withdrawal of insurers from high-risk zones of floods, wildfires, coasts, and drought, many properties may be uneconomically offered insurance or may have premiums beyond the repayment capacity of the mortgage holder. For retail banks, uneconomically insured properties pose an existential threat to one of the very pillars of mortgage banking: without adequate collateral, the risk of single event loss of collateral, and consequently default, is very high. This erosion of insurance availability creates second-order risks, including declining property prices, stranded mortgage portfolios, higher loan-to-value breaches, and growing concentrations of geographic exposure in climate-vulnerable districts. Hybrid institutions must now incorporate insurance fragility into credit assessment, pricing models, and early-warning systems—not as a peripheral factor but as a core determinant of long-term asset quality. Branch teams and risk officers require new playbooks to support affected customers: restructuring options, advice on mitigation measures, guidance on local risk-reduction schemes, and partnerships with micro-insurance providers in emerging markets. Regulators in the UK, EU, Australia, and Asia Pacific are signalling that banks must stress-test mortgage portfolios against insurance retreat, aligning climate-adjusted capital expectations with real-world exposure patterns. For hybrid banks, integrating insurance withdrawal into risk intelligence strengthens resilience, protects community stability, and ensures that lending decisions reflect the true environmental, financial, and social realities shaping modern retail portfolios.

Green Branches and Energy Design

Green branch transformation begins with reframing physical infrastructure as a strategic asset that directly shapes cost efficiency, brand credibility, and long-term resilience. Branches account for a substantial share of a retail bank's energy footprint through lighting, climate control, legacy ATMs, ageing electrical systems, and outdated building materials. Modernising these environments requires more than aesthetic upgrades; it demands a systematic shift towards energy-efficient design, sensor-driven optimisation, and climate-aligned operations. Leading institutions are now deploying passive cooling, advanced insulation, LED retrofits, solar rooftops, and smart HVAC systems that adjust airflow and temperature based on occupancy patterns. These investments reduce the bank's operational expenditure while improving environmental performance, aligning with global net-zero pathways and national energy-efficiency mandates. For hybrid institutions, green branches reinforce public trust because they help to embed sustainability into everyday operations rather than just placing it into corporate reports. Branch modernisation initiatives support both financial and ESG outcomes: reduced energy costs, reduced emissions, healthier indoor environments, and improved customer perception. This also places a premium on location-specific design: using urban, rural, and climate-sensitive regions to make sure buildings can keep operating during heatwaves, storms, or grid instability. Green branch design, then, falls right to the foundational precepts of the modern hybrid network, joining environmental responsibility with institutional credibility and long-term operational resilience.

A green branch network needs a transformation from an episodic upgrade approach towards a formalised design philosophy aimed at integrating a long-term ecological approach into the physical infrastructure lifecycle. Throughout the arc, the necessity for retail banks to move beyond episodic upgrade approaches towards long-term planning, including energy audits, predictive maintenance, and lifecycle costing in the design of the retail branch infrastructure will be discussed. Banks still largely approach infrastructure as a necessary evil, pursuing reactive repairs or legacy procurement practices that do not consider the long-term effects of energy savings or environmental impact. However, the high-performing global retail banks have developed a sustainability roadmap for each of the retail branch locations based on the age, material, ventilation, energy profile, and exposure to regional climatic influences. Modern lifecycle approaches incorporate recyclable materials, modular interiors, low-VOC paints, solar-ready roofing, and energy-efficient façades designed to reduce heat ingress and improve daylight utilisation. They also factor in the environmental footprint of vendor selection, transport logistics, and waste disposal, ensuring that sustainability is embedded end-to-end. For hybrid banks, lifecycle-based design enhances operational resilience by reducing the likelihood of energy outages, equipment failures, and cooling breakdowns—issues that disproportionately affect rural and emerging markets. Customers increasingly associate sustainable environments with responsible institutions, making lifecycle-aligned branch design a contributor to brand trust. By treating branch infrastructure as a living system that evolves with climate demands, energy standards, and customer expectations, banks strengthen both their cost efficiency and their ESG credibility.

This transformation is most effective when energy intelligence is built directly into the operating environment, allowing institutions to monitor, predict, and optimise consumption in real time. Hybrid banks can integrate smart-building technologies—such as IoT sensors, energy-management platforms, AI-driven optimisation engines, and automated controls—to convert physical branches into intelligent, self-regulating environments. Modern systems continuously track temperature, footfall, humidity, natural-light availability, equipment heat output, and air-quality levels to determine the most efficient way to run lighting, cooling, ventilation, and digital signage. Instead of fixed schedules, branches operate on dynamic, data-based patterns that align energy use with customer traffic and ambient conditions. This reduces costs significantly, especially in hot-weather geographies where cooling loads dominate operational expenditure. The value of predictive-maintenance capabilities should also be highlighted: sensors detect early signs of malfunction in HVAC units, ATMs, and UPS systems, allowing timely intervention and preventing failures that can disrupt service in vulnerable markets. Importantly, data collected from intelligent branches helps banks refine their sustainability roadmaps by identifying high-consumption clusters, inefficient design patterns, and opportunities for solar integration or insulation upgrades. Intelligent energy systems strengthen operational resilience by ensuring that branches remain functional even under fluctuating grid conditions—a common challenge in emerging economies. For customers, energy-smart environments communicate efficiency, responsibility, and technological readiness, enhancing trust and reinforcing the bank's ESG credibility. This data-driven foundation is essential for institutions aiming to meet net-zero commitments while maintaining a cost-effective and reliable branch footprint.

Case Study: DBS Bank—Net Zero Branch Transformation

DBS Bank has implemented large-scale green-branch programme across Asia, integrating energy-efficient architecture, smart building management systems, and renewable energy sourcing into its retail footprint. Branches were redesigned with LED lighting, intelligent cooling systems, occupancy-based energy controls, and solar integration where feasible. DBS reported material reductions in energy consumption and operational emissions while improving customer comfort and service reliability in high-heat and high-footfall environments. The programme demonstrates how ESG-aligned branch design delivers simultaneous environmental, cost, and resilience benefits, reinforcing the role of physical infrastructure as a strategic ESG asset rather than as a legacy liability.

Designing green branches requires banks to move beyond isolated retrofits and adopt a whole-system architectural approach that links physical materials, layout, equipment, and energy logic into a unified design philosophy. Environmentally aligned branch architecture integrates sustainable construction materials, efficient spatial planning, and climate-responsive layouts to reduce long-term energy demand without compromising customer comfort or operational workflow. Modern branches increasingly rely on insulated wall assemblies, low-VOC paints, recycled flooring, reflective roofing systems, and double-glazed facades that naturally regulate temperature and reduce reliance on mechanical cooling. Spatial zoning separates high-traffic areas from service-intensive back-office sections, allowing for targeted cooling instead of using energy uniformly in the full footprint. Landscaping also plays a strategic role; using shade trees, pergolas, and green buffers decreases heat absorption, which has the effect of lowering branch temperatures in hot climates. Self-service kiosks, teller counters, and advisory pods are placed in ergonomic spots to cluster energy-intensive devices in zones with efficient airflow and cooling. A strategy of solar daylighting—skylights, light shelves, and reflective interior paints—can greatly reduce artificial lighting needs while enhancing ambiance and security. For hybrid banks, this efficient architectural design is supportive of resilience during energy outages; well-ventilated branches maintain reasonable comfort levels even during temporary power shortages. This integrated architectural philosophy enhances operation efficiency, lessens the carbon footprint, and solidifies public perception of the bank as a responsible institution committed to environmental stewardship.

Operations increasingly depend on intelligent building-management systems (BMS) that use data to optimise energy performance in real time. Smart sensors, automated controls, and integrated energy dashboards enable retail banks to reduce wastage, enhance operational predictability, and maintain consistent environmental standards across large branch networks. Modern BMS platforms combine temperature sensors, occupancy detection, daylight sensors, and equipment-level monitoring to regulate heating, cooling, ventilation, and lighting with a precision that manual processes cannot achieve. In many markets, banks are installing IoT-enabled meters that track energy peaks, identify abnormal consumption patterns, and trigger automated shutdowns of idle equipment such as ATMs, display screens, and kiosks outside business hours. Air-conditioning units are increasingly linked to centralised command centres, ensuring that cooling cycles adjust to real-time weather fluctuations and branch occupancy levels. Beyond energy savings, integrated BMS systems improve resilience: early detection of equipment strain reduces the risk of breakdowns and predictive maintenance models extend the lifecycle of HVAC systems, lighting grids, and security infrastructure. Data collected from BMS platforms feeds into ESG reporting frameworks, helping banks substantiate energy-efficiency claims with verifiable metrics. The cultural shift required should also be highlighted: frontline teams must be trained to interpret energy dashboards, adhere to operational protocols, and escalate anomalies promptly. For hybrid institutions, intelligent energy management reinforces both sustainability and cost efficiency, showcasing how technology, governance, and operational discipline converge to deliver measurable environmental impact.

The transformation of green branches is significantly influenced by the redesign of physical layouts to enable maximum efficiency using natural light, air, and warmth, reducing the need to use artificial air conditioners and light sources. This means the transformation of banking institutions towards bioclimatic architectural concepts to ensure that the use of artificial air conditioners and light sources is reduced through techniques such as the use of windows, shades, reflective coatings, and intelligent insulation to provide consistent indoor conditions despite the changing outside climate. In this regard, bank branches have resorted to the use of open-plan layouts to eliminate the need to have many enclosed spaces and to enable the free circulation of air through tellers' sections, advisory sections, and waiting areas. Additionally, bank branches in hot climates are using overhangs, pergolas, and greening to reduce the amount of absorbed heat, while those in cold climates are using triple-glazed windows and retention materials to ensure the retention of warmth within the facilities despite the cold climate. Also worth highlighting is how interior material choices—such as bamboo composites, recycled aluminium, and low-carbon concrete—reduce embodied emissions while improving durability. Beyond design elements, branch workflows are being reconfigured to ensure that high-energy activities, such as printing or ATM servicing, occur in optimised zones that minimise overall power demand. Staff engagement plays a crucial role: energy-conscious layout design must be accompanied by operational behaviours such as keeping doors closed during peak cooling hours, adhering to temperature guidelines, and promptly escalating maintenance issues. Through thoughtful layout engineering, banks achieve not only environmental gains but also quieter, healthier, and more welcoming spaces that reinforce trust and customer satisfaction.

Energy optimisation in branch operations increasingly depends on intelligent monitoring systems that analyse consumption patterns in real time and automatically adjust energy use across lighting, cooling, heating, and equipment loads. Banks are deploying smart meters, IoT-enabled sensors, and predictive-analytics platforms to identify inefficiencies and correct them without manual intervention. These systems track temperature fluctuations, occupancy levels, and peak-usage cycles, enabling branches to modulate energy demand dynamically rather than rely on static schedules. For instance, motion-sensitive lighting can automatically dim or switch off in low-traffic zones, while adaptive HVAC algorithms can adjust airflow and temperature based on the number of customers present, local weather conditions, and time of day. Worth mentioning too is how predictive maintenance models reduce energy waste by detecting faults in cooling units, ATMs, UPS systems, and server rooms before they escalate, preventing leaks, over-heating, or unnecessary power draw. Branches in regions with unstable grids increasingly use hybrid energy systems—solar rooftops paired with battery storage or grid-tie inverters—to smooth consumption patterns and reduce dependency on fossil-fuel electricity. In addition, dashboards provide branch managers and facilities teams with clear visibility of consumption trends, allowing them to benchmark performance across locations and identify high-opportunity sites for retrofits. Customer-facing transparency, such as digital displays showing carbon savings or energy-efficiency achievements, strengthens institutional credibility and reinforces the message that sustainability is part of everyday operations. By integrating technology, behaviour, and monitoring, smart-energy systems help hybrid retail banks transition from reactive to anticipatory energy management, reducing costs while advancing net-zero commitments.

Retrofitting existing branches for sustainability requires a structured approach that balances environmental ambition with operational practicality. Hybrid institutions are modernising legacy buildings through phased upgrades that target the highest-impact components: insulation, glazing, ventilation, lighting, and material use. Many older branches were designed in eras with limited awareness of energy optimisation, resulting in inefficient heat retention, outdated electrical layouts, and heavy reliance on artificial lighting. Modern retrofit programmes increasingly focus on installing double-glazed windows, reflective roofing, thermal-efficient wall panels, and low-emission flooring materials to create stable internal climates that reduce the load on HVAC systems. Alongside physical upgrades, banks are redesigning internal layouts to maximise natural light, repositioning service counters and self-service zones to minimise artificial illumination needs. Additionally, retrofitting entails the replacement of energy-consumption-intensive machines such as ATMs, servers, and security systems with energy-friendly ones that are certified to the latest energy efficiency standards. In places with high solar irradiance, solar roof tops and solar carports are integrated into the older bank branches to reduce the level of dependence on the public grid. What is intriguing in this shift, however, is the emphasis on the fact that an effective retrofitting programme depends on the predominance of "effective governance" regarding the determinations of procurement policies, lifecycle-cost analysis, vendor selection aligned to sustainability, and periodic assessments to review the energy performance. Hybrid banks are developing inter-professional groups consisting of facilities managers, sustainability specialists, risks managers, and branch supervisors to ensure that the retrofitting does not compromise service performance. A well-structured retrofitting programme not only reduces the footprint on the environment but equally emphasises a positive image by being able to "measure" the commitment to sustainable practices.

Designing green branches increasingly depends on intelligent energy-management systems that automate, monitor, and optimise consumption patterns across the full retail network. Hybrid banks are adopting sensor-led architectures that continuously track temperature, humidity, footfall, lighting needs, and equipment utilisation to create dynamic energy profiles for each location. Modern branches employ occupancy sensors that dim or switch off lights in unused areas, smart thermostats that adjust cooling and heating based on real-time weather data, and AI-enabled controllers that learn daily usage patterns to reduce waste. These systems also synchronise with ATM uptime requirements, security lighting schedules, and digital-signage displays to ensure energy is consumed only when operationally necessary. A critical aspect of intelligent energy design is the integration of branch-level dashboards with enterprise-wide sustainability platforms. This allows banks to benchmark branches against each other, identify anomalies such as excessive HVAC usage, detect faulty equipment early, and allocate budget for targeted upgrades. Energy-management intelligence enables branches in hot climates to regulate cooling loads without compromising customer comfort, while branches in colder regions optimise heating cycles during low-footfall periods. Importantly, automated systems require robust governance: clear accountability for overrides, periodic calibration, cybersecurity safeguards for sensor networks, and continuous training for facilities teams. Intelligent energy-management not only lowers the environmental footprint but also strengthens operational resilience by reducing power dependency, improving equipment lifespan, and enhancing overall cost-efficiency across the retail network.

Green branch design increasingly extends beyond energy efficiency into the broader concept of environmental stewardship, where physical locations act as visible demonstrations of a bank's sustainability commitments. Thus, hybrid institutions are incorporating sustainable construction materials, water-conservation systems, and circular-economy principles into both new builds and retrofits. Banks are using low-carbon concrete, recycled composites, responsibly sourced timber, and non-toxic paints to reduce embedded emissions. Water-saving fixtures, rainwater-harvesting units, and grey-water recycling are being integrated into branches in drought-prone geographies, lowering operational risk linked to water scarcity. Furthermore, landscaping choices—native plants, permeable pavements, and pollinator-friendly micro-gardens—help branches manage stormwater runoff while enhancing their role as community-centric spaces. Increasingly, banks are adopting "design for disassembly" principles, ensuring fixtures, partitions, and furniture can be reused or recycled at end of life. The dimension of governance should also be taken into consideration, where the implementation of sustainable procurement policies and the use of lifecycle assessments, along with the mandatory implementation of environmental audits, ensure that the green design elements are not merely superficial, but they impact the actual architectural design of the buildings. What is interesting, however, is the manner in which the organisation's customers perceive such design features of the retail bank's outlets as determinants of integrity, where the physically manifested green conscience of the branch maintains the credibility of the ESG efforts of the organisation as a whole. Thus, through the manner in which the retail banks have implemented green design into the construction, water management, and material specifications, they can effectively build infrastructure that not only enhances efficiency in operations but also exhibits environmental responsibility in the hybrid banking landscape.

Ethical AI in Credit and Lending

Ethical AI in credit and lending begins with re-examining how retail banks define fairness, accuracy, and accountability in a world where algorithms increasingly influence who receives access to financial opportunity. Hybrid institutions must recognise that traditional credit models—built on historical data, rigid scorecards, and narrow behavioural assumptions—often embed structural biases that disadvantage low-income groups, women, migrants, informal-sector workers, and digitally limited customers. As banks transition to AI-driven risk engines, the potential for both improvement and harm expands significantly. Ethical design requires an institutional commitment to re-engineering data foundations: ensuring training sets reflect diverse demographics, incorporating alternative data responsibly, and correcting for patterns that reproduce past inequities. It also demands transparent model governance, where every AI system has clear lineage documentation, human-validated decision thresholds, and audit trails that regulators and customers can understand. This highlights the need for interdisciplinary oversight—bringing together risk teams, data scientists, compliance officers, behavioural experts, and community voices—to prevent blind spots created by purely technical perspectives. Ethical AI also extends to frontline practice: staff must be able to explain algorithmic outcomes, escalate anomalies, and recognise when model outputs conflict with inclusion principles. For hybrid institutions, the credibility of AI depends on embedding fairness checks throughout the lifecycle—data collection, model training, validation, deployment, and ongoing monitoring. By treating ethical AI as both a governance responsibility and a social contract, retail banks can ensure that automation enhances mobility and trust rather than deepening inequality.

Fairness in AI must be experienced by customers as dignity, where decisions are not only accurate but also understandable and respectful.

AI must also address some degree of opacity that surrounds algorithmic decisions, especially when these decisions, in the form of automated credit denials, limit cuts, or even suspected fraud blocks, seem to happen without a customer's full comprehension. What follows will look at how, as a result, explainability has emerged as a major issue in the ethical applications of AI, as UK, European, Singaporean, and North American banking supervisors increasingly demand that these systems show how AI-generated outcomes were produced, validated, and scrutinised. In the case of hybrid banking, there's an added dimension here because, within these systems, explainability is not just a question of complying with legislation—it's one of creating a customer-centricity that starts with a customer's feeling that their life is being managed by an accountable, rather than invisible, hand. To achieve this, banks must invest in model-interpretability tools, maintain documentation that traces input variables to final decisions, and train frontline teams to communicate AI outcomes in clear, human-centred language. Equally important is the recognition that explainability must coexist with security and fraud-prevention safeguards; banks must strike the right balance between revealing enough to build trust while protecting models from manipulation. This also stresses the importance of customer journey design, ensuring that digital interfaces provide meaningful explanations, appeal mechanisms, and pathways to human review for customers experiencing distress or confusion. When combined with strong governance and regular fairness audits, transparent AI empowers customers, strengthens institutional credibility, and reinforces the principle that technology should serve human needs with dignity and clarity.

In today's world, ethical AI also demands stronger accountability structures that ensure model development, deployment, and monitoring are governed with the same discipline applied to financial risk and compliance. Hybrid institutions must thus establish clear lines of ownership for AI outcomes, assigning defined responsibilities to data scientists, risk teams, model validators, and business leaders rather than allowing accountability to diffuse across departments. Effective oversight requires independent model-risk committees, periodic fairness testing, scenario-based stress evaluations, and end-to-end documentation that tracks model evolution over time. Also worth highlighting is the importance of cross-functional governance: AI cannot be managed solely by technology teams; risk, compliance, legal, behavioural experts, and frontline leaders must collectively shape the frameworks that determine what is acceptable, what is prohibited, and how emerging risks are escalated. At the same time, institutions must address the cultural risks surrounding AI adoption—over-reliance on automated outputs, inadequate challenge from human reviewers, and the misconception that algorithmic systems are inherently objective. Strong accountability mechanisms help counter these tendencies by reinforcing the principle that AI supports decision-making but does not replace institutional judgment. By embedding accountability into governance structures, hybrid banks demonstrate that ethical AI is not an afterthought but a strategic commitment to fairness, transparency, and responsible innovation.

Similarly, the issue of ethical AI in the context of lending requires the same utmost scrutiny in regard to the quality, origin, and completeness of the data sets fed into the system to make credit determinations. The discussion so far in this chapter traces the concept of how historical data sets in banking carry inbuilt biases that have been programmed over decades of differential access, lack of proper documentation, incomplete credit history, and demographic factors. Unless addressed, there may be further worsening of the position of the poor, those with credit-inexperience, migrants, and communities with limited digital footprints. In response, hybrid institutions need to invest in data cleansing, representative sampling, and the inclusion of alternative data sources such as transaction patterns, rental payments, community banking activity, and behavioural signals that collectively paint a more accurate and inclusive picture of customer risk. Worth emphasising is that improving data quality is both an ethical and commercial imperative: better data reduces credit losses, expands profitable segments, and lowers misclassification risks. Banks must also maintain strict controls around data privacy, consent, and retention, ensuring that the drive for richer data does not compromise customer rights. By elevating data quality as a core pillar of ethical AI, hybrid institutions move towards credit systems that are fairer, more transparent, and better aligned with social and regulatory expectations.

Ethical deployment of AI in lending also requires that banks create transparent, explainable pathways for customers to understand how decisions affecting their financial lives are being made. This highlights that opacity in algorithmic decisions—from automated credit scoring to fraud alerts and portfolio rebalancing—can erode trust and create feelings of unfairness, especially when customers do not receive clear reasoning for approvals, rejections, or limit changes. Hybrid institutions must therefore invest in explainable-AI frameworks that convert complex model outputs into simple, human-readable explanations. This includes outlining the key variables considered, clarifying how behavioural or transactional patterns influence risk assessment, and offering customers meaningful avenues to dispute inaccuracies or request reconsideration. It should be emphasised that transparent communication strengthens regulatory compliance under emerging global guidance on fairness and explainability, while also protecting vulnerable customers who may not be familiar with digital systems. Noteworthy too is that clear explanations improve customer satisfaction and reduce grievance volumes, directly supporting conduct-risk management. By embedding explainability into the lending journey, banks demonstrate accountability, reinforce ethical standards, and create a more dignified and trustworthy credit experience for every customer.

Besides, the quality, diversity, and completeness of the data fed to the AI system also play an important role in ethical AI for lending. When there is an overrepresentation of specific groups in the lending dataset and an underrepresentation of other groups, the AI system may end up "hardcoding" potential biases into the lending process. Accordingly, the list of gaps in terms of demographic data, thin files, informal income groups, women-led households, migrant communities, and those who are digitally constrained is just a hint at the fact that hybrids need to step up and correct these issues by addressing the need for greater data sources and exploring alternative measures of creditworthiness. Another matter to highlight is the importance of continuously monitoring model outputs to detect emerging biases as customer behaviour and macroeconomic conditions evolve. In parallel, banks must ensure that data science teams collaborate with frontline staff, compliance officers, and social-impact specialists to review outcomes from multiple lenses, not only statistical performance. By treating data diversity as a core ethical responsibility rather than a technical afterthought, retail banks can build AI systems that support broader financial inclusion, reduce credit misclassification, and ensure that lending decisions reflect a fair and representative view of the communities they serve.

Another component of ethical AI usage is that lending decisions need to be transparent to customers, regulators, and internal governance structures. With more complex machine learning models being used within hybrid financial institutions, there remains the potential for decisions on lending approvals or denials to become non-transparent or non-explainable if these institutions fail to adhere to strict guidelines related to model explanation or interpretability. This analysis has been presented to identify key reasons why it remains critical for customers to be able to understand simple reasons or rationale for lending decisions, particularly for denials or reduced lending thresholds. Explainability also strengthens internal oversight: risk committees, auditors, and board members can only discharge their duties effectively when AI models provide interpretable insights rather than black-box outputs. Explainable AI is not a compromise on model accuracy; rather, it ensures that technological sophistication remains aligned with fairness, accountability, and customer confidence. Institutions that invest in explainability tools, governance workflows, and staff training build credit systems that are not only compliant but trusted. For hybrid banks, this transparency becomes a competitive differentiator, demonstrating that technology is being used to support—not replace—responsible judgement.

Ethical AI in credit decision-making also demands rigorous stress-testing of models across demographic, geographic, and socioeconomic segments to ensure that outcomes do not diverge unfairly for vulnerable groups. Hybrid banks must simulate diverse scenarios—such as income volatility, limited digital footprints, irregular employment patterns, and varying regional data availability—to detect biases that conventional validation methods may overlook. We should also highlight that stress-testing AI models is no longer limited to accuracy under normal conditions; regulators increasingly expect banks to demonstrate how models behave under atypical customer journeys, thin-file profiles, or incomplete transaction histories. Furthermore, the quality of training data is often the root cause of AI-driven exclusion, making it essential for banks to incorporate synthetic data augmentation, cross-segment benchmarking, and periodic dataset reviews to correct skewed patterns. For governance teams, these stress tests offer a transparent basis for approving or recalibrating AI systems before deployment. For customers, they translate into more reliable and equitable access to credit, especially in communities historically underserved by formal financial systems. Through disciplined stress-testing, hybrid banks ensure that AI strengthens institutional fairness rather than amplifying structural inequalities.

Another ethical AI consideration for banks revolves around the explanation of the determinations made with the help of AI systems, especially in the case of unfavourable outcomes. Herein lies the significance of explanation as the basis of the legitimacy of an institution, as the customer now expects an explanation as to why the loan was sanctioned, changed, or denied. Also relevant is the process of devising the explanation mechanism for the customers of the hybrid banks so that the complex reasoning is transformed into a simple one with the help of the AI system deployed by the banks. We should also note how frontline teams must be trained to interpret algorithmic outputs, challenge questionable decisions, and escalate cases that appear inconsistent with fairness expectations. This relates to the need for continuous learning loops, where customer feedback, appeal patterns, and dispute outcomes are fed back into model refinement processes. By embedding explainability into both the customer journey and internal governance, hybrid banks ensure that AI-driven credit systems remain accountable, intelligible, and aligned with ethical and social expectations.

Finally, ethical AI for credit and lending models depends on the overall governance culture, where fairness is not seen as a milestone within the compliance process but rather as an ongoing operation. We have thus far covered the overall process where hybrid institutions need to develop structures for ongoing reviews of model behaviour through the financial cycles, customer segments, and regulatory environments. The chapter has also emphasised the overall need for multi-disciplinary skills in those models. An example would be AI governance committees that include risk specialists, data scientists, frontline representatives, and social-impact experts who collectively review model drift, fairness indicators, escalation trends, and customer-experience outcomes. Also outlined is how banks must maintain rigorous documentation that captures model assumptions, training-data sources, validation results, override patterns, and audit findings to ensure traceability and dependability in supervisory reviews. Ethical AI must evolve with market behaviour, new data sources, and emerging fairness risks, making periodic recalibration and independent testing essential. And, as customers increasingly perceive algorithmic decisions as reflections of institutional intent, ethical governance must be embedded in everyday operational choices, shaping how decisions are explained, challenged, and corrected. By institutionalising fairness as a living governance function, hybrid banks create AI systems that are resilient, trustworthy, and consistent with the social purpose of retail banking.

Boards and senior leadership must treat AI governance as a standing agenda item, ensuring continuous oversight of fairness, risk, and customer impact.

Financial Literacy and Inclusion Gaps

Financial literacy forms the foundation of meaningful economic participation, yet it remains unevenly distributed across age groups, income levels, geographies, and cultural contexts. Low financial awareness directly shapes customer vulnerability, influencing savings habits, borrowing behaviour, digital adoption, and long-term financial resilience. As a result, hybrid banks must recognise literacy not as a peripheral social initiative but as an operational priority that affects delinquency rates, service quality, product suitability, and regulatory expectations. Many customers struggle to interpret fees, interest structures, credit terms, or digital-service paths, leading to confusion, mistrust, and avoidable risk exposures. It is also important to underscore some of the underlying causes of low literacy, for example, inconsistent income, lack of access to well-informed guides, language, and the intricacies of contemporary financial services. For hybrid banking organisations, tackling these literacy gaps demands a sophisticated response, where product experience, communication, personalised persuasion, community programmes, and training for customer service representatives to demystify finance become essential steps to instilling confidence within customers while solidifying the social purpose of retail banking.

Improved literacy must translate into measurable outcomes, including reduced complaints, better repayment behaviour, and increased product suitability.

Financial inclusion and literacy are deeply interlinked, and hybrid banking models must address both simultaneously to ensure genuine access. Customers who are underserved or newly connected to formal finance often lack the contextual knowledge required to evaluate product choices, manage repayment obligations, or navigate digital platforms confidently. Literacy gaps manifest differently across segments: older adults may struggle with authentication steps; women in certain communities may face social barriers to financial decision-making; rural customers may have limited exposure to formal banking norms; and migrants may be unfamiliar with regulatory protections in their new country. These barriers create a cycle in which low literacy discourages usage, and low usage prevents customers from building confidence and trust. For hybrid institutions, the responsibility is twofold: designing products that assume low literacy as a default, and enabling advisory pathways that combine digital simplicity with human support. This includes multilingual materials, visual cues for complex decisions, transparent fee structures, and service journeys that avoid hidden conditions. When literacy-informed design becomes part of the operating model, banks can reduce grievances, improve repayment outcomes, and strengthen the ethical core of ESG by ensuring equitable access to financial capability.

The financial literacy challenges are often compounded by the increasing digital divide, where the inability of vulnerable groups to engage meaningfully in hybrid banking ecosystems shows up. Less digitally comfortable customers struggle not only with app navigation or authentication but also with understanding digital transaction logs, assessing automated prompts, or interpreting algorithm-driven recommendations. These gaps increase the risk of errors, fraud exposure, and dependency on informal advisers who may not act in the customer's best interest. For hybrid institutions, literacy therefore cannot be separated from digital capability. Banks must anticipate where users may hesitate, misinterpret information, or abandon a process, and design safeguards that simplify decision-making. This includes intuitive interface layouts, step-by-step confirmations, low-literacy modes, assisted-digital support at branches, and frontline staff trained to guide customers without overwhelming them. When banks recognise that digital literacy is a prerequisite for safe participation in modern retail finance, their ESG strategy becomes more grounded, ensuring that technology does not widen inequality but instead expands access through thoughtful design and responsible engagement.

Financial behaviour is shaped not only by knowledge gaps but by deep cultural patterns, collective memory, and the informal financial systems on which many households rely. In many parts of Asia, Africa, and Latin America, choices about borrowing, saving, and risk-taking are made according to community norms, family duties, religious imperatives, and long-standing informal practices. Even in the developed economies, migrant families, multigenerational households, and digitally cautious customers continue to rely on word-of-mouth advice, peer experience, or community intermediaries rather than written disclosures or online calculators. Hybrid banks must treat this cultural variability as a core ESG priority because financial literacy cannot be meaningfully improved without first understanding the "mental models" through which customers interpret money, institutions, and trust. This calls for frontline teams to use relatable analogies, locally contextualised examples, and multilingual formats that understand how different groups see debt, investment, and risk. It also requires banks to recognise that in many communities, mistrust of formal financial systems is inherited rather than experienced—shaped by stories of hidden charges, denied claims, or insensitive recovery practices that linger for decades. For hybrid institutions, addressing these behavioural norms is not a soft initiative but a structural requirement for long-term inclusion. ESG-aligned banks must therefore embed cultural awareness into product explanations, digital onboarding flows, advisory models, and grievance-redress pathways, ensuring that the institution meets customers where they are rather than expecting them to navigate unfamiliar financial landscapes alone. When banks design literacy interventions with cultural intelligence, they close inclusion gaps, reduce misunderstanding-driven delinquency, and strengthen the social fabric that underpins resilient, community-rooted retail banking.

Hybrid retail banking cannot advance meaningful inclusion without addressing the structural barriers that prevent customers from understanding, comparing, and safely using financial products. Many households operate with fragmented information: they know the price of a product but not the total cost of credit; they understand the convenience of digital payments but not the consequences of recurring fees; they recognise the appeal of savings instruments but not the implications of early withdrawal or inflation. These gaps are not a reflection of capability but of asymmetry: banks possess full knowledge, while customers receive only fragments of it within complex, jargon-heavy disclosures. This pillar argues that literacy initiatives must evolve beyond pamphlets, workshops, or digital tutorials; they must be woven into the product architecture itself. Transparent pricing dashboards, intuitive risk explanations, personalised nudges, and step-by-step decision journeys can convert transactional interfaces into learning environments. For vulnerable customers—the elderly, migrants, first-time borrowers, young adults, and those with limited digital confidence—such embedded literacy reduces anxiety and prevents misinformed decisions that lead to debt traps or overreliance on informal lending. ESG-aligned banks must recognise that simplification is not dilution; it is empowerment. Every product—from a basic savings account to a buy-now-pay-later plan—carries behavioural risks when misunderstood. Therefore, literacy must be engineered into onboarding flows, mobile interfaces, branch conversations, and complaint-resolution pathways. When customers understand products clearly, they make choices that align with long-term well-being, reducing portfolio stress for banks and improving economic stability for communities. Financial literacy, thus, becomes both a social responsibility and a strategic risk-management tool, reinforcing the ESG commitment to fairness, transparency, and inclusive growth.

Responsibility for understanding cannot rest solely with the customer; institutions must design for clarity as a default condition.

For any kind of effective financial inclusion to be achieved, the institutions have to understand that literacy is not just about individual ability; the context in which one lives is equally important. How any individual uses financial information is based on the realities that they have learned to deal with over the years, such as the nature of income earned, the nature of work done, peer group pressures, community group pressures, and family responsibilities. Informal influences like family opinion, peer group opinion/pressure, and community opinion/pressure are the conventional driving forces that any individual in the market will be used to if they have to make financial decisions. The key challenge that the hybrid retail banks will be presented with will be that a "one-size-fits-all" type of textbook explanation on proper financial literacy will not work because any given individual will have unique financial worldviews based on the above factors. The delivery mechanism matters as much as the content: community branches, school partnerships, workplace programmes, women-led collectives, and vernacular digital channels can dramatically increase reach and comprehension. Regulated markets increasingly expect banks to prove that customers genuinely understand the products they adopt, especially loans, insurance, and digital-credit offerings. Embedding comprehension checks, simplified terms, and prompt-based clarifications helps close the gap between intention and understanding. For ESG-aligned institutions, literacy becomes a measurable outcome—demonstrated through improved repayment behaviour, reduced complaints, lower fraud vulnerability, and stronger customer retention. When banks design literacy around the lived contexts of their customers rather than abstract financial theory, they strengthen trust and ensure that inclusion becomes a practical reality rather than a policy aspiration.

Digitalisation has created a new literacy divide that is often misunderstood by institutions. The issue is not merely whether customers can operate a mobile app, but whether they can interpret digital cues, distinguish legitimate requests from fraudulent ones, and navigate multi-step journeys without anxiety. Many first-time or low-confidence users experience cognitive overload when screens present dense text, complex menus, or unclear error messages. This can lead to abandonment, incorrect selections, or unintentional consent to features they do not fully understand. Hybrid banks must therefore build digital interfaces that assume low literacy by default—reducing jargon, sequencing information gradually, providing visual reinforcement, and offering clear options to pause or seek help. Assisted-digital models, where frontline staff guide customers through live transactions, can serve as a bridge for those transitioning from physical to digital channels. At the same time, banks must recognise that literacy and trust are interlinked: customers who feel unsure about digital interactions often distrust the institution itself, fearing hidden charges, irreversible mistakes, or data misuse. Strengthening digital literacy therefore reduces institutional risk, particularly fraud, conduct complaints, and repetitive service failures. Regulators across multiple jurisdictions now expect banks to demonstrate that digital journeys are fair, accessible, and inclusive—especially for older adults, rural populations, migrants, and individuals with limited formal education. This pillar argues that hybrid institutions must treat digital literacy not as customer support, but as a strategic capability embedded in design, training, communication, and community outreach. When banks proactively build digital confidence, customers engage more consistently, navigate services safely, and deepen their relationship with the institution.

Poor financial literacy often manifests as subtle behavioural patterns that retail banks misinterpret as disinterest or irresponsibility. Customers who avoid digital statements may not be hiding from obligations; they may not understand the terminology or the layout. Those who would rather visit branches for basic inquiries may not be resisting digitalisation; they may be seeking reassurance because they cannot confidently navigate self-service tools. Literacy gaps also drive repayment behaviour, savings discipline, product choices, and susceptibility to fraud. For instance, those with limited exposure to formal finance may mistake credit limits for available income, misunderstand variable interest structures, or fail to distinguish between secure and insecure digital channels. These patterns raise vulnerability to predatory schemes, push customers toward high-cost alternatives, and create avoidable financial stress. Hybrid banks must therefore build ecosystems that reduce misunderstanding before it occurs—using predictive analytics to identify literacy-linked behaviours, simplifying product disclosures, redesigning transaction flows, and ensuring every digital journey includes contextual guidance. Community-based outreach can deepen this effort, especially in markets where banking relationships are influenced by family structures, local networks, or informal intermediaries. Partnering with schools, employers, cooperatives, and local councils can help banks reach populations that do not naturally engage with institutional finance. Crucially, literacy initiatives must avoid a paternalistic tone; customers respond better when education is framed as empowerment rather than correction. By addressing literacy proactively, banks support healthier financial habits, reduce operational strain, and strengthen long-term trust across demographic segments that often feel overlooked or excluded by traditional banking systems.

Financial inclusion is not only influenced by knowledge gaps but also by structural and psychological barriers that shape how different communities perceive formal banking. Many customers hesitate to use financial products because they fear making irreversible mistakes, misinterpreting fees, or triggering unintended obligations. This hesitation is often reinforced by past negative experiences, cultural norms that favour cash over formal channels, or a lack of trust in institutions that have historically overlooked certain groups. Thus, hybrid banks must redesign engagement models to acknowledge and respond to these realities. Clear, empathetic communication can transform complex processes such as onboarding, loan applications, and dispute resolution into accessible pathways rather than intimidating hurdles. Digital tools can support this by offering explainers, simulations, and multilingual guidance that help customers understand consequences before taking action. However, digital advancement alone is not enough; frontline staff must be trained to recognise signs of confusion or anxiety and respond with patience, clarity, and culturally informed support. The role of community advocates becomes vital in this context, as trusted intermediaries can bridge the gap between formal institutions and customers who rely on informal advice networks. Banks can also collaborate with civic bodies, religious institutions, and local organisations to build confidence among populations that rarely engage with traditional financial systems. By treating inclusion as an ongoing conversation rather than a compliance requirement, hybrid institutions create an environment where customers feel seen, respected, and supported. This reduces attrition, enhances portfolio quality, and strengthens the social legitimacy of retail banking in diverse and evolving communities.

Closing the literacy and inclusion gap also requires retail banks to rethink how products are designed, communicated, and supported throughout a customer's financial journey. Many individuals who are classified as "unbanked" or "underbanked" are not disengaged by choice; they are navigating lives shaped by irregular incomes, sudden expenses, and limited buffers against shocks. Traditional financial products often assume stability, predictability, and digital fluency—assumptions that do not hold true across large segments of society. Hybrid institutions must design flexible, transparent, low-friction products that adapt to the realities of customers whose financial patterns move in cycles rather than straight lines. For example, credit products can embed variable repayment triggers, micro-savings can be embedded into daily behaviours, and insurance can be offered in modular, low-ticket formats that adjust to income seasonality. Beyond design, banks must adopt language that demystifies fees, timelines, and obligations through visually intuitive statements, interactive digital dashboards, and personalised nudges. Local branch staff, call-centre teams, and digital assistants must align on product explanation so that customers receive consistent, confidence-building messaging across channels. Institutions can further reinforce inclusion by analysing behavioural data for early signs of distress, enabling proactive outreach before small challenges escalate into defaults or account closures. Such practice changes the role of retail banks from being mere passive providers to active enablers of financial resilience. When customers see that institutions anticipate their needs, support their circumstances, and communicate sans jargon, trust deepens and participation expands. Literacy, therefore, becomes an educational and structural commitment strewn across every touchpoint of hybrid retail banking.

Global Reporting and Assurance Models

Global reporting and assurance have become the backbone of credible ESG integration in retail banking, transforming transparency from a reputational preference into a structural obligation. Retail institutions today operate in an environment where regulators, investors, and customers expect not only disclosures but disclosures that are accurate, comparable, and decision-useful. This section examines how reporting frameworks such as ISSB, TCFD, CSRD in the European Union, and emerging national taxonomies across Asia and Africa are reshaping governance behaviours inside banks. These frameworks require institutions to map climate exposure across lending portfolios, quantify social-impact indicators, and articulate governance practices with a level of clarity that can withstand external scrutiny. As a result, reporting now demands unified data architecture: banks must integrate environmental data, credit information, operational risk metrics, and third-party performance indicators into a coherent reporting layer. This complexity elevates the role of assurance. Internal audit teams, independent reviewers, and regulated external auditors are increasingly required to verify climate metrics, validate data lineage, and assess whether reported ESG claims align with actual practices. For hybrid banks, whose operations span physical branches, digital platforms, and outsourced ecosystems, the accuracy of reporting becomes a key determinant of institutional trust. When disclosures are fragmented or inconsistent, confidence erodes; when they are robust, comparable, and externally assured, institutions gain legitimacy with regulators, investors, and communities. This positions reporting and assurance as more than compliance activities—they are the mechanisms through which hybrid banks signal reliability, demonstrate accountability, and strengthen their long-term social licence to operate.

As ESG expectations intensify, the quality of reporting increasingly depends on how effectively banks integrate data across diverse operational layers, business units, and geographies. Hybrid retail banks must build unified reporting architecture that connects frontline systems, lending platforms, digital channels, branch operations, and partner ecosystems into a single source of truth. Fragmented data remains one of the biggest obstacles to credible ESG disclosures; environmental metrics may sit in facilities teams, inclusion metrics with community units, and governance records with compliance or risk. When these sources are not standardised, disclosures become inconsistent and vulnerable to challenge. Regulators have begun to focus on data provenance, requiring banks to evidence how data was collected, verified, processed, and protected. Reporting teams must therefore work closely with technology, risk, and operations functions to create structured data pipelines that support traceability and auditability. These models now rely on these pathways to test climate-related risks, emissions calculations, social impact measures, and compliance with their governance models. For hybrid banks, which frequently outsource cloud services, digital onboarding, and analytics, the integrity of their respective reports will be influenced by their ability to satisfy these requirements effectively. This narrative demonstrates that the integrity of reporting cannot be established towards the close of the year as companies release their reports; rather, it requires consistent and effective governance and operational disciplines, as well as accountability at every step. For retail banks with effective system support, their respective reports will be released with confidence, despite the increased scrutiny from external forces such as regulators, investors, and civil society groups.

The disclosures have become more reliable based on the effectiveness of internal assurance processes, which provide assurance on data quality before it is released to the public. There are various ways that hybrid retail banks have had to redesign assurance systems based on the complexity of ESG measurement, which is no longer limited to climate modelling, workforce diversity, or community impact, but has become comprehensive, as shown in green-branch performance, the need to consider the ethics of artificial intelligence, and the results of governance assurance. The traditional internal approach, which has relied merely on the accuracy of the figures as well as ensuring regulatory compliance, is no longer comprehensive in meeting the needs of ESG assurance. Therefore, the assurance team should be multidisciplinary in nature in ensuring the completeness, accuracy, and rationale of the disclosed data. As climate-risk expectations evolve under frameworks such as TCFD, ISSB, and national supervisory guidance, assurance teams must verify that scenario methodologies are consistent, model assumptions are defensible, and stress-testing results are reproducible. For social metrics, assurance must confirm that inclusion, literacy, digital accessibility, and customer-vulnerability data reflect real behaviour and are not influenced by sampling biases or definitional inconsistencies. Hybrid institutions also require assurance over third-party data flows, ensuring that outsourced processes, digital partners, and cloud providers maintain controls equivalent to internal standards. This emphasises that internal assurance is not simply a gatekeeping function—it is a capability that strengthens institutional credibility, improves regulatory trust, and ensures that ESG disclosures stand up to peer and public scrutiny. When built into everyday operations, strong assurance models create a culture of accuracy and accountability that protects the bank's reputation and reinforces long-term confidence in its ESG commitments.

ESG reporting increasingly requires retail banks to harmonise multiple disclosure standards, each with different expectations, measurement boundaries, and audit philosophies. Hybrid institutions must build a unified reporting architecture that can accommodate ISSB's investor-centric metrics, the EU's CSRD (Corporate Sustainability Reporting Directive) double-materiality model, national climate-risk guidelines, and voluntary frameworks such as the TCFD and GRI (Global Reporting Initiative). The challenge is not only technical—it is strategic. Retail banks operate across diverse markets, products, and regulatory regimes, which means emissions data, social-impact indicators, governance metrics, and climate-risk assessments originate from different systems, timelines, and operational owners. To produce coherent disclosures, institutions must develop centralised ESG data hubs, standardise definitions, and align internal reporting calendars with external submission requirements. This includes reconciling portfolio-level climate exposure with branch-level energy use, integrating HR datasets for diversity and conduct, validating operational-resilience indicators, and tracing data lineage across core-banking, risk, and treasury systems. Hybrid banks face the additional complexity of digital channels, where usage patterns, accessibility metrics, and inclusion outcomes have to be measured with the same rigour as financial and environmental indicators. Regulators increasingly expect transparent methodologies, consistent unit boundaries, and clear explanations of why particular metrics change over time. A unified reporting architecture allows banks to meet such expectations without duplication, ensuring that all ESG disclosures are internally consistent, comparable year-on-year, and of sufficient robustness for external assurance. Well-executed, harmonised reporting strengthens institutional legitimacy, reduces regulatory friction, and positions the bank as a credible participant in global sustainability conversations.

Boards must ensure that ESG disclosures are aligned with actual institutional behaviour, not only with reporting standards.

Assurance now represents the gold standard by which the viability and trustworthiness of a retail bank's sustainability promises are judged by regulators, markets, and communities. This trajectory has led hybrid models to transcend their positions on disclosure and pressurise their resources into well-designed assurance infrastructures to prove the validity, completeness, and accuracy of respective ESG data. Herein lies the challenge and opportunity for assurance professionals to engage effectively with sustainability data just as they would with any other data set, including the climate-related data, social outcomes, and governance processes for which assurance is now required. In the case of hybrid models, assurance is more complex because of the interaction between digital platforms, physical branches, vendors, and cloud-based infrastructures. Data often flows across third-party systems, requiring banks to demonstrate control over sources, transformation logic, and storage environments. Regulators have begun to ask for explainability—why certain assumptions were used, how qualitative judgments were applied, and how uncertainties are handled in climate modelling. Assurance also reinforces discipline: when teams know that reported metrics will be independently tested, data quality improves, operational ownership strengthens, and sustainability becomes integrated into everyday decision-making rather than treated as a specialised reporting exercise. Ultimately, credible assurance strengthens market confidence by showing that the bank's ESG claims withstand scrutiny, align with global standards, and rest on verifiable evidence.

Global reporting frameworks are evolving rapidly, and hybrid retail banks must navigate a landscape where multiple standards overlap, diverge, and continually expand in scope. Institutions can, however, build coherent reporting systems that satisfy international requirements without overwhelming internal teams. The shift toward global baseline standards—driven by ISSB's climate and sustainability disclosures and reinforced by TCFD-aligned expectations—demands that banks harmonise their data models, redefine materiality assessments, and document their environmental and social impacts with far greater precision. For retail banks operating across borders, the complexity increases: EU CSRD mandates granular value-chain reporting; UK regulators emphasise climate scenario analysis; and emerging markets are building their own regional disclosure rules that still expect compatibility with global frameworks. Hybrid institutions must therefore create a unified reporting backbone capable of supporting diverse regulatory submissions, investor questionnaires, climate-risk filings, and community-impact reports. This requires integrated data warehouses, standardised taxonomy mapping, and clearer accountability between sustainability teams, finance functions, and risk units. Without such integration, ESG reporting becomes fragmented, inconsistent, and reputationally risky. Importantly, global reporting is not only a compliance process but a narrative of institutional maturity. Banks that disclose their limitations, transition plans, and capability gaps often gain more credibility than those presenting overly polished stories. By aligning reporting with transparent governance, evidence-based metrics, and forward-looking commitments, retail banks can position themselves as trustworthy actors within the global financial system. Effective reporting signals that the institution understands its environmental and social footprint and is prepared to manage it responsibly in a world demanding far greater accountability.

As sustainability disclosures become more comprehensive, assurance models are emerging as the backbone of credibility, transforming ESG reporting from a narrative exercise into a verifiable statement of institutional responsibility. As such, hybrid retail banks must strengthen both internal and external assurance processes to ensure that disclosed information is accurate, consistent, and decision-useful. Regulators and investors increasingly expect sustainability data to undergo the same level of scrutiny traditionally applied to financial statements—requiring robust internal audit reviews, independent validation of climate metrics, and transparent methodologies for social-impact measurement. For retail banks, this means building cross-functional assurance capabilities that bring together risk officers, auditors, data specialists, and ESG domain experts to examine underlying datasets, validate assumptions, and confirm compliance with global standards such as ISSB, CSRD, and TCFD. External assurance is equally significant: independent auditors, sustainability consultancies, and accredited verification bodies play a critical role in confirming that disclosures reflect real performance rather than aspirational targets. This is especially important in areas such as financed emissions, climate-risk modelling, diversity metrics, and community-impact reporting, where methodologies remain evolving and prone to inconsistency. Assurance also mitigates the growing reputational and regulatory risks associated with greenwashing, helping banks avoid misstatements that could trigger penalties, stakeholder backlash, or loss of public confidence. Crucially, strong assurance frameworks reinforce the institution's ethical posture: they demonstrate openness to scrutiny, willingness to improve, and commitment to transparency. In hybrid banking environments—where digital footprints, customer expectations, and regulatory oversight intersect—assurance becomes a strategic asset, enabling banks to present ESG claims that are trusted, verifiable, and aligned with long-term societal expectations.

Integrated reporting has become a defining expectation for modern retail banks, reflecting a shift from siloed financial statements to holistic disclosures that capture environmental, social, governance, and economic performance in a unified narrative. Thus, hybrid institutions must build reporting systems that bring together climate metrics, social-impact measures, governance indicators, operational resilience data, and financial results into a single, coherent structure. Integrated reporting demands that banks explain how ESG considerations influence strategy, resource allocation, risk management, and long-term value creation, moving beyond compliance checklists to demonstrate how sustainability is embedded in institutional decision-making. For retail banks, this means creating cross-functional reporting teams capable of synthesising insights from sustainability officers, financial controllers, data-science specialists, risk managers, and frontline units. It also requires the adoption of common taxonomies and interoperable data structures so that ESG indicators remain consistent across business lines, geographies, and regulatory regimes. As global standards converge through ISSB, CSRD, and regional frameworks, integrated reporting enables banks to speak a language that investors, regulators, rating agencies, and customers can trust. Importantly, integrated reporting also strengthens internal governance: once sustainability metrics are tied to business performance and executive accountability, ESG becomes a strategic driver rather than an afterthought. Hybrid institutions, which operate across physical branches, digital platforms, and partner ecosystems, benefit significantly from this approach because integrated reporting provides a unified view of impact across all channels. By presenting a clear, comprehensive, and verifiable picture of how the bank creates value, integrated reporting enhances transparency, builds stakeholder confidence, and positions the institution as credible and forward-looking in an increasingly sustainability-conscious world.

Assurance has become the backbone of credible ESG reporting, transforming sustainability disclosures from self-declared statements into independently validated evidence of performance. Hybrid retail banks must strengthen both internal and external assurance mechanisms to meet rising expectations from regulators, investors, and communities. Internal assurance begins with robust data-governance controls: clear ownership of ESG metrics, consistent data definitions, disciplined documentation, and audit trails that enable verification of every reported figure. As ESG data increasingly originates from multiple systems—credit engines, climate-risk models, HR platforms, supplier databases, and third-party fintech integrations—hybrid banks must establish governance structures that validate data accuracy before it reaches formal reporting cycles. At the external level, market expectations are shifting towards independent sustainability audits conducted by accredited firms that follow globally recognised assurance standards. These audits test the reliability of disclosures across emissions, energy usage, inclusion metrics, conduct indicators, and governance performance, providing stakeholders with confidence that the bank's claims are grounded in fact. Assurance also strengthens strategic discipline: when sustainability metrics undergo external scrutiny, leadership teams are compelled to align operational behaviour with stated commitments rather than treating ESG as a branding exercise. Importantly, assurance plays a stabilising role in hybrid architectures by examining not only internal processes but also third-party arrangements, cloud environments, and data-sharing interfaces that contribute to ESG outcomes. In a world where ESG performance increasingly influences capital markets, regulatory goodwill, and customer trust, strong assurance frameworks ensure that retail banks communicate with integrity, defend their reputation with evidence, and demonstrate accountability across every layer of their business model.

The concept of integrated reporting is the upcoming frontier of ESG performance, which necessitates retail banks to make effective connections between financial performance, ESG performance, and value added within a cohesive report. Hybrid banks need to transform from fragmented ESG performance to a cohesive and integrated approach to reporting, which includes an effective explanation of "what" ESG performance looks like for the bank, as well as "why" ESG performance matters. Integrated reporting requires banks to articulate the impact of exposure to climate risks on credit profiles, the impact of inclusion strategies on customer delinquencies, the impact of ethical AI management on customer performance, and how leader behaviours impact operational integrity. This approach forces institutions to articulate the interdependencies between environmental impact, social responsibility, and governance quality—moving beyond checklists into genuine strategic transparency. Hybrid banks are uniquely positioned to lead this shift because the hybrid model naturally spans digital channels, physical branches, community engagement, and multi-layered data systems. Integrated reporting therefore becomes a strategic discipline: mapping how energy-efficient branches reduce costs, how climate risk assessments shape mortgage pricing, how literacy initiatives strengthen repayment behaviour, and how conduct standards protect brand credibility. Globally, regulators and investors are increasingly rewarding organisations that provide integrated, forward-looking disclosures supported by scenario analysis and clear performance indicators. For customers, integrated reporting offers visible evidence that their bank acts responsibly and invests in long-term community well-being. As ESG standards continue to converge across jurisdictions, integrated reporting will define which institutions earn trust and which fall behind—making it a core capability for every future-ready retail bank.

Institutional Perspective: A Global Lens on Customers, Society, and Being Human in Responsible Banking

When Responsibility Becomes Institutional

For most of modern banking history, responsibility was interpreted narrowly. Profitability, compliance, and shareholder returns defined success. Environmental impact, social inclusion, and ethical technology deployment were treated as secondary—important for reputation, but rarely central to strategy.

That's changing fundamentally.

Responsibility is no longer an external obligation sitting alongside banking operations. It's becoming embedded into how institutions are judged, governed, and trusted within society. ESG expectations now influence lending models, digital systems, customer treatment, operational resilience, and executive accountability. ESG is evolving from disclosure language into institutional behaviour.

Customers don't experience this through sustainability reports. They experience it through everyday interactions. A mortgage customer encounters it when climate risks are explained honestly. A vulnerable customer encounters it when collections processes remain humane during hardship. A digitally inexperienced customer encounters it when systems are accessible rather than confusing. Communities encounter it when institutions remain dependable during disruption.

This is why responsibility increasingly functions as institutional architecture rather than corporate messaging.

Climate exposure affects mortgage portfolios. Ethical AI affects lending fairness. Financial literacy influences fraud vulnerability. Governance quality affects public confidence during institutional stress. These aren't peripheral concerns—they're operational realities.

Different societies interpret responsible banking differently. In Europe, it centres on climate accountability, transparency, and data governance. In emerging economies, it focuses more on inclusion, accessibility, and community resilience. Across Asia, operational safety and infrastructure continuity are emphasised. In North America, scrutiny around algorithmic fairness and consumer protection continues intensifying.

Despite regional differences, one principle is emerging globally: customers increasingly expect institutions to behave responsibly even when systems become complex, digital, and invisible. Responsibility is becoming inseparable from resilience—societies increasingly expect financial institutions to operate not only efficiently, but ethically and dependably under pressure.

Climate Risk as a Human and Household Experience

Climate risk is often discussed through institutional language—transition exposure, stress testing, portfolio alignment. These dimensions matter, but they obscure how climate disruption is actually lived. People encounter it through homes, livelihoods, rising insurance costs, energy prices, infrastructure disruption, and growing economic uncertainty.

A homeowner affected by flooding doesn't process this through ESG terminology. The experience is immediate: insurance delays, repair costs, displacement, and uncertainty about future affordability. A small business facing supply disruption from extreme weather isn't thinking about sustainability frameworks. It's thinking about survival and liquidity.

As climate instability increases, banks are sitting at the intersection between environmental disruption and household economic security. Customer expectations will shift accordingly. Individuals may increasingly expect institutions not only to finance growth but to support resilience during environmental stress. Climate resilience may become part of how institutional trust itself is experienced.

Different regions will encounter these pressures differently. In Europe, climate transition policy is already reshaping financial sector strategy. In the UK, climate resilience intersects with property markets, flood exposure, and insurance affordability. Across Africa and South Asia, more immediate pressures emerge through agriculture disruption, food security, and infrastructure vulnerability—where climate resilience is directly tied to community livelihoods.

Climate transition also introduces social complexity. The shift toward greener economies may create new inequality if costs fall unevenly across populations. Responsible banking requires balancing sustainability goals with fairness and social stability—not just environmental ambition.

AI and data systems are increasingly valuable here. Climate analytics and predictive risk tools allow institutions to evaluate environmental exposure with far greater sophistication. But they also raise important questions about transparency and fairness when climate-related risk begins influencing lending decisions or insurance availability in ways that disadvantage vulnerable populations.

The deeper tension is this: how can banks strengthen climate resilience without unintentionally weakening inclusion or affordability? Banks may increasingly be judged not only by environmental commitments, but by how fairly and transparently they support individuals and communities adapting to environmental uncertainty.

Fairness, Inclusion, and the Social Meaning of Banking

Banking has always carried a social dimension beyond transactions. Access to savings, payments, credit, and advice determines whether individuals can participate fully in economic life. Historically, inclusion was interpreted narrowly—account ownership and physical reach. Increasingly, it's becoming broader, more behavioural, and more deeply connected to dignity, digital capability, and societal trust.

Modern exclusion no longer happens only through absence of banking services. It can occur inside highly advanced financial systems themselves.

A customer may technically have a bank account while struggling to navigate digital platforms confidently. A migrant worker may have payment access but face difficulty establishing credit history. Older customers may experience growing anxiety around authentication and automated servicing. Vulnerable individuals may become overwhelmed by financial complexity even where services are digitally available.

Financial inclusion is not only about access. It's about whether human beings can participate confidently and with dignity within increasingly digital financial environments.

In developed economies, exclusion increasingly intersects with ageing populations, digital literacy gaps, mental health pressures, and regional inequality. Branch closures illustrate this tension clearly—their disappearance creates genuine feelings of institutional withdrawal even where digital alternatives technically exist.

Across emerging economies, mobile ecosystems have significantly expanded participation, yet inclusion remains tied to affordability, infrastructure reliability, and trust in the systems themselves. In Latin America, access alone may not generate trust where customers remain uncertain about institutional reliability. In the Gulf, rapidly modernising ecosystems coexist with diverse expatriate populations requiring accessible, varied forms of engagement.

Financial literacy is becoming increasingly important. Modern systems are deeply interconnected with embedded finance, subscription models, algorithmic marketing, and AI-assisted behavioural environments. Fraud ecosystems increasingly target behavioural weaknesses rather than technical gaps.

Customers may lose confidence not because banking is unavailable, but because digital complexity creates fear or fatigue.

AI introduces additional dimensions of fairness. Algorithmic systems can improve access—accelerating onboarding and expanding credit visibility. They can also reproduce exclusion if models reflect biased historical data or disadvantage certain populations. Concerns emerge when outcomes feel inconsistent, difficult to challenge, or emotionally disconnected from lived circumstances.

Inclusion ultimately concerns whether institutions continue treating individuals as participants within society rather than as operational data points inside automated environments. As financial systems become more digital and interconnected, fairness and inclusion may become among the most important foundations of institutional legitimacy itself.

Being Human in an Age of Ethical AI and Data Responsibility

AI is now embedded across nearly every layer of modern banking—fraud detection, onboarding, credit assessment, customer servicing, cybersecurity, and behavioural analysis. The operational advantages are real: improved efficiency, stronger fraud prevention, faster servicing, and broader access to financial products.

But as AI becomes more deeply integrated, a more important question emerges: what does fairness look like when financial life is increasingly interpreted through data and algorithms?

Historically, banking decisions involved visible institutional judgement. Customers may not always have agreed with outcomes, but they understood that human processes existed within the system. Increasingly, financial decisions are shaped through automated environments where behavioural data, predictive models, and algorithmic interpretation influence outcomes continuously in the background.

These systems remain invisible during normal operation. But invisibility creates emotional distance when customers don't understand how important financial outcomes are being determined. A customer declined for credit may not know whether the decision reflects affordability, historical data patterns, or algorithmic weighting. A fraud classification may interrupt access to funds without clear explanation. Automated collections may escalate distress if they fail to recognise sensitive human circumstances.

People generally accept institutional complexity when systems appear fair, explainable, and recoverable. Trust weakens when individuals feel reduced to behavioural outputs that can't be questioned meaningfully. AI may improve operational capability while unintentionally weakening emotional legitimacy if institutions fail to preserve human reassurance alongside automation.

Different societies approach these questions differently. In Europe, explainability, privacy, and ethical AI frameworks are central to public trust. In North America, rapid AI innovation sits alongside growing scrutiny around bias and data concentration. Across Asia, established digital integration may support faster adoption, yet institutional trust expectations remain critically important. In emerging markets, AI may expand inclusion through alternative data models—while also risking amplifying exclusion if behavioural assumptions aren't managed carefully.

Ethical AI is not only about avoiding harm. It's about preserving human dignity inside increasingly automated systems.

Financial systems may know more about behavioural patterns than customers consciously recognise. This creates extraordinary capability alongside profound responsibility. Data responsibility therefore becomes inseparable from institutional trust. Confidence weakens when individuals feel observed without understanding, profiled without clarity, or influenced without awareness.

The deeper question isn't whether institutions can automate decisions—they clearly can. It's whether human beings continue feeling respected, recognised, and protected inside systems shaped by invisible algorithmic interpretation.

Why Responsible Institutions Will Define Long-Term Trust

Institutional strength was historically measured through scale, profitability, and operational efficiency. These factors remain important. But as societies become increasingly digital, environmentally exposed, and behaviourally complex, another dimension of legitimacy is growing more significant: whether financial institutions are perceived as responsible under pressure.

Historically, trust emerged through institutional permanence—large branch networks, long-established brands, visible market presence. Increasingly, legitimacy is judged through behavioural evidence: how institutions respond during crises, how transparently they communicate risk, how fairly systems treat customers, how responsibly data is governed, and whether accountability remains visible when systems fail.

Responsibility becomes operational trust in practice.

Climate disruption illustrates this. Customers affected by flooding or insurance stress evaluate institutions through whether support feels timely, understandable, and fair—not through product features. Customers encountering fraud or algorithmic rejection judge institutions less by technological sophistication and more by whether human reassurance and accountability remain accessible when needed most.

Despite regional differences in how these expectations are expressed, a common global pattern is emerging: people increasingly expect institutions to behave responsibly inside highly automated and complex systems.

Modern banking ecosystems are deeply interconnected—institutions depend on third-party platforms, cloud infrastructure, AI systems, and embedded finance environments operating continuously across borders. Responsibility cannot be confined to isolated sustainability programmes or annual disclosures. It must exist across the entire institutional operating environment.

Institutions combining innovation with fairness, resilience, and human legitimacy may strengthen public confidence over time. Those pursuing scale and efficiency while neglecting societal trust may face growing reputational and regulatory pressure even when short-term performance remains strong.

Responsible institutions are often better positioned to maintain trust during disruption precisely because governance, transparency, and ethical discipline strengthen legitimacy before crises emerge. Responsibility, in this sense, functions as a form of institutional resilience.

Banking systems are becoming more intelligent, more connected, and more operationally sophisticated. Human expectations around dignity, fairness, accountability, and trust are not. The institutions that endure will likely be those demonstrating that technological advancement and human responsibility can continue existing within the same financial system.

Reflection

The evolution of ESG from a peripheral reporting exercise into a core operating philosophy signals a fundamental shift in how retail banks define responsibility, resilience, and long-term value. As climate volatility increases, as AI influences credit decisions, and as customers demand fairness and transparency, institutions can no longer treat environmental, social, and governance considerations as separate from their commercial strategies. ESG has become the architecture through which hybrid banks understand risk, design products, govern technology, and strengthen inclusion. It shapes how branches are built, how algorithms are supervised, how portfolios are priced, how communities are served, and how trust is earned. This chapter has demonstrated that true ESG integration requires discipline: climate intelligence embedded into credit models; green design in physical networks; ethical AI frameworks that prevent exclusion; literacy programmes that empower customers; and reporting systems that communicate transparently across regulators, investors, and society. These are not compliance obligations—they are strategic capabilities that reinforce a bank's licence to operate. Across markets, institutions that embed ESG into their decision-making architectures demonstrate stronger customer loyalty, better risk-adjusted performance, and greater adaptability to regulatory change. Those that neglect ESG increasingly face reputational challenges, regulatory scrutiny, and internal inconsistencies that weaken operational stability. For hybrid banks operating across digital and physical environments, ESG provides the unifying framework that aligns frontline behaviour, technological governance, leadership intent, and community expectations. As global standards converge, and as customers become more aware of environmental impact, social fairness, and institutional integrity, banks that invest in ESG as a structural discipline will set the benchmark for trust and credibility. The future of retail banking will belong to institutions that integrate ESG into every layer of their architecture—making sustainability, equity, and governance central to how they grow and how they serve society. The credibility of ESG is most visible during periods of stress, where institutions must demonstrate that governance, ethics, and sustainability remain intact under operational and financial pressure.

Framework

Framework Overview

This framework summarises the structural forces that shape ESG integration in hybrid retail banking. It consolidates the insights from all five pillars into a single, practical model that senior leaders, regulators, and practitioners can use to align environmental responsibility, social inclusion, and governance integrity with operational realities. The framework shows how ESG shifts from a reporting requirement to a design principle—influencing product architecture, branch systems, risk intelligence, technology governance, and customer engagement.

ESG Banking Architecture

CLIMATE EXPOSURE INTEGRATION

Retail institutions must embed climate risk into product design, credit models, portfolio planning, and frontline decision-making. Climate-adjusted assessments strengthen resilience and ensure customer outcomes remain stable across environmental volatility.

SUSTAINABLE BRANCH AND ENERGY SYSTEMS

Hybrid banks must reduce operational energy intensity by modernising branch infrastructure. Green materials, efficient systems, and adaptive energy design lower cost-to-serve while aligning with national and international net-zero commitments.

ETHICAL INTELLIGENCE IN DECISION SYSTEMS

AI models used for lending, fraud, and collections must operate under transparent, fair, and inclusive governance. Ethical AI ensures technology supports mobility, protects vulnerable groups, and upholds institutional integrity.

SOCIAL INCLUSION AND LITERACY ALIGNMENT

Banks must recognise literacy, access, and digital-comfort gaps as structural barriers. Designing intuitive, supportive, multilingual service pathways expands financial participation and reduces risk across retail portfolios.

TRANSPARENT REPORTING AND ASSURANCE

Credible ESG performance requires clear disclosures, unified data, and independent assurance. Consistent reporting builds trust with customers, investors, and regulators, reinforcing accountability across hybrid operating models.

Purpose of the Framework

This framework establishes the foundational ESG architecture for hybrid retail banking. It shows that sustainability cannot be achieved through isolated initiatives; it must be engineered through structural alignment across climate strategy, branch operations, decision systems, social inclusion, and reporting integrity. It provides leaders with a clear structure for diagnosing ESG gaps and building institutions that are resilient, responsible, and trusted. Each component must translate into consistent customer outcomes, including fairness in decision-making, clarity in communication, reliability in service, and confidence in institutional behaviour.

Table 5.1 Checklist: ESG Banking Model Readiness

1	Climate Risk Are climate risks embedded into credit, pricing, and portfolio decisions?
2	Exposure Do we clearly understand sectoral and geographic exposure to climate and transition risk?
3	Operations Are we actively reducing emissions and resource consumption across our operations?
4	Infrastructure Is our physical and digital infrastructure aligned with long-term environmental sustainability?
5	Data Ethics Are customer data practices transparent, consent-driven, and aligned with trust?
6	AI Governance Do our algorithms operate with fairness, explainability, and accountability?
7	Responsible Lending Are credit products designed to support long-term customer resilience?
8	Inclusion Are we addressing financial inclusion, literacy, and access for underserved segments?
9	Ecosystem Responsibility Are third parties and partners aligned with our ESG standards and expectations?
10	Governance Is ESG owned at board level with clear accountability and measurable outcomes?

Table 5.2 Template: ESG Banking Architecture Mapping

No.	*Dimension*	*Current State*	*Risk / Gap*	*Target State*	*Owner*
1	Climate Risk Integration	Limited or reporting-led	Underestimated long-term risk	Embedded in credit, pricing, and capital allocation	CRO
2	Portfolio Exposure	Partial visibility	Concentration and transition risk	Dynamic climate and sectoral mapping	Risk / Data
3	Operational Sustainability	Fragmented initiatives	Inconsistent impact	Integrated emissions and energy management	COO
4	Infrastructure Alignment	Legacy infrastructure	High cost and inefficiency	Sustainable, energy-efficient design	COO
5	Data Ethics and Privacy	Compliance-focused	Trust erosion risk	Transparent, consent-driven data architecture	CDO
6	AI Governance	Model-driven, limited oversight	Bias and regulatory risk	Explainable and audited AI systems	CIO / CRO
7	Responsible Lending	Product-centric	Customer stress and conduct risk	Lifecycle-based, resilience-oriented lending	Business Heads
8	Financial Inclusion	Peripheral focus	Exclusion and low engagement	Embedded inclusion and literacy frameworks	Retail / COO
9	Third-Party Alignment	Contractual oversight	Hidden ESG exposure	Continuous ESG monitoring of partners	CRO / Procurement
10	Governance and Accountability	ESG siloed	Weak oversight and execution	Board-level ownership and integration	Board / CEO

Bibliography

Bank for International Settlements (2021). *Principles for Operational Resilience*. BIS.

Bank of England and Prudential Regulation Authority (2021). *Climate Biennial Exploratory Scenario (CBES)*. Bank of England.

DBS Bank (2023). *Sustainability Report 2023*. DBS Group Holdings.

European Commission (2023). *Corporate Sustainability Reporting Directive (CSRD)*. European Union.

Financial Stability Board (2022). *Supervisory and Regulatory Approaches to Climate-Related Risks*. FSB.

International Sustainability Standards Board (2023). *IFRS S1 General Requirements for Disclosure of Sustainability-related Financial Information*. IFRS Foundation.

International Sustainability Standards Board (2023). *IFRS S2 Climate-Related Disclosures*. IFRS Foundation.

National Institute of Standards and Technology (2023). *Artificial Intelligence Risk Management Framework (AI RMF 1.0)*. U.S. Department of Commerce.

OECD (2021). *Research on Responsible Artificial Intelligence and Society*. OECD Publishing.

Task Force on Climate-related Financial Disclosures (2021). *Implementing the Recommendations of the TCFD*. TCFD.

United Nations Environment Programme Finance Initiative (2023). *Principles for Responsible Banking Guidance Document*. UNEP FI.

World Bank (2022). *The Global Findex Database 2021: Financial Inclusion, Digital Payments, and Resilience in the Age of COVID-19*. World Bank.

World Economic Forum (2022). *Research on Digital Trust and Responsible Banking Technology*. World Economic Forum.

World Economic Forum (2023). *Global Risks Report 2023*. World Economic Forum.

6 The Intelligent Branch Network

Context

Hybrid retail banking has revived the strategic relevance of the physical branch, not by returning to traditional formats, but by redefining what a branch is expected to do in a digitally dominant world. Customers may initiate most transactions online, but they continue to rely on branches for reassurance, complex problem resolution, sensitive financial discussions, identity validation, and navigating moments of vulnerability. This shift has created a new design logic: branches must operate as intelligent, data-enabled nodes that complement digital channels rather than compete with them. Branch transformation is thus not a cosmetic upgrade but a structural redesign that reshapes cost models, operational flows, technology layers, and talent strategy. Retail banks across markets are discovering that without intelligent physical infrastructure, digital strategies become fragile—unable to support customers during disruption, unable to manage exceptions effectively, and unable to reinforce trust consistently across channels. While the strategic intent of hybrid branching is well established, execution maturity varies significantly across institutions. Many networks demonstrate strong design ambition but face inconsistency in delivery at the branch level, where systems, processes, and frontline behaviour determine the actual customer experience.

Also worthy of highlighting is how future-ready institutions are using sensors, automation, workflow orchestration, and redesigned layouts to build branches that are leaner, greener, and deeply integrated with enterprise systems. In markets such as India, Kenya, Brazil, and the UK, branches are being reconfigured into micro-formats, advisory studios, low-cost self-service hubs, and hybrid service centres that adjust to local demand. Staff roles are evolving as frontline teams become digital guides, problem-solvers, and community anchors who understand both the emotional and practical needs of diverse customers. These shifts reflect a broader architectural movement: the physical branch is no longer the centre of banking operations, but it remains the centre of customer confidence. When branches are designed intelligently—with automation supporting humans, data supporting decisions, and layouts supporting accessibility—they become a structural enabler of trust, inclusion, and institutional resilience. This chapter builds the case that

DOI: 10.4324/9781042021765-7

intelligent branch networks are not optional; they are essential to the long-term stability and social legitimacy of retail banking. Trust remains the integrating measure across all elements of the intelligent branch. Customers do not distinguish between digital and physical failure; they experience the institution as one system. Consistency across channels therefore becomes essential to sustaining confidence.

The Sensor-Enabled Branch

A sensor-enabled branch transforms what was once a static physical environment into a living, responsive, intelligence-driven space that continuously adapts to customer demand, operational needs, and risk conditions. Motion sensors, queue-intelligence systems, biometric gateways, thermal scanners, ambient-energy monitors, and real-time diagnostic sensors embedded in ATMs and service terminals allow the bank to understand how the branch is functioning at any given moment. These insights help managers forecast traffic

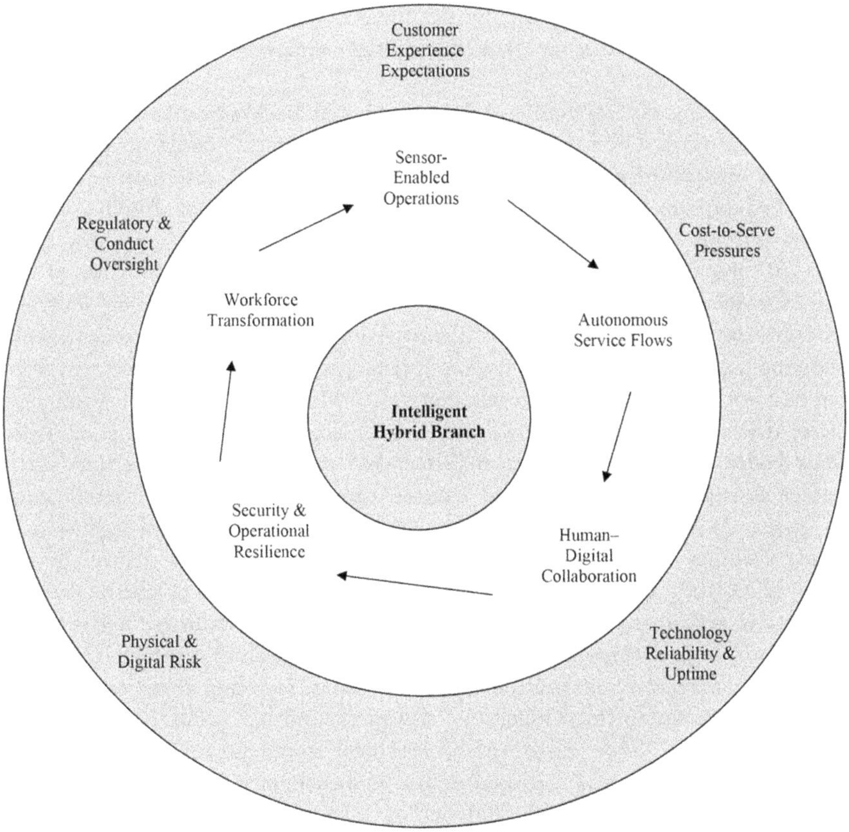

Figure 6.1 The Architecture of the Intelligent Branch Network

surges, adjust staffing patterns, identify service bottlenecks, and maintain optimal energy consumption. In European markets, for example, occupancy analytics now drive heating and lighting automation, cutting energy costs significantly while ensuring customer comfort. In Asia, biometric-enabled entry points help frontline teams prioritise vulnerable customers and guide them quickly to advisory zones. The broader impact is that the branch becomes predictable, efficient, and safer—creating the conditions for trust. Customers feel reassured when they experience smooth flows, reduced waiting times, and proactive assistance during busy periods. For hybrid banks, sensors also play a bridging role by connecting digital pre-journeys with in-branch interactions: online appointments trigger preparation workflows, mobile apps provide indoor navigation, and backend systems sync customer histories before they speak to staff. The sensor-enabled branch enhances resilience as well, alerting teams to malfunctioning devices, unusual movement patterns, or environmental irregularities that may signal security risks or service breakdowns. Through these capabilities, sensors stop being gadgets; they become a structural asset that helps the branch operate with intelligence, integrity, and customer-centric precision. For customers, these capabilities must remain largely invisible but consistently effective, ensuring that technology enhances experience without creating complexity.

Sensor intelligence strengthens the operational backbone of the branch by creating real-time visibility that traditional branch models could never achieve. In legacy environments, managers often relied on manual observation, instinct, or end-of-day reports to understand service flow challenges. Today, sensor-driven systems provide continuous, data-rich insights that reshape how branches are managed. Occupancy sensors reveal footfall patterns by time of day and customer type, enabling more accurate scheduling of frontline staff and advisory specialists. Queue sensors identify congestion before it becomes visible, allowing supervisors to deploy floor walkers, open alternate counters, or redirect customers to self-service zones. Smart ATMs and kiosks send automated alerts when cash levels run low, when paper supplies need refilling, or when error codes indicate impending malfunction—reducing downtime and costly service disruption. Environmental sensors add a further layer of intelligence: air-quality monitors help maintain safe indoor conditions, ambient-light sensors adjust visibility for elderly customers, and temperature sensors ensure comfort while minimising energy waste. For hybrid institutions, this operational transparency is transformative. It reduces friction, prevents failures, and elevates service reliability—three factors directly tied to customer trust. It also frees frontline managers from routine troubleshooting, enabling them to focus on coaching staff, supporting vulnerable customers, and maintaining a calm, well-run environment. When integrated with central command centres, sensor analytics allow regional and national teams to benchmark branch performance, identify systemic issues early, and deploy targeted support. Thus, real-time sensing becomes a quiet but powerful force that elevates operational discipline across the entire network.

Case Study: BBVA Smart Branches and Real-Time Branch Intelligence

BBVA has progressively redesigned its branch network using real-time occupancy analytics, queue-management systems, and device-health monitoring to improve service predictability and staff deployment. Sensors embedded across branch environments track customer footfall, waiting times, and utilisation of self-service devices, allowing branch managers to adjust staffing dynamically and reduce congestion during peak periods. Device telemetry alerts central teams to ATM or kiosk issues before failures affect customers. This data is aggregated at regional command centres, enabling consistent service standards across locations. BBVA's experience demonstrates how sensor-enabled visibility transforms branches from reactive service points into disciplined, data-driven operational units that strengthen reliability, customer confidence, and cost control.

A sensor-enabled branch will also revolutionise security management by adopting a proactive approach to security, as opposed to the reactive approach in traditional branches. In traditional branches, CCTV cameras and manual checks were mainly used for post-event verification, where security personnel would be informed of a potential threat only after the event had taken place. Sensors have completely turned this concept around. Biometric access controls will ensure that only authorised personnel are allowed into secure areas, while door status and vault temperature sensors will alert security personnel to any irregularities the moment they happen. Motion and perimeter sensors identify unusual activity after hours or during low-footfall periods, prompting automated alerts to security teams or local law enforcement. Smart panic buttons linked to centralised dashboards reduce response times during emergencies, and ATM-vibration sensors detect tampering before substantial damage occurs. For hybrid institutions, cybersecurity and physical security intersect: device-integrity sensors protect connected terminals, Wi-Fi access points, and backend systems against unauthorised interference. These layers create a security architecture that constantly scans for deviations, making the branch environment safer for customers and staff. Importantly, this intelligence does not create an intrusive atmosphere; when designed well, the technology remains invisible while enhancing the sense of safety. Branch teams gain confidence knowing risks are identified early, enabling them to serve customers with composure and focus. Customers, in turn, perceive the branch as a place where their personal and financial safety is respected. Sensor-driven security therefore becomes a trust-building mechanism—quiet, consistent, and integral to the credibility of the physical network in a world where risk is increasingly multidimensional.

Case Study: State Bank of India—Integrated Branch Security Systems

State Bank of India has deployed integrated sensor-based security systems across large parts of its branch network, combining CCTV analytics, intrusion detection, biometric access controls, and ATM-tamper sensors. These systems enable early detection of abnormal activity, faster incident response, and improved safety for customers and staff, particularly in high-traffic and rural locations. Centralised monitoring allows security teams to coordinate with branch leadership and local authorities in real time. The SBI case highlights how sensor-driven security shifts branch protection from reactive investigation to proactive risk management, reinforcing trust in environments where physical presence remains critical.

They also play a crucial role in creating a branch environment that is operationally predictable and aligned with real customer demand rather than assumptions or historical averages. In most traditional settings, staffing models, queue layouts, and service counters are designed based on outdated footfall patterns, leading to under-utilisation at some times and overwhelming congestion at others. Sensor-driven footfall analytics correct this imbalance by continuously measuring entry counts, dwell times, queue lengths, and heat maps of customer movement. These insights allow managers to dynamically adjust staffing, open or close counters, and prioritise advisory roles during peak demand. Environmental sensors further support operational predictability by monitoring temperature, air quality, noise levels, and lighting conditions, ensuring that the branch remains comfortable, safe, and aligned with energy-efficiency goals. Maintenance sensors integrated into ATMs, kiosks, printers, and cash recyclers detect early signs of malfunction, enabling pre-emptive servicing before breakdowns affect customers. For hybrid banks, this operational intelligence synchronises physical and digital delivery—when sensors detect unusual crowding, banks can push in-app notifications encouraging customers to book appointments or use assisted-digital channels. The result is a branch network that responds fluidly to real-world conditions: less waiting, fewer disruptions, and a smoother interplay between people, processes, and technology. In this way, sensor analytics become a foundation for operational excellence, giving banks the ability to run leaner, smarter, and more resilient networks without compromising human experience.

A sensor-enabled branch will also make the institution more resilient to challenges by creating a feedback loop between what is happening in the branch and how the bank reacts. Conventional reporting mechanisms depend on end-of-day reports, observations, or audits, which may not pick up warning signs in time. Sensors, on the other hand, provide real-time information that enables banks to detect anomalies as soon as they occur. Sudden drops in footfall may indicate a service outage in digital channels; unusual clustering near cash machines may signal a potential security concern; extended dwell times in advisory zones may suggest complexity in customer queries that requires additional staff training or process redesign. Environmental fluctuations, such as rising temperature or excessive humidity, can alert facilities teams to HVAC issues before they escalate into safety risks or equipment failures. For banks operating a hybrid model, these signals integrate into central operations dashboards, enabling cross-functional teams—security, IT, facilities, branch leadership—to coordinate responses quickly. This real-time situational awareness improves business continuity, reduces operational losses, and enhances customer safety. Most importantly, it embeds a culture of proactive management rather than reactive firefighting. When branches behave like intelligent nodes within a wider network, the institution becomes more adaptive, predictable, and reliable. In a world where customer trust depends on uninterrupted service and visible control, the sensor-enabled branch becomes a foundational asset that strengthens both resilience and reputation.

Nor do these branches operate in isolation; they become part of a coordinated, multi-branch intelligence network that strengthens decision-making at the institutional level. A good point to focus on is that aggregated sensor data, when analysed centrally, provides leaders with a powerful view of operational patterns across regions, customer groups, and time periods. Daily footfall trends, occupancy surges, heat-mapping of congestion points, and device-usage patterns help banks decide which branches require staffing changes, which layouts need redesign, and which locations can transition to smaller or more automated formats. For example, consistent data showing low counter usage but high advisory demand may justify converting a traditional branch into an advisory-first model. Similarly, patterns of early-morning or late-evening footfall can inform extended or reduced operating hours. When multiple branches report simultaneous stress signals—rising queues, device failures, or cash-machine pressure—the central command centre can dynamically deploy mobile staff, technical teams, or security support. Over time, these insights also influence long-term network strategy, including consolidation, expansion, and new-format pilots. By converting what was once guesswork into evidence-based planning, sensor networks help banks allocate resources with precision, reduce operational waste, and maintain service continuity. This data-driven branch intelligence strengthens hybrid delivery by ensuring that physical infrastructure evolves alongside changing customer behaviour, creating a network that is agile, efficient, and strategically aligned with institutional goals. Senior management must retain clear visibility of network-wide patterns, ensuring that operational intelligence translates into structured decision-making rather than isolated optimisation.

A sensor-enabled branch with a fully developed sensor system employs real-time analytics not only for managing operations but also for improving the safety, confidence, and emotional comfort of customers as they step into the branch. Worth highlighting in this regard is the role of intelligent sensing in improving the psychological aspect of customer experience, which is commonly neglected in the design of a traditional branch. Customers, especially the elderly and those who are not familiar with digital technology, feel nervous when they step into a contemporary branch. Sensors tracking queue size, waiting time, and foot traffic density enable the system to dynamically manage service processes so that customers never feel lost, neglected, or overwhelmed. Digital displays can show approximate waiting times, directing customers to less crowded areas or available self-service stations. Subtle environmental signals, including lighting changes, temperature control, and sound level management, can provide a welcoming ambiance without requiring staff intervention. In high-stress situations, such as payment deadlines or seasonal crowding, sensors can trigger targeted support: additional counters opening, queue marshals being deployed, or advisory staff stepping in for vulnerable customers. Safety is reinforced through continuous monitoring of unusual movements, unauthorised access attempts, or unattended objects, enabling proactive intervention before incidents escalate. These features collectively build a sense of predictability, reassurance, and care—key drivers of trust in a hybrid world where customers expect both efficiency and human sensitivity. By elevating invisible operational intelligence into an enhanced emotional experience, sensor-enabled branches strengthen a bank's social presence and demonstrate the institutional empathy that customers value deeply.

As the maturity of sensor-enabled environments increases, branches begin to have the capability to function as predictive service hubs instead of reactive service points. This trajectory examines the impact of predictive intelligence on management and planning at the branch level. Data from occupancy sensors, queue analytics, device health monitoring, and environmental systems can be combined to reveal trends that are often overlooked by the frontline staff: off-peak arrival times, service bottlenecks, underutilised spaces, or seasonal customer behaviour. Once these trends are recognised, predictive systems can provide recommendations on staffing, advisory appointments, and resource allocation that are much more accurate than current models. For instance, if the data from the sensors reveals a consistent trend of senior customers between 10 am and 12 pm, banks can automatically allocate more staff with advisory skills to this time slot. If ATM diagnostics indicate a recurring failure pattern before a weekend or holiday, maintenance can be triggered proactively to avoid downtime. Predictive insights also strengthen operational resilience: environmental sensors may flag rising temperatures in ATM rooms, prompting early intervention before equipment overheats; footfall data may reveal sudden spikes that could signal fraud attempts, community events, or emergency situations. Over time, this intelligence enables branches to become more disciplined, efficient, and stable, reducing operational risk and improving customer satisfaction. Importantly, predictive systems do not replace managerial judgement—they enhance it by giving teams clearer visibility and more precise decision tools. In a hybrid architecture, this predictive capability becomes a cornerstone of long-term readiness, allowing branches to evolve continuously as customer needs and market conditions change.

As sensor ecosystems expand, the branch evolves into a coordinated environment where every component—people, devices, workflows, and spaces—interacts intelligently. Orchestration platforms use sensor data to synchronise multiple branch functions in real time, creating a seamless service experience. For example, when occupancy sensors detect rising footfall, queue-management systems can automatically reallocate staff from back-office tasks to front-of-house roles, while digital signage adjusts to guide customers toward available service points. If biometric gateways observe an increase in authentication failures, the system can instantly alert a supervisor to assist vulnerable customers. Similarly, environmental sensors can adjust lighting and air circulation when branch activity rises, creating a more comfortable and energy-efficient setting. Orchestration integrates all these micro-responses into one coordinated rhythm, ensuring that the branch behaves like an intelligent, adaptive organism rather than a static physical space.

This orchestration also strengthens governance. Every action taken by the system—from staff redeployment to equipment reset—is logged, time-stamped, and auditable, providing a transparent trail that supports compliance, operational reviews, and continuous improvement. Over time, these logs help institutions build a deep understanding of customer behaviour, failure patterns, and service opportunities, enabling more precise decision-making at regional and head-office levels. Most importantly, orchestration preserves the human centre of the branch: instead of replacing frontline teams, it frees them from routine interventions and allows them to focus on reassurance, empathy, and advisory conversations. In hybrid architectures, this coordinated intelligence becomes a critical differentiator, enhancing efficiency while reinforcing trust and service consistency.

The true benefit of a sensor-enabled branch comes into play when institutions begin to transition from reactive management to predictive management, where they can predict their needs based on data patterns before they actually happen. This trajectory will examine how predictive intelligence can help branches predict peak hours, service bottlenecks, security risks, and equipment failures with a high level of accuracy. For example, occupancy trends and transaction flow patterns can help managers determine staffing levels weeks in advance, ensuring that experienced staff are available during high complexity hours while lower complexity hours are staffed with leaner teams. Predictive diagnostics of ATMs, cash recyclers, kiosks, and connectivity equipment can detect early warning signs of equipment failure before it happens, allowing for proactive maintenance that prevents service disruptions.

Predictive operations also strengthen resilience in hybrid institutions by integrating branch intelligence with digital-channel data. When mobile-banking logs indicate rising error messages in a particular geography, the branch can prepare for a temporary increase in walk-ins. When regional weather alerts suggest flood risks or heat-stress events, branches can adjust staffing, cash levels, and security protocols accordingly. These anticipatory behaviours reflect a branch network that thinks, learns, and adapts in alignment with customer needs and environmental conditions. Crucially, predictive intelligence supports a more human-centred experience: vulnerable customers receive smoother journeys, staff experience less stress from unexpected spikes, and communities benefit from branches that remain reliable even during volatility. In this way, predictive operations become the final layer of the sensor-enabled branch—transforming physical spaces into forward-looking, resilient, and trusted service hubs.

Autonomous Service Flows

Service flows that are self-contained re-engineer the way and means of customer movement within a branch by migrating mundane, high-volume activities into optimised, self-directed experiences that minimise reliance on human intervention while maintaining the human touch of reassurance where necessary. This trajectory reviews the underlying infrastructure that supports these flows—an integrated system of smart kiosks, biometric or QR-coded authentication, automated document scanning, real-time backend verification, and digital workflows that strip away redundancies conventionally built into counter-centric services. The goal is not to do away with human presence but to re-engineer the operating tempo of the branch to ensure that human attention is reserved for consultative dialogue, at-risk customers, complex problem-solving, and relationship-building. In hybrid organisations, autonomous service flows are the great equaliser—they ensure consistency across big-city branches, micro-formats in rural areas, and shared-infrastructure hubs by providing predictable levels of service regardless of staffing limitations or branch layout. Another positive is the behavioural impact of autonomy. When customers experience a frictionless journey—quick authentication, clear prompts, no duplication of forms, instant confirmation, and visible pathways for escalation—their confidence in the institution rises. Equally, staff benefit from reduced transaction fatigue, fewer repetitive tasks, and real-time visibility of system queues, enabling them to focus on value-added support. Globally, banks in Asia and Africa have demonstrated how autonomous service pods can handle the majority of simple transactions, freeing branches to act as advisory centres rather than processing hubs. The essential lesson is that autonomy succeeds only when the design is humane: flows must be intuitive, multi-lingual, accessible for older customers, and supported by staff who can step in without judgement or delay. In this sense, autonomous service flows become a structural capability—one that drives efficiency while strengthening the dignity and trust embedded in every customer interaction. Autonomy must preserve customer dignity, ensuring that independence does not translate into isolation or confusion.

Case Study: ICICI Bank Digital Branches and Self-Service Journeys

ICICI Bank has implemented digital-first branch formats that rely heavily on autonomous service flows, including self-service kiosks, assisted-digital onboarding, automated cheque and cash services, and tablet-based advisory workflows. Customers complete routine tasks independently, while staff focus on advisory support and complex issue resolution. Backend integration ensures that transactions initiated in-branch are reflected instantly across digital channels. These branches demonstrate how autonomous service flows reduce queue pressure, improve consistency, and allow large networks to scale hybrid delivery without sacrificing customer reassurance or governance control.

Self-sufficient service flow is only possible if the underlying architecture is designed in a way that reduces friction intelligently, enabling customers to perform mundane tasks with minimal cognitive overload while still feeling served, protected, and in control. It is important to look at the operational choreography that lies beneath an effective autonomous branch experience: the backend infrastructure that pre-validates customer data even before it reaches the branch, appointment engines that forecast probable service requirements, AI-driven forms that auto-populate data based on consent, and queue management systems that dynamically manage self-service and staff-assisted lines. An effective autonomous ecosystem is not an achievement of machines alone but a delicate mix of behaviour design and operational rigor. Screens must speak in clear, human language; error messages must guide rather than alarm; authentication steps must feel natural; and every pathway must offer the option to seek help instantly without embarrassment. When these elements work together, the automation is invisible—customers simply experience a swift, intelligent journey that "just works". The deeper value emerges behind the scenes: real-time analytics help managers understand peak patterns, machine performance, failure points, and staffing needs with far greater precision than traditional counters ever allowed. This data becomes the backbone of hybrid delivery, informing decisions on branch layout, staffing rosters, service redesign, and cost-to-serve optimisation. Autonomous flows also strengthen risk management by ensuring standardised processing, automated audit trails, and consistent controls across locations. For hybrid institutions seeking scale, these flows are a structural advantage: they allow large networks to maintain uniform quality, reduce operational dependency on local expertise, and deliver reliable service even in resource-constrained or high-volume environments. In doing so, they redefine the branch not as a place of queuing and paperwork but as a space of empowered, confident self-service supported by thoughtful human oversight.

Autonomous service flows transform the daily rhythm of a branch by reducing unnecessary handoffs and allowing customers to complete tasks at their own pace, but their success depends on how seamlessly they integrate with human-led pathways. Relevant to explore here is the importance of designing automation that complements rather than competes with the frontline role. When a customer initiates a journey through a kiosk, QR check-in, or mobile pre-booking, branch systems must instantly synchronise the information so staff can step in at any point without asking the customer to repeat details. This continuity builds confidence, particularly for vulnerable or digitally hesitant individuals who often fear losing control when interacting with technology. At the same time, autonomous flows must be built with empathy: clear on-screen reassurance, visible help buttons, multilingual instructions, and quiet physical spaces that give customers the comfort to navigate digital tasks without feeling rushed. In many markets, elderly customers, migrants, and small-business owners value the privacy and dignity that well-designed automation can offer when completing sensitive tasks. For the institution, the advantage is structural. As automated flows handle predictable, high-volume activities with consistency, frontline teams are released to focus on high-value advisory work, complex cases, and trust-building conversations. Managers gain visibility through dashboards that track transaction performance, customer drop-off points, and machine utilisation—enabling more intelligent placement of devices, smarter rostering, and stronger controls. Over time, autonomous flows reshape the operational culture of the branch, moving it away from transactional firefighting and toward proactive, insight-led service. Ultimately, autonomy becomes a quiet but powerful enabler of hybrid excellence, strengthening reliability while preserving the relational heart of retail banking.

However, independent service flows will only reach their true potential when they are rooted in robust backend connectivity, since the customer experience at the front of the branch is directly impacted by the resilience and smarts of the systems behind it. Relevant to this is the role of real-time integration between kiosks, core banking systems, authentication tiers, and workflow engines in determining whether the customer experience of automated journeys is smooth or frustrating. When systems are perfectly in sync—updating account balances, authenticating documents, sending notifications, or directing service requests—customers feel the confidence that comes with a modern, reliable bank. However, when latency, system unavailability, or disparate data sources disrupt these processes, the onus moves back to the frontline worker, who must manually step in and compensate for the gaps in automation. This is why hybrid-ready institutions invest heavily in middleware, API orchestration, and network resilience to ensure that autonomous flows do not operate in isolation but form part of a shared enterprise architecture. Also significant is how backend intelligence supports operational decision-making: automated categorisation of service requests, fraud-pattern detection, and dynamic risk scoring all help route tasks to the right engine—machine or human—in real time. For customers, this means fewer repeated steps, faster completion times, and reduced cognitive load; for staff, it means clearer dashboards, prioritised queues, and the ability to focus on issues that genuinely require judgment and empathy. Over time, strong backend connectivity transforms autonomous flows from mere convenience tools into dependable service pathways that reinforce trust. When customers see that automation consistently "just works", their willingness to adopt digital tools increases, creating a virtuous cycle that strengthens both operational efficiency and customer confidence.

Autonomous service flows work best when they are coupled with helpful customer guidance systems that eliminate any doubts at every stage of the process. Thus, hybrid-ready banks create self-service routes that are natural even for customers who are not tech-savvy. Helpful customer guidance starts with the physical setting. Customer kiosks and self-service stations need to be visibly accessible, placed at an optimal height, well-lit, and accompanied by simple visual signals that point to where to begin and what to do next. Once a customer embarks on the process, the system needs to provide step-by-step guidance in simple terms, accompanied by multilingual facilities, progress tracking, and the ability to pause or resume without any negative consequences. Visual signals, touchscreen guidance, and voice assistance can also be used to improve the process, especially for seniors and nervous customers. Another feature to highlight is how predictive prompts—for example, suggesting documents to keep ready, warning about common errors, or offering smart suggestions based on previous visits—reduce friction and build confidence. Crucially, guidance must be designed with empathy: customers should always feel that help is available, either through an easily accessible "call staff" button or through a frontline employee who monitors the self-service zone and intervenes only when needed. This balanced choreography ensures that customers experience autonomy without feeling abandoned. When guidance is thoughtfully designed, automated flows become inclusive rather than intimidating, allowing a broader range of customers to engage with hybrid services comfortably. Over time, this builds familiarity, strengthens digital adoption, and reinforces the branch's role as a supportive environment where technology and human presence coexist seamlessly.

A mature autonomous service flow depends on deep integration between branch-level devices and the bank's core systems, ensuring that every automated interaction is accurate, secure, and instantly reflected across channels. This explains why back-end synchronisation is the true backbone of automation: without real-time alignment between kiosks, mobile banking, CRM platforms, risk engines, and operations hubs, even the best-designed self-service experience will produce errors, delays, or customer frustration. When integration is strong, automated tasks such as debit-card replacement, address updates, cheque processing, or e-KYC verification flow seamlessly from the branch terminal to central systems without manual intervention. This reduces operational load, lowers error rates, and accelerates fulfilment times. It also enhances transparency by ensuring that customers see real-time updates in their mobile apps or receive instant confirmations via SMS or email. Another aspect to highlight is the security dimension: integrated systems enable consistent fraud checks, audit trails, and risk triggers across automated journeys, giving institutions confidence that autonomy does not weaken controls. For frontline teams, integration provides visibility into what customers have completed on their own, allowing them to step in only for exceptions or advisory needs. Integration also unlocks new service possibilities—such as pre-staging transactions on mobile and completing them in branch, or enabling automated issue resolution across interconnected service nodes. Ultimately, integrated automation transforms the branch from a standalone service point into a connected node within a hybrid ecosystem. When executed well, it enhances reliability, improves customer trust, and delivers an operational rhythm that is faster, safer, and more consistent across the entire retail-banking network.

Self-aware service flows will only thrive if customers feel supported throughout the self-service process; guided automation is thus important in gaining confidence and adoption. Guided automation is a design element that foresees customer inquiries, eliminates uncertainty, and reassures customers at every step—from on-screen instructions to visual guides, support for multiple languages, audio assistance, and immediate access to human support when needed. In some markets, poorly guided digital interfaces have been identified as a major factor in low adoption rates, particularly among older customers, first-time users, or those who are less digitally literate. Successful banks in hybrid retail design understand that automation should not only work well but also communicate effectively and with empathy. Guided flows include features such as "Are you sure?" confirmations, real-time error feedback, automatic form completion based on existing data, and simple explanations of why certain information is required. They also incorporate adaptive prompts that respond to customer behaviour—slowing down when hesitation is detected, offering help when steps are repeated, or enabling staff to receive alerts when customers appear stuck. These design choices reduce abandonment rates, prevent mistakes, and increase trust in automated systems. Guided automation also supports inclusion: customers who might otherwise avoid digital channels feel empowered to complete tasks independently, strengthening their long-term relationship with the bank. For frontline teams, guided flows reduce intervention demand, allowing staff to focus on more complex cases while still maintaining a watchful, supportive presence. When implemented thoughtfully, guided automation becomes a bridge between autonomy and human reassurance—enabling branches to deliver efficient service without compromising empathy, clarity, or accessibility.

A truly autonomous branch environment depends on the reliability and resilience of the underlying systems that power self-service journeys, in which the role of backend integration and real-time synchronisation is critical. Even the most intuitive customer interface will fail if data does not update instantly, if there are delays between channels, or if back-office systems cannot process transactions without manual intervention. Many institutions still operate legacy cores, fragmented workflows, and siloed operational teams, which create friction the moment customers attempt to complete tasks independently. The hybrid-ready branch, by contrast, uses integrated workflow engines, real-time data synchronisation, automated ticketing, and unified service logs to ensure that every autonomous action—from updating contact details to issuing a debit card—is captured and reflected across the system without delay. This reliability builds trust: customers learn that self-service channels "just work", reducing reliance on staff and increasing willingness to use automation for a wider range of transactions. For frontline teams, backend strength reduces exceptions, minimises correction work, and eliminates operational noise. It also supports advisory quality, as staff can see real-time customer activity and intervene appropriately when support is genuinely needed. Operationally, strong system integration enables banks to scale automation across branches, ensuring that even small or rural locations can deliver the same experience as a flagship urban centre. When backend systems are well-designed, autonomous service flows become predictable, consistent, and safe—reinforcing confidence in digital channels and strengthening the overall hybrid architecture.

The success of autonomous service flows is ultimately dependent on how intuitively customers can navigate these flows, and this is concerned with the role of assisted digital guidance in the branch environment. Even the most confident digital users may feel uncertain when engaging with new interfaces or complex processes, and many customers, particularly older consumers, first-time users, or those with low literacy levels, need to be reassured before they are fully confident in automation. Assisted digital guidance fills this gap by providing a supportive environment in which customers feel in control but are still able to leverage the benefits of technology. This includes visual guidance, multilingual support, voice-assisted flows, and help buttons that alleviate fears and prevent mistakes. But equally important is the physical choreography around the machines—including signage, privacy panels, and staff visibility—that convey a sense of safety and customer-friendliness. In leading hybrid institutions, frontline teams are trained to observe quietly, stepping in only when a customer struggles or signals discomfort—preserving dignity while ensuring success. This guidance builds confidence quickly, and once a customer completes a task independently, they are far more likely to use digital options again. Over time, assisted-digital support reduces queue pressure, improves throughput, and shifts staff capacity toward higher-value advisory work. At a system level, it also increases adoption rates, allowing banks to scale automation more effectively across locations. By blending human reassurance with digital convenience, assisted-digital design strengthens customer trust and helps create a branch environment where technology feels empowering rather than intimidating.

A mature autonomous service environment must also include strong resilience and contingency measures to ensure uninterrupted customer experience, even when individual devices or systems encounter problems. Leading hybrid institutions design redundancy into their self-service architecture so that no single point of failure can disrupt branch operations. This includes deploying dual-network connectivity, automated health diagnostics for machines, remote reboot capability, and standby kiosks that activate when primary terminals are offline. Equally important is building clear fallback pathways for customers: if a kiosk becomes temporarily unavailable, the system should immediately redirect them to another device, trigger a staff alert, or offer a simplified manual option without increasing wait times. These contingency processes must be invisible to customers, preserving their confidence in the reliability of digital tools. Resilience planning also requires continuous monitoring of usage patterns to identify peak times, bottlenecks, and latent issues that may cause service friction. Banks that integrate predictive maintenance—using sensor data, error logs, and machine-learning models—can anticipate downtime and intervene before disruptions occur. In rural or low-connectivity environments, offline-capable workflows or delayed-sync mechanisms ensure that automation remains functional even during network fluctuations. By embedding resilience into every automated touchpoint, hybrid institutions transform autonomous service flows from isolated machines into dependable infrastructure. This reinforces customer trust, enhances operational stability, and ensures that automation contributes to—rather than compromises—the overall quality of service in the intelligent branch ecosystem. Clear fallback pathways are essential to maintaining trust, ensuring that customers always have a reliable alternative when automation encounters limitations.

Human–Machine Interaction Design

The starting point for human—machine interaction design is that customers will only adopt digital technology in a branch if it feels intuitive, respectful, and safe. This pillar examines the significance of the emotional experience of interacting with a machine as much as the outcome. Customers come to kiosks, tablets, ATMs, or biometric scanners with different levels of confidence—some are curious and confident, while others are nervous, uncertain, or unfamiliar with digital processes. A good interaction design expects this variety. It provides strong visual signals, soothing screen designs, and guided instructions that require little cognitive processing. Even the physical location of the machine is important—machines should be located at convenient heights, with sufficient privacy, lighting, and enough room for staff to help without invading the space. This design language conveys respect and care, reiterating that technology is there to assist, not test or exclude the customer. Equally, accessibility features such as multilingual interfaces, text-to-speech capability, large-font options, and simplified pathways for common tasks ensure that every customer can participate with dignity. For hybrid institutions, the branch is where digital confidence is built; poor interaction design can erode trust not only in the machine but in the entire bank. This underscores that human-centred design is not an aesthetic exercise but a strategic imperative. When customers feel in control, supported, and comfortable, they are more willing to adopt digital channels outside the branch as well—strengthening long-term engagement and helping the institution deliver service at scale with empathy and reliability.

Human–machine interaction in the branch is also dependent on the choreography between staff and technology—the "dance" that will determine whether customers feel supported or abandoned. This explains why frontline staff need to be trained not only in the mechanics of the technology but also in how customers are likely to feel when using it. Customers, particularly older people or technophobes, may be concerned about making errors, proceeding too slowly, or obstructing others in a line. A good branch design will anticipate this emotional environment. Staff will be trained to approach in a supportive way, without pressure, and to enable customers to maintain a sense of control. Small behaviours—standing at the right distance, speaking in a reassuring way, showing a step rather than doing it—will help to reassure and calm. The physical design of the space reinforces this: screens angled for privacy, clear signage indicating where help is available, and visible fallback options for customers who prefer human interaction. Importantly, staff must learn to interpret signals: when to step forward gently, and when to step back and let autonomy grow. This balance ensures that automation does not feel like forced migration but an invitation to learn. For hybrid institutions, this human–machine partnership is foundational. If customers experience dignity, patience, and clarity inside the branch, they are far more likely to trust digital channels at home—reducing operational load and strengthening long-term loyalty. This positions frontline mediation as a skill that blends emotional intelligence with digital fluency, enabling technology to enhance customer experience rather than overshadow it.

The intuitiveness of branch technologies in catering to customers with different physical, cognitive, and linguistic abilities is also essential for effective human–machine interaction. Inclusive design can change digital technology from being mere equipment to a confidence and independence enabler. The interface should be readable in different lighting conditions, with high contrast text, large font size, and simplified menus that do not use technical terms unnecessarily. Multilingual functionality is also essential in branches that cater to different communities, enabling customers to access services in a language they understand. Accessibility for customers with mobility, vision, or hearing impairments is also crucial. This includes adjustable screen heights, tactile keypads, audible guidance, induction loops, and layouts that ensure wheelchairs can approach machines comfortably without compromising privacy. Beyond the physical interface, inclusive design requires iterative testing with real customers—not theoretical personas—so institutions can understand where confusion arises, where anxiety builds, and where a small design tweak can meaningfully reduce friction. Branch staff play a key role in reinforcing inclusivity by offering clear explanations, demonstrating alternative access options, and signalling that support is available without judgment. For hybrid institutions, such inclusive design standards do more than improve usability; they communicate institutional values. When customers feel seen and respected in their unique needs, trust grows, digital confidence expands, and complaints reduce. This establishes inclusive interaction design as a practical and ethical requirement for modern retail banking—ensuring that hybrid systems serve every customer, not only the digitally fluent.

A mature human–machine interaction model requires frontline teams to become confident facilitators of digital adoption, not passive observers of technology. Similarly, staff behaviour determines whether customers perceive automation as empowering or intimidating. When employees demonstrate calm familiarity with kiosks, tablets, biometric tools, and assisted-digital stations, customers naturally mirror that confidence. Conversely, if staff appear hesitant, rushed, or unsure about when to intervene, customers often withdraw from digital channels altogether. Effective human–machine interaction therefore demands structured capability-building: frontline employees must be trained not only on the technical steps of using each device, but also on behavioural techniques such as pacing support, reading non-verbal cues, and offering timely reassurance without taking over the process prematurely. For elderly or anxious customers, this may include slow verbal guidance, step-by-step demonstrations, or standing alongside them during their first few automated transactions. Staff should also understand backend processes—knowing how data flows, how authentication works, and why certain security steps are non-negotiable—so they can explain these confidently in plain language. This level of clarity strengthens trust and reduces escalation rates. In hybrid institutions, frontline teams effectively orchestrate the interplay between digital and human service: encouraging customers to use automation where appropriate, stepping in with empathy where needed, and providing accurate, real-time problem resolution when technology fails. By embedding this facilitative mindset, banks transform human–machine interaction from a technical experiment into a seamless, trusted, and dignified customer experience that supports broad adoption across demographics.

Human–machine interaction within a contemporary branch setting will only be beneficial if the physical space is deliberately designed to facilitate ease of understanding, comfort, and smooth navigation. An important point is how physical design decisions, such as sight lines, lighting, device spacing, accessible routes, and signage placement, have a direct correlation to customer confidence and adoption rates. If self-service machines are placed in tight corners, dark areas, or areas where customers' screens are visible to the general public, it is only natural that adoption rates will be low. However, when institutions design welcoming spaces that are easy to navigate, customers feel more comfortable. This also highlights the need for smooth navigation, where customers can easily determine where to go, what to press, and where to go for assistance without any hesitation. Multilingual signage, high-contrast displays, and intuitive icons help in catering to a wider audience, including senior citizens, immigrants, and people with low digital literacy. Additionally, the sensory experience—sound cues, device responsiveness, ambient noise levels, and ergonomic placement—plays a significant role in whether customers perceive the branch as modern yet human-centred. For staff, clear lines of visibility and short walking distances enable timely interventions without appearing intrusive. This thoughtful environmental design allows hybrid institutions to blend automation with dignity, ensuring that customers never feel exposed, confused, or rushed. When design reduces friction, customers view digital tools not as barriers but as supportive extensions of the branch, strengthening both adoption and trust.

This interaction is heavily influenced by the emotional experience customers carry into a branch, particularly those who feel anxious, unsure, or intimidated by digital tools. A focus is needed on the behavioural dimension of hybrid service and how frontline teams can create calm, confidence, and psychological safety around automated journeys. Many customers, especially elderly individuals, first-time users, and vulnerable groups, approach machines with hesitation because they fear making mistakes or being judged. Effective hybrid institutions train staff to recognise these emotional cues early—observing body language, hesitation / pauses, repeated scanning of the environment, or customers quietly stepping out of queues. Staff are taught to intervene with soft prompts, empathetic reassurance, and guidance phrased in plain language rather than technical terminology. Small gestures, such as demonstrating the first step, standing at a respectful distance, or verbally confirming each stage, can transform anxiety into empowerment. The also explains how emotionally aware support reduces operational pressure by preventing errors, abandoned transactions, and repeated assistance requests. For digitally advanced customers, staff behaviours shift towards unobtrusive availability—stepping forward only when a machine flags an error or when a customer explicitly signals the need for help. This behavioural choreography ensures that every customer, regardless of digital skill, feels respected and supported. By embedding emotional intelligence into human–machine interaction, hybrid banks create an environment where technology feels approachable, human presence remains visible, and customers perceive the branch as a place of reassurance rather than complexity.

Human–system engagement in branches also depends on how intuitively the physical environment supports movement, visibility, and comfort during digital use. This leads us on to how layout, lighting, acoustics, signage, and spatial flow directly influence whether customers feel confident enough to engage with automated services. In many legacy branches, machines are placed in corners, poorly lit areas, or high-traffic zones that unintentionally increase stress and hesitation. Future-ready hybrid branches redesign these spaces deliberately: kiosks are positioned with clear sightlines, screens are angled to reduce glare, and privacy panels are installed to give customers a sense of security while entering personal information. Simple environmental elements—like calm lighting, soft flooring to reduce noise, and intuitive directional markings—help customers understand where to stand, where to queue, and where to seek help. Thoughtful placement of advisory desks near self-service equipment also reassures customers that support is close by without creating a sense of surveillance. For visually impaired or elderly users, tactile guides, larger font sizes, and audio-assisted navigation ensure equitable access. Importantly, the physical environment becomes part of the service choreography: it guides customers gently, reduces confusion, and encourages adoption without verbal prompting. When human–machine interaction is supported by a well-designed physical space, branches experience fewer bottlenecks, less frustration, and higher satisfaction. This environmental intelligence reinforces the message that hybrid banking is not about forcing digital behaviour but about creating a welcoming and accessible ecosystem where customers of all abilities feel comfortable using technology at their own pace.

Machine interaction in branches also depends on how intuitively customers understand the purpose of each digital touchpoint, and this clarity must be engineered into the visual and verbal language of the branch. Effective communication design—signage, micro-instructions, tone of voice, iconography, and even colour coding—plays a decisive role in reducing hesitation and improving adoption. Many customers, especially older adults or those with limited digital exposure, abandon self-service journeys simply because they are unsure what the machine does, how long the process will take, or whether assistance is available if something goes wrong. Future-ready hybrid branches therefore adopt a communication style that is simple, reassuring, and transparent. Machines display plain-English prompts, estimated completion times, and clear error messages that avoid technical jargon. Colour-coded pathways help customers recognise whether a kiosk is for deposits, passbook updates, advisory appointments, or service requests. On-screen support features—such as "Need Help?" buttons, multilingual guidance, and visual demonstrations—reduce anxiety and empower customers to proceed independently. Staff training is equally critical: frontline teams learn to use consistent phrases, calm assurance, and unobtrusive guidance that protects customer dignity. By treating communication as part of service choreography, banks reduce bottlenecks, shorten queues, and build confidence among customers who may have previously avoided digital tools. This positions communication design as a foundational component of hybrid branches: when customers understand what to do, how to do it, and who will help if needed, digital adoption rises naturally, and trust in the institution deepens.

The next level of human–machine interaction is accessibility engineering, where every customer, regardless of age, physical ability, or technology savvy, can fully engage with the hybrid banking experience. We need to emphasise the importance of incorporating accessibility into branch technology, rather than viewing it as an afterthought or an add-on. Screen positioning, contrast, touch-sensitive buttons, font size, voice assistance, accessible designs for wheelchair users, and queue management systems all impact whether customers feel included or excluded. In most international markets, branches are still using machines designed for a specific demographic, which inadvertently creates a barrier for older customers, visually impaired customers, customers with cognitive impairments, and customers with mobility impairments. An accessible hybrid branch would resolve this issue by providing customers with flexible screen positioning, high contrast and large font options, voice instructions through headphones, slow navigation speed options, and simplified menu paths for customers who struggle with complex menus. Employees would also be trained to identify when a customer requires subtle help without drawing attention to them or invading their privacy. The branch layout itself must reinforce accessibility: clear walking paths, non-slip flooring near machines, visible seating for those who need rest, and logical placement of kiosks so that customers do not feel exposed or rushed. By embedding accessibility into both design and behaviour, banks send a strong signal that every customer matters—not just those who are digitally fluent. Accessibility engineering is a strategic requirement for hybrid banking: it improves service quality, reduces customer frustration, and strengthens institutional legitimacy by ensuring that modernisation does not leave anyone behind.

The final element of human–machine interaction design is emotional reassurance, a subtle but critical factor in building confidence within hybrid branches. Even when technology is intuitive and efficient, customers often seek a sense of safety, acknowledgement, and human presence—especially when handling money, resolving problems, or navigating unfamiliar digital steps. Emotional reassurance ought thus to be engineered through layout, staff behaviour, and interface cues. Simple design choices—such as warm lighting, privacy-friendly kiosk placement, visible support buttons, progress indicators, and confirmation screens written in clear human language—reduce uncertainty and lower stress during transactions. Staff training reinforces this atmosphere: frontline teams learn how to observe hesitation, step forward gently, offer calm explanations, and celebrate small digital milestones with customers who are learning new behaviours. Emotional reassurance is equally important for digitally confident customers who experience outages or confusing flows; in these moments, the branch becomes a stabilising environment where human support restores trust in the institution. For hybrid banks, emotional reassurance is an operational capability, not a soft add-on. It reduces abandonment rates, improves digital adoption, enhances fraud awareness, and strengthens long-term customer relationships. When customers feel emotionally safe in a hybrid branch, they return with confidence, recommend the bank to others, and view the institution as a dependable partner in moments of uncertainty. In this way, emotional reassurance becomes a strategic differentiator—one that blends technology with humanity to create a branch experience that is modern, inclusive, and deeply trusted. Institutions must periodically review interaction design outcomes to ensure accessibility, fairness, and consistency across customer segments.

Reskilling Frontline Staff

Reskilling frontline staff begins with establishing a clear institutional philosophy about the evolving purpose of the branch workforce in a hybrid environment. This pillar explains that frontline roles are no longer defined by manual processing or transactional volume; they are now centred on advisory capability, digital facilitation, risk awareness, and human reassurance. Hybrid branches require staff who can guide customers through automated journeys, interpret data-driven prompts, recognise vulnerability, and solve complex issues with confidence. To achieve this, banks must redesign training from the ground up, moving away from product-heavy modules toward structured learning pathways that build digital fluency, behavioural sensitivity, and ethical decision-making. Global institutions increasingly incorporate simulation labs, guided digital walkthroughs, and scenario-based assessments that mirror real customer situations. Reskilling also requires a cultural shift: staff must feel supported, not threatened, by technology. When employees understand how automation reduces routine workload, creates time for meaningful conversations, and helps them serve customers more effectively, adoption becomes natural rather than forced. Such situations have organisational benefits too—fewer errors, faster service flows, improved digital adoption, and stronger customer trust—all of which contribute to hybrid readiness. When frontline teams are reskilled with intention and clarity, the branch becomes a high-performance environment where human competence and digital tools work in harmony, strengthening the bank's presence, reputation, and community value. Reskilling must be measured through outcomes, including improved resolution quality, higher digital adoption, and reduced customer dependency on manual processes.

Frontline staff increasingly function as the bridge between customers and technology, guiding them through self-service journeys, mobile app installations, biometric authentication, and secure digital payments. This requires not only technical knowledge but also patience, clarity of communication, and the ability to identify when a customer is struggling or anxious. Effective digital coaching reduces branch queues, improves adoption rates, and builds customer trust in hybrid systems. Leading banks across India, the UK, and Southeast Asia have introduced structured "digital buddy" programmes where trained staff support elderly customers, new-to-digital individuals, and small businesses transitioning to online tools. This form of high-touch digital assistance strengthens the social role of the branch and reduces vulnerability among those who feel left behind by rapid technological shifts. We must emphasise that digital coaching is not an additional task; it is a strategic capability that determines whether hybrid banking is inclusive or exclusionary. By equipping staff with techniques such as guided demonstration, simple-language explanation, and protective oversight during sensitive transactions, institutions create a safer and more empowering customer experience. When digital coaching is embedded into the frontline culture, the branch becomes not only a service point but a confidence-building environment that helps communities navigate the modern financial system with dignity and assurance.

Case Study: DBS Bank—Frontline Reskilling for Hybrid Branches

DBS Bank has invested heavily in reskilling frontline employees to operate confidently within hybrid branch environments. Staff are trained as digital coaches, problem-solvers, and advisers rather than transaction processors. Structured programmes focus on guiding customers through self-service tools, resolving digital-journey failures, and supporting vulnerable customers with empathy and clarity. By aligning frontline capability with automation, DBS has reduced service friction while strengthening human trust. This case illustrates that intelligent branch networks depend as much on people capability as on technology architecture.

A modern frontline workforce must also be equipped with advanced problem-resolution skills, as branches increasingly become escalation points for complex, multi-channel customer issues that cannot be resolved digitally. Hybrid delivery has thus shifted the nature of branch interactions: customers now arrive with backend discrepancies, digital-journey failures, payment reversals, identity mismatches, fraud alerts, or regulatory queries that require structured reasoning and cross-team coordination. Frontline staff therefore need a deeper understanding of workflows, risk signals, compliance expectations, and the logic behind digital systems. Banks in markets such as the UK, Singapore, and the Middle East are creating "resolution pods" where trained frontline employees collaborate with risk, IT, and operations units to diagnose issues in real time, reducing repeat visits and improving customer satisfaction. This problem-solving capability demands analytical thinking, documentation discipline, and the confidence to make judgment calls within defined governance boundaries. It also requires emotional resilience, as customers facing digital failures or financial distress often bring heightened anxiety into the branch environment. Institutions that invest in structured problem-resolution training—including scenario practice, regulatory awareness, fraud-pattern recognition, and clear escalation pathways—see significant improvements in trust, efficiency, and service stability. When frontline staff become capable problem solvers rather than mere transaction handlers, the branch transforms into a reliable safety net for the hybrid institution, ensuring that customer issues are resolved accurately, empathetically, and with institutional accountability.

Reskilling frontline staff also requires building strong digital-facilitation capability, enabling employees to guide customers confidently through mobile banking, self-service tools, automated journeys, and assisted-digital interactions inside the branch. As hybrid delivery expands, many customers—especially elderly users, first-time digital adopters, migrants, and low-literacy segments—rely on branch staff to bridge the gap between physical reassurance and digital efficiency. This explains why banks across India, the UK, and Africa are training employees to become "digital coaches" capable of demonstrating app navigation, authentication steps, biometric onboarding, QR-based payments, and grievance-logging tools directly alongside the customer. Effective facilitation requires more than technical knowledge; it demands patience, emotional intelligence, and clarity of communication. Employees need to be aware of the typical areas of confusion, identify symptoms of digital discomfort, and intervene actively without making the customer feel inadequate or reliant. Organisations that integrate digital coaching into the daily work of employees experience increased adoption, decreased operational stress, and increased trust in digital channels. Digital facilitation competencies also safeguard vulnerable customers from misinformation and fraud by ensuring that they are provided with accurate and responsible advice from a trusted human anchor. As a hybrid bank, this competency is a strategic imperative because it ensures that technology investments are leveraged to drive real behavioural change, it sustains inclusion, and it turns the branch into an enabling environment rather than a declining one. A frontline workforce competent in digital facilitation enhances the entire hybrid framework by empowering confident, capable, and digitally empowered customers.

A critical dimension of frontline reskilling is strengthening advisory capability, enabling staff to handle more complex financial needs as routine transactions move into automated and digital channels. As hybrid banking matures, customers increasingly walk into branches not for simple services but for guidance on mortgages, small-business financing, retirement planning, debt restructuring, digital-fraud concerns, and sensitive grievance resolution. Global banks are thus redefining frontline roles to function as informed advisers who can translate institutional policies, product features, and risk considerations into clear, human conversations. Advisory capability is not only technical; it requires staff to interpret behavioural cues, practise empathetic listening, and tailor explanations to different levels of financial literacy. Modern advisory training also includes scenario-based learning, role-play modules, and real-time decision—support tools that help staff provide consistent and compliant guidance. Strengthening advisory capability directly improves customer outcomes by reducing mis-selling risks, clarifying product suitability, and supporting vulnerable customers who may struggle with digital confidence or financial planning. For institutions, this shift enhances trust, deepens relationships, and differentiates the branch as a place of reassurance and expertise rather than simply a transactional site. In hybrid banking, the frontline adviser becomes the human face of the institution—bridging digital intelligence with grounded, real-world judgment—and this capability is now essential for any bank aspiring toward long-term relevance and customer confidence.

A second pillar of frontline reskilling is building digital coaching capability, enabling staff to guide customers in using mobile apps, self-service kiosks, authentication tools, and assisted-digital journeys confidently and safely. As hybrid banking expands, many customers—including older adults, first-time users, migrants, and individuals with limited digital familiarity—require patient, step-by-step support to adopt digital channels. The leading banks are those training frontline teams to become digital facilitators who can simplify instructions, demonstrate features, reassure anxious users, and highlight security precautions without overwhelming them. Digital coaching also reduces long-term dependency on branch counters, lowers service bottlenecks, and accelerates the shift toward more resilient, autonomous service flows. The most successful institutions integrate coaching into their everyday service model: staff proactively identify customers who might benefit from learning, offer short "micro-lessons", and use tablets or shared screens to demonstrate processes in real time. This capability is especially valuable in rural or low-connectivity markets, where customers may have limited exposure to formal digital finance. For the bank, strong digital coaching strengthens adoption rates, reduces operating costs, and builds trust by showing that technology is introduced with care and human support. For customers, it enhances confidence, safety, and a sense of empowerment—reinforcing hybrid banking as an accessible, inclusive architecture rather than a barrier.

A third dimension of frontline reskilling is strengthening problem-resolution capability, ensuring staff can handle complex, emotionally sensitive, and high-stakes cases that automated systems cannot resolve. Hybrid banking has increased the volume of issues that begin digitally but escalate to human intervention: disputed transactions, fraud concerns, failed onboarding attempts, credit-limit challenges, account freezes, or technical breakdowns during a transaction. This explains why frontline teams must be equipped with deeper diagnostic skills, clearer decision pathways, and a structured escalation model that allows them to act confidently within defined risk boundaries. Leading institutions train their staff to listen attentively, find the root cause quickly, check facts accurately, and coordinate efforts across operations, fraud, and digital support without requiring customers to tell their story multiple times. Excellent problem-solving skills also mean that staff members are emotionally intelligent, able to comfort customers in need, stay calm during complaints, and explain their decisions clearly, especially when they are not in the customer's favour. Leading banks across the world that invest in this capability see improved customer retention, reduced complaints, and reduced escalations to regulators. For customers, excellent problem-solving capabilities mean that the institution has reinforced its commitment to accountability even when technology lets them down. For hybrid banks, this becomes a source of strength: a highly trained customer-facing team becomes the shock-absorbing layer that safeguards the brand, fills gaps in services, and ensures that the digital transformation does not weaken the safety net that customers are still dependent on.

A fourth dimension of frontline reskilling is building fraud-awareness and digital-risk competence, a capability that has become essential as hybrid banks operate across multiple channels and threat surfaces. Frontline staff increasingly serve as the first line of defence against scams, social-engineering attempts, identity misuse, and suspicious behavioural patterns that automated systems may not immediately detect. Customers often approach branches when they feel uncertain, anxious, or confused about unusual account activity, and staff must know how to respond with clarity, speed, and caution. Leading institutions train employees to recognise red flags such as coerced withdrawals, unusual third-party influence, mismatched instructions, or customers being coached via phone while at the counter—all common indicators of authorised push-payment fraud globally. Staff must also understand digital-journey vulnerabilities: SIM-swap risks, device compromise, spoofed communication, and payment-link manipulation. This capability is not merely technical; it requires confidence, empathy, and the ability to intervene respectfully while safeguarding customer dignity. All this highlights how global regulators increasingly expect frontline teams to play an active role in fraud prevention, with obligations to warn customers, halt suspicious transactions, and escalate concerns through defined risk channels. For hybrid institutions, fraud-aware frontline staff form a critical protective layer that complements analytics, authentication tools, and back-office controls. When branches and digital channels work together in this way, institutions reduce losses, strengthen public trust, and demonstrate their commitment to keeping customers safe in an increasingly complex financial landscape. Frontline capability must be supported by clear governance, ensuring that staff decisions align with risk, compliance, and customer protection standards.

A fifth pillar of frontline reskilling focuses on digital-adoption coaching, recognising that millions of customers across age groups, income levels, and regions still rely on staff to bridge the gap between traditional banking and digital tools. Frontline teams are becoming "digital guides" who help customers understand mobile banking features, navigate authentication steps, use self-service kiosks, manage card controls, and complete high-risk journeys such as payments or dispute submissions. For many customers—especially elderly individuals, first-time digital users, migrants, or those with limited literacy—confidence does not come from the app design alone; it comes from a human being who explains, reassures, and walks them through the process. Effective digital coaching reduces fear, prevents errors, and significantly decreases dependency on manual counters. It also accelerates digital-migration strategies without abandoning vulnerable groups. Leading banks now embed structured coaching into frontline routines through micro-training modules, scenario-based practice, and accessibility-focused service scripts. Staff learn how to identify digital hesitation, tailor instructions to different abilities, and encourage safe digital habits, such as avoiding public-Wi-Fi logins, recognising fraudulent messages, and securing devices. Digital coaching also reduces operational load: customers who receive high-quality guidance return to branches less frequently for routine transactions and become more confident in managing their financial lives independently. For hybrid institutions, this capability is both a trust-builder and a cost-lever, ensuring that digital transformation is inclusive rather than exclusionary. A branch network where frontline staff can translate technology into human understanding becomes a powerful enabler of long-term customer empowerment and institutional relevance.

A final dimension of frontline reskilling is the development of community-centric service capability, recognising that branches often operate as social anchors within their local geography. In this context, frontline staff increasingly serve as community advisors who understand hyper-local customer needs, demographic patterns, small-business realities, and the socioeconomic pressures that shape financial behaviour. Community-centric capability equips staff to support vulnerable customers, identify early signs of financial stress, guide individuals toward responsible products, and collaborate with local organisations such as schools, councils, small-business networks, and social-care groups. In many regions, especially semi-urban and rural markets, customers still rely on in-person reassurance before adopting digital tools, making borrowing decisions, or resolving complex issues. Staff trained in community-awareness can listen with empathy, adjust communication styles, and provide culturally aligned guidance that strengthens trust. This strength also enables the prevention of fraud against elderly consumers, enhances outcomes in early intervention for borrowers in distress, and mitigates reputation risk by ensuring that consumers feel truly supported, not simply processed. The best hybrid players have begun to integrate community mapping exercises, market immersion, and behavioural awareness modules into employee training, allowing frontline staff to identify changes in sentiment, service requirements, or digital exclusion patterns. When the front line is grounded in local knowledge, customer relationships are strengthened, branch relevance rises, and digital inclusion improves. In the hybrid banking world, a community-focused frontline represents a competitive strength because it combines technology with human understanding, ensuring that banking modernisation does not diminish the human element of banking but raises it as a force for resilience, loyalty, and lasting reputation.

Adaptive Branch Models (Urban vs Rural)

Adaptive branch models recognise that retail banking operates across diverse geographies where customer needs, infrastructure maturity, financial behaviour, and service expectations differ significantly. This explains why a single, standardised branch format cannot meet the requirements of both densely populated urban centres and dispersed rural regions. In metropolitan cities, high footfall, complex service needs, and digitally confident customers demand compact, technology-rich formats with strong automation, fast-processing capabilities, and advisory-centric spaces. These branches often operate with reduced back-office load because routine workflows are digitised, allowing staff to focus on financial planning, SME support, investment queries, and problem resolution. In contrast, rural and semi-urban locations require branches designed around accessibility, human reassurance, cash availability, multilingual support, and flexible layouts that accommodate community engagement. These branches often serve customers with limited digital confidence, making human-assisted journeys, education zones, and extended advisory time imperative. In Africa, India, and Latin America, banks have adopted micro-branches, shared-infrastructure hubs, solar-powered kiosks, and mobile vans to overcome distance. Adaptive models also need customised staffing, risk management, and cycles to ensure that cost-to-serve is optimised without sacrificing inclusion. By creating formats that are attuned to local conditions instead of imposing institutional sameness, hybrid institutions enhance relevance, foster greater trust, and provide better access. Adaptive branch models thus become a tool of strategy, allowing banks to responsibly scale, optimise cost, and improve customer outcomes in different economic and geographical environments. Adaptation must be structured, not ad hoc, ensuring that local flexibility aligns with enterprise strategy and governance.

Adaptive branch strategy requires banks to understand not only where customers live, but how they live, transact, and seek financial support. Demographic patterns, mobility trends, income cycles, and community behaviours shape branch design across different regions. In urban centres, customers often expect extended hours, rapid resolution, seamless appointment systems, and strong digital-branch integration that allows them to transition easily between mobile banking and in-person advisory. These branches rely heavily on queue intelligence, behavioural analytics, and real-time data to manage congestion and optimise staffing. Rural and semi-urban markets operate differently: customers may rely on cash flows tied to agriculture, seasonal work, or informal labour cycles. Service patterns may cluster around market days, festivals, or wage distribution dates, requiring branches to plan capacity with far more sensitivity to local rhythms. Connectivity gaps in remote locations mean branches must support offline contingencies and provide trusted human touchpoints for transactions that urban users might complete digitally. Local partnerships—with post offices, schools, cooperatives, and panchayat centres—often become essential for distributing services efficiently. In regions with low digital literacy, the branch also becomes a classroom for financial education, digital onboarding, and fraud-prevention awareness. Adaptive design therefore blends institutional capabilities with community realities, ensuring that every branch operates as part of a broader social and economic ecosystem. By aligning branch functionality with lived behaviour rather than generic corporate templates, banks enhance both service effectiveness and community engagement.

Cost-to-serve also varies dramatically across geographies and traditional branch economics—built on uniform formats and fixed staffing—cannot support hybrid retail banking. In dense urban markets, high rental costs and heavy footfall justify investment in automation, advisory specialists, and advanced queue-management systems that enhance productivity. These branches often rely on modular layouts that can be reconfigured quickly as service demand fluctuates. In rural or low-income regions, however, sustainability depends on lightweight infrastructure: micro-branches, shared premises, low-energy equipment, and multi-skilled staff who can manage both service and community engagement. Here, the emphasis shifts from speed and convenience to trust-building, inclusion, and continuity of cash services. Banks also evaluate cost efficiency through partnerships, using agent networks, correspondent bankers, and community intermediaries to extend reach without heavy capital expenditure. In many markets, mobile branches, solar-powered kiosks, and shared ATM hubs significantly reduce fixed costs while maintaining service access. Adaptive cost models integrate technology, local workforce availability, and community needs rather than imposing a standard footprint across regions. By doing so, banks achieve a balanced economic profile: high-productivity urban branches that anchor brand presence, and low-cost rural formats that uphold accessibility and social responsibility. This approach ensures that hybrid delivery remains financially viable, equitable, and strategically aligned with the institution's long-term purpose.

Designing adaptive branch models also requires banks to analyse demographic patterns, behavioural expectations, and cultural norms that shape how different communities interact with financial institutions. Urban customers often prefer speed, autonomy, and digital-first engagement, meaning branch layouts must prioritise efficient self-service flows, rapid advisory access, and seamless integration with mobile journeys. These customers typically value extended hours, multilingual digital interfaces, and specialist advisers capable of addressing complex needs such as mortgages, SME financing, or wealth products. By contrast, rural and semi-urban customers frequently associate banking with relationship, reassurance, and personal guidance. In these locations, the physical branch serves as a trusted anchor—a place where customers can ask questions freely, clarify documentation, and learn how to use digital tools in a safe environment. Cultural norms may require private spaces for conversations, staff who understand local customs, and service routines that accommodate seasonal income patterns and community rhythms. Many rural branches also play an educational role, offering demonstrations on mobile banking, fraud awareness, and financial planning. Demographic sensitivity must thus be embedded into branch design—influencing staffing profiles, service scripts, queue flows, signage styles, and community engagement efforts. Adaptive models ensure that each branch feels relevant to the people it serves: a high-speed advisory hub in metropolitan areas, a comfort-driven, relationship-led environment in smaller towns, and a capability-building centre in villages where digital confidence is still emerging. When institutions design with demographic intelligence, hybrid banking becomes not just efficient, but genuinely inclusive and culturally aligned.

Branch models that adapt must also account for infrastructure disparities that influence how reliably customers can access digital services across different geographies. In urban centres with strong connectivity, customers often move fluidly between mobile channels and branch environments, allowing institutions to design branches that assume high levels of digital readiness. These locations can adopt lighter physical formats supported by powerful backend systems—digital appointment queues, remote advisory pods, interactive dashboards, and seamless handoffs from app to branch. However, in rural and semi-urban regions, inconsistent network availability, device limitations, and lower digital familiarity require branches to act as infrastructure stabilisers rather than mere service points. Here, branches may need offline-capable systems, manual fallback options, robust cash management facilities, and staff trained in assisted-digital support. They may also need partnerships with local post offices, schools, community halls, or panchayat centres to extend reach during outages or seasonal service disruptions. Also worth highlighting here is how infrastructure-aware design enables banks to build branch clusters that complement each other—for instance, a digitally advanced hub supporting smaller satellite branches or agent touchpoints across a wider rural radius. By aligning physical layouts, staffing levels, energy systems, and service menus with real infrastructure conditions, hybrid banks create a resilient distribution architecture that does not force customers into digital journeys they cannot reliably complete. Instead, institutions meet customers where they are, ensuring continuity of service, safety of transactions, and dignity of access. This infrastructure-led adaptability becomes a defining strength of hybrid retail banking in diverse markets.

In urban centres, customer activity tends to be stable across the week, with predictable peaks linked to salary cycles, SME working hours, and digital-service handovers. Branch formats here can therefore rely on appointment-led advisory, streamlined self-service zones, and modular staffing models that adjust to demand. In contrast, rural and semi-urban regions experience far more pronounced fluctuations: agricultural cycles, remittance inflows, festival seasons, market days, and government-benefit disbursements can trigger sudden surges in branch traffic. Adaptive branches must therefore be engineered to absorb these spikes without compromising service quality or customer dignity. This often means flexible queue systems, temporary service counters, reservist staff pools, and enhanced cash-handling capability during critical periods. Also worth emphasising is that economic-cycle sensitivity allows hybrid banks to align digital nudges with local behaviours—encouraging pre-booking, remote balance checks, or automated bill payments during high-pressure days, while ensuring human support remains readily available for complex needs. When branches are synchronised with local economic patterns, customers perceive the bank as a reliable partner that understands their realities rather than an institution imposing uniform processes. This sensitivity builds trust, reduces operational risk, and strengthens the bank's role as a stable anchor within the community.

Adaptive branch models also require banks to calibrate service design around the varied digital maturity of local populations, ensuring that hybrid delivery remains genuinely inclusive and not inadvertently exclusionary. Urban branches typically serve customers who are more familiar with mobile banking, self-service tools, and automated journeys; here, the design focus can tilt toward advanced kiosks, QR-enabled workflows, and seamless transitions between branch and app. However, in rural and low-access environments, digital literacy levels, device availability, and connectivity constraints differ significantly. Branches in these regions must therefore integrate human-assisted digital services, staffed guidance counters, simplified interface designs, and multilingual support to ensure customers can navigate hybrid journeys confidently. This emphasises how adaptive models must avoid a "digital-first bias" that isolates those who rely on face-to-face support. Instead, the most effective branches blend automation with culturally grounded engagement—such as digital ambassadors, community educators, or rotating advisory sessions that help customers build capability over time. When digital adoption is encouraged through empathy rather than pressure, customers experience a sense of empowerment rather than fear or inadequacy. Also noteworthy is that regulators in several markets increasingly expect banks to demonstrate how their branch strategies support digital-inclusion mandates. By aligning design with local digital realities, hybrid banks not only reduce operational strain but also build long-term trust and credibility, positioning the branch as a gateway to both participation and progress.

Branch models that are flexible must also account for variations in economic activity, local business ecosystems, and community financial behaviours, ensuring that each branch contributes meaningfully to its surrounding environment. In urban areas, branches often serve a high density of SMEs, professionals, and digitally active customers who expect speed, specialised advisory support, and extended service windows. These branches can integrate relationship-management pods, SME advisory desks, and segmented service hours aligned to business rhythms. Conversely, rural and semi-urban branches typically operate within slower economic cycles marked by agriculture, informal trade, and seasonal incomes. Here, the branch must be designed as a stabilising local institution—offering support for cash-flow challenges, government-benefit distributions, micro-enterprise credit, and financial-literacy programmes that enhance long-term resilience. This highlights that the branch's value is not defined by transaction volumes alone but by its ability to strengthen the financial wellbeing of its community. Adaptive models therefore require banks to analyse local patterns—harvest cycles, remittance flows, small-business seasonality, and community income structures—and then align staffing, product design, and service availability accordingly. By fitting the economic tempo of each locality rather than imposing a uniform operating rhythm, hybrid institutions ensure deeper engagement, stronger trust, and better portfolio outcomes. Ultimately, the adaptive branch becomes an anchor for both economic participation and institutional legitimacy, reinforcing the bank's presence not as a distant provider but as a committed partner in the everyday life of its customers.

Adaptive branch models also play a decisive role in strengthening the long-term sustainability of hybrid retail banking, because they allow institutions to respond intelligently to differences in population density, income distribution, cultural expectations, and infrastructure maturity. A metropolitan branch may require sophisticated queue-management systems, multi-language advisory pods, high-speed connectivity, and strong interaction between digital screens and human advisors, while a rural or semi-urban branch must emphasise reliability, cash availability, community presence, and accessible human support. These differences are structural and cannot be managed through cosmetic design; they must be embedded in the operating model from the start. In India, Kenya, and parts of Latin America, the success of micro-branches and agent-enabled service points demonstrates how smaller, technology-light formats can drive both inclusion and viability. In contrast, dense European and Asian urban markets show the value of compact advisory hubs supported by automation and real-time data flows. The adaptive branch also becomes a key source of institutional trust: rural branches reassure customers who rely heavily on face-to-face guidance, while urban advisory hubs provide confidence for complex financial decisions. This emphasises that adaptability is not simply about size or cost—it is about designing a service logic that respects geography, behaviour, digital readiness, and socioeconomic context. Hybrid retail banking succeeds only when its physical network acknowledges that different communities require different forms of presence. Institutions that treat branch design as a flexible, context-driven capability, rather than a standard template, achieve stronger outreach, lower cost-to-serve, and deeper relevance across diverse customer groups.

Branch models that can adapt also define the bank's ability to scale responsibly across different economic environments, because they allow leadership teams to adjust service intensity, staff mix, and infrastructure investment based on local conditions rather than applying a uniform, headquarters-driven template. In mature urban centres, branches increasingly operate as specialised advisory hubs supported by automation, offering services such as SME consultations, retirement planning, mortgage structuring, and problem-resolution support that customers prefer to discuss in person. These hubs rely on digitally skilled staff, data-enabled insights, and coordinated appointment flows. Meanwhile, in rural or economically diverse regions, the priority shifts toward accessibility, frequent outreach, multilingual assistance, and the presence of trusted human advisors who help customers navigate both digital tools and financial decisions. In many markets, shared-infrastructure branches, solar-enabled micro-units, and agent-assisted kiosks have allowed banks to maintain presence without incurring the heavy fixed costs that traditional formats require. Adaptive models also reinforce regulatory confidence because they demonstrate that institutions are designing networks with awareness of inclusion obligations and community needs. When implemented well, adaptive branching becomes a structural advantage: it enables the bank to optimise cost-to-serve, deepen local trust, expand market coverage, and maintain service continuity even during environmental disruptions or economic shocks. To conclude: the future hybrid institution will not operate a single type of branch; it will operate a portfolio of formats, each designed intentionally for the geography, culture, and customer behaviour it serves.

Institutional Perspective: A Global Lens on Customers, Society, and Being Human in the Intelligent Branch

When Physical Presence Becomes Intelligent

For decades, the bank branch was the public face of retail banking—where customers deposited cash, resolved issues, sought approvals, and interacted directly with the institution. Large branch networks symbolised stability, scale, and trust. Banking wasn't just digital or procedural; it had a visible, physical presence.

That role has changed dramatically. Mobile banking, digital payments, and automated workflows have shifted most routine activity away from counters, leading many to predict the end of the branch.

But branches haven't disappeared. They're evolving into intelligent hybrid environments built less around processing transactions and more around guidance, reassurance, and trust.

This shift matters because even in highly digital societies, customers still want human support during moments of uncertainty or emotional stress. Fraud incidents, account freezes, bereavement, mortgage decisions, business distress, or failed digital experiences often push people toward physical interaction. In those moments, the branch becomes more than a service point—it becomes proof that the institution is still reachable.

Modern branches operate very differently from traditional ones. Sensors, occupancy analytics, biometric systems, predictive diagnostics, and integrated platforms shape how the environment functions. A customer entering a future-ready branch may experience appointment recognition, intelligent queue management, seamless continuity between their mobile activity and in-branch interaction, and staff who already understand the context of the visit before the conversation begins.

Yet the real significance of the intelligent branch isn't the technology itself. Its value lies in preserving confidence inside increasingly invisible financial systems.

People are comfortable with automation when systems work smoothly. Trust becomes fragile when something goes wrong. A failed payment, fraud alert, or account restriction can feel stressful because digital systems often seem distant and difficult to interpret under pressure. Physical branches provide something digital systems cannot fully replicate: visible reassurance that the institution is present and accountable.

Different regions are approaching this transition in different ways. In places like Singapore and parts of East Asia, branches are becoming compact advisory spaces supported heavily by automation. Customers use them selectively for complex discussions or problem resolution. In emerging markets, branches still perform wider social and infrastructural roles—acting as service centres, digital-support hubs, cash-access points, and local trust anchors. In rural communities worldwide, branch closures are often seen not as operational streamlining but as institutional withdrawal.

That highlights an important shift: the value of branches increasingly lies not in transaction volume, but in trust infrastructure.

AI and automation will continue reducing the operational need for large branch networks. But as financial systems become more algorithmic and embedded into daily life, people may place even greater emotional value on spaces where accountability remains visible. Intelligent branches succeed because they combine automation with human reassurance—technology manages predictable tasks, while people handle uncertainty.

Branches of the future will likely be smaller, leaner, and more data-driven. Yet their importance may grow precisely because digital banking has made visible institutional reassurance more psychologically valuable. In increasingly automated societies, branches endure because they continue serving a deeply human need: knowing someone is still there behind the system.

The Branch as a Place of Reassurance, Not Transactions

For most of the 20th century, bank branches were designed for transaction processing—deposits, cash withdrawals, transfers, approvals, and paperwork. Their layouts, staffing, and operating hours were built around handling high volumes efficiently.

Digital banking changed that. Mobile apps, ATMs, digital wallets, and embedded finance platforms now handle most routine banking activity. Customers no longer need branches for everyday transactions, yet branches still matter. The reason is increasingly emotional rather than operational.

When customers visit a branch today, it's often during moments of stress or uncertainty: fraud incidents, financial hardship, bereavement, identity issues, mortgage decisions, or failed digital experiences. In those situations, people want more than technical resolution. They want reassurance that the institution understands the problem and remains accountable.

The branch is becoming a place of reassurance rather than routine processing.

That changes how branches must be designed. Historically, banks focused on throughput and transactional efficiency. The future branch must instead prioritise clarity, accessibility, and emotional confidence. A branch only creates value if customers leave feeling more secure and supported than when they arrived.

Different customer groups experience this differently. Older customers may find digital systems overwhelming. Vulnerable individuals facing financial pressure often need visible human interaction before trusting major decisions. Small business owners value direct conversations during uncertain economic periods. Fraud victims want immediate confirmation that their identity and finances can be recovered.

Even highly digital customers often turn to physical interaction when stakes become emotionally significant. Mortgages, inheritance matters, or major financial transitions can create a strong desire for face-to-face engagement. People may embrace digital convenience operationally while still relying on physical reassurance psychologically.

Countries are adapting in different ways. In the UK and parts of Europe, branches increasingly focus on advisory services, vulnerable-customer support, and assisted digital journeys. In Asia, highly advanced digital ecosystems often remain closely tied to relationship-based service cultures. Across emerging markets, branches continue serving broader community roles tied to accessibility, financial inclusion, and human guidance.

Ironically, AI and automation may increase the importance of reassurance-focused branches. As more decisions happen inside invisible systems and algorithms, physical spaces where customers can speak to accountable people become more psychologically important.

This creates a difficult balance. Banks naturally want efficiency through automation and digital migration. But removing physical support too aggressively can weaken trust, especially among customers already uncertain about automated systems.

The branch is increasingly part of a wider trust architecture. Its role is to absorb complexity, restore confidence when systems become confusing, and provide visible accountability when digital infrastructure feels emotionally distant.

Customers rarely remember seamless digital transactions. What they remember are the moments when something went wrong—and whether the institution felt present when reassurance mattered most.

How Branch Networks Feel Different Across Societies

Branch networks are usually discussed in terms of cost, efficiency, and transaction migration. But branches also carry social and cultural meaning that varies across societies. Expectations around accessibility, institutional visibility, and personal interaction are shaped by local history, infrastructure, economic conditions, and cultural ideas about trust.

The future of branch banking can't be understood through technology alone.

In the UK, digital banking adoption is high, yet people still value visible institutional presence. Customers may happily use mobile banking daily while expecting physical access during moments of vulnerability or complexity. Branch closures often trigger reactions that go beyond inconvenience, especially in smaller towns or economically fragile regions where closures can feel like institutional retreat.

Across Europe, debates around branches frequently involve accessibility, ageing populations, regional equality, and inclusion. In many places, branches still function as visible civic infrastructure that reinforces confidence that institutions remain reachable.

North America has developed varied models because of its scale and competitive banking environment. Urban branches may operate as highly automated advisory centres, while suburban branches maintain broader retail formats. Physical presence still matters for wealth management, business relationships, and problem resolution.

Singapore and parts of East Asia have created highly integrated systems where digital and physical channels work together seamlessly. Branches operate less as standalone destinations and more as intelligent extensions of digital ecosystems.

Japan presents a different challenge. Older populations continue valuing personal interaction, procedural familiarity, and service continuity, forcing institutions to balance digital progress with cultural expectations around stability and reassurance.

China's digital ecosystem has transformed financial behaviour at massive scale, reducing physical interaction significantly in many cities. Yet branches still matter during disputes, trust-related issues, and complex financial situations.

Across the Gulf, banking cultures remain strongly relationship-oriented. Physical interaction continues to signal trust, credibility, and service quality, particularly among business customers.

In many African markets, branches still play critical infrastructural and social roles. Mobile finance has expanded access dramatically, but physical branches and agent networks remain important for identity support, cash services, financial literacy, and trust-building.

Latin America adds another layer shaped by histories of inflation, volatility, and institutional instability. Visible banking infrastructure often reinforces confidence that financial systems remain tangible and accessible during uncertain periods.

These differences matter because branch networks reflect how societies interpret trust. A highly automated model that works in one country may feel emotionally distant in another. Compact digital advisory spaces may fit dense urban environments while feeling inadequate in communities where institutional confidence depends on permanence and personal familiarity.

This creates a challenge for global banks. Branch transformation can't follow one universal efficiency model. AI and digital servicing may standardise operations, but expectations around dignity, reassurance, and trust remain deeply local.

The future branch network will likely become more differentiated, not more uniform. Some societies will prioritise automation and advisory capability; others will continue valuing community presence, cash access, and relationship continuity. But the core question remains the same everywhere: how visible should trust remain in a world where banking increasingly operates invisibly?

Branches survive not only because of operational need, but because physical presence still carries human meaning.

Being Human Inside Automated Service Environments

Retail banking is moving steadily toward environments shaped by automation. Self-service kiosks, biometric authentication, AI-assisted servicing, predictive queue management, automated onboarding, and real-time analytics increasingly define how customers interact with institutions across digital and physical channels.

The operational benefits are clear. Automation reduces waiting times, improves consistency, strengthens fraud protection, and handles routine activity more efficiently. Intelligent systems can also improve accessibility through multilingual interfaces and adaptive customer journeys.

But automation raises a deeper question: how do people continue feeling recognised inside systems built around efficiency and prediction?

This matters because banking interactions are often emotionally significant. Customers approach institutions during periods of stress—fraud incidents, financial hardship, bereavement, business uncertainty, or identity problems. In those moments, operational efficiency alone is not enough. People accept automation when systems feel understandable and predictable. Frustration emerges when automated environments appear emotionally indifferent or inflexible.

A customer may move through an intelligent branch with seamless authentication and AI-assisted servicing, yet still leave frustrated if the experience feels cold or procedural. The issue isn't whether automation works. It's whether customers still feel supported within system-led environments.

Banking relationships are never purely transactional. Financial interactions touch security, identity, dignity, and personal stability. A mortgage discussion represents aspiration. Fraud creates fear. Debt conversations affect self-worth. Automated systems can process workflows, but people experience these situations emotionally.

Different societies balance this differently. In Singapore and parts of East Asia, customers may adapt comfortably to automation-rich environments because digital coordination is already embedded into daily life. In Europe and the UK, people often embrace automation for routine tasks while still expecting easy escalation to human support during complex or sensitive situations.

In emerging economies, automation can greatly improve accessibility and scale, especially where infrastructure previously struggled with demand. But literacy differences, language diversity, and uneven digital confidence make hybrid models essential.

AI intensifies these dynamics. Systems increasingly predict customer needs, analyse sentiment, and personalise journeys in real time. Yet excessive automation can create emotional fatigue if people feel processed rather than understood.

This is especially important for vulnerable populations—older customers, migrants, financially distressed individuals, or fraud victims—who may need patience, empathy, and visible accountability in moments where automated systems feel intimidating.

The intelligent branch therefore becomes a carefully balanced human-technology environment. Technology handles speed, authentication, routing, and operational coordination. Humans absorb ambiguity, emotional complexity, and trust repair.

Automation doesn't eliminate the need for people. It changes where people matter most.

Routine banking fades into digital infrastructure. Human interaction becomes concentrated around complexity, vulnerability, judgement, reassurance, and accountability. Staff roles shift away from processing transactions and toward guidance, problem-solving, and trust management within increasingly automated systems.

Customers value speed and convenience. But underneath those expectations remains something more enduring: the need to feel understood when financial situations become uncertain or deeply personal.

Why Intelligent Branches Will Remain Trust Anchors

As banking becomes more digital, automated, and embedded into everyday life, traditional assumptions about physical infrastructure are being challenged.

Transactions now happen through mobile apps, digital wallets, embedded commerce, and invisible payment systems. AI is reshaping customer servicing at enormous scale.

From a purely technological perspective, it may seem inevitable that physical branches will steadily lose importance.

But that view may underestimate the deeper role branches continue playing in society.

Branches are unlikely to survive because customers need help with routine transactions. They may survive because people still need visible trust anchors inside increasingly invisible financial systems.

Modern banking runs through infrastructure most customers never see or fully understand: AI fraud engines, behavioural monitoring systems, cloud platforms, embedded finance ecosystems, and automated authentication systems. These systems work smoothly most of the time. But trust becomes fragile during moments of disruption or uncertainty.

That's when physical presence matters most.

Customers dealing with fraud, identity theft, bereavement, business distress, or operational failure often seek more than technical fixes. They want visible confirmation that the institution is still accountable, reachable, and capable of human judgement when automated systems fall short.

Paradoxically, the more invisible banking becomes operationally, the more psychologically valuable visible reassurance may become.

Different societies will express this differently. In highly digital economies like Singapore, branches may evolve into compact advisory and trust-recovery spaces. In Europe and the UK, they may increasingly function as visible accountability centres during periods of digital stress or complexity. Across emerging markets, branches may continue supporting financial inclusion, literacy, and community trust while also providing cash access and local economic participation. In rural regions worldwide, physical presence remains closely tied to perceptions of institutional commitment.

AI strengthens this dynamic. As algorithms increasingly mediate customer journeys and automate decisions, customers may place greater emotional value on environments where accountability still feels tangible and human.

Future branches will not resemble the large transaction halls of the past. They'll become smaller, more specialised, more automated operationally, and more integrated with digital systems. Their role changes fundamentally: not processing predictable activity, but absorbing uncertainty on behalf of customers.

That means resolving complex situations, rebuilding trust after fraud, supporting vulnerable individuals, guiding customers through major life transitions, and providing reassurance when invisible systems feel emotionally insufficient.

Banks that remove physical presence too aggressively may gain short-term efficiency while weakening long-term emotional legitimacy. Institutions that preserve intelligent, well-positioned physical environments may strengthen trust precisely because they continue balancing technological efficiency with human accessibility.

The future challenge for banks is not choosing between digital systems and physical branches. It's designing ecosystems where technology handles scale and efficiency while physical spaces preserve confidence, accountability, and reassurance when trust matters most.

Intelligent branches may ultimately endure because they satisfy something deeper than operational necessity. They provide visible evidence that behind increasingly invisible systems, the institution itself remains present, reachable, and accountable.

Reflection

The intelligent branch network represents a fundamental rethinking of how physical presence contributes to the strength, trust, and long-term relevance of retail banking. Branches are no longer the primary centres of transaction processing; they are the institutional anchors that provide reassurance, capability, and continuity in a world where most interactions occur digitally. This chapter has shown that the future branch is defined less by its size and more by its intelligence—its ability to sense, adapt, and support customers through a blend of automation and human guidance. Sensors, autonomous flows, intuitive interfaces, and redesigned layouts make the branch more efficient and predictable, while frontline reskilling ensures that human engagement remains empathetic, responsible, and value-adding. The result is a physical network that enhances hybrid delivery rather than competing with it.

The strength of the branch network is most visible during disruption, when customers rely on physical presence for reassurance, resolution, and continuity.

What emerges clearly is that branches continue to hold a unique social and institutional role. They provide a tangible point of trust for vulnerable customers, a specialised resource for complex decisions, and a community presence that digital channels alone cannot replicate. The future network is therefore not about reducing branches, but about redesigning them to fit the service expectations, demographic diversity, and economic realities of different regions. Adaptive models—from high-density advisory hubs in urban centres to micro-branches and shared-service nodes in rural areas—demonstrate how institutions can remain accessible without compromising cost discipline or operational resilience.

Ultimately, the intelligent branch network strengthens the hybrid architecture by offering stability where customers expect it most and innovation where efficiency demands it. Banks that successfully modernise their physical footprint will not only reduce operational friction but also reinforce institutional credibility in an increasingly automated financial landscape. The branch of the future becomes a strategic asset: lean, local, data-informed, accessible, and deeply aligned with the bank's long-term purpose.

Framework: The Intelligent Branch Network

Framework Overview

This framework explains the structural foundations that enable branch networks to operate as intelligent, adaptive components of hybrid retail banking. It consolidates insights from all five pillars to show how branches can evolve from cost-heavy legacy units into smart, sensor-enabled, human-centred hubs that strengthen trust, inclusion, and operational resilience. It outlines how data, automation, environment design, and frontline capability converge to create branches that are efficient, responsive, and aligned with modern customer expectations.

The framework demonstrates how the future branch must blend automation with empathy, digital fluency with physical presence, and standardised service flows with local relevance. It positions the intelligent branch network not as an optional upgrade but as a core architectural requirement for hybrid retail banking—enabling strong customer experience, safer operations, lower environmental impact, and more consistent institutional reliability across diverse geographies.

Intelligent Branch Network Architecture

THE SENSOR-ENABLED BRANCH

A sensor-enabled branch uses real-time data to monitor customer movement, service demand, energy use, and security patterns, enabling a dynamic and responsive operational environment. Sensors support workforce planning, enhance safety, reduce consumption costs, and create predictable service experiences across channels.

AUTONOMOUS SERVICE FLOWS

Autonomous service flows shift routine transactions to automated touchpoints such as smart kiosks, self-service terminals, and AI-guided processes. These flows free frontline teams to focus on advisory work, reduce wait times, improve accuracy, and create scalable, consistent service across branch formats.

HUMAN–MACHINE INTERACTION DESIGN

Future-ready branches depend on intuitive, inclusive interaction design that helps customers engage confidently with digital tools. Clear interfaces, accessible layouts, and supportive staff behaviours create a seamless experience where automation enhances trust rather than replacing human connection.

RESKILLING FRONTLINE STAFF

Frontline employees must transition from transactional work to advisory, digital coaching, and complex-case handling. Reskilling enables staff to guide customers across hybrid journeys, support vulnerable groups, reduce error rates, and strengthen institutional credibility.

ADAPTIVE BRANCH MODELS (URBAN VS RURAL)

Branch formats must be tailored to geographic and demographic realities. Urban branches prioritise automation and advisory zones, while rural locations emphasise accessibility, multilingual support, and community presence. Adaptive models ensure cost efficiency, inclusion, and relevance across diverse markets.

Purpose of the Framework

This framework shows how intelligent branch networks form a structural pillar of hybrid retail banking. It demonstrates that a future-ready branch system must be environmentally efficient, digitally integrated, operationally resilient, and deeply human-centred. It provides leaders with a practical model for designing branch networks that uphold trust, expand access, and deliver consistent, high-quality service across all geographies. Each element of the intelligent branch must translate into measurable customer outcomes, including reliability, clarity, accessibility, and confidence in institutional behaviour.

Table 6.1 Checklist: Intelligent Branch Readiness

1	Purpose Is the branch designed for advisory, resolution, and reassurance, not routine transactions?
2	Integration Is the branch fully integrated with digital channels to support seamless customer journeys?
3	Intelligence Do we use real-time data (sensors, analytics) to manage flow, demand, and operations?
4	Automation Are routine services handled through autonomous, self-service, or assisted-digital flows?
5	Continuity Can customers move between digital and branch channels without repeating steps?
6	Experience Is the branch environment intuitive, calm, and accessible for all customer segments?
7	Human Role Are frontline teams focused on advisory, problem-solving, and digital guidance?
8	Resilience Can the branch maintain service continuity during system failures or disruptions?
9	Adaptability Are branch formats tailored to local demand, geography, and customer behaviour?
10	Trust Does the branch consistently reinforce safety, confidence, and institutional credibility?

Table 6.2 Template: Intelligent Branch Architecture Mapping

No.	*Branch Purpose*	*Transaction-led model*	*Low relevance, high cost*	*Advisory and resolution-led branch role*	CEO / COO
1	**Channel Integration**	Partial integration with digital	Fragmented journeys	Seamless hybrid integration	CIO / COO
2	Data and Intelligence	Limited real-time visibility	Reactive operations	Sensor-enabled, data-driven branch	CIO
3	Autonomous Service Flows	Manual or staff-heavy processes	Inefficiency, queues	Self-service and assisted-digital flows	COO
4	Journey Continuity	Repetition across channels	Customer frustration	End-to-end journey continuity	COO
5	Customer Experience Design	Functional, not intuitive	Low adoption, confusion	Human-centred, inclusive design	CX Head
6	Frontline Capability	Transaction-focused staff	Low value engagement	Advisory, digital coaching capability	HR / COO
7	Operational Resilience	Basic fallback mechanisms	Service disruption risk	Integrated resilience and contingency	CRO / COO
8	Adaptive Branch Models	Standardised formats	Misalignment with local needs	Context-driven branch formats	Strategy / COO
9	Trust and Confidence Layer	Implicit, not designed	Inconsistent experience	Deliberate trust-building environment	CEO / Board
10	Branch Purpose	Transaction-led model	Low relevance, high cost	Advisory and resolution-led branch role	CEO / COO

Bibliography

Accenture (2023). *Insights on Platformisation and Customer Experience in Banking*. Accenture Banking Research.

Bank for International Settlements (2021). *Principles for Operational Resilience*. BIS.

DBS Bank (2023). *Sustainability Report 2023*. DBS Group Holdings.

Deloitte (2023). *Insights on Hybrid Banking and Human-Centred Digital Transformation*. Deloitte Insights.

European Banking Authority (2021). *Guidelines on ICT and Security Risk Management*. EBA.

Gartner (2023). *Research on Intelligent Branch Transformation and Future Retail Banking Models*. Gartner Research.

International Monetary Fund (2023). *Digital Financial Services and Financial Inclusion: Global Trends and Policy Challenges*. IMF.

McKinsey & Company (2023). *Global Banking Annual Review 2023*. McKinsey Global Banking Practice.

National Institute of Standards and Technology (2023). *Artificial Intelligence Risk Management Framework (AI RMF 1.0)*. U.S. Department of Commerce.

OECD (2021). *Digital Transformation in Financial Services and Consumer Protection*. OECD Publishing.

PwC (2023). *Insights on Retail Banking Ecosystems and Future Financial Services Models*. PricewaterhouseCoopers.

State Bank of India (2023). *Annual Report 2022–23*. SBI.

World Bank (2022). *The Global Findex Database 2021: Financial Inclusion, Digital Payments, and Resilience in the Age of COVID-19*. World Bank.

World Economic Forum (2022). *Digital Identity Systems: Balancing Innovation, Security and Privacy*. World Economic Forum.

World Economic Forum (2023). *Global Cybersecurity Outlook 2023*. World Economic Forum.

7 The Future of Risk

Cybersecurity and Infrastructure Gaps

Cybersecurity now defines the operating stability, credibility, and operational integrity of hybrid retail banks, yet the risk landscape has shifted from protecting a perimeter to securing a constantly moving digital operating environment. As retail banking expands across mobile channels, API connections, cloud platforms, ATM networks, and merchant interfaces, every node becomes a live access point that attackers can probe for vulnerabilities. The legacy infrastructure that once served predictable volumes and centralised environments struggles when exposed to real-time, multi-device, cross-border interactions. Threat actors no longer rely on brute force; they exploit misconfigurations, weak vendor controls, unmonitored endpoints, and gaps between digital and physical service layers. Phishing attacks now leverage behavioural analytics; ransomware operators use automated reconnaissance to locate unpatched pathways; and coordinated fraud rings exploit timing mismatches between customer authentication, transaction routing, and backend verification. Customers, meanwhile, experience none of this complexity; they expect the bank to be secure everywhere, at all times, without delay or friction. A single breach—whether caused by a compromised vendor credential, a cloud misconfiguration, or a social-engineering attack—can erode trust built over decades. For hybrid institutions, cybersecurity can no longer be treated as a technical domain; it is a design responsibility that must shape governance, operational design, and customer experience. Zero-trust verification, continuous monitoring, encrypted data pathways, active red-teaming, strong endpoint discipline, and coordinated incident-response structures must operate as one integrated system. Cyber resilience is therefore the foundation on which every other risk capability—credit, operational, conduct, climate, and reputational—ultimately depends.

For customers, cybersecurity must remain invisible but consistently reliable, ensuring protection without friction or uncertainty.

Hybrid retail banks now operate within technology environments where complexity itself becomes a source of vulnerability, because modern banking architecture is no longer a single system but a closely linked mesh of cloud workloads, API gateways, mobile applications, ATM networks, payment

DOI: 10.4324/9781042021765-8

processors, vendor services, and data-analytics layers that all depend on one another to function smoothly. This interdependence means that the security of the institution is only as strong as the weakest element in the chain, whether that is an outdated patch on a server, insufficient monitoring of an API endpoint, a poorly governed vendor connection, or an overlooked interface between legacy and cloud systems. Attackers exploit precisely these seams, using automated scanning tools and AI-driven reconnaissance to identify misalignments, privilege gaps, and hidden backdoors that human teams often miss. At the same time, many retail banks carry the burden of parallel technology stacks—old systems designed for closed environments running alongside new systems built for continuous integration and rapid updates. When these worlds collide, security controls become uneven, making it harder to maintain consistent encryption, authentication, and access management across platforms. Customers, meanwhile, are transacting more frequently and across more devices, increasing the volume and speed at which threats can materialise. Regulators are responding by demanding integrated resilience testing, cross-border data safeguards, and evidence that banks can contain and recover from breaches without operational downtime. In such an environment, cybersecurity must evolve into a discipline of continuous orchestration—aligning technology, governance, and behaviour so that every layer of the hybrid operating environment remains secure, predictable, and trusted.

Hybrid environments face escalating risk because modern cyber threats are no longer isolated attacks but coordinated, multi-stage campaigns designed to exploit both digital and physical touchpoints simultaneously. A single intrusion attempt might begin with credential harvesting through phishing, move into lateral movement across internal networks, trigger transactional fraud through compromised APIs, and then escalate into a full-scale ransomware event targeting core banking systems. Retail banks—once protected by perimeter firewalls and closed networks—must now defend dynamic environments where customers authenticate from multiple devices, staff access systems remotely, and third-party vendors integrate directly into operational workflows. This complexity increases exposure: an overlooked configuration on a cloud instance, an unencrypted data flow between systems, or a poorly governed vendor connection can become an unexpected entry point for attackers. At the same time, customer expectations for instant service reduce the tolerance for multi-layer verification or service slowdowns, creating a tension between speed and security. Regulators across the UK, EU, and Asia are responding by mandating zero-trust principles, multi-factor authentication across all privileged access, real-time anomaly detection, and robust incident-response drills that simulate data loss, payment-system compromise, and operational shutdowns. For hybrid banks, cyber resilience can no longer rely solely on defence; it must be built into architecture itself—into systems designed to absorb shocks, isolate compromised components, and recover quickly without disrupting customer journeys.

Cybersecurity risk intensifies when legacy systems are forced to coexist with modern cloud-based architectures, because the older components were never designed for today's transaction speeds, authentication demands, or integration patterns. Core banking platforms—built decades ago—often operate on batch-processing logic, rigid data structures, and limited monitoring tools, yet they now sit behind mobile applications, open APIs, and real-time payment rails. This mismatch creates hidden vulnerabilities: authentication checks may not propagate across systems consistently, encryption standards may differ between environments, and audit trails may be incomplete when data flows between old and new layers. Attackers actively exploit these seams because they represent blind spots where neither the legacy system nor the new platform has full visibility or control. Hybrid banks must therefore treat infrastructure modernisation as a risk priority, not merely an IT investment. Strengthening this environment requires continuous penetration testing across both legacy and cloud systems, standardising encryption protocols end-to-end, and creating unified monitoring dashboards that can track behaviours across the entire technology estate. Just as importantly, boards and executive committees must recognise that infrastructure risk is strategic: an outdated core or poorly governed integration can compromise trust more quickly than any individual cyber-attack. In a hybrid world, resilience depends on eliminating architectural inconsistency and ensuring that every system—old or new—meets the same standard of security, transparency, and controllability.

Banks are increasingly exposed to coordinated, multi-vector attacks that move fluidly across digital and physical channels. Criminal networks no longer rely on isolated techniques such as phishing or card skimming; instead, they orchestrate attacks that blend social engineering, device compromise, API exploitation, and real-time fraud manipulation. An attacker may begin by targeting a customer's mobile device, escalate through weaknesses in SMS-based authentication, probe API endpoints for inconsistent validation rules, and finally exploit back-office process gaps to execute unauthorised transactions. These chains of attacks succeed when institutions treat cyber risks in silos rather than as interconnected threats that evolve dynamically. Retail banks must therefore redesign their defences around behavioural intelligence, anomaly detection, and real-time decision engines that can detect abnormal patterns across multiple channels simultaneously. This requires integrating fraud teams, cybersecurity teams, and data-science capabilities so that signals from one domain immediately influence responses in another. It also demands that frontline operations are trained to recognise escalation cues that may originate digitally but manifest in branch or call-centre interactions. A modern hybrid bank is only as strong as its ability to connect dots quickly; without this integrated vigilance, a sophisticated attacker can exploit the gaps between organisational functions. Cyber resilience in this environment is the product of continuous learning, rapid escalation, and an architecture that treats every channel as part of one unified security perimeter.

Hybrid banking environments depend on a complex mesh of cloud platforms, data exchanges, authentication layers, and third-party services, making infrastructure resilience a frontline risk rather than a background concern. A single outage in a cloud region, payments processor, or telecom network can interrupt customer journeys across millions of users, instantly eroding confidence in the institution's reliability. These breakdowns are rarely the result of one failure; they emerge from subtle interactions between legacy systems, custom integrations, and modern cloud-native components that were never originally designed to operate together. As transaction volumes grow and customer expectations intensify, the tolerance for disruption narrows dramatically, pushing banks to rethink how they engineer continuity into their systems. This requires eliminating hidden dependencies, building redundancy across geographies, and ensuring that critical workloads can shift seamlessly when one part of the infrastructure is under strain. It also calls for rigorous stress testing that simulates real-world conditions such as telecom failures, cloud throttling, or sudden spikes in digital traffic. For customers, any period of unavailability feels like a breach of trust; for institutions, it exposes structural weaknesses in architecture and governance. A future-ready retail bank must therefore design resilience into every layer, ensuring that service continuity is not an aspiration but an operational guarantee in an increasingly unpredictable environment.

These environments demand an operating model where cybersecurity teams and technology teams work in continuous alignment, yet in many institutions these functions still operate in parallel rather than as an integrated discipline. This gap becomes visible during incidents, where response times slow because system owners, risk leads, vendors, and security analysts do not share a unified operating picture. As attack surfaces expand across mobile apps, APIs, ATMs, cloud workloads, and partner platforms, fragmentation of responsibility becomes a structural vulnerability. Threat actors exploit precisely these seams—targeting overlooked integrations, legacy modules, or vendor-maintained components that fall outside daily oversight. To counter this, banks must build a single, institution-wide security posture rooted in shared dashboards, coordinated escalation paths, and round-the-clock monitoring that blends behavioural analytics with threat intelligence. Modern resilience also requires an architecture that anticipates failure rather than assuming stability: sandboxed environments for testing, near-real-time configuration management, and adaptive protection rules that change automatically when risk levels rise. When cybersecurity becomes an embedded, organisation-wide capability instead of a specialised function, institutions can respond to incidents before customers feel the impact. In a hybrid landscape where breaches can originate anywhere, coherence is not optional; it is the defining marker of a secure and trustworthy retail bank.

Senior leadership must maintain a unified view of cyber posture across all systems, ensuring that accountability is clear and response is coordinated.

The rise of cloud-based infrastructure has transformed scalability and efficiency, yet it has also introduced new forms of concentration risk that many retail banks underestimate. When critical workloads are hosted on a small number of global cloud providers, operational resilience becomes dependent on infrastructure that lies outside the bank's direct control. Outages, configuration errors, or regional service disruptions at a cloud provider can cascade rapidly across digital channels, payments, authentication services, and call-centre systems. At the same time, hybrid environments where legacy systems coexist with cloud platforms create complex security layers, making it difficult to maintain consistent controls, encryption standards, and patch cycles. This emphasises that banks must design cloud strategies with realism rather than optimism: multi-zone redundancy, distributed failover models, continuous verification of provider controls, and contractual clarity on incident-response obligations. Cloud governance is not simply a procurement or IT decision; it is an architectural responsibility that determines how reliably customers can access their money. For hybrid institutions that promise uninterrupted digital service, resilience at the cloud layer becomes as critical as capital adequacy or credit quality.

Case Study: Cloud Concentration Risk and Systemic Exposure

Capital One (United States)

In 2019, Capital One experienced a major data breach linked to a misconfigured cloud firewall within its public cloud environment. While the underlying cloud infrastructure remained operational, the incident exposed how configuration errors, identity management gaps, and insufficient monitoring can create significant security failures in shared cloud architectures. The breach affected over 100 million customer records and led to regulatory scrutiny, financial penalties, and reputational damage. The case reinforced that cloud adoption does not transfer accountability to providers; banks remain fully responsible for governance, configuration discipline, and continuous oversight of cloud-hosted environments.

Increasingly sophisticated fraud operating environments exploit the very speed and convenience that hybrid banking enables. Attackers now combine social engineering, credential harvesting, SIM-swap techniques, malware, and real-time reconnaissance to bypass both customer vigilance and institutional controls. What makes this threat landscape especially challenging is the blurring of boundaries: fraudsters target customers, staff, devices, and third-party platforms simultaneously, knowing that a single weak point can compromise an entire service journey. Legacy fraud-monitoring systems often struggle to keep pace because they rely on rule-based detection suited to older transaction patterns rather than to today's rapid, multi-channel behaviour. Modern institutions must therefore treat fraud prevention as an intelligence function, integrating behavioural analytics, device profiling, biometric verification, and adaptive authentication into a unified risk engine. This approach demands continuous data sharing across channels and tight coordination between cybersecurity teams, fraud units, and frontline operations. For customers, the experience must remain intuitive, yet beneath the surface the bank must operate a high-velocity defence system capable of detecting anomalies within seconds. In hybrid banking, fraud resilience does not emerge from technology alone; it requires culture, oversight, and the discipline to update controls as quickly as attackers evolve.

The final layer of cybersecurity risk in hybrid banking arises from the growing dependence on cloud environments and distributed infrastructure. While cloud platforms offer unmatched scalability, resilience, and cost efficiency, they also introduce architectural blind spots when banks lack full visibility into how data moves across regions, availability zones, and multi-tenant systems. Misconfigured storage buckets, weak API permissions, and inconsistent encryption policies remain among the most common sources of breach exposure globally. At the same time, regulators now expect institutions to demonstrate not only operational soundness but also sovereignty over critical data assets, especially when third-country service providers are involved. This requires hybrid banks to maintain a clear, continuously updated map of their technology estate: what is hosted where, who has access, how backups are managed, and how failover processes behave under stress. A mature cloud-risk posture integrates automated configuration checks, rigorous change-management controls, workload segmentation, and independent assurance testing. It also demands the capability to isolate compromised components without disrupting essential services. For retail banks seeking to operate securely at scale, cloud governance is no longer an IT topic; it is a core element of institutional resilience and a determinant of long-term customer trust.

AI Risk Models and Bias

AI-driven risk models are reshaping how retail banks assess creditworthiness, detect fraud, and allocate resources, but their growing influence introduces a new class of institutional vulnerability: algorithmic opacity. Traditional scorecards allowed risk teams to trace every decision, examine each variable, and explain outcomes to customers and regulators. Modern machine-learning systems, by contrast, often rely on complex, non-linear patterns drawn from high-dimensional datasets, making their internal logic difficult to interpret even for specialists. This loss of transparency becomes a governance concern when model behaviour cannot be fully explained, especially in adverse decisions such as credit declines or payment blocks. The danger intensifies when historical training data embeds structural inequalities, leading models to reproduce patterns that regulators classify as discriminatory. Hybrid banks must therefore integrate robust oversight mechanisms that treat AI models as living systems requiring continuous validation, recalibration, and stress testing. This includes independent challenge functions, bias-detection protocols, guided model documentation, and escalation paths when outputs deviate from expected ranges. In a hybrid operating environment, the credibility of AI depends not on technical sophistication alone but on an institution's ability to show that every automated decision is fair, accountable, and aligned with regulatory expectations.

AI systems increasingly shape frontline customer experiences—from credit approvals and fraud alerts to payment routing and collections—and this expanding influence introduces a subtle but serious risk: behavioural misinterpretation. Many algorithms infer risk from digital behaviour patterns such as device usage, login frequency, typing speed, or transaction sequencing. While these signals can strengthen fraud detection, they can also penalise legitimate customers whose circumstances do not match expected digital norms, including the elderly, migrants, rural users, or individuals with inconsistent connectivity. When behavioural risk scores decline silently in the background, decisions may appear arbitrary or unfair, creating frustration that frontline staff cannot easily resolve because the model's logic is opaque. This erodes trust at the point where customers are most vulnerable. To mitigate this, hybrid banks must embed explainability standards into model operations, ensuring every automated action can be articulated in plain language and verified through independent review. They must also design feedback loops where human oversight can override or escalate questionable outputs, particularly when behavioural data intersects with protected characteristics. The credibility of AI hinges on an institution's willingness to ensure that efficiency does not override equity, and that risk models strengthen—rather than undermine—the principles of fairness and inclusion in retail banking.

Automated decisioning must preserve dignity, ensuring that efficiency does not lead to exclusion or misinterpretation.

The greatest structural weakness in AI-driven banking emerges when models trained on historical data are deployed into rapidly changing economic and social environments. Legacy datasets often encode outdated behaviours, past market conditions, or incomplete customer journeys, resulting in risk assessments that fail to reflect present-day realities. For example, small businesses adapting to post-pandemic volatility or individuals with fragmented income streams may appear "high risk" simply because their patterns differ from pre-2020 norms. Similarly, communities affected by climate stress, rising housing costs, or digital-access constraints may be misclassified due to structural factors rather than financial misconduct. When these distortions are baked into AI-driven credit scoring, fraud detection, or collections workflows, the system inadvertently magnifies exclusion, even when frontline staff attempt to support customers in good faith. Hybrid banks must therefore treat data quality as a core component of risk governance. This includes continuously refreshing datasets, monitoring drifts in model behaviour, and integrating contextual variables such as regional volatility or emerging vulnerability patterns. Independent assurance teams should routinely test how models behave across different demographic and geographic groups, ensuring that bias is detected and corrected before decisions affect real households and businesses. A modern risk function is defined not by the sophistication of its models, but by its commitment to ensuring that those models evolve with society—not lag behind it.

AI risk in hybrid banking intensifies when decision systems operate as "black boxes", producing outcomes that neither customers nor frontline teams can easily interpret. When a payment is blocked, a loan declined, or a fraud alert triggered, customers increasingly expect clear, respectful explanations—not technical ambiguity. Yet many algorithmic models rely on complex feature interactions or proprietary vendor logic that make their decisions difficult to explain in human terms. This opacity creates operational, regulatory, and reputational exposure. Customers who feel unfairly treated escalate complaints more rapidly; regulators scrutinise institutions that cannot justify automated outcomes; and internal teams struggle to intervene when errors cascade through interconnected systems. Hybrid banks must therefore embed explainability as a foundational design principle. This includes constructing models with interpretable features, maintaining documentation that translates technical reasoning into plain language, and equipping staff with the tools to provide meaningful explanations without breaching security protocols. Strong governance requires periodic audits that assess not only model accuracy but also narrative clarity, ensuring that automated systems align with principles of fairness, transparency, and public accountability. In a future shaped by AI, trust will depend not simply on whether decisions are correct, but on whether institutions can clearly articulate how those decisions were made.

Case Study: Algorithmic Opacity and Public Trust

Apple Card (United States)

Following the launch of Apple Card, regulators investigated allegations that its credit-decision algorithm produced gender-based disparities in credit limits. Although no intentional discrimination was proven, the issuing bank was unable to clearly explain how the model arrived at specific outcomes. The episode triggered public criticism, regulatory inquiry, and reputational strain, illustrating that opaque algorithms can damage trust even when technical compliance is met. The case highlighted that explainability, auditability, and narrative clarity are essential safeguards when AI systems directly affect customer financial outcomes.

AI-driven decisioning introduces significant governance challenges when models drift from their intended behaviour due to changing data patterns, market conditions, or customer behaviour. In hybrid banking, this drift can occur rapidly because data flows are continuous, multidimensional, and influenced by external events—from economic shocks to fraud innovations to seasonal repayment cycles. When a model begins to infer new patterns that were not present in its training data, its outputs may inadvertently disadvantage certain customer groups, increase false positives, or elevate systemic risk without immediate human detection. Effective governance requires continuous monitoring frameworks that track model performance across demographic segments, product types, and behavioural cohorts. Risk teams must employ real-time dashboards, early-warning indicators, and exception triggers that surface anomalies before they turn into customer-impacting failures. Equally important is establishing structured escalation pathways so that when drift is detected, accountability is clear and corrective action is immediate. Hybrid banks must combine technical oversight with ethical review—ensuring that drift is not only a data-science issue but a board-level concern linked to fairness, inclusion, and institutional integrity.

These systems increasingly operate within complex hybrid environments where data originates from multiple channels, devices, and partner operating environments, making explainability a central requirement for trust and regulatory acceptance. When customers receive an automated decision—whether it is a declined payment, an adjusted credit limit, or a fraud alert—they expect to understand the rationale behind it. In the absence of clear explanations, even accurate models can appear arbitrary or discriminatory, triggering complaints, reputational risk, and regulatory scrutiny. For hybrid banks, explainability is not merely a technical feature; it is a conduct obligation that links customer rights with institutional transparency. This requires designing models with interpretable features, creating human-readable outputs, and integrating explanation modules into frontline systems so staff can articulate decisions with confidence. Regulators globally are tightening expectations—requiring banks to document how models work, the data they use, the assumptions they embed, and how often they undergo independent validation. A robust explainability framework therefore strengthens accountability, builds customer confidence, and ensures that automated decisions reinforce rather than undermine institutional credibility.

AI-driven decision systems demand continuous monitoring because risk profiles, customer behaviour, and environmental conditions evolve rapidly, and static models can become unsafe within weeks. As hybrid banks integrate AI into credit scoring, fraud analytics, collections, and service personalisation, model drift becomes a major vulnerability: changes in economic cycles, demographic patterns, or transaction characteristics can quietly distort outputs and generate unfair or inaccurate decisions. Continuous monitoring requires disciplined pipelines that track performance metrics, stability indicators, bias signals, and data-quality anomalies in real time, supported by escalation protocols when deviation thresholds are breached. It also requires alignment between data-science teams, risk committees, and frontline operations, ensuring that emerging issues are detected early, understood properly, and addressed before they manifest as customer harm or regulatory breaches. For hybrid institutions operating across multiple jurisdictions, monitoring must also reflect local market conditions and regulatory expectations. A strong continuous-monitoring framework turns AI from a static tool into a managed, living system—enabling banks to maintain fairness, safeguard trust, and uphold consistent service quality across all customer segments.

AI systems introduce a new category of operational fragility when institutions fail to maintain full transparency over how models behave, evolve, and influence customer outcomes. As hybrid banks expand the use of machine-learning engines in credit, fraud prevention, marketing, collections, dispute management, and customer segmentation, decision chains become increasingly complex—often spanning multiple vendors, datasets, and embedded algorithms. This opacity creates significant institutional risk: bank leaders may not fully understand the logic driving key decisions, frontline teams may be unable to interpret why certain customers receive specific outcomes, and regulators may expect levels of explainability that legacy systems were never designed to provide. This emphasises that explainability must become a formal governance requirement rather than a retrospective compliance activity. Hybrid institutions need structured documentation, accessible model summaries, rationale logs, and clear accountability pathways for how automated decisions are produced and challenged. Also worth highlighting is the importance of building interpretability tools that can simplify complex model behaviour for non-technical stakeholders, enabling risk managers, audit teams, and senior executives to identify early warning signs of bias, drift, or unintended exclusion. In a hybrid banking environment where decisions are distributed across digital and human pathways, transparency becomes a cornerstone of fairness, trust, and institutional legitimacy—protecting customers, enhancing governance discipline, and strengthening regulatory credibility.

AI-driven systems can rapidly amplify small errors into large-scale institutional risks when retail banks lack robust mechanisms for monitoring model drift and ensuring continuous performance integrity. In hybrid environments, data patterns evolve quickly—driven by shifting customer behaviour, emerging fraud vectors, macroeconomic changes, and seasonal or geographic variations. When models trained on historical data encounter new patterns, their predictive accuracy can decline without warning, resulting in unfair credit decisions, inaccurate risk scores, higher false positives in fraud prevention, or misaligned customer engagement journeys. This highlights that hybrid institutions must treat model drift as an operational inevitability rather than a rare event, embedding continuous validation, periodic recalibration, challenger models, stability thresholds, and automated alerts into their governance structures. The also emphasises that drift is not only mathematical but also socio-behavioural—customer groups evolve, financial stress fluctuates, and economic conditions reshape risk signals. Banks therefore need multidisciplinary oversight that unites data scientists, risk managers, compliance officers, and behavioural specialists to evaluate how models respond to real-world dynamics. Without these safeguards, AI systems can become misaligned with institutional values and regulatory expectations, creating material customer harm and eroding trust. In the hybrid future, proactive drift detection becomes a critical component of responsible AI governance, ensuring decisions remain fair, resilient, and aligned with strategic intent.

As AI becomes deeply embedded across credit, fraud, collections, service design, and customer experience, retail banks must build governance structures that treat algorithms as living systems requiring continuous oversight, ethical scrutiny, and operational accountability. This emphasises that responsible AI is not achieved through technical controls alone; it demands institutional discipline that spans board-level understanding, cross-functional ownership, transparent escalation pathways, and clear lines of accountability for model outcomes. Hybrid banks must ensure that every AI-driven decision can be explained in plain language—not only to regulators but to customers whose financial wellbeing is directly shaped by automated judgments. This requires model documentation, interpretability tools, fairness testing, redress mechanisms, and inclusion checks that prevent structural bias from being embedded into automated processes. Responsible AI governance extends to vendor models, cloud-based AI services, and fintech-provided algorithms, making external assurance, contractual safeguards, and independent validation essential components of the risk framework. In a multi-channel hybrid environment, responsible AI becomes a core institutional capability, demonstrating that technology can enhance fairness, strengthen trust, and support long-term resilience when governed with clarity, transparency, and human-centred accountability.

Board-level oversight is essential to ensure that AI systems align with institutional values, regulatory expectations, and long-term trust objectives.

Third-Party and Vendor Risk

Hybrid banking depends on a dense web of external providers. Modern banks rely on cloud infrastructures, payment rails, cybersecurity firms, API intermediaries, data-analytics platforms, facilities-management providers, and fintech collaborators—each introducing dependency chains that can compromise resilience if not governed rigorously. Given this, third-party and vendor risk must now be treated as a core institutional exposure rather than an operational afterthought. The risk profile of a vendor is no longer limited to service quality; it includes financial stability, technology maturity, information-security posture, regulatory alignment, and their own network of sub-contractors. Failures such as outages, cyber incidents, or data-handling lapses at even a minor supplier can cascade across customer journeys and create reputational and regulatory consequences for the bank. To manage this exposure, institutions must shift from periodic due-diligence exercises to continuous monitoring frameworks supported by real-time dashboards, incident-reporting obligations, contractual clarity, and shared-resilience testing. It's important to position third-party risk as a structural component of hybrid architectures—one that requires disciplined oversight, consistent assurance, and strong board-level visibility to protect institutional integrity and safeguard customer trust.

Third-party relationships in hybrid banking introduce multi-layered operational exposure. This leads to a focus on why traditional outsourcing controls are no longer adequate for modern dependency chains. As banks integrate cloud services, API gateways, fraud-monitoring engines, video-KYC platforms, and external data sources, they inherit not only the vendor's strengths but also their vulnerabilities. As a result, a vendor's internal controls, encryption standards, patch-management discipline, and incident-response maturity directly influence the bank's resilience. A lapse within a sub-vendor—for example, an analytics tool hosted on an inadequately protected cloud instance—can trigger service disruptions, regulatory breaches, or data-leak obligations for the bank, even when the bank has no direct operational visibility into that environment. This interconnected reality demands stronger upstream and downstream assurance: clear service-level definitions, mandatory reporting of cyber events, performance telemetry, cross-border compliance reviews, and coordinated drills involving key vendors. This shows that banks must design governance structures where third-party oversight is continuous, data-driven, and deeply embedded into hybrid operating models, ensuring that institutional reliability does not depend on blind trust in external partners.

Hybrid retail banking now operates on dense, interdependent networks of cloud providers, payment processors, cybersecurity partners, API gateways, infrastructure vendors, fintech collaborators, and outsourced operational teams. This explains why continuous, real-time oversight of every external partner has become a non-negotiable element of institutional resilience. Traditional vendor reviews—annual questionnaires, periodic compliance attestations, and static documentation checks—are fundamentally inadequate in a world where a single misconfigured API, outdated software library, or unresolved vulnerability can escalate into a large-scale service disruption. Continuous monitoring requires banks to integrate live telemetry from vendors into risk systems, tracking uptime, authentication errors, latency, data-flow anomalies, policy breaches, and cyber alerts that may indicate hidden stress. Financial resilience must be monitored with equal discipline: if a fintech partner faces liquidity issues, layoffs, governance changes, or investor exits, those pressures often translate into operational shortcuts that heighten risk. Cross-border vendors add further complexity, as local regulations, data-residency requirements, and supervisory expectations differ sharply. Real-time dashboards, joint incident-response rehearsals, automated alerts, and collaborative escalation protocols help banks detect problems before they propagate across customer journeys. Vendor oversight is no longer an administrative exercise but a core strategic capability, requiring technology integration, governance maturity, and constant situational intelligence. A hybrid bank that treats vendor monitoring as continuous rather than episodic is far better positioned to protect customers, uphold regulatory expectations, and maintain operational integrity across its entire operating environment.

Vendor failures rarely occur in isolation; they emerge from a chain of subtle weaknesses that accumulate over time across people, processes, and technology. Early-warning indicators can help hybrid banks identify vulnerabilities long before they materialise as outages, data breaches, or customer-impacting incidents. Weak audit findings, delayed penetration-test remediation, unexplained staff turnover, increasing ticket backlogs, postponed maintenance windows, or sudden changes in technology roadmaps often signal that a partner's internal environment is under strain. Likewise, shifts in ownership, leadership departures, funding pressures, or rapid expansion can destabilise operational discipline, especially within younger fintechs still maturing their governance capabilities. Early-warning detection requires banks to assess vendors not only on the basis of SLAs but on behavioural markers that indicate whether a partner is becoming reactive rather than proactive. Advanced banks also analyse metadata such as authentication failures, spikes in API throttling, integration latency, and deviations in encryption standards, all of which can reveal stress within a vendor's infrastructure. As such, hybrid banks must build predictive intelligence into vendor-risk processes, combining human judgement with real-time technical signals. When early-warning indicators are captured and escalated consistently, institutions can intervene collaboratively, provide remediation support, activate temporary safeguards, or prepare contingency arrangements. Treating vendor fragility as a predictable pattern rather than a sudden shock strengthens resilience and ensures that customer journeys remain stable even in complex multi-partner environments.

A defining challenge in hybrid banking is that third-party incidents escalate faster than internal teams can react, particularly when banks rely on multiple vendors for critical services such as payments, cloud hosting, fraud analytics, cybersecurity monitoring, and customer-experience platforms. This reveals the importance of real-time visibility across vendor environments, highlighting that traditional quarterly reviews or annual certifications are no longer sufficient. Hybrid operating models require continuous telemetry: uptime trends, API error codes, failed authentications, latency spikes, patch compliance, and deviations from baseline performance. Banks must integrate vendors into a unified observability layer that provides operational, security, and compliance signals without exposing sensitive proprietary information. This creates a shared responsibility model where both parties monitor the same indicators and respond quickly to anomalies. It also emphasises that real-time oversight must be accompanied by clear, pre-agreed escalation pathways. During an incident, delays often occur because vendors operate through layered internal teams, offshore support groups, or fragmented ticket queues. By establishing joint command structures, named escalation contacts, runbooks, and decision rights beforehand, hybrid banks can respond within minutes rather than hours. Furthermore, regulators increasingly expect banks to demonstrate how they maintain situational awareness across outsourced environments, especially in cross-border arrangements where local laws, data-sovereignty constraints, and time-zone differences add complexity. Real-time oversight is therefore not merely a technical capability; it is a structural requirement for institutional resilience. When banks and vendors operate from a shared operational picture, they reduce customer impact, strengthen regulatory confidence, and build trust across the operating environment.

Hybrid banking depends on a landscape of specialised providers whose technologies, data practices, and operational maturity directly shape the institution's own resilience. A factor worth examining is the governance challenge created when critical services sit outside the bank's physical and regulatory perimeter and must therefore be controlled through disciplined, contract-based, and risk-sensitive oversight. As payment processors, cloud operators, authentication partners, and analytics firms become embedded in day-to-day customer journeys, banks must treat these entities not as suppliers but as extensions of their own risk environment, subject to the same standards of security, continuity, and ethical conduct that would apply internally. This requires continuous validation of vendor capabilities through live resilience tests, code-level assessments, threat-intelligence sharing, and regular evidence of financial stability and incident-response readiness. It also demands clarity about data pathways—who stores what, where it is processed, how it is encrypted, and what happens when access must be revoked. Herein lies the importance of structured escalation routes, joint crisis protocols, and real-time performance dashboards that allow banks to detect degradation early and intervene decisively. By elevating vendor relationships into a formal governance construct rather than a procurement arrangement, hybrid banks create a coordinated risk perimeter in which every external dependency is monitored, benchmarked, and capable of withstanding systemic shocks.

Accountability for customer outcomes always remains with the bank, regardless of where the failure originates.

As hybrid banking expands across cloud architectures and API-driven operating environments, the stability of third-party vendors becomes inseparable from the stability of the bank itself. An important point in this regard is how concentration risk—the dependence on a small number of dominant cloud providers, payment gateways, authentication engines, or infrastructure companies—has become a major structural vulnerability. When a critical vendor services hundreds of institutions, a single outage or misconfiguration can ripple across markets, disrupting payments, locking customers out of accounts, or exposing data flows to unintended failures. For retail banks, managing concentration risk requires a far more proactive posture: mapping all points of dependency, assessing single-provider exposure, and developing dual-vendor or federated-service strategies where feasible. It also demands deeper assessment of geopolitical exposure, including data-sovereignty vulnerabilities, cross-border hosting arrangements, and the risk that regulatory or political developments in one jurisdiction may affect operational continuity elsewhere. Banks must establish clear thresholds for acceptable dependency, stress-test vendor resilience against extreme but plausible scenarios, and build robust exit strategies that allow critical services to be migrated without destabilising customer journeys. This reinforces that concentration risk is not an abstract regulatory concern but an operational reality that shapes the everyday functioning of hybrid banking, making transparent oversight and alternative pathways essential to long-term institutional resilience.

Case Study: Vendor Dependency and Customer Harm

TSB Bank (United Kingdom)

TSB's 2018 core-banking migration failure revealed the operational and reputational risks created by deep vendor dependency and insufficient transition governance. Customers experienced prolonged service outages, restricted account access, and transaction failures over several weeks. Regulatory penalties and remediation costs followed, alongside long-term reputational damage. The incident demonstrated that third-party technology decisions are strategic risk decisions and that accountability for customer impact remains with the bank, regardless of vendor involvement.

The complexity of modern vendor operating environments means that banks now face significant fourth-party risk—exposure arising not from their direct suppliers, but from the suppliers of those suppliers. One thing to examine is how these hidden dependencies can undermine operational resilience, especially when banks rely on fintech platforms or cloud-based services that themselves subcontract critical components such as analytics engines, identity-verification modules, fraud-detection tools, or hosting infrastructure. A disruption at any layer can cascade quickly: a downstream analytics provider suffering an outage may compromise credit decisioning; a subcontracted authentication service may prevent customers from logging in; a fragile API aggregator may break a core product journey. The challenge is that banks often lack complete visibility of these nested arrangements, leaving governance gaps that are only discovered during incidents. To manage fourth-party risk effectively, hybrid banks must establish requirements for supply-chain transparency, insisting that primary vendors disclose their material subcontractors, control frameworks, and continuity mechanisms. They must also implement contractual obligations requiring prompt notification of incidents, independent certifications, and adherence to security standards across all tiers. Regular scenario testing should include downstream providers, ensuring that business continuity plans account for failures beyond the immediate vendor perimeter. This underscores that in a deeply interdependent operating environment, the resilience of a retail bank is only as strong as the weakest, most distant actor in its digital supply chain—making structured oversight, end-to-end visibility, and enforceable accountability essential components of hybrid-era risk management.

Institutions must extend visibility beyond direct vendors to ensure that downstream dependencies do not create hidden vulnerabilities.

Vendor concentration risk has become one of the most significant structural vulnerabilities in hybrid retail banking, as institutions increasingly depend on a small number of dominant providers for cloud hosting, payments processing, cybersecurity, and core banking platforms. Over-reliance on a single supplier—even one with strong credentials—creates systemic exposure that can disrupt entire markets if an outage, cyber incident, regulatory sanction, or geopolitical shock affects that provider. When multiple banks are concentrated on the same cloud platform or the same identity-verification engine, a technical failure can cascade across regions, undermining customer access, transaction flow, and public confidence. As a result, regulators in the UK, EU, and other jurisdictions have begun raising concerns about "critical third parties," signalling that banks must diversify strategically rather than assume resilience through scale alone. Effective mitigation requires a careful redesign of technology architecture to support portability, multi-cloud readiness, and the ability to switch vendors without long interruptions—capabilities that many legacy systems lack. It also demands internal governance structures that assess concentration exposure regularly, run stress scenarios on dependency failures, and evaluate alternative suppliers for backup capacity. Partnerships should include exit clauses, data-retrieval guarantees, and reciprocal obligations that ensure continuity even in adverse scenarios. By viewing concentration as a structural risk rather than a procurement issue, hybrid banks can build operating environments that remain stable even when dominant vendors face pressure—protecting customers, preserving trust, and strengthening market-wide resilience.

A resilient vendor operating environment depends not only on evaluating suppliers at the point of onboarding but on maintaining continuous, intelligence-led oversight throughout the relationship lifecycle. This highlights that modern vendor risk must operate as an always-on capability, supported by real-time monitoring tools, periodic reassessment of contractual obligations, updated security attestations, and refreshed scenario testing that reflects new market threats. Hybrid banks increasingly face risks that evolve far more quickly than traditional annual review cycles can accommodate: a supplier may become financially unstable, adopt weaker security practices, experience rapid staff turnover, or become the target of geopolitical restrictions that compromise data hosting or service continuity. This requires institutions to build integrated oversight processes that bring together procurement, technology, operational risk, and legal teams under a unified governance model. Effective oversight includes continuous log visibility from external platforms, proactive detection of anomalous performance patterns, and early escalation to internal leadership when red flags emerge. Banks must also insist on transparency from vendors regarding subcontractors, offshore delivery units, and any changes to the environments where customer data is processed. When external partners operate in jurisdictions with weaker regulatory protections, banks must compensate with stronger controls, stricter audit rights, and more rigorous testing of failover mechanisms. To summarise, third-party oversight is ultimately a trust function: customers depend on a bank to choose and supervise partners responsibly, and regulators expect clear evidence that the institution fully understands and manages each dependency. For hybrid institutions, continuous, structured, and multi-disciplinary monitoring is therefore the cornerstone of safe and accountable vendor operating environments.

Climate-Adjusted Retail Risk

Climate-driven volatility is reshaping the foundations of retail banking. It is no longer an abstract environmental concern—it is a direct retail-portfolio issue affecting mortgage markets, agricultural lending, SME survival, insurance affordability, and customer vulnerability. Extreme weather events disrupt incomes, damage assets, inflate operating costs, and increase credit stress, creating ripple effects across entire communities and local economies.

Retail banks must treat climate exposure as a core input to risk modelling, segmentation, and local-market strategy. This means integrating climate data into credit scoring, updating property valuations in risk-prone geographies, reassessing insurance dependencies, and calibrating pricing models to reflect new patterns of volatility. Regulators across the UK, EU, and Asia are already requiring banks to incorporate climate scenarios into probability-of-default, loss-given-default, and stress-testing frameworks. Climate risk has moved firmly into supervisory expectations.

For hybrid institutions, climate-adjusted risk also intersects with inclusion. Vulnerable groups are disproportionately exposed to environmental shocks, amplifying delinquency risks and widening financial gaps. Banks need early-warning indicators that combine financial and environmental signals, frontline protocols for supporting affected customers, and local-market strategies that anticipate climate-related stress before it manifests as default.

Climate-related shocks are altering household stability, business continuity, and everyday financial behaviours in ways that traditional scorecards cannot capture. Rising insurance premiums, property devaluations in high-risk zones, agricultural volatility, and supply-chain disruptions affecting micro-enterprises all reshape repayment capacity and liquidity patterns invisibly—until it's too late.

Retail banks need multi-layered climate intelligence that blends geospatial data, local economic indicators, environmental-impact projections, and behavioural insights. The shift is not merely analytical—it is operational and cultural. Hybrid institutions must redesign frontline processes, onboarding flows, product suitability checks, and early-warning signals to ensure climate exposure is recognised in real time rather than detected after delinquency emerges.

Climate-related vulnerability also interacts with other forms of fragility—income shocks, health issues, digital access constraints—creating compounding risks requiring more holistic supervisory oversight. Integrating climate sensitivity into retail decision-making means strengthening dialogue with regulators, insurers, housing authorities, and local councils, as these institutions increasingly co-govern the risk environment. The competitive advantage will shift toward banks that can blend data science, empathy, and local-market intelligence into customer-centric risk design.

The volatility in climate is forcing banks to rethink how collateral, affordability, and long-term customer stability are modelled across different geographies. Traditional methods underestimate how environmental disruption erodes financial resilience over time. Mortgages in coastal or flood-prone areas face accelerated depreciation. Small businesses dependent on climate-sensitive supply chains encounter unpredictable cost cycles. Agricultural borrowers experience rising variability in yields, insurance coverage, and market access.

Static credit policies are increasingly inadequate. Retail institutions must incorporate forward-looking climate projections, scenario-based valuations, and stress-tested affordability assessments. Customers grappling with climate stress often alter spending, saving, and repayment patterns in ways traditional models fail to detect, delaying instalments during seasonal shocks or drawing down savings earlier than expected. Hybrid banks must redesign early-warning systems using integrated data from payments, transaction patterns, local climate alerts, and insurance environments to anticipate stress points before they become arrears.

Properties in flood-prone areas are beginning to show volatility in insurance availability, premium affordability, and long-term asset stability—all of which directly influence a bank's risk position. When insurers withdraw coverage or impose prohibitive excesses, effective collateral value declines even if the physical structure remains intact. In many regions, properties are becoming functionally uninsurable for parts of the year, creating a mismatch between book valuation and real-world market appetite. Hybrid banks must update valuation methodologies to include climate-adjusted risk weights, future insurance trajectories, and local environmental projections rather than relying solely on historical price trends.

This insurance disruption is emerging as one of the most immediate and underestimated risks for households and small businesses. As insurers reassess viability of covering high-risk zones, premiums are rising sharply, deductibles are widening, and in some regions coverage is being withdrawn entirely. A customer whose home is no longer insurable becomes significantly riskier to lend to. A small business facing insurance volatility may struggle to maintain liquidity buffers or secure affordable protection for inventory and equipment.

For hybrid banks, this requires a redesign of affordability assessments, mortgage renewal policies, and branch-level advisory models. Customers may not fully understand the long-term financial implications of diminishing coverage—frontline teams must identify early signals of insurance distress and guide borrowers through mitigation options. Institutions must also integrate insurance-market intelligence into risk dashboards, tracking regional withdrawal patterns, price spikes, and regulatory interventions.

Climate-driven insurance instability is not only a financial issue—it's a trust issue. Customers expect banks to anticipate vulnerabilities and act with foresight. Retail institutions that pre-emptively adjust lending criteria and engage customers proactively will be better positioned to manage this new layer of systemic risk. Those that delay will face higher defaults, reputational strain, and deeper exposure to climate-related market volatility.

Climate volatility is reshaping household financial behaviour in ways retail banks can no longer treat as peripheral. Extreme weather events, rising utility costs, heat-related income disruptions, and climate-linked inflation directly influence repayment patterns, savings buffers, and consumer resilience. Families facing repeated climate shocks experience irregular expenses—emergency repairs, temporary relocation, medical needs—that erode liquidity and shorten the financial runway households rely on during stress.

These behavioural adaptations create silent deterioration in credit quality long before arrears appear. Families may defer home maintenance, reduce insurance coverage, increase short-term borrowing, and rely more heavily on informal credit. Digital channels offer early signals through rising complaint volumes, missed micro-payments, shifts in spending patterns, or increased requests for short-term credit.

Hybrid banks must integrate climate-sensitive behavioural analytics into early-warning systems, combining geospatial exposure data, income stability profiles, insurance gaps, and community-level resilience indicators. Branches and frontline teams play a critical role in spotting early distress, especially in rural and semi-urban regions where climate impact shows unevenly. Advisory models must adapt to guide customers through insurance choices, government schemes, emergency funds, and financial planning options designed for climate resilience.

Retail risk in climate-adjusted circumstances ultimately requires banks to rethink how products, pricing, and long-term customer engagement are designed—particularly in geographies where environmental volatility is becoming structural rather than exceptional.

Mortgages in flood-risk zones may require dynamic loan-to-value adjustments as collateral strength shifts. Small-business borrowers dependent on climate-sensitive supply chains may need flexible repayment calendars. Personal-loan borrowers in heat-affected labour markets may require redesigned grace-period structures. Conventional credit-scoring models anchored in historical behaviour are increasingly misaligned with emerging physical-risk realities.

Hybrid banks must embed climate intelligence directly into underwriting tools, credit-decision engines, and frontline advisory journeys, ensuring products adapt to real environmental conditions rather than outdated assumptions. This also strengthens customer trust: when banks proactively recognise climate-related hardship and provide tailored support, they position themselves as long-term partners to communities navigating a rapidly changing world.

Climate risk must be integrated into core banking decisions rather than treated as a parallel analytical exercise. Institutional response must align credit policy, customer engagement, and regulatory expectations within a unified climate-risk framework. Banks that embed climate intelligence into everyday operations will be better positioned to safeguard both customers and balance sheets in an increasingly volatile world.

Reputation and Digital Conduct Risk

Reputational and digital conduct risk has become one of the most volatile and consequential risk domains for hybrid retail banks, shaped by real-time information flows, algorithmic decisioning, heightened regulatory scrutiny, and rising public expectations of fairness. A single negative customer experience—a declined payment, an unexplained account freeze, an inaccessible digital interface, or a miscommunicated product condition—can escalate into viral public criticism within minutes, affecting customer trust across entire regions. For hybrid banks, the risk lies not only in operational failures but in how customers perceive the fairness, clarity, and intent behind digital interactions. Conduct is now interpreted through interfaces, chatbots, automated decisions, and online engagement pathways, making design choices effectively ethical choices. This highlights how retail banks must reconsider the governance of digital conduct, ensuring product journeys are transparent, terms are understandable, grievance channels are visible, and decisions are communicated with empathy. It also highlights the pressures created by algorithmic opacity: customers increasingly expect explanations even when models are complex. Reputational stability now depends on consistent omnichannel service quality, proactive escalation frameworks, and leadership cultures that prioritise accountability. Institutions that treat conduct as a technical compliance function risk systemic erosion of trust; institutions that recognise conduct as a reflection of institutional values will strengthen resilience, reduce regulatory exposure, and differentiate themselves in a highly scrutinised marketplace.

Digital conduct risk increasingly originates from the design and behaviour of automated systems that customers interact with daily, making interface architecture an essential component of reputational protection. When customers encounter unclear navigation, misleading button labels, algorithmically driven rejections without explanation, or service flows that feel punitive or opaque, they interpret these experiences as intentional decisions by the institution rather than design flaws. In a hybrid environment where most interactions occur without human involvement, the bank's "conduct culture" is projected entirely through digital touchpoints. As such, banks must treat interface design, copywriting, notification structures, chatbot behaviour, and automated decisions as core conduct decisions—each requiring transparency, empathy, and fairness embedded into the user journey. Poorly designed journeys, such as making cancellation difficult, hiding fees in drop-down menus, or issuing template-based denial messages, trigger reputational harm even when the underlying decision is legally sound. Regulators across jurisdictions are increasingly framing these issues under consumer fairness, digital suitability, and algorithmic accountability. Hybrid institutions must therefore adopt proactive oversight mechanisms: regular UX conduct audits, behavioural testing for vulnerable customers, explainability layers that translate technical decisions into human language, and review committees that assess whether digital pathways align with the organisation's values. Reputational resilience now stems from how well the institution anticipates emotional, cognitive, and behavioural responses to digital interactions. Banks that design systems with humility, clarity, and inclusiveness will strengthen public trust; those that overlook the conduct implications of digital design will face escalating complaints, social backlash, and regulatory intervention.

Hybrid banking increasingly reflects how institutions manage moments of friction—declined transactions, delayed payments, identity mismatches, or verification failures that customers often interpret as personal judgments rather than system-driven safeguards. These "critical moments" shape long-term trust, especially when customers lack visibility into the logic behind automated decisions. When a card is blocked abroad, a mortgage application stalls due to missing data, or an online transfer is halted for security checks, the absence of timely, empathetic communication can transform a routine risk-control action into a reputational event. Hybrid banks must therefore redesign incident-handling pathways so they feel supportive rather than accusatory. This includes crafting plain-language notifications that explain the reason for the interruption, providing immediate self-service remedies, and ensuring staff are trained to resolve issues without technical jargon or defensive behaviour. Regulators now expect institutions to anticipate the stress, embarrassment, or financial risk customers face during such interruptions, especially vulnerable groups who may lack digital confidence or linguistic familiarity. Internally, banks must strengthen cross-functional collaboration between risk, operations, customer-service, and digital teams to ensure that automated safeguards are complemented by human-centred escalation models. A well-managed friction moment can reinforce trust by showing the bank's protective intent; a poorly handled one can trigger complaints, social-media amplification, and long-lasting stigma. The institutions that excel will be those that integrate emotional intelligence into digital safeguards, ensuring that security interventions are understood as care, not obstruction.

Every customer interaction must preserve dignity, particularly during moments of friction or vulnerability.

Hybrid banking has amplified the speed at which reputational harm can spread, making transparency and consistency fundamental elements of institutional credibility. Even minor service failures—a delayed refund, an ambiguous notification, an inconsistent response from customer support—can escalate into broader trust concerns when customers share their experiences instantly across digital channels. The hybrid environment creates a visibility gap: customers can see the outcomes of automated decisions, but not the reasoning behind them. When these outcomes appear arbitrary or contradictory across channels, customers assume systemic unfairness, even when the underlying controls are sound. Banks must therefore build coherent conduct pathways that ensure decisions made by algorithms, frontline staff, and digital service flows align in tone, rationale, and customer impact. This requires strengthening product governance, refining customer-journey testing, and adopting real-time monitoring tools that detect patterns of dissatisfaction before they crystallise into reputational events. Cultural tone is equally critical; institutions must avoid defensive behaviours when customers challenge decisions, responding instead with clear explanations and empathetic reassurance. In hybrid systems, trust depends not only on accuracy but on perceived intention—whether the bank appears to act with fairness, predictability, and respect. By embedding conduct integrity across processes, interfaces, and interactions, banks can reduce reputational volatility and demonstrate that digital-era efficiency does not come at the expense of accountability or human dignity.

In a hybrid banking environment, reputational resilience increasingly depends on how well institutions manage moments of customer vulnerability—the points at which financial stress, confusion, or fear collide with automated systems that may not fully understand context. Reputational damage often arises not from major failures but from everyday interactions where customers feel unheard or unfairly treated. Automated declines, delayed fraud alerts, unexpected account holds, or confusing dispute processes can create a sense of institutional indifference that travels quickly across digital channels. To mitigate this, banks must redesign conduct pathways to recognise and respond to vulnerability signals, using behavioural analytics, frontline training, and escalation frameworks that prioritise empathy and clarity. Hybrid institutions must ensure that algorithms do not unintentionally penalise customers during periods of temporary hardship—for example, misinterpreting irregular income patterns or seasonal cash-flow dips as credit deterioration. At the same time, reputational strength depends on consistent transparency: customers should always understand why a decision was made, what steps they can take to resolve it, and how the bank is ensuring fairness. This requires closer integration between risk teams, digital designers, and customer-experience specialists to build decision journeys that uphold dignity and minimise friction. Ultimately, reputational conduct becomes a structural capability when institutions treat every interaction—digital or human—as a moment to reinforce trust, fairness, and institutional intent.

It responds when things go wrong. The rising expectations of real-time accountability in a world where service failures, payment glitches, security alerts, or misinformation can spread across social networks within minutes. Customers now expect instant acknowledgement, clear explanations, and visible corrective action. Silence, delays, or vague responses are interpreted as evasiveness and can amplify negativity far beyond the scale of the incident itself. To meet this new standard, banks must build crisis-response protocols that integrate digital communication teams, operational leaders, risk managers, and frontline staff into a single coordinated system. This includes pre-approved message templates, automated alerts that trigger senior oversight, and a clear chain of command for public communication. Hybrid institutions also need a unified dashboard that captures customer pain signals across channels—complaints, drop-off patterns, abandoned journeys, social feedback, and dispute escalations—enabling early detection of reputational risks before they become viral issues. Importantly, the bank's cultural posture matters: acknowledging mistakes early and showing a willingness to fix problems strengthens credibility far more than defensive communication. By treating transparency as an operational discipline rather than a public-relations tactic, hybrid banks can convert incidents into opportunities to reinforce institutional character and demonstrate respect for customers' time, concerns, and emotional experience.

Reputational strength increasingly depends on how consistently a hybrid bank demonstrates fairness, empathy, and clarity across automated decision-making systems. Similarly, customers interpret digital decisions—declined payments, flagged transactions, credit-limit reductions, account freezes, or algorithmic credit rejections—as reflections of institutional integrity. When these experiences occur without explanation, the customer perceives the institution as opaque or uncaring, regardless of whether the underlying decision was technically correct. As such, hybrid banks must embed "decision transparency" directly into their systems: real-time reasoning summaries, clear next steps, and accessible human escalation paths. Also worth highlighting is the moral responsibility attached to automated outcomes. A poorly tuned fraud model that blocks genuine transactions during emergencies, or an AI credit model that disproportionately disadvantages young borrowers or migrants, creates reputational damage that spreads quickly through online communities. To address this, banks must implement oversight routines that combine model-governance committees, ethical-risk reviews, and routine customer-impact audits. They must also maintain human override capability for cases requiring contextual judgement. The hybrid bank's reputation will increasingly depend on how respectfully its systems treat customers at moments of vulnerability, ensuring that automation accelerates service without diminishing dignity, fairness, or the customer's sense of agency.

Resilience now hinges on how effectively hybrid banks manage incidents in real time, especially when digital channels amplify every service disruption. Outages, payment delays, login failures, data-access problems, and system slowdowns create cascading trust shocks when customers cannot distinguish between a minor glitch and a serious breach. In the hybrid environment, reputation is shaped less by the incident itself and more by how transparently, quickly, and empathetically the bank responds. This argues that institutions must operate with a "public-first" incident posture, providing rapid status updates, clear cause explanations, expected resolution timelines, and accessible alternative channels. Silence or generic apologies deepen frustration and encourage speculation across social media, harming long-term credibility. There is thus a need for pre-approved communication templates, empowered incident leaders, and coordinated response teams across IT, operations, risk, compliance, and customer care. Hybrid banks should treat every disruption as a reputational event, not a technical event, recognising that customers judge stability based on how well they are informed and supported. A reputation-first incident model reinforces the perception of competence, accountability, and respect—all essential qualities in a banking landscape where digital transparency is non-negotiable.

Hybrid banking increasingly depends on how fairly and transparently automated decisions are communicated to customers. The focus here is on the rising expectation that institutions must explain the rationale behind declined transactions, credit rejections, fraud flags, and service restrictions in language that is clear, humane, and free from technical ambiguity. Customers today experience these outcomes in real time, often through mobile interfaces, meaning that poorly worded system messages or generic rejection notices can be perceived as discriminatory, careless, or disrespectful. This means that digital conduct now requires banks to embed "explainability layers" directly into customer journeys, ensuring that automated decisions are accompanied by contextual reasoning, guidance on next steps, and a route to human support where needed. It also highlights how customers judge fairness not only by outcomes but by the transparency and empathy of the communication surrounding those outcomes. Hybrid institutions must therefore design decision flows that are consistent, bias-aware, and sensitive to vulnerable users. Poorly executed messaging can escalate into public complaints and regulatory scrutiny, whereas well-crafted, transparent communication strengthens institutional integrity and promotes long-term trust.

Reputational resilience in hybrid banking ultimately depends on how consistently an institution demonstrates accountability when things go wrong. To end this pillar, we shall focus on the critical expectation that banks must acknowledge errors quickly, take visible corrective action, and maintain open channels for customers to escalate concerns. In a world where service disruptions, payment delays, system outages, and algorithmic misclassifications can spread instantly across social media, silence or defensive messaging can severely damage institutional credibility. Instead, hybrid banks must adopt a proactive conduct posture: real-time incident notifications, clear status updates, and publicly communicated remediation steps. This includes establishing crisis playbooks that integrate technology teams, legal advisers, frontline staff, and communication specialists to ensure a unified response. Emphasis ought also be placed on the need for transparent root-cause explanations—not technical jargon, but accessible language that reassures customers that the issue is understood and being addressed. Accountability must extend beyond incidents to include ongoing learning, with insights from complaints, service failures, and digital-behaviour patterns feeding back into product design and governance reviews. When institutions demonstrate humility, responsiveness, and integrity during moments of stress, they convert potential reputational damage into evidence of reliability. In a hybrid world, accountability is not a defensive strategy; it is a core component of digital conduct that strengthens long-term trust and reinforces the bank's standing within the communities it serves.

Consistent accountability in moments of failure is a defining indicator of institutional integrity.

Institutional Perspective: A Global Lens on Risk, Trust, and Being Human in an Age of Invisible Systems

When Risk Becomes Invisible

For most of banking history, risk was visible. Customers could see branches, vaults, security staff, and physical procedures that signalled institutional control. When something went wrong—a delayed payment or a branch closure—the disruption was usually localised and understandable.

Modern banking works very differently.

Today's financial systems run through invisible digital infrastructure spread across cloud platforms, APIs, AI-driven decision systems, telecommunications networks, authentication layers, and data centres operating far beyond any bank's physical walls. Customers interact with simple mobile interfaces, but underneath sits a deeply interconnected system functioning in real time.

Risk no longer emerges from visible processes. It increasingly comes from hidden complexity customers rarely see or fully understand. A cloud outage in one region can disrupt payments across multiple countries. A compromised API may expose data without obvious signs of intrusion. An AI fraud model can silently block legitimate transactions. A vendor failure may interrupt services while customers still blame the bank itself.

Risk becomes invisible long before it becomes operationally visible.

This changes how trust works. In the past, people associated safety with physical scale and visible control—branches, vaults, formal procedures. Today, trust depends on infrastructure customers cannot observe directly. Most people are comfortable with that invisibility when systems run smoothly. Anxiety appears when hidden systems fail unexpectedly.

A payment outage, authentication problem, or cyberattack creates stress because customers often don't know where the failure began or how widespread it is. Invisible systems suddenly become emotionally visible.

Different societies experience this differently. In highly digital economies like Singapore, South Korea, and parts of Northern Europe, customers tend to show strong behavioural trust in integrated digital infrastructure because digital coordination is already embedded in daily life. In regions shaped by inflation, banking instability, or weak infrastructure, customers may adopt digital services while still carrying underlying doubts about reliability during periods of stress. Across emerging markets, trust often depends heavily on practical consistency because mobile banking supports everyday economic activity.

AI deepens this shift. Financial decisions are increasingly shaped by systems customers cannot see—fraud detection models, behavioural analytics, predictive monitoring, and automated authentication. People usually experience only the outcome, not the reasoning behind it. As a result, customers depend on systems they neither fully understand nor directly observe, even though those systems influence access to money, credit, and financial continuity.

The challenge for banks now goes beyond cybersecurity or operational resilience. Institutions must preserve confidence in environments where complexity itself creates vulnerability. Customers expect uninterrupted access, secure transactions, fair treatment, fast recovery during disruption, and clear accountability when failures occur—even as the infrastructure behind those expectations becomes more distributed and harder to interpret.

The strongest institutions may not simply be the ones that prevent failures most effectively, but those that maintain transparency and reassurance when hidden systems break down. As banking becomes increasingly embedded in digital life, invisible risk is becoming one of the defining realities of modern finance.

Why Human Beings Still Expect Safety

Despite the rapid digitisation of finance, one expectation has remained constant: people still expect banks to keep them safe.

That expectation sits at the emotional core of retail banking.

Customers may embrace mobile payments, biometric authentication, digital wallets, and invisible payment systems, but beneath the technology remains a basic human assumption: banks will protect identity, safeguard money, maintain continuity, and restore order when uncertainty appears.

Banking systems evolved because societies needed trusted institutions to protect economic value over time. Digital technology has changed how banking operates, but it hasn't changed that emotional requirement. Customers still expect salaries to arrive on time, payments to clear, savings to remain accessible, fraud to be controlled, and systems to recover quickly during disruption. The difference is that these expectations now depend on invisible digital infrastructure.

People rarely think about cloud architecture, operational resilience, or AI governance during normal banking activity. But when systems fail, even briefly, the emotional reaction can be immediate because financial continuity is closely tied to feelings of stability and control.

A delayed salary payment creates anxiety far beyond the transaction itself. A blocked account can trigger panic because individuals suddenly feel excluded from everyday economic life. Fraud feels personally invasive because financial identity is now deeply connected to digital identity.

Modern banking safety therefore goes beyond technical security. Customers judge it emotionally through questions like: can I still access my money? Is the institution still in control? Can someone help if systems fail? Will the bank resolve this fairly?

Different societies interpret financial safety differently. In stable economies with mature infrastructure, customers often assume digital reliability automatically, which is why major outages trigger strong reactions when they occur. In countries shaped by economic instability or weak banking systems, trust may coexist with greater awareness of fragility. Across emerging markets, mobile banking has expanded access dramatically, but confidence still depends heavily on practical reliability because digital finance supports essential daily activity.

Cybercrime has intensified these concerns. Fraud increasingly targets behaviour, identity, and trust rather than purely technical weaknesses. Customers must constantly manage passwords, verify activity, and protect their digital identities. That creates a subtle shift: people are now expected to participate actively in maintaining their own financial security, which can generate fatigue alongside genuine risk.

AI adds another layer of complexity. Automated systems can improve fraud prevention and operational resilience, but they can also create unease when decisions happen invisibly without clear explanations or meaningful recourse.

This highlights an important reality: people tolerate complexity when they believe institutions remain accountable during uncertainty. Safety depends not only on preventing disruption, but on preserving confidence when disruption occurs. Customers may forgive isolated failures if institutions appear transparent, responsive, and committed to restoring stability. Trust erodes faster when organisations seem distant, procedural, or unable to communicate clearly during stressful moments.

The institutions that maintain long-term trust may not simply be those with the strongest security systems, but those that make customers feel safe inside systems they increasingly cannot see or fully understand.

How Risk Feels Different Across Societies

Risk is often discussed through technical frameworks—probabilities, resilience controls, cybersecurity, and regulation. But people don't experience risk through institutional terminology. They experience it through memory, confidence, fear, and trust.

The emotional meaning of financial risk varies widely across societies depending on history, infrastructure, economic conditions, and collective experience with institutional reliability.

Modern financial systems may use similar technologies globally—AI, digital payments, cloud platforms, biometric authentication—but public confidence in those systems remains deeply shaped by local conditions.

In the UK and Northern Europe, banking exists within relatively stable institutional environments. Customers interact with digital banking confidently during normal conditions, but because continuity is strongly assumed, major disruptions trigger intense public reactions. A prolonged outage quickly becomes a trust issue because reliability is considered part of the institutional contract.

Across continental Europe, concerns around privacy, governance, and accountability strongly shape how digital risk is viewed. Customers may welcome technological progress while still expecting visible safeguards around data use, AI systems, and transparency.

In North America, rapid digital innovation has accelerated adoption, but repeated cyber incidents and data breaches have also increased awareness of vulnerability. Customers experience risk through a mix of technological dependence and concern about systemic exposure.

Singapore and parts of East Asia operate within highly coordinated digital ecosystems where payments, mobility, identity systems, and financial services function with exceptional continuity. Trust remains relatively strong as long as institutional performance continues meeting expectations.

Japan adds another cultural dimension. Stability, procedural discipline, and operational precision carry deep social value, making risk management closely tied to preserving confidence through predictability.

China's deeply integrated digital ecosystems create extraordinary convenience while also increasing dependence on platform continuity. Disruptions in such environments can have broad social and economic consequences.

Across many emerging economies, financial risk is experienced more directly through practical vulnerability. Infrastructure inconsistency, fraud exposure, or currency instability often shape trust more powerfully than abstract operational concepts. In parts of Africa and South Asia, payment outages can have immediate consequences because mobile finance supports everyday survival and commerce. In Latin America, historical memories of inflation and instability still influence public attitudes toward financial systems.

These differences matter because risk management now depends not only on technical resilience, but also on societal confidence. The same cyber incident may trigger very different reactions depending on how societies historically view institutions and financial vulnerability.

AI complicates this further. While customers may value efficiency and security improvements, perceptions of fairness, transparency, and accountability vary significantly across cultures.

The broader insight is simple: risk is never purely technical because trust is never purely rational. Financial systems may become increasingly global and standardised, but perceptions of vulnerability remain deeply local and human.

Being Human in an Age of Algorithmic Risk

Modern banking increasingly operates through systems where algorithms identify and manage risk long before people become aware of it. Fraud detection tools monitor behaviour continuously. Authentication systems analyse devices, locations, and behavioural signals in seconds. Predictive systems scan for cyber threats across massive streams of data moving through interconnected infrastructure.

Operationally, this is a major leap forward. Banks can detect suspicious activity faster, improve resilience dynamically, and manage complexity at scales impossible through human processes alone.

But there's a deeper human reality beneath this sophistication: customers now live inside systems that constantly evaluate them without visible interaction.

In the past, risk decisions were easier to identify. Customers dealt with branch managers, underwriters, or fraud investigators exercising human judgement. Today, algorithms continuously classify behaviour, assign risk scores, and trigger actions invisibly in the background.

Most customers only notice these systems when something interrupts daily life: a payment gets declined while travelling; an account is restricted because of unusual activity; digital onboarding suddenly fails. Customers see the outcome, not the reasoning behind it.

People generally accept automation when decisions feel understandable, fair, and reversible. Anxiety grows when outcomes seem opaque, unpredictable, or impossible to challenge.

Algorithmic risk management now extends beyond fraud prevention. Digital systems increasingly influence lending visibility, identity verification, behavioural trust assessments, and access to financial services. Individuals operate inside environments where digital behaviour constantly shapes institutional judgement, often without fully realising it.

Different societies respond differently. In highly digitised economies like Singapore and parts of East Asia, people may adapt relatively comfortably because integrated digital systems are already part of everyday life. In Europe, stronger sensitivity around privacy and surveillance creates greater concern about invisible behavioural analysis. In North America, rapid AI adoption overlaps with debates around bias, discrimination, and data concentration. Across emerging markets, AI can expand inclusion through alternative data models, but it can also unintentionally exclude people whose economic behaviour falls outside formal digital patterns.

AI intensifies these concerns because modern systems often work probabilistically rather than through fixed rules. Decisions emerge through predictive inference and pattern recognition, making them harder to explain even as they become more powerful.

This creates one of modern banking's central tensions: how can institutions maintain human trust inside increasingly autonomous systems?

The answer may depend on recognising that risk is experienced emotionally, not just technically. People accept strong security and intelligent controls when they believe systems remain transparent, recoverable, and accountable. Trust weakens when customers feel trapped inside automated environments without meaningful explanation or human support.

Being human in an age of algorithmic risk means living inside systems that constantly interpret behaviour and shape access to economic life. The institutions that preserve trust will likely be those that manage digital risk intelligently while still ensuring people feel recognised, protected, and fairly treated.

Why Trust Will Become the Most Important Risk Control

Banks invest heavily in cybersecurity, fraud prevention, operational resilience, AI governance, and regulatory compliance. These capabilities are essential. But another reality is becoming just as important: trust itself is emerging as one of the most critical forms of resilience.

Traditionally, risk management focused on measuring and controlling operational or financial exposure. In modern digital ecosystems, institutions increasingly depend on whether customers continue believing systems remain reliable during uncertainty.

Risk now extends beyond technical failure into the preservation of public confidence.

This matters because digital finance runs largely on invisible trust. Customers don't inspect cloud systems, AI models, or resilience frameworks themselves. Instead, they operate on the assumption that institutions remain competent, accountable, and capable of maintaining continuity during disruption.

Trust acts as a stabilising force that allows complex financial systems to function at scale without constant public fear.

People generally tolerate invisible systems when they believe institutions remain in control. Confidence weakens rapidly when that belief starts to collapse.

A major outage, cyberattack, or fraud wave therefore creates consequences far beyond the technical event itself. Customers begin questioning whether systems are truly safe, whether institutions are being transparent, and whether recovery can still be trusted. The emotional impact of disruption often lasts longer than the operational incident.

That's why trust increasingly functions as risk infrastructure. Institutions that communicate clearly, respond transparently, restore continuity quickly, and visibly support customers during crises tend to recover confidence more effectively, even after serious incidents. Technical failures become trust crises when organisations appear defensive, distant, or emotionally disconnected from customer experience.

Different societies experience this differently. In highly stable banking environments like Northern Europe or Singapore, resilience is assumed as part of the institutional contract, so disruptions provoke strong reactions. In societies shaped by economic instability, trust may remain more conditional and sensitive to signs of fragility. Across emerging markets, confidence often depends heavily on practical reliability and visible institutional responsiveness.

AI makes trust even more important. As systems become more autonomous and less visible, customers increasingly rely on institutional trust rather than personal understanding of how technology works.

People are willing to accept complexity they cannot fully understand if institutions continue appearing fair, transparent, accountable, and human during moments of uncertainty.

This is why future risk management will become increasingly interdisciplinary. Cybersecurity, AI governance, operational resilience, fraud prevention, communications, and customer experience are converging into a single trust architecture.

The institutions that endure may not simply be those with the strongest technology, but those capable of preserving human confidence under pressure. Customers may forgive occasional disruption. They are far less likely to forgive institutions that appear indifferent, opaque, or absent when trust matters most.

In an era of invisible infrastructure and algorithmic dependency, trust may become the most important risk control banks possess.

Reflection

The evolution of risk in retail banking is no longer a technical adjustment; it is a structural reset that demands a deeper, more integrated mindset across the entire institution. This chapter has shown that hybrid banking introduces a level of interdependence that blurs the old boundaries between technology, governance, customer experience, and societal responsibility. Cybersecurity is no longer simply an IT discipline; it is the frontline expression of institutional trust. AI is no longer just an analytical tool; it is a moral and regulatory obligation that determines fairness and inclusion. Vendor relationships are no longer transactional; they shape the bank's operational resilience. Climate volatility is not an external variable; it directly influences household stability, collateral reliability, and long-term credit performance. And reputational conduct is no longer about communications; it is the behavioural signature of the entire hybrid operating environment.

The strength of a bank's risk architecture becomes most visible during disruption, when systems, decisions, and communication are tested simultaneously.

A critical insight emerging across all pillars is that modern risk cannot be managed only through controls—it must be designed into the architecture of the bank. Hybrid institutions must operate with continuous visibility: real-time monitoring of systems, constant evaluation of third-party performance, adaptive AI oversight, climate-aware decision models, and a reputation strategy that anticipates how customers interpret digital interactions. Risk becomes a living capability, shaped by the institution's ability to sense, respond, learn, and correct at speed.

Equally important is the shift from departmental ownership to shared accountability. Cyber teams, data scientists, frontline employees, product owners, compliance officers, and board members must operate with a unified understanding of systemic risk. This collective discipline transforms risk from a back-office concern into a strategic leadership function—integral to trust, competitiveness, and long-term institutional resilience.

Resilience is not created by individual controls but by the coherence of the entire system working together under pressure.

The chapter concludes that the future of risk is not about predicting every threat but about building an operating model capable of adapting to any threat. Hybrid banks that internalise this principle will not only withstand volatility; they will emerge as trusted financial institutions for the next generation.

Framework

Context

Retail banking has always operated on a foundation of risk management, but the contours of that foundation have changed dramatically. The hybrid era has dissolved the clear boundaries that once separated internal systems from external environments, physical processes from digital flows, and institutional responsibilities from operating environment dependencies. A retail bank today is not a standalone organisation; it is a distributed architecture of cloud services, partner platforms, API pathways, automated decision engines, mobile interfaces, and physical branches. This interconnected reality has expanded the risk surface exponentially. Vulnerabilities now emerge from multiple directions at once: cyber intrusions, algorithmic errors, data leakage, climate extremes, operational disruptions, and sudden shifts in public sentiment. The traditional three-lines-of-defence model, while still relevant, no longer captures the dynamic nature of these threats. Risk has shifted from being a controlled function to becoming a living system that touches every part of the institution.

While the structural shift in risk is widely recognised, execution maturity varies significantly across institutions. Many banks demonstrate strong policy frameworks but face inconsistency in implementation across technology, operations, and frontline environments.

In this new environment, the speed and transparency of digital interactions have elevated customer expectations and sharpened reputational exposure. A service disruption that once remained local now becomes instantly visible across online channels. A flawed algorithm can marginalise entire customer segments before the issue is detected. A data breach, even if contained, can undermine trust across demographics and geographies. Hybrid delivery also introduces new asymmetries: while digital channels increase convenience, they also concentrate risk in underlying infrastructure that may not be under the bank's direct ownership or control. Cloud outages, vendor failures, and fintech integrations can disrupt core operations in ways that traditional business-continuity plans were never designed to handle. This chapter highlights that institutional resilience must now account for this complex risk mesh—one where dependency risk, data risk, and trust risk are intertwined.

Customers experience risk as a single institutional behaviour. They do not distinguish between cyber failure, operational disruption, or vendor breakdown. Consistency across these domains therefore becomes central to maintaining confidence.

Regulators across the world are responding to these structural shifts with new expectations. Supervisory focus is widening beyond compliance processes to include operational resilience, model governance, climate-adjusted risk, third-party oversight, and systemic transparency. Frameworks emerging from the UK, EU, Singapore, and Australia reflect a shared understanding: retail banks must demonstrate the ability to withstand disruptions, recover quickly, and maintain customer confidence regardless of where the failure originates. This regulatory recalibration signals a move toward architecture-level scrutiny. Boards and executive teams are expected to understand technology pathways, assess concentration risks, evaluate vendor dependencies, and ensure that AI systems operate with fairness and integrity. Risk is no longer a specialist conversation; it is a leadership obligation that shapes strategy, culture, and organisational identity.

The context also recognises that risks do not operate independently. A cyber incident can escalate into a reputational crisis; a climate event can affect household incomes and portfolio quality; a third-party system failure can erode trust in services that customers perceive as the bank's responsibility. These interconnected pathways require a shift from siloed risk categories to a holistic view of institutional fragility. Hybrid banks must design for continuity across digital, physical, and operating environment layers, recognising that customer expectations of safety, fairness, and reliability remain constant even when delivery models change. The chapter thus emphasises that risk intelligence must be embedded into the everyday architecture of retail banking: this includes identity systems built for resilience, AI governed with accountability, vendor networks monitored continuously, climate risks integrated into credit and portfolio thinking, and conduct standards reflecting the realities of digital engagement.

Retail banking is now judged not only by its profitability but by its integrity—by how well it protects customers, anticipates disruptions, and strengthens societal trust. The chapter positions risk as a forward-looking capability that determines whether institutions can sustain relevance in a world where shocks are more frequent, expectations are higher, and systems are deeply interdependent.

Cyber Integrity

Hybrid banking demands strong cyber foundations that remain reliable under high transaction volumes, complex integrations, and evolving threat patterns. Cyber integrity requires multi-layered controls for authentication,

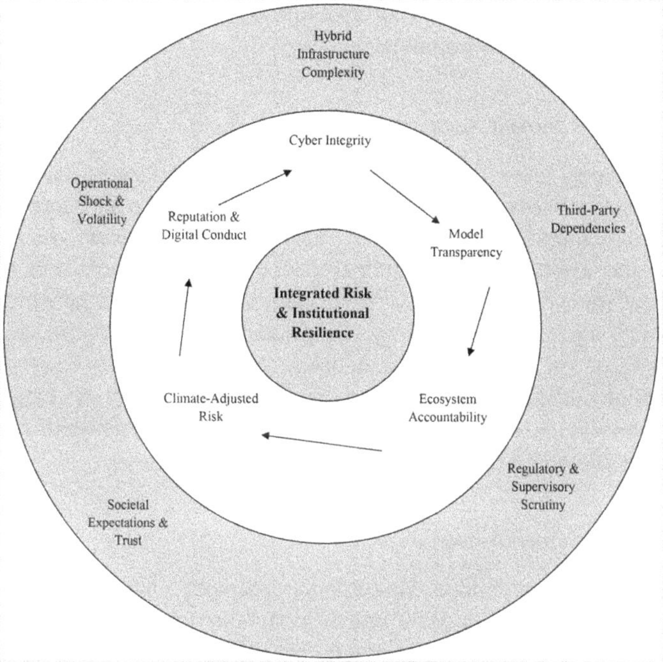

Figure 7.1 Risk and Resilience Architecture for Hybrid Banking

encryption, network segmentation, and real-time monitoring, ensuring that digital channels, cloud platforms, and interconnected systems work securely at scale. Institutions must anticipate ransomware, coordinated fraud, and API-level attacks, embedding resilience into architecture rather than relying on perimeter defence. When cyber integrity is weak, operational disruption, reputational damage, and regulatory exposure escalate simultaneously. A stable risk architecture begins with secure digital infrastructure that protects data, identity, and core services.

Model Transparency

AI-driven systems increasingly influence risk classification, fraud detection, decision automation, and customer interactions. Model transparency ensures that these systems remain explainable, testable, and accountable, reducing the risk of bias, misclassification, or opaque decision flows. Clear documentation, independent validation, and structured governance allow institutions to understand how models behave across diverse customer groups and market conditions. When predictive systems are transparent, banks can manage regulatory expectations, strengthen fairness, and calibrate decisions with precision. Transparency therefore becomes essential for institutional credibility and operational reliability in hybrid environments.

Operating Environment Accountability

Hybrid banking relies on cloud providers, fintech partners, payment networks, data processors, cybersecurity vendors, and cross-border service operators. Operating environment accountability extends governance beyond the institution, ensuring that resilience, compliance, and security standards apply consistently across all partners. This anchor demands clear contractual rights, shared testing, coordinated incident response, and real-time oversight of high-risk dependencies. Weakness in any external node can disrupt customer journeys, compromise data integrity, or trigger systemic instability. A resilient architecture requires a unified governance model that spans the entire operating environment.

Climate–Operational Convergence

Climate-related disruptions increasingly intersect with operational risk, affecting credit portfolios, local branch continuity, supply chains, and customer vulnerability. Climate–operational convergence recognises that extreme weather, insurance gaps, and environmental degradation now influence financial stability. This anchor emphasises the need for climate-adjusted stress testing, geographic exposure mapping, and integration of climate intelligence into retail decision-making. By embedding environmental variables into operational resilience planning, institutions can anticipate disruptions, support vulnerable communities, and safeguard long-term financial viability.

Cultural Resilience

Long-term stability depends on leadership culture, organisational behaviour, and the capacity of staff to respond effectively in moments of stress. Cultural resilience requires institutions to build risk awareness, ethical decision-making, transparent communication, and disciplined escalation practices. Strong cultures support early detection of weak signals, encourage responsible use of data and technology, and maintain service integrity across hybrid channels. When the leadership models accountability and trust, institutions are better equipped to navigate crises and sustain resilience during periods of uncertainty.

Purpose of the Framework

This framework establishes the structural foundation for modern risk and resilience in hybrid banking. It demonstrates that risk cannot be managed through compliance routines alone; it must be engineered into systems, decisions, partnerships, and organisational behaviour. By integrating cybersecurity, predictive analytics, climate intelligence, cultural strength, and operating environment governance, the model provides leaders with a clear architecture for diagnosing vulnerabilities and designing long-term resilience. It offers a practical reference point for boards, regulators, and executive teams seeking to protect institutional stability, support customer trust, and prepare for an increasingly complex operating environment.

Each component of the framework must translate into observable outcomes, including stability, fairness, transparency, and sustained customer confidence.

Table 7.1 Checklist: Hybrid Risk Architecture Readiness

1	Cyber Integrity Are security controls embedded across all systems, channels, and integrations—not treated as perimeter defence?
2	Real-Time Monitoring Do we operate continuous visibility across systems, transactions, and external dependencies?
3	AI Governance Are AI models explainable, monitored for bias, and governed with clear accountability?
4	Model Drift Control Do we actively detect and correct changes in model behaviour over time?
5	Third-Party Oversight Are vendors monitored continuously with real-time risk intelligence—not periodic reviews?
6	Concentration Risk Awareness Do we understand and actively manage dependency on critical providers (cloud, payments, APIs)?
7	Climate Risk Integration Is climate exposure embedded into credit, portfolio, and customer-risk decisioning?
8	Operational Resilience Can we maintain continuity during cyber events, system failures, or vendor disruptions?
9	Digital Conduct Discipline Are customer-facing decisions transparent, fair, and clearly communicated across all channels?
10	Unified Risk Ownership Is risk treated as a shared leadership responsibility across the institution—not a siloed function?

Table 7.2 Template: Risk And Resilience Architecture Mapping

No.	*Cyber Architecture*	*Fragmented controls across systems*	*Exposure to multi-channel attacks*	*Integrated zero-trust, end-to-end security*	CIO / CISO
1	Monitoring and Visibility	Periodic reporting	Delayed risk detection	Real-time monitoring and alerts	CRO / CIO
2	AI Model Governance	Limited transparency	Bias, opacity, regulatory risk	Explainable, audited, continuously monitored models	CRO / Data Head
3	Model Lifecycle Control	Static deployment	Model drift and misalignment	Continuous validation and recalibration	CRO
4	Vendor Risk Management	Annual/periodic reviews	Hidden dependencies and failures	Continuous, intelligence-led oversight	COO / CRO
5	Concentration Risk	Unmapped dependencies	Systemic disruption exposure	Diversified, stress-tested provider ecosystem	Strategy / CRO
6	Climate Risk Integration	Treated as external factor	Mispriced credit and exposure	Embedded climate-adjusted risk models	CRO / Credit Head
7	Operational Resilience	Basic continuity planning	Inability to absorb shocks	Architecture-level resilience design	COO
8	Digital Conduct and Reputation	Reactive issue handling	Rapid trust erosion	Proactive, transparent conduct design	CX / Compliance
9	Risk Governance Model	Function-based ownership	Fragmentation and slow response	Integrated, enterprise-wide risk architecture	Board / CEO
10	Cyber Architecture	Fragmented controls across systems	Exposure to multi-channel attacks	Integrated zero-trust, end-to-end security	CIO / CISO

Bibliography

Accenture (2023). *Research on Cybersecurity and Operational Resilience in Financial Services*. Accenture Financial Services Research.

New York Department of Financial Services (2021). *Research on Algorithmic Decisioning, Explainability and Consumer Fairness in Financial Services*. NYDFS.

Bank for International Settlements (2021). *Principles for Operational Resilience*. BIS.

Deloitte (2023). *Insights on Risk Management and Operational Resilience in Financial Services*. Deloitte Insights.

European Banking Authority (2021). *Guidelines on ICT and Security Risk Management*. EBA.

European Central Bank (2022). *Guide on Climate-Related and Environmental Risks*. ECB.

Financial Stability Board (2023). *Enhancing Third-Party Risk Management and Operational Resilience*. FSB.

Gartner (2023). *Research on Cybersecurity Trends in Hybrid Financial Services Infrastructure*. Gartner Research.

International Monetary Fund (2023). *Research on Climate Risk and Financial Stability in Banking Systems*. IMF.

McKinsey & Company (2023). *Insights on AI, Cybersecurity and Operational Resilience in Banking*. McKinsey Global Banking Practice.

National Institute of Standards and Technology (2023). *Artificial Intelligence Risk Management Framework (AI RMF 1.0)*. U.S. Department of Commerce.

National Institute of Standards and Technology (2024). *Cybersecurity Framework (CSF 2.0)*. U.S. Department of Commerce.

New York Department of Financial Services (2021). *Research on Algorithmic Decisioning, Explainability and Consumer Fairness in Financial Services*. NYDFS.

Organisation for Economic Co-operation and Development (2023). *Digital Financial Services, AI Governance and Consumer Protection*. OECD Publishing.

PwC (2023). *Research on Third-Party and Concentration Risk in Modern Banking*. PricewaterhouseCoopers.

Singapore Monetary Authority (2022). *Technology Risk Management Guidelines*. MAS.

TSB Bank plc (2019). *Independent Review of the TSB IT Migration Programme*. TSB.

World Economic Forum (2023). *Global Cybersecurity Outlook 2023*. World Economic Forum.

World Economic Forum (2024). *Global Risks Report 2024*. World Economic Forum.

8 Customer Inclusion

Context

Hybrid banking has created powerful new possibilities for reach, speed, and efficiency. Customers can open accounts from home, move money instantly, check balances at any time, and access services without travelling to a branch. At the same time, the shift to digital has exposed a difficult reality: a significant share of the population still struggles with access, confidence, or suitability. Older customers may be uncomfortable with apps and scared of fraud. People with disabilities often face interfaces and branches that are not designed for their needs. Women and other groups can be constrained by income patterns, social norms, or safety concerns. Many people across income levels still prefer to talk to another human being before making important financial decisions.

Despite progress in digital adoption, inclusion outcomes remain uneven across institutions. Many banks demonstrate strong intent but lack consistent execution across channels, products, and frontline environments.

When banks design primarily for the "average digital customer", these realities are easy to overlook. Internal metrics tend to celebrate adoption rates and transaction volumes rather than ask who is not using a service and why. Product design may assume stable incomes, good connectivity, and high literacy. Risk models may penalise those with irregular cash flows or no digital footprint. Contact-centre journeys may require long waits and complex menu navigation that are difficult for older, anxious, or vulnerable customers. The result is a silent form of exclusion: people technically have access to banking, but they cannot use it comfortably, safely, or with a sense of control.

Inclusion must be measured through observable outcomes, including usage patterns, drop-off rates, complaint themes, and customer confidence indicators across segments.

At the same time, regulators and policymakers are bringing inclusion into the mainstream of supervisory agendas. Central banks, financial-conduct authorities, and development agencies are all asking how banks support vulnerable customers, how they protect those at risk of digital exclusion, and how they design for fair outcomes. In parallel, civil-society organisations and consumer groups are highlighting practical barriers that traditional metrics overlook: the difficulty of remembering passwords,

DOI: 10.4324/9781042021765-9

the stress of dealing with chatbots, the fear of making a mistake online, or the absence of local help when something goes wrong. These concerns are no longer reputational only; they translate into regulatory expectations and strategic risk.

Inclusion directly shapes institutional trust. Where customers feel excluded, confused, or unsupported, confidence erodes regardless of product availability.

Global practice shows that inclusive banking is not achieved through a single flagship initiative. It is built through hundreds of design decisions across channels, products, language, staffing, training, and local partnerships. Some institutions are experimenting with ageing-friendly app modes, disability-accessible branches, women-focused advisory programmes, and agent networks embedded in trusted community settings. Others are using behavioural insights to simplify choices, reduce mistakes, and support better financial habits without being manipulative. The common pattern is intentionality: inclusion does not happen by default. The purpose of this chapter is to provide a structured lens—customer inclusion—that helps boards, executives, and operational teams reframe inclusion from a set of projects into a core element of institutional architecture.

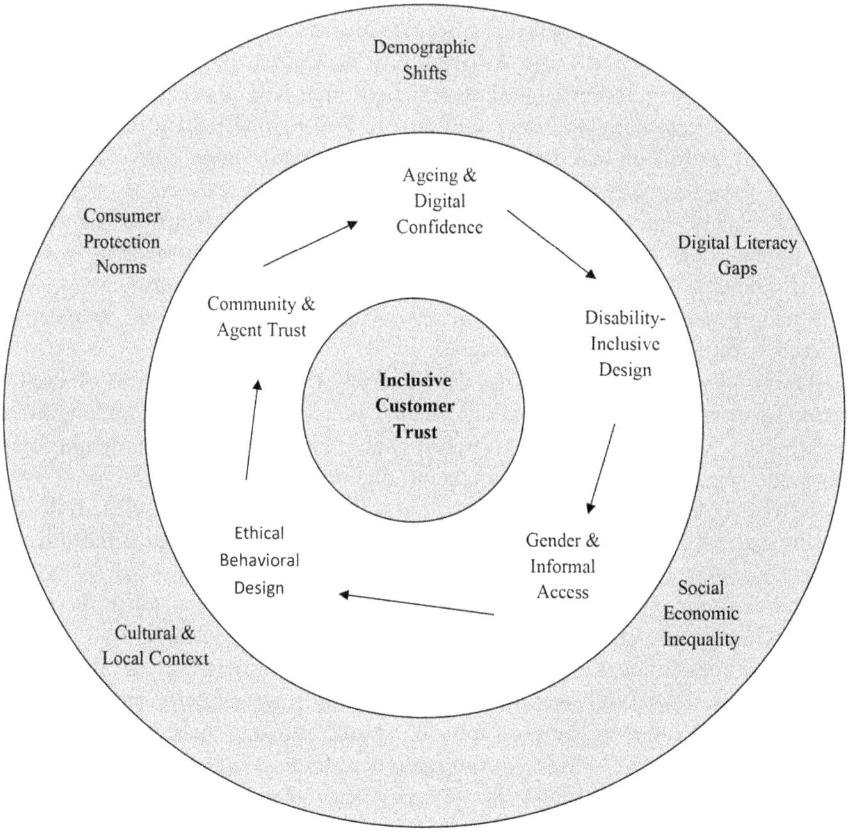

Figure 8.1 Inclusive Customer Trust

Ageing Populations and Digital Access

Ageing populations are reshaping the foundations of retail banking, not only because older customers hold a significant share of deposits and long-term savings, but because their behavioural relationship with banking is fundamentally different from that of younger generations. Many older adults approach digital systems with caution, shaped by concerns about fraud, worries about making irreversible mistakes, and a lifetime of relying on branches, paper trails, and human reassurance. The complexity of modern authentication—one-time passwords, biometric prompts, device switching, app updates, and layered security messages—can create confusion and anxiety rather than empowerment. Hybrid banks must recognise that digital access for older adults is not merely a matter of training; it requires thoughtful design that reduces cognitive load, supports slower decision rhythms, and offers help that feels respectful rather than rushed. Ageing-friendly attributes like simplicity modes, text size options, transaction confirmation, and access to human support are critical. The physical branch is also important, but no longer as a transactional channel, more as an advice, digital coaching, and reassurance tool. As Europe, Japan, South Korea, and other parts of Asia and Latin America face an increasingly aged population, the imperative to design digital experiences that are predictable, safe, and emotionally reassuring to users will grow. For hybrid institutions, it is no longer a question of whether older adults will engage with digital technologies, as many already are. Rather, it is whether they can do so with confidence, clarity, and a sense of partnership. Financial institutions that design for ageing users demonstrate dignity, empathy, and commitment to societal trust. They thereby enhance their own relevance as institutions.

Ageing-inclusive design must preserve dignity, ensuring that support is offered without reducing independence.

Ageing customers often face a dual barrier: the rapid evolution of digital banking interfaces and the gradual decline in physical, sensory, or cognitive capabilities that naturally accompany age. This creates a widening gap between the design speed of financial technology and the everyday lived experience of older adults. Many digital journeys assume quick reflexes, strong eyesight, confident navigation, and the ability to manage simultaneous tasks—such as reading an SMS code while switching screens—all of which can be challenging for senior customers. Hybrid institutions must recognise that inclusive service begins with predictable, forgiving design: fewer steps, slower timeouts, clearer error messages, and alternatives to multi-step authentication that still protect security. Equally important is the emotional environment. Older customers often fear being judged, rushed, or dismissed when asking for help, which discourages them from trying digital tools in the first place. Branch staff therefore play a critical role in digital enablement by offering patient, non-technical explanations, hands-on demonstrations, and reassurance that mistakes are normal and recoverable. International evidence from Europe, Japan, and the UK shows that when banks invest in sustained digital coaching—not one-off sessions—adoption rates among older adults increase significantly. Furthermore, a hybrid design must recognise life events that disproportionately affect senior customers, such as bereavement, fraud vulnerability, or limited mobility, and should offer tailored pathways that reduce stress and uncertainty. A bank that understands the rhythms, concerns, and practical realities of ageing not only designs more humane systems but strengthens multi-generational loyalty.

As populations age, hybrid institutions must rethink not only user interfaces but the entire service ecosystem that surrounds older customers. Many seniors rely on blended routines: checking balances on the phone but preferring to resolve issues in a branch, or using an ATM for cash but depending on staff for more complex needs. Banks that force a fully digital transition risk alienating a segment that still values human reassurance as a core part of financial security. This emphasises the importance of multi-pathway design: ensuring that every essential journey—such as resetting a password, disputing a transaction, updating a mandate, or understanding fees—can be completed through digital, assisted-digital, or human-led options without friction or judgement. Empathy is a design principle here, not an afterthought. Seniors often navigate grief, illness, reduced income, and caregiving responsibilities, which can heighten anxiety around money and technology. Hybrid institutions must therefore design processes that slow down at moments of vulnerability and offer more time, clearer explanations, and proactive follow-up. Community partnerships are also part of this picture. Partnerships with libraries, seniors' organisations, healthcare organisations, and municipal governments can extend the reach of digital confidence far beyond the branch walls. Research in the UK, Canada, and Singapore demonstrated that when banks partner with community organisations to deliver sustained digital skills training, their older customers become much more confident and secure. In short, ageing-inclusive design is not an accessibility issue; it's an issue of trust, dignity, and relevance.

Designing hybrid banking for ageing populations requires institutions to move beyond surface-level adjustments and embed accessibility into the deeper architecture of customer journeys. Many older adults experience a combination of cognitive load, reduced dexterity, visual strain, and anxiety around fraud—which means that even simple digital tasks can feel overwhelming without thoughtful support. Banks must therefore design predictable, low-stress pathways that reduce the number of decisions required at each step, offer clear confirmation messages, and minimise the risk of accidental errors. Equally important is the emotional experience: older customers value reassurance, continuity, and a sense that the institution is patient rather than hurried. Successful hybrid models introduce "slow lanes" for guidance at branches, dedicated helpline routes for seniors, and call back systems that eliminate the frustration of waiting on hold. This also highlights the importance of transition design. As institutions digitise more services, they must ensure that older customers are never left behind—offering side-by-side options rather than sudden migration to new systems. Pilot programmes from Europe and East Asia show that when banks run structured transition loops, where seniors can test new features with staff support before they go live, digital confidence increases dramatically. Family-inclusive design is equally powerful: giving customers the option to add trusted delegates, receive shared notifications, or seek help jointly builds a safety net against mistakes and scams. By treating ageing customers as long-term partners rather than late adopters, hybrid banks can preserve intergenerational trust and strengthen the social contract that underpins retail banking.

Supporting ageing customers in a hybrid banking environment requires institutions to recognise that digital adoption is not a single event—it is a gradual journey shaped by confidence, familiarity, and trust. Many older adults engage with digital tools only when a specific need arises, such as checking pension credits or paying a bill, and then disengage until the next necessity. This episodic usage means banks must build systems that are forgiving, simple to restart, and easy to recover when customers forget passwords, misplace devices, or become uncertain about on-screen messages. A well-designed hybrid model anticipates these realities by providing layered entry points: biometric authentication for ease, assisted-digital zones in branches, and step-by-step voice-guided flows for customers who prefer auditory cues. Banks also need to develop fraud prevention journeys that are not only effective but also non-intimidatory, as the fear of being defrauded is one of the biggest inhibitors to digital adoption among the elderly population. Trust is also built when the staff are able to spot vulnerable customers and provide the necessary support without being judgmental or pushy. The successful banks also run multi-touch engagement strategies such as phone walkthroughs and in-branch workshops, as well as collaborating with local community groups to conduct workshops at the customers' homes, rather than relying on one-off training sessions to address the digital divide. Another important factor that the banks should not overlook is the fact that ageing does not happen at the same pace for all people. An active 65-year-old in an urban centre and an 85-year-old in a rural centre would have vastly different digital capabilities and concerns. By developing flexible and human-centred paths that respect the dignity and independence of the elderly, the banks not only reduce the strain on their operations but also become an integral part of the lives of the elderly population, who require stability and security.

For ageing customers, trust in banking is shaped less by the sophistication of digital tools and more by the predictability and emotional comfort that the experience provides. Many seniors approach technology with caution because they fear making irreversible mistakes, such as transferring money to the wrong account or unintentionally approving a fraudulent request. As a result, hybrid institutions must design digital environments that reduce perceived risk at every step. Clear confirmations, visible cancellation options, slow-paced screen transitions, and empathetic language make an enormous difference to customer confidence. Equally important is building "no shame" support pathways, where older adults can ask questions freely without feeling embarrassed or rushed. Branch staff and call-centre teams play a central role here, especially when they are trained to recognise hesitation, confusion, or frustration and respond with patience and clarity. Proactive outreach is another critical component: banks can analyse interaction patterns to identify seniors who suddenly reduce digital usage, exhibit repeated authentication failures, or switch back to branch-only behaviour, signalling potential discomfort or early cognitive decline. In these cases, gentle follow-up through a trusted staff member can rebuild confidence and ensure continued safe access. Designing for ageing populations also means considering physical realities, such as diminished eyesight, slower motor response, and reduced hearing, which require larger touch zones, optional voice prompts, and clear contrast settings. When digital and physical channels work together to compensate for these limitations, seniors experience banking as a supportive, stable system rather than a source of anxiety. Institutions that invest in these thoughtful, anticipatory design choices not only deepen loyalty but also protect some of society's most vulnerable customers, delivering inclusion in its most essential form.

As societies age, hybrid banks must prepare for a future in which a significant share of daily financial activity is conducted by customers who manage multiple health, mobility, and cognitive constraints. Many older adults live alone, depend on carers, or rely on family members for occasional support, creating both privacy concerns and practical challenges in routine banking. With this in mind, institutions can design respectful, secure solutions that allow seniors to retain autonomy while enabling trusted assistance when needed. Features such as tiered account permissions, view-only access for caregivers, controlled transaction limits, and temporary support modes give older customers flexibility without compromising safety. At the branch level, priority seating zones, low-noise service areas, slow-lane counters, and extended appointment durations ensure that seniors can engage without feeling pressured. The sensitivity required for these types of communication channels is just as great as that needed for video banking, with increased font size, slower speech, and the option to replay instructions. The institution also needs to take into consideration the fact that older people are at a higher risk of being taken advantage of financially. Banks can protect their customers in this way through early detection of suspicious behaviour, such as unusual withdrawal patterns, sudden online activity, or repeated requests for OTP. Working with community organisations, elderly organisations, and volunteers in the community helps to create a safety net for older people. In doing this, banks are reaffirming their position as the rock of their customers' lives. The most successful types of hybrid banks will be those that have incorporated the values of dignity, patience, and protection in every interaction with their older customers.

Ageing customers often manage a complex mix of emotional, cognitive, and financial pressures that shape how they interact with banks, and hybrid institutions must recognise these realities with empathy and design maturity. Many seniors worry about making mistakes online, forgetting passwords, or clicking the wrong option, which leads to hesitation or complete avoidance of digital channels. Banks can replace that fear with confidence through structured digital-coaching programmes delivered in branches, community halls, libraries, and senior-care centres. These programmes work best when rooted in repetition and practice rather than one-time demonstrations, giving older adults the time and reassurance they need to absorb new behaviours. Banks can also introduce "safe practice modes" within apps—simulated environments that allow seniors to explore features without the risk of completing a real transaction. At the same time, communication must be redesigned to avoid cognitive overload: plain-language alerts, step-by-step instructions, and calm, unhurried voice prompts help customers feel in control. For those with memory challenges, optional reminders for bill payments, benefit credits, or upcoming maturities provide stability and reduce anxiety. Hybrid institutions should also recognise the emotional dimension of ageing: many seniors value routine, personal relationships, and a sense of being known by their bank. Scheduled check-ins, named relationship contacts, and the ability to speak to familiar staff—whether in the branch or via remote video—reinforce continuity and trust. By creating a service environment that respects ageing as a natural life stage rather than a problem to be solved, banks help older customers participate securely and comfortably in an increasingly digital world.

Populations with ageing also require hybrid banks to rethink risk, security, and fraud-prevention models through a more compassionate and anticipatory lens. Older adults are disproportionately targeted by social-engineering scams, remote-access fraud, and impersonation attempts, often because fraudsters exploit trust, politeness, or confusion during high-pressure moments. Institutions can, however, create protective layers that support seniors without making them feel restricted or monitored. Risk engines can be tuned to recognise unusual behavioural patterns—sudden large transfers, new payees added late at night, or transactions initiated from unfamiliar devices—and prompt the customer with calm, conversational warnings such as "This seems unusual. Are you sure you meant to do this?" rather than alarming red flags. Branch teams and call-centre staff must be trained to detect subtle signs of coercion, fear, or hesitation, enabling early intervention before losses occur. At the same time, communication campaigns designed for seniors, using language, scenarios, and examples that resonate with them, also contribute to this. Family-assisted banking, which allows users to nominate a supporter with restricted visibility but no transactional authority, is another approach that strikes a balance. For seniors who prefer voice-based interactions, voice biometric authentication can be used to provide an added layer of security without requiring an additional password. Perhaps more important is that the bank maintains dignity while serving this customer segment. There should be no assumption of risk on the basis of age. The approach to risk management should be behavioural, not demographic. The hybrid bank is able to provide an environment that is secure enough for seniors to feel comfortable participating in digital as well as physical channels.

A final dimension of inclusion for ageing populations is the creation of hybrid service pathways that offer genuine choice, allowing older adults to decide how, where, and when they engage with their bank. This explains why choice architecture is critical: seniors have widely varied preferences, comfort levels, and physical capabilities, and a one-size model inadvertently excludes large segments of this group. Some older customers may rely heavily on branches for reassurance, while others, especially those familiar with smartphones through family support, may prefer simple digital interactions. Banks can support this diversity by offering parallel service modes—fully digital journeys, assisted-digital journeys in branches, voice-led journeys through call centres, and home-visit options for customers with mobility challenges. Each mode must be designed with equal dignity and quality, ensuring that no customer feels pushed toward a channel they are uncomfortable with. Predictable appointment systems, dedicated senior-support queues, visual guidance tools, and simplified digital pathways allow older adults to navigate services at their own pace. Meanwhile, community partnerships—with libraries, senior centres, and local councils—can create safe environments for digital-skill building without pressure. Importantly, hybrid banks must avoid the common pitfall of designing only for "younger digital users" and retrofitting accessibility later; senior-centred inclusion must be embedded from the first line of design. When older adults see that their needs are anticipated, not marginalised, trust deepens and engagement increases. By institutionalising choice and flexibility, hybrid banks build long-term relationships grounded in respect, enabling ageing populations to participate confidently in the financial system.

Senior leadership must maintain clear oversight of ageing-customer outcomes across digital, assisted, and physical channels.

Disability-Inclusive Design

Accessibility is not a feature to be added later: it's a structural commitment embedded into every product, channel, policy, and customer journey from the outset.

Customers with visual impairments need interfaces compatible with screen readers, high-contrast modes, and tactile branch cues. Those with hearing limitations benefit from captioned videos, text-first service pathways, and induction loops at counters. Customers with mobility challenges require barrier-free layouts, lowered kiosks, and digital journeys that don't demand excessive typing or navigation. Cognitive diversity calls for simplified flows, plain-language forms, and optional human support at key decision points. Underpinning all of this is one paramount requirement: dignity. Customers should feel respected and empowered, not required to ask for special accommodation each time they interact with their bank.

The business case is as compelling as the moral imperative. Inclusive design reduces digital drop-off, improves customer confidence, and broadens participation. When institutions design for disability inclusion from the beginning rather than retrofitting it, they create banking environments where all customers can participate fully and independently.

True inclusion requires a unified design system not isolated accessible touchpoints. Fragmentation is one of the biggest barriers: a customer may find the mobile app accessible but struggle with PDF statements, or navigate branch counters comfortably but face incomprehensible digital forms.

Institutions need institution-wide accessibility standards covering typography, colour contrast, alt-text, keyboard navigation, audio description, quiet-service zones, and staff protocols. Crucially, inclusive design must be tested with people who actually live with disabilities rather than relying on internal assumptions. Co-design models, accessibility councils, and periodic audits ensure that lived experience guides design decisions.

Emotional accessibility matters here too—reducing anxiety, creating predictable flows, and providing reassurance during authentication, password resets, and error messages. Many customers with disabilities report that the most stressful moments aren't the transactions themselves but the fear of making a mistake or being rushed. When accessibility becomes part of operating culture rather than a compliance exercise, the bank becomes an institution that welcomes every customer with consistency and respect.

Many banking tasks—filling forms, navigating menus, interpreting alerts—require sustained attention and working memory. For customers who experience dyslexia, ADHD, memory challenges, anxiety, or other neurodivergent conditions, this creates real stress and disengagement.

Plain-language communication, linear task flows, reduced jargon, and visual cues significantly lower the mental effort required for everyday tasks. Optional "guided modes" that break complex actions into smaller steps, adaptive interfaces that slow transitions, and audio explanations all help. Branch environments need quieter waiting areas, clear signage, reduced clutter, and staff trained to support customers without rushing them.

For neurodivergent customers, routine matters profoundly. Changes to app design or authentication processes should never happen without prior notification. Banks that make cognitive accessibility a fundamental design principle prevent abandonment, reduce errors, and allow more customers to manage their finances independently.

Physical accessibility is often approached narrowly as a compliance exercise rather than a holistic design responsibility. Every stage of the branch experience—arrival, movement, interaction, and exit—should be safe, dignified, and predictable.

Accessible branches require ramps, non-slip surfaces, automatic doors, height-adjusted counters, wheelchair-friendly queue systems, and seating layouts with sufficient turning radius and clear sightlines. ATMs and kiosks positioned too high or too deep create unnecessary exclusion. Staff training is critical—

employees must know how to offer assistance respectfully, without assumptions or overstepping personal boundaries, and must understand how different disabilities affect pace, posture, and spatial requirements. Accessibility must also extend to emergency procedures, ensuring evacuation routes and assistance protocols account for customers with hearing, mobility, or sensory challenges.

When physical design is thoughtful and predictable, customers feel welcomed rather than merely tolerated.

Banking environments can unintentionally heighten emotional pressure. Long queues, time-bound interactions, authoritative communication styles, dense forms, and rapid decisions can create fear of making mistakes, being judged, or losing financial control—particularly for customers experiencing anxiety, stress sensitivity, trauma histories, or mental-health conditions.

Institutions must design emotionally safe pathways that allow customers to proceed at their own pace, ask questions without hesitation, and receive support without stigma. In branches, private consultation spaces, calm reassurance, and the ability to pause or revisit decisions make a significant difference. Digital channels can reinforce this through "help me decide" tools, step-by-step visual cues, and easy access to human advisors at any stage. Notification wording must be sensitive—aggressive calls to action erode trust. Major financial events like bereavement, serious illness, or job loss require specific attention, slower pacing, and dedicated hardship pathways.

Emotionally secure environments foster disclosure, lower error rates, and create the confidence needed for full economic participation. This isn't only good practice—it's good business.

As digital channels increasingly serve as the primary entry point for everyday financial activity, inclusive technology must go beyond basic compliance and embrace universal design principles.

Screen-reader compatibility, high-contrast modes, adjustable text sizes, and keyboard-only navigation are essential for customers with visual impairments. Captioned videos, vibration alerts, and sign-language-enabled support assist customers with hearing limitations. Voice-enabled authentication, facial recognition, and touch-free transaction flows reduce physical strain for customers with mobility challenges. AI-based tools—real-time language simplification, predictive text assistance, adaptive screen layouts—are expanding what's possible.

Strong governance must support all of this: continuous accessibility testing, diverse user panels, and rapid remediation systems ensure new product releases don't unintentionally exclude specific groups. Staff must be trained to troubleshoot accessibility features without making customers feel dependent or singled out. Treating accessibility as a design priority rather than a retrofit genuinely broadens participation and ensures that people with disabilities experience the same dignity, autonomy, and safety as every other customer.

Many customers with disabilities encounter barriers not in products but in processes—onboarding, verification, grievance handling, and loan applications, where rigid documentation requirements or inflexible procedures create disproportionate difficulty.

Banks can introduce video-KYC for customers who cannot travel, assisted-digital form completion guided by frontline staff, and simplified authentication for those with cognitive or memory challenges. Grievance channels must offer multiple touchpoints—customers with disabilities often require more time, clearer communication, or non-digital submission formats. Loan and credit processes should allow contextual assessment where income documentation is informal or where a disability affects employment patterns.

Many global banks are now implementing "Accessibility by Default" checklists ensuring all new products and operational changes are assessed from a disability perspective before launch. When inclusivity is embedded into operational processes, customers experience fewer friction points and greater confidence in the institution's intentions. Process inclusion is ultimately a governance requirement, ensuring customers with disabilities are served with dignity, efficiency, and fairness throughout the entire banking relationship.

Disability-inclusive banking requires stronger collaboration between institutions, regulators, technology partners, and disability-rights organisations. Co-design models, customer advisory panels, and structured feedback loops help banks understand real barriers—screen-reader inconsistencies, confusing gesture controls, inaccessible branch layouts, cognitive overload in digital forms—that conventional usability testing often misses.

Partnerships with NGOs and accessibility experts help develop guidelines for ATM placement, branch signage, emergency protocols, and remote-service options. Regulators increasingly encourage industry-wide accessibility standards so that a person with disabilities can move across institutions without relearning entirely different systems. Technology vendors play a critical role in ensuring assistive-technology compatibility is built into core platforms from the beginning, not added later as an optional feature.

These partnerships improve product quality, reduce exclusion risk, and build genuine trust. Customers with disabilities gain confidence when they see that their needs are understood, respected, and reflected in the services offered.

Accessibility failures represent institutional gaps, not customer limitations. Boards must ensure that accessibility standards are embedded across all customer journeys and continuously monitored.

A fully disability-inclusive bank isn't simply one that meets regulatory requirements or deploys the right technology. It's one that brings together technology and empathy, designing systems that are safer, more accessible, and more humane for all users, including those who may be cognitively or emotionally less able due to illness, stress, or digital unfamiliarity. That is the larger mandate of hybrid banking, and disability inclusion sits squarely at its heart.

Gendered Financial Access

Gendered financial access remains one of the most persistent structural barriers in global retail banking, and its causes run deeper than product design or marketing outreach. This pillar examines how social norms, household decision dynamics, informal labour patterns, caregiving roles, and safety concerns fundamentally shape the way women engage with financial services. In many markets, women earn income irregularly, hold fewer formal assets, and face restrictions on mobility that limit their ability to visit branches or complete KYC requirements; in others, cultural expectations reduce confidence in navigating digital channels or seeking advisory support. These barriers are amplified when products are designed around assumptions that reflect male income patterns, documentation norms, or risk profiles. Hybrid banking must therefore adopt an intentional design philosophy that recognises the lived realities of women in different economic and cultural settings. This includes flexible onboarding processes, privacy-sensitive digital journeys, micro-savings and micro-credit pathways tailored to informal earners, and advisory environments that feel safe, respectful, and judgement-free. Evidence from South Asia, Latin America, and Africa shows that women-led agent networks, peer groups, and community anchors significantly increase comfort, uptake, and long-term financial confidence. At the same time, gender inclusion requires institutions to examine internal biases—in credit scoring, data models, frontline behaviour, and product suitability assessments—to prevent unintentional exclusion. By prioritising gendered access as a structural pillar of hybrid architecture, banks strengthen not only inclusion but also portfolio quality, household resilience, and multi-generational customer relationships.

Financial inclusion must enable agency, allowing women to participate independently and securely.

Gender disparities in financial access are often rooted in documentation gaps, limited collateral ownership, and structural constraints that prevent women from meeting traditional underwriting standards. Hybrid institutions can redesign credit pathways to recognise alternative forms of financial identity: informal income patterns, group guarantees, community references, or transaction histories derived from mobile usage. In many regions, women operate home-based enterprises or participate in informal labour networks that generate stable cash flows but leave few formal records; conventional credit-scoring models overlook this economic contribution, creating an artificial perception of higher risk. Forward-looking institutions are now developing inclusive scoring systems that use behavioural signals, savings patterns, utility payments, and micro-transaction data to build a more accurate picture of repayment capacity. At the same time, privacy and dignity should remain central to the gender-inclusive approach—the digital journey should facilitate discreet onboarding, secure authentication, and options that avoid exposing personal circumstances in a shared family environment. Also worth underscoring is the increasing need for advisory models for first-time borrowers, particularly for women who may not have been previously exposed to budgeting tools, loan products, or grievance redressal mechanisms. Cases from East Africa, Bangladesh, and Brazil show that for financial institutions that provide structured financial advisories and product explanations to women borrowers, the performance of the portfolio is better, household stability is improved, and savings behaviour is enhanced. For hybrid banks, the imperative is obvious: credit architectures need to be re-designed to mirror the lived realities of women and not the conventional assumptions made about them. In doing so, they unlock a huge and resilient segment of the population base for themselves and make a meaningful impact on the development landscape.

Gender gaps in financial confidence are often underestimated but play a decisive role in product uptake, digital adoption, and long-term financial behaviour. Many women report lower confidence in navigating financial jargon, comparing products, or using digital interfaces, even when their actual capability is equal to or higher than male counterparts. Hybrid institutions can address this through intentional design: simplified product explanations, transparent fee structures, visual decision aids, and step-by-step digital journeys that reduce anxiety and promote autonomy. Confidence grows when customers feel respected, understood, and empowered—and this is especially true for women who have historically been underserved or excluded from formal financial systems. The importance of safe spaces for financial engagement should also be highlighted. Women-only workshops, community sessions led by female bankers, and peer-learning circles have proven effective in building familiarity with digital tools and enabling informed decision-making. In markets such as India, Kenya, and the Philippines, confidence-building programmes have led to higher usage of savings accounts, micro-insurance products, and digital payments among women who initially perceived banking as intimidating. Beyond customer-facing initiatives, internal culture also matters. When women see themselves represented among frontline staff, branch managers, product designers, and grievance-handling teams, institutional trust deepens. Hybrid banks must therefore integrate confidence-based design into customer journeys and organisational practices—not as special treatment, but as an acknowledgement that confidence is a barrier shaped by social norms rather than capability. By treating confidence as a structural factor, institutions unlock higher engagement, improve financial resilience within households, and strengthen multi-generational customer relationships.

These kinds of security concerns significantly influence how women engage with digital and physical banking channels, and such concerns must be treated as structural design inputs rather than peripheral issues. Many women hesitate to use mobile banking due to fears of data misuse, device theft, social surveillance, or unauthorised access by family members. Others avoid travelling to distant branches or ATMs due to safety concerns, especially in rural or low-lit urban environments. We need to examine how hybrid institutions can respond with thoughtful, dignity-oriented safeguards: privacy-protected login flows, discreet account-balance displays, app-level lock features, geo-safe ATM routing, and time-bound transaction limits that enhance personal security without reducing autonomy. An example to highlight is how several African and South Asian banks have introduced "safe mode" interfaces for women, enabling confidential savings, controlled sharing of financial information, and alerts that flag unusual activity. Physical environments also matter—branches designed with clear sight lines, separate advisory rooms, and women-staffed service counters increase comfort and reduce intimidation. Here we should stress the importance of security extending beyond the technical domain to the cultural domain as well, with the frontline staff being aware of situations wherein the customer may be under social pressure, financial duress, or uncomfortable in mixed gender situations. Through the incorporation of gender-sensitive security principles in the design of the channels, authentication processes, and customer service environments, hybrid banks are thus showing their respect for the reality of women. This not only fosters trust, promotes the adoption of digital channels, and helps in the safe exercise of financial independence, but also creates more secure, more inclusive, more resilient, and more socially aware financial ecosystems.

Women entrepreneurs represent one of the most underserved and highest-potential customer segments in retail banking, yet their financial journeys are frequently constrained by structural barriers that have little to do with capability and everything to do with institutional design. Many women-led micro and small businesses operate in informal ecosystems where revenue is cyclical, documentation is limited, and collateral ownership is restricted due to prevailing social norms. Traditional underwriting models, built around formal income proofs and asset-backed security, systematically disadvantage these entrepreneurs. Hybrid institutions can redesign credit pathways that recognise real economic activity rather than penalise informal patterns. Cash-flow-based lending, household-income assessments, digital-footprint scoring, community references, and flexible instalment structures aligned with business cycles help reduce exclusion without compromising prudence. Advisory support is also important: women entrepreneurs often benefit from dedicated relationship managers, group-based financial literacy sessions, and simplified digital tools that help them separate personal and business cash flows. Examples from East Africa, India, and Latin America show that when banks collaborate with women-led cooperatives, self-help groups, or community networks, repayment performance improves significantly, and financial independence grows. At the same time, safety and privacy considerations must be embedded into digital channels to protect women who manage finances in sensitive household contexts. By treating women entrepreneurs not as a marginal segment but as a strategic growth driver, hybrid banks strengthen inclusion, unlock new portfolio opportunities, and build multi-generational customer loyalty. Institutions that redesign credit architecture with gender reality in mind contribute directly to economic resilience and social progress.

Women's long-term financial security is shaped not only by access to products, but by the design of those products and the institutional assumptions embedded within them. Across many regions, women have fragmented work histories, career breaks due to caregiving, lower average earnings, and reduced access to formal pension schemes. Traditional savings, insurance, and retirement products often fail to accommodate these realities, resulting in lower coverage, inadequate protection, and long-term vulnerability. Hybrid institutions can redesign financial products that reflect women's lived economic patterns rather than expecting women to fit into legacy financial templates. Flexible saving tools with variable contribution schedules, micro-pension products, insurance policies with simplified onboarding, bundled protection plans for informal workers, and family-centric financial planning modules can significantly strengthen women's financial resilience. At the same time, the digital interface also needs to facilitate privacy, simplicity, and trust through explanations, plain language, planning tools, and assisted-digital services in branches to empower women to take up long-term financial decisions without intimidation. There is also evidence from markets such as the UK, Kenya, and India that if retirement and insurance products are specifically targeted at women, their take-up increases, household resilience increases, and trust across generations increases. Banks also gain as long-term savings relationships with women show loyalty and stability in product engagement over long periods. Retail financial institutions can now rethink their products through a gender architecture that combines behavioural, risk, and hybrid delivery to create equitable financial futures and bridge the long-standing structural gap.

Women entrepreneurs is one of the fastest-growing segments in retail and micro-enterprise banking, yet they continue to face structural barriers that limit credit access, business stability, and long-term economic participation. Hybrid institutions can redesign lending pathways that recognise the realities of women-led enterprises, many of which operate in informal settings, rely on cash-flow rather than collateral, and balance business commitments with household responsibilities. Traditional underwriting models often disadvantage women because they rely heavily on documented income, asset ownership, or formal credit history—areas where women, particularly in emerging markets, have historically had limited presence. A more inclusive model incorporates cash-flow analytics, alternative data, behavioural indicators, community-verified profiles, and relationship-based assessments conducted through branches or agent networks. It also requires advisory support: financial-planning assistance, mentorship programmes, risk-awareness workshops, and digital-skills training that help women operate confidently in hybrid environments. Successful case studies from Africa, Southeast Asia, and Latin America demonstrate that when banks blend data-driven insights with human engagement, repayment rates among women entrepreneurs are consistently strong, fraud risks are lower, and customer loyalty is higher. For hybrid institutions, women-focused enterprise banking is not a social initiative; it is a commercially sound growth segment that strengthens community resilience. By designing credit journeys that honour women's realities—stable but undocumented income, shared household responsibilities, limited mobility, and safety concerns—banks can unlock a large, under-served market while advancing inclusive economic development.

Financial confidence is a critical but often overlooked dimension of gendered access, shaping how women perceive risk, engage with products, and make long-term financial decisions. Across many markets, women report lower confidence in navigating digital tools, interpreting financial information, or challenging inappropriate product offerings, even when their actual capability is equal to or higher than male counterparts. Hybrid institutions can close this confidence gap by redesigning customer education, advisory interactions, and digital interfaces through a gender-sensitive lens. Practical interventions include clear product explanations, transparent fee structures, guided onboarding, simplified investment journeys, and human-assisted channels where women can ask questions without judgement. Safety is another major factor: privacy controls, discreet communication options, and fraud-awareness modules tailored to women substantially improve comfort with digital banking. Evidence from South Asia, East Africa, and Latin America shows that when banks invest in confidence-building—through financial-literacy circles, women-led advisory teams, peer networks, and community-based digital demonstrations—product adoption rises sharply, loan performance improves, and multi-generational trust is established. Confidence is not a behavioural nicety; it is a structural enabler of inclusion, determining whether customers feel safe to save, borrow, invest, and seek help when needed. For hybrid banks, closing the confidence gap strengthens portfolio quality, enhances digital adoption, and deepens long-term customer relationships. By treating confidence as a design variable within hybrid architecture, institutions create environments where women can engage fully and independently with financial services, reinforcing inclusion as both a strategic priority and a societal commitment.

Economic agency plays a decisive role in shaping women's access to formal financial systems, and its absence often restricts long-term financial stability. Within this context, uneven labour-force participation, informal income patterns, caregiving responsibilities, and unequal asset ownership create structural barriers that limit women's ability to qualify for loans, accumulate savings, or build credit history. In many markets, women work in sectors where income is irregular, seasonal, or unrecorded, resulting in thin or non-existent financial profiles that algorithmic models struggle to interpret. Hybrid institutions must therefore redesign credit evaluation frameworks to recognise diverse income realities, incorporating community references, transaction behaviour, savings discipline, and ecosystem touchpoints rather than relying solely on traditional documentation. Economic agency also extends to negotiable power within households: women frequently lack autonomy over financial decisions, making product usage and repayment vulnerable to external pressures. Banks can play a role in agency by creating safe spaces for advisory, women-friendly digital wallets, micro-saving platforms, and debt management opportunities that can facilitate independent financial participation for women. Studies conducted in Kenya, Bangladesh, and Brazil indicate that banks that invest in structures that enhance economic agency, such as group lending approaches, micro-enterprise platforms, and cash flow-based credit scoring, can significantly enhance women's repayment capabilities and loyalty to these banks. For hybrid retail banks, enabling economic agency for women is not only a moral imperative but also a market opportunity that can tap into a large and loyal market with high-risk performance and intergenerational influence.

Digital safety has emerged as a critical determinant of women's financial participation, shaping how confidently they use mobile banking, payments, and online advisory services. Safety concerns—ranging from privacy breaches and unauthorised surveillance to online harassment and fraud—disproportionately affect women across markets. Many women hesitate to adopt digital channels because shared devices, unsafe networks, or household oversight expose their financial information to others. In some communities, even the act of downloading a banking app can attract scrutiny, limiting women's autonomy and discouraging independent financial management. Hybrid institutions must address these barriers through safety-first design: discreet login methods, secondary PIN layers, privacy-opting features, gender-sensitive alerts, selective notifications, and secure communication channels that protect confidentiality. Another important aspect to highlight is financial-safety education: teaching women how to recognise scams, protect passwords, navigate consent, and use fraud-response pathways confidently. Evidence from India, Nigeria, and Indonesia shows that when banks deploy women-centric safety programmes, digital adoption rises, abandonment rates fall, and long-term account activity strengthens. Staff training plays an equally important role; frontline teams must be capable of offering judgement-free support, understanding cultural sensitivities, and guiding customers through secure usage patterns. For hybrid banks, building digital safety for women is not an optional enhancement but a structural requirement. It reduces systemic vulnerability, widens digital inclusion, and solidifies the institution's reputation as a responsible, protective service provider. Above all, it ensures that the digital revolution does not widen gender gaps but instead enables every woman to engage with financial systems on her own terms, with confidence and dignity.

Responsibility for safe participation rests with the institution, not with the customer navigating structural constraints.

Behavioural Nudges and Choice Architecture

Hybrid retail banking increasingly relies on behavioural insight to simplify complex decisions for customers, especially those who feel overwhelmed by financial choices or digital interfaces. This section explains how well-designed nudges help customers navigate saving, borrowing, payments, and problem resolution without feeling pressured or judged. Simple interventions—clear defaults, staged prompts, spending summaries, gentle reminders, or structured goal-setting—reduce cognitive load and help customers make decisions that align with their long-term interests. Yet nudges must be grounded in ethics: a responsible institution uses behavioural design to support customers, not to maximise product uptake or obscure true costs. International evidence shows that when nudges are transparent and respectful, repayment patterns improve, fraud exposure declines, and vulnerable customers face fewer moments of panic or confusion. In hybrid environments, choice architecture becomes even more important because digital pathways often operate without human reassurance, while branch or call-centre interactions rely on speed and clarity. This highlights the value of consistent messaging across channels, intuitive sequencing of steps, and "pause-and-review" options that give customers room to think before committing. It also stresses the importance of removing friction that penalises low-confidence users: complex menus, hidden fees, overly technical language, or pathways that push customers toward unwanted products. When behavioural nudges are used with care and integrity, they create a service experience that feels calm, predictable, and respectful. They support customers through emotionally stressful decisions and reinforce the bank's role as a trusted partner rather than a transactional vendor. In an era where attention is fragmented and financial anxiety is widespread, choice architecture becomes a core capability that strengthens inclusion, improves outcomes, and reduces avoidable risk.

Behavioural design must remain transparent, ensuring that customer autonomy is preserved at all times.

Behavioural design becomes particularly powerful when it helps customers overcome moments of hesitation, fear, or confusion that typically lead to financial mistakes. In this context, hybrid institutions can use small, well-timed interventions to support customers at the exact moment they are most vulnerable—such as when they are about to miss a repayment, fall for a phishing attempt, abandon a digital journey, or withdraw savings impulsively. Rather than relying on generic alerts, hybrid-ready banks use data patterns, behavioural cues, and contextual insight to craft personalised prompts that gently guide customers back to a stable decision path. The purpose is not to control behaviour, but to give customers a clearer frame of reference at moments where stress narrows their ability to think rationally. Equally important is the way these nudges are delivered: respectful tone, simple phrases, and non-technical language help customers feel supported rather than scrutinised. It is important to highlight that digital-only nudges must be complemented by human-assisted options—for instance, allowing customers to speak to an advisor quickly when they feel anxious about a transaction or need reassurance before taking a financial step. It is also worth explaining how predictable choice patterns differ across age groups, income segments, and digital comfort levels, making behavioural insight a strategic tool for inclusion. By designing nudges that calm rather than pressure, clarify rather than confuse, and guide rather than direct, banks create decision environments that reduce risk for customers and for the institution. Done responsibly, behavioural architecture becomes a quiet but transformative capability that improves financial resilience, builds confidence in digital channels, and strengthens long-term trust.

Behavioural patterns in retail banking are shaped not only by personal habits but also by the broader emotional context in which decisions are made. Stress, uncertainty, social pressure, and information overload can distort customer choices, particularly for vulnerable groups who may already feel intimidated by financial systems. Hybrid institutions must recognise that customers do not arrive at a decision point with a blank slate; they bring their anxieties, past experiences, cultural cues, and cognitive limitations into every interaction. When a customer faces a long form, a sudden warning message, or an unexpected request for authentication, the emotional response can overshadow logical reasoning and lead to abandonment or errors. Banks can soften these emotional spikes by simplifying pathways, spacing information more gently, and using calm, friendly language at moments where fear tends to rise. Important in these contexts is positive reinforcement, such as recognition of progress or a simple explanation of the need for a process, in reducing cognitive burden and re-establishing a sense of control. For the customer who is uneasy about technology, the behavioural architecture must provide rapid exit routes to human support, prominent "I need help" buttons, and unambiguous routes that avoid humiliation or bewilderment. In hybrid organisations, these behavioural safeguards are just as important as the robustness of the technology or the bank's compliance. When customers feel emotionally secure, they make more confident decisions, use digital channels more consistently, and avoid unnecessary financial stress. In designing a space that acknowledges the importance of emotional reality, banks can enhance inclusion and engender a trust that goes beyond the practicalities of convenience.

This works most effectively when they are embedded into the natural rhythm of a customer's financial life rather than presented as occasional prompts. Given this, banks can use timing, context, and relevance to make nudges meaningful rather than intrusive. A reminder to save, for example, has more impact when sent just after a salary credit rather than at a random point in the month; a prompt to review spending patterns is more helpful when delivered after a major festival, school-fee cycle, or seasonal expense period. This approach respects the customer's lived reality and reduces the sense of being "told what to do". It also highlights how hybrid institutions can use journey mapping to anticipate moments where small interventions can prevent bigger future problems—such as suggesting a repayment plan before a loan instalment is missed, flagging unusual account activity early to prevent fraud shocks, or offering budgeting tools when spending volatility increases. Nudges must remain transparent and non-coercive: customers should always understand why a message has appeared and how it benefits them. In branch settings, advisors can use gentle verbal nudges—simplified explanations, step-by-step cues, and confidence-building dialogue—to complement digital interventions. When digital and human nudges reinforce each other, customers feel supported rather than managed. This alignment of timing, tone, and context transforms nudges from isolated features into a long-term behavioural architecture that helps customers make better decisions, reduces institutional risk, and strengthens the overall inclusion agenda.

Architecture becomes truly powerful when banks design environments that make the better choice the easier choice. Subtle structural decisions influence customer outcomes without restricting freedom. For example, setting sensible defaults—such as automatic savings sweep-ins, safer transfer limits, or pre-selected fraud-alert settings—helps customers who might otherwise struggle with configuration. Choice simplification also plays a major role: when too many options are presented, customers often freeze or choose the quickest path rather than the most suitable one. By reducing cognitive load through clearer menus, consolidated product categories, and plain-language explanations, banks help customers act with confidence instead of confusion. This method is especially relevant to vulnerable customers, who can feel swamped by digital interfaces or pressured into making decisions they do not fully comprehend. In the context of hybrid branches, behavioural design means physical signage of advisory areas, step-by-step guidance through kiosks, staff intervening only when needed, and quiet areas to reduce decisional stress. Good nudges are ethical nudges, encouraging customers towards stability, well-informed decision-making, and long-term security rather than product take-up. The more an institution successfully integrates behavioural design into its digital and physical infrastructure, the more customers learn to manage their finances well over time. This increases household resilience while alleviating operational stress on the bank. The institution becomes not only a source of financial services but a behavioural ally in the customer's financial lives.

Behavioural nudges become even more effective when they are personalised to the customer's financial reality, communication style, and cultural context. Thankfully, banks can use responsible data signals—spending rhythm, income patterns, repayment behaviour, digital fluency, and preferred modes of interaction—to tailor nudges that feel supportive rather than intrusive. A well-timed reminder before a bill is due, or an alert about an unusually high transaction, helps customers avoid fees, prevent fraud, and maintain control. Equally important are "positive friction" techniques: inserting a brief confirmation step before risky actions such as large transfers or high-interest borrowing. These gentle pauses protect customers from impulsive decisions and reduce error-driven grievances. In hybrid environments, personalised nudges also support branch staff, who can view contextual prompts on advisory screens and provide clearer, more empathetic guidance. However, the design of these nudges must remain transparent, with explicit consent and easy opt-out mechanisms to preserve trust. Ethical nudging is not about influencing behaviour covertly—it is about helping customers act in their own long-term interest. When behavioural architecture is aligned with transparency, relevance, and customer agency, it reduces delinquency, strengthens adoption of digital tools, and improves operational resilience. Over time, the institution becomes known not only for efficiency but for steady, human-centred guidance that helps diverse population groups navigate financial complexity with confidence and dignity.

Behavioural design also plays a critical role in supporting vulnerable customers who face cognitive overload, financial stress, or limited digital confidence. To combat these, banks can create calmer, more predictable decision environments by reducing unnecessary choices, simplifying language, and presenting information in digestible steps. Many customers abandon digital journeys not because the task is complex, but because the interface triggers anxiety or confusion. Hybrid institutions can counter this by using progressive disclosure—revealing information gradually rather than overwhelming the user at once—and by integrating reassurance signals such as clear success messages, human-support options, and transparent explanations of fees or consequences. Within physical branches, behavioural design can be used to support customers in advisory interactions with structured prompts that help them articulate their needs, make comparisons, and understand the consequences of their choices without pressure. In the case of financial distress, for example, empathetic nudges that encourage early engagement for those who have made a mistake with their payments or who need to get back on the road to savings can prevent problems from worsening. Crucially, these behavioural interventions should never be used to exploit the biases they target but should always be designed to enhance the customer's ability to make better choices. In all these ways, the argument suggests that the quality of the decision environment is just as important as the question of access in the definition of inclusive banking, and behavioural design is one of the strongest tools that institutions have to achieve it.

Behavioural interventions become especially powerful when they are embedded across both digital and physical channels in a consistent, transparent manner. Accordingly, banks can build integrated behavioural pathways that guide customers through long-term financial habits rather than isolated transactions. Digital channels on the other hand can reinforce saving and budgeting through soft nudges such as automated round-ups, progress visualisations, and personalised reminders that encourage steady behaviour without creating pressure. Branches, in turn, can complement these nudges by offering human conversations that translate complex choices into simple, actionable steps—particularly for customers with low confidence or limited financial literacy. When these two environments work together, customers experience continuity: the advice they receive in person is echoed subtly in the digital journey, reinforcing clarity and reducing cognitive load. This alignment also strengthens trust because customers feel supported rather than pushed. Importantly, the design must respect autonomy. Nudges should offer customers the freedom to opt out, control their settings, and understand why certain prompts appear. Hybrid institutions that strike this balance see higher adoption of savings tools, lower delinquency rates, and improved engagement among vulnerable groups who often fall out of the system due to confusion or fear. By embedding behavioural alignment across channels, banks move from reactive problem-solving to proactive capability-building—helping customers navigate the complexity of modern finance with confidence, stability, and dignity.

Financial decisions often fail not because customers lack intention, but because they face cognitive overload at critical moments of choice. Many customers abandon digital journeys because they encounter too many options, too much text, or unclear instructions. Likewise, in-branch conversations can become overwhelming when financial terms, eligibility criteria, and product rules are delivered too quickly or in excessive detail. However, banks can design hybrid environments that reduce mental effort, simplify comparisons, and support customers through clear, structured decision pathways. Reducing cognitive load requires institutions to break information into digestible steps, use plain language, and present options in formats that make comparisons intuitive rather than stressful. Successful models across the UK, India, and Southeast Asia show how simplified forms, guided screens, progressive disclosure, and visual tools reduce customer anxiety and improve follow-through rates. Reducing cognitive load is especially important for vulnerable groups: older adults, customers with low digital confidence, people under financial stress, and those managing multiple family responsibilities often struggle with complex instructions or decision-heavy environments. Hybrid banks can support these groups by using prompts that highlight the "next best step", providing short summaries before detailed explanations, and offering consistent assistance across digital, phone, and branch channels. Behaviourally aware design ensures customers feel in control rather than overwhelmed. For institutions, the benefits are equally significant: fewer abandoned journeys, fewer errors, improved compliance, and stronger long-term relationships. By consciously removing friction and simplifying tasks, banks create environments that respect how people think, process information, and make choices under pressure. This approach strengthens trust, deepens inclusion, and helps customers make decisions that are sustainable and well understood.

Vulnerable customers often face emotional, cognitive, and practical barriers that make financial decisions particularly difficult, yet guided journeys can offer stability, reassurance, and clarity at moments when people feel least confident. Vulnerability can arise from bereavement, illness, sudden unemployment, debt pressure, domestic instability, or low financial capability. In these situations, customers can feel overwhelmed by paperwork, deadlines, jargon, authentication steps, or the fear of making an irreversible mistake. Guided journeys—whether delivered through a branch advisor, a helpline specialist, or a digital assistant designed with empathy—help break down complex processes into manageable, step-by-step actions. They reassure customers by clarifying what will happen next, what information is required, and what choices they have. The global examples of the UK, Australia, and Singapore demonstrate that banks that design guided journeys for vulnerable customers have fewer drop-offs, higher satisfaction, and fewer complaints. For older customers, guided journeys alleviate fears of fraud. For customers in distress, guided journeys provide a sense of safety. For customers who are less digital-savvy, guided journeys alleviate embarrassment. The hybrid model takes this further. The customer can begin a journey online, then move to assisted digital support, and then to a branch when reassurance is needed. The support of bank staff, who are able to communicate empathetically and explain things simply, can make a profound difference to customer outcomes. Guided journeys do not reduce customer independence. They create the conditions in which independence can grow. Guided journeys support vulnerable customers through respectful design. They reinforce the social role of banks. They support customer wellbeing. They build trust that lasts longer than the present moment.

Institutions must ensure that behavioural interventions are governed, monitored, and aligned with fair customer outcomes.

Agent Networks and Community Banking

Local trust is the anchor of every successful agent-network model, and this explains why communities often engage more comfortably with familiar, accessible intermediaries than with distant or impersonal banking channels. In many regions across Africa, India, Indonesia, and Latin America, formal banking infrastructure may exist, but customers hesitate to use it due to language barriers, documentation challenges, cultural norms, or fear of making mistakes in unfamiliar environments. Agents—shopkeepers, community leaders, small business owners, or trained micro-entrepreneurs—bridge this trust gap by offering services in settings that feel familiar and safe. Customers approach them for cash withdrawals, deposits, onboarding, bill payments, grievance support, or digital-tool guidance because the interaction feels human, respectful, and grounded in local understanding. When an elderly customer trusts the neighbourhood agent, or when a migrant worker feels comfortable asking questions without judgement, financial participation becomes possible. This trust is reinforced by continuity; agents are part of the same daily ecosystem as their customers and often share the same lived experiences. For hybrid banks, these trust anchors become strategic assets, extending the institution's reach far beyond its branch network. However, trust does not emerge automatically; it requires rigorous training, oversight, liquidity management, fraud controls, and identity-verification systems to ensure safety and consistency. When trust is broken, community networks collapse quickly; when trust is protected, agents become ambassadors of inclusion, guiding customers confidently into digital systems and formal banking pathways. By recognising the foundational role of local trust, retail institutions can design agent networks that are resilient, respected, and deeply aligned with the communities they serve.

A resilient agent network is built not on scale alone, but on the strength of its governance, standards, and daily operational discipline. This explains why agent banking succeeds only when institutions design clear rules, reliable processes, and strong accountability systems that ensure consistency across thousands of decentralised touchpoints. An agent may operate from a small shop or community centre, but the standards guiding that agent must match those of a formal branch: secure identity verification, accurate record-keeping, transparent pricing, and strict protocols for handling cash and sensitive customer data. Without these controls, even a single weak link can create fraud risks, customer dissatisfaction, or regulatory breaches that undermine the entire network. Leading global institutions therefore invest in structured certification programmes, continuous training modules, remote-monitoring dashboards, and periodic on-site audits to ensure agents meet service expectations. Liquidity management is another critical component; agents must have predictable cash flows and settlement mechanisms to avoid service disruptions. This not only increases the grip of the organisation over the employees through enhanced control over their activities in the field but also helps in tracking every transaction in real-time, geo-tagging, biometric identification, and sending alerts in case of suspicious behaviour. At the same time, the governance structure also needs to take into account the ground reality of the agents. There should be flexibility in escalation procedures and culturally sensitive communication channels, as well as an efficient dispute resolution processes to ensure that the agents do not feel "policed" but rather "governed" in a good sense. In the case of hybrid banks, a well-governed agent network is a source of strength for the organisation, helping them penetrate markets that were previously not served while at the same time being compliant with regulations.

The institution remains accountable for all outcomes delivered through agent networks.

Agent networks succeed not only because they offer convenience, but because they operate through human anchors who hold cultural trust within their communities. Indeed, agents become credible intermediaries precisely because they share the same language, customs, routines, and social environment as the people they serve. In many regions, customers feel more comfortable approaching a familiar local shopkeeper or community representative than walking into a distant bank branch or navigating a digital interface alone. This familiarity reduces fear, lowers perceived risk, and encourages first-time users to engage with formal financial systems. Cultural proximity also improves communication: agents can explain products in simple, locally relevant terms, interpret documentation requirements, support customers with limited literacy, and provide reassurance during complex processes such as onboarding, loan applications, or digital enrolment. At the same time, the human role of agents extends beyond transactions. Agents help customers build confidence in digital tools by demonstrating how to use mobile apps, guiding them through authentication steps, and offering a safe environment to learn without judgment. They also act as informal advisers, identifying vulnerable customers, detecting early signs of financial stress, and directing individuals toward appropriate services or support. In rural or low-income areas, agents often become the face of the bank, shaping perceptions of fairness, reliability, and respect. Because of this influence, institutions must invest in selecting agents carefully, ensuring they represent community values and uphold service ethics. By combining cultural trust with institutional backing, agent networks bridge the emotional and cognitive barriers that traditional banking channels often struggle to overcome. They create a sense of belonging and legitimacy that strengthens financial inclusion in a way technology alone cannot achieve.

Strong governance determines whether an agent network becomes a trusted extension of the bank or a point of vulnerability that undermines customer confidence. As such, hybrid retail institutions must apply clear accountability structures, risk controls, and service standards to every agent touchpoint, ensuring that each transaction reflects institutional integrity. Agents handle activities such as cash-in, cash-out, onboarding support, digital enrolment, and grievance resolution, which makes them critical risk nodes. Without disciplined oversight, challenges such as liquidity shortages, mis-selling, fraud attempts, identity breaches, or inconsistent service behaviours can emerge quickly. Effective governance therefore requires continuous training, transparent incentive systems, unambiguous operational guides, and live monitoring systems that monitor transactions, settlement activities, and consumer complaints. Liquidity management is another key area that the agents need to manage properly. Agents need to have predictable levels of float, timely channels for replenishment, and mechanisms to avoid cash stress from affecting the trust levels in the area. Institutions also need robust authentication systems to ensure that the process of identity verification is done properly. Of key importance is the fact that the service discipline should extend to the customer as well. Agents should have the ability to communicate properly, respect consumer privacy, and be able to break down complex ideas into simple terms for the consumers. Audits, feedback from the consumers, and mystery consumer evaluations help the banks to identify the gaps before they become systemic risks for the bank. When the governance is robust, the agent networks not only serve the purpose of operation but also act as credibility multipliers for the bank. This disciplined backbone makes the networks robust, scalable, and aligned to the long-term goals of the bank.

Community trust is the true engine that powers successful agent networks, and this explains why the strongest inclusion models emerge when local leadership, cultural understanding, and social credibility come together. Agents are often embedded in neighbourhoods where personal familiarity matters more than brand recognition, and their behaviour directly shapes whether customers feel safe engaging with formal banking systems. When agents come from the same community, speak the local language, understand cultural nuances, and share lived experiences, they become bridges that make digital tools less intimidating and formal processes more approachable. This local legitimacy is especially important for first-time users, elderly customers, women with mobility constraints, migrants unfamiliar with documentation, and low-income households that depend on daily liquidity. Strong community-led models also create informal learning spaces where customers receive guidance on digital payments, fraud awareness, savings habits, and grievance escalation. Hybrid banks that nurture these relationships often invest in long-term agent capacity building, leadership development, financial literacy sessions, and community events that reinforce trust. Importantly, community trust must be supported by institutional systems—transparent pricing, clear dispute mechanisms, reliable uptime, and fast issue resolution. When local agents consistently deliver on these expectations, the bank becomes part of the community's fabric, not an external institution. This strengthens resilience during crises, increases adoption of digital channels, and deepens customer loyalty. Ultimately, community leadership transforms agent networks from distribution channels into social infrastructure, enabling hybrid banks to serve remote and underserved populations with dignity, continuity, and cultural relevance.

Liquidity management sits at the heart of every successful agent network, yet it is often the least understood component of last-mile financial delivery. This explains why reliable cash availability is the single biggest determinant of customer trust in community-based models. When customers arrive at an agent location and cannot withdraw money, confidence erodes immediately—not because of the agent, but because the institution appears unreliable. Hybrid banks must therefore treat liquidity forecasting, float limits, digital reconciliation, and emergency replenishment protocols as core operational infrastructure rather than administrative overhead. In high-traffic rural and peri-urban markets across India, Kenya, and Brazil, leading banks use predictive analytics to anticipate cash-in and cash-out patterns, supported by automated alerts and real-time dashboards that help agents manage float proactively. No less important is the design of settlement systems that reduce downtime to a minimum and allow agents to access working capital as easily and securely as possible, often through mobile-linked overdraft facilities or digital top-ups. Here we can also underscore the role of security, from dual-control operations to discreet cash handling and tamper alert mechanisms that safeguard agents and customers. Where liquidity is stable, community networks become solid service anchors. Where it is not, the whole model suffers, regardless of digital capability. For hybrid institutions, the objective is straightforward: to make certain that local cash systems are solid, stable, and intelligently managed. Stable liquidity turns agents into true extensions of the bank, building on trust, extending reach, and generating everyday utility with dignity.

Effective agent networks depend on disciplined training and governance systems that create consistency, reliability, and customer confidence across diverse local contexts. Training must thus go far beyond operational instructions: agents need a structured understanding of product features, onboarding protocols, fraud risks, grievance handling, accessibility norms, and digital-system navigation. In many regions, agents serve as the first and sometimes only point of contact for vulnerable customers, making their competence a direct reflection of the institution's integrity. Banks in Africa, South Asia, and Latin America increasingly use blended training models—digital micro-learning, in-person workshops, practical demonstrations, and periodic refresher modules—to build capability and reduce errors. Governance frameworks are equally essential: clear service standards, mystery-shopping audits, performance dashboards, biometric log-ins, and centralised escalation channels ensure that customer experiences remain predictable, secure, and aligned with regulatory expectations. Quality control mechanisms must be sensitive to local realities; rural agents may require more flexible support, while high-volume urban agents need stronger controls and faster supervision cycles. The importance of values and behaviour should also be underscored: respectful communication, accurate guidance, privacy awareness, and fairness in cash handling build deeper customer trust than technology alone. Where governance is weak, agent networks can drift into inconsistent practices, exposing customers to misinformation or exploitation. Where governance is strong, agents become disciplined extensions of the retail bank—capable, confident, and aligned with institutional purpose. For hybrid institutions, well-trained and well-governed agents form the backbone of inclusive and trustworthy financial systems.

Liquidity management determines whether an agent network can function reliably, particularly in regions where customers depend on agents for cash-in and cash-out services. Operational stability hinges on an agent's ability to maintain adequate float, access replenishment channels, and manage cash securely throughout the day. When agents run out of liquidity, customers experience service failure, travel costs, stress, and sometimes complete exclusion from the financial system. Leading hybrid institutions address this challenge by creating structured liquidity frameworks, including tiered float limits, automated alerts, real-time dashboards, and partnerships with local merchants who serve as cash-rebalancing points. Some markets use mobile treasury vans or designated partner branches for end-of-day balancing, while others rely on digital settlements that reduce the need for physical cash movement. Important in this context are forecasting tools that anticipate peak demand days, seasonal patterns, and community-cash cycles, particularly in rural economies tied to harvest periods or social-protection disbursement dates. Security protocols are equally critical: tamper-proof deposit bags, secure storage, dual-verification logs, and discreet cash-handling practices protect both agents and customers. Liquidity stability also depends on incentives—agents who earn predictable commissions, receive timely settlements, and operate within supportive ecosystems are far more likely to maintain required float. The reliability of cash access reinforces public trust in the banking system, especially among households that operate in mixed cash-digital environments. For hybrid institutions, strong liquidity management transforms agent networks into dependable, resilient extensions of the branch infrastructure, ensuring that inclusion is not disrupted by operational failures.

Training and governance determine whether an agent network delivers safe, consistent, and trustworthy service across diverse communities. Strong agent ecosystems are built on clear operating standards, structured onboarding, and continuous capability development. Agents often serve customers who are first-time users of formal finance, which means even small errors in explanation, documentation, or transaction handling can erode confidence. Leading institutions therefore invest in systematic training that covers digital literacy, product understanding, fraud awareness, grievance handling, and ethical selling. Many banks use blended methods: classroom sessions for foundational skills, on-site coaching for practical reinforcement, and mobile learning modules for ongoing updates. Governance structures complement training by creating clear accountability. These include agent scoring models, routine audits, mystery shopping, complaint-pattern analysis, and periodic certification renewals to ensure that quality does not decline over time. The importance of escalation frameworks ought also to be highlighted: agents must know how to route complex issues, protect vulnerable customers, and manage disputes without improvisation. Robust governance protects both customers and agents through fair contract terms, transparent commission structures, and timely settlement processes. It also creates early-warning systems that flag non-compliance, liquidity risks, or behavioural issues before they turn into systemic failures. When agents are supported with high-quality training and governed through respectful but firm oversight, they act as trusted ambassadors of the institution. For hybrid banks, well-governed agent networks extend reach, uphold brand integrity, and anchor customer inclusion at the last mile.

Community trust is the anchor that determines whether an agent network becomes a transactional convenience or a long-term inclusion engine. Agents succeed not only because they offer proximity, but because they reflect the identity, language, and cultural rhythms of the communities they serve. Customers often approach agents with personal questions, anxieties, and uncertainties they would hesitate to raise in a formal branch. This emotional comfort enables deeper engagement: agents help elderly customers navigate digital steps, reassure first-time users during onboarding, and guide low-income households through product choices they do not fully understand. Over time, the agent becomes a local financial adviser, mediator, and problem-solver—roles that build loyalty far beyond the transaction itself. Agents also play a role in in strengthening community trust by participating in local activities, partnering with schools or cooperatives, participating in digital literacy initiatives, or working with women's or youth collectives. This not only positions the bank as a social entity rather than an institution, but it also shows the importance of the continuity of the relationship between the agent and the bank and the household and the agent. In summary, community trust turns the agent network from a distribution channel into a social infrastructure because, when grounded in local identity and backed by strong institutional systems, the agents become long-term bridges between households and the formal financial system, helping to drive financial inclusion in a manner that digital channels cannot reach.

Community-based delivery models must be supported by strong risk visibility and control frameworks.

Institutional Perspective: A Global Lens on Inclusion, Dignity, and Being Human in Banking

From Access to Belonging—Redefining What Inclusion Means

For years, financial inclusion meant access. Open more accounts, expand payment systems, extend digital services—and inclusion would follow. Governments, regulators, and financial institutions poured resources into infrastructure, account ownership, and digital reach. The results were real: mobile banking swept across Africa and South Asia, digital payments accelerated across multiple continents, agent networks reached remote communities, and millions entered formal banking for the first time.

But a harder truth emerged underneath that progress.

Access doesn't guarantee meaningful participation.

People can own bank accounts and still struggle to use financial systems with any real confidence. Elderly customers may have smartphones and avoid online banking anyway. People with disabilities hit inaccessible interfaces. Women in certain environments face privacy, mobility, or documentation barriers.

Customers under financial stress abandon digital journeys not because they lack access, but because the systems feel emotionally overwhelming.

Exclusion, in other words, is often a design problem—not a distribution problem.

What makes this tricky is that most institutions don't exclude people deliberately. Exclusion creeps in through accumulated assumptions: a mobile app that presumes strong literacy, a fraud process that assumes you have your personal device on hand, a credit model built around formal employment, a branch layout that never considered mobility limitations. Each individually seems like a reasonable design choice. Together, they quietly lock people out.

This is why inclusion has to become part of institutional architecture—not a standalone programme.

Digital transformation intensifies the problem. As banks digitise, efficiency improves—but digital systems naturally reward customers who already have confidence, literacy, stable connectivity, and tech fluency. Everyone else may stay technically "inside" the system while gradually disengaging from it. That's the crucial gap: access means the service exists. Inclusion means someone can use it safely, confidently, and with dignity.

The distinction plays out differently around the world. In Singapore or Northern Europe, headline adoption figures look strong, yet elderly populations, migrants, and digitally anxious customers still experience hidden friction. Across emerging economies, mobile-first growth has been remarkable, but gaps around literacy, language, gender, and disability persist. In Latin America, Africa, and South Asia, informal income structures often don't align with the assumptions baked into traditional underwriting.

Banking doesn't operate in a vacuum. It interacts constantly with ageing populations, inequality, gender norms, disability, migration, cultural trust systems, and education levels. A bank that doesn't understand this isn't just missing a social obligation—it's missing a strategic one.

AI makes the stakes higher still. Algorithms now influence onboarding, fraud detection, credit scoring, and customer prioritisation. Used well, they expand access dramatically. Used carelessly, they scale invisible biases. A model trained on narrow financial patterns may quietly disadvantage informal earners. Automated systems may not recognise cognitive diversity or emotional vulnerability as anything other than suspicious deviation.

The most resilient banks going forward may not be the ones with the largest customer base. They may be the ones that have designed environments where diverse populations can participate without fear, confusion, or humiliation.

The Geography of Exclusion—How Place Shapes Financial Participation

Financial inclusion gets measured in numbers—accounts opened, digital penetration, payment adoption, credit expansion. These metrics matter. But they don't capture how banking actually feels to the people inside it.

People don't experience banking only through availability. They experience it through confidence, respect, independence, and dignity.

A customer who technically has access but feels intimidated by digital processes isn't fully included. An elderly person who avoids online banking out of fraud anxiety isn't fully included. A migrant worker who holds an account but struggles with language barriers and identity verification isn't fully included. Someone who stops contacting their bank entirely because past interactions felt dismissive—they've been lost too, and it may never show up in the data.

This is modern exclusion: not the visible kind, where people lack branches or accounts entirely, but the quiet kind, where people remain connected to systems they no longer trust enough to use.

The consequences compound over time. Customers who feel respected and understood engage more confidently. Those who feel confused, judged, or dependent on others for basic tasks gradually withdraw—even when services remain technically available. Sometimes the outcome isn't formal exclusion. It's silent retreat.

What's at stake isn't just convenience. Banking connects to how people experience their own independence and social standing. The ability to manage money privately, without asking for help, is tied to self-worth in ways that don't appear in any access metric.

Different societies feel this differently. In the UK and Europe, dignity increasingly intersects with ageing, disability, and the anxiety of keeping pace with systems that evolve quickly. Across Asia, strong digital adoption coexists with cultural expectations around respect and relationship continuity—systems that feel impersonal can erode confidence even when they work efficiently. In emerging economies, basic financial inclusion is often inseparable from personal agency and economic mobility.

AI-driven systems create a specific risk here. When institutions optimise heavily for efficiency and standardisation, customers can start feeling processed rather than served. Dignity erodes when explanations become inaccessible, when there's no clear path for recourse, when systems become emotionally cold. People generally accept digital systems when they feel understandable, fair, and recoverable. They disengage when participation starts to feel humiliating.

The future task for retail banking isn't just reaching more people. It's designing systems where people can participate with genuine confidence and self-respect—regardless of age, ability, literacy, income, or familiarity with technology. People remember not just whether they had access, but how they felt while trying to use it.

Vulnerability as a Universal Condition, Not a Minority Experience

Inclusion is often discussed as a universal goal. But what it means—and how it feels—varies enormously across societies.

In digitised economies like Singapore or Northern Europe, inclusion largely means seamless digital participation: mobile ecosystems, biometric authentication, embedded payments, interconnected infrastructure. But even there, beneath strong adoption figures, hidden exclusion persists. Elderly people, migrants, and digitally anxious customers experience friction that aggregate metrics simply don't surface.

In the UK and Europe more broadly, inclusion intersects with ageing, regional inequality, branch closures, disability access, and digital literacy gaps. Customers may have access to sophisticated banking products while still feeling disconnected because systems move too fast or feel too procedural. Public expectations increasingly include fairness, accessibility, and the notion that institutions remain reachable in moments of vulnerability.

In North America, inclusion is tightly bound to credit visibility and financial history. Those with stable employment and established records enjoy considerable convenience. Those with fragmented histories or economic instability hit invisible structural barriers—not through deliberate exclusion, but through systems calibrated around assumptions they don't meet.

Latin America carries a different set of historical associations: economic volatility, institutional instability, deep inequality. Trust isn't assumed there the way it might be elsewhere. Customers evaluate whether institutions are genuinely stable and supportive over time, and informal economic activity is significant enough that traditional banking models often fail to reflect real-life behaviour.

In much of Africa, mobile-first ecosystems filled a gap that conventional banking never reached, enabling millions to participate without ever needing a branch. Inclusion there is practical and community-based—affordability and local usability matter enormously. But challenges around literacy, infrastructure, gender access, and digital safety remain real.

South Asia presents scale, linguistic diversity, and varied digital maturity across regions. Digital identity and mobile banking have expanded reach substantially, yet barriers tied to literacy, gender norms, rural infrastructure, and informality continue to shape who participates and how.

The Gulf adds another layer: rapidly modernising financial systems serving diverse expatriate populations, multilingual communities, and relationship-oriented service cultures. Balancing sophisticated digital infrastructure with genuinely varied demographic realities is itself an inclusion challenge.

These differences matter because trust is shaped locally. An authentication method that feels natural in one country may feel alienating in another. Communication styles, onboarding requirements, branch expectations, and digital behaviour are all shaped by social and historical context. AI doesn't change this—if anything, it amplifies the risk. Systems trained on narrow behavioural assumptions can quietly disadvantage populations whose economic patterns or digital footprints don't match the dominant institutional norm.

The insight is straightforward even if the execution isn't: inclusion can't be standardised globally through technology alone, because human experience isn't standardised globally. Customers carry different histories, anxieties, and expectations into every financial interaction. Institutions that ignore this may expand digital access while widening emotional and behavioural exclusion at the same time.

Dignity, Design, and the Human Cost of Getting It Wrong

Modern banking systems are built around speed, efficiency, and automation. Mobile onboarding, biometric verification, AI-assisted servicing, predictive fraud detection—operationally, these advances are substantial. But underneath the technological progress sits an uncomfortable question: *what happens to people whose lives don't fit the assumptions the system was built around?*

Most financial systems aren't intentionally exclusionary. The problem is subtler. Banking environments are typically designed around assumptions of literacy, digital fluency, stable connectivity, standard income patterns, predictable documentation, and physical ability. Customers who don't match those assumptions remain technically inside the system while experiencing continuous, quiet friction.

That friction adds up. An elderly customer struggles repeatedly with authentication designed for digitally confident users; a visually impaired person navigates an interface that meets formal accessibility standards but is still hard to use independently; someone under cognitive or emotional pressure abandons a financial task because the automated journey is unforgiving; a migrant faces documentation requirements that don't account for the complexity of transnational identity; an informal worker gets flagged as high-risk by an underwriting model built for payslips. In each case, the institution looks operationally successful. The customer quietly adapts—or gives up.

The psychological cost of that adaptation shouldn't be underestimated. Occasional inconvenience is tolerable. What erodes trust is the repeated feeling of not belonging naturally within the system. Customers who consistently need extra effort, external help, or workarounds to manage basic financial tasks can start feeling invisible. That's a form of exclusion, even when access technically remains.

In highly digitised economies, this often surfaces through procedural speed and complexity. In emerging markets, infrastructure, literacy, and informal economic behaviour add further dimensions. In multicultural societies—the UK, Canada, the Gulf—diversity itself is the complicating factor. Standardised journeys unintentionally privilege some groups and create friction for others.

AI escalates all of this. Automated systems increasingly shape onboarding, credit visibility, fraud interpretation, and servicing pathways. If those systems learn from historical data that already reflects social inequality, they may reproduce that inequality at scale while appearing perfectly objective. An irregular income pattern looks like risk. Limited digital history creates verification problems. Emotional distress or cultural communication differences get read as anomalies.

The fundamental mindset shift required is this: instead of asking *how do customers fit the system*, institutions need to ask *how does the system adapt to human difference*. That's not a cosmetic change. It's a different philosophy of banking.

People are shaped by age, ability, language, trauma, culture, education, confidence, and circumstance. Systems designed without recognising that complexity may function efficiently while quietly weakening trust across large parts of society—and the damage may not become visible until the withdrawal is already well underway.

Inclusion as Institutional Responsibility—Building Systems That Serve Everyone

Technology will keep reshaping banking—AI, embedded finance, digital identity, predictive analytics, automated servicing. Efficiency and scale will remain important. But a different reality is sharpening into focus: institutions that can't include society broadly may struggle to sustain trust over time.

Historically, banking trust came from permanence—branch networks, established brands, regulated continuity. That still matters. But increasingly, trust is also shaped by whether people feel able to participate meaningfully in systems that are growing more digital, automated, and complex. Exclusion today is rarely absolute. It's gradual, emotional, and behavioural. Customers stay connected to financial systems while feeling confused, anxious, dependent, or simply not seen. Trust erodes quietly under those conditions.

People engage confidently with systems when they feel recognised, respected, capable, and able to recover when things go wrong. Inclusion is therefore not just a social objective—it's connected directly to institutional legitimacy.

The way this plays out varies. In digitised economies, inclusive institutions will be judged partly on whether they preserve human support and dignity alongside automation. In emerging markets, inclusion remains tied to practical usability, identity access, and economic participation. In multicultural societies, it depends on whether institutions genuinely understand different languages, behaviours, and cultural contexts, not just accommodate them formally.

What's converging globally is a rising expectation: financial systems should adapt to human complexity, not the other way around. AI sharpens this expectation. Customers increasingly sense that invisible systems influence their access to opportunity and financial visibility. They may accept automation operationally while still expecting accountability, fairness, and meaningful human oversight when it matters.

That makes inclusion a governance question as much as a customer experience one. Institutions that overlook hidden exclusion face growing risks—reputational, regulatory, and social. Institutions that design for diversity intentionally tend to build stronger participation, because customers who feel confident and respected engage more consistently, adopt new services more readily, and maintain more stable long-term relationships.

The aging of populations, the complexity of migration, the persistence of economic vulnerability—all of these make this more urgent, not less. Banking touches everyday life in fundamental ways: income, housing, healthcare, education, mobility. Customers who feel excluded from financial systems often experience something deeper than inconvenience. They feel excluded from full participation in society.

The institutions that endure won't necessarily be the ones with the most advanced technology. They'll be the ones that ensure their technology remains navigable across the full diversity of human experience. Speed, intelligence, and automation will keep advancing. But the human expectation—to be treated with dignity, to belong within the system, to participate without fear—doesn't really change.

Ultimately, inclusive institutions may define the future of trust because trust depends on one simple belief: that the system still has a place for you.

Reflection

Customer inclusion is not a peripheral activity for retail banks; it is the backbone of institutional relevance in a society that is ageing, diversifying, and digitally fragmenting at a rapid pace. This chapter shows that inclusion is not a list of programmes but an architecture of thinking—one that requires banks to look beyond channels and products into lived realities, daily behaviours, cultural constraints, and emotional barriers that shape how individuals interact with money. Ageing customers, people with disabilities, women managing complex socio-economic pressures, and individuals navigating behavioural biases all represent segments that traditional banking models have struggled to serve well. Hybrid banking offers a renewed opportunity to correct these gaps, but only if institutions design systems with care, patience, and empathy. The analysis across the five pillars reveals that inclusion is not achieved through one grand intervention; it emerges through hundreds of small structural decisions—interface clarity, language support, guided journeys, safe in-branch environments, gender-sensitive credit approaches, local advisory networks, and behavioural design that reduces complexity rather than increases it. The examples drawn from India, Africa, Latin America, Europe, and Southeast Asia also demonstrate a simple truth: inclusion grows fastest when banks blend institutional capability with community understanding. Agent networks work because they offer human reassurance; accessible design works because it respects dignity; behavioural nudges work because they meet customers where they are; gender-intentional models work because they recognise structural constraints, not just preferences. The reflection therefore brings the chapter to a single conclusion: customer inclusion is the strategic foundation of the future retail institution. Banks that embed inclusion into their architecture—not as CSR, not as outreach, but as operational principle—will build deeper trust, stronger resilience, and multigenerational loyalty in an environment where customers reward institutions that see them, hear them, and design for them.

Framework

Framework Overview

This framework outlines the structural components required to embed customer inclusion within hybrid retail banking. It brings together insights from all five pillars in this chapter to show how demographic shifts, behavioural realities, accessibility needs, gendered constraints, and community-led service models shape financial participation. It explains how institutions can redesign products, channels, support systems, and local ecosystems to ensure equitable access for all customer groups.

The framework positions inclusion as a design principle rather than a social add-on—demonstrating how accessibility, relevance, trust, and human-centred pathways must be engineered into the operating model of the hybrid bank. Each component must translate into measurable outcomes, including access, usability, confidence, and sustained engagement.

Customer Inclusion Architecture

AGEING POPULATIONS AND DIGITAL ACCESS

Hybrid banks must design journeys that meet the needs of older adults who experience usability, cognitive, physical, and security barriers. Age-friendly digital interfaces, assisted-digital support, simplified authentication, and predictable service pathways strengthen confidence and enable safe adoption.

DISABILITY-INCLUSIVE DESIGN

Accessibility must be universal across digital channels, branches, documentation, and service environments. Inclusive design standards—screen-reader compatibility, audio tools, tactile guidance, simplified flows, and trained frontline staff—ensure equitable access for customers with diverse physical, sensory, or cognitive needs.

GENDERED FINANCIAL ACCESS

Women and gender-disadvantaged groups face structural barriers in credit, savings, mobility, and digital adoption. Banks must adopt gender-intentional product design, culturally grounded advisory models, and privacy-respecting digital pathways to expand meaningful participation.

BEHAVIOURAL NUDGES AND CHOICE ARCHITECTURE

Customer behaviour is shaped by cognitive biases and contextual triggers. Applying ethical behavioural design—such as reminders, simplified options, friction-balanced journeys, and goal-based tools—helps customers make confident financial decisions and reduces vulnerability in hybrid environments.

AGENT NETWORKS AND COMMUNITY BANKING

Local agent ecosystems extend the reach of hybrid banking into communities where digital or branch access is limited. Strong governance, training, liquidity management, and culturally grounded service models allow community intermediaries to deliver trust, guidance, and last-mile accessibility.

Purpose of the Framework

This framework shows how inclusion must be engineered, not assumed, within modern retail banking. It demonstrates that equitable access arises from deliberate design choices—across channels, products, branch formats, digital interfaces, behavioural cues, and community partnerships. It gives leaders a clear structure for diagnosing inclusion gaps and building human-centred retail institutions that reflect the needs of diverse populations while strengthening trust, participation, and long-term institutional relevance. The effectiveness of inclusion must be evaluated through real customer experience, not design intent.

Table 8.1 Checklist: Customer Inclusion Architecture Readiness

1	Ageing-Friendly Design Are digital and physical journeys designed for slower pace, clarity, and reassurance for older customers?
2	Multi-Channel Access Equality Can every critical service be completed through digital, assisted, and human channels without disadvantage?
3	Disability Accessibility Standards Are accessibility features (visual, auditory, cognitive, physical) embedded across all channels by default?
4	Cognitive Simplicity Are products, forms, and journeys simplified to reduce confusion, anxiety, and drop-offs?
5	Gender-Inclusive Product Design Do products reflect real income patterns, privacy needs, and mobility constraints faced by women?
6	Behavioural Safety and Ethics Are nudges used to support customers' decisions—not to influence or pressure them?
7	Digital Confidence Support Do customers receive continuous support (not one-time training) to build comfort with digital tools?
8	Community and Agent Trust Layer Are local agents or community channels integrated to support last-mile confidence and access?
9	Safe and Dignified Customer Journeys Do customers feel respected, unhurried, and secure across all interactions?
10	Inclusion as Governance Priority Is inclusion embedded into risk, product, operations, and board-level oversight?

Table 8.2 Template: Customer Inclusion Architecture Mapping

No.	*Ageing Customer Design*	*Standard digital journeys*	*Low confidence, high drop-off among seniors*	*Age-friendly, assisted, and flexible journeys*	CX / COO
1	Channel Accessibility	Digital-first bias	Exclusion of low-confidence users	Equal quality across digital, assisted, and branch channels	COO
2	Disability Inclusion	Partial compliance	Fragmented accessibility	End-to-end inclusive design across channels	CIO / Compliance
3	Cognitive Load Management	Complex interfaces and processes	Customer confusion and abandonment	Simplified, guided, low-friction journeys	Product / CX
4	Gender Inclusion	Neutral product design	Structural exclusion in access and credit	Gender-intentional products and safe digital pathways	Product / Risk
5	Behavioural Design	Basic alerts and prompts	Misaligned or intrusive nudges	Ethical, transparent behavioural support systems	CX / Data
6	Digital Confidence and Literacy	One-time onboarding/training	Low sustained adoption	Continuous coaching and assisted digital support	COO
7	Community and Agent Networks	Limited local engagement	Lack of last-mile trust	Strong agent ecosystem with governance and training	COO
8	Customer Dignity and Experience	Transaction-focused delivery	Stress, anxiety, disengagement	Calm, respectful, human-centred experience design	CX
9	Inclusion Governance	Treated as CSR or compliance	Lack of ownership and accountability	Embedded into strategy, risk, and board oversight	Board / CEO
10	Ageing Customer Design	Standard digital journeys	Low confidence, high drop-off among seniors	Age-friendly, assisted, and flexible journeys	CX / COO

Bibliography

Accenture (2023). *Research on Financial Inclusion and Human-Centred Banking in the Digital Era.* Accenture Financial Services Research.

Asian Development Bank (2022). *Digital Financial Inclusion and Gender Equality in Asia.* ADB.

Bank for International Settlements (2022). *Inclusive Digital Finance and Financial Stability.* BIS.

CGAP (2023). *Research on Customer-Centric Financial Inclusion and Vulnerable Communities.* Consultative Group to Assist the Poor.

European Banking Authority (2022). *Guidelines on Customer Protection, Accessibility and Fair Treatment in Financial Services.* EBA.

Financial Conduct Authority (2021). *Guidance for Firms on the Fair Treatment of Vulnerable Customers.* FCA.

Gartner (2023). *Research on Human-Centred Digital Banking and Customer Accessibility Trends.* Gartner Research.

International Labour Organization (2022). *Gender Gaps in Financial Inclusion and Informal Work Economies.* ILO.

International Monetary Fund (2023). *Research on Financial Inclusion, Digital Access and Economic Participation.* IMF.

McKinsey & Company (2023). *Insights on Inclusive Banking, Human-Centred Design and Digital Participation.* McKinsey Global Banking Practice.

Organisation for Economic Co-operation and Development (2023). *Financial Literacy, Consumer Vulnerability and Digital Inclusion.* OECD Publishing.

Reserve Bank of India (2022). *Financial Inclusion and Customer Protection in a Digital Banking Environment.* RBI.

Singapore Monetary Authority (2022). *Principles for Fair Digital Banking and Customer Accessibility.* MAS.

United Nations Development Programme (2022). *Gender, Digital Inclusion and Financial Participation.* UNDP.

United Nations Department of Economic and Social Affairs (2023). *World Social Report: Ageing, Accessibility and Inclusive Societies.* United Nations.

World Bank (2022). *Global Findex Database 2021: Financial Inclusion, Digital Payments and Resilience in the Age of COVID-19.* World Bank.

World Economic Forum (2023). *Insights on Financial Inclusion in Digital Economies.* World Economic Forum.

World Health Organization (2021). *Global Report on Ageism and Healthy Ageing.* WHO.

9 The Institutional Design Lens

Context

Retail banking is entering a period where technology alone cannot sustain transformation. Institutions that built their operating logic around branches, hierarchical structures, and product silos are now required to deliver seamless experiences across distributed channels, fragmented customer needs, and rapidly evolving regulatory environments. This shift exposes a critical reality: the institution itself must be redesigned. Hybrid models challenge how decisions are made, how accountability is defined, how talent is organised, and how governance frameworks support or constrain innovation. A bank may invest heavily in digital tools, cloud platforms, and automated workflows, but without mature institutional design these investments generate complexity instead of capability. The gap between technological ambition and organisational readiness has become one of the most visible barriers to progress in global retail banking. Across markets, many institutions demonstrate strong strategic intent but uneven execution. The gap between ambition and institutional capability remains one of the most persistent constraints in hybrid transformation.

Across markets, supervisors and policymakers have increasingly linked customer harm, service breakdowns, and strategic failures to weaknesses in governance and internal oversight. These failures rarely emerge from technology alone; they emerge when institutions lack the structures that enable disciplined decision-making, forward-looking risk assessment, and coordinated execution. Many retail banks still operate with legacy processes that reward short-term achievements, prioritise departmental interests, and struggle to adapt to multi-partner ecosystems. In hybrid environments, customer journeys often depend on multiple teams, external vendors, and real-time data flows. When responsibilities are unclear, when committees operate in silos, and when leadership lacks the diversity of perspectives needed to challenge prevailing assumptions, the entire system becomes vulnerable.

The modern institution must therefore be designed with the same precision that is applied to technology architecture. This involves rethinking board composition, strengthening strategic foresight, building multidisciplinary operating models, and nurturing leadership environments where challenge and debate are encouraged rather than suppressed. Technology has expanded the scope of what institutions

DOI: 10.4324/9781042021765-10

can offer, but has also expanded the scope of what they must manage: cyber risks, AI ethics, cross-border data rules, cloud concentration risks, and ecosystem dependencies. These complexities require governance structures capable of understanding and responding to them with speed, clarity, and integrity.

International examples illustrate this point clearly. In the UK and EU, regulatory interventions following conduct scandals, operational outages, and thematic reviews have repeatedly emphasised board capability, culture, and governance maturity as indicators of institutional strength. In Singapore and Australia, supervisors expect banks to demonstrate foresight—not merely to comply with requirements, but to anticipate emerging risks and societal expectations. India's experience with large-scale digital infrastructure has shown the importance of aligning institutional design with public-purpose objectives, ensuring that innovation supports inclusion rather than widening disparities. African markets highlight the need for leadership teams that reflect local realities and understand the constraints of diverse customer segments. Across these examples, one lesson stands out: transformation that ignores internal architecture ultimately undermines itself.

The hybrid era also introduces new types of institutional risk linked to culture, behaviour, and learning. When decision-making is centralised, organisations become slow and reactive. When it is fragmented, customer outcomes become inconsistent. When leadership lacks technological fluency, oversight becomes superficial. When diversity is absent, blind spots widen. When professional standards are weak, misconduct becomes harder to detect and prevent. These risks cannot be addressed through technology upgrades or policy documents alone. They require a deeper commitment to institutional maturity—continuous learning, ethical leadership, transparent communication, and a shared understanding of purpose.

Customer expectations reinforce this need for institutional redesign. Hybrid customers experience banks not as departments but as a single service journey that must remain coherent regardless of platform, geography, or partner. When internal structures fail to support this coherence, trust erodes. A mobile-app failure becomes a governance issue; a delayed complaint becomes a leadership issue; an opaque algorithm becomes a conduct issue. Institutions that recognise this linkage between internal design and external trust are better placed to navigate the pressures of modern retail banking.

Finally, the chapter highlights the growing importance of cross-border regulatory alignment. As retail banks expand through digital services, partnerships, and cloud platforms, they must operate across multiple supervisory regimes—each with its own rules for privacy, resilience, AI oversight, and consumer protection. Institutions that develop coherent regulatory-intelligence capabilities and harmonised internal standards will gain strategic flexibility. Those that rely on localised, fragmented compliance approaches will face escalating operational and reputational risks.

This chapter therefore argues that the future institution is one that is designed deliberately: strong in governance, confident in foresight, modern in operating logic, diverse in leadership, disciplined in standards, and aligned with global regulatory expectations. Without this institutional foundation, hybrid banking becomes unstable, innovation becomes risky, and customer trust becomes fragile. With it, retail banks can transform with clarity, responsibility, and long-term resilience.

Board Design and Strategic Foresight

Boards today sit at the centre of institutions that are far more complex, interconnected, and exposed than anything the traditional banking environment ever demanded. A hybrid retail bank operates across digital channels, physical networks, ecosystem partnerships, outsourced infrastructures, and regulatory regimes that change with increasing speed. In this context, board design cannot remain anchored in legacy expectations of financial oversight alone; it requires a structure that brings together technological fluency, behavioural insight, risk intelligence, and a deep understanding of customer realities. Modern boards must be composed of individuals who can interrogate data-driven decision

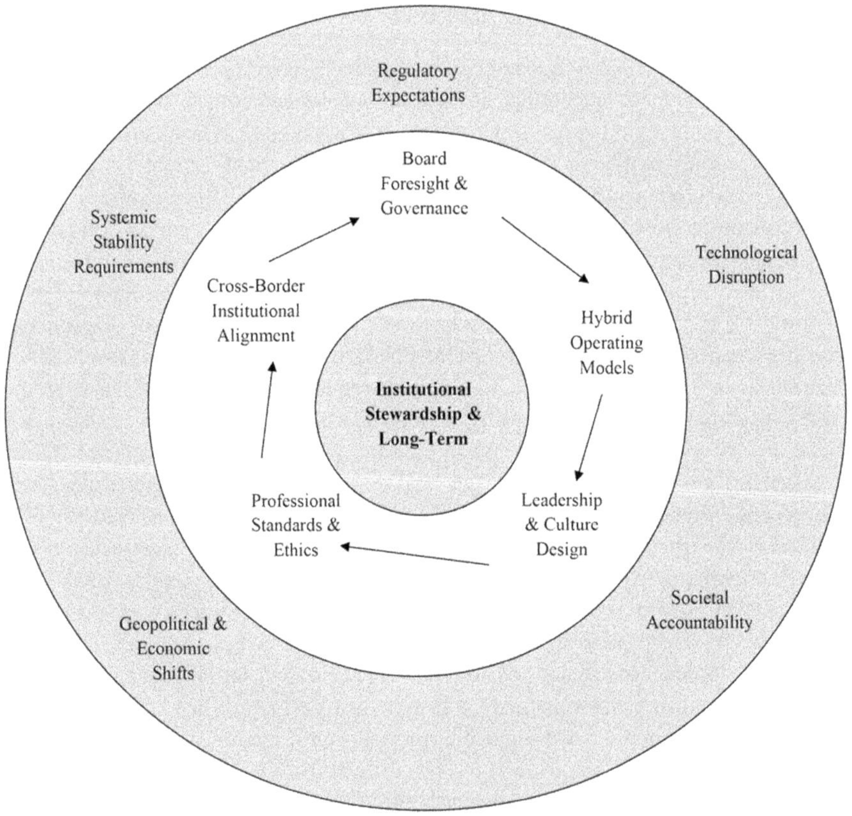

Figure 9.1 Institutional Design Architecture for Hybrid Banking

models, understand the implications of cloud and API architecture, and appreciate how conduct risk manifests in hybrid journeys. Strategic foresight becomes equally important, because institutions that rely on backward-looking indicators struggle to anticipate systemic changes in regulation, demographics, climate exposure, and digital competition. Effective boards maintain disciplined horizon-scanning processes, integrate independent expertise where needed, and challenge management to ensure long-term purpose remains aligned with near-term execution. They understand that transformation is not a project but a continuous redesign of the institution itself, and they provide a stabilising anchor when the organisation moves through periods of uncertainty or rapid change. A well-designed board therefore becomes a structural capability: it shapes organisational culture, strengthens resilience, and ensures that hybrid delivery is supported by thoughtful governance rather than fragmented decision-making. Boards remain ultimately accountable for institutional outcomes, regardless of technological or operational complexity.

In hybrid retail banks, boards must operate with a far stronger grasp of how technology, regulation, and customer expectations intersect to shape institutional stability. Traditional committee structures centred on audit, risk, and remuneration are no longer sufficient when banks depend on cloud platforms, real-time data flows, and third-party ecosystems. This explains why boards must redesign their internal rhythms—meeting agendas, escalation pathways, information dashboards, and oversight routines—to ensure they are receiving timely, relevant, and forward-looking intelligence. Effective boards demand integrated reporting that connects financial outcomes with operational resilience, cyber exposure, customer behaviour, and technology strategy, enabling directors to make decisions with a holistic view of risk. They also prioritise independent challenge by encouraging dissenting views, inviting external experts, and ensuring the chair creates an environment where complex issues can be examined without defensiveness. Strategic foresight becomes part of the board's culture: directors regularly assess emerging regulatory directions, geopolitical dynamics, demographic shifts, and climate-related stresses to anticipate how these external forces will influence business models over time. The most effective boards are those that stay close to institutional purpose while remaining adaptable, balancing prudence with innovation and long-term value with immediate execution. In a hybrid environment where service failures can become public crises within hours, strong board design is what keeps institutions anchored, prepared, and capable of navigating uncertainty with clarity and confidence.

Today boards cannot rely solely on periodic updates or retrospective reporting; they need a continuous, real-time view of how the institution is performing across channels, regions, and risk domains. Boards must demand data that is timely, integrated, and decision-ready, rather than rely on fragmented insights delivered too late to influence outcomes. Modern governance requires dashboards that link technology incidents with customer impacts, financial indicators with operational stress, and regulatory developments with strategic priorities. Directors must be able to see how small failures accumulate into systemic risks, how changes in customer behaviour alter service demand, and how third-party dependencies influence overall resilience. This level of visibility is not merely a technical upgrade—it is a shift in board mindset. Directors need to become fluent in reading operational signals, understanding data-quality issues, and asking questions that go beyond compliance to examine institutional capability. To support this, banks are investing in board education programmes covering cyber risk, AI ethics, cloud governance, digital identity, and cross-border regulation. These structured learning pathways ensure that directors are not dependent solely on management interpretations but can exercise independent judgment grounded in contemporary knowledge. By embedding continuous visibility and strengthening director capability, boards are better positioned to anticipate risks, challenge assumptions, and shape strategies that protect customers, maintain trust, and allow hybrid institutions to adapt confidently to a fast-changing financial environment.

Effective boards in hybrid retail banking must move beyond annual strategy cycles and adopt a dynamic foresight approach that continuously scans for weak signals, structural shifts, and emerging risks. This explains why foresight is not prediction—it is the disciplined practice of preparing the institution for multiple plausible futures. Boards must regularly test how their strategy holds up against changes in customer expectations, geopolitical volatility, climate shocks, regulatory tightening, technology breakthroughs, and disruptions from new market entrants. Scenario planning becomes an essential governance tool: directors must explore what happens if cyber incidents escalate, if climate events reshape local markets, if fintech collaborations fail, or if demographic shifts change product demand. The value is not in selecting the "correct" future, but in strengthening the institution's ability to adapt. This requires boards to integrate foresight into committee agendas, mandate management to run cross-functional stress tests, and ensure that strategy discussions include long-term societal and technological forces rather than short-term financial pressures alone. Boards must also cultivate psychological readiness—the ability to challenge optimistic assumptions, confront uncomfortable possibilities, and make decisions under uncertainty without losing clarity of purpose. Markets such as the UK, Singapore, and the EU increasingly expect boards to demonstrate active foresight in regulatory filings, operational resilience frameworks, and strategic governance reviews. By institutionalising foresight, boards shift from passive oversight to active stewardship, guiding the bank towards a resilient, adaptive, and mission-aligned future in an era where the pace of change is accelerating.

Case Study: Bank of England—Systemic Scenario Planning as Institutional Design

The Bank of England institutionalised long-horizon scenario planning through exercises such as the Biennial Exploratory Scenario (BES) and climate stress testing, embedding foresight directly into governance rather than treating it as an academic exercise. These scenarios are used to test capital resilience, operational continuity, and behavioural responses under multiple plausible futures rather than a single forecast. The approach has reshaped how boards and senior leadership across UK financial institutions engage with uncertainty, shifting governance from reactive oversight to anticipatory stewardship. This case demonstrates that institutional foresight is not limited to banks alone but is a governance capability increasingly expected across systemically important institutions.

A board's ability to provide meaningful oversight depends on the quality, diversity, and readiness of information it receives. This highlights why modern retail-banking boards must redesign their information flows to support sharper, more independent judgment. Traditional board packs are often retrospective, overloaded with operational detail, and disconnected from real-time market signals. In a hybrid environment, this creates blind spots that weaken decision-making. Boards need forward-looking dashboards that integrate customer behaviour trends, cyber-risk indicators, climate-exposure metrics, partner-dependency risks, and early warning insights from frontline teams. They also require clarity on the assumptions behind management recommendations, the trade-offs being made between innovation and resilience, and the alternative options that were considered but not taken. High-quality board information is not about volume; it is about precision, coherence, and relevance. Leading institutions in the UK and EU are introducing structured "insight reports" that combine analytics with strategic interpretation, enabling directors to challenge more effectively and identify systemic risks earlier. This argues that information governance becomes a core pillar of institutional architecture, ensuring that directors are not simply recipients of polished reports but informed custodians of long-term stability. Strengthening information flows also builds trust between boards and executive teams, as decisions are grounded in shared understanding rather than fragmented interpretations. For hybrid banks navigating rapid regulatory, technological, and societal shifts, the discipline of providing clear, anticipatory, and strategically aligned information is essential. It enables boards to maintain oversight with confidence and ensures that decisions reflect both present realities and future possibilities.

Effective board leadership depends not only on individual expertise but on the collective dynamics that shape how directors think, debate, and make decisions. This examines why board culture—often overlooked in governance discussions—is a structural determinant of institutional strength. In many retail banks, boards inherit legacy behaviours: deference to hierarchy, reluctance to challenge management, and a narrow focus on compliance rather than long-term transformation. These patterns become liability risks in a hybrid banking environment where rapid technological change, cyber threats, and shifting customer expectations demand sharper questions and more open debate. Modern boards require cultures that encourage constructive challenge, welcome dissenting views, and reward intellectual curiosity. Chairs play a central role in setting this tone by ensuring balanced participation, inviting diverse perspectives, and creating space for independent thinking. Regulators in the UK, Australia, and Singapore increasingly evaluate board culture during supervisory reviews, recognising that culture shapes accountability as much as formal structures do. A healthy board culture strengthens foresight by enabling directors to explore emerging risks, question optimistic assumptions, and pressure-test strategic options without fear of friction. It also reinforces institutional integrity by ensuring decisions reflect genuine scrutiny rather than procedural approval. As hybrid delivery models widen operational complexity, a strong board culture becomes a competitive advantage: it helps institutions navigate uncertainty with resilience, adapt to market changes more quickly, and maintain public trust through transparent, principled leadership.

Boards that excel in strategic foresight build disciplined mechanisms for learning—not only from internal reports, but from external shifts that reshape the banking landscape. As such, continuous learning is now a structural requirement for board effectiveness. Hybrid banking models evolve quickly, influenced by changes in technology, customer behaviour, regulatory expectations, and global economic conditions. Many institutional failures in recent years were not caused by a lack of information, but by boards that did not adapt their understanding to new realities. Progressive boards therefore invest in structured learning agendas: periodic deep dives on cyber risk, scenario sessions on climate exposure, briefings on demographic change, and external insights from regulators, technologists, and consumer bodies. These inputs help directors recalibrate their mental models, move beyond outdated assumptions, and better anticipate the second-order effects of innovation. It should be emphasised that board learning is not a passive process; it requires intellectual humility, curiosity, and a willingness to examine institutional blind spots. It also requires deliberate design: curated reading lists, external speakers, cross-market visits, and regular refreshers on key risk domains. Regulators are increasingly assessing whether boards demonstrate evidence of continuous learning as part of governance evaluations. For hybrid institutions, where risk and opportunity are tightly interlinked across digital and physical channels, board learning becomes a strategic capability. It strengthens oversight quality, enhances decision-making speed, and prepares institutions to respond confidently to unexpected developments. Ultimately, a learning-oriented board becomes a stabilising force—one that anchors long-term strategy in informed judgment rather than legacy habits.

These cannot exercise effective oversight unless the flow of information they receive is clear, timely, and genuinely decision-enabling. Information architecture has thus become a critical part of board design in hybrid banking institutions. Traditional board packs often overwhelm directors with hundreds of pages of operational detail but provide little insight into underlying risks, emerging patterns, or forward-looking indicators. In a hybrid environment where systems, channels, and partners operate simultaneously, the complexity increases dramatically. Boards require structured dashboards that combine financial metrics with customer-experience signals, risk-intelligence insights, technology-health indicators, vendor performance updates, and early-warning markers across cyber, conduct, and resilience domains. Effective information design filters noise, highlights exceptions, and allows directors to understand where pressure is building in the institution. It ensures that oversight conversations shift from retrospective reporting to anticipatory governance. Information quality, then, is not a reporting problem alone; it is a cultural discipline. Management teams must be willing to surface issues early, acknowledge uncertainties, and present balanced views without defensive framing. Boards, in turn, must demand clarity, ask probing questions, and establish expectations for transparency and accountability. Across global markets, regulators increasingly review board papers to assess whether institutions are equipping directors with appropriate information for sound judgment. For hybrid banks, disciplined information design strengthens institutional integrity by ensuring that directors see the institution as it truly is—not as a filtered or sanitised version. It enables better challenge, sharper decisions, and more resilient long-term strategy.

Today boards must navigate a world where uncertainty is continuous rather than episodic, and this requires a disciplined commitment to strategic foresight built into the rhythm of governance. How boards can operationalise foresight as a structured practice rather than an occasional exercise deserves exploration. Leading institutions, for instance, conduct regular horizon-scanning sessions, where directors review emerging regulatory shifts, geopolitical risks, demographic transitions, climate-related pressures, and technological changes that may shape customer expectations or institutional vulnerabilities. Scenario planning becomes a standing capability: boards test the organisation's readiness under multiple futures, from rapid digital acceleration to supply-chain disruptions, cyber-attacks, or socioeconomic stress in local communities. This forward-looking posture enables directors to identify latent risks before they crystallise and to anticipate strategic inflection points that may require shifts in business models, investment priorities, or leadership competencies. Diverse perspectives in foresight work are also important—a homogeneous board will naturally miss signals that fall outside its shared experience. Boards with gender, cultural, generational, and professional diversity pick up weak signals earlier and ask more penetrating questions. Regulators in the UK, EU, Singapore, and Australia increasingly view foresight capability as a marker of strong governance, especially in hybrid institutions where interdependencies multiply risk. Finally, it ought to be underlined that foresight is not about predicting the future; it is about building institutional posture, agility, and confidence to act decisively amid uncertainty. Boards that embed foresight into governance create institutions that are steadier, more adaptive, and better aligned with long-term societal and financial stability.

Boards must also ensure that foresight translates into disciplined strategic execution, supported by clear accountability and regular performance dialogue with the executive team. Strong boards, in these circumstances, close the gap between long-horizon thinking and day-to-day operational reality. Effective boards do not stop at scenario discussions; they require management to demonstrate how strategic risks, technology transitions, regulatory expectations, and customer-behaviour shifts are being translated into concrete plans, resourcing decisions, and measurable outcomes. This includes reviewing investment cases for digital infrastructure, monitoring the progress of hybrid-delivery initiatives, and ensuring that operating models evolve in line with customer needs and systemic pressures. Boards must also scrutinise culture, leadership effectiveness, and succession planning, all of which directly influence institutional resilience. Strong governance creates clear lines of escalation, enabling emerging issues to reach the board early rather than after they become failures visible to regulators or the public. This further underscores the importance of continuous board education: directors must stay current with developments in cyber risk, AI governance, climate exposure, data ethics, and cross-border regulatory trends. This learning mindset prevents complacency and strengthens the board's ability to challenge constructively. Ultimately, board design and oversight must blend foresight with disciplined follow-through, ensuring that strategy does not remain conceptual but becomes embedded in systems, behaviours, and business decisions. Boards that achieve this integration help create institutions that are governed with clarity, prepared for volatility, and aligned with the expectations of customers, regulators, and society. Effective governance requires continuous visibility across risk, operations, and customer outcomes, not periodic oversight.

Operating Models for Hybrid Delivery

Hybrid delivery demands operating models that move beyond traditional departmental silos and create a unified institution capable of serving customers consistently across channels, geographies, and partners. This explains why many retail banks struggle with hybrid transformation: their internal structures were built for a world where branches, call centres, and digital channels functioned as separate units with limited coordination. In the hybrid era, such fragmentation creates delays, duplication, inconsistent decision-making, and service failures that customers immediately experience. Modern operating models must therefore shift towards end-to-end journey ownership, where accountability is tied to customer outcomes rather than departmental metrics. This requires integrated teams that bring together product specialists, risk officers, technology staff, frontline advisors, and data analysts to work on shared problems using common information systems. In this context, leading institutions are adopting centralised operations hubs for complex tasks, while empowering local teams to handle customer-facing decisions with clarity and confidence. The importance of unified data flows, which allow staff to access the same customer history, risk signals, and service status regardless of channel, should also be stressed. At the same time, hybrid models require adaptive staffing: the mix of physical and digital volumes shifts continuously, making flexibility essential. Vendor partnerships must also be embedded directly into operating procedures, ensuring that third-party performance aligns with the bank's own standards. Hybrid delivery thus succeeds only when operating models are redesigned with cross-functional collaboration, shared intelligence, and institutional coherence at their core, making the bank feel seamless to customers, stable to regulators, and efficient in its daily execution.

This type of delivery cannot function without end-to-end ownership of customer journeys, and this helps show why journey ownership is now a structural requirement rather than an operating choice. Traditional operating models distribute accountability across product units, channel teams, and risk departments, which often results in fragmented decisions, unclear responsibilities, and slow resolution when issues arise. In a hybrid environment, customers expect continuity; they may begin a process online, seek clarification in a branch, escalate through a call centre, and receive follow-up on a mobile app—all within one journey. When ownership is split, customers experience the gaps: repeated explanations, inconsistent advice, and contradictory outcomes. Successful hybrid institutions re-architect operating models by assigning full journey responsibility to multi-disciplinary teams that are accountable for quality, speed, risk, and customer satisfaction from start to finish. These teams are supported by unified dashboards, common data stores, and shared service platforms that allow them to monitor journey health in real time, address emerging friction points, and adjust flows quickly when new regulatory or operational requirements arise. Good examples are banks that have implemented journey squads, agile review cycles, and cross-functional decision rights that significantly improve customer experience and risk control. Also noteworthy is that journey ownership strengthens inclusivity and fairness: when one team sees the whole journey, it is easier to identify points where vulnerable customers face barriers or where algorithmic rules may unintentionally disadvantage certain groups. Fundamentally, journey ownership is central to hybrid excellence because it eliminates fragmentation, accelerates service design, and builds a culture where teams take responsibility not for tasks, but for outcomes—the defining quality of a modern retail institution.

Case Study: HM Revenue and Customs (UK)—End-to-End Digital Service Ownership

HM Revenue and Customs redesigned its operating model around end-to-end digital service ownership, assigning multidisciplinary teams' responsibility for entire citizen journeys such as tax registration, self-assessment, and benefits interaction. Rather than operating through functional silos, teams integrate policy, technology, operations, and service design to deliver consistent outcomes across digital and assisted channels. This model has reduced duplication, improved response times, and strengthened accountability in high-volume public services. The HMRC example shows that journey-based operating models are not exclusive to banks but represent a broader institutional shift in how complex organisations deliver hybrid services at scale.

Operating hybrid models depend on unified data flows, and this explains why institutions cannot deliver consistent service when data is scattered across legacy systems, product silos, and partner platforms. Customers expect that the bank "remembers" them across every touchpoint: their preferences, history, pending queries, risk flags, and behavioural patterns. But in many institutions, each channel holds its own version of customer information, resulting in duplication, errors, and delays. In contrast, hybrid-ready banks redesign data architecture to create a single view of the customer through integrated data lakes, event-driven systems, and real-time synchronisation across physical and digital channels. By enabling staff, systems, and partners to access unified data, institutions reduce friction, improve fraud detection, and personalise service more effectively. Governance should also be discussed: unified data flows require strong data standards, classification rules, and quality controls to prevent inconsistencies and ensure regulatory compliance. Furthermore, banks use API gateways and middleware to connect old and new systems without compromising security, allowing branches, call centres, mobile apps, and third-party platforms to draw from the same source of truth. Real examples from global markets show how unified data flows help resolve long-standing pain points such as conflicting KYC records, mismatched addresses, and inconsistent credit histories. Unified data flows are also essential for vulnerability detection, identifying early signs of financial stress or accessibility challenges that may not be visible when data resides in isolated systems. Hybrid delivery, then, is not a matter of channel design alone; it is fundamentally a data problem, and institutions that address this will unlock faster decisions, stronger resilience, and deeper customer trust.

Hybrid delivery succeeds only when institutions move from fragmented responsibilities to true end-to-end journey ownership. This explains why traditional structures—where product teams, operations, risk, IT, and frontline units work in isolation—cannot support seamless customer journeys. Each department optimises its own tasks, but the customer experiences the gaps between them: repeated document requests, inconsistent advice, slow handovers, and contradictory information. End-to-end ownership solves this by assigning full responsibility for a journey, such as onboarding, payments, lending, or service recovery, to a single cross-functional "journey team." These teams include members from technology, operations, risk, compliance, design, analytics, and frontline roles, ensuring decisions reflect the full picture rather than narrow departmental interests. Another aspect to highlight is how journey teams use shared dashboards, unified KPIs, and real-time service metrics to identify bottlenecks early and adjust processes quickly. It's clear then that governance must evolve—instead of multiple committees approving small steps, one accountable owner ensures clarity, speed, and alignment with customer outcomes. Practical examples from global institutions show how journey teams have shortened onboarding times, reduced complaints, and improved fraud controls by eliminating handover gaps. The behavioural impact can also be explored: when teams see the whole journey, they develop empathy for customers, understand the sequencing of risks better, and coordinate more effectively with external vendors. End-to-end ownership also enhances the institution's ability to adapt to regulatory change, because journey teams can update processes holistically rather than making piecemeal adjustments. In summary, hybrid banking requires institutions to shift mindset from "managing departments" to "managing journeys", enabling faster delivery, clearer accountability, and a more predictable customer experience across physical and digital channels.

This is because the success of the hybrid operating models relies on the strength of internal/external integration, and no better manifestation of this is evident than in the way in which banks are managing partnerships with vendors. This helps illustrate the reasons why the traditional models of outsourcing are no longer relevant in a world in which the data flows are in real time, cloud-based infrastructures are the new normal, and API-based interactions are the new reality for the way in which banking is conducted. Also relevant here is the way in which the new hybrid models of delivery are demanding that banks have a constant view of the way in which the technology partners, payment processors, cloud providers, KYC providers, and the service platform collaborators are delivering services, as any failure in these models is a failure in the bank's own ability to deliver the customer experience. There is a cultural shift required, too: vendor management can no longer be treated as a procurement function; it must be embedded into operations, risk, and technology, with shared responsibilities and decision rights. Examples from global institutions demonstrate how integrated vendor governance reduces downtime, improves regulatory audit readiness, and strengthens resilience during high-volume periods. In addition, transparency is essential: vendors must share audit logs, security protocols, and performance indicators openly, enabling the bank to maintain consistent standards across the ecosystem. This integration also shapes customer experience—when partners are aligned, service flows become faster, errors reduce, and customers feel greater reliability even during peak demand. Hybrid institutions must treat vendors as operational extensions of the bank, supported by real-time monitoring, clear accountability, and a collaborative governance model that keeps the entire delivery chain stable, predictable, and trusted. Responsibility for outcomes delivered through partners remains fully with the institution.

For hybrid delivery to be successful, retail banks have to rethink their approach to decision-making to align with the pace, complexity, and interconnectedness of the new service environment. The limitations of the traditional approach to hierarchical escalation, where decisions are made at a slow pace from the front office to the mid-office and finally to the head office, are made more apparent. In a hybrid model, the customer could start the journey in-app, move to the call centre, and end up in the branch; if each has its own approach to decision-making and separate decisioning flows, the customer experience is fragmented. Leading institutions are thus replacing rigid hierarchies with delegated authority frameworks, multi-disciplinary "journey teams," and real-time decision matrices that guide frontline staff clearly and safely. By empowering staff with clearer parameters, banks reduce avoidable escalation, improve service speed, and strengthen accountability at the point of interaction. To give an example from banks in the UK, EU, and Asia, agile decision environments have reduced processing times, cut operational volumes, and improved customer trust. It is also worth emphasising that empowerment cannot exist without safeguards: institutions must align delegated powers with risk thresholds, automated controls, and transparent monitoring so that decisions remain consistent with regulatory and ethical expectations. This model requires investment in training and culture, of course; staff must understand not just rules, but the purpose behind them, allowing for sound judgment across different customer scenarios. A hybrid operating model thrives when decision rights mirror customer journeys instead of organisational charts, enabling the bank to respond quickly to emerging risks, evolving expectations, and operational disruptions. Overall, institutions with empowered, well-guided decision structures are better positioned to deliver seamless hybrid experiences, reduce internal bottlenecks, and maintain resilience in a fast-changing environment.

This also puts considerable pressure on legacy workflow systems, which were often designed for linear and paper-based processes, and single-channel customer interactions. The chapter thus far has outlined the reasons why legacy workflow systems act as structural constraints for retail banking, where journeys are now fluidly delivered across mobile applications, contact centres, branches, and third-party platforms. When each channel has its own workflow and, in many cases, its own technology stack, it can lead to re-keying of information, duplication of information for the customer, and errors building up across the interaction. To address this, leading retail banking organizations are now moving towards unified workflow engines that can manage journeys end-to-end, irrespective of where the initial interaction started. These engines integrate with API layers, CRM systems, and risk-management tools to ensure that data is captured once, validated centrally, and used across the lifecycle of the service. Banks in the UK, EU, and India are consolidating dozens of disconnected processes into streamlined, modular workflows that dramatically reduce friction. Workflow redesign must also be accompanied by governance clarity—every step of a journey requires an owner, a defined service standard, and an escalation path. Without this discipline, even the best workflow technology can reproduce old problems in a new system. Furthermore, hybrid workflows demand continuous tuning based on error patterns, customer feedback, and frontline insights. Institutions that maintain rigid, one-time process designs struggle to adapt; those that review workflows continuously are more resilient and responsive. Ultimately, unified, well-governed workflows form the operational backbone of hybrid delivery, reducing cost, strengthening compliance and creating a more coherent customer experience across all channels.

This is because hybrid delivery relies on the operating models that provide the frontline teams with the clarity and autonomy needed to resolve issues without going through the complexities within the organisation. The above illustrates the reasons why the traditional hierarchical structure, which often includes approval procedures and strict departmentalisation, creates a barrier to the prompt decision-making needed in a hybrid environment that demands responses in real time. When staff lack the authority to make routine decisions or must escalate simple matters through several managers, customer journeys become fragmented and frustration rises on both sides. To address this, leading retail banks are adopting what is often called “controlled empowerment”: frontline teams receive clearly defined decision rights supported by risk-aligned guardrails, while managers focus on coaching and oversight rather than gatekeeping. This approach works only when supported by strong data visibility. Staff must have access to complete, reliable customer information, real-time transaction updates, and clear policy guidance embedded directly into their workflow tools. Without this foundation, empowerment becomes unsafe. Banks in markets such as the UK, Australia, and Singapore are restructuring branch, call-centre, and digital-support teams into multi-skilled units capable of handling sales, service, and advisory functions with minimal handover. Behavioural consistency is important in this context: empowered teams must be trained in judgement, empathy, and ethical decision-making to uphold customer trust. Furthermore, controlled empowerment requires robust feedback loops so that recurring issues, policy gaps, and customer pain points can be escalated quickly to design teams. Institutions that invest in this operating discipline find that hybrid delivery becomes more seamless, with reduced service errors, faster cycle times, and more confident customer interactions. In contrast, those that maintain rigid hierarchies and centralised control struggle to deliver a unified hybrid experience, regardless of how advanced their technology may be.

For the hybrid operating models to be successful, there is a need to develop a rhythm of coordination among the central teams, branches, digital teams, and partners. This requires the operating discipline to sustain the alignment of the different parts of the organisation. At many retail banks, failures of the hybrid models are not necessarily caused by the banks’ technology but by the fact that different teams have different timelines, priorities, or receive the same information at different rates. To address this challenge, leading retail banks are using various structured operating cadences such as a daily stand-up meeting for issue resolution, a weekly review for the performance of the journey, and a monthly forum for bringing together the leaders of the risk, technology, operations, and customer experience teams. These routines ensure that emerging problems are surfaced early, responsibilities are clear, and decisions are made before small issues escalate into customer-facing failures. The importance of shared measurement systems should also be highlighted: hybrid delivery requires common KPIs and SLAs across physical and digital channels so that teams are not optimising in silos. When branch teams, call-centre teams, and digital teams work toward the same metrics—response time, resolution quality, customer satisfaction, error rates—coordination becomes natural rather than forced. Equally important is the integration of vendor participation in operating rhythms. Fintech partners, cloud providers, and API suppliers must adhere to the same review cycles and escalation pathways to ensure transparency and accountability. We can conclude that hybrid operating models function best when institutions develop predictable routines, unified dashboards, and collaborative decision forums that allow every unit to operate as part of a single system.

Without this, even the best-designed hybrid models break down under operational friction, leaving customers with inconsistent experiences and frontline teams with limited clarity.

Sustaining a high-performing hybrid operating model requires a continuous learning environment that helps teams adapt to shifting customer expectations, evolving regulatory demands, and new technology cycles. Institutions can build learning systems into day-to-day operations rather than treating training as a periodic intervention. Successful hybrid banks create feedback loops where frontline insights, customer complaints, operational incidents, and digital-journey analytics feed directly into process refinement and staff capability development. For example, patterns observed in branch interactions may reveal accessibility gaps in mobile apps, while digital-channel complaints may highlight gaps in branch advice or product explanation. Embedding structured learning cycles—such as monthly skill refreshers, cross-channel shadowing programmes, and micro-learning modules triggered by real incidents—ensures teams remain agile and aligned across environments. We should also emphasise the importance of leadership behaviours: managers must model curiosity, openness, and accountability so that teams feel safe reporting errors and proposing improvements. In hybrid settings, learning cannot be linear or hierarchical; institutions must cultivate a culture where operational teams, product designers, data analysts, and risk specialists learn from each other continuously. Also of importance is data-enabled coaching: unified dashboards allow managers to guide teams using real performance signals rather than anecdotal impressions. A final aspect to stress is that hybrid operating models evolve only when learning is treated as part of operational governance—embedded in KPIs, linked to performance reviews, and supported by digital learning platforms. When learning becomes structural rather than optional, hybrid institutions stay resilient, reduce operational friction, and consistently deliver experiences that reflect customer expectations and regulatory standards. Sustained hybrid performance depends on disciplined operating routines rather than isolated improvements.

Diversity in Governance and Leadership

Diversity in governance and leadership is now recognised as a structural requirement for institutional strength, not a peripheral social initiative. This explains why decision-making in hybrid retail banks demands a wide range of lived experiences, professional backgrounds, and cognitive strengths. As hybrid models connect digital channels, physical networks, ecosystem partnerships, and cross-border regulatory expectations, leadership teams must be able to interpret signals from different communities, demographic groups, and customer segments. Institutions that rely on narrow leadership profiles often miss early warning signs—such as shifts in customer trust, accessibility barriers in digital journeys, or emerging conduct-risk concerns—simply because the people making decisions do not reflect the diversity of the customers they serve. Diversity also contributes to stronger oversight by reducing blind spots in risk evaluation and enhancing the collective ability to question assumptions. Boards and leadership teams that bring together technologists, frontline operators, community representatives, economists, behavioural experts, and experienced bankers create a richer dialogue and a more balanced governance environment. With this backdrop, there is a growing regulatory focus: supervisors in the UK, EU, and Australia increasingly expect institutions to demonstrate how diversity supports risk management, culture, and customer outcomes. Finally, diversity is meaningful only when it is paired with inclusion. Leaders must build cultures where different voices are heard, challenge is encouraged, and psychological safety is embedded in everyday interactions. When diversity is institutionalised as a governance strength, retail banks become more adaptive, trusted, and capable of managing the complexity of hybrid transformation. Diversity without influence does not strengthen governance.

It strengthens governance only when institutions move beyond symbolic representation and embed inclusion into the rhythm of everyday decision-making. This explains why hybrid retail banks need leadership teams that reflect the socioeconomic, cultural, and generational realities of their customer base, particularly as digital channels widen the gap between those who can navigate complex systems and those who struggle with access, language, or confidence. A leadership group composed of similar backgrounds often designs services based on assumptions rather than lived realities, leading to product misalignment, inaccessible digital journeys, and policies that unintentionally disadvantage vulnerable groups. This highlights that meaningful diversity must span gender, ethnicity, disability, professional expertise, frontline exposure, and community knowledge. It also brings forward an emerging requirement: banks increasingly need leaders who understand behavioural design, ethical technology, and inclusion psychology just as much as they understand credit and financial management. Regulators in markets like the UK and Canada now assess diversity outcomes as part of culture reviews, insisting that banks demonstrate how leadership composition affects fairness, customer treatment, and institutional integrity. Another important area to stress is inclusive leadership behaviours—these include creating space for challenge, valuing dissent, building transparent pathways for internal progression, and ensuring that individuals from underrepresented groups see real opportunities to influence strategy. Hybrid banking multiplies points of risk, judgement, and customer impact, making homogeneity a structural weakness. When leadership reflects society, institutions build deeper trust, anticipate risks more accurately, and deliver services that genuinely meet the needs of diverse communities.

Diversity becomes meaningful in governance only when institutions recognise its direct impact on risk management, innovation, and customer fairness. Monocultural leadership teams, in contrast, often miss early warning signals in areas such as digital exclusion, product suitability, and emerging community vulnerabilities, simply because these issues fall outside their lived experience. In hybrid retail banking, where decision-making shapes digital journeys, automated outcomes, and cross-channel service flows, the absence of diverse perspectives can produce blind spots that escalate into regulatory breaches or reputational harm. Boards and executive teams that include individuals from varied socioeconomic backgrounds, genders, ethnicities, and professional disciplines tend to identify risks earlier, debate more constructively, and adapt faster to market transitions. Integrating diversity into senior-level recruitment practices is also important: widening talent pipelines, assessing leadership potential beyond traditional markers, and valuing frontline, technology, and community experience on equal terms with classical banking careers. Regulators in regions such as the EU and Australia increasingly tie governance assessments to evidence of diversity outcomes, recognising its influence on consumer protection and institutional resilience. At an operational level, diverse leadership teams help design better digital interfaces, reduce discriminatory algorithmic patterns, and ensure product strategies work for both digitally fluent customers and vulnerable groups. Ultimately, this positions diversity not as a moral imperative alone, but as a structural lever that strengthens judgement, widens institutional awareness, and positions hybrid banks to serve society with fairness, empathy, and long-term integrity.

Case Study: Monetary Authority of Singapore—Diversity and Supervisory Expectations

The Monetary Authority of Singapore has repeatedly emphasised leadership diversity as a governance and risk-management issue rather than a social initiative. Through supervisory guidance and board-level engagement, MAS expects financial institutions to demonstrate how leadership composition improves challenge management, decision quality, and oversight of technology and conduct risk. Institutions operating in Singapore have responded by broadening board expertise to include technology, behavioural risk, and regional market experience. This case illustrates how diversity is increasingly viewed by regulators as a structural control that strengthens institutional judgement and resilience.

Diversity in governance must translate into everyday leadership behaviours for it to have any real organisational effect. Indeed, institutions often recruit diverse leaders but fail to create the conditions in which their perspectives can influence strategy, risk decisions, and customer-facing policies. In many retail banks, hierarchical cultures, legacy power structures, and informal networks suppress dissenting views, even when those views reflect lived experience from communities that the institution is meant to serve. Hybrid banking requires a different approach: decision-making must be open, evidence-based, and willing to challenge long-standing assumptions about customer behaviour, workforce capabilities, and technology adoption. Inclusive leadership supports this by fostering psychological safety, encouraging debate during critical reviews, and removing the penalties associated with disagreeing with senior voices.

Regulators and professional bodies increasingly view inclusion as a governance indicator, linking it to conduct outcomes, staff confidence, and quality of escalation. At a practical level, inclusive leadership creates stronger digital-journey testing, better responses to complaints, and more balanced product designs because teams feel empowered to raise concerns early. This positions inclusion not as an HR initiative but as a governance discipline that affects institutional stability. Without inclusive cultures, diversity becomes symbolic; with it, diverse leaders help improve decisions, reduce blind spots, and strengthen the organisation's ability to navigate complex hybrid environments.

Diversity strengthens institutional decision-making only when it filters into how the organisation interprets risk, designs products, and supports customers across different life situations. Thus, hybrid banking environments require leadership teams that reflect the communities they serve; particularly as digital channels reshape how customers interact with institutions. Retail banks today support a spectrum of needs spanning vulnerable customers, migrant families, digitally limited populations, and emerging segments such as gig-economy workers. Leaders who bring varied socioeconomic backgrounds, generational experiences, and cultural perspectives are better positioned to understand these groups and anticipate where service gaps or conduct risks may arise. In many markets, the most severe customer-experience failures have occurred not due to technology issues but because leadership underestimated the impact of language barriers, digital anxiety, or cultural hesitations around borrowing and saving. A more representative leadership approach reduces this disconnect by embedding real-world insights into strategy, product reviews, and operational planning. Regulators across the UK, Canada, and the EU increasingly expect boards to demonstrate how diversity informs governance, particularly in vulnerability frameworks and conduct-risk oversight. Diversity is not just a social obligation; it is an operational requirement for delivering fair, accessible, and trustworthy hybrid services. When leadership teams mirror the diversity of their customer base, institutions make better decisions, build deeper trust, and minimise the blind spots that often lead to regulatory scrutiny or reputational damage.

Diversity becomes meaningful only when it shapes how decisions are made, whose voices are heard, and how challenge is encouraged within the institution. Hybrid banking environments demand leadership teams that can balance technology-driven change with deep sensitivity to human behaviour, inclusion gaps, and social expectations. Diverse leaders improve institutional resilience by broadening the organisation's interpretation of risk, ensuring that decisions are not filtered through a single cultural or professional lens. In many banks, governance failures have emerged when leadership teams shared similar backgrounds, career paths, or worldviews, resulting in groupthink and an underestimation of emerging risks. Diverse perspectives counter this pattern by introducing alternative ways of analysing customer journeys, evaluating partner relationships, and interpreting regulatory expectations. For example, leaders with experience in community finance may identify gaps in digital-access planning, while those from technology or entrepreneurial backgrounds may challenge operational bottlenecks more effectively. Diversity also improves an institution's cultural intelligence—an essential capability as banks serves increasingly multicultural and multigenerational customer bases. Regulators across mature markets emphasise the importance of diversity in risk committees, conduct oversight, and remuneration governance to avoid uniform thinking. Accordingly, diversity strengthens institutions by fostering constructive debate, widening the leadership bandwidth, and ensuring that decisions are grounded in both analytical judgment and lived experience. When properly embedded, diversity transforms governance from a compliance requirement into a strategic advantage that enhances institutional integrity and customer trust.

This must be supported by institutional systems that recognise, reward, and protect constructive challenge. In many banks, diverse leaders enter the organisation but struggle to influence decisions because legacy hierarchies, informal power structures, or unspoken cultural norms limit their ability to speak openly. Hybrid institutions must deliberately redesign their governance processes to ensure that challenge is not only permitted but expected. Boards and executive committees must reinforce behaviours that welcome dissenting views, encourage evidence-based debate, and protect individuals who raise concerns about conduct, customer fairness, or operational risk. Without these safeguards, diversity becomes symbolic rather than structural. Institutions with strong challenge cultures actively rotate meeting chairs, anonymise certain decision inputs, and create multiple entry points for raising concerns—from internal forums to independent risk teams. Hybrid delivery amplifies the need for these mechanisms because decisions are made faster, across more partners, and with greater reliance on digital systems that can malfunction or produce unintended outcomes. When leaders from varied backgrounds feel empowered to challenge assumptions, the institution becomes more resilient, less prone to blind spots, and more aligned with community expectations. Diversity, however, only succeeds when the organisation creates the psychological safety required for honest dialogue. In practice, this means embedding challenge into training, performance evaluation, succession planning, and everyday leadership routines. True diversity is therefore not measured by representation alone but by whether leaders can influence decisions, shape strategy, and safeguard the institution's long-term credibility.

It also demands that institutions examine how power is distributed across their leadership structures and whether decision-making genuinely reflects the varied perspectives present in the organisation. Many banks still operate with narrow circles of influence, where key decisions are shaped by a small group with similar backgrounds or experiences. This explains why hybrid institutions must adopt governance mechanisms that broaden decision inputs, reduce concentration of authority, and create more balanced representation across committees. This requires transparent appointment processes, rotation of leadership roles, structured succession pipelines, and deliberate identification of high-potential talent from underrepresented groups. When authority is shared more equitably, organisations are less vulnerable to groupthink and better positioned to anticipate risks arising from technology shifts, demographic changes, and new customer expectations. It also sends a clear cultural signal: leadership is not confined to one type of profile, career path, or social background. Institutions across the UK, EU, and Asia are increasingly building cross-functional councils, independent advisory panels, and multi-disciplinary project boards to distribute influence and ensure that expertise—not hierarchy—shapes decisions. For hybrid banks, this is critical: operating across physical and digital channels requires leaders who understand community realities, digital ethics, frontline pressures, and ecosystem dependencies. By diversifying the centre of gravity within governance, banks strengthen accountability, embed a broader understanding of customer needs, and create a more adaptive institutional culture. Diversity in power structures is therefore not an HR initiative—it is a foundation of institutional design.

Diversity in governance must also extend beyond internal structures to include the voices and expectations of the communities that banks serve. Retail institutions increasingly operate in multicultural environments where customer needs, risk sensitivities, and digital behaviours vary widely across demographic groups. This highlights why hybrid banks must build governance mechanisms that bring community insight into decision-making in a structured and meaningful way. Institutions in the UK, Europe, and parts of Africa are evolving towards advisory forums, community councils, customer-experience panels, and stakeholder-engagement groups that provide direct feedback to boards and executive committees. These mechanisms ensure that policy decisions, digital-journey redesign, and service-quality expectations are grounded in real lived experiences rather than assumptions. Diversity at the governance level also means being attentive to vulnerable groups—the elderly, migrants, low-income households, and digitally limited users—whose needs are often overlooked in traditional board discussions. For hybrid banks, understanding these segments is essential for designing safe interfaces, inclusive products, and responsible AI-driven decision flows. With regard to community-centred governance, it improves risk identification, enhances institutional legitimacy, and strengthens long-term trust. It also reduces regulatory friction, as supervisors increasingly expect firms to demonstrate how customer perspectives influence strategic and operational decisions. Ultimately, governance diversity is not only about who sits at the table inside the institution but also whose voices shape the institution from outside. Banks that embed this outward-looking approach are better positioned to anticipate social shifts, strengthen inclusion, and build models of leadership that reflect the realities of the markets they serve.

It becomes meaningful only when it is embedded into the institution's decision-making systems, leadership behaviours, and organisational routines. This explains why hybrid banks must move beyond representation metrics and focus on how diverse voices influence strategy, risk oversight, product governance, and customer outcomes. Many institutions create diversity policies, but the real test is whether different viewpoints are genuinely heard, respected, and integrated into decisions that affect millions of customers. This requires deliberate leadership practices: structured challenge sessions, cross-functional decision forums, transparent succession planning, and evaluation processes that reward inclusive behaviour rather than reinforce traditional hierarchies. Global evidence from the UK, Canada, and South Africa shows that institutions with inclusive cultures experience fewer conduct failures, stronger innovation outcomes, and higher customer trust. Diversity also influences how effectively banks navigate emerging responsibilities—from ethical AI governance to inclusive digital design and climate-risk decisions that disproportionately affect vulnerable communities. As hybrid models expand, institutions must ensure that leadership teams have lived experience across technology, community engagement, financial inclusion, and frontline operations, not only corporate or regulatory backgrounds. In sum, diversity is an institutional capability: it strengthens resilience by broadening the organisation's field of vision, reduces blind spots by challenging assumptions, and builds credibility with customers who expect fairness and representation. For hybrid banks, embedding diversity into governance is both an ethical responsibility and a competitive advantage. It creates institutions that learn continuously, adapt faster, and lead with sensitivity to the real social and economic contexts in which they operate. Boards must ensure that diversity is reflected not only in composition but in decision outcomes.

The Role of Professional Standards

Professional standards are the bedrock of trust in retail banking, and this is certainly the case with the hybrid approach, which combines digital channels, human judgment, and decisioning technology. It's the rationale for the bank's approach to professional accreditation, ethical codes, and ongoing learning and development as not just an operational nicety but an operational necessity. The customer may interact through an app, a branch, or a contact centre, but they still expect competence, integrity, and fairness. As banking becomes increasingly mediated by algorithms, staff must balance technical understanding with strong ethical judgment, ensuring that decisions made by systems are escalated, interpreted, or corrected when necessary. Global regulators—including the FCA, MAS, and APRA—expect institutions to demonstrate not only compliance but also evidence of professional capability across frontline roles, product governance teams, cyber-risk units, and leadership groups. Professional standards help create this coherence: they align behaviours across departments, reduce misconduct risk, and ensure that customers receive consistent outcomes regardless of who serves them or which channel they use. The role of professional bodies such as the Chartered Banker Institute, LIBF, CFA Institute, and governance associations that shape competency expectations for modern bankers should also be highlighted. Their influence is growing as hybrid delivery demands new skills—from digital literacy and data ethics to vulnerability awareness and cross-sector communication. For hybrid institutions, embedding professional standards into recruitment, promotion, appraisal, and training ensures that institutional behaviour remains predictable, responsible, and trustworthy. It signals to customers and regulators that the institution takes its obligations seriously and is building a workforce capable of meeting the demands of a rapidly changing financial landscape. Professional standards define how institutional intent is translated into customer outcomes.

Professional standards also provide a stabilising force in hybrid retail banking, where decisions increasingly blend automated processes with human oversight. Institutions must adopt a structured approach to competence, ensuring that every role—from frontline advisers to risk analysts, product designers, algorithm auditors, and branch leaders—operates with clarity, discipline, and ethical grounding. In traditional banking, experience and tenure were often seen as proxies for capability, but hybrid delivery exposes the limitations of informal knowledge transfer. Staff now navigate digital-first journeys, evolving fraud patterns, new identity models, and sensitive customer situations that require both technical fluency and human sensitivity. Professional standards create a baseline of expected competence so that customers receive predictable, fair, and responsible service even when channels differ or staff vary in experience. Global institutions are embedding accredited pathways into workforce strategy through structured learning programmes, scenario-based ethical training, and mandated refresher modules tied to regulatory priorities. The operational benefits should also be emphasised: well-trained staff reduce complaints, improve customer outcomes, and lower institutional risk by recognising vulnerabilities, escalating issues correctly, and interpreting data responsibly. For leadership teams, professional standards serve as signals of organisational maturity, helping boards demonstrate to regulators that the institution has a disciplined culture rooted in competence and accountability. Ultimately, professional standards ensure that hybrid transformation is anchored in human capability, allowing technology to enhance—not erode—the quality and fairness of financial services.

As hybrid banking expands, frontline and operational staff are increasingly required to interpret complex digital signals, manage sensitive customer interactions, and operate within evolving regulatory expectations. As such, professional standards must evolve beyond traditional classroom training into continuous capability-building frameworks that reflect the realities of hybrid delivery. Staff today must understand how automated decisions are made, how algorithmic recommendations should be validated, how customer vulnerabilities manifest in digital journeys, and how to maintain judgment in environments where technology performs much of the initial triage. Institutions that rely on outdated competencies risk creating service gaps, mismanaging complaints, or mishandling data—all of which lead directly to regulatory scrutiny and public distrust. Global banks are adopting modular training ecosystems anchored in recognised professional bodies, integrating micro-credentials, digital ethics modules, and scenario-based simulations that mirror real hybrid service contexts. Behavioural expectations are also becoming codified: fairness, transparency, listening skills, and cultural sensitivity are now treated as professional competencies rather than soft skills. By anchoring staff development in these structured standards, hybrid institutions can create more consistent customer outcomes, reduce operational risk, and enhance the credibility of their service models. Professional standards ultimately serve as a governance mechanism—ensuring that as technology accelerates, the institution retains a strong, human-centred backbone capable of safeguarding trust and delivering responsible financial services across every channel.

These standards increasingly function as a stabilising anchor in environments where decision-making is distributed across technology, frontline teams, outsourced partners, and automated workflows. This explains why hybrid institutions must embed clear ethical codes and conduct expectations into every layer of the organisation, ensuring that staff understand not just what to do, but why these principles matter. As digital journeys accelerate, many key decisions—such as payment declines, fraud flags, credit recommendations, and suitability checks—are triggered algorithmically. Yet regulators across the UK, EU, Australia, and Singapore have made it clear that accountability for outcomes remains fully with the institution and its people. This requires staff who can challenge automated decisions, escalate anomalies, and recognise when a customer outcome may be technically correct but practically unfair. Professional standards create the shared behavioural baseline that allows staff to act confidently and consistently in these situations. Also worth highlighting is how institutions are incorporating ethical-risk lenses into recruitment, appraisal, and leadership development, ensuring that integrity is measured with the same seriousness as technical capability. As hybrid banking introduces more external partners and distributed delivery chains, common standards ensure coherence across teams that may never meet physically but must deliver a unified experience. Ultimately, professional standards become a governance tool that strengthens institutional culture, reduces misconduct risk, and reinforces public confidence in a banking model where trust relies as much on human judgment as it does on technology.

Professional standards can also be considered as that which holds together the relationship between institutional intent and day-to-day frontline practice, especially in a hybrid world where customers can interact in many different ways and expect high quality across all those ways. Standards thus play a key role in helping an institution deliver on its values by providing staff with clear expectations around fairness, transparency, communication, and responsible practice. In hybrid banking, customers may receive advice through a branch one day, a chatbot the next, and a call-centre representative soon after; without shared standards, these journeys quickly become fragmented and inconsistent. Regulators in the UK, EU, and Asia increasingly assess organisations not only on policy frameworks but on whether customer outcomes show clear evidence of professional judgement, ethical reasoning, and cultural alignment across teams. This pushes banks to embed standards into daily routines, from onboarding training to performance reviews and leadership pathways. Many institutions now combine technical accreditations with behavioural assessments to ensure employees understand their responsibilities around data privacy, vulnerable customers, digital inclusion, and mis-selling risks. Professional standards must also evolve alongside technology: staff must be confident managing digital tools, interpreting algorithmic decisions, and identifying situations where human intervention is required. By integrating standards into both digital and human delivery, hybrid institutions can build a culture where accountability is shared, customer interests are protected, and staff consistently uphold the institution's reputation.

Such professional standards assume even greater importance as hybrid banks continue to build their dependence on automation, platforms, and algorithms. This section has been an overview of how standards are a stabilising influence in situations where technology provides a speed and scale that cannot be matched by human capabilities. In areas like digital lending, approvals, and fraud detection, employees may not even be involved, but they are still accountable. Clear professional expectations guide teams on how to interpret automated alerts, when to challenge an algorithmic recommendation, and how to escalate anomalies that may signal customer harm or system failure. Supervisors across the UK, EU, Singapore, and Australia increasingly expect banks to demonstrate that staff understand their responsibilities even when technology performs the first layer of analysis. This requires structured training that blends digital literacy, ethical judgement, and regulatory awareness, ensuring teams can identify bias, safeguard vulnerable customers, and spot operational risks masked by automation. Professional standards therefore evolve into a framework for human–technology partnership: staff must complement digital systems with integrity, caution, and contextual understanding. Institutions that invest in this blend reduce the risk of over-reliance on systems, strengthen internal challenge, and create a culture where employees feel responsible for outcomes rather than just processes. This commitment reassures regulators and customers that despite rapid digital transformation, the institution remains grounded in competence, fairness, and human accountability.

Professional standards also play a role in how institutions can build credibility with their regulators, auditors, and their communities. Thus, this shows that in a hybrid model, regulators are also looking beyond systems and policies to assess the quality of the people who are making decisions within that bank. As a result, when misconduct, poor judgment, or poor oversight are identified as part of a supervisory review, it's not that technology was missing; it's that standards were missing. Institutions that are able to provide robust accreditation, role, and capability assessments are showing that their workforce understands what's expected of them in terms of fairness, data, vulnerability, and product. This is particularly important in areas such as collections, complaints management, and dispute resolution, where customers interact with staff during moments of stress or confusion. Professional standards ensure consistency: the same level of care, respect, and accuracy is maintained whether the interaction occurs in a branch, contact centre, or digital channel. For regulators, these standards provide confidence that the institution can deliver reliable outcomes even when volumes spike or external conditions deteriorate. For customers, they reinforce the belief that the bank's values are lived through everyday actions rather than expressed only in reports. In hybrid banking, where trust is influenced by both human service and digital journeys, professional standards act as the common thread that ties conduct, judgement, and accountability together. They elevate the institution from compliance-driven behaviour to principled decision-making, strengthening long-term trust while reducing the likelihood of operational or reputational failures.

Case Study: NHS England—Professional Standards as System Stability

NHS England operates one of the world's largest hybrid service systems, combining digital platforms, physical facilities, outsourced partners, and frontline professionals. Professional standards governed by bodies such as the General Medical Council and Nursing and Midwifery Council provide a common behavioural and ethical framework across this complex environment. These standards ensure consistency of judgment, accountability, and escalation even when services are delivered through different channels and organisations. The NHS case demonstrates how professional standards function as institutional infrastructure, stabilising large-scale hybrid systems where technology alone cannot guarantee trust or safety.

These standards gain even greater importance as hybrid operating models become more complex and distributed across internal teams, outsourced partners, and technology-driven processes. Such standards act as a stabilising mechanism in environments where decisions are increasingly guided by algorithms, automated workflows, and data-led triggers. When staff understand the principles behind fairness, transparency, vulnerability assessment, and responsible product delivery, they are better equipped to challenge algorithmic outputs, escalate anomalies, and intervene when automated systems produce unintended outcomes. This strengthens institutional resilience by ensuring that human judgement continues to play a critical role in protecting customers. Professional standards also support consistent interpretation of policies across geographies and business lines. As retail banks expand through cross-border partnerships, shared services, and multi-country compliance frameworks, standards create a common language for conduct and ethics. They reduce ambiguity in grey areas, helping teams navigate situations that fall outside procedural checklists. This is particularly valuable in emerging markets, where local norms, digital maturity, and regulatory expectations may differ from the bank's home jurisdiction. Embedding professional standards through mandatory certification pathways, refresher programmes, and supervisory reinforcement helps institutions maintain coherence across a diverse workforce. In hybrid retail banking, standards therefore function not only as an ethical compass but as a practical tool for ensuring stability, reducing operational risk, and promoting a culture where responsible innovation is encouraged and routinely practised.

Standards of professionalism also feature prominently in the response to misconduct, operational failures, and customer-impact events. In a hybrid model, where incidents originate from a variety of places, be it algorithmic failures, digital products sold to customers in a mis-selling capacity, or even direct interactions, banks have to develop a framework to address responses to those incidents. This section has sought to explain the importance of strong standards in eliminating ambiguity in the heat of the moment, where employees know what to do in terms of documentation, communication, cooperation, etc. Banks with strong standards of professionalism tend to have a stronger discipline in terms of incident response. They are less defensive, more open to learning, and more effective at preventing recurrence. Professional standards also influence how organisations treat vulnerable customers when processes go wrong. Instead of relying on rigid scripts, employees trained in ethical judgement are more likely to provide tailored support, acknowledge institutional responsibility, and offer fair outcomes without delay. This reinforces trust at a time when customer confidence can erode quickly. For leadership teams, professional standards create a bridge between culture and compliance; they translate abstract values into observable behaviours. They also help boards assess whether the organisation is operating with integrity across channels and geographies. In hybrid retail banking, where institutions depend on distributed teams and automated systems, professional standards act as the resilience layer that keeps customer treatment consistent, reinforces fairness, and strengthens overall institutional credibility.

Ultimately, it is the professional standards that will ensure that the translation of hybrid transformation into public trust is achieved. As banks introduce AI-driven decision systems, develop partnerships, digitalise frontline services, and decentralise delivery, the customer will increasingly be able to relate with the institution via digital means. This is the rationale behind the need for professional standards to be dynamic in ensuring that there is clarity in terms of how professionals should engage with algorithmic indicators of customer vulnerability, and how to balance efficiency with fairness when systems escalate cases for manual review. Institutions that invest in continuous professional development create teams that understand both the technical and human dimensions of hybrid banking. They are better equipped to recognise unintended bias, anticipate customer confusion, and intervene early when products or interfaces risk causing harm. The role of standards in shaping organisational identity should also be emphasised. When banks uphold high standards consistently—through transparent communication, responsible product design, and empathetic customer handling—they cultivate a reputation for reliability that endures beyond individual channels or technologies. This reputation becomes a strategic advantage in markets where trust is fragile. Finally, professional standards help institutions bridge internal silos: risk, operations, technology, frontline, and compliance align around shared expectations. This collective discipline strengthens institutional cohesion and ensures that hybrid transformation enhances, rather than dilutes, the organisation's ethical foundation. Leadership must ensure that standards are continuously reinforced through systems, training, and accountability mechanisms.

Cross-Border Regulatory Alignment

Operating across multiple regulatory regimes has become a defining reality for modern retail banks, even for institutions that historically served domestic markets alone. Global payment rails, cloud-hosting arrangements, digital identity frameworks, cross-border data dependencies, and multinational fintech partnerships all expose banks to supervisory expectations shaped outside their home jurisdiction. This explains why cross-border regulatory alignment is no longer an optional compliance exercise but a structural design requirement. Hybrid institutions must ensure that their internal policies, technology stacks, data-handling processes, and risk controls remain consistent with global standards such as GDPR for data protection, ISO security frameworks, international open-banking rules, and climate-disclosure guidelines. The challenge is not just about meeting multiple checklists; it is about harmonising principles—privacy, consent, operational resilience, customer fairness, cloud governance, and technology risk. As institutions scale digital products or adopt global platforms, even small misalignments can create systemic gaps: a vendor may comply with EU cloud-sovereignty rules but fall short of Asian cybersecurity mandates; a payment partner may meet UK fraud-reporting norms but lack alignment with emerging African consumer-protection requirements. Regulators increasingly expect banks to anticipate these divergences and demonstrate how their governance models manage them proactively. Cross-border alignment, this section argues, strengthens institutional integrity: it reduces operational surprises, enables smoother market expansion, and reinforces a culture of disciplined, future-oriented compliance. Institutions that embed global regulatory intelligence into their design become more adaptive, trustworthy, and resilient in a world where financial ecosystems transcend geographical borders.

In terms of cross-border regulatory alignment, banks have to shift their focus from a rule-based approach to a systems-based approach, where compliance is actually embedded into the systems rather than being seen as a series of separate compliance obligations. This is about how banks have to rethink their internal policy processes in terms of ensuring that data flows, API interactions, cloud deployments, and customer processes are all continuously compliant across multiple jurisdictions without manual intervention. A traditional compliance team would have worked on a periodic basis, dealing with country-specific issues, but in the world of hybrid banking, there is a need for real-time compliance because digital customer journeys are often operating across multiple jurisdictions simultaneously. A simple event—such as a customer initiating a payment through an app hosted on overseas cloud infrastructure—can activate a chain of regulatory obligations across data residency, encryption, fraud reporting, and consumer-consent rules. Institutions that rely on reactive controls face escalating operational risks, conflicting requirements, and duplicated effort. Forward-looking banks are therefore building unified compliance architectures, where core policies, data taxonomies, retention rules, and risk protocols are standardised at the enterprise level and then adapted locally only where necessary. This reduces fragmentation and ensures that operational teams, technology partners, and global vendors all work from the same structural blueprint. The importance of cross-functional governance must also be highlighted—legal, technology, operations, risk, and product teams must collaborate to interpret global regulations consistently and translate them into practical controls. When regulatory alignment is designed into workflows from the start, institutions operate with greater confidence, deliver smoother customer experiences, and avoid costly remediation cycles. This design-based approach to compliance becomes a competitive differentiator, enabling hybrid institutions to innovate safely and scale across markets with clarity and discipline. Compliance must be embedded into systems rather than applied after execution.

In the current scenario, the ability of cross-border regulatory alignment is also being driven by the ability of banks to address data residency and cloud-hosting obligations, which are sharply differentiated across markets and are resulting in complex tensions in terms of architecture. One point to address is how hybrid banks are being forced to rethink the foundational architecture of their data management strategies in a manner that enables the free flow of information while still addressing regional privacy regulations, localisation mandates, and sectoral regulations. Markets such as the EU, India, the Gulf, and parts of Africa mandate that certain forms of financial data be stored within the country or be processed by certified cloud service providers. The challenge becomes more pronounced in hybrid environments where customer journeys cross channels, partners, and geographies. For example, a UK customer making an international remittance through a fintech partner may generate data that flows through multiple regulatory zones, each with its own expectations on retention, access rights, and incident reporting. Institutions that do not understand these nuances face operational breaches even when their intent is compliant. Leading banks respond by establishing cross-border data councils, harmonising data dictionaries, creating layered access-control systems, and deploying automated compliance-checking tools that validate every transfer, API call, and storage location against local rules. These practices allow banks to innovate without exposing themselves to regulatory fragmentation. When data residency is treated as a structural design principle rather than a policy memo, institutions safeguard customer trust, reduce supervisory friction, and maintain the flexibility required to scale digital services globally in a compliant, future-proof manner.

In addition, cross-border regulatory alignment is increasingly demanding that banks develop structured intelligence capabilities that monitor supervisory advancements across multiple jurisdictions in real time. Hybrid institutions must evolve beyond periodic updates for regulatory compliance and instead embrace continuous forms of regulatory intelligence that interpret emerging regulations, predict directional shifts, and translate external expectations into internal actions. As global regulators tighten standards around open finance, cloud concentration risk, operational resilience, climate disclosures, and consumer protection, banks operating across borders face the challenge of aligning policies with frameworks that evolve at different speeds. The UK may prioritise data portability and consumer rights, while the EU sharpens its focus on digital operational resilience, and Asian regulators emphasise national digital infrastructure and cybersecurity localisation. Without a structured intelligence function, institutions risk fragmented responses—one division updating its controls while another continues operating under outdated guidance. Leading global banks address this through central regulatory-intelligence teams equipped with legal, policy, and technology expertise; automated rule-tracking platforms that scan supervisory updates; and scenario tools that map how new regulations may affect products, data flows, outsourcing arrangements, and capital requirements. These teams maintain close engagement with supervisors, participate in industry consultations, and translate cross-border developments into internally aligned operating manuals and board-level briefings. By embedding regulatory intelligence into institutional design, banks create a more anticipatory posture: they reduce implementation shocks, avoid reactive compliance spending, and protect customer trust by ensuring policies remain consistent across markets. In hybrid banking, regulatory alignment is ultimately a leadership discipline—one that ensures the institution remains globally coherent, strategically agile, and fully prepared for the shifts shaping tomorrow's financial architecture.

Hybrid retail banks increasingly depend on cloud platforms, cross-border data centres, international payment rails, and global technology vendors, which means compliance cannot stop at national boundaries. Institutions must redesign internal policies so that data flows, technology choices, and outsourcing decisions remain compliant across multiple jurisdictions simultaneously. Regulators in the UK, EU, Singapore, Australia, and India are strengthening expectations around cloud concentration, data localisation, third-party risk, and digital-operational-resilience testing. For banks operating or partnering across borders, these differences can quickly create misalignment: a cloud configuration approved in one jurisdiction may violate retention rules or localisation requirements in another, while a fintech partner compliant with one supervisory regime may fall short under a stricter regulatory standard elsewhere. Institutions with outdated or siloed compliance models struggle the most, because each business unit interprets rules in isolation. Leading banks resolve this through harmonised policy frameworks that define a global minimum standard for data protection, cybersecurity controls, outsourcing governance, incident reporting, and model risk management—standards that apply everywhere unless local law requires something higher. These global baselines reduce duplication, simplify vendor oversight, and give technology teams a stable design reference when architecting hybrid systems across markets. They also help boards fulfil their cross-border responsibilities by ensuring oversight is anchored in a unified compliance map rather than fragmented local interpretations. Banks that invest in harmonised standards strengthen operational predictability, accelerate product deployment across geographies, and build a culture where compliance is understood as a shared institutional responsibility. In a world where data moves instantly and regulators expect accountability across entire ecosystems, cross-border alignment becomes a design principle—a way to protect customers, reduce friction, and keep the institution's hybrid infrastructure safe, coherent, and globally trusted.

The cross-border alignment of regulations is now heavily influenced by the institution's capacity to sustain data governance discipline in multiple environments, especially with the integration of hybrid delivery models, cloud-based platforms, global networks of APIs, and analytics models. The arcs discussed in this chapter outline the reasons for the need to standardise data lineage, classification, and retention frameworks, rather than adjusting them to respond to each market's regulations. When data is being moved from one country to another, the regulators' expectations from banks include the location of the data, its protection, access, and retention, which is heightened with the EU's GDPR, India's Digital Personal Data Protection Act, Australia's CDR, and Singapore's PDPA. Without a unified data-governance foundation, hybrid institutions risk contradictory interpretations, duplicated controls, and accidental non-compliance as data travels between business units or external partners. Leading banks address this by mapping all data assets through a single enterprise inventory, tagging sensitive information consistently, and deploying automated controls that enforce masking, tokenisation, encryption, and access governance regardless of geography. This approach reduces the operational burden on local teams, improves audit readiness, and allows technology platforms to be configured once and scaled globally. Strong data-governance alignment also enables better collaboration with fintechs and cloud providers, who can plug into a predictable compliance framework rather than tailoring integrations market by market. For boards and senior leaders, unified data governance offers clarity: it becomes easier to monitor risks, approve expansion into new markets, and engage with regulators confidently. In a hybrid world where customer journeys often span multiple systems, channels, and countries, cross-border compliance cannot rely on manual interpretation. It requires a coherent data-governance architecture that makes regulatory alignment a natural consequence of good design—protecting consumers, enabling innovation, and giving the institution long-term resilience.

Cross-border alignment increasingly requires institutions to strengthen how they manage cloud-sovereignty expectations, particularly as regulators tighten controls on where data can be stored, processed, and backed up. Hybrid institutions must thus design cloud architectures that respect jurisdictional boundaries while still enabling seamless customer experiences and operational continuity. Many regulators now demand that banks maintain local data copies, use region-specific cloud zones, or demonstrate the ability to rapidly repatriate data during crises. These expectations differ across markets: the EU prioritises data-residency guarantees, India enforces stringent localisation norms for financial data, and jurisdictions like the UAE, Japan, and South Korea impose sector-specific sovereignty requirements. For banks operating across these regions, cloud strategy becomes a matter of regulatory design rather than pure technology choice. Leading institutions respond by adopting multi-cloud or hybrid-cloud models with built-in localisation controls, encrypted regional storage, and automated routing that ensures sensitive data never crosses a restricted boundary. They also implement "sovereign cloud overlays": governance layers that provide visibility into data movement, enforce policy compliance, and support regulator audits with real-time evidence. Such architectures prevent unintentional breaches, reduce the risk of sanctions, and build regulator confidence in the bank's operational discipline. For senior leadership, cloud sovereignty introduces a new responsibility—ensuring technology investment does not outpace compliance capability. Boards must ask whether the bank can trace data flows across all markets, demonstrate operational separation where required, and maintain resilience if a cloud region becomes unavailable. When designed well, cloud-sovereignty alignment shifts from a constraint to a strategic advantage, enabling hybrid banks to scale responsibly across borders while protecting customer rights and strengthening institutional legitimacy.

This regulatory alignment increasingly depends on how effectively institutions manage financial-crime obligations that vary sharply across jurisdictions but operate through interconnected transaction flows. Given this, hybrid banks must build financial-crime frameworks that remain consistent in principle yet adaptable in execution. Regulators in the UK, EU, Singapore, and Australia emphasise robust anti-money-laundering (AML) monitoring, real-time sanctions screening, and clear auditability, while countries across Africa, the Middle East, and South Asia often require enhanced due-diligence steps for high-risk sectors or regions. When transactions move across borders, differing definitions of suspicious activity, reporting thresholds, and politically exposed persons (PEP) classifications can introduce operational friction and regulatory vulnerability. Hybrid institutions must therefore design multi-layered AML systems that interpret local rules without creating conflicting outcomes for customers using multiple channels. Leading banks address this through unified case-management platforms, shared transaction-monitoring engines, and risk-based segmentation that adapts automatically to local regulatory conditions. They also invest in cross-border typology intelligence—learning from fraud patterns, sanctions-evasion methods, and predicate-offence trends observed in partner markets—so that risk controls remain dynamic rather than static. Governance plays a critical role: periodic cross-jurisdiction calibration reviews, regulator-to-regulator engagement, and "global minimum standard" policies ensure the institution never falls below the highest expectation among its markets. This reduces the likelihood of breaches, protects correspondent-banking relationships, and enhances the institution's reputation for proactive compliance. For hybrid banks, sophisticated financial-crime alignment is not simply a protective measure; it is a foundation for global participation. By ensuring that every transaction, partner interface, and customer journey adheres to the strongest AML standards across borders, institutions reinforce trust, maintain operational integrity, and secure long-term access to international financial networks.

The extent to which cross-border regulatory alignment is dependent on institutions' handling of rapidly evolving expectations around data sovereignty, cloud hosting, and localisation regulations is also an issue under this arc. This is therefore an explanation of the reasons why hybrid banks must shift their thinking from merely viewing cloud adoption as a purely tech-centric decision to one that is more regulatory-centric. Different regulations have different expectations regarding the placement of customer data, encryption, backups, and even regulators' access in times of crisis. The EU prioritises strict data-protection standards under GDPR and emerging financial-data access rules; countries like India and the UAE emphasise local data storage and real-time supervisory access; and the UK follows a risk-based approach focused on operational resilience and multi-cloud diversification. For retail institutions operating across borders, these differences create architectural tension: a single technology stack may not be compliant everywhere, yet fragmented systems can undermine efficiency and customer experience. Leading banks address this by building modular cloud architectures with jurisdiction-specific controls, region-restricted data pods, and policy-driven routing that ensures sensitive information never crosses prohibited boundaries. They also embed regulatory observability into their systems—automated logs, audit trails, access monitoring, and reporting dashboards that give supervisors confidence in how data is managed. Vendor governance becomes critical, as cloud providers must meet the highest applicable regulatory standard rather than the lowest. Cross-border coordination teams work closely with regulators to clarify expectations before launching new services, reducing compliance risk and strengthening institutional credibility. When executed well, cloud-alignment strategies allow hybrid banks to maintain global scale while meeting local obligations without compromise. This capability becomes a competitive advantage: institutions that align cloud governance intelligently can innovate faster, deploy services consistently across markets, and offer customers reliable, secure, and regulation-ready experiences everywhere they operate.

The final element of cross-border regulatory alignment is contingent upon the institution's capacity to operationalise global standards. The final part of this section explores the manner in which hybrid banks seek to consolidate supervisory requirements, such as anti-money laundering regulations and financial crime intelligence, climate-related disclosures, consumer protection, and cyber-incident reporting, to name a few, into a cohesive operating blueprint. Fragmented approaches to compliance have the potential to generate costly duplication, inconsistent customer experiences, and heightened regulatory risk, whereas a harmonised operating blueprint enables institutions to sustain trust and growth. Leading banks adopt a "global standard, local execution" model: core policies, risk appetites, escalation thresholds, and conduct expectations are defined centrally, while country teams adapt implementation to local laws, cultural norms, and market realities. This reduces ambiguity, strengthens resilience, and ensures that frontline staff, vendors, and partners understand their responsibilities no matter where they operate. Technology plays a central role in reinforcing alignment. Global case-management platforms, shared transaction-monitoring engines, cross-jurisdiction KYC frameworks, and consolidated regulatory-intelligence systems enable teams to respond quickly to emerging rules or supervisory guidance. Training programmes are designed to reflect multi-market ethics and compliance principles, ensuring that staff can navigate differences in privacy laws, open-banking rules, reporting obligations, and consumer-rights frameworks. Importantly, strong alignment requires proactive relationships with regulators: hybrid banks that engage early-sharing pilots, risk assessments, and operational insights-build credibility and reduce the likelihood of enforcement action or operational disruption. Regulatory consistency, then, is not simply a defensive posture; it is a foundation for institutional trust. Banks that manage alignment effectively can launch new products confidently, enter partnerships with lower risk, and offer customers clarity even in complex markets. In a hybrid era defined by interconnected ecosystems and rapid regulatory evolution, cross-border alignment becomes a strategic capability that directly influences institutional stability, reputation, and long-term competitiveness. Regulatory alignment is a strategic capability that enables safe growth, not merely a compliance requirement.

Institutional Perspective: A Global Lens on Stewardship, Governance, and Being Human in Banking

Banking as a Civilisational Responsibility—What Institutions Owe Society

Banking discussions usually focus on technology—AI, cloud infrastructure, digital identity, embedded finance, open banking, real-time data. All of that matters. But underneath it sits a less discussed reality: technology alone doesn't create trust, stability, or resilience. Institutions do.

A bank can invest heavily in advanced systems and still struggle if governance is weak, accountability is fragmented, or leadership loses sight of emerging risks. At the same time, institutions with disciplined governance, strong culture, and operational clarity often navigate disruption far more effectively, even without having the most sophisticated technology.

The institution itself becomes a form of infrastructure.

Customers may never see governance frameworks directly, but they experience governance constantly through outcomes. A failed payment reflects institutional weakness. A cyber breach becomes a governance problem. A misleading product points to leadership failure. Poor complaint handling reveals cultural weakness. An inaccessible digital journey exposes flawed institutional design.

Technology is what customers see on the surface. Institutional maturity is what shapes the experience underneath.

Different societies experience this differently. In countries with long traditions of institutional continuity, operational reliability is treated as part of the social contract. Banks are expected not only to function, but to behave responsibly. In emerging economies, trust often depends on visible consistency because rapid transformation can coexist with uneven infrastructure. Across Asia, the Gulf, and parts of Europe, deeply digitised ecosystems require institutions to coordinate payments, identity systems, telecoms, cloud providers, and public infrastructure simultaneously. Institutional capability there becomes essential to maintaining broader societal confidence.

AI makes this even more important. Algorithms can improve fraud detection, servicing, and risk analysis dramatically. But their effectiveness depends entirely on the institutional discipline surrounding them. Weak governance doesn't disappear when advanced technology is introduced—it becomes amplified.

Customers understand this instinctively, even if they don't describe it in those terms. Long-term trust depends on fundamentally institutional questions: Is leadership accountable? Can problems be resolved fairly? Does the organisation learn from failure? Can it still be trusted when systems break?

Those questions cannot be solved through software alone.

Modern institutions now operate inside environments where complexity moves faster than traditional hierarchies were designed to manage. Decisions are spread across vendors, platforms, cloud environments, partners, and algorithmic systems simultaneously. Without institutional coherence, complexity becomes fragile.

Many recent operational failures in banking didn't happen because institutions lacked technology. They happened because organisations failed to coordinate responsibility and accountability effectively across interconnected systems.

The future institution may therefore be judged less by how much technology it owns and more by how well it governs complexity. Strong institutions are not simply large institutions. They are institutions capable of absorbing uncertainty, adapting continuously, and sustaining trust through rapidly changing environments.

Governance, in that sense, becomes part of the customer experience—even when customers never see it directly.

Governance Across Generations—How Leadership Shapes Institutional Memory

Governance is often discussed through structures—boards, committees, controls, reporting lines, and regulatory frameworks. Those things matter. But customers don't experience governance through organisational charts. They experience it through outcomes.

That distinction is becoming increasingly important.

A payment failure. A cyber incident. A mishandled vulnerable-customer complaint. A delayed fraud response. An inaccessible digital process. Customers don't need to understand governance frameworks to judge whether an institution seems prepared, accountable, and capable of responding responsibly under pressure.

Governance becomes emotionally visible when something goes wrong.

This matters because banking systems are woven into everyday life. Salaries, housing, healthcare, education, and business activity all depend on financial systems functioning reliably. Customers don't just expect innovation; they expect institutions to manage complexity responsibly.

When that expectation breaks down, the consequences extend far beyond operational inconvenience.

Different societies interpret governance differently. In the UK and much of Europe, customers expect transparency, procedural fairness, and visible accountability during disruption. Across highly coordinated Asian financial ecosystems, institutional credibility is closely tied to operational precision and reliability at scale. In emerging markets, governance is often judged more pragmatically: does the institution consistently protect customer interests while delivering dependable service in a rapidly changing environment?

Across all these contexts, one pattern remains consistent: customers judge institutions by how they behave under pressure.

AI intensifies this challenge. Automated systems increasingly shape fraud decisions, onboarding, servicing, and risk management. When those systems produce unfair or confusing outcomes, customers still hold the institution responsible—not the algorithm.

That is a critical governance reality. Accountability cannot be outsourced to technology.

Customers still expect explanations, fair treatment, escalation pathways, and human oversight when systems behave unexpectedly.

Modern governance frameworks are now under real strain because banking complexity evolves faster than traditional structures were built to handle. Cloud ecosystems, embedded finance, third-party dependencies, and real-time operations create interconnected risks that siloed organisations struggle to manage effectively.

Strong governance increasingly depends on organisational clarity, learning culture, leadership transparency, and cross-functional coordination. It requires institutions willing to confront complexity openly rather than simply contain it operationally.

Customers often recognise institutional maturity before they can explain why. Institutions that communicate clearly during disruption, resolve problems consistently, and remain visibly accountable tend to build stronger long-term trust than those relying primarily on brand reputation or technological sophistication.

In highly interconnected societies, trust is no longer built through promises alone. It is built through repeated demonstrations of competence and accountability when conditions become difficult.

The Human Architecture of Accountability—People, Culture, and Judgement

Institutional maturity is usually measured internally through governance standards, resilience frameworks, leadership capability, and financial strength. Externally, though, people experience it through confidence and trust—and those are shaped as much by culture and history as by organisational design.

People often recognise institutional maturity emotionally before they understand it technically. They notice whether institutions feel stable, fair, responsive, and dependable, especially during uncertainty.

In the UK and Northern Europe, maturity is closely associated with continuity, transparency, and procedural fairness. Customers expect clear escalation pathways, visible accountability, and strong oversight during disruption. Across continental Europe, there is also a strong emphasis on inclusion, ethical responsibility, and data protection.

In North America, maturity is often associated with capability, responsiveness, and innovation. Customers expect advanced digital experiences and rapid execution, while remaining highly sensitive to governance failures, data misuse, or market concentration.

Singapore and parts of East Asia present a different model, where institutional maturity is experienced through operational precision, coordination, and long-term strategic discipline. In Japan, institutional credibility is tied closely to consistency, procedural integrity, and social stability over time.

China represents another distinct environment where maturity is linked to platform integration and technological coordination at extraordinary scale. Convenience and speed shape customer expectations, but that scale also creates stronger demands for continuity and control.

Across the Gulf, maturity is often connected to visible service quality, relationship continuity, and support for rapidly modernising economies. In Africa, South Asia, and Latin America, mobile ecosystems have transformed participation, but institutional maturity depends less on technological sophistication and more on whether institutions remain understandable, accessible, and dependable across varied social realities.

These differences matter in practical terms. A governance approach that feels reassuring in one society may appear bureaucratic or emotionally distant in another. A highly automated customer experience may signal efficiency in one market while weakening trust in another where personal interaction still carries strong emotional importance.

AI magnifies these differences further. Public expectations around privacy, fairness, transparency, and algorithmic oversight vary widely depending on cultural attitudes toward authority and autonomy. A system viewed as trustworthy in one environment may feel opaque or intrusive in another.

The key insight is simple: institutional maturity cannot be measured purely internally because trust is experienced socially and culturally.

Institutions need more than operational capability. They need societal awareness—an understanding of how different populations interpret accountability, responsiveness, fairness, and institutional behaviour.

The institutions that endure globally may be those capable of translating internal discipline into public confidence across very different human environments.

Designing for Complexity—When Institutions Must Hold Multiple Truths at Once

Modern banks carry enormous influence. They shape access to credit, housing, payments, savings, business formation, and identity verification. Increasingly, they also shape how people move through digital society itself, because financial systems now intersect with behavioural data, digital infrastructure, and algorithmic decision-making almost everywhere.

Banking is no longer just a financial service. It has become part of the architecture of modern life.

As institutions become larger, more interconnected, and more data-driven, a deeper human question emerges: how do people continue feeling recognised inside systems shaped by concentrated institutional power?

Customers rarely interact with financial institutions as equals. Banks possess information asymmetry, legal authority, technological capability, and behavioural data far beyond what ordinary individuals can see. Most people accept this imbalance because they assume institutions will exercise power responsibly and within accountable frameworks.

When that assumption weakens, trust can collapse quickly.

This is why accountability matters emotionally as well as operationally. A customer unexpectedly denied access to funds feels powerless, even when the underlying control is justified. Someone trapped in an automated complaint process becomes frustrated not only because of delay, but because the institution feels unreachable. A vulnerable customer navigating rigid systems feels invisible when procedures matter more than human understanding.

People generally accept institutional authority when decisions feel explainable, escalation feels possible, and responsibility still appears human.

Historically, branches and relationship managers provided visible accountability. Customers knew where to go and who to speak to. Today, banking interactions increasingly happen through distributed digital ecosystems—apps, outsourced operations, AI systems, third-party platforms, and automated workflows—where customers often struggle to identify where responsibility actually sits.

The result is a subtle but important emotional shift: systems begin to feel as though they govern people rather than serve them.

AI intensifies this further. Automated systems now influence fraud detection, onboarding, behavioural interpretation, customer prioritisation, collections activity, and escalation pathways. These systems improve efficiency and risk management significantly, but they also create environments where people may not understand how decisions affecting their financial lives are made.

Power becomes harder to recognise when it operates invisibly through algorithms.

Customers only experience the consequences: a declined payment, restricted functionality, delayed access, or repeated verification requests. Without transparency and meaningful human oversight, automated systems create emotional distance between institutions and society—not intentionally, but through opacity.

That is why governance must include visible human accountability alongside technological sophistication. Institutions need to show not only that systems work operationally, but that decisions remain challengeable, fairness remains reviewable, escalation remains accessible, and responsibility ultimately remains human.

This extends beyond customer service. Public trust in large institutions increasingly depends on whether they appear governable, ethical, and socially accountable.

Banking has become part of a much broader societal question about how institutional power operates inside digitally mediated life.

The institutions most likely to sustain long-term legitimacy may be those ensuring people continue feeling respected, heard, and protected inside systems far larger than themselves.

Stewardship and the Long View—Building Institutions That Outlast Their Leaders

Technology will continue transforming banking through AI, automation, embedded finance, open banking, and real-time infrastructure. Institutions will become faster, smarter, and more interconnected. But alongside that transformation, another requirement is becoming more important: societies increasingly need institutions capable of responsible stewardship in environments defined by growing complexity.

Banks are no longer simply financial intermediaries. They have become critical infrastructure supporting payments, digital identity, economic participation, and social stability. As banking becomes more deeply embedded in daily life, institutional behaviour carries consequences far beyond commercial performance.

This is where stewardship becomes essential.

Management focuses on execution, efficiency, and operational delivery. Stewardship is broader. It means protecting long-term institutional legitimacy while navigating uncertainty responsibly across generations, technologies, and social change.

A stewarding institution asks different questions: how does this system affect society over time? What happens to vulnerable groups during rapid transformation? Does innovation remain governable? Will customers still trust the institution during disruption? Does the organisation strengthen social stability, or unintentionally weaken it?

These questions matter because modern financial systems are too interconnected for purely short-term thinking.

AI illustrates this clearly. It can dramatically improve fraud prevention, servicing, and resilience. But without careful stewardship, the same systems can also increase opacity, exclusion, bias, and emotional disconnection between institutions and society. Embedded finance creates similar tensions: convenience improves while accountability becomes harder for customers to locate when something fails.

Stewardship is ultimately the discipline of preserving trust inside increasingly invisible systems.

Different societies interpret stewardship differently. In the UK and Europe, it often centres on governance quality, ethical technology deployment, and visible accountability during uncertainty. Across much of Asia, stewardship is closely associated with continuity, infrastructure coordination, and long-term institutional discipline. In emerging markets, it frequently carries a developmental role focused on inclusion, accessibility, and societal trust-building.

Across all these environments, one expectation is becoming clearer: people increasingly expect institutions to manage complexity responsibly on behalf of society, not just shareholders.

That creates enormous leadership pressure, especially in a world shaped by cyber threats, geopolitical instability, AI acceleration, climate disruption, and growing scrutiny around institutional accountability.

The institutions that endure will not be the ones that avoid failure entirely. They will be the ones that remain transparent, adaptive, and visibly responsible when complexity becomes difficult to manage.

There is also an emotional dimension to stewardship. Customers now live inside systems they cannot fully see or understand. They depend on the assumption that institutional leaders remain disciplined, thoughtful, and accountable behind the surface of financial technology.

That assumption is fragile. It has to be reinforced continuously through behaviour, not marketing.

Technology can be replicated. Products can be replicated. Operational processes can be replicated.

Long-term institutional trust is far harder to replicate.

The next generation of banking institutions may ultimately be defined less by technological capability and more by whether they can govern transformation responsibly while preserving human confidence across society.

In increasingly algorithmic environments, stewardship may become the defining factor separating institutions that remain trusted for decades from those that succeed only temporarily.

Reflection

Institutional transformation is often described in terms of technology modernisation, digital acceleration, and customer-centric redesign. Yet the deeper truth emerging across global markets is that hybrid banking succeeds or fails based on the strength of its internal architecture. This chapter has shown that governance, leadership, operating models, professional standards, and regulatory alignment are not background enablers; they are the structural foundations that determine whether a retail bank can evolve with confidence, resilience, and integrity. Institutions built around legacy hierarchies, siloed responsibilities, and narrow leadership pipelines struggle to respond to the speed, complexity, and interdependence of the hybrid era. By contrast, institutions with strong boards, diverse leadership teams, disciplined risk intelligence, and coherent operating principles can adapt more quickly and make better long-term decisions. Institutional strength becomes most visible during moments of stress, when systems, leadership, and governance are tested simultaneously.

The analysis demonstrates that hybrid delivery reshapes everything inside the bank. Decision-making becomes distributed; risk oversight becomes continuous; talent requirements become multidisciplinary; and board accountability extends beyond internal operations to entire ecosystems of partners, vendors, and cross-border regulatory expectations. In this environment, professional standards serve as an anchor, ensuring that staff behaviours remain consistent even as channels, technologies, and customer expectations evolve. At the same time, cross-border regulatory alignment ensures that these behaviours are reinforced by coherent policies, transparent processes, and a shared understanding of supervisory expectations.

Above all, institutional design shapes trust. Customers may not see governance structures, operating models, or talent strategies, but they experience the consequences through service reliability, ethical decision-making, transparent communication, and responsible product design. Regulators, investors, and communities draw similar conclusions. A bank with strong internal architecture demonstrates discipline, foresight, and public responsibility-qualities that increasingly determine long-term legitimacy. As retail banking moves further into a hybrid, multi-partner, data-driven future, institutional excellence becomes a strategic differentiator. The banks that succeed will be those that redesign themselves with clarity of purpose, strength of governance, and a deep commitment to institutional integrity.

Framework

Framework Overview

This framework explains the institutional foundations that enable hybrid retail banking to function with consistency, accountability, and long-term resilience. It consolidates the insights from all five pillars to show how governance, leadership capability, organisational culture, operating discipline, and regulatory alignment must work together as a coherent system. Retail banking is increasingly shaped by cross-border rules, rapid technology shifts, and multi-partner ecosystems. Institutions cannot rely on outdated structures. The framework highlights how strategic foresight, professional competence, and adaptive models form the internal architecture that supports every customer-facing transformation. Each component must translate into measurable institutional outcomes, including resilience, decision quality, and customer trust.

The Institutional Design Lens

BOARD FORESIGHT AND STRATEGIC GOVERNANCE

Hybrid banking requires boards that can oversee complex service flows, digital infrastructures, and multi-market regulatory expectations. Institutions must ensure that board composition, committee structures, and decision pathways are equipped for technology-driven environments. Effective governance depends on clear accountability, informed challenge, long-term purpose, and continuous education. Strategic foresight—scenario planning, horizon scanning, and cross-jurisdictional intelligence—becomes a structural requirement, not an optional discipline.

OPERATING MODEL INTEGRATION

Institutional resilience depends on operating models that unify physical and digital delivery, central and local functions, and internal and external partners. Fragmented structures weaken service reliability and increase risk. Integrated journey ownership, consistent process standards, shared data environments, and collaborative teams form the backbone of hybrid delivery. Strong operating models reduce friction, improve responsiveness, and allow institutions to scale innovation safely.

LEADERSHIP DIVERSITY AND CULTURAL INTEGRITY

Diverse leadership strengthens governance quality, reduces blind spots, and improves institutional legitimacy. Institutions must build teams that reflect the markets they serve and encourage challenge, transparency, and inclusive decision-making. Culture becomes infrastructure: behaviours, incentives, and norms determine how effectively institutions respond to technology, risk, and customer expectations. A healthy culture enables ethical judgment, operational discipline, and sustained trust.

PROFESSIONAL STANDARDS AND INSTITUTIONAL COMPETENCE

Professional standards anchor consistency across hybrid operations. Accreditation, conduct expectations, ethical codes, and continuous learning create a baseline for competence and customer protection. As decision-making shifts into digital channels and algorithmic environments, these standards ensure fairness, responsibility, and technical capability. Embedding professional disciplines into recruitment, training, and leadership pathways strengthens integrity and reduces misconduct risk.

CROSS-BORDER REGULATORY ALIGNMENT

Hybrid institutions increasingly operate across regulatory regimes with different expectations for data sharing, cloud use, customer protection, cybersecurity, and sustainability. Consistent alignment with global standards is now essential. Institutions must harmonise internal policies, build regulatory-intelligence capabilities, and maintain transparent engagement with supervisors. Regulatory alignment is not only about avoiding sanctions—it is the structural mechanism that enables scale, partnership, innovation, and public trust. Alignment must be evidenced through consistent execution, not policy intent.

Purpose of the Framework

This chapter's framework establishes the governance and design foundations required

for a modern hybrid retail bank to operate with coherence, accountability, and long-term institutional strength. It shows that resilience is not solely a technology question but a leadership and design question—one that requires boards, executive teams, operating models, and cultures to function as a single, aligned system. When institutional design is strong, banks can absorb complexity, sustain customer confidence, and fulfil their obligations to communities and regulators across cycles of change.

Table 9.1 Checklist: Institutional Design Maturity Readiness

1	Board Capability and Foresight Does the board demonstrate technological, regulatory, and strategic fluency beyond financial oversight?
2	Clarity of Accountability Are decision rights, escalation pathways, and ownership clearly defined across the institution?
3	Integrated Operating Model Do physical, digital, and partner ecosystems operate as one coherent system?
4	Decision-Making Discipline Are decisions timely, informed, and aligned across risk, operations, and customer outcomes?
5	Leadership Depth and Diversity Does leadership reflect varied perspectives, capabilities, and real-world customer understanding?
6	Culture of Challenge and Transparency Is constructive challenge encouraged, and are issues surfaced early without defensiveness?
7	Professional Standards and Competence Are behaviours, ethics, and capabilities consistently applied across all roles and channels?
8	Regulatory Alignment Capability Can the institution operate seamlessly across multiple regulatory regimes without fragmentation?
9	Data and Information Governance Is decision-making supported by timely, integrated, and reliable information flows?
10	Institutional Learning and Adaptability Does the organisation continuously learn, evolve, and respond to emerging risks and shifts?

Table 9.2 Template: Institutional Design Architecture Mapping

No.	*Board Design and Foresight*	*Traditional oversight focus*	*Limited forward-looking capability*	*Strategically foresighted, technology-aware board*	*Chair / Board*
1	Governance and Accountability	Fragmented ownership	Delays and unclear escalation	Clear decision rights and accountability structures	CEO / Board
2	Operating Model Integration	Channel and function silos	Inconsistent delivery	Unified, journey-aligned operating model	COO
3	Decision-Making Architecture	Hierarchical and slow	Bottlenecks and inconsistency	Delegated, real-time, risk-aligned decisions	COO / CRO
4	Leadership Composition	Homogeneous leadership	Blind spots and narrow perspective	Diverse, multi-disciplinary leadership	CEO / Nomination Committee
5	Culture and Behaviour	Compliance-driven culture	Weak challenge and escalation	Open, transparent, challenge-led culture	CEO / HR
6	Professional Standards	Uneven capability and ethics	Inconsistent outcomes	Institution-wide professional discipline and accreditation	HR / Compliance
7	Data and Information Flows	Fragmented reporting	Delayed or partial visibility	Integrated, real-time, decision-grade information	CIO / Data
8	Regulatory Alignment	Localised compliance approach	Cross-border risk exposure	Harmonised global standards with local adaptation	CRO / Compliance
9	Institutional Learning	Reactive adjustments	Slow adaptation to change	Continuous learning embedded in governance and operations	CEO / Board
10	Board Design and Foresight	Traditional oversight focus	Limited forward-looking capability	Strategically foresighted, technology-aware board	Chair / Board

Bibliography

Accenture (2023). *Research on Banking Operating Models and Digital Transformation.* Accenture Financial Services Research.

APRA (2022). *Prudential Practice Guide on Governance, Risk Culture and Accountability.* Australian Prudential Regulation Authority.

Bank for International Settlements (2023). *Principles for Operational Resilience and Digital Governance in Financial Services.* BIS.

Bank of England (2022). *Biennial Exploratory Scenario (BES): Climate and Systemic Risk Framework.* Bank of England.

Chartered Banker Institute (2023). *Research on Professional Standards and Ethical Banking Practices.* Chartered Banker Institute.

Deloitte (2023). *Insights on Governance in Hybrid Financial Institutions.* Deloitte Insights.

European Banking Authority (2022). *Guidelines on Internal Governance under Directive 2013/36/EU.* EBA.

European Union (2022). *Digital Operational Resilience Act (DORA).* European Commission.

Financial Conduct Authority (2021). *Guidance on Operational Resilience and Consumer Duty.* FCA.

Gartner (2023). *Research on Board Governance, AI Oversight and Institutional Foresight in Financial Services.* Gartner Research.

HM Revenue & Customs (2022). *Research on Digital Service Transformation and Operational Integration.* HMRC.

International Monetary Fund (2023). *Research on Governance, Institutional Resilience and Financial Stability in Digital Economies.* IMF.

LIBF (2023). *Research on Professional Banking Standards and Conduct in Digital Financial Services.* LIBF.

McKinsey & Company (2023). *Insights on Future Operating Models for Retail Banking.* McKinsey Global Banking Practice.

Monetary Authority of Singapore (2022). *Information Paper on Corporate Governance and Board Diversity in Financial Institutions.* MAS.

NHS England (2022). *Research on Professional Standards, Accountability and Hybrid Service Governance.* NHS England.

Organisation for Economic Co-operation and Development (2023). *Governance, Trust and Institutional Resilience in the Digital Economy.* OECD Publishing.

Reserve Bank of India (2022). *Governance and Digital Operating Frameworks in Banking.* RBI.

World Economic Forum (2023). *Insights on Financial Governance and Institutional Trust.* World Economic Forum.

10 Designing the Bank of the Future

It also highlights why long-lived institutions must balance continuity with renewal. Designing the bank of the future anticipates climate pressures, cybersecurity threats, shifting customer expectations, and the consequences of open ecosystems—while remaining grounded in values that anchor public trust. It must learn continuously, modernise responsibly, invest in people, and maintain clarity of purpose even as operating models transform. The chapter concludes by presenting the Future Architecture Manifesto, which integrates trust, governance, hybrid delivery, inclusion, resilience, and institutional purpose into a unified design philosophy. This final chapter sets out the mindset, capabilities, and structural principles required for retail banks to serve society with integrity for the next century. Longevity therefore becomes a matter of institutional discipline, where governance, technology, and culture operate together to protect public trust.

Context

Designing a retail bank that can remain relevant for the next century requires a very different mindset from designing an institution for the next five years. Most banks today manage transformations around product cycles, regulatory timelines, digital programmes, or market competition. But a 100-year bank must think in decades—not quarters. It must be built on foundations that can absorb shocks, adapt to new societal demands, and remain trusted even when technologies, customers, and economic conditions change dramatically. This section explains why long-term institutional design is now essential, and why hybrid banking, in particular, demands an institution that is resilient, reflective, and deeply anchored in purpose.

A long-lived institution is not one that stays the same; it is one that evolves continuously without losing its identity. Retail banking has become deeply interconnected with climate risk, demographic transitions, cyber exposure, open data ecosystems, and global regulatory shifts. Banks must therefore operate as adaptive systems. They must learn from failures, recalibrate strategies, and redesign processes while preserving the cultural integrity and governance discipline that anchor public trust. This chapter places

DOI: 10.4324/9781042021765-11

emphasis on institutional behaviour- decision-making, leadership quality, organisational learning, and operational coherence as the true determinants of longevity. Institutional capability must be visible in execution quality, including decision consistency, operational stability, customer experience outcomes, and responsiveness under stress.

Another defining feature of designing the bank of the future is its ability to remain relevant across generations. Few industries span such diverse customer groups: Gen Z digital natives, mid-career families navigating financial complexity, ageing populations requiring advisory support, and vulnerable groups needing stability and reassurance. A future-ready bank must build systems and services that are inclusive, intuitive, and adaptable to these varying needs. It must avoid the trap of designing solutions only for the digitally fluent or the high-income segment. Instead, it must approach customer design with humility, empathy, and a long-term commitment to capability-building.

Institutional longevity also depends on resilience—not just operational resilience, but multi-dimensional resilience that spans governance, technology, culture, partnerships, and societal responsibility. Designing the bank of the future cannot treat resilience as a compliance requirement. It must embed resilience into decision-making, strategy development, vendor dependencies, crisis response, and talent planning. Major global banks that have withstood decades of disruption have done so because they invested in strong governance, disciplined risk frameworks, transparent leadership, and organisational culture long before crises emerged.

Systems thinking is another critical capability for longevity. Retail banks today operate in an ecosystem where small decisions in technology, product, or risk can create large effects across the institution. Hybrid delivery amplifies this complexity because digital channels influence branch behaviour, partner ecosystems influence customer experience, and AI-driven decisions influence trust. Designing the bank of the future must cultivate a leadership culture that sees connections, anticipates unintended consequences, and aligns decisions across departments.

Finally, longevity requires purpose. A bank cannot thrive for 100 years without a clear understanding of its responsibility to customers, communities, and the economy. Purpose shapes culture, anchors decision-making, and provides stability in times of uncertainty. This chapter argues that long-term institutions are those that treat banking as a societal obligation, not just a commercial activity—balancing innovation with prudence, technology with humanity, and efficiency with fairness.

This context section sets up the five pillars that follow, each offering a structural building block for designing the future 100-year bank.

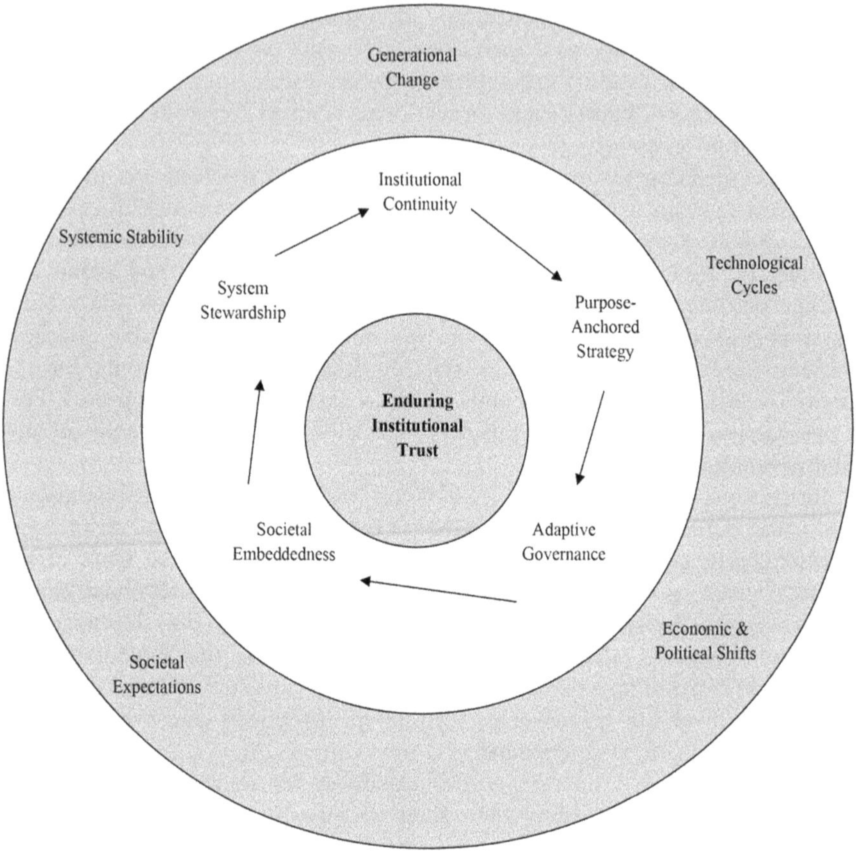

Figure 10.1 The Architecture of a 100-Year Financial Institution

Designing for Institutional Longevity

Case Study: Mitsubishi UFJ Financial Group—Banking Across Centuries

Mitsubishi UFJ Financial Group traces its institutional roots back more than 350 years, evolving from merchant banking origins into one of the world's largest financial institutions. Its longevity has not been driven by constant reinvention, but by disciplined adaptation across political regimes, economic cycles, and technological eras. The group has consistently preserved core principles of prudence, relationship banking, and long-term capital stewardship while selectively modernising governance, risk management, and digital capability. This case illustrates that a "100-year bank" is not defined by disruption, but by the capacity to evolve without losing institutional memory or societal trust.

Designing a bank for 100-year relevance requires leadership teams to adopt a fundamentally different orientation toward risk, investment, and organisational culture. Long-lived institutions demonstrate a consistent ability to make steady, patient decisions even when markets around them reward short-term gains. They resist the temptation to over-optimise for quarterly results and instead focus on preserving financial strength, maintaining customer goodwill, and nurturing internal talent over long horizons. A central element of longevity is governance discipline: clear committee structures, transparent decision-making, and active oversight that prevents operational weaknesses from accumulating silently over time. Equally important is the bank's ability to refresh itself. Institutions that survive across generations deliberately introduce new skills, new leadership perspectives, and new operating models before they become outdated. They modernise technology platforms proactively, cultivate digital and analytical talent, and strengthen risk systems in anticipation of future regulatory standards. Longevity also depends on cultural integrity. Staff at all levels must feel connected to the bank's purpose and understand the responsibilities that come with safeguarding customer trust. This culture must withstand external turbulence—economic downturns, political change, or technological disruption—without losing its ethical centre. Finally, designing for longevity requires organisations to invest in inclusive service models that ensure relevance across evolving societal needs. A 100-year bank does not lock itself into serving one demographic or market condition; it adapts to the needs of youth, migrants, ageing populations, and digitally hesitant customers. By embedding long-term thinking into governance, strategy, culture, and capability building, retail banks create the foundations to remain credible, competitive, and trusted for generations.

Institutional longevity depends heavily on a bank's ability to maintain strategic coherence across leadership transitions, market cycles, and regulatory shifts. Many institutions falter not because they lack capability, but because their long-term vision becomes fragmented each time leadership changes. A 100-year bank ensures continuity by embedding its purpose and strategic priorities into governance documents, board charters, executive mandates, and performance frameworks that outlive individual personalities. This institutionalisation of purpose protects the organisation from short-term swings in leadership style or market pressure. At the same time, longevity requires disciplined adaptability—the ability to pivot thoughtfully without abandoning core principles. Banks that endure across decades integrate structured horizon scanning into board discussions, regularly assess technology pathways, and keep their operating models flexible enough to embrace new delivery formats. They also maintain institutional memory through well-documented processes, strong internal audit functions, and leadership-development systems that prepare future executives to understand past decisions without being bound by them. The culture within a long-lived bank reinforces collective accountability, rewarding teams for responsible stewardship rather than isolated heroics. Additionally, institutions designed for longevity nurture deep stakeholder relationships—with regulators, community groups, local businesses, and global partners—recognising that multi-decade trust is built through consistent behaviour, not marketing. A 100-year bank views customers not as short-term revenue opportunities but as long-term relationships that must be earned and re-earned across generations. By building continuity into structures, adaptability into systems, and responsibility into culture, the bank develops the strategic coherence needed to withstand disruption and remain relevant over extended time horizons. Continuity must be embedded in structures rather than dependent on individual leadership.

Institutional longevity also depends on how effectively a bank balances prudence with innovation—two forces that can easily conflict if not managed deliberately. Long-lived institutions recognise that innovation without discipline leads to instability, while discipline without innovation leads to irrelevance. They therefore create governance structures that allow controlled experimentation, ensuring that new technologies, partnerships, and business models are tested within clear risk parameters before being scaled. This balance is reinforced through investment principles that prioritise long-term capability-building rather than short-lived efficiency gains. Successful century-ready institutions invest steadily in core infrastructure: secure data foundations, resilient systems, talent development, and customer-trust mechanisms. These investments may not produce immediate financial returns, but they pay off over decades by reducing operational shocks and strengthening credibility. At the same time, longevity requires institutions to avoid becoming inward-looking or overconfident in their legacy. Banks that survive across generations cultivate external awareness through engagement with regulators, academia, technology leaders, and community bodies, continually reassessing their position within a changing world. They also adopt adaptive capital strategies—balancing stable, low-risk portfolios with measured exposure to emerging sectors that reflect evolving customer needs. Another hallmark of enduring institutions is their approach to crisis management: instead of reacting defensively, they use crises as catalysts to improve systems, sharpen leadership capability, and strengthen governance. By institutionalising learning from disruptions, they ensure that each challenge enhances, not weakens, their long-term trajectory. Ultimately, a 100-year bank matures in cycles: it preserves what is essential, discards what is outdated, experiments with what is emerging, and reforms what is misaligned. This disciplined evolution is what makes longevity an attainable and repeatable organisational outcome.

A defining feature of institutions that endure for a century or more is their ability to design leadership pipelines that evolve with the times while preserving the organisation's core character. How long-lived banks create leadership continuity without becoming static or dependent on a single generation of executives is an important focus. Sustainable institutions invest in structured succession planning that looks beyond titles and hierarchy, identifying individuals with judgment, humility, resilience, and a genuine understanding of customer realities. They recognise that future leadership requires a blend of domain expertise, digital fluency, ethical reasoning, and the capacity to operate in diverse, multi-stakeholder environments. Long-term institutions therefore build leadership capability deliberately—through formal governance training, exposure to cross-functional areas, rotations across geographies, and mentorship that emphasises institutional purpose alongside performance metrics. They also create transparent systems that prevent leadership concentration, groupthink, or over-reliance on legacy networks. This includes encouraging challenge in boardrooms, inviting external voices, and fostering environments where decisions are tested, debated, and stress-checked rigorously. Leadership renewal becomes a cultural discipline rather than an occasional event. The most resilient institutions also recognise that leadership is not confined to senior executives; they nurture talent across all levels, ensuring that frontline teams, risk managers, technologists, and community partners understand their role in shaping the bank's long-term direction. By decentralising responsibility and reinforcing shared purpose, these institutions avoid fragility and create a deep bench of future-ready leaders. This sustained investment in people—guided by values, strengthened by governance, and tested through real-world complexity—ensures that the organisation can retain its identity while continually renewing itself. In a world defined by rapid change, it is this leadership architecture that gives a bank the clarity, adaptability, and credibility required to thrive for 100 years.

Institutions that aspire to last 100 years treat culture not as a slogan but as an operating system that guides behaviour, decision-making, and customer engagement across generations. Cultural architecture becomes a long-term asset when it is deliberately shaped, continuously reinforced, and deeply connected to the bank's purpose. A future-ready culture emphasises integrity, accountability, service, and humility—values that anchor trust even as technology and market expectations evolve. Long-lived banks recognise that culture is most vulnerable during periods of rapid growth, mergers, regulatory scrutiny, or digital transformation. To counter this, they create clear behavioural standards, transparent communication routines, and leadership practices that make culture visible in everyday actions. Institutions with longevity actively measure cultural health through staff engagement, customer sentiment, conduct indicators, and decision patterns across departments. They provide mechanisms for employees to challenge poor behaviour, raise concerns early, and escalate risks without fear. They also embed cultural expectations into recruitment, promotions, performance reviews, and vendor relationships, ensuring that external partners uphold the same standards. A strong culture supports resilience by helping teams respond consistently during crises—protecting customers, prioritising stability, and maintaining service quality even under stress. It also fosters adaptability: people who feel valued and empowered are more willing to learn, embrace new tools, and support organisational change. Critically, culture becomes a bridge between generations of employees, keeping the institution grounded in its founding principles while encouraging renewal. In designing the bank of the future, culture is not a static ideal; it is a living framework that evolves with society, strengthens trust, and ensures that institutional behaviour remains aligned with long-term purpose and public responsibility.

Long-lived institutions recognise that leadership succession is one of the most decisive factors determining whether a bank can maintain relevance across decades. Succession must be treated not as an episodic event triggered by retirements or crises, but as a continuous organisational discipline that safeguards institutional memory, strategic direction, and public trust. Future-ready banks build structured succession pipelines that identify talent early, develop leaders through cross-functional exposure, and ensure that potential successors understand technology, risk, customer behaviour, governance, and societal expectations. Effective succession frameworks blend technical capability with values, judgement, and integrity—qualities that sustain credibility during transitions. Institutions with longevity also prioritise transparency in leadership changes, communicating clearly with regulators, staff, and customers to minimise uncertainty and maintain stability. They build redundancy in leadership capabilities so that no single individual becomes a point of institutional dependency. This includes developing multiple successors for critical roles, investing in continuous leadership development, and ensuring diverse perspectives in executive teams. Long-lived banks also expose emerging leaders to external ecosystems—regulators, fintech partners, community stakeholders, and global markets—so that future leadership remains outward-looking and attuned to shifts in society and technology. Importantly, succession planning extends beyond the executive tier: sustainable institutions ensure operational continuity at every level, from branch leadership to technology governance. A disciplined approach to succession prevents abrupt cultural shifts, reduces strategic volatility, and preserves the bank's long-term purpose during transitions. In designing the bank of the future, leadership renewal becomes a strategic capability, enabling the institution to remain stable yet adaptive as it journeys through generations of change.

Longevity also depends on an institution's ability to balance heritage with reinvention—preserving the values that anchor trust while updating the systems, behaviours, and structures that shape everyday performance. Banks with long-term resilience consciously maintain a stable core identity while allowing for continuous evolution at the edges. The most enduring institutions articulate a clear purpose that transcends market cycles: enabling financial security, supporting community prosperity, safeguarding trust, and acting responsibly in society. This purpose serves as a stabilising force during periods of technological disruption, regulatory change, or economic stress. At the same time, long-lived banks avoid the trap of institutional nostalgia. They modernise product portfolios, streamline processes, adopt new delivery models, and refresh customer engagement approaches without losing sight of the principles that define who they are. This balance between constancy and reinvention becomes a cultural discipline embedded in leadership behaviour, staff training, and strategic planning. Institutions that manage this duality well often establish dedicated innovation units, continuous improvement teams, and cross-functional forums that encourage experimentation while protecting core governance. They regularly review legacy practices, question past assumptions, and retire outdated processes that hinder agility. By doing so, they prevent the gradual stagnation that often weakens long-established organisations. Crucially, designing the bank of the future builds a culture where employees understand both the weight of institutional history and the need to evolve with customer expectations. This creates a stable yet adaptive organisation—one that honours its past but is not constrained by it, ensuring that it remains relevant and trusted as society, technology, and financial landscapes continue to evolve.

It also relies on a bank's ability to cultivate leadership continuity without allowing leadership stagnation. Accordingly, future-ready institutions design leadership pathways that ensure smooth transitions, protect institutional memory, and maintain cultural stability while still bringing in new thinking at the right moments. Long-lived banks avoid over-reliance on a single leadership style or a narrow pool of executives. Instead, they build structured succession pipelines that identify talent early, develop leaders through cross-functional exposure, and rotate high-potential individuals through risk, operations, technology, and customer-facing roles. This broadens institutional understanding and prevents siloed thinking. At the same time, resilient institutions recognise the value of external infusion—bringing in leaders with new perspectives on digital architecture, regulatory change, behavioural economics, or community engagement. The strongest long-term organisations blend internal continuity with strategic external appointments to maintain balance. Leadership continuity also requires systems that institutionalise learning: after-action reviews, crisis debriefs, scenario exercises, and knowledge-capture routines that ensure insights do not leave with retiring leaders. Equally important is leadership culture—long-lived banks nurture leaders who are humble, ethically grounded, and open to challenge, not simply technically strong. These behaviours set the tone for accountability, collaboration, and long-term decision-making across the organisation. By designing leadership development as a structural capability rather than an HR activity, banks create a pipeline of leaders who understand both legacy responsibilities and future ambitions. This ensures that the institution does not depend on luck or personality, but on a disciplined, renewable leadership model capable of carrying the bank confidently into the next century.

This ultimately depends on how well an institution balances stability with reinvention, ensuring that its long-term purpose remains intact even as its operating reality transforms. With this knowledge, future-ready banks build disciplined renewal cycles—structured moments where strategy, culture, technology, and customer needs are reassessed without waiting for a crisis to trigger change. Long-lived institutions establish formal review rhythms that look beyond annual business plans: multi-year strategic refreshes, periodic culture diagnostics, deep dives into customer relevance, and independent evaluations of governance, inclusion, and risk posture. These cycles act as early-warning systems, identifying shifts in behaviour, regulation, technology, and societal expectations before they erode competitiveness. At the same time, enduring organisations preserve foundational anchors: a clear sense of purpose, a commitment to public responsibility, and values that guide behaviour across generations. This combination of renewal and continuity allows institutions to evolve without losing identity. The importance of long-term investment should also be highlighted—whether in community relationships, staff capability, resilient infrastructure, or ethical technology—recognising that the return on such investments often spans decades rather than quarters. Finally, longevity requires institutions to embrace humility: acknowledging what is no longer working, learning from external benchmarks, and being willing to redesign entrenched practices. Banks that embed this balance into their institutional DNA become capable of navigating uncertainty while strengthening trust over time. They do not merely survive change—they shape it.

Figure 10.2 presents the "Singh Framework for Designing the Bank of the Future." This framework brings together the institutional principles developed throughout this book into a single institutional architecture for designing resilient, trustworthy, and future-ready banking institutions.

Institutional longevity begins with clarity of purpose, disciplined governance, and a deep commitment to public trust. A retail bank that aims to survive for 100 years must anchor its identity in values that endure beyond market cycles, leadership changes, or technology shifts. Longevity is not achieved through scale or profitability alone; it is earned by institutions that cultivate resilience in their culture, protect customer interests consistently, and maintain a steady focus on long-term value creation. Banks that have endured for decades typically exhibit one characteristic above all others: they do not allow short-term pressures to distort strategic judgment. They prioritise early investment in risk controls, customer relationships, and organisational capability even when such investments are not immediately profitable. Longevity also requires adaptability. Institutions must treat every technological transition, regulatory change, and economic shock as an opportunity to modernise, not a threat to stability. This means leadership teams must encourage learning, allow space for new ideas, and avoid becoming rigid in structure or thinking. Organisational memory plays a vital role: retaining lessons from past crises helps prevent repeat failures, while allowing younger talent to bring fresh perspectives prevents complacency. A 100-year bank recognises that the world its customers live in changes rapidly - climate patterns shift, demographics evolve, digital expectations accelerate - and therefore it builds systems, governance processes, and leadership mindsets that evolve continuously. By balancing heritage with renewal, prudence with ambition, and tradition with innovation, institutions lay the groundwork for multi-decade relevance and stability. Longevity ultimately reflects the institution's ability to deliver consistent outcomes, not its stated ambition.

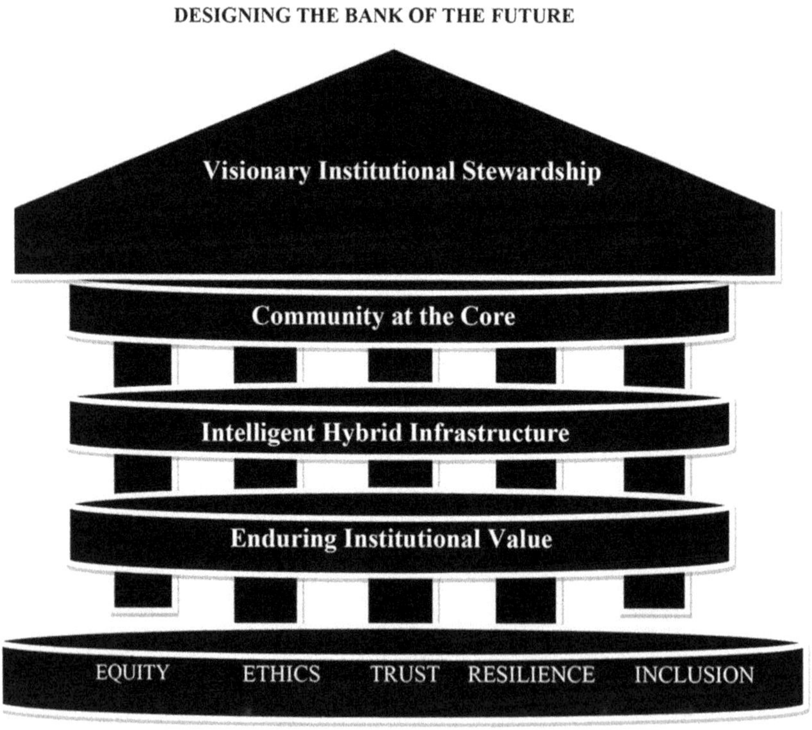

Figure 10.2 The Singh Framework for Designing the Bank of the Future

The Adaptive Resilience Cube

Resilience in a 100-year institution must be conceived as a living system, not a static checklist, and this establishes why long-term survival depends on multi-dimensional strength rather than isolated controls. Retail banks historically treated resilience as a narrow operational function—continuity plans, backup sites, and crisis-response manuals—but hybrid banking demands a far broader architecture. This section introduces the notion of the "Adaptive Resilience Cube" as a way of viewing resilience across interconnected dimensions: structural, technological, operational, cultural, and societal. Structural resilience covers capital adequacy, liquidity depth, balance-sheet composition, and governance clarity. Technological resilience focuses on secure digital platforms, interoperable infrastructure, and the ability to recover rapidly from cyber incidents. Operational resilience encompasses continuity of service, vendor stability, multi-site redundancy, and the ability to maintain customer journeys even during disruption. Cultural resilience reflects leadership behaviour, staff adaptability, and the institution's ethical maturity under pressure. Societal resilience recognises that banks must retain legitimacy, uphold their public role, and support communities during stress. When banks view resilience through this cube, they recognise that a weakness in any dimension can cascade into failures across the others—for example, a cyber breach triggering reputational loss, or cultural indiscipline undermining operational controls. The Adaptive Resilience Cube provides an integrated, long-term lens for testing, strengthening, and aligning the institution's ability to absorb shocks, adapt intelligently, and continue delivering trustworthy services for decades to come. Resilience is measured through continuity of service, protection of customers, and stability under stress.

The first dimension of the Adaptive Resilience Cube is structural resilience: the capacity of the institution to maintain operational continuity, governance coherence, and customer confidence under conditions of stress, disruption, or transformation. Structural resilience is not achieved through redundancy alone. It is built through clear accountability frameworks, disciplined capital planning, coherent operating models, and a leadership culture that prioritises long-term stability over short-term optimisation. A structurally resilient bank can absorb regulatory change, withstand economic shocks, and navigate technology transitions without losing clarity of purpose or control of customer outcomes. It is the foundation upon which every other dimension of the Adaptive Resilience Cube rests. The second dimension of the Adaptive Resilience Cube focuses on technological resilience, recognising that digital infrastructure now forms the central nervous system of every hybrid retail bank. This form of resilience can no longer be achieved through occasional upgrades or fragmented cybersecurity investments; it demands a coherent, end-to-end technology architecture built for continuity, transparency, and recovery. A future-ready institution must maintain interoperable platforms, real-time monitoring systems, robust encryption standards, and cloud arrangements that ensure service availability even when individual components fail. Such modern resilience requires layered defence: continuous authentication, automated threat detection, partner-level visibility, and active stress-testing of digital assets. It should also be highlighted that many technology breakdowns stem not from cyber-attacks but from poor configuration, vendor dependency, or failure to align legacy systems with new digital capabilities. Hybrid delivery makes this even more complex, as APIs, mobile journeys, and third-party services create chains of interdependency where a single weak link can disrupt entire customer flows. It should be stressed that technological resilience is not solely a technical function; it is a governance responsibility that must engage the board, the risk committee, and frontline units that rely on digital tools. Institutions that invest in resilient technology—real-time dashboards, redundant systems, interoperable data models, and secure cloud-native frameworks—are better positioned to maintain trust, protect customer data, and recover swiftly from incidents. By embedding technological resilience into long-term planning, banks strengthen their capacity to operate confidently in an increasingly volatile, digital-first financial ecosystem. Technological resilience remains a board-level accountability, not a technical function.

The third dimension of the Adaptive Resilience Cube is operational resilience, which ensures that the institution can continue delivering essential services even when faced with disruption, uncertainty, or external shocks. Operational resilience goes well beyond business continuity plans kept on a shelf; it is an organisational discipline grounded in clarity of roles, robust processes, tested playbooks, and the ability to mobilise quickly when systems, people, or partners come under stress. Hybrid retail banking introduces additional complexity, as operations now span physical branches, digital channels, centralised hubs, outsourced processes, and real-time interactions with fintech partners. A breakdown in any one node—whether a payment processor, a cloud service, a call centre, or a core-banking function—can trigger consumer anxiety, regulatory attention, and reputational damage. As a result, leading institutions build resilience by mapping critical services, identifying single points of failure, embedding redundancy, and running end-to-end simulations that test real-world scenarios such as cyber incidents, vendor outages, climate-related disruptions, or unexpected surges in customer demand. It should be emphasised that operational resilience depends on people as much as systems: staff must be trained to respond calmly, escalate issues quickly, and collaborate across departments without bureaucracy slowing down decisions. The importance of vendor stability, contract clarity, data-recovery arrangements, and shared responsibility models across ecosystems should also be underscored. For hybrid banks, operational resilience becomes a strategic capability—one that preserves trust, protects vulnerable customers, and ensures continuity in a world where disruptions are frequent, visible, and unforgiving.

Case Study: Rabobank—Cooperative Purpose at Scale

Rabobank was founded as a cooperative institution to support agricultural communities and local enterprises, a purpose that continues to shape its governance and operating model today. Member ownership, regional accountability, and reinvestment into community development have allowed the bank to scale internationally without abandoning its cooperative roots. Through crises, consolidation, and digital transformation, Rabobank has maintained trust by aligning profitability with long-term societal contribution. The case of Rabobank demonstrates how purpose, when structurally embedded rather than rhetorically stated, becomes a stabilising force that enables institutions to survive and remain relevant over generations.

The fourth dimension of the Adaptive Resilience Cube is cultural resilience, the internal strength that enables institutions to respond constructively to pressure, uncertainty, and rapid change. Systems, processes, and technologies can only go so far if the underlying culture is rigid, fearful, or disconnected from purpose. Cultural resilience is built when leadership encourages openness, cross-functional collaboration, and honest escalation rather than blame or avoidance. In a hybrid retail-banking environment, teams must routinely work across disciplines—risk, technology, operations, compliance, branches, and digital—to solve complex problems under time pressure. Institutions that cultivate psychological safety, ethical behaviour, and responsibility at every level are better equipped to adapt during crises, maintain service quality, and protect customer trust. Cultural resilience also depends on leadership humility, ethical decision-making, and role-modelling-leaders who listen, communicate clearly, and convey stability in periods of volatility. Such leaders have a direct impact on staff confidence and customer experience. Also worth stressing is the importance of continuous learning: staff must be encouraged to build new skills in digital systems, customer vulnerability, data literacy, climate exposure, and operational governance. Cultural resilience is therefore not about maintaining a "positive atmosphere"; it is about equipping people with the mindset, tools, and authority to respond effectively when the unexpected happens. In designing the bank of the future, culture becomes a strategic asset: it strengthens institutional memory, accelerates adaptation, and ensures that values such as fairness, inclusion, prudence, and integrity remain visible in day-to-day behaviour. Through this cultural backbone, hybrid institutions build resilience that is deeply human, authentically grounded, and aligned with long-term institutional purpose.

The fifth dimension of the Adaptive Resilience Cube is societal resilience, which emphasises the bank's responsibility to contribute positively to the communities it serves. A 100-year institution must be embedded in the social and economic fabric of society, not positioned above it. Societal resilience recognises that the strength of a bank is linked to the stability, confidence, and capability of the households and small businesses around it. When communities face financial stress—rising debt, climate disruption, unemployment, digital exclusion—the bank feels the impact directly through credit losses, reduced deposits, reputational strain, and operational disruption. Therefore, the most forward-looking institutions invest actively in financial literacy, digital inclusion, climate preparedness, and local economic participation. Banks that support households during difficult periods, especially vulnerable groups such as the elderly, migrants, low-income families, and small business owners, build long-term trust that withstands competitive and economic pressure. Societal resilience also includes ethical data use, transparent communication, fair pricing, and responsible product design. Hybrid banking amplifies these responsibilities: automated decisions must remain fair, digital journeys must be accessible, and partnerships across ecosystems must uphold consumer protection. Additionally, societal resilience requires institutions to maintain strong environmental stewardship, reducing carbon footprints across branches, operations, and supply chains. In sum, a 100-year bank views society not as a market, but as a shared environment where institutional stability depends on community well-being. By reinforcing societal resilience, banks strengthen their licence to operate, deepen trust, and create a foundation that supports longevity far beyond economic cycles or technological eras.

The sixth dimension of the Adaptive Resilience Cube is leadership resilience, which reflects how the behaviour, discipline, and emotional steadiness of senior leaders shape the institution's long-term stability. A 100-year bank cannot be built on technical expertise alone; it requires leaders who demonstrate judgement under pressure, clarity during uncertainty, and humility when decisions affect millions of customers. Leadership resilience is defined by how effectively executives and board members absorb external shocks, communicate with transparency, and steer the institution through moments of complexity without eroding trust. Resilient leaders maintain a calm, reasoned approach during crises—system outages, regulatory findings, reputational incidents, or economic stress—ensuring that staff at all levels remain aligned and focused on customer protection. The importance of ethical decision-making ought also be stressed: leaders must uphold fairness, prudence, and accountability even when commercial pressure is high. They must promote cultures where teams feel empowered to raise concerns, challenge weak assumptions, and escalate risks early. Leadership resilience also includes succession planning, knowledge continuity, and the ability to blend experience with new perspectives from digital, risk, inclusion, and behavioural disciplines. In hybrid institutions, leaders must understand frontline conditions, technology systems, regulatory expectations, and customer realities, rather than operating from a distance. When leaders model discipline, authenticity, and constructive behaviour, the organisation becomes more stable, adaptive, and trusted. To conclude, leadership resilience is not about charismatic personalities; it is about consistent, principled conduct that sustains the institution's integrity over decades. A 100-year bank is built on leaders who embody responsibility, protect the public interest, and make decisions with an eye on long-term institutional health rather than short-term visibility.

The seventh dimension of the Adaptive Resilience Cube is financial and capital resilience, which determines whether a retail bank can withstand prolonged stress, absorb unexpected losses, and continue supporting customers through economic volatility. A 100-year institution must be built on disciplined capital planning, diversified income streams, prudent provisioning, and the ability to maintain liquidity even during market shocks. Financial resilience is not only about regulatory ratios; it is about the judgement behind how capital is allocated, how risks are priced, and how buffers are maintained over time. Long-lived banks avoid the temptation of excessive short-term growth and instead invest steadily in technology, trust systems, people, and infrastructure. Resilient institutions also run rigorous stress tests that incorporate climate shocks, cyber incidents, geopolitical tensions, demographic pressures, and prolonged low-margin environments, ensuring they are prepared for both cyclical and structural risks. Also important in financial resilience are balanced portfolios, responsible lending, transparent pricing, and diversified revenue models that do not rely heavily on a single geography, product, or customer segment. Strong treasury practices, liquidity coverage planning, and early-warning indicators help detect stress long before it becomes visible to the public. Another aspect to highlight is the connection between capital resilience and customer confidence: communities trust banks that remain stable during downturns and continue lending when households and small businesses need support the most. Finally, financial resilience must be reviewed independently, overseen by informed boards, and embedded into everyday decision-making. A 100-year bank treats capital strength as a public responsibility, ensuring that institutional stability, customer protection, and long-term value creation remain at the centre of its strategy across generations.

The eighth dimension of the Adaptive Resilience Cube is ecosystem and partner resilience, recognising that modern retail banks no longer operate as isolated institutions but as nodes within large, interdependent networks of fintechs, technology vendors, payment processors, cloud providers, and regulatory infrastructures. This means a 100-year bank must be capable of absorbing shocks not only within its own operations but across the wider ecosystem that supports its services. Modern hybrid delivery relies on API integrations, outsourced functions, shared cloud environments, biometric authentication partners, and embedded-finance collaborations, any of which can become points of systemic vulnerability if not governed correctly. To remain resilient, institutions must create strong partner-governance frameworks built on transparent contracts, shared incident protocols, joint testing cycles, and clear accountability for data protection, uptime, and customer outcomes. Mapping all critical dependencies is important, including sub-contractors and concentration risks that may emerge when too many services rely on a small set of vendors. Resilience requires more than vendor monitoring; it demands active collaboration through scenario simulations, live failover exercises, and coordinated recovery planning. Leading banks globally are now adopting ecosystem dashboards that provide real-time visibility into partner performance, latency, error rates, and risk alerts, ensuring early detection and swift response. The cultural side of ecosystem resilience also needs stressing: partners must share values around ethics, transparency, and customer protection, otherwise operational alignment becomes fragile. For a 100-year bank, resilience extends beyond internal strength; it is about ensuring the entire network can withstand disruption without compromising trust, service continuity, or regulatory expectations. Institutions that manage ecosystem resilience proactively build stronger reputations, reduce long-term risk, and create more reliable customer experiences across all channels and markets.

The ninth dimension of the Adaptive Resilience Cube is leadership and decision-making resilience, recognising that no amount of capital strength or technological investment can compensate for weak judgment during moments of uncertainty. Long-lived institutions differentiate themselves through leadership behaviours that remain steady under pressure, transparent in communication, and consistent in values even when decisions must be taken at speed. Effective leaders in a 100-year bank demonstrate the discipline to weigh long-term implications over short-term optics, the humility to seek expertise beyond their own domains, and the courage to act decisively when early signals of risk appear. Decision-making resilience requires governance routines that slow down impulsive actions while accelerating informed ones: structured escalation paths, real-time risk dashboards, pre-agreed crisis triggers, and cross-functional decision forums where operations, technology, risk, customer, and compliance leaders assess scenarios as a single institutional team. Leadership resilience is not about individual heroism; it is about institutionalising good judgment through culture, training, and shared expectations. Leading banks now invest heavily in leadership capability programmes that combine crisis simulations, behavioural coaching, ethical reasoning, and exposure to emerging risks such as cyber events, climate shocks, and misinformation-driven reputational crises. This prepares leaders to handle situations where information is incomplete, public pressure is high, and consequences are far-reaching. Another aspect to stress is the importance of emotional resilience—the ability to remain calm, empathetic, and people-centred during operational disruption. In a 100-year institution, leadership resilience becomes a stabilising force that guides staff, reassures customers, and upholds trust even when the external environment is volatile. Institutions that build this capability are better equipped to navigate complexity, maintain service continuity, and preserve long-term confidence in their mission and purpose.

The final dimension of the Adaptive Resilience Cube is societal and community-level resilience, recognising that a 100-year bank cannot sustain longevity unless the communities it serves remain stable, confident, and economically secure. Modern retail banks now operate in an environment where financial shocks, environmental events, digital vulnerabilities, and social inequality directly influence customer behaviour, portfolio risk, and institutional reputation. A future-ready institution therefore invests in strengthening the resilience of households, small businesses, and local ecosystems—not as philanthropy, but as a strategic necessity. This includes designing safety-net products for vulnerable segments, supporting community credit pathways, promoting financial literacy, and offering recovery support after climate-related disruptions or economic downturns. Leading banks today collaborate with local councils, educational institutions, small-business networks, and civil-society organisations to address structural challenges that affect customer stability, such as digital exclusion, rising living costs, or climate-impacted housing markets. Societal resilience also depends on transparent communication during crises. Customers expect timely updates, empathetic guidance, and clear explanations when disruptions occur. Institutions that communicate honestly and proactively maintain trust even in difficult moments. This dimension of resilience also requires ethical behaviour: responsible marketing, fair product design, unbiased AI systems, and supportive treatment of customers in hardship all reinforce long-term legitimacy. A 100-year institution views itself not simply as a financial entity but as a long-term partner in community well-being. By investing in the resilience of the wider environment in which it operates, the bank protects its own stability, strengthens intergenerational relationships, and reinforces its role as a trusted anchor in society across decades.

Multi-generational Customer Thinking

A future-ready retail bank cannot think in short cycles; it must understand that customer needs evolve over decades, not quarters, and that each generation brings its own expectations, anxieties, and behavioural patterns. Multi-generational thinking begins with recognising that the financial lives of people are shaped by their stage in life, their digital confidence, their income stability, and their cultural environment. Young customers often focus on affordability, flexibility, and digital convenience; mid-career households look for stability, credit access, and long-term planning; older customers prioritise clarity, trust, personal guidance, and physical reassurance. This diversity requires institutions to design journeys that remain relevant across life transitions rather than creating isolated products for isolated moments. A 100-year bank sees every customer as a long-term relationship that must adapt as they study, work, build families, manage responsibilities, retire, and plan legacies. It invests in behavioural insight, demographic analysis, and inclusive service design so that its channels evolve with the changing capabilities of each age group. It builds advisory pathways that support intergenerational financial management, recognising that families increasingly manage money collaboratively across borders, digital platforms, and multiple identities. It ensures that automation does not marginalise elderly customers and that human service does not limit the confidence of younger, digitally fluent segments. Multi-generational design becomes a strategic lens through which a retail bank strengthens loyalty, reduces friction, and remains relevant across decades. By carefully aligning digital tools, human engagement, and long-term product pathways, the institution positions itself not just as a service provider, but as a lifelong partner that can support families across three or four generations with dignity, consistency, and trust. Customer design must translate into consistent and fair outcomes across all generations.

A multi-generational retail bank must recognise that customer expectations are no longer fixed within age groups; they are shaped by technology exposure, employment patterns, cultural norms, social mobility, and life-stage transitions that vary widely across societies. Younger customers may adopt digital-only routines, yet many still value human guidance when making their first investments or taking their first loan. Middle-aged households increasingly juggle dual responsibilities—supporting children entering adulthood while caring for ageing parents—creating demand for advisory models that integrate saving, credit, insurance, and long-term planning in a more coordinated way. Older customers, especially those who grew up in branch-first environments, often seek reassurance, clarity, and continuity from familiar staff. This diversity demands that institutions move away from one-size-fits-all segmentation and adopt dynamic profiling that evolves with household realities. Hybrid delivery becomes essential because it allows customers to choose their preferred mode of interaction based on context rather than demographic assumptions. A simple transaction may be handled digitally, while sensitive decisions, such as restructuring a loan or managing a retirement portfolio, may require human presence. Multi-generational thinking also calls for inclusive product design—interfaces that are easy to read, advisory tools that are intuitive, and service scripts that respect cultural and emotional nuances. A 100-year bank invests in capability-building for staff so they can support customers across all generations with confidence and sensitivity. It builds internal systems that learn, adapt, and personalise without compromising fairness. By adopting this long-term, human-centred view, the bank earns the trust of families who remain with the institution not because of short-term incentives, but because they feel understood, respected, and supported throughout the different phases of life.

Case Study: The Bank for International Settlements—Quiet Institutional Stewardship

The Bank for International Settlements has operated for nearly a century as a neutral institutional anchor for central banks, providing coordination, research, and stability across changing monetary regimes. It does not compete, advertise, or scale in the commercial sense, yet it has remained indispensable through wars, financial crises, and systemic transformation. Its endurance stems from clarity of mandate, restrained governance, and a long-term orientation that prioritises system stability over short-term outcomes. The BIS demonstrates that institutional longevity is often built through restraint, credibility, and continuity rather than visibility or growth.

Serving multiple generations effectively requires institutions to design journeys that reflect how families make decisions together. Financial choices are often shared across age groups—children rely on parents for guidance on their first bank account, young professionals consult elders when making large purchases, and older customers increasingly depend on younger family members for digital tasks. A 100-year bank recognises these interdependencies and builds service paths that allow customers to collaborate safely and smoothly. This means creating permission-based access for family members, clearer support channels for carers, and advisory models that consider household-level realities rather than treating each customer as an isolated profile. It also requires the institution to understand how financial pressures differ across generations. Younger customers face volatile employment and high living costs; middle-aged families manage education expenses and mortgages; older customers prioritise stability, healthcare, and fraud protection. By embedding these nuances into product design and risk assessment, the bank ensures that solutions are not only relevant but also empathetic. Multi-generational design must also prepare for demographic transitions: rising longevity, smaller households, delayed retirement, and growing cross-border mobility. These shifts create new service needs that cannot be met with outdated assumptions. A 100-year bank therefore invests in continuous customer research, redesigns its digital interfaces for accessibility, and equips frontline teams with practical skills to support customers who may struggle with technology, language, or complex financial concepts. By aligning its systems and behaviours to the realities of multi-generational life, the institution builds a durable bond with customers that extends across families and decades, reinforcing the stability and social value of the bank.

A genuinely multi-generational institution must recognise that customer expectations are shaped not only by age, but by life events that demand different forms of support. Key transitions such as entering the workforce, starting a business, buying a home, raising a family, accessing credit for education, managing mid-career financial stress, or planning for retirement each require thoughtful engagement. A 100-year bank designs its architecture around these life milestones rather than around products. This approach ensures that services feel intuitive, timely, and genuinely helpful. Younger customers may need simple guidance, budgeting tools, or help building credit histories; mid-life customers may require streamlined mortgage options, flexible savings plans, or advisory support during economic uncertainty; older customers value dependable human contact, fraud-safe channels, and predictable service. The differences can be stark, but they are also predictable when banks invest in behavioural insight and long-term customer analysis. Multi-generational thinking also calls for inclusive design—digital channels must be accessible for customers with limited digital confidence, while physical branches must remain welcoming for those who rely on personal reassurance. At the same time, banks must offer digitally fluent customers efficient, self-directed pathways that reduce friction. Balancing these needs demands a hybrid model where human and digital strengths reinforce each other. The institutional mindset also matters: staff must be trained to understand generational differences without stereotypes, approaching every interaction with empathy and clarity. By embedding life-stage thinking into product development, risk models, customer journeys, and frontline culture, the bank stays relevant across decades. This creates a deeper form of loyalty—rooted not in transactions but in long-term partnership—which is essential for institutions aspiring to remain trusted through generations.

A bank that intends to remain relevant for 100 years must treat generational diversity as an operating principle, not a marketing theme. This requires investing in deep behavioural insight to understand how different cohorts make decisions, process information, and experience financial stress. As noted, younger customers often face income volatility, rising living costs, and uncertain career paths; they value flexible products, transparent pricing, and digital autonomy. Mid-career customers juggle mortgages, childcare costs, and long-term savings pressure; they need stability, personalised advisory support, and products that adapt to shifting responsibilities. Older customers prioritise security, clarity, and continuity; they depend more heavily on trusted human support, predictable service environments, and robust fraud protection. These differences shape expectations of service speed, communication style, and the balance between self-service and human assistance. For a 100-year institution, designing for these variations is not optional—it is central to maintaining trust and relevance. This pillar also underscores the importance of generational empathy within frontline teams and leadership. Staff must be trained to recognise behavioural cues, avoid unconscious bias, and provide clear explanations that meet each customer's comfort level. Technology must complement, not replace, human reassurance. For instance, a frictionless digital journey may be ideal for younger cohorts but may create confusion for older customers unless paired with accessible support. Equally, advisory-led interactions for seniors must be honest, transparent, and free from misselling—a critical trust requirement in ageing markets. Banks that bridge these generational expectations effectively create lasting relationships that survive leadership changes, market cycles, and technology transitions. They ensure that customers do not outgrow the institution—instead, the institution grows with them.

A multi-generational institution must build service pathways that recognise how each cohort interprets risk, opportunity, and financial stability. Younger customers typically engage with money through short-term horizons, subscription-based consumption, and digitally mediated decisions. They expect proactive alerts, immediate resolution, and financial tools that simplify budgeting and savings. Middle-aged customers, balancing family responsibilities and long-term commitments, seek reliability, credit flexibility, and advisory guidance that clarifies complex choices such as refinancing, wealth transfer, or retirement planning. Older customers, by contrast, prioritise service continuity, personal assurance, and fraud protection, especially as digital fatigue increases. A 100-year bank must design these journeys holistically, ensuring that segmentation does not become stereotyping but instead supports personalised, respectful engagement. This includes designing intuitive interfaces for younger cohorts, hybrid advisory models for midlife customers, and assisted-service environments for seniors where clarity and trust remain paramount. Importantly, product structures must evolve as customers age: a young professional who starts with a digital savings tool may need mortgage advice, then long-term investment planning, and later estate support. Each transition requires consistency of experience and recognition of customer history, so the institution becomes a lifelong anchor rather than a transactional provider. Banks that fail to integrate this multi-stage continuity often face churn, fragmented relationships, and reputational risk. A multi-generational strategy therefore depends on integrated data, consistent communication, and a frontline culture that respects differing comfort levels with technology and financial language. By designing for these diverse life patterns, hybrid banks build emotional resilience into the customer relationship, creating an institution that is not only relevant across generations but trusted to accompany families through multiple chapters of their financial lives.

A 100-year bank must recognise that generational expectations are shaped not only by age but by the social and economic events each cohort has lived through. Customers who experienced economic crises, inflation cycles, or major technology shifts often carry distinct attitudes toward borrowing, savings, and digital risk. Older generations who lived through branch-centric banking value face-to-face assurance and written confirmations, while younger customers raised in mobile-first environments assume instant access, zero friction, and personalised nudges. Middle-generation customers, balancing both worlds, want digital convenience supported by human guidance at critical decision moments. To remain relevant across these differing worldviews, the institution must adopt a service philosophy that offers choice rather than forcing uniformity. This means enabling customers to toggle between channels, choose their preferred interaction style, and escalate to human assistance whenever they feel uncertain. Generational sensitivity also requires adapting communication: concise, visual content works well for younger segments; structured explanations and clear documentation build confidence for older ones; while personalised, scenario-based support helps mid-life customers plan ahead. The institution must also recognise that financial vulnerability manifests differently across generations. Young adults may face income instability, rising housing costs, or limited credit history. Older adults may face cognitive decline, digital scams, and isolation. A multi-generational strategy must therefore embed safeguards—fraud alerts, concierge support, simplified flows, and proactive guidance—to ensure fairness and protection. By respecting these generational realities and designing an operating model that adapts rather than dictates, the hybrid bank strengthens long-term loyalty, builds intergenerational trust, and positions itself as a stable, empathetic presence throughout each customer's life journey.

A bank designed for a 100-year horizon must build systems that understand how financial capability evolves over a lifetime, and how these changes influence behaviour, vulnerability, and trust. Younger customers typically focus on short-term needs such as budgeting, digital payments, credit-building, and early career planning, requiring intuitive tools, simple insights, and nudges that encourage responsible habits without feeling intrusive. As individuals move into mid-life, their financial lives become more complex—mortgages, children's education, caregiving responsibilities, savings gaps, and business aspirations. This segment values stability, transparency, and flexible advisory support that helps them navigate uncertainty. Older customers often prioritise security, dignity, and human reassurance, especially in an environment where digital fraud, financial abuse, and cognitive fatigue are rising sharply. A 100-year bank must design for all these transitions seamlessly so that customers never feel left behind as their circumstances change. This means creating adaptive service layers where digital journeys automatically become simpler, clearer, or more supportive based on customer signals; where frontline staff are trained to recognise behavioural cues; and where policies, interfaces, and communications can adjust as customers age. It also requires the institution to maintain continuity of relationships over time-through shared data histories, trusted advisory channels, and consistent service delivery across generations. Institutions that build this intergenerational continuity gain not only loyalty but also stability: families stay with banks that understand their long-term story. By recognising that financial needs shift with age, identity, mobility, and capability, the hybrid institution strengthens public trust and becomes a lifelong anchor for individuals navigating a changing world.

Designing for multiple generations requires banks to understand not only life stages but also the broader socioeconomic transitions shaping financial behaviour across different groups. Younger customers are entering adulthood during a period of rising living costs, income volatility, and changing work patterns, which makes traditional financial milestones—home ownership, long-term savings, business formation—far harder to achieve. This cohort values transparency, fairness, and services that reduce friction rather than add complexity. Mid-career customers, in contrast, face competing pressures: caring for ageing parents, supporting children, managing debt, and planning for retirement while navigating uncertain job markets. These demands require flexible credit structures, personalised advisory support, and tools that simplify long-range planning. Older customers need stability, predictability, and protection from digital and social vulnerability; yet they also represent one of the fastest-growing adopters of online banking when systems are designed with clarity, safety, and human touchpoints. A 100-year bank must recognise these distinct pressures and build systems that can flex without fragmenting—using unified data models, inclusive interface design, and adaptive risk controls that adjust to capability levels.

A multi-generational strategy becomes meaningful only when banks translate demographic understanding into practical service models that evolve over time. Given this, hybrid institutions can design lifecycle-based financial pathways that adjust as customers progress through education, early employment, family formation, career shifts, entrepreneurship, retirement planning, and later-life care needs. Rather than offering isolated products, designing the bank of the future connects these milestones through integrated journeys supported by advisory tools, behavioural nudges, and contextual interventions—such as early savings guidance for students, credit-building pathways for young workers, cash-flow planning for mid-career households, and simplified, fraud-resistant interfaces for seniors. It also recognises that generational patterns are no longer linear: career breaks, remote work, gig incomes, caregiving responsibilities, and immigration-related complexities all require flexible, empathetic systems. Banks must balance automated service with human reassurance, ensuring that customers receive personalised support during moments of vulnerability or major financial decisions. Multi-generational thinking further demands that institutions develop outreach models tailored to local communities—faith groups, cultural associations, migrant networks, and senior-support organisations—where trust is shaped through sustained presence rather than digital convenience alone. By approaching customer relationships as multi-decade partnerships grounded in stability, adaptability, and dignity, designing the bank of the future positions itself as an enduring anchor in people's financial lives. Over generations, this long-term orientation strengthens trust, deepens relevance, and transforms the bank from a transaction provider into a true institutional companion. Multi-generational relevance is sustained through continuity of experience, not isolated product innovation.

Systems Thinking in Retail Strategy

Systems thinking enables retail banks to move beyond siloed optimisation and recognise the institution as a single, interconnected organism where decisions in one domain inevitably shape outcomes elsewhere. This explains why hybrid banking requires leadership teams to understand how technology choices influence risk models, how customer-experience design affects operational load, how branch strategy interacts with digital adoption, and how regulatory expectations ripple across product architecture and data governance. In many institutions, fragmentation persists because decisions are made in isolation—technology teams prioritise speed, risk teams prioritise control, frontline teams prioritise simplicity, and finance teams prioritise cost. Systems thinking helps reconcile these tensions by encouraging leaders to analyse whole-system consequences, identify structural bottlenecks, and anticipate second-order effects before they manifest as customer pain points or operational failures. Designing the bank of the future relies on integrated planning cycles, cross-functional governance forums, shared data models, and institution-wide visibility dashboards that link customer journeys to financial, operational, and risk outcomes. By adopting systems thinking as a leadership discipline, banks create coherence between strategy, culture, and execution—allowing innovation to scale safely and consistently. Institutions that master this discipline are better equipped to adapt to regulatory shifts, customer expectations, demographic changes, and technological transitions, giving them the structural agility required for long-term relevance. System-wide coherence is a governance responsibility, not an operational by-product.

It strengthens strategic decision-making by helping institutions visualise how customer behaviour, economic conditions, operational capacity, and regulatory shifts interact within a single ecosystem. Even small policy choices—such as tightening credit criteria, redesigning KYC journeys, modifying branch layouts, or introducing new digital features—can trigger downstream effects across risk, compliance, operations, and customer trust. Many banks struggle with unintended consequences because decision pathways are linear, departmental, or based on short-term pressures rather than integrated institutional logic. Systems thinking introduces structured mapping tools, feedback-loop analysis, and scenario-based planning that reveal hidden dependencies and vulnerabilities early. For hybrid banks, this discipline becomes essential: digital enhancements increase demand on back-office processes; automation changes frontline roles; ESG expectations influence disclosure systems; and regulatory tightening reshapes data architecture. By embedding systems thinking into leadership routines, institutions improve coherence between long-term vision and day-to-day execution. Leaders begin to focus on institutional health rather than departmental optimisation, ensuring that every strategic choice enhances resilience, customer confidence, and operational stability.

This encourages banks to move away from fragmented decision-making by creating shared visibility across functions, enabling leaders to recognise how operational performance, customer sentiment, and regulatory compliance are interconnected. Institutions often pursue digital upgrades, branch optimisation, risk adjustments, or cost-reduction measures in isolation, unintentionally creating imbalances elsewhere in the organisation. For example, accelerating digital onboarding without strengthening fraud controls increases vulnerability; reducing branch staff without redesigning service flows weakens experience quality; and launching new products without aligning risk models can damage long-term trust. Systems thinking introduces structured routines—end-to-end journey reviews, integrated planning cycles, cross-functional problem-solving forums, and unified performance dashboards—that transform how decisions are made. For hybrid institutions, this approach prevents siloed interventions from undermining resilience or customer confidence. It helps leadership teams anticipate second-order effects, design controls that support innovation, and prioritise investments that balance efficiency with stability. Most importantly, systems thinking strengthens institutional agility: leaders learn to adjust strategy based on real-time patterns rather than static planning, ensuring that the bank evolves coherently as customer behaviour, technology, and regulatory expectations continue to shift.

Systems thinking becomes especially powerful when institutions recognise that customer experience is not the responsibility of a single department but the cumulative outcome of dozens of interconnected decisions across technology, risk, product design, branch operations, vendor systems, and regulatory interpretation. Customer journeys often break not because teams lack capability, but because institutional structures do not allow them to see the full picture. A glitch in a payments API may originate from a vendor update, but it manifests as customer frustration; a credit decision that appears "unfair" to the customer may be the result of mismatched data fields between legacy systems and new scoring models; delays in complaint resolution often reflect fragmentation between compliance, servicing, and frontline teams. Systems thinking encourages banks to redesign governance around these interdependencies, creating mechanisms such as journey owners with cross-functional authority, shared-service agreements between digital and physical teams, and escalation pathways that cut across organisational boundaries. It emphasises that hybrid banking is a living system—changes in one channel inevitably influence behaviour in another, and customer trust is shaped by the weakest link, not the strongest. Institutions that apply systems thinking learn to diagnose root causes instead of symptoms, balancing customer needs with regulatory expectations and operational discipline. This approach also enhances strategic clarity: leadership teams can prioritise investments that deliver compound value across departments, minimise unintended consequences, and reduce operational friction. Over time, systems thinking embeds a culture of coherence, enabling the bank to evolve as a unified institution rather than a collection of disconnected units.

It also reshapes how retail banks plan and sequence transformation. Traditional change programmes often operate in silos, with technology upgrades, risk enhancements, branch renovations, and product launches running in parallel but without alignment. This fragmentation leads to cost overruns, duplicated work, and uneven customer experiences. A systems-oriented institution, then, designs transformation as an interconnected roadmap, recognising that improvements in one domain influence capacity and outcomes in others. For example, a new mobile-banking interface should not be treated as a standalone technology project; it must be coordinated with fraud-risk adjustments, call-centre scripts, staff training, and updates to branch advisory workflows. Similarly, shifting to cloud-based infrastructure affects vendor-risk assessments, cybersecurity controls, and regulatory notifications. By applying systems thinking, leadership teams create integrated planning cycles that bring together product, risk, technology, operations, and compliance teams around shared objectives and shared timelines. This ensures that transformation is not just fast but structurally sound. It also embeds continuous feedback loops: frontline staff can signal emerging issues, customers can provide real-time insights, and risk teams can recalibrate thresholds as patterns evolve. Over time, these mechanisms reduce operational surprises, strengthen institutional discipline, and support the long-term architecture required for hybrid banking.

Systems thinking also helps decision-making by helping leaders understand second-order effects—the consequences that emerge only after a decision interacts with other parts of the institution. For example, tightening underwriting rules may reduce credit losses in the short term but could unintentionally drive vulnerable customers toward high-cost lenders, increasing long-term delinquency risks when they eventually return to the bank. Similarly, accelerating digital adoption without preparing frontline staff can create service pressures in branches, erode customer confidence, and harm vulnerable groups who rely on assisted channels. These second-order effects rarely show up in dashboards or governance papers; they are revealed only when institutions examine how policies, technologies, and behaviours interact as part of a wider system. A systems-oriented bank maps feedback loops, identifies where decisions may create strain, and evaluates cross-channel consequences before committing to change. This approach encourages leadership teams to test ideas through pilots, shadow modelling, customer panels, and internal simulations that explore how different functions react under real conditions. It also embeds a culture of shared accountability: risk teams, product teams, and operations units collaborate to anticipate bottlenecks rather than escalating issues after they arise. By understanding second-order effects, the institution strengthens resilience, reduces unintended harm, and makes decisions that balance innovation with responsibility—core qualities of a future-ready 100-year bank.

How institutions measure performance is another area reshaped by systems thinking, moving them away from narrow, siloed indicators toward integrated dashboards that reflect the full customer and operational journey. Traditional metrics—such as product sales, call-centre handling time, or branch footfall—often encourage fragmented behaviour because they reward local optimisation rather than system-wide improvement. This highlights that a 100-year bank must design measurement systems that reveal how different functions influence one another, such as how digital-channel defects increase branch workload, how poor credit journeys affect long-term trust, or how delays in risk approvals slow innovation cycles. Integrated dashboards connect data from product, risk, technology, operations, and customer-experience teams into cohesive insights that show the true health of the institution. This allows leaders to spot structural frictions early, allocate resources more intelligently, and reduce waste created by duplicated efforts. It also fosters a culture where teams work toward shared outcomes—customer resilience, operational stability, and long-term value creation—rather than competing for performance scores. By redesigning performance measurement around system-wide coherence, retail banks strengthen alignment, reduce organisational noise, and create a disciplined foundation for sustained transformation across decades.

Systems thinking also requires institutional leaders to recognise the compounding effect of small structural weaknesses that, over time, can undermine resilience and customer confidence. Indeed, many failures in retail banking are not caused by dramatic breakdowns but by accumulated friction: disconnected policy updates, inconsistent customer journeys, unclear escalation routines, and misaligned incentives between digital and physical teams. These small gaps create operational drag, increase error rates, and push customers into avoidable service loops. A 100-year bank treats these friction points as signals of deeper system issues rather than isolated incidents. By mapping interdependencies across processes, leaders can identify where policy, technology, and human behaviour collide in unintended ways. This enables targeted interventions—such as revising approval chains, redesigning workflows, or simplifying decision-making thresholds—that strengthen the entire architecture. Institutions that excel in this discipline adopt routines such as cross-functional retrospectives, journey-based audits, and systemic root-cause analysis to ensure continuous improvement. Over decades, the ability to detect and correct small issues before they escalate becomes a defining marker of institutional maturity, supporting long-term trust and operational coherence.

Another effect of systems thinking is its reshaping how retail banks anticipate and manage risk by integrating early-warning signals across operational, technological, customer, and regulatory domains. While traditional risk frameworks treat incidents as discrete events—a cyber alert here, complaints spike there, a service outage somewhere else—in a 100-year bank, these signals are viewed collectively, revealing patterns that point to deeper structural vulnerabilities. A rise in digital-channel complaints, for instance, may be connected to staffing shortages in call centres, outdated middleware, or policy changes that unintentionally increased customer effort. Similarly, a regulatory challenge may reflect not just compliance gaps but weaknesses in data governance, vendor oversight, or leadership alignment. This pillar highlights that long-lived institutions build integrated dashboards, cross-domain risk councils, and shared intelligence routines that dissolve silos and produce a unified picture of organisational health. By combining behavioural analytics, operational telemetry, customer sentiment, and compliance indicators, banks can detect emerging stress long before it appears in financial results. This predictive capability allows institutions to allocate resources proactively, intervene with precision, and maintain stability even in volatile conditions. Over the long term, banks that cultivate this holistic risk view are far better positioned to sustain trust, reduce crisis frequency, and deepen resilience across generations.

Systems thinking ultimately transforms how strategy is executed, ensuring that long-term ambitions are not undermined by fragmented decisions or short-term pressures. In a 100-year bank, strategic plans are not treated as static documents but as living systems that evolve through continuous feedback loops across the entire organisation. Product launches are assessed not just for revenue potential but for implications on risk, customer trust, operational load, and regulatory alignment. Technology investments are evaluated for how they influence branch behaviour, staff capability, future scalability, and cross-market expansion. Cultural initiatives are designed with an understanding of how leadership behaviour, incentives, and everyday practices interact. This interconnected view prevents local optimisations—such as a faster digital journey or a cost-saving automation step—from creating unintended consequences elsewhere. Leading institutions build shared architecture councils, cross-functional strategy forums, and integrated planning cycles that maintain coherence across functions and markets. By aligning long-term purpose with everyday decisions, systems thinking helps institutions avoid drift, maintain strategic integrity, and build competitive advantage that strengthens over decades. Ultimately, designing the bank of the future succeeds because every decision, whether technical or human, reflects a disciplined understanding of how the whole system works together to create lasting public value. Strategy must be continuously validated through execution outcomes across the institution.

Ecosystem Coordination and Institutional Interoperability

This also requires institutions to coordinate increasingly complex ecosystem relationships across platforms, partners, AI-enabled workflows, and open digital infrastructures. As retail banking evolves toward interconnected operating models, institutions increasingly depend on external technology providers, cloud environments, fintech ecosystems, data-sharing frameworks, and orchestration layers that sit across multiple systems simultaneously. In this environment, the challenge is no longer limited to technology adoption alone; it is also the ability to govern integration, accountability, interoperability, and operational trust across highly distributed ecosystems.

AI-enabled banking environments further amplify this complexity. Intelligent servicing systems, real-time decision engines, embedded-finance models, API-based ecosystems, and agentic AI workflows are accelerating how institutions interact with customers, process information, and coordinate services across organisational boundaries. While these developments create opportunities for speed, efficiency, and personalisation, they also increase operational dependency, governance exposure, and systemic interconnectedness. A future-ready institution must therefore ensure that innovation remains aligned with transparency, resilience, explainability, and responsible oversight.

Industry collaborations such as FINOS (Fintech Open Source Foundation), alongside broader open-source financial ecosystems, illustrate how modern financial institutions are increasingly exploring shared interoperability standards, common governance models, open collaboration frameworks, and reusable technology architectures to support secure and scalable transformation across banking environments. Initiatives associated with FINOS around interoperability, cloud governance, data standards, and ecosystem collaboration reflect a wider institutional movement toward coordinated operating models within regulated financial systems. These developments are important not only because of the technologies involved, but because they demonstrate how long-term trust, resilience, and operational consistency increasingly depend on collaborative governance across interconnected digital ecosystems.

Emerging orchestration approaches within modern banking ecosystems also demonstrate how workflow coordination layers may increasingly support integration across customer journeys, operational systems, partner environments, and AI-assisted service models. Over time, these orchestration capabilities may help institutions reduce fragmentation, improve operational visibility, strengthen resilience, and create more explainable governance structures across increasingly complex banking architectures.

For a 100-year bank, ecosystem coordination becomes a strategic capability rather than a technical exercise. Institutions must be able to manage interconnected systems without weakening accountability, trust, or operational discipline. As banking ecosystems become increasingly intelligent, distributed, and automated, long-term institutional stability will depend not only on digital capability, but on the ability to govern complexity responsibly across technology, operations, partnerships, and customer experience.

The Future Architecture Manifesto

The Future Architecture Manifesto begins with a simple premise: a retail bank that hopes to remain relevant over the next century must redefine itself as a public-service institution built on trust, purpose, and long-term accountability.

This section explains that the manifesto is not a vision statement or a set of aspirations; it is a structural commitment to how the institution will behave, evolve, and serve society across generations. It asserts that every architectural choice—whether related to technology, governance, risk, talent, or customer service—must reinforce transparency, fairness, and resilience. The manifesto states that a bank's legitimacy is earned daily through consistent conduct, ethical data use, clear communication, and decisions that protect customers even when it is commercially inconvenient. It also emphasises that future-ready banks cannot rely solely on digital efficiency or scale; they must retain humanity at the centre of their systems, ensuring that vulnerable customers, ageing populations, migrants, and digitally limited groups are not left behind. This first positions the manifesto as a long-term contract between the bank and the communities it serves, grounded in the belief that institutional longevity depends on public trust, societal contribution, and an unwavering commitment to doing what is right—not only what is profitable. The manifesto must be visible in institutional behaviour, not limited to stated principles.

The manifesto reinforces that a future-ready bank must treat trust as infrastructure, embedding reliability, clarity, and accountability into every system rather than relying on marketing narratives or brand heritage. Trust is created through the design of processes—how decisions are made, how data is handled, how complaints are resolved, and how customers are treated when something goes wrong. It argues that in a world of rapid digital interactions, customers judge institutions less by their promises and more by the consistency of their experience: seamless transactions, transparent disclosures, predictable service, and responsible use of automation. The manifesto calls for eliminating friction that undermines confidence and closing gaps between frontline practices and executive intentions. It also emphasises that modern trust relies on resilience: customers expect banks to withstand outages, cyber events, economic shocks, and ecosystem failures without compromising safety or access. A 100-year bank must therefore invest continuously in secure platforms, strong data foundations, and disciplined governance so that trust becomes a measurable, engineered output rather than an intangible sentiment. This positions trust not as an abstract value but as a structural design principle that shapes the institution's long-term relevance.

A 100-year bank must anchor inclusion as a non-negotiable design mandate, not as a community initiative or a CSR statement. Genuine inclusion requires institutions to redesign products, channels, data models, and service pathways so that every customer—regardless of age, income, ability, geography, or digital confidence—can participate meaningfully in the financial system. In turn, exclusion often emerges not from intent, but from design choices: complex interfaces, inaccessible language, rigid eligibility criteria, algorithmic bias, or branch strategies that overlook vulnerable groups. The manifesto calls for a holistic inclusion architecture, blending digital simplicity with human support, locally attuned branch formats with multilingual content, and credit models that recognise diverse income patterns. It positions inclusion as essential for long-term legitimacy: societies trust institutions that serve them fairly. As demographics shift, work becomes more fragmented, and digital ecosystems expand, the banks that embed inclusion into every design decision will maintain resilience, loyalty, and relevance across generations. This therefore frames inclusion as a structural pillar of durability—an investment in societal stability that strengthens institutional continuity.

Ethical data stewardship is one of the most defining responsibilities of a 100-year bank, because data has quietly become the institution's most powerful and most sensitive asset. This argues that the way a bank collects, stores, processes, protects, and interprets data is no longer a technical exercise; it is a reflection of its moral compass and its long-term credibility. Retail banks increasingly depend on interconnected digital ecosystems, AI-driven decisions, cross-border data flows, and continuous authentication layers. Every one of these elements introduces risks that can erode customer trust if not managed with discipline and humility. A future-ready institution must therefore adopt data practices that are transparent, fair, and aligned with society's expectations of dignity, rights, and accountability. Ethical stewardship begins with clarity: customers must understand how their information is used, why it is used, what benefits they receive, and how they can withdraw consent without penalty. It extends into strong governance—independent oversight, rigorous model testing, bias detection, data-minimisation policies, privacy-by-design protocols, and explainable algorithms that do not treat people as data points but as individuals with unique circumstances. It also involves cultural leadership, where staff across functions appreciate the ethical implications of data handling and recognise that trust can be lost through a single lapse. For a 100-year bank, data is not merely a competitive advantage; it is a shared responsibility between the institution and the community it serves. Ethical data practice becomes an anchor for public confidence, a safeguard against reputational volatility, and a long-term investment in institutional integrity. When a bank demonstrates that it uses data responsibly, transparently, and with respect, it strengthens its legitimacy and earns the type of deep, intergenerational trust that no technology or marketing can manufacture.

A 100-year bank cannot treat technology as a series of upgrades, channel improvements, or efficiency programmes; it must treat technology as an expression of institutional purpose. Purpose-driven technology is the discipline of ensuring that every digital investment, every automation layer, every AI model, and every interface strengthens the bank's long-term commitment to trust, inclusion, fairness, and customer well-being. Technology becomes human-centred when it is guided not by what is easiest to implement, but by what genuinely improves people's financial lives—offering clarity rather than complexity, confidence rather than confusion, and meaningful support rather than transactional convenience. A future-ready institution designs systems that reduce anxiety for vulnerable users, improve access for individuals with limited digital confidence, and simplify journeys for customers who navigate financial stress, life transitions, or language barriers. Purpose-driven innovation requires leadership teams to step back from quarterly pressures and evaluate digital transformation through a wider lens: does this technology reinforce transparency? Does it widen access? Does it reduce friction for customers who need help the most? Does it protect people from unintended harm or algorithmic exclusion? It also demands that institutions place ethical guardrails around experimentation, ensuring that agility never compromises accountability. When technology is rooted in purpose, it becomes a quiet stabiliser of trust, a protector of rights, and an enabler of opportunity. For a 100-year bank, this alignment between purpose and technology becomes essential: it prevents the institution from becoming overly mechanised, emotionally distant, or driven purely by optimisation logic. Instead, it ensures that innovation serves society, strengthens relationships, and positions the bank as a long-term partner in the financial lives of every generation it aims to serve.

Ethical governance is not a policy document or an annual report requirement for a 100-year bank—it is a daily operating discipline that shapes every interaction, every decision, and every customer outcome. Enduring institutions protect their legitimacy by embedding ethics into the smallest details of how they function: how frontline staff communicate with vulnerable customers, how automated systems treat edge cases, how complaints are escalated, how data is handled, and how leaders behave when no one is watching. Ethical governance becomes visible in the consistency of service quality, the fairness of products, the clarity of disclosures, and the dignity with which customers are treated during moments of stress. It requires leaders to maintain a culture where employees feel responsible for doing the right thing, even when shortcuts appear easier. In hybrid environments—where digital systems make thousands of decisions instantly—ethical governance means ensuring algorithms do not disadvantage certain groups, ensuring consent is meaningful rather than symbolic, and ensuring that commercial targets do not overshadow customer welfare. It also requires boards to set out clear expectations on transparency, conflict-of-interest management, whistleblowing protections, and accountability pathways. A long-lived institution strengthens ethical governance through routine behaviours: reflective reviews after failures, honest communication during crises, respectful treatment of customers and staff, and a willingness to correct mistakes proactively rather than defensively. In a rapidly changing world, where public trust fluctuates and scrutiny is constant, ethical governance acts as an anchor that stabilises the bank's reputation across decades. For a 100-year bank, this discipline is not an idealistic aspiration—it is a practical necessity for maintaining credibility and ensuring that longevity is supported by character, not just capability.

This system survives not by choosing between global standards and local presence, but by mastering both simultaneously. Long-lived institutions thrive when they uphold the highest global expectations in governance, security, resilience, and ethics, while remaining deeply rooted in the needs, culture, and realities of the communities they serve. Global standards give the bank its backbone: strong data governance aligned with GDPR and international privacy frameworks; secure cloud and cyber practices benchmarked against leading digital economies; responsible lending aligned with global ESG and conduct expectations; and transparent reporting that meets international assurance norms. However, longevity also depends on local legitimacy—understanding neighbourhood economics, regional vulnerabilities, linguistic diversity, demographic patterns, and cultural expectations. The 100-year institution designs products that work for elderly customers in rural areas as effectively as they do for young digital users in urban centres. It supports local job creation, community resilience, and financial literacy by partnering with councils, cooperatives, schools, and local enterprises. It adapts its advisory models to reflect local needs—whether those are migration-driven remittances, agricultural seasonality, small-business volatility, or climate-related risks that vary by region. The blend of "local empathy + global discipline" creates institutions that are both trusted and future-proof. This duality also shapes leadership capability: decision-makers must understand global risk frameworks while staying sensitive to the lived realities of the customers who walk into their branches. For hybrid banks, this multi-level consciousness is essential—digital systems may scale globally, but trust is earned locally. Designing the bank of the future protects its future by ensuring that international standards never become detached from community relevance, creating an institution that is sophisticated in its design yet grounded in its humanity.

A 100-year bank must treat data not as an asset to be exploited, but as a responsibility to be honoured across generations. This frames ethical data stewardship as a long-term institutional commitment that extends far beyond regulatory compliance or competitive advantage. As digital footprints expand, hybrid banks accumulate unprecedented volumes of behavioural, transactional, and identity-related information. How this data is governed—collected, used, shared, protected, and eventually retired—will determine whether the institution remains trusted decades into the future. Ethical stewardship demands clear boundaries: data must only be used in ways customers understand, consent to, and benefit from. It requires restraint in an era when predictive analytics, AI-driven nudges, and behavioural profiling can tempt institutions into practices that cross ethical lines, even if technically permissible. A future-ready bank builds transparent algorithms, ensures explainability in automated decisions, and maintains strong oversight of data-sharing arrangements with fintechs, insurers, and ecosystem partners. It embeds rigorous privacy standards, supports customer rights to portability and deletion, and designs systems that minimise unnecessary data retention. Ethical stewardship also requires empathy: consumers at different life stages—elderly customers, young adults, small businesses, migrants—have varying levels of literacy, digital comfort, and vulnerability. A 100-year bank calibrates its data practices to protect these groups thoughtfully, ensuring fairness and safeguarding dignity at every interaction. When institutions treat data as a long-term custodial duty, they reinforce enduring trust and build reputational capital that outlives technology cycles. This mindset ensures that, long after today's systems are replaced, the institution remains respected for its integrity, restraint, and unwavering commitment to using data in ways that empower rather than exploit customers.

It sustains its relevance by ensuring that purpose is not confined to mission statements or board discussions, but is translated into everyday decisions across the institution. Long-term purpose anchors behaviour, aligns leadership, and guides decision-making in moments of uncertainty, especially when commercial pressures push organisations toward short-term optimisation. Purpose becomes the compass that shapes how products are designed, how customers are treated, how risks are assessed, and how partnerships are chosen. It prevents "mission drift"—the gradual erosion of values that occurs when institutions chase quarterly results at the expense of societal trust. Embedding purpose means creating mechanisms that make it visible and actionable: governance committees that evaluate strategic proposals against purpose-alignment criteria, performance frameworks that reward long-term outcomes, and leadership behaviours that reinforce integrity and accountability in day-to-day operations. Purpose-driven institutions are deliberate about ensuring that digital innovations do not compromise human dignity, that automation does not exclude vulnerable groups, and that cost efficiencies do not undermine service accessibility. They place equal weight on customer well-being, staff culture, community outcomes, and financial prudence. When employees at every level understand why the bank exists—not only what it does—they make decisions that strengthen consistency, fairness, and credibility. This internal coherence becomes a powerful source of stability, enabling the institution to navigate crises, adapt to disruptive technologies, and maintain stakeholder confidence over decades. A bank that embeds purpose deeply into everyday action builds a cultural foundation capable of sustaining trust across generations, ensuring that its long-term relevance is upheld not by slogans but by continuous, principled practice.

A century-forward retail bank is built on the recognition that institutions survive when they are structurally coherent, socially grounded, and strategically adaptive. This following section brings together the full architecture developed across the book—trust, inclusion, resilience, governance, hybrid delivery, and purpose—into a unified long-term blueprint. It emphasises that future-ready institutions do not simply respond to change; they design themselves to evolve with it. A 100-year bank builds its systems with modularity so that technology can be upgraded without disruption, develops risk frameworks that anticipate climate, cyber, demographic, and geopolitical shocks, and invests in leadership that can navigate cross-sector ecosystems with maturity and humility. It commits to genuine financial inclusion by ensuring that every customer—from digitally confident professionals to elderly citizens and newly arrived migrants—can access banking safely and with dignity. It prioritises ethical data use, transparent decision-making, and fair treatment embedded at every touchpoint. Most importantly, the century-forward bank positions itself as a societal anchor rather than a transactional entity. It supports the real economy, strengthens communities, and contributes to broader national goals such as resilience, sustainability, and digital capability. It recognises that long-term legitimacy comes from being dependable in crises, empathetic in service, and principled in governance. The blueprint concludes that the institutions that endure are those that combine strong architecture with a clear moral core—banks that are built to last because they are built to see. Long-term architecture must translate into measurable institutional performance and trust outcomes.

Institutional Perspective: A Global Lens on the 100-Year Bank, Society, and Being Human in the Future of Retail Banking

When the Bank Becomes a Social Institution

For most of modern banking history, banks were judged mainly by financial strength, scale, profitability, and operational capability. Those things still matter. But as banking becomes more deeply woven into daily life, banks are increasingly functioning not just as financial institutions, but as long-term social institutions.

That changes how they must think about purpose, responsibility, and design.

Banking has always played a social role. It safeguards assets, supports trade, finances infrastructure, and helps societies navigate uncertainty. It was never purely transactional. Banks became part of the trust infrastructure that allowed economies and communities to function.

Today that role is broader than ever. Retail banks influence salaries, housing, healthcare access, pensions, education, payments, digital identity, and small-business creation. Financial systems now sit inside larger ecosystems of platforms, algorithms, data, and digital infrastructure that shape everyday life.

The modern bank is no longer simply a place where money moves. It has become part of the operating architecture of society itself.

That creates a fundamental institutional shift. A short-term institution can optimise for efficiency and growth alone. A long-term institution must also optimise for resilience, continuity, legitimacy, and public trust across generations.

This is where the idea of the "100-year bank" becomes important. Longevity is not simply survival. Institutions can continue operating while losing public confidence or social relevance. A truly enduring bank evolves continuously while preserving trust through changing technologies, political environments, economic cycles, and demographic shifts.

The future bank must therefore think beyond quarterly performance and isolated transformation projects. It has to behave like a durable institutional system—one capable of adapting responsibly while remaining socially legitimate during uncertainty.

Different societies will experience this differently. In highly digitised economies, banks increasingly operate as invisible infrastructure embedded into commerce, mobility, identity, and payments. In emerging economies, they still play a developmental role through inclusion and economic formalisation. In ageing societies, accessible and dependable financial systems become closely tied to social stability and independence.

AI expands this responsibility further. As algorithms shape onboarding, fraud detection, credit decisions, customer servicing, and operational management, banks gain greater influence over how people participate economically and digitally.

That raises a critical question: can banks become more technologically powerful while remaining socially trusted?

The institutions that endure may not be the ones that digitise fastest or scale largest. They may be the ones that understand banking is ultimately about preserving social continuity during constant change.

Why the 100-Year Bank Must Preserve Human Continuity

Modern banking transformation is driven by speed. Faster payments, real-time data, AI-driven servicing, embedded finance, and automation are reshaping the industry at extraordinary pace.

Yet beneath this acceleration, one human need remains remarkably stable: continuity.

People still want continuity of access, identity, trust, security, and institutional reliability during uncertain moments.

Historically, the institutions that survived periods of upheaval weren't the ones that resisted change. They were the ones that adapted without breaking public confidence. Societies have already endured industrial revolutions, financial crises, political instability, and technological disruption. The institutions that lasted were those able to evolve while preserving trust.

The future bank faces the same challenge.

Digital transformation often focuses heavily on innovation and efficiency. But institutions designed only around speed and automation risk weakening the emotional continuity people still expect from financial systems. Customers may value convenience while still wanting institutions that feel dependable, understandable, recoverable, and accountable when things go wrong.

That matters because modern banking operates inside permanent change. AI evolves continuously. Cyber threats shift constantly. Platform ecosystems move quickly. Regulation expands. Climate disruption increases complexity. Geopolitical instability affects global financial systems.

In this environment, banks cannot rely on static business models or occasional transformation programmes. They need adaptive resilience—the ability to evolve continuously while preserving trust over long periods of time.

Most customers do not understand cloud infrastructure, AI governance, or resilience frameworks. What they judge instinctively is whether the institution still feels stable, whether support remains accessible, and whether problems can still be resolved during stress.

Different societies define continuity differently. In ageing societies like Japan and parts of Europe, it relates to predictability, accessibility, and institutional reliability. In highly digital economies, continuity depends on whether digital ecosystems operate smoothly across payments, commerce, and public services. In emerging economies, continuity is closely linked to financial participation and protection from volatility.

AI intensifies the challenge. If customers begin feeling disconnected from institutions because systems appear opaque or excessively automated, trust may weaken even when operational performance improves.

The 100-year bank must therefore balance intelligence with explainability, automation with accountability, efficiency with dignity, and innovation with reassurance.

The future bank cannot simply optimise transactions. It must sustain public confidence through long periods of technological and societal change.

The institutions that endure may not be those changing fastest, but those capable of evolving responsibly without creating instability in the lives of the people who depend on them.

Why the Future Bank Will Feel Different Across Societies

The future of retail banking is often discussed as though technology will create a single global model. AI, embedded finance, digital identity, cloud infrastructure, and real-time payments are certainly reshaping financial systems everywhere.

But technology may converge globally while human experience does not.

The future bank will not feel the same across societies because banking is shaped by culture, history, governance, and local expectations around trust.

In highly digitised societies like Singapore or South Korea, banking may become almost invisible operationally. Financial services blend seamlessly into commerce, mobility, healthcare, and digital public infrastructure. Customers experience trust through continuity and systemic reliability.

In Northern Europe and parts of the UK, digital ecosystems are likely to coexist with strong expectations around accountability, transparency, accessibility, and consumer protection. Customers may embrace automation as long as institutions remain visibly responsible during disruption.

Across continental Europe, debates around privacy, digital rights, and ethical technology deployment will shape how future banking systems are governed.

In North America, future banking will likely be driven heavily by platform ecosystems, convenience, personalisation, and competitive innovation. At the same time, public concern around data concentration, cyber risk, and algorithmic influence is increasing.

China represents another model entirely. Banking increasingly operates inside highly integrated digital ecosystems connecting commerce, communication, payments, mobility, and identity. Financial services become less of a standalone institution and more of a continuous societal layer.

Across the Gulf, rapid digital modernisation exists alongside strong relationship-oriented expectations around service and trust. Technological sophistication must coexist with human accessibility and institutional reputation.

In Africa, mobile-first financial participation continues reshaping banking around inclusion, accessibility, and practical utility. Trust depends heavily on reliability and usability rather than institutional heritage.

In South Asia, future banking may evolve at extraordinary scale through mobile infrastructure, digital identity systems, and AI-driven participation models serving highly diverse populations with varying levels of literacy and digital maturity.

In Latin America, historical experiences with inflation and instability still shape emotional expectations around trust and resilience.

These differences matter because banking is never experienced purely through technology. It is experienced through lived social reality, historical memory, and cultural expectations around institutions and authority.

There will not be one future bank. There will be many versions shaped by different relationships with trust, governance, and technology.

The strongest institutions may not be those imposing uniform global models, but those capable of combining technological capability with deep understanding of the societies they serve.

Technology scales globally. Trust scales locally.

Staying Human Inside the Future Bank

The future bank will almost certainly be more intelligent, predictive, automated, and interconnected than any institution before it. AI will shape decisions continuously.

Embedded finance will make transactions nearly invisible. Behavioural analytics and real-time systems will operate constantly beneath everyday activity.

Operationally, this is a remarkable achievement.

But it raises a deeper question: what does it mean to remain human inside increasingly algorithmic systems?

Historically, banking involved visible human interaction. Customers entered branches, spoke with staff, signed documents, and dealt with identifiable institutional processes. Today, much of financial life happens through invisible systems operating silently in the background.

Payments complete automatically. Fraud systems assess behaviour continuously. Lending models evaluate eligibility instantly. Identity verification happens digitally. Customers often see only the outcome, not the institutional processes behind it.

That changes how people experience financial life. Individuals increasingly exist inside systems that monitor behaviour, classify patterns, assess legitimacy, and influence economic participation through algorithmic interpretation.

Most customers accept this because it improves convenience and efficiency. But human expectations have not disappeared. People still need reassurance during uncertainty, fairness during disputes, explanation during confusion, and accountability when systems behave unexpectedly.

This tension between algorithmic efficiency and emotional reality may become one of the defining challenges of future banking.

Different societies respond differently. In highly digitised environments, customers may adapt comfortably to invisible systems if reliability remains strong. In societies more sensitive to surveillance or institutional opacity, customers may demand greater explainability and governance. In emerging economies, intelligent systems may expand inclusion while simultaneously raising concerns around fairness and accessibility.

Technology evolves quickly. Human emotional expectations evolve much more slowly.

AI makes this more significant because institutions increasingly interpret customers through behavioural data rather than direct human interaction. Financial trustworthiness, fraud suspicion, and customer visibility may all become continuously inferred through systems operating beyond normal human awareness.

This creates new institutional responsibilities.

Banks must ensure people do not feel reduced to behavioural signals inside systems optimised only for prediction and efficiency. That is why explainability, ethics, oversight, accountability, and human recourse are becoming strategically important.

Customers experiencing fraud still need reassurance beyond automated workflows. Elderly individuals still need patient support navigating digital systems. Vulnerable customers still need empathy during hardship. Small-business owners still seek confidence through responsive human interaction.

The future bank cannot be built around technology alone. It must preserve human dignity and emotional continuity alongside operational intelligence.

The institutions that endure may not simply possess the best technology. They may be the ones ensuring technology continues serving people without weakening trust, fairness, or reassurance.

Why Trust Architecture Is the Final Blueprint

Throughout history, banking has repeatedly transformed itself alongside changing societies and technologies. Institutions evolved from merchant networks to industrial finance, from paper-based systems to global digital infrastructure, and from physical branches to intelligent ecosystems operating continuously across modern life.

Yet one requirement has remained constant: banking survives only when trust survives.

Modern retail banking now operates inside systems shaped by AI, embedded finance, cloud infrastructure, digital identity, behavioural analytics, cyber dependency, geopolitical instability, and constantly shifting societal expectations.

Technology can improve capability, speed, and scale. But technology alone cannot sustain legitimacy.

That is why trust architecture becomes the defining blueprint of the future bank.

Trust architecture is not a marketing slogan or a single initiative. It is the institutional design through which confidence is preserved across changing technological and social conditions. It combines governance, operational resilience, accountability, inclusion, ethics, customer experience, and long-term stewardship into one coherent system.

This matters because modern financial life increasingly depends on invisible infrastructure that customers cannot directly verify or fully understand. People simply assume payments will work, identities will remain secure, systems will recover, and institutions will behave fairly during uncertainty.

Trust becomes the hidden operating system beneath financial life itself.

Different societies will define this differently. In highly digital economies, trust architecture may depend heavily on cybersecurity, operational continuity, and coordinated infrastructure. In ageing societies, it may focus more on accessibility and reassurance. In emerging markets, it may depend more strongly on reliability, inclusion, and institutional legitimacy.

Despite these differences, one principle remains universal: people still need institutions that feel dependable during uncertainty.

AI intensifies this need. As algorithms shape decisions, servicing, fraud detection, and behavioural interpretation, institutional power becomes more invisible. Customers may no longer understand how financial decisions are made even while depending on those systems daily.

Future institutions must therefore preserve not only technical resilience, but emotional legitimacy. Customers need to believe systems remain governable, fairness remains possible, and accountability still exists behind automated environments.

Trust architecture is ultimately the discipline of ensuring technological complexity does not erode human confidence.

This is where the major themes shaping the future of retail banking converge: intelligent branches, operational resilience, inclusion, governance, adaptive systems, institutional longevity, and responsible AI. All connect back to one central question: can banks remain trusted human institutions inside increasingly algorithmic societies?

The institutions that endure for the next century may not be those that innovate fastest. They may be the ones that balance intelligence with humanity, efficiency with dignity, and transformation with continuity.

Because even as technology changes constantly, human beings still seek institutions they can rely on when uncertainty arrives.

Reflection

The journey toward a 100-year bank is ultimately a journey toward institutional purpose, discipline, and humility. This chapter reflects on the deeper truth that longevity in banking is not an outcome of technology, capital, or scale alone; it is the result of values expressed consistently over time through decisions, behaviours, and relationships. A bank becomes worthy of a century only when it understands the responsibility it carries in shaping people's financial lives, supporting communities, and contributing to a nation's economic resilience. Designing the bank of the future entails treating trust not as a sentiment but as a public asset that must be protected every single day. It recognises that hybrid delivery models, data-driven systems, and digital infrastructure are only meaningful when they enhance fairness, access, and customer well-being. This reflection also reinforces that the future institution must embrace adaptability without losing its anchor. It must be modern enough to lead in open finance, AI governance, platform ecosystems, and cross-border standards, while remaining grounded enough to safeguard vulnerable customers, ensure transparency, and preserve institutional memory. The chapter has highlighted that leadership character will be as important as technology capability: boards, executives, and frontline teams must demonstrate judgement, empathy, and foresight in a world where risks are interconnected and expectations are rising. It reminds us that retail banking, at its heart, is a human institution—a trusted companion in people's life journeys. The banks that endure for a century will be those that stay close to real needs, understand social context, and strengthen the link between innovation and responsibility. This reflection closes with a simple, enduring message: a 100-year bank is built not by predicting the future, but by designing an institution capable of evolving with integrity, relevance, and purpose over every generation it serves.

Framework: Designing the Bank of the Future Architecture

Framework Overview

This framework brings together the design principles developed across the entire book and translates them into a long-horizon institutional blueprint. It explains how retail banks can build the structures, disciplines, and cultural foundations necessary to remain relevant, trusted, and resilient across generations. A 100-year bank does not survive on technology cycles or product innovation alone. It survives because its purpose is clear, its systems are adaptive, its governance is strong, and its connection to society is genuine. The framework consolidates fifty design pillars into a single, coherent model that senior leaders, boards, regulators, and practitioners can use to diagnose long-term readiness. It highlights that longevity is engineered—through discipline, foresight, and institutional character—not inherited.

100-Year Bank Architecture

DESIGNING FOR INSTITUTIONAL LONGEVITY

Long-lived institutions maintain clarity of purpose, embed disciplined risk frameworks, and invest continuously in customer trust. Longevity is achieved through intergenerational thinking, stable governance, and a culture that balances tradition with renewal.

THE ADAPTIVE RESILIENCE CUBE

Resilience must be multi-dimensional—structural, technological, operational, cultural, and societal. The Adaptive Resilience Cube provides a practical guide for integrating these pillars so that institutions can absorb shocks, adapt intelligently, and protect public confidence.

MULTI-GENERATIONAL CUSTOMER THINKING

Future-ready banks design for customers across life stages, demographics, and digital capabilities. Multi-generational thinking ensures services remain relevant, inclusive, and accessible as societies age, youth populations expand, and expectations evolve.

SYSTEMS THINKING IN RETAIL STRATEGY

Retail banks must operate as integrated systems. Systems thinking links product design, risk decisions, technology investment, customer experience, ESG commitments, and regulatory alignment into a unified strategy that reduces fragmentation and strengthens coherence.

THE FUTURE ARCHITECTURE MANIFESTO

The manifesto synthesises the full architecture of the book: trust as infrastructure, inclusion as a design responsibility, resilience as a core institutional capability, governance as public duty, and hybrid delivery as the operating system. It sets out the enduring commitments required for institutions to serve society for the next century.

Purpose of the Framework

This framework provides leaders with a structured, long-horizon guide for designing institutions capable of thriving for the next 100 years. It shows that longevity is not about age or market dominance, but about purpose, discipline, governance, and adaptability. It offers a practical architecture they can use to evaluate strategic readiness, strengthen institutional character, and build a bank that remains relevant across generations. It positions the future retail bank as a living institution—stable, trusted, and deeply connected to the communities it serves. Each pillar must translate into observable outcomes across resilience, governance effectiveness, and customer trust.

Table 10.1 Checklist: 100-Year Bank Architecture Readiness

1	Clarity of Enduring Purpose Is the institution anchored in a purpose that remains relevant across generations?
2	Balance Between Continuity and Renewal Can the bank evolve without losing its identity, values, and institutional memory?
3	Embedded Trust Architecture Is trust engineered into processes, decisions, and customer interactions consistently?
4	Multi-dimensional Resilience Does resilience extend across governance, technology, operations, culture, and society?
5	Multi-generational Customer Relevance Are services designed to remain relevant across life stages and demographic shifts?
6	System-Wide Strategic Coherence Are decisions aligned across functions, avoiding fragmentation and unintended consequences?
7	Purpose-Driven Technology Deployment Is technology aligned to customer well-being, inclusion, and long-term institutional goals?
8	Ethical Governance and Data Stewardship Are ethics, transparency, and responsible data practices embedded into daily operations?
9	Leadership Continuity and Renewal Is there a structured pipeline ensuring leadership evolves without destabilising the institution?
10	Societal Embeddedness and Responsibility Does the bank actively contribute to community resilience, financial inclusion, and economic stability?

Table 10.2 Template: 100-Year Bank Architecture Blueprint

No.	*Institutional Purpose*	*Implicit or evolving*	*Lack of clarity across organisation*	*Clearly articulated, lived across all levels*	*Board / CEO*
1	Trust Architecture	Experience-led trust	Inconsistent delivery	Trust embedded into systems, processes, and decisions	COO / CRO
2	Resilience Model	Compliance-driven resilience	Fragmented resilience layers	Integrated multi-dimensional resilience architecture	CRO
3	Customer Relevance	Segment-based design	Limited life-cycle continuity	Multi-generational, lifecycle-driven service model	CCO
4	Strategic Coherence	Functional alignment gaps	Siloed decisions	System-wide aligned decision-making architecture	CEO / COO
5	Technology Orientation	Efficiency-focused	Disconnected from purpose	Purpose-driven, human-centred technology architecture	CIO
6	Governance and Ethics	Policy-driven	Limited behavioural embedding	Ethical governance embedded in daily decision-making	Board / Compliance
7	Data Stewardship	Regulatory compliance focus	Trust vulnerability risks	Transparent, ethical, customer-aligned data governance	CIO / Data
8	Leadership Model	Role-based succession	Leadership fragility	Continuous, diverse, institution-aligned leadership pipeline	Board / HR
9	Societal Role	Peripheral engagement	Weak community integration	Deep societal embeddedness and public responsibility	CEO / Board
10	Institutional Purpose	Implicit or evolving	Lack of clarity across organisation	Clearly articulated, lived across all levels	Board / CEO

Bibliography

Accenture (2024). *Research on Trust, Institutional Design and Future Banking Models.* Accenture Financial Services Research.

Asian Development Bank (2023). *Digital Financial Inclusion and Long-Term Institutional Resilience in Asia.* ADB.

Bank for International Settlements (2023). *Principles for Operational Resilience, Governance and Digital Trust in Financial Services.* BIS.

Bank of England (2023). *Financial Stability in a Digital Financial System.* Bank of England.

European Banking Authority (2023). *Guidelines on ICT and Security Risk Management in Financial Institutions.* EBA.

European Union (2022). *Digital Operational Resilience Act (DORA).* European Commission.

Financial Conduct Authority (2023). *Consumer Duty and Long-Term Customer Outcomes Framework.* FCA.

FINOS (2023). *Research on Open Source Collaboration and Interoperability in Financial Services.* Fintech Open Source Foundation.

Gartner (2024). *Research on Future Banking Operating Models, AI and Institutional Architecture.* Gartner Research.

Harvard Business Review (2023). *Research and Insights on Leading Institutions Through Technological and Societal Change.* Harvard Business Publishing.

IBM Institute for Business Value (2024). *Research on Trust, AI and Human-Centred Banking Design.* IBM.

International Monetary Fund (2023). *Research on Financial Stability, Institutional Governance and Digital Transformation.* IMF.

McKinsey & Company (2024). *Insights on Retail Banking Resilience, Trust and Institutional Adaptability.* McKinsey Global Banking Practice.

Monetary Authority of Singapore (2023). *Principles of Responsible AI and Data Governance in Financial Services.* MAS.

Organisation for Economic Co-operation and Development (2023). *Trust, Digital Governance and Institutional Resilience.* OECD Publishing.

PwC (2024). *Research on Governance, Culture and Institutional Longevity in Banking.* PricewaterhouseCoopers.

Reserve Bank of India (2023). *Digital Banking, Governance and Financial Inclusion Frameworks.* RBI.

World Bank (2023). *Financial Inclusion, Resilience and the Future of Banking Systems.* World Bank.

World Economic Forum (2024). *Insights on the Future of Financial Services, Trust Architecture and Intelligent Institutions.* World Economic Forum.

Closing Reflections

The Future of Retail Banking Will Not Ultimately Be Determined by Technology Alone

It will be determined by whether banking institutions remain trusted, resilient, accountable, and human in an environment increasingly shaped by automation, data, operational complexity, and continuous change.

Across this book, the discussion has deliberately remained institutional rather than fashionable. The objective has not been to predict the next technology cycle or present digital transformation as an end in itself. Instead, the focus has been on the deeper institutional foundations required for retail banking institutions to remain credible, stable, operationally resilient, and socially legitimate over time.

Again and again, the same lesson emerges: strong banking institutions are not built through innovation alone. They are built through governance, operational discipline, leadership judgement, institutional memory, and the consistent ability to earn public confidence across changing economic and societal conditions.

Retail banking occupies a unique position within society. Unlike many industries, banks do not simply provide products or services. They operate as part of the daily infrastructure of economic life. Customers experience banking through moments that directly affect security, livelihoods, families, businesses, savings, homes, and long-term financial confidence. Trust therefore becomes more than a commercial advantage. It becomes an institutional responsibility.

As retail banking systems evolve, trust itself increasingly becomes the core infrastructure of finance.

Customers may experience banking through applications, platforms, algorithms, automation, embedded finance ecosystems, or digital interfaces, yet confidence in banking institutions will continue to depend on far more fundamental questions:

How decisions are made.
How risks are governed.
How institutions behave under pressure.
How consistently they support customers and communities.
And whether accountability remains visible within increasingly complex systems.

Technology will continue to reshape retail banking. Artificial intelligence, open banking, embedded finance, automation, cloud infrastructure, digital identity systems, and data-led operating models will all continue to influence

DOI: 10.4324/9781042021765-12

how institutions function. However, no technological capability can permanently compensate for weak governance, institutional fragility, poor judgement, operational inconsistency, or the erosion of trust.

The retail banks that endure over the coming decades are unlikely to be defined simply by speed, scale, efficiency, or digital sophistication. They will be defined by their ability to combine innovation with responsibility, operational resilience with human judgement, and institutional capability with long-term public confidence.

The challenge for banking leaders therefore is not merely technological adaptation. It is institutional stewardship.

This requires more than investment in platforms or operating models. It requires clarity of purpose, disciplined governance, operational accountability, responsible leadership, and institutions capable of balancing commercial ambition with long-term societal credibility.

Throughout this book, one broader principle remains constant: retail banking institutions do not operate separately from society. They influence economic participation, business confidence, financial inclusion, community resilience, and public trust itself. Their decisions shape not only markets, but everyday human experience.

As banking becomes increasingly digital, the human dimension of banking may in fact become more important rather than less. Customers will continue to value clarity, continuity, accessibility, responsible judgement, and institutions capable of remaining dependable during periods of uncertainty and change.

If this book leaves one lasting reflection, it is this: retail banking remains, fundamentally, a trust institution.

Its future will depend not only on what banking institutions build, automate, digitise, or scale, but on what they protect, sustain, and preserve for the businesses, communities, and individuals who continue to depend upon them.

The future of retail banking will therefore belong not simply to the most technologically advanced institutions, but to those capable of remaining trusted through change.

Dr Gulzar Singh
United Kingdom

Index

Note: Locators in italic and bold refer figures and tables respectively.

accessibility 279, 281; emotional 280; engineering 212
accountability 310; human architecture of 344–345
Account Aggregator (AA) framework 113, 115, 118, 121, 143
adaptive branch models (urban vs. rural) 218–223
Adaptive Resilience Cube 363–369
advisory-centric branches 51
Africa, hybrid banking in 69
ageing populations/customers 274–279, 304
agent networks 294–299
AI risk models 240–245
algorithmic opacity 242, 253
algorithmic risk 261–263
anti-money-laundering (AML) monitoring 17, 340
API 119–123, 130; and agile integration layers 121; governance 124, 127; interactions 125; management frameworks 126–127; operating platform 129
architecture 4–5; consistent identity 41; design 132; of 100-year financial institution 356; of hybrid banking 17, 38, 75; of intelligent branch network 195; modular 128; open finance 111, 152; retail reinvention 6; trust 15, 104; trust infrastructure shift 79, 106–107; unified data 178–179
assisted channels 41
assisted-digital models/workflows 53–57, 176
authentication 41, 77–78; digital identity and 78–83; in hybrid banking 81
automation 57, 60; AI and 226; guided 205, 206; service environments 227–228; systems 29; well-designed 48; workflow 48
autonomous service flows 202–207

back-end processes 8
balanced approach 13
bank boards, strategic challenges for 137–143
Bank for International Settlements 370
banking institutions: branch vs. digital evolution 5–10; consumer confidence and institutional trust 10–15; context 3–5; cost–inclusion dilemma 15–19; customers interact with 3; institutional perspective 26–31; post-pandemic behavioural shifts 19–22; reflection 31–34; reinvention of 3–34; structural barriers in emerging economies 23–26
Bank of England 314–315
banks/banking 1; Adaptive Resilience Cube 363–369; boards 137–143; as civilisational institution 26–27; designing 354–394; fintech–bank collaboration 92–93; Future Architecture Manifesto 380–385; in India 37; multi-generational customer thinking 369–375; in North America 28; responsible 184–189; systems thinking 375–379; trust 304; trust in 104
behavioural nudges/design 288–293
behavioural risk 241
behavioural shifts, post-pandemic 19–22
Biennial Exploratory Scenario (BES) 314–315
biometric authentication 79, 276
board design 312–318

branch 8, 54, 58; vs. digital evolution 5–10; and digital platforms 8; evolution of 10; formats 51; machine interaction in 211; networks 9; operations 17; relevance 8; smart design 55; strategy 8; transactions 16; transformation 194
branch-dependent models 38
building-management systems (BMS) 165

capital resilience 367
cash dependency 16
channel strategy 56–62
choice architecture 288–293
civilisation: institution 26–27; responsibility 342–343
civil-society organizations 272
climate: risk 156–162, 185–186; stress testing 159; volatility 158, 160, 162, 250–253
climate-adjusted retail risk 250–253
Climate Biennial Exploratory Scenario (CBES) 159
climate change 154, 162
climate-driven migration 161
climate–operational convergence 268
cloud adoption 47, 48
cloud-based ecosystems 45
cloud governance 239
cloud migration 46–48
cloud sovereignty 340
cognitive diversity 279, 300
communication 15; channels 277
community banking 294–299
community-based scrutiny 96
community-centric service capability 218
community partnerships 275
community spaces 53
community trust 295, 299
competitive advantage 72
competitive differentiation 4
compliance 337
confidence 11
consent architecture 83–88
consistency 44; end-to-end 44; in service quality 41–42
consistent identity 40–41
consumers: confidence 10–15; groups 272; protection 118, 135
contact-centre journeys 272
contemporary authentication methods 79
context visibility 43
continuous authentication 80, 82
continuous monitoring systems 122, 246
continuous testing 49
controlled empowerment 323
convergence 117
core banking platforms 237
core modernisation 45
Corporate Sustainability Reporting Directive (CSRD) 180, 181
cost design 56–62
cost–inclusion dilemma 15–19
cost optimisation 61
cost-to-serve intelligence 58–61
cost transparency 61
credit infrastructure 25
criminal networks 237
cross-border regulatory alignment 336–342
cross-channel synchronisation 86–87
cross-functional governance 337
cultural alignment 93
cultural proximity 295
cultural resilience 268, 363, 365
cultural risks 170
customer confidence 122
customer data 144–145
customer inclusion 272–308; ageing populations and digital access 274–279; agent networks and community banking 294–299; architecture readiness 307; "average digital customer" 272; behavioural nudges and choice architecture 288–293; disability-inclusive design 279–282; framework 305–307; gendered financial access 283–288; geography of exclusion 300; mapping 308; in North America 302; redefining 299–300; trust 273; vulnerability as universal condition 301–302
customers 5, 7, 11, 77; ageing 274; behaviour 9; data rights 114; expectations 20; expect consistent experiences 111; gain convenience 144; harm 248; outcome 4; risk 135; trust institutions 49; trust technology 20; value institutions 22
cybercrime 260
cybersecurity 122, 127, 235–240

data: architectures 110; continuity 46; governance 43, 90; portability 119–122, 149; quality 124; responsibility 187–188; rights 83–88, 114–115
data-sharing: in China 145; controls systems 78; expansion of 111; partnerships 86; transparent 125
DBS Bank 164
decentralised identity systems 81–82

demographic sensitivity 220
"design for disassembly" principles 168
digital: access 274–279; adoption 69; banking 5; channels 18, 37, 42, 44, 57, 59, 61, 69, 155, 162, 292; coaching 216; conduct risk 253–258; convenience 99; economy 3; exclusion 16; and human service 209; identity 78–83, 100–101; literacy 19, 21, 50–51, 142, 176; and physical channels 9; platforms 8; safety 288; systems 70; technology 259; transformation 28, 70, 300, 387; trust 20
digitalisation 176
digital-only models 37, 38
disability-inclusive design 279–282
distributed ecosystems 124
diversification process 156
diversity, in governance 324–330
dynamic consent model 85

e-commerce platform 111
economic agency 287
economic instability 25
economic volatility 24
ecosystem: coordination 379–380; design 131–137; platforms 131; resilience 368
effective governance 89, 91, 130, 167, 179, 242, 295, 389
efficiency 27
embedded finance: and ecosystem design 131–137; society 146–147
emerging economies 31; structural barriers in 23–26
emerging technologies 16
emotion: accessibility 280; reassurance 212; resilience 214
empathetic communication 177
empathy 275
empowerment 323; controlled 323
end-to-end consistency 44
end-to-end ownership 319–320
energy design 163–168
energy optimisation 166
environmental sensors 196, 198
environmental, social, and governance (ESG): architecture mapping 192; banking architecture 190–191; banking model 154–192, **191**; climate risk and retail portfolios 156–162; credibility of 189; ethical AI in credit and lending 168–173; financial literacy and inclusion gaps 173–178; global reporting and assurance models 178–184; green branches and energy design 163–168; as institutional banking architecture 156; measurement 179; performance 183; reporting 180, 181; responsible banking 184–189
environmental stewardship 168
episodic upgrade approach 163
ethical AI 189; in credit and lending 168–173; and data responsibility 187–188
ethical governance 383
ethical nudging 291
ethical stewardship 382–384
European banks 37
EU's Financial Data Access Framework 114, 116
explainable AI 171
external assurance 182
extreme weather events 160

fairness 14, 186–187
family-assisted banking 278
family-inclusive design 276
FCA 115, 116, 118
financial behaviour 174
financial confidence 283, 284, 286
Financial Data Access Framework 112, 114–116, 143
financial identity 283
financial inclusion 177, 283, 299
financial institutions 23, 110, 274
financial judgement 103
financial literacy 23, 173–178, 186
financial resilience 367
financial systems 28, 31, 146, 188
financial technology innovations 113
fintech–bank collaboration models 92–94
Fintech Open Source Foundation (FINOS) 380
fintech partnerships 155
formal financial systems 175
fragmentation 25
fragmented data environments 46
fraud: classification 187; detection 29, 43, 102, 261; ecosystems 186; incidents 147; patterns 78, 111; prevention 104
frontline reskilling 213–218
Future Architecture Manifesto 380–385

gendered financial access 283–288
gender-sensitive security principles 285
generational sensitivity 373

global reporting and assurance models 178–184
governance 45, 54, 88, 90, 320; API 124, 127; cloud 239; complexity 128; cross-functional 170, 337; dimension of 168; effective 89, 91, 130, 167, 179, 242, 295, 389; frameworks 50, 297; in hybrid banking 89, 91; institutionalising 124; open-source adoption 96; operational 324; resilience 89; in retail banking 129; robust 298; strong 15, 50, 53, 84, 86, 88, 91, 96, 122, 124, 155, 169, 242, 281, 295, 318, 382; structures 86, 110, 131; teams 132; third-party 86, 88; training and 298
green branch design 163–168
green financing 155
grievance channels 282
guided automation 205, 206
guided journeys 293

harmonised journeys/harmonisation 41
HM Revenue and Customs 319
human agency 144–145
human-assisted digital journeys 43
human being 29–30
human–machine interaction design 207–213
human reassurance 19
100-year financial institution 356, 393, 394
hybrid banking/retail banking 4, 24, 25, 38, 45, 50, 62, 73, 164, 175; in Africa 69; for ageing populations 275; architecture of 17, 38, 75; authentication in 81; consent architecture in 84; consistency in service quality 41–42; cybersecurity risk in 240; defining feature of 40; demands governance structures 91; effective boards in 314; environment 276; governance in 89; harmonised journeys/harmonisation 41; human being in 66–72; hybrid infrastructure readiness 44–50; identity infrastructure 80; institutional design architecture for 312; institutions 37; journey continuity 40; literacy 174; physical and digital delivery 36; physical–digital integration models 39–44; reflection 72–73; retail 7; rise of 36–75; in Singapore model 64, 73; trust in 77; in United Kingdom 63, 68
hybrid delivery, operating models for 318–324
hybrid institutions 49, 50, 58, 71, 161, 162, 166–168, 171, 178, 182; customer inclusion 272–308; infrastructure readiness 44–50
hybrid-ready institution 46, 47, 51
hyperlocal branch models 54

identity systems 80–81
inclusion 16, 18
inclusion gaps 173–178
inclusive consent models 85
India: Account Aggregator (AA) framework 113, 115, 118, 121, 143; Digital Public Infrastructure 116
infrastructure gaps 235–240
infrastructure governance models 88–92
innovation 28
institutional behaviour 98
institutional design 1, 4; architecture mapping 352; board design and strategic foresight 312–318; civilisational responsibility 342–343; cross-border regulatory alignment 336–342; designing for complexity 345–347; diversity in governance and leadership 324–330; effectiveness of 4; human architecture of accountability 344–345; institutional memory 343–344; lens 310–352; maturity readiness 351; operating models for hybrid delivery 318–324; professional standards, role of 330–335; stewardship 347–348
institutional ecosystem 10
institutional perspective 26–31
institutional resilience 31
institutional risk 311
institutional steadiness 11
institutional trust 10–15, 27
institutions 42, 60, 101, 105; banking see banking institutions; ethical posture 182; foundations 3; hybrid 49, 50; hybrid-ready 43, 46, 47; interoperability 379–380; legitimacy 104–105; longevity 356–362; long-lived 354, 357–359, 361, 368; maturity 344–345; memory 343–344; people and 99; retail banking 111
integrated branch security systems 198
integrated design 19
integrated reporting 183
intelligent branch network 194–233; adaptive branch models (urban vs. rural) 218–223; architecture mapping 233; architecture of 195; automated service environments 227–228; autonomous service flows 202–207; framework 231–232; human–machine interaction design 207–213; physical

branches 224–225; readiness 232; reskilling frontline staff 213–218; sensor-enabled branch 195–201; strength 230; transaction processing 225–226
intelligent energy-management systems 167, 168
internal data integration 157
International Sustainability Standards Board (ISSB) 154
interoperability 47, 49, 95, 120–122; consent architecture 87; critical effects of 121; identity infrastructure 81; institutional 379–380
invisible digital systems 101–102

journey continuity 40

KYC techniques 134

Latin American banks 37–38
leadership 88, 238, 311, 335, 359; continuity 361; diversity in governance and 324–330; institutional memory 343–344; resilience 366, 368; senior 279; teams 66, 325–326
legacy: cost models 8; fraud-monitoring systems 239; governance models 122; systems 17, 110
liability 122
licensing regimes 23
liquidity: management 294, 296; stability 298
longevity 354–358, 360, 361, 383; institutions 356–362
long-lived institutions 354, 357–359, 361, 368
long-term institutions 358
long-term stewardship 131

machine-learning systems 240
maintenance sensors 198
market competition 18
measurement discipline 155
micro-processing pods 53
migrant worker 301
Mitsubishi UFJ Financial Group 356
mobile banking 7
mobile financial systems 28, 102
mobile-led financial systems 26
modern authentication 81
modern resilience 238
Monetary Authority of Singapore 326
mortgage banking 162
mortgage portfolios 160
multi-generational customer thinking 369–375
multilingual functionality 209

national digital ecosystems 25
national digital identity infrastructure 80
net zero branch transformation 164
NHS England 334
non-banking platforms 133
North America, customer inclusion in 302

occasional inconvenience 303
occupancy sensors 196
omnichannel identity orchestration 82
one-size-fits-all approach 8, 155, 176, 370
Open Banking framework 84
open finance: architecture 111, 152; banking 143–144; customer data 144–145; embedded finance and ecosystem design 131–137; embedded financial society 146–147; environment 118, 141; experience 145–146; human agency and new ownership question 144–145; as institutional architecture 112; liability 118; mandate 110–152; platform setup of retail banks 125–131; portability 119–120; readiness 151; regulation 117; regulatory mandates 112–125; strategic challenges for bank boards 137–143; supervisory convergence of 119; ultimate infrastructure of 147–148
open financial ecosystems 148
open-source technology/adoption 94–98
operating models, for hybrid delivery 318–324
operational assurance 49
operational efficiency 54, 104
operational governance 324
operational resilience 48, 49, 60, 164, 364
operational risk 136
operational stability 298
orchestration platforms 200–201
overcoming fragmentation 25

paper-based control systems 45
physical channels 9, 37, 57, 59, 292
physical–digital convergence 73
physical–digital integration models 39–44
physical environment 10, 285
physical risks 156
platformisation 125, 127, 128, 130, 149
platform risk management 129
political instability 25

politically exposed persons (PEP) 340
portability 119–120
"positive friction" techniques 291
post-pandemic behavioural shifts 19–22
predictive analytics 58
professional standards, role of 330–335
public infrastructure 3
public trust 94–98, 242

quality control mechanisms 297
queue sensors 196

Rabobank 365
real-time data orchestration 127–128
real-time systems 4
reassurance 27
reflection 31–34
regulatory alignment 338
regulatory expectations 38, 47, 48, 50, 63, 78, 87, 98, 129, 158
regulatory mandates 112–125
reinvention readiness 34
reputation risk 253–258
resilience 49–50, 82–83, 87, 204, 256, 265, 367; Adaptive Resilience Cube 363–369; agent network 294; architecture 267, 270; cultural 363, 365; cyber 235, 237; decision-making 368; dimension of 369; financial 367; governance 89; leadership 366, 368; of open finance 149; operational 48–49, 60, 164, 364; planning 131, 207; reputational 257; sensor-enabled branch 196; societal 363, 365, 369; structural 363; technological 363; vendor operating environment 250
reskilling frontline staff 213–218
responsible banking institutions 184–189
responsiveness 14, 15
retail banking 1, 19, 78, 95, 310; banking institutions see banking institutions; behavioural patterns in 289; challenge for 71; evolution of 5; fragmentation forces 23; future of 2; hybrid 38, 50, 62; inclusive 23; institutions 111, 117; platform-based ecosystems 126; trust in 11, 13, 77; unit economics of 16
retail portfolios 156–162
retail reinvention architecture 6, 32–33
risk: age of invisible systems 258–264; AI risk models and bias 240–245; algorithmic 261–263; architecture readiness 269; assessment techniques 134; climate 156–162, 185–186; climate-adjusted retail risk 250–253; credit 135; cybersecurity and infrastructure gaps 235–240; engines 278; framework 265–269; future of 235–270; management process 129, 158; operational 136; reputation and digital conduct risk 253–258; and resilience architecture 267, 270; third-party and vendor risk 245–250; vendor 245–250
robust economic model 130
robust governance 298
robust resilience governance 89
routine transactions 54, 56

Santander Work Café 52
seamless data continuity 46
seamless digital participation 301
seamless transitions 42
secure branch 12
self-management 20
self-service tools 41
self-sufficient service flow 203
sensor-enabled branch 195–201
shifts: post-pandemic behavioural 19–22; structural 32; trust infrastructure see trust infrastructure shift
Singapore: digital identity 100; model 64
smart branch configurations 50–56
smartphones 7
social institution 385–386
societal resilience 363, 365, 366, 369
"sovereign cloud overlays" 340
staff 15
static consent models 85
stewardship 347–348; ethical 384
strategic foresight 312–318
strong governance 344
structural resilience 363
structural shifts 32
supervisory convergence 119
systems thinking 375–379

Task Force on Climate-Related Financial Disclosures (TCFD) 154, 180, 181
technical resilience 261
technological assurance 11
technological resilience 363
technology-driven change 1
telecom-led platforms 63
third-party: ecosystems 84; governance 86, 88; participants 123; risk 245–250
traditional on-premise systems 46, 47
traditional operating models 7
transaction processing 225–226
transition risks 156

transparent value articulation 86
trust 1, 14; architecture 15, 104; banking 304; in banks 104; community 295; in coordinated institutions 29; customer inclusion 273; in Europe 148; fundamental redefinition of 77; hybrid banking environment 14, 77; imbalance 3; in retail banking 11, 13; unified data models 123
"Trust as Institutional Infrastructure" 2
trust infrastructure shift 77–108; age of invisible trust 99–105; architecture 79, 106–107; consent architecture and data rights 83–88; digital identity and authentication 78–83; fintech–bank collaboration models 92–94; infrastructure governance models 88–92; mapping 108; open source and public trust 94–98; readiness 107; reflection 105–107; in retail banking 77

UK retail banking 159
unified consent governance model 85
unified data models 123
unified data visibility 43
United Kingdom: digital banking adoption 226; hybrid banking in 63, 68; regulatory architecture 118

vendor: contracts 91; dependency 248; partnerships 318; risk 245–250
vulnerable customers 293

well-constructed resilience model 83
well-rounded investment strategy 59
women: economic agency 287; empowerment 286; entrepreneurs 285–286; financial participation 288; long-term financial security 285
workflow automation 48

zones/zoning 52–53

For Product Safety Concerns and Information please contact our EU
representative GPSR@taylorandfrancis.com
Taylor & Francis Verlag GmbH, Kaufingerstraße 24, 80331 München, Germany

www.ingramcontent.com/pod-product-compliance
Ingram Content Group UK Ltd.
Pitfield, Milton Keynes, MK11 3LW, UK
UKHW022016111026
476504UK00011B/451

* 9 7 8 1 0 4 1 4 0 2 1 9 0 *